Global Passages

Sources in World History

VOLUME II: SINCE 1500

Roger Schlesinger

Washington State University

Fritz Blackwell

Washington State University

Kathryn Meyer

Washington State University

Mary Watrous-Schlesinger

Washington State University

HOUGHTON MIFFLIN COMPANY   Boston   New York

In Memory of Donna (1937–2002)

Editor-in-Chief: Jean Woy
Senior Sponsoring Editor: Nancy Blaine
Development Editor: Julie Dunn
Senior Project Editor: Ylang Nguyen
Editorial Assistant: Wendy Thayer
Production/Design Assistant: Bethany Schlegel
Senior Marketing Manager: Sandra McGuire
Senior Manufacturing Coordinator: Marie Barnes

Cover image: Sadahide, Utagawa (1807–1873). *Sailing from a California Port in America.* (triptych) Polychrome woodblock print; ink and color on paper. Credit: The Metropolitan Museum of Art, Gift of Lincoln Kirstein, 1959. (JP 3268) Photograph by Otto E. Nelson. Photograph © 1986 The Metropolitan Museum of Art.

Printed in the U.S.A.

Library of Congress Catalog Card Number: 2001131550

ISBN: 0-618-06796-5

123456789-EB-06 05 04 03

Contents

CHAPTER 4   The Americas and Oceania, 1500–1800   *87*

CHAPTER 5   Europe, 1500–1800   *121*

Part II: *On the Eve of Modernity, 1800–1918*   *149*

CHAPTER 6   East and Southeast Asia, 1800–1918   *151*

CHAPTER 7   South and Southwest Asia, 1800–1918   *181*

Preface

A graduate student's remark provided the conceptual framework for this project. A few years ago, one of the authors of this book had a student from the People's Republic of China as a teaching assistant. One day he showed her a memo written by a university administrator. The professor was interested in the content, but the Chinese student focused on a grammatical mistake the administrator had overlooked. When the professor commented on the student's sharp eye, she responded, "Perhaps when you learn a language as a foreigner, you look more carefully at it than a native does." The same notion, we believe, is true of observers who describe a given society's culture. Foreigners or travelers are more likely to take careful notice of customs, manners, and rituals than native inhabitants, who often tend to take them for granted.

We decided students and instructors needed a primary source reader for World Civilizations courses that focused on foreigners' accounts of societies and cultures. We included all parts of the world from ancient times to the present. The sources in *Global Passages* emphasize daily life—marriage and funeral customs, food, social and religious rituals and ceremonies—rather than the behavior or policies of political elites. Frankly, we believe that the daily lives and customs of a people reveal their society's collective beliefs and values more clearly and accurately than any discussion of elite political behavior. Moreover, most of the selections in this reader serve a second function: they describe some facet of a society and illuminate and exemplify the values and beliefs of the observer.

Not all of the selections in *Global Passages*, however, were written by foreigners or travelers. We have included natives' observations as well because they serve to illustrate the different ways that foreigners, travelers, and "insiders" might

view the same or similar cultural phenomena. These writers also had a variety of motivations: entertainment, social commentary, rebuttal of criticism, and justification of their socioeconomic systems. When reading both types of accounts, students should keep in mind the authors' motivations, backgrounds, and prejudices.

While most of the readings in this collection are non-fiction, in a few cases we have incorporated literary materials that are especially effective in conveying cultural values or perspectives. In addition to literary materials and narrative accounts, *Global Passages* includes illustrations. We have used these sources especially for societies that have left no written sources, or whose writings were strictly political in nature (e.g., Mayan, Andean, and early sub-Saharan African), as illustrations provide the best evidence of social values and belief systems.

ORGANIZATION

The two volumes of *Global Passages* are divided into three chronological sections. Only Part I of Volume I, "Foundations of Civilization," departs somewhat from this organizational principle. Focusing on the religious and philosophical beliefs of peoples at early stages of their development, the myths, legends, and travel accounts in Part I illustrate time periods ranging from the twenty-first century B.C.E. to the twentieth century C.E. Parts II and III of Volume I, however, adhere to specific chronological divisions: "Classical Civilizations, 800 B.C.E.–800 C.E.," and "Expanding Civilizations, 800–1550." In Part II, selections describe well-established civilizations that instituted distinct patterns of life that prevailed for at least a millennium, and in many cases, longer. In Part III, selections document changes that civilizations experienced primarily in response to increasing intercultural contacts, especially overland ones. The theme of contact is continued in Volume II, which opens with "The Early Modern World, 1500–1800." In Part I, sources reveal that maritime exploration laid the foundation for the global civilization in which we live today—by 1800 the peoples of the earth had a thorough knowledge of the size of the planet, its major bodies of water and land masses, and its diverse inhabitants. Part II of Volume II, "On the Eve of Modernity, 1800–1918," illustrates the rapid increase in contact among the earth's peoples that followed; and Part III, "Toward the Contemporary World, 1918 to the Present," brings even previously isolated areas into a mutually dependent global network. Finally, each of the chronological sections in both volumes has been further subdivided by region. These are Africa, the Americas and Oceania, East and Southeast Asia, South and Southwest Asia, and Europe.

LEARNING AIDS

In addition to the selections themselves, *Global Passages* includes a number of learning aids. There is an introduction to each Part, Chapter, and selection in these volumes as well as suggested discussion questions for each selection and an annotated list of relevant websites for further investigation at the end of each volume. Our introductions to the individual selections vary in length according to the nature and complexity of each source. We have tried to provide enough context to facilitate understanding but also to avoid furnishing the very ideas that classroom discussion and debate should themselves elicit. Some selections include bracketed editorial definitions or explanations, our own footnotes (indicated by symbols, for example, *, †), or footnotes from the original edited source (indicated by number). The date cited for any selection is that of its actual composition; when that cannot be ascertained, we have used the date of the publication of the work from which the selection was taken. Although limited by the need to include selections in the English language, we have chosen narratives from a variety of fields, languages, and periods of time. Unless specifically noted, we have not attempted to modernize spelling, syntax, or punctuation.

ACKNOWLEDGMENTS

Any work of such a broad scope usually necessitates expert advice. *Global Passages* is no exception. Among our colleagues in the Department of History at Washington State University, we thank Lydia Gerber, Candice Goucher, Thomas Kennedy, John Kicza, Thomas Pesek, Robert Staab, Heather Streets, Orlan Svingen, Marina Tolmacheva, Richard Williams, and Baodi Zhou. From Washington State University's Department of Anthropology we thank Peter Mehringer, and formerly from the Libraries we thank Mary Jane Engh. From Houghton Mifflin we thank Peter Atwood (for encouragement at an early stage), Nancy Blaine, Julie Dunn, and Ylang Nguyen. Finally, we thank the following reviewers for their helpful comments and suggestions: Deborah D. Buffton, University of Wisconsin-LaCrosse; Timothy Coates, College of Charleston; Joan L. Coffey, Sam Houston State University; Anna Dronzek, University of Minnesota-Morris; Bruce Garver, University of Nebraska-Omaha; Mary Halavais, Sonoma State University; William V. Hudon, Bloomsburg University; David M. Kalivas, Middlesex Community College; Joy Kammerling, Eastern Illinois University; Donald L. Layton, Indiana State University; Matthew Lenoe, Assumption College; Mark W. McLeod, University of Delaware; Robert J. Rowland, Jr., Loyola University; Peter von Sivers, University of Utah; Anthony J. Steinhoff, University of Tennessee-Chattanooga; and Alexander Zukas, National University.

Map Index

(continued at top of next column)

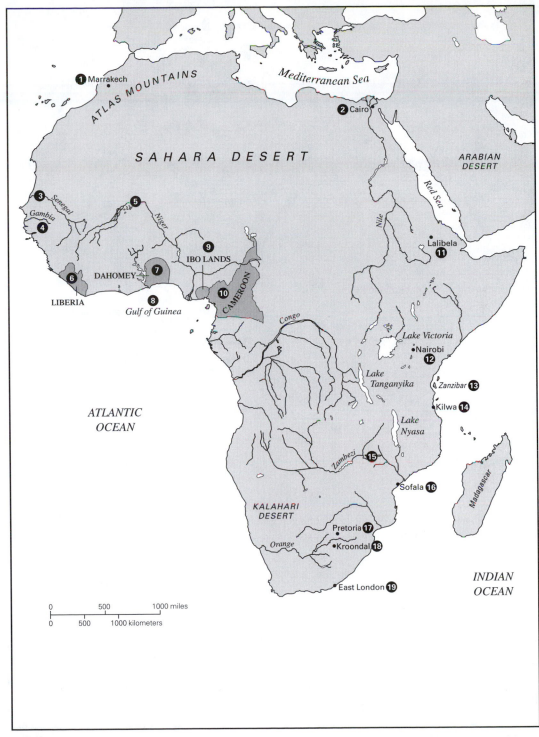

AFRICA

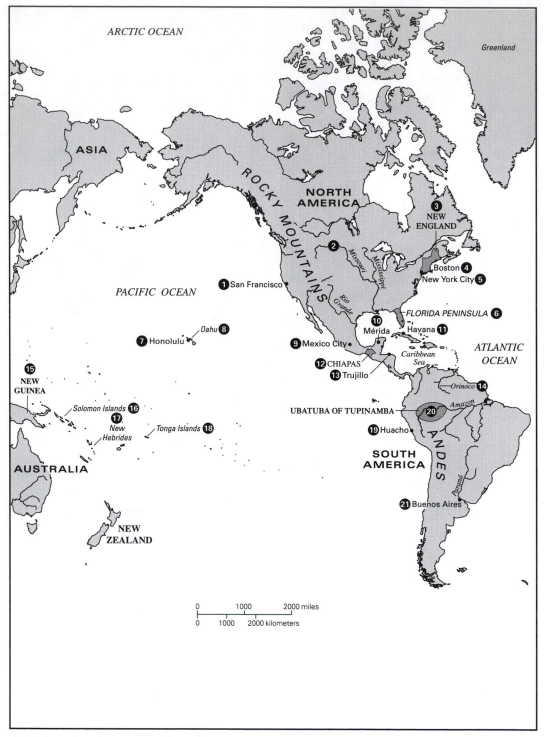

AMERICAS AND OCEANIA

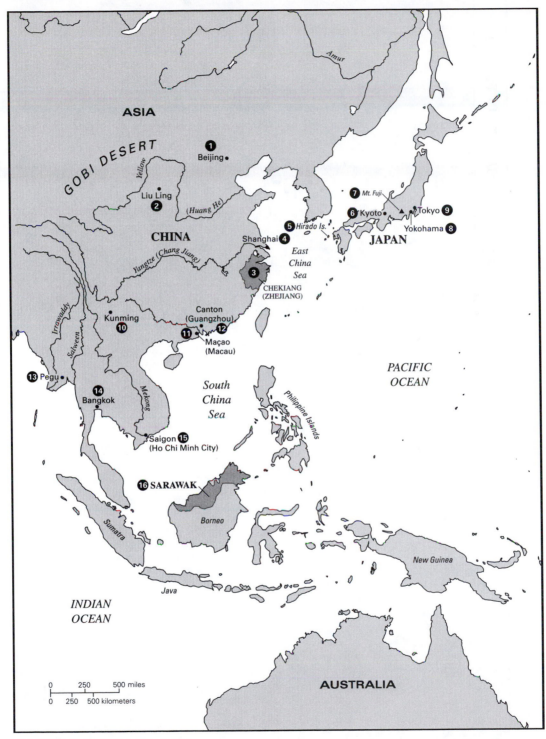

EAST/SOUTHEAST ASIA

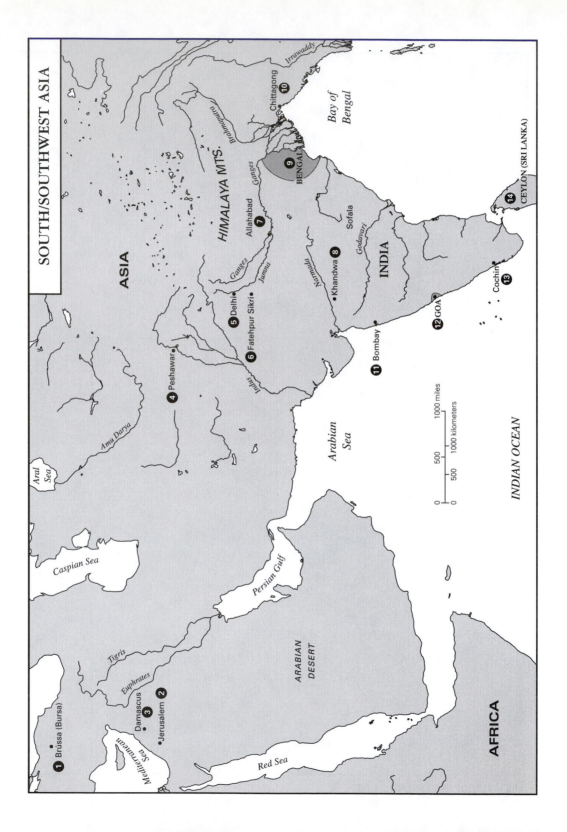

SOUTH/SOUTHWEST ASIA

ASIA

AFRICA

INDIA

HIMALAYA MTS.

Aral Sea

Caspian Sea

Mediterranean Sea

Red Sea

Persian Gulf

Arabian Sea

INDIAN OCEAN

Bay of Bengal

ARABIAN DESERT

Tigris

Euphrates

Amu Darya

Indus

Ganges

Ganges

Jumna

Narmada

Godavari

Brahmaputra

Irrawaddy

Sofala

1 Brússa (Bursa)

2 Jerusalem

3 Damascus

4 Peshawar

5 Delhi

6 Fatehpur Sikri

7 Allahabad

8 Khandwa

9 BENGAL

10 Chittagong

11 Bombay

12 GOA

13 Cochin

14 CEYLON (SRI LANKA)

0   500   1000 miles

0   500   1000 kilometers

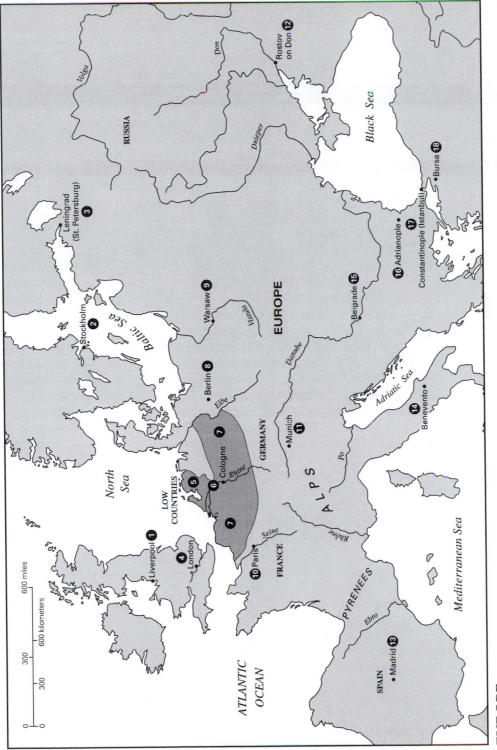

EUROPE

Part I

The Early Modern World, 1500–1800

The three centuries following the turn of the sixteenth century witnessed fundamental changes in all areas of human activity. Perhaps the most important of these was increased contact among the peoples of the earth. Improvements in technology—especially in shipbuilding, navigation, and cartography—enabled Europeans in particular to travel to, explore, and exploit areas that were previously difficult (or in the case of the Americas, impossible) to reach by overland routes. Thus the interdependence of various countries, the salient feature of modern society, actually began in the period covered in Part I.

A second notable theme for this time period is the rise of Europe to a position of economic and political dominance. At least one historian has explained this phenomenon by arguing that the relatively small European states were in constant competition with one another, whereas the large Chinese, Mughal, and Persian Empires faced no challenges to their hegemony. Believing they were culturally superior (as they may well have been), each of these empires demonstrated little or no interest in lands beyond their spheres of influence. On the other hand, Europeans manifested an unprecedented interest in other civilizations. For example, although the Mughal emperor Akbar entertained English envoys and visitors, he exhibited no inclination whatsoever to send representatives in return to the court of Queen Elizabeth I.

The Europeans who visited Akbar and the heads of other major Asian states usually were motivated by commercial, personal, and/or religious objectives—and the new technologies facilitated their aspirations. The creation of large-scale merchant associations in both the East and West Indies by the leading European powers (for example, the Netherlands and its Dutch East India Company) testifies to the importance that individuals and government officials placed on commerce. Not only were great fortunes and reputations made, but some Europeans found their foreign experiences stimulating and exhilarating. For example, the German physician Engelbert Kämpfer simply had adventure in mind when he traveled to Persia, Java, and Japan. Finally, both Catholic and Protestant missionaries hoped to make converts and spread Western values and beliefs in Asia, Africa, and the Americas. Typically Westerners had an arrogant, condescending, and condemnatory attitude toward the people they encountered.

Thus, the process of interaction came at a high price for the people of Africa, Asia, and the Americas. In the Americas and the Caribbean, millions of natives lost their lives as a result of contact with Europeans. American Indians also lost much of their culture. Because zealous missionaries destroyed records of native culture and religion, scholars like Diego Durán had to labor to restore native traditions and histories.

In Asia the threat posed by Western ideas may have been more subtle, but it still elicited the hostility and suspicion of the ruling elite. Toyotomi Hideyoshi clearly believed that Christianity was a subversive and dangerous ideology. Indeed, as a result of this fear, foreigners were either prohibited from entering Japan or, in the case of the Dutch, were confined to a small area in Nagasaki harbor; native converts to Christianity were massacred. In Africa, the most obvious consequence of the encounter with Europeans was the Atlantic slave trade. For example, J. Crassons de Medeuil and Olaudah Equiano provide detailed information about this reprehensible practice.

Not only did Europeans try to export their values to other areas, but they also had trouble dealing with each other. Their differences were exacerbated by religious, national and political, and cultural variations. The arrogant Englishman Thomas Coryat, who traveled with the express purpose of experiencing other cultures, nevertheless failed to appreciate the values of other Europeans. Europeans who shared the same religion sometimes were no better. Antonio de Beatis, an Italian cleric, found the Catholic French to be considerably less cultured than they claimed. His attitude may be best described by the phrase "condescendingly amused."

Part I considers events from the Age of Exploration to the end of the pre–industrial world, a period that lasted from approximately 1500 to 1800. Although the choice of these dates may appear to be Eurocentric, in fact they both have worldwide significance. Columbus's encounter with America and the voyages of exploration that followed in his wake changed the history of the world and certainly transformed the lives of millions of people, as the selections that follow demonstrate. Part I ends just before the spread of the Industrial Revolution from England to other parts of the globe. This event likewise changed the lives of people all over the world, and its impact will be illustrated in the selections that constitute Parts II and III of this volume.

1

East and Southeast Asia, 1500–1800

On the heels of the explorers came merchants and missionaries. Although earlier Europeans had traveled (see selections in the first volume of this reader), Asia, especially eastern Asia, was an almost entirely new experience for most Westerners. Their intrusions were usually received with disquiet and suspicion, as is aptly shown in Toyotomi Hideyoshi's letter to the Portuguese viceroy at Goa. Even native merchants, let alone foreign ones, were often resented, as can be seen from Chang Han's essay.

The foreign travelers' accounts in this chapter predominantly deal with China. There are several reasons for this imbalance. China was physically much larger than Japan and more accessible geographically, and internal security was of greater concern in the much more compact area of Japan than in the hugeness of China. Although some places were off limits to foreigners, in general foreigners could roam much of the vastness of China relatively unobserved. In contrast, the island nation of Japan was not amenable to foreigners, particularly after what its rulers considered a very bad experience with Christianity. Indeed, Toyotomi Hideyoshi's letter shows that Christianity came to be viewed as subversive. The merchant François Caron was an exception for a while, but eventually even he was banished from Japan. Englebert Kämpfer, a physician attached to the Dutch embassy, also had some access to Japanese subjects and produced a history from private interviews. But most of the following accounts deal with China. Martin de la Herrada (in the account by Juan Gonzalez de Mendoza) was a Roman Catholic missionary eager to convert the Chinese. He even contemplated posing as a slave in order to gain entrance into China.

Other accounts deal with East Asia. John Bell, a physician, diplomat, and merchant, was one of the better travel authors in early modern times, providing entertainment and objective reporting to Western readers. In contrast, the observations of Fray Manrique in Arakan (upper Burma or Myanmar) are loaded with condemnatory and pejorative value judgments. At the end of the period, 1793–1794, a diplomat, George Macartney, expressed respect and genuine interest in China. Like Bell, Macartney also knew what he was writing about, and his observations were well informed.

A Chinese Official Criticizes Commercial Practices in His Native Land (1580)

CHANG HAN, *Essay on Merchants*

Traditional societies—even modern societies for that matter—have often been suspicious of merchants. Japan considered them lowly, China considered them unproductive (being mere traders, not producers), and the Aryans in ancient India ranked them below priests and guardians or warriors.

From 1279 to 1368 China had been under the influence of the Mongol Yuan dynasty, viewed by the Chinese as an alien dynasty. The Ming dynasty, which replaced the Yuan, was founded by a man of peasant descent in a period of famine and disorder. The first Ming emperor ruled ruthlessly. When order was restored, so was bureaucracy, but there was a break with past tradition. Old values were challenged, wealth became more important, and commercialism flourished. With stability came arts and crafts and an appreciation for the finer things in life. As in Europe (such as during the Renaissance in Florence), merchants and commerce made it all possible.

However, Confucian ideals deprecated the motives of merchants and the transactions of commerce. This age-old distrust may well have energized the Communist revolution of the twentieth century; yet the Chinese today seem to be returning to, perhaps rediscovering, the need for merchants. Historically, as today, the general attitude seemed to be ambivalence: merchants and commerce may be necessary, unfortunately, but they are suspect. There is resentment, as the author of this selection puts it, toward "merchants {who} eat fine food and wear elegant clothes." "The foot peddler, the cart peddler, and the shopkeeper" are also mistrusted.

In the following selection, a government official—Chang Han, 1511–1593—who is heir to a merchant family's fortune, makes some acute observations and expresses some reservations about commerce as it was then practiced. Yet although he raises concerns, he does not suggest anything but minor corrective measures, and it is unclear if he even deems any to be necessary. How to control commerce—that is the question—and, as today, there is no clear answer. Han's writings also mention salt and tea as important commodities. Well after this date, the British, especially in India, were to find these same items extremely troublesome.

ESSAY ON MERCHANTS

Money and profit are of great importance to men. They seek profit, then suffer by it, yet they cannot forget it. They exhaust their bodies and spirits, run day and night, yet they still regard what they have gained as insufficient. . . .

Those who become merchants eat fine food and wear elegant clothes. They ride on beautifully caparisoned, double-harnessed horses—dust flying as they race through the streets and the horses' precious sweat falling like rain. Opportunistic persons attracted by their wealth offer to serve them. Pretty girls in beautiful long-sleeved dresses and delicate slippers play string and wind instruments for them and compete to please them.

Merchants boast that their wisdom and ability are such as to give them a free hand in affairs. They believe that they know all the possible transformations in the universe and therefore can calculate all the changes in the human world, and that the rise and fall of prices are under their command. They are confident that they will not make one mistake in a hundred in their calculations. These merchants do not know how insignificant their wisdom and ability really are. As the *Chuang Tzu* says: "Great understanding is broad and unhurried; little understanding is cramped and busy."

Because I have traveled to many places during my career as an official, I am familiar with commercial activities and business conditions in various places. The capital is located in an area with mountains at its back and a great plain stretching in front. The region is rich in millet, grain, donkeys, horses, fruit, and vegetables, and has become a center where goods from distant places are brought. Those who engage in commerce, including the foot peddler, the cart peddler, and the shopkeeper, display not only clothing and fresh foods from the fields but also numerous luxury items such as priceless jade from K'un-lun, pearls from the island of Hainan, gold from Yunnan, and coral from Vietnam. These precious items, coming from the mountains or the sea, are not found in central China. But people in remote areas and in other countries, unafraid of the dangers and difficulties of travel, transport these items step by step to the capital, making it the most prosperous place in the empire. . . .

South of the capital is the province of Honan, which is the center of the empire. Going from K'ai-feng, its capital, northwards to Wei-chung, one can reach the Yangtze and Han rivers. Thus, K'ai-feng is a great transportation center; one can travel by either boat or carriage from this spot to all other places, which makes it a favorite gathering place for merchants. The area is rich in lacquer, hemp, sackcloth, fine linen, fine gloss silk, wax, and leather. In antiquity, the Chou dynasty had its capital here. The land is broad and flat, the people are rich and prosperous, and the customs are refined and frugal. . . .

In general, in the Southeast area the greatest profits are to be had from fine gauze, then silk, cheap silk, and sackcloth. San-wu in particular is famous for them. My ancestors' fortunes were based solely on such textile businesses. At the present time, a great many people in San-wu have become wealthy from the textile industry.

In the nation's Northwest, profits are greatest in wool, coarse woolen serge, felt, and fur garments. Kuan-chung is especially famous for these items. There is a family named Chang in that area which has engaged in the animal-breeding business generation after generation. They claim to have 10,000 sheep. Their animal-breeding enterprise is the largest in the Northwest and has made them the richest family in

the area. In the surrounding areas of Yen, Chou, Ch'i, and Chin, many other people have also become rich from animal breeding. From there, merchants seeking great profits go west to Szechwan and south to Kwangtung. Because of the nature of the special products from the latter area—fine and second-grade pearls, gold, jade, and precious woods—profits can be five- or tenfold or more.

The profits from the tea and salt trades are especially great but only large-scale merchants can undertake these businesses. Furthermore, there are government regulations on their distribution, which prohibit the sale of tea in the Northwest and salt in the Southeast. Since tea is produced primarily in the Southeast, prohibiting its sale to the non-Chinese on the northern border is wise and can be enforced. Selling privately produced salt where it is manufactured is also prohibited. This law is rigidly applied to all areas where salt was produced during the Ming dynasty. Yet there are so many private salt producers there now that the regulation seems too rigid and is hard to enforce.

Profits from selling tea and the officials' income from the tea tax are usually ten to twenty percent of the original investment. By contrast, merchants' profits from selling salt and the officials' income from the salt tax can reach seventy to eighty percent of the original invested capital. In either case, the more the invested capital, the greater the profit; the less the invested capital, the less the profit. The profits from selling tea and salt enrich the nation as well as the merchants. Skillful merchants can make great profits for themselves while the inept ones suffer losses. This is the present state of the tea and salt business.

In our Chekiang province it appears that most of the rich gain their wealth from engaging in salt trade. But the Chia family in Wuling became rich from selling tea and have sustained their prosperity for generations. The "Book of Chou" says: "If farmers do not work, there will be an insufficiency of food; if craftsmen do not work, there will be an insufficiency of tools; if merchants do not work, circulation of the three necessities will be cut off, which will cause food and materials to be insufficient."

As to the foreign trade on the northwestern frontier and the foreign sea trade in the Southeast, if we compare their advantages and disadvantages with respect to our nation's wealth and the people's well-being, we will discover that they are as different as black and white. But those who are in charge of state economic matters know only the benefits of the Northwest trade, ignoring the benefits of the sea trade. How can they be so blind?

In the early years of the frontier trade, China traded sackcloth and copper cash to the foreigners. Now we use silk and gold but the foreigners repay us only with thin horses. When we exchanged sackcloth and copper cash for their thin horses, the advantage of the trade was still with China and our national wealth was not endangered. But now we give away gold and silk, and the gold, at least, will never come back to us once it flows into foreign lands. Moreover, to use the silk that China needs for people's clothing to exchange for useless, inferior horses is clearly unwise.

Foreigners are recalcitrant and their greed knows no bounds. At the present time our nation spends over one million cash yearly from our treasury on these foreigners, still we cannot rid ourselves of their demands. What is more, the greedy heart is unpredictable. If one day they break the treaties and invade our frontiers, who will be able to defend us against them? I do not think our present trade with them will ensure us a century of peace.

As to the foreigners in the Southeast, their goods are useful to us just as ours are to them. To use what one has to exchange for what one does not have is what trade is all about. Moreover, these foreigners trade with China under the name of tributary contributions. That means China's authority is established and the foreigners are submissive. Even if the gifts we grant them are great and the tribute they send us is small, our expense is still less than one ten-thousandth of the benefit we gain from trading with them. Moreover, the Southeast sea foreigners are more

concerned with trading with China than with gaining gifts from China. Even if they send a large tribute offering only to receive small gifts in return, they will still be content. In addition, trading with them can enrich our people. So why do we refrain from the trade?

Some people may say that the Southeast sea foreigners have invaded us several times so they are not the kind of people with whom we should trade. But they should realize that the Southeast sea foreigners need Chinese goods and the Chinese need their goods. If we prohibit the natural flow of this merchandise, how can we prevent them from invading us? I believe that if the sea trade were opened, the trouble with foreign pirates would cease. These Southeast sea foreigners are simple people, not to be compared to the unpredictable Northeast sea foreigners. Moreover, China's exports in the Northwest trade come from the national treasury. Whereas the Northwest foreign trade ensures only harm, the sea trade provides us with only gain. How could those in charge of the government fail to realize this?

Turning to the taxes levied on Chinese merchants, though these taxes are needed to fill the national treasury, excessive exploitation should be prohibited. Merchants from all areas are ordered to stop their carts and boats and have their bags and cases examined whenever they pass through a road or river checkpoint. Often the cargoes are overestimated and thus a falsely high duty is demanded. Usually merchants are taxed when they enter the checkpoint and are taxed again at the marketplace. When a piece of goods is taxed once, the merchant can still make some profit while complying with the state's regulations. But today's merchants often are stopped on the road for additional payments and also suffer extortions from the clerks. Such exploitation is hard and bitter enough but, in addition, the merchants are taxed twice. How can they avoid becoming more and more impoverished?

When I was Vice-President of the Board of Public Works in Nanking, I was also in charge of the customs duties on the upper and lower streams of the Black Dragon River. At that time

I was working with Imperial Censor Fang K'o-yung. I told him: "In antiquity, taxes on merchants were in the form of voluntary contributions based on official hints, not through levies. Levying taxes on merchants is a bad policy. We should tax people according to their degree of wealth or poverty. Who says we cannot have good government!" Fang agreed with me, so we lowered the taxes on the merchants some twenty percent. After the taxes were lowered, merchants became willing to stop at the checkpoints. All boats stop when they should and the total tax income received from merchants increased fifty percent. From this example one can see that the people can be moved by benevolent policies.

REVIEW QUESTIONS

1. What do you find timeless (or at least contemporary) about the author's concerns?
2. How would you characterize Chang Han's attitude toward merchants? Is he personally antagonistic toward them?
3. Does Chang Han have a complaint about the accumulation of wealth? What might such an accumulation do to society?
4. How much did Han rely on the government bureaucracy to correct the problems that he saw? Was he realistic?
5. Why do you think a scion of a merchant family would write such an essay?

A Spanish Missionary Collects Observations of Chinese Society (1580s)

Juan Gonzalez de Mendoza, *The History of the Great and Mighty Kingdom of China*

The History of the Great and Mighty Kingdom of China by Juan Gonzalez de Mendoza (1550–1620) had a curious genesis. In 1574, the Spanish governor-general of the Philippines, Lopez de Legaspi, met with a Chinese official and took advantage of what he thought was a good opportunity to introduce Christianity to China. He chose Martín de la Herrada, or de Rada, to lead the mission. This turned out to be an excellent choice. Rada, a dedicated missionary, had already studied the Chinese language and at one point had even asked (without success) some Chinese merchants he encountered in the Philippines to take him to China as a slave so he could begin his work. The group under de Rada's leadership landed in China in July 1575. The mission, however, failed, and de Rada's group left China only two months later. The Chinese captain who took them back to the Philippines, and who had learned the main points of Christian theology from his passengers, said that they would easily succeed in converting the Chinese if they could first win over the emperor, by means of an embassy sent to him by the king of Spain.

De Rada, prevented from preaching in China, spent his time there collecting Chinese books, visiting pagodas, and composing a vocabulary of the Chinese language. He also wrote a brief account of his voyage, which was presented to King Philip II in 1576. Philip then nominated three ambassadors, including Juan Gonzalez de Mendoza, to go to Mexico to plan the next missionary expedition to China and to collect suitable presents for Chinese leaders. This embassy did not depart from Mexico until 1584. At this point, Mendoza decided to collect the various accounts of Portuguese and Spanish priests who had been to China and publish them together in one volume. His work was well received and quickly went through several editions and translations. Following an English translation of Marco Polo's *Travels* in 1579, it is the first detailed account of China to be published in English. As a reward for his service to the church, Mendoza received several important ecclesiastical positions in Mexico.

Manie things of great gouernment hath beene and shall be declared in this historie worthy to be considered: and in my opinion, this is not the least that is contained in this chapter, which is such order as the king and his counsell hath giuen, that the poore may not go a begging in the streetes, nor in the temples whereas they make orations vnto their idols: for the auoiding therof the king hath set downe an order, vpon great and greeuous penaltie to be executed vpon the saide poore, if they do begge or craue in the streetes, and a greater penaltie vpon the citizens or townes men, if they do giue vnto any such that beggeth; but must incontinent go and complaine on them to the justice, who is one that is called the justice of the poore, ordayned to punish such as doo breake the lawe, and is one of the principallest of the citie or towne, and hath no other charge but only this. And for that the townes be great and many, and so full of people, and an infinite nomber of villages, whereas it cannot be chosen but there is many borne lame, and other misfortunes, so that he is not idle, but alwaies occupied in giuing order to remedie the necessities of the poore without breaking of the lawe. This iudge, the first day that hee doth enter into his office, hee commandeth that whatsoeuer children be borne a creeple in any part of his members, or by sicknes be taken lame, or by any other misfortune, that incontinent their fathers or mothers doo giue the iudge to vnderstande thereof, that he may

prouide for all things necessarie, according vnto the ordinance and will of the king and his counsell; the which is, the man child or woman child, being brought before him, and seene the default or lacke that it hath, if it be so that with the same it may exercise any occupation, they giue and limit a time vnto the parents, for to teach the child that occupation ordayned by the iudge, and it is such as with their lamenes they may vse without any impediment, the which is accomplished without faile; but if it so be, that his lameness is such that it is impossible to learne or exercise any occupation, this iudge of the poore doth command the father to sustaine and maintaine him in his owne house all the dayes of his life, if that hee hath wherewithall; if not, or that hee is fatherlesse, then the next rich kinsman must maintaine it; if he hath none such, then doth all his parents and kinsfolkes contribute and pay their partes, or giue of such thinges as they haue in their houses. But if it hath no parentes, or they be so poore that they cannot contribute nor supply any part therof; then doth the king maintaine them in verie ample manner of his owne costes in hospitalles, verie sumptuous, that he hath in euerie citie throughout his kingdome for the same effect and purpose: in the same hospitalles are likewise maintayned all such needie and olde men as haue spent all their youth in the wars, and are not able to maintaine themselues: so that to the one and the other is ministered all that is needefull and necessarie, and that with great diligence and care: and for the better accomplishing of the same, the iudge doth put verie good order, and dooth appoint one of the principallest of the citie or towne, to be the administrator, without whose licence, there is not one within that hospitall that can goe foorth of the limittes: for that license is not granted vnto anie, neyther doo they demand it, for that there they are prouided of all thinges necessarie so long as they doo liue, as well for apparell as for victualles. Besides all this, the olde folkes and poore men within the hospitall, doo bring vpp hennes, chickens, and hogges for their owne recreation and profit, wherein they doo delight themselves. The iudge doth visite often times the administrator by him appointed. Likewise the iudge is visited by an other that commeth from the court, by the appointment of the king and the counsell to the same effect: and to visite all such hospitalles as bee in the prouinces limited in his commission, and if they doo finde any that hath not executed his office in right and iustice, then they doo displace them, and punish them verie rigorouslie: by reason

whereof all such officers haue great care of their charges and liue vprightly, hauing before their eyes the straight account which they must giue, and the cruell rewarde if to the contrarie.

The blinde folkes in this countrie are not accounted in the number of those that of necessitie are to bee maintayned by their kinsfolkes, or by the king; for they are constrayned to worke; as to grind with a querne wheate or rice, or to blowe smythes bellowes, or such like occupations, that they haue no neede of their sight. And if it be a blind woman, when she commeth vnto age, she doth vse the office of women of loue, of which sorte there are a great number in publike places, as shall be declared in the chapter for that purpose. These haue women that doo tende vpon them, and doo paint and trim them vp, and they are such that with pure age did leaue that office. So by this order in all this kingdome, although it be great, and the people infinite, yet there is no poore that doo perish nor begge in the streetes, as was apparent vnto the Austen and Barefoote fryers, and the rest that went with them into that countrie.

REVIEW QUESTIONS

1. How did Mendoza judge the treatment of the poor in China? Did he approve or disapprove of Chinese policy? What evidence supports your opinion?
2. Were poor men and women treated differently in China?
3. How did the Chinese authorities expect the poor to help themselves?
4. What does this selection tell you about the role of the family in Chinese life? About the role of the government?

A Scottish Diplomat Visits China in the Service of Russia (1719–1722)

JOHN BELL, *A Journey from St. Petersburg to Pekin*

John Bell (1691–1780) spent much of his life visiting foreign countries. After becoming a physician in his native Scotland, he obtained a recommendation to the chief physician of the Russian czar Peter I (Peter the Great). Bell arrived in Russia in 1714, just in time to join a diplomatic mission to Persia (Iran). Upon his return to St. Petersburg in 1718, he learned that another diplomatic mission was ready to leave for China. Bell used his influence with highly placed Russians to secure a place for himself in this venture. After this second mission ended in January 1722, Bell continued his travels. Only a few months later, he accompanied the czar on an expedition to the city of Derbent, on the western shore of the Caspian Sea. In 1737 he went on a mission to Constantinople (Istanbul), where he resided as a merchant for ten years before returning to Scotland in 1747.

Sixteen years after his return to Scotland, Bell published a two-volume narrative of his journey under the title *Travels from St. Petersburg in Russia to Diverse Parts of Asia* (1763). The book, modeled after Jonathan Swift's *Gulliver's Travels,* was well received. It went through several subsequent English editions (1764, 1788, 1806) and was translated into French in 1766. In 1817 a reviewer in the *Quarterly Review* described Bell's book as "the best model perhaps for travel-writing in the English language." The part of *Travels* that describes his journey to and observations about China, from which the following selection is drawn, made Bell's reputation as an authority on China and as a good storyteller. His vivid accounts of Chinese customs and institutions did much to enlighten Westerners in an age when few of them had traveled to these regions.

It may easily be imagined, that, in so populous a city, there must be many idle persons of both sexes; though, I believe, fewer than in most other cities of the world, even in those of much less extent than that of Pekin. In order to prevent all disorderly practices, as much as possible, the government have thought fit to permit, or connive at, certain places, in the suburbs, for the reception and entertainment of prostitutes, who are maintained by the landlords of the houses in which they dwell; but not allowed to straggle abroad. I have been informed, that these ladies of pleasure have all separate apartments; with the price of each lady, describing, at the same time, her beauties and qualities, written, over the door of her apartment, in fair legible characters; which price is paid directly by the gallant; by which means, these affairs are conducted without noise in the houses, or disturbances in the neighbourhood. Noisy brawls are very seldom, hardly ever, known at Pekin; those who are found offending, in this way, undergo very severe penalties. It is likewise to be observed, that these houses are calculated for the meaner sort of people only; so that any person, who hath the least regard to his credit or reputation, carefully avoids being seen in them.

I must, however, take notice of one shocking and unnatural practice; which appears more extraordinary in a country so well regulated and governed as China. I mean, that of exposing so many new-born infants in the streets. This, indeed, is only done by the poor, who have more wives than they can maintain. To prevent the death of these children, there are publick hospitals appointed for their reception, and people sent out through the streets, every morning, to pick up, and carry thither, such children as they find exposed. The missionaries also send out people to take up such as have been neglected, who are carried to a private hospital, maintained at their charge, and educated in the Christian religion. And of such persons do the greatest part of the Chinese Christians consist.

I shall now make a few remarks upon the ladies, who have many good qualities besides their beauty. They are very cleanly, and modest in their dress. Their eyes are black, and so little, that, when they laugh, you can scarce see them. Their hair is black as jet, and neatly tied up, in a knot, on the crown of the head, adorned with artificial flowers of their own making; which are very becoming. The better sort, who are seldom exposed to the air, have good complexions. Those who are inclined to the olive, take care to add a touch of white and red paint, which they apply very nicely.

The ladies of distinction are seldom permitted to stir abroad, except to visit their nearest relations; and, on these occasions, they are always carried in close chairs, and attended by their servants. The women of all ranks stay pretty much at home. The smallness of their feet, which renders them unable to walk to any considerable distance, makes their confinement less disagreeable. As soon as a girl comes into the world, they bind her tender feet with tight bandages, which are renewed as occasion requires, to prevent their growing. This custom prevails universally, the Tartar ladies, residing in China, only excepted, who appear to have no inclination to conform to this fashion.

This fashion was introduced into China by a great Princess, who lived some ages ago. She was a lady of extraordinary beauty and virtue, and has obtained the reputation of a saint; but, it is reported, her feet resembled those of birds; on which account she kept them always carefully wrapped up, and concealed even from the Emperor her husband. The ladies of the court followed her example; which, of course, soon became general. The Chinese women never pare their nails; but suffer them to grow to the full length. This proves no impediment in embroidery, and other needle-work, in which they are constantly employed. These they finish with extraordinary neatness, as fully appears from some specimens of them brought to Europe.

The Chinese deserve great praise for their patience in finishing, completely, every thing they undertake. And, what is still a greater recommendation, their labours are not the effect of whim or caprice, but calculated to serve some useful purpose. The publick works, about the city of Pekin, are instances of these observations. The streets, in particular, are the finest in the world. They are spacious, neat, and straight. The canals, which supply the city with water, have, at proper distances, commodious stone-bridges over them; and these canals are not only built with free-stone, on the sides, but the bottoms of them paved with broad cut-stones, in the neatest manner imaginable. There are but few springs of soft water in Pekin. And the water, in general, though a little brackish, is by no means unwholesome.

The Chinese are generally of a middle size, and slender make; but very active. They are honest, and observe the strictest honour and justice in their dealings. It must, however, be acknowledged, that not a few of them are much addicted to knavery, and well skilled in the arts of cheating. They have, indeed, found many Europeans as great proficients in that art as themselves. And if you once cheat them, they are sure to retaliate on the first opportunity.

As to the religion of the Chinese, I cannot pretend to give a distinct account of it. According to the best information I could procure, they are divided into several sects; among which, that of the Theists is the most rational and respectable. They worship one God, whom they call Tien, the Heaven or the highest Lord, and pay no religious homage to the images of their countrymen. This sect has subsisted for many ages longer than Christianity, and is still most in vogue; being embraced by the Emperor himself, and most of the grandees, and men of learning. The common people are generally idolaters. The few Jews and Mahometans, residing here, are supposed to have entered China about six or seven hundred years ago, in company with the western Tartars. There is a very inconsiderable sect, called Cross-worshippers. They worship the holy cross; but have lost all other marks of Christianity; which makes it probable the gospel was preached in this country before the arrival of the missionaries; but by whom is uncertain. The Christians, at present, are computed to amount to one hundred thousand, of both sexes. I have been told, the Chinese have also some Atheists among them.

I had several opportunities of talking with their physicians. They, generally, both prepare and administer their own prescriptions, and are very little acquainted with the medicinal system practised in Europe. As they have but few chymical preparations, their chief study is the virtues of plants, which they apply on all occasions, and often with success. They feel the patient's pulse for four or five minutes, and very seldom let blood, even in high fevers. They compare a fever to a boiling pot, and chuse rather to take the fire from it than diminish the quantity of liquor it contains, which would only make it boil the faster. Bathing and cupping are much practised; and they even apply fire in some cases, particularly for pains in the joints, and gouty disorders. On these occasions they apply a lighted match, composed of the downy substance that grows on mugwort, to the part affected; which, making a scar, either entirely removes or considerably mitigates the pain.

I cannot but take notice, on this occasion, of a famous plant, called gingsing, which grows in the province of Leotong. The root of this plant is so much esteemed for its physical virtues, that it is gathered by people, appointed by the Emperor, for this purpose only; and is valued at the rate of about twenty five pounds Sterling the pound weight. It is so rare, that the Emperor sent two pounds of it only in a present to his Czarish Majesty. There are two sorts of it; one looks as if candied; the other like small parsley roots, and has something of the same taste. They slice down or pound it; and, after infusion and slight boiling, give it to the patient. I could never learn from their physicians, what specific qualities this plant possessed, only that it was of universal use. I have heard many stories of strange cures performed by it; that persons, seemingly dead, have, by its means, been restored to health. I believe, indeed, it may be a good restorative plant; but, if it really has any extraordinary virtues, I could never discover them, though I have made many experiments on it, at different times. I should imagine this rare plant might be cultivated, with success, in the country where it grows naturally; and it appears improbable the Chinese would neglect such a sovereign remedy.

The great men in China follow the example of the western Asiatics, in keeping eunuchs to attend them; who are their counsellors, and chief confidants, on all occasions. Their business is to take care of the women; and, being in a manner detached from the world, they are much respected. Castrating is a trade in China; and so skilful and dexterous are the performers that few die under their hands. I knew a man, who, being reduced to low circumstances, sold himself to be made a eunuch, after he was thirty years of age.

REVIEW QUESTIONS

1. What particular features of Chinese society impressed Bell most favorably? Least favorably?
2. How did Bell evaluate the character of Chinese women and their role in society?
3. Do you think Bell had a positive or negative opinion of Chinese religion? How can you tell?
4. Do you think Bell had a positive or negative opinion of Chinese medicine? How can you tell?
5. Why do you think late-eighteenth- or early-nineteenth-century Europeans would find the material in this book interesting?

A British Diplomat Depicts Daily Life in China (1793–1794)

GEORGE MACARTNEY, *An Embassy to China*

George Macartney (1737–1806), a British diplomat, was awarded several titles for his service in Ireland, the Caribbean, India, and southern Africa. In each region he held a high-ranking office. In 1793–1794 he was sent on an embassy to China, during which he kept a journal. The purpose of the embassy was to seek expansion of British trading privileges. These were denied by the Chinese imperial court, which viewed his mission as tributary. He was told that such trading rights as had been granted were considered a favor and that China did not need British trade.

Macartney's observations on various aspects of Chinese life go into considerable detail; they show a depth of interest beyond what one might expect from a British aristocrat of the period. Understandably, the bias for his comparisons is his own culture, yet the entries also reveal a sympathy for the Chinese way of life.

A Chinese family is regulated with the same regard to subordination and economy that is observed in the government of a state; the paternal authority, though unlimited, is usually exercised with kindness and indulgence. In China children are indeed sometimes sold, and infants exposed by the parents, but only in cases of the most hopeless indigence and misery, when they must inevitably perish if kept at home; but where the thread of attachment is not thus snapped asunder by the anguish of the parent, it every day grows stronger and becomes indissoluble for life.

There is nothing more striking in the Chinese character through all ranks than this most respectable union. Affection and duty walk hand in hand and never desire a separation. The fondness of the father is constantly felt and always increasing; the dependence of the son is perfectly understood by him; he never wishes it to be lessened. It is not necessary to coax or to cheat the child into the cutting off an entail, or the charging his inheritance with a mortgage; it is not necessary to importune the father for an irrevocable settlement. According to Chinese ideas, there is but one interest in a family; any other supposition would be unnatural and wicked. An undutiful child is a monster that China does not produce; the son, even after a marriage, continues for the most part to live in the father's house; the labour of the family is thrown into one common stock under the sole management of the parent, after whose death the eldest son often retains the same authority, and continues in the same union with his younger brothers.

The houses of the better sort exhibit a certain show of grandeur and magnificence, and even of taste and elegance in their decorations, but at the same time discover, at least to our eyes, evident marks of discomfort and inconvenience. There is a want of useful furniture. They have indeed lanterns of gauze and paper and horn and diaphanous gum, most beautifully coloured and disposed, and they have tables, couches, and chairs, loosely covered with rich carpeting, with gold and silver damasks, and other silks; but they have no bureaux, commodes, lustres, or looking-glasses; they have no sheets to their beds, neither does their bedding itself seem well adapted or agreeable. They don't undress themselves entirely as we do, when they go to rest, but lay themselves down upon alcoved benches, which are spread with a single mat or thin mattress, and adjusted with small pillows and cushions. Their apartments are not well contrived or distributed, according to our ideas of utility and propriety, having seldom any doors that shut with locks or proper fastenings, but in lieu of them screens and curtains, which are removed or drawn back as occasion requires. In the cold weather they are warmed by flues under the floor, for there are neither stoves, fire-places, nor fire-grates in the rooms; but sometimes braziers filled with charcoal are brought in and occasionally renewed.

The people, even of the first rank, though so fond of dress as to change it usually several times in a day, are yet in their persons and customs frowzy and uncleanly. Their outward garment of ceremony is richly embroidered with silks of different colours (those of the highest class of all with golden dragons), and their common habit it of plain silk, or fine broadcloth; but their drawers and their waistcoats (of which they usually wear several according to the season) are not very frequently shifted. They wear neither knit nor woven stockings, but wrap their legs round with a coarse cotton stuff, over which they have constantly drawn a pair of black satin boots without heels, but with soles nearly an inch in thickness. In summer everybody carries a fan in his hand, and is flirting it incessantly.

They wear but little linen or calico, and what they do wear is extremely coarse and ill washed, soap being never employed by them. They seldom have recourse to pocket handkerchiefs, but spit about the rooms without mercy, blow their noses in their fingers, and wipe them with their sleeves, or upon anything near them. This practice is universal, and what is still more abominable, I one day observed a Tartar of distinction call his servant to hunt in his neck for a louse that was troublesome to him.

At their meals they use no towels, napkins, table-cloths, flat plates, glasses, knives nor forks, but help themselves with their fingers, or with their chopsticks, which are made of wood or ivory, about six inches long, round and smooth,

and not very cleanly. Their meat is served up ready cut in small bowls, each guest having a separate bowl to himself. Seldom above two sit together at the same table, and never above four. They are all foul feeders and eaters of garlic and strong-scented vegetables, and drink mutually out of the same cup which, though sometimes rinsed, is never washed or wiped clean. They use little vinegar, no olive oil, cyder, ale, beer, or grape wine; their chief drink is tea, or liquors distilled or prepared from rice and other vegetables, of different degrees of strength according to their taste, some of which are tolerably agreeable and resemble strong Madeira.

They almost all smoke tobacco and consider it as a compliment to offer each other a whiff of their pipes. They also take snuff, mostly Brazil, but in small quantities, not in that beastly profusion which is often practised in England, even by some of our fine ladies.

They have no water-closets nor proper places of retirement; the necessaries are quite public and open, and the ordure is continually removing from them, which occasions a stench in almost every place one approaches.

They have no wheel-carriages for travelling on a better construction than that of a higler's cart; the best are set upon four clumsy wheels, and drawn by five horses or mules, two abreast in the shafts and three leaders abreast before them. They are without springs, consequently very uneasy. The saddles, bridles and accoutrements of their horses are inelegant and ill-contrived, much heavier than is requisite, and equally inconvenient to the beast and his rider. Although so much prejudiced in favour of their own customs and fashions they could not, after some time, withstand the superiority of ours in a variety of instances. The lightness, neatness, and commodiousness of my post-chaise, in which I travelled to Jehol, they were quite delighted with; but the fearlessness and celerity and safety with which my postilions drove it along almost petrified them with astonishment. The elegance and finishing of our saddles and other parts of horse-furniture particularly struck the Tartars, some of whom I think are likely to adopt them by degrees.

Our knives and forks, spoons, and a thousand little trifles of personal conveniency were singularly acceptable to everybody, and will probably become soon of considerable demand, although the government is certainly averse to all novelties, and wishes to discountenance a taste for any foreign article that is not absolutely necessary; but luxury is stronger than law, and it is the prerogative of wealth to draw from abroad what it can't find at home. One great advantage indeed of the embassy is the opportunity it afforded of showing the Chinese to what a high degree of perfection the English nation had carried all the arts and accomplishments of civilized life; that their manners were calculated for the improvement of social intercourse and liberal commerce; that though great and powerful they were generous and humane, not fierce and impetuous like the Russians, but entitled to the respect and preference of the Chinese above the other European nations, whom they have any knowledge of. This favourable impression of us may be confirmed and improved in them by a continuance of our own attention and cautious conduct. The restriction and discipline of our seamen at Canton are among the proper regulations for this purpose, not to mention some other arrangements that will naturally be made there, in consequence of the ground we now stand upon.

The common people of China are a strong hardy race, patient, industrious, and much given to traffic and all the arts of gain; cheerful and loquacious under the severest labour, and by no means that sedate, tranquil people they have been represented. In their joint efforts and exertions they work with incessant vociferation, often angrily scold one another, and seem ready to proceed to blows, but scarcely ever come to that extremity. The inevitable severity of the law restrains them, for the loss of a life is always punished by the death of the offender, even though he acted merely in self-defence, and without any malice prepense.

Superstitious and suspicious in their temper they at first appeared shy and apprehensive of us, being full of prejudices against strangers, of whose cunning and ferocity a thousand ridiculous tales had been propagated, and perhaps industriously encouraged by the government, whose political system seems to be to endeavour to persuade the people that they are themselves already perfect and can therefore learn nothing from others; but it is to little purpose. A nation that does not advance must retrograde, and finally fall back to barbarism and misery.

REVIEW QUESTIONS

1. How would you describe Macartney's comments on the Chinese family?
2. Macartney's observations are over two hundred years old; how are they similar to or different from what a modern traveler might see?
3. What characteristics of Chinese life does Macartney disapprove of? Do you think he is fair? Why or why not?
4. Compare Macartney's account of Chinese life with that of Juan Gonzalez de Mendoza. What are the most significant similarities and differences?

A Japanese Ruler Criticizes European Attitudes (1591)

TOYOTOMI HIDEYOSHI, *Letter to the Viceroy of the Indies*

Toyotomi Hideyoshi (1536–1598) was the second in a succession of three strong men who united Japan. He rose from being a peasant to become the foremost general under Oda Nobunaga (1534–1582), a ruthless warlord who virtually eliminated all of his opposition. After Oda's death, Hideyoshi (who had grown up without a surname, hence is generally referred to as Hideyoshi) gained nominal control of Japan. He was not strong enough to eliminate the *daimyo,* or local feudal lords, but he did take control of the government and reorganized it.

The following selection reveals two of Hideyoshi's principal concerns: conquering Korea and China, and suppressing foreign influence in Japan. Regarding the former, the Japanese invaded Korea in 1592, but their lines of supply proved inadequate; they invaded again in 1597 but withdrew on the news of Hideyoshi's death. Imperial ambitions then became dormant until the end of the nineteenth century.

Perhaps because they were insular, the Japanese frequently exhibited distrust and hostility toward foreigners. Their contact had been slight and probably only with other East Asians. Thus Europeans constituted a new experience. The Portuguese reached Japan in 1543, and six years later the Jesuit missionary Francis Xavier arrived. Almost immediately concern arose about the role and purpose of Christianity, which soon became viewed as a tool of subversion. Hideyoshi, as the beginning of the letter shows, had problems with internal security and was trying to impose his hegemony on the country. He came to view Christianity as a political threat. As is also expressed in the letter, he had serious religious reservations about Christianity, which—in contrast to Confucianism, Buddhism, and Shinto—must have repelled him by its exclusivity and absolutism.

The letter is dated 1591. In 1597 Hideyoshi wrote a similar letter to the governor-general of the Philippines. Also in 1597 the Japanese government started persecuting Christians, vigorously so in 1614, with executions of missionaries and converts in 1622. The Japanese people were required to disavow Christianity, and in 1635 an edict prohibited Japanese from going abroad. Spaniards and Portuguese were excluded from Japan in 1624 and 1637, respectively. Then, in 1641, trade was restricted to the Chinese and the Dutch, and that only in Nagasaki harbor. This prohibition followed the execution in 1640 of Portuguese from a mission on Macao who were seeking reversal of the exclusionary policy. The "closed door" policy was in effect until the forced "opening of Japan" by U.S. Commodore Matthew Perry in 1853. Thus the following letter is of great historical significance. It expresses an early dislike of European intentions and uncanny foresight about later European imperialism.

LETTER TO THE VICEROY OF THE INDIES

Reading your message from afar, I can appreciate the immense expanse of water which separates us. As you have noted in your letter, my country, which is comprised of sixty-odd provinces, has known for many years more days of disorder than days of peace; rowdies have been given to fomenting intrigue, and bands of warriors have formed cliques to defy the court's orders. Ever since my youth, I have been constantly concerned over this deplorable situation. I studied the art of self-cultivation and the secret of governing the country. Through profound planning and forethought, and according to the three principles of benevolence, wisdom, and courage, I cared for the warriors on the one hand and looked after the common people on the other; while administering justice, I was able to establish security. Thus, before many years had passed, the unity of the nation was set on a firm foundation, and now foreign nations, far and near, without exception, bring tribute to us. Everyone, everywhere, seeks to obey my orders. . . . Though our own country is now safe and secure, I nevertheless entertain hopes of ruling the great Ming nation. I can reach the Middle Kingdom aboard my palaceship within a short time. It will be as easy as pointing to the palm of my hand. I shall then use the occasion to visit your country regardless of the distance or the differences between us.

Ours is the land of the Gods, and God is mind. Everything in nature comes into existence because of mind. Without God there can be no spirituality. Without God there can be no way. God rules in times of prosperity as in times of decline. God is positive and negative and unfathomable. Thus, God is the root and source of all existence. This God is spoken of by Buddhism in India, Confucianism in China, and Shinto in Japan. To know Shinto is to know Buddhism as well as Confucianism.

As long as man lives in this world, Humanity will be a basic principle. Were it not for Humanity and Righteousness, the sovereign would not be a sovereign, nor a minister of state a minister. It is through the practice of Humanity and Righteousness that the foundations of our relationships between sovereign and minister, parent and child, and husband and wife are established. If you are interested in the profound philosophy of God and Buddha, request an explanation and it will be given to you. In your land one doctrine is taught to the exclusion of others, and you are not yet informed of the [Confucian] philosophy of Humanity and Righteousness. Thus there is no respect for God and Buddha and no distinction between sovereign and ministers. Through heresies you intend to destroy the righteous law. Hereafter, do not expound, in ignorance of right and wrong, unreasonable and wanton doctrines. A few years ago the so-called Fathers came to my country seeking to bewitch our men and women, both of the laity and clergy. At that time punishment was administered to them, and it will be repeated if they should return to our domain to propagate their faith. It will not matter what sect or denomination they represent—they shall be destroyed. It will then be too late to repent. If you entertain any desire of establishing amity with this land, the seas have been rid of the pirate menace, and merchants are permitted to come and go. Remember this.

As for the products of the south-land, acknowledgment of their receipt is here made, as itemized. The catalogue of gifts which we tender is presented on a separate paper. The rest will be explained orally by my envoy.

REVIEW QUESTIONS

1. In what ways does the letter express Hideyoshi's concerns about internal security?
2. Although the term *Christianity* does not appear in the selection, in what ways

does Hideyoshi express his distrust and disdain for Christianity as experienced in Japan?

3. How does Hideyoshi describe Japanese religious attitudes as inclusive and Christianity as exclusive?

A French Employee of the Dutch East India Company Describes Japanese Family Customs (1619–1641)

FRANÇOIS CARON, *A True Description of the Mighty Kingdoms of Japan and Siam*

Very few Europeans went to or were allowed into Japan before 1853. Those who did enter the country experienced a culture that was so different from their own that they were amazed; it was literally the other end of the world for Europeans. Likewise, the Japanese found Europeans to be strange: self-absorbed, self-assured, and self-centered to the point of arrogance. The difference was that the Europeans were trying to exploit the Japanese—and not vice-versa.

François Caron (1600–1673), originally a cook's assistant in the Dutch East India Company, worked at a Japanese trading post from 1619 to 1641. In 1639 he became director, only to be banished by the shogunate two years later. Nevertheless, he continued to hold key positions in the company. Caron's family were Huguenots who had fled France to avoid persecution; yet he ended his career as a director of the French East India Company. The following description shows his ability to notice details of Japanese homes and hospitality, as well as of Japanese social patterns.

HOW THIS NATION LIVES IN THEIR HOUSES AND FAMILIES

All the houses in this Country are built of wood and timber, which is likewise their fewel; hence their houses are much subject to burning, one of the plagues very frequent in their Towns; for this cause each house hath its pack-house of proof against the fire, wherein they keep their best and choice goods. The houses are all built four foot high from the earth, made of planks closely covered with thick mats very artificially joyned, resembling each other and uniform; they dwell most below, their upper rooms being employed to keep their smaller household stuffs; but their best Chambers, where they receive and entertain their Friends, are neat and sumptuous, according to their several abilities. The Souldiers and Gentry have their houses divided, one side for their Wives, and the other for them, for their Friends and their ordinary vocation. The Marchants and Citizens Wives dwell promiscuously with their Husbands, governing and ordering their families as with us; but are very modest, and never spoken to but with respect, none presuming to use any freedom in discourse with them, although otherwise innocent and harmless, for both the man that took, and the woman that permitted this familiarity would be equally slighted, and blamed and looked upon as culpable and scandalous. Their household-stuff consists ordinarily in fine painted gilt dishes, instead of pictures; the walls of their chambers are also for the most part painted with variety of figures, and laid with gilt paper so curiously, as if it were but one large sheet; the boards round about being beautified with lists of black Wax, very artificially wrought; most of their rooms are divided with shuts, prepared and painted as the walls are, which being taken out, enlarges the rooms at pleasure. In the upper end of this partition they have a picture with a pot full of flowers, which they have ready all the year long; and at the lower end there is alwaies a gallery, with stairs to descend into their gardens, which are alwaies green, and so placed, that they in the hall have the full prospect of it. They do not furnish and adorn their Houses with Chests, Cupboards, Wax-works, and the like, these are alwaies in their free-Chambers, or pack-houses, where none is suffered to enter, but their familiar and most intimate Servants and Friends. Their chief furniture which they expose, are *Tsia* Cups and Pots, Pictures, Manuscripts, and Sables, which each provides himself of, rich and goodly, according to his condition and might.

HOW THEY RECEIVE EACH OTHER, AND OF THEIR HOSPITALITY

The Japanners are very hospitable and civil to such as visit them, they treat them with Tobacco and with *Tsia,* and if the friend be more then ordinary, with Wine: They cause them first to sit down, and setting a Lack bowl before them, will not suffer them to depart before they have tasted of it; they sing, they pipe, and play upon such stringed instruments as they have, to rejoyce their Guests, omitting no manner of carouses and kindnesses to testifie their welcome, and the value they put upon their conversation. They never quarrel in their debauches, but he that is first drunk retires and sleeps, until the fumes of

the wine be evaporated. There is no such thing as Tavern or publick drinking House in all the Countrie; they eat, drink and are merry, but all in their own houses, not refusing lodging and refreshment for the traveller and stranger.

OF THEIR CONJUGAL STATE

These People neither make love nor woo, all their marriages being concluded by their Parents, or for want of such near relations, by the next of kin. One Man hath but one Wife, though as many Concubines as he can keep; and if that Wife do not please him, he may put her away, provided he dismiss her in a civil and honorable way. Any Man may lie with a Whore, or common Woman, although he be married, with impunitie; but the Wife may not so much as speak in private with another Man, as is already said, without hazarding her life. What is said of divorce, relates only to the Citizen, Marchant and common Souldier; a Gentleman or Lord may not put away his Wife, although she should not please him, and that out of respect to her quality and his own Person; he must maintain her according to her condition and necessities; but may freely divert himself with his Concubines and Women, and when the Humour takes him with his own Wife again. This liberty that the Men have, obliges the Woman to observe their Husbands, and endeavour to endear them to them, by an humble compliance and submission to their humors, being sure else to lose them, and see their Rivals preferred before them. Open Whorehouses are publickly allowed of, as well for the use and conveniency of Batchelors, as to prevent the debauching of young Maids and married Women.

OF THE BRINGING UP OF THEIR CHILDREN

Children are carefully & tenderly brought up; their Parents strike them seldom or never, and though they cry whole nights together, endeavour to still them with patience; judging that

Infants have no understanding, but that it grows with them as they grow in years, and therefore to be encouraged with indulgence and examples.

It is remarkable to see how orderly and how modestly little Children of seven or eight years old behave themselves; their discourse and answers savouring of riper age, and far surpassing any I have yet seen of their times in our Country. None go to School under seven or eight years of age, as being until then uncapable of its rules, and more inclined to play then to learn, unless it be waggishness and wantonness. At School they begin by degrees, by sweetness and not by force, the Masters imprinting an ambition and desire in each of them to out-go his fellow; they lead them likewise by examples, telling them that such and such learned so much in so little Time, whereby his Honour and Family was so highly advanced. The Children are so accustomed to this way, that they learn sooner and more then by any correction or whipping; for generous spirits, and an obstinate Nation, such as this is, are not to be forced, but rather won with gentleness and emulation.

WHAT SUCCESSION *AB INTESTATO*

When the Parents are grown old, and the Children come to be Men, the Father then quits his Government, Commerce, Shop or Trade, placing his eldest Son in his room, and giving him the greatest part of his Estate; the younger Children are likewise provided for by the indulgent Parents, although their portions return to the eldest in case they die before them. Daughters have no portions at all, nor nothing given them at their marriage; sometimes it happens that rich Parents send a good sum of money with their Daughters, upon their marriage day, to their Son in law; which present is returned by the Bridegroom & his Parents with much thanks, being unwilling that the Bride should have any colourable excuse to raise her into an opinion of having obliged her Husband: The poorer sort do but seldom return these offers as needing them, and glad of any augmentation of their Friends. They have a common saying, that a Woman hath no constant dwelling, living in her youth with her parents, being married with her Husband, and when she is old with her Childe.

REVIEW QUESTIONS

1. How would you characterize the manner in which Japanese children were raised? How does it compare with your own upbringing?
2. What is Caron's attitude toward arranged marriages? Do you agree or disagree? Why?
3. What features or characteristics of Japanese life interested Caron the most?

A German Physician Describes Travelers' Lodgings in Japan (1690–1692)

ENGLEBERT KÄMPFER, *History of Japan*

The German physician Englebert Kämpfer (1651–1716) published no travel accounts during his lifetime, but he nevertheless became one of the most important sources of information about Japan during the eighteenth century.

After completing his formal education in Germany, he spent four years in Köningsberg, Prussia, studying medicine and natural science. His career as a traveler began in 1681 with a visit to Sweden. Although he remained there for two years, Kämpfer declined the opportunity to settle permanently in Uppsala. Instead, he joined an embassy sent by King Charles XI to Persia (Iran) in 1683. After a stay of little more than a year in Isfahan, the Persian capital, the Swedish ambassadors returned home. Kämpfer, however, took the position of chief surgeon to the fleet of the Dutch East India Company operating in the Persian Gulf. In this capacity, he visited Arabia and the western coast of India. In September, 1689, he visited Batavia (Jakarta), Java, and spent the following winter studying Javanese natural history. In May 1690 Kämpfer went to Japan as the physician to the embassy sent annually to that country by the Dutch. He remained there for two years.

Upon his return to Westphalia (Germany) in 1693, Kämpfer became court physician to the Count of Lippe. Apparently the burden of these duties prevented him from publishing his travel accounts during his lifetime. At his death, his unpublished manuscripts were purchased by the great English collector and naturalist Sir Hans Sloane and brought to England. Included among them was a description of Japan ("History and Description of Japan"), which was first published in English in 1727 under the title *History of Japan.* The work appeared in German only in 1779, after it had already been translated into Latin, Dutch, and French. In the preface of his *History,* Kämpfer offered the following insight about his methods of obtaining information about Japanese history and society.

> Liberally assisting them, as I did, with my advice and medicines, with what information I was able to give them in Astronomy and Mathematicks, and with a cordial and plentiful supply of European liquors, I could also, in my turn, freely put to them what questions I pleased, about the affairs of their Country, whether relating to the government in Civil or Ecclesiastical affairs, to the customs of the natives, to the natural and political history, and there was none that ever refused to give me all the information he could, even when we were alone, in such things, which they are otherwise strictly charged to keep secret. These private informations I procured from those who came to visit me, were of great use to me in collecting materials for my intended history of this Country, but yet they fell far short of being altogether satisfactory, and I should not perhaps have been able to compass that design, if I had not, by good luck, met with other opportunities, and in particular the assistance of a discreet young man, by whose means I was richly supplied with whatever notice I wanted, concerning the affairs of Japan.

Thus informed, Kämpfer recorded detailed descriptions of Japanese geography, climate, flora and fauna, and the customs of the people. His *History* is particularly important for its account of the two journeys that he made to the residence of Tokugawa Tsunayoshi, the ruling shogun, in Edo (Tokyo). Here Kämpfer described such details as the condition of the roads, the various means of travel, the customs of Japanese travelers from different social strata, and, as the following selection illustrates, the forms of accommodation available to travelers. It is obvious that he had the opportunity to observe Japanese life closely. As a result, for over a century after its publication in 1727, Kämpfer's *History* remained the chief source of information for Europeans about Japan.

They keep their plate, china ware, and other household goods rang'd upon the floor in a curious and very particular order, according to their size, shape and use. Most of these goods are made of wood, thin, but strongly varnish'd, the greatest part upon a dark red ground. They are wash'd with warm water every time they are used, and wip'd clean with a cloth, and so laid by, against the next time. By this means, if they be lacker'd, and the varnish good, they will, though constantly used, keep clean and neat, and in their full lustre for several years.

The small gallery, or walk, which jets out from the house towards the garden, leads to the house of office, and to a bathing-stove, or hothouse. The house of office is built on one side of the back part of the house, and hath two doors to go in. Going in you find at all times, a couple of new small mats, made either of straw or spanish broom, lying ready, for the use of those persons, who do not care to touch the ground with their bare feet, although it be kept neat and clean to admiration, being always cover'd with mats. You let drop what you need, sitting after the Asiatic fashion, through a hole cut in the floor. The trough underneath is fill'd with light chaff, wherein the filth loses it self instantly. Upon the arrival of people of quality, the board, which is opposite to your face, sitting in this necessary posture, is cover'd with a clean sheet of paper, as are also the bolts of the two doors, or any other part they are likely to lay hold of. Not far from the little house stands a bason fill'd with water, to wash your hands after this business is over. This is commonly an oblong rough stone, the upper part whereof is curiously cut out, into the form of a bason. A new pail of bambous hangs near it, and is cover'd with a neat fir, or cypress board, to which they put a new handle every time it hath been us'd, to wit

a fresh stick of the bambou cane, it being a very clean sort of a wood, and in a manner naturally varnish'd.

The bagnio, or bathing place, is commonly built on the backside of the garden. They build it of cypress-wood. It contains either a Froo, as they call it, a hot house to sweat in, or a Ciffroo, that is, a warm bath, and sometimes both together. It is made warm and got ready every evening, because the Japanese usually bath, or sweat, after their days journey is over, thinking by this means to refresh themselves and to sweat off their weariness. Besides, as they can undress themselves in an instant, so they are ready at a minute's warning to go into the bagnio. For they need but untie their sash, and all their cloaths falls down at once, leaving them quite naked, excepting a small band, which they wear close to the body about their waste. For the satisfaction of the curious, I will here insert a more particular description of their Froo, or hothouse, which they go into only to sweat. It is an almost cubical trunk, or stove, rais'd about three or four foot above the ground, and built close to the wall of the bathing place, on the outside. It is not quite a fathom high, but one fathom and a half long, and of the same breadth. The floor is laid with small plan'd laths or planks, which are some few inches distant from each other, both for the easy passage of the rising vapours, and the convenient out-let of the water people wash themselves withal. You are to go, or rather to creep in, through a small door or shutter. There are two other shutters, one on each side, to let out the superfluous damp. The empty space beneath this stove, down to the ground, is enclos'd with a wall, to prevent the damps from getting out on the sides. Towards the yard is a furnace just beneath the hot-house. The fire-hole is shut up towards the bathing stove, to prevent the smoke's getting in there. Part of the furnace stands out towards the yard, where they put in the necessary water and plants. This part is shut with a clap-board, when the fire is burning, to make all the damp and vapours ascend through the inner and open part into the hot-house. There are always two tubs, one of warm, the other of cold water, put into these hot-houses, for such as have a mind to wash themselves, either for their diversion, or out of necessity.

The garden is the only place, we Dutchmen, being treated in all respects little better than prisoners, have liberty to walk into. It takes in all the room behind the house. It is commonly square, with a back door, and wall'd in very neatly, like a cistern, or pond, for which reason it is call'd Tsubo, which in the Japanese language signifies a large water-trough, or cistern. There are few good houses and inns, but what have their Tsubo. If there be not room enough for a garden, they have at least an old ingrafted plum, cherry, or apricock tree. The older, the more crooked and monstrous this tree is, the greater value they put upon it. Sometimes they let the branches grow into the rooms. In order to make it bear larger flowers, and in greater quantity, they commonly cut it to a few, perhaps two or three branches. It cannot be denied, but that the great number of beautiful, incarnate, and double flowers, which they bear in the proper Season, are a surprizingly curious ornament to this back part of the house, but they have this disadvantage, that they bear no fruit. In some small houses, and Inns of less note, where there is not room enough, neither for a garden, nor trees, they have at least an opening or window to let the light fall into the back rooms, before which, for the amusement and diversion of travellers, is put a small tub, full of water, wherein they commonly keep some gold or silver fish, as they call them, being fish with gold or silver-colour'd Tails alive. For a farther ornament of the same place, there is generally a flower-pot or two standing there. Sometimes they plant some dwarf-trees there, which will grow easily upon pumice, or other porous stones, without any

ground at all, provided the root be put into the water, from whence it will suck up sufficient nourishment. Ordinary people often plant the same kind of trees before the street-doors, for their diversion, as well as for an ornament to their houses. But to return to the Tsubo, or Garden, if it be a good one, it must have at least 30 foot square, and consist of the following essential parts. 1. The ground is cover'd partly with roundish stones of different colours, gather'd in rivers or upon the sea-shore, well wash'd and clean'd, and those of the same kind laid together in form of beds, partly with gravel, which is swept every day, and kept clean and neat to admiration, the large stones being laid in the middle, as a path to walk upon, without injuring the gravel, the whole in a seeming but ingenious confusion. 2. Some few flower-bearing plants planted confusedly, tho' not without some certain rules. Amidst the Plants stands sometimes a Saguer, as they call it, or scarce outlandish tree, sometimes a dwarf-tree or two. 3. A small rock or hill in a corner of the garden, made in imitation of nature, curiously adorn'd with birds and insects, cast in brass, and placed between the stones, sometimes the model of a temple stands upon it built, as for the sake of the prospect they generally are, on a remarkable eminence, or the borders of a precipice. Often a small rivulet rushes down the stones with an agreeable noise, the whole in due proportions and as near as possible resembling nature. 4. A small bush, or wood, on the side of the hill, for which the gardiners chuse such trees, as will grow close to one another, and plant and cut them according to their largeness, nature, and the colour of their flowers and leaves, so as to make the whole very accurately imitate a natural wood, or forest. 5. A cistern or pond, as mention'd above, with alive fish kept in it, and surrounded with proper plants, that is such, as love a watry soil, and would lose their beauty and greeness if planted in a dry ground. It is a particular profession to lay out these gardens, and to keep them so curiously and nicely, as they ought to be, as I shall have an opportunity to shew more at large in the sequel of this history. Nor doth it require less skill and ingenuity to contrive and fit out the rocks and hills above-mention'd, according to the rules of art. What I have hitherto observ'd will be sufficient to give the reader a general Idea of the Inns in Japan. The accommodation travellers meet with in the same, I intend to treat of in a chapter by itself.

There are innumerable smaller Inns, Cook-shops, Sacki, or Ale-houses, Pastry-cook's, and Confectioner's shops, all along the road, even in the midst of woods and forests, and at the tops of mountains, where a weary foot-traveller, and the meaner sort of people, find at all times, for a few farthings, something warm to eat, or hot Tea-water, or Sacki, or somewhat else of this kind, wherewithal to refresh themselves. 'Tis true, these cook-shops are but poor sorry houses, if compar'd to larger Inns, being inhabited only by poor people, who have enough to do to get a livelihood by this trade: and yet even in these, there is always something or other to amuse pas-sengers, and to draw them in; sometimes a gar-den and orchard behind the house, which is seen from the street looking thro' the passage, and which by its beautiful flowers, or the agreeable sight of a stream of clear water, falling down from a neighbouring natural or artificial hill, or

by some other curious ornament of this kind, tempts People to come in and to repose them-selves in the shadow; at other times a large flower-pot stands in the window, fill'd with flowering branches of trees, (for the flowers of plants, tho' never so beautiful, are too common to deserve a place in such a pot,) dispos'd in a very curious and singular manner; sometimes a handsom, well-looking house-maid, or a couple of young girls well dress'd, stand under the door, and with great civility invite people to come in, and to buy something. The eatables, such as cakes, or whatever it be, are kept before the fire, in an open room, sticking to skewers of Bambous, to the end that passengers, as they go along, may take them, and pursue their journey without stopping. The landladies, cooks, and maids, as soon as they see any body coming at a distance blow up the fire, to make it look, as if the victuals had been just got ready. Some busy themselves with making the tea, others prepare the soop in a cup, others fill cups with Sacki, or other liquors to present them to passengers, all the while talking, and chattering, and com-mending their merchandize with a voice loud enough to be heard by their next neighbours of the same profession.

REVIEW QUESTIONS

1. Was Kämpfer a careful observer? What evidence supports your opinion?
2. Was Kämpfer biased either for or against Japanese society? How can you tell?
3. What evidence of class distinctions is presented here?
4. What generalizations about the values of Japanese society does this selection encour-age you to make?
5. Based on the information supplied here by Kämpfer, would you feel comfortable and secure traveling in late-seventeenth-century Japan? Why or why not?

A Portuguese Friar Describes Religion in Upper Burma (1629–1643)

Travels of Fray Sebastien Manrique

Much of what we know about the life of Fray {Friar} Sebastien Manrique (1587?–1669) comes from his *Travels.* A native of Oporto, Portugal, he took holy orders in Portuguese-controlled Goa in 1604. In 1629, he was sent from India to Arakan (Myanmar, or Burma), where he lived for eight years. From 1637 to 1640 he traveled to the Philippines and China, returning to India in 1640–1641. There Asaf Khan, the father-in-law and powerful minister of Emperor Shah Jahan, befriended Manrique and entrusted him with official business. Asaf Khan's death in 1641 left Manrique without a patron; perhaps for this reason, Manrique departed from India for Europe in the same year. By the time he reached Rome in 1643, he had been away from Europe for almost forty years, fifteen of which had been devoted to missionary work. It is certainly ironic that, after living through numerous hardships in Asia, Manrique was murdered in London by his own Portuguese servant in the course of a robbery attempt in 1669.

Manrique's *Itinerario de las Missiones Orientales (Travels of Fray Sebastien Manrique),* written in Spanish, first appeared in 1649. It found a receptive audience, and a second edition quickly followed in 1653. It recounts his experiences in India, his trip to Arakan (Myanmar), his visits to the Philippines, Java, and China, and his return trip to India. Manrique's detailed depictions of life in Arakan are particularly notable because they deal with people, places, and customs that were little known in other parts of the world. The selection that follows, for example, offers a vivid description of the Sansaporau festival, a local variant of a Buddhist ceremony.

The people of Pegu, Burma and the Maghs,[*] of whom I am treating, call the feast Sansaporau, which means in our language "Feast in commemoration of the dead." This eight-day feast is celebrated with such rites and so much devotion that it produced in me the three effects which I mentioned above, of astonishment, edification, and regret. My astonishment was roused, as I say, by seeing the great blindness of these Pagans and the many wiles by which the universal Enemy conceals our true faith from them, in attracting to himself honour which is due only to God. I was edified by seeing their very complete rejoicings, the carrying out of so many pious acts and so much charity, such as the giving of alms, payment of debts, the provision of free tables bearing every kind of food and delicacy, bestowed for the love of God on whatever people might come to share them, irrespective of class. Such acts are indeed more to be expected of Christians than infidels, but in them, incidentally, they surpass many Christians. But they do these good works under the influence of a false faith, whereas if done in the name of our sacred religion for the love of God, they would doubtless be acceptable to God Himself. But they are, as products of a false faith, fruitless and lacking in all merit, serving only to elicit human approbation and present us, who live in hopes of obtaining true glory and happiness, with an

[*]Pegu is in southern Myanmar.

example for edification and imitation. The acts which drew forth my compassion and sorrow took place during the procession which was held on the eighth day of this festival of Sansaporau. In it the Idol of Poagrī, a god over many gods, was carried in a triumphal car four stories high, accompanied by ninety-six Raulins[*] belonging to the three orders, episcopal, priestly and clerical, that is thirty Pungrīs, thirty Panjans and thirty-six Moxans.[†] They were all dressed in damasks, satins and yellow taffetas, their robes falling to the feet. On the fourth and the highest story of the chariot was a throne, reached by twelve small steps. On this was the statue of Poagrī. It was of silver, about eleven palms high, with a tiara of gold set with many valuable pearls and rubies, one large pearl between two rubies. The Idol was shown standing. Below it was a snake made of bronze, its scales being all coloured green.

The Idol held in its hands a large silver partisan with a cross-piece, with which he was said to have killed the serpent the *"Swallower* of the house of smoke,"* such being their name for the Devil. The snake is supposed to come yearly to steal the relics of their sainted martyrs, men who had given up their lives in sacrifice at this procession, which is held in remembrance of these dead. This theft prevents the souls of these men from going to heaven.

On the twelve steps twenty-four Raulins of Moxan rank were kneeling, holding as many silver censers in their hands, with which they perfumed their false god. Twelve more Moxans were kneeling beside the lowest step of the throne playing musical instruments, to the sounds of which the twenty-four Panjans, in four choirs, were singing hymns of praise to the Idol. Behind this chariot came nine more chariots, but of only three stories each, full of many tiny Idols made of metal or coloured wood.

Many Raulins were in these chariots also, singing to various instruments. This Idol-scum proceeded between two rows of priests, numbering over three thousand, while a huge crowd of people accompanied them. The streets along which this superstitious procession passed were well decorated with boughs of trees as well as with cloths of silk and cotton of many hues. In these streets stood certain houses better ornamented than the others, especially allotted for the assembling of such of these Barbarians as desired to offer themselves in sacrifice. On the arrival of the chariots these men came out. They were naked from the waist upwards, anointed and marked with stripes of sweet-smelling substances, with gold bracelets on their arms. On their appearance the crowd opened up so as to let them reach the centre of the procession; here they prostrated themselves before the principal chariot in which the God of many gods was travelling, or as we should more truthfully say, the Devil of devils. After making numerous obeisances and prostrations they threw themselves down on their faces on the earth at full length, and while lying in this position the chariot passed over them, crushing them to pieces with its metal-shod wheels. Thus did these unhappy folk voluntarily offer themselves in sacrifice to that diabolical deity. As soon as he had obtained certain possession of these wretched souls the chariots were stopped and the chief priests of that false priesthood, the Pungrins, descended with golden and silver dishes in their hands. They gathered up those remains, firebrands of hell, with the utmost reverence and placing them in the dishes put these upon their heads and remounted the principal chariot. They then presented these wretched remains of human flesh to the Idol, with all ceremony: truly a pretty offering, as the flesh of all mankind could not satisfy his greed. On these offerings being made by those hellish priests the whole concourse, with loud and terrifying shouts, exclaimed: *O Lord, accept these pure and holy offerings and stay thy wrath from our dead and from us the living when we too die.* In some of the streets passed through were wooden poles from

---

[*]Manrique uses this word as a general name for Buddhist priests in Arakan.
[†]Pungrīs, or Pungrins, are fully ordained monks, Panjans are fully ordained monks with no monastery, and Moxans are novices.

twenty-five to thirty palms high. At the top of these were streamers of various colours, and four or five palms lower down iron or steel hooks made very sharp and penetrating. On them certain of these Barbarians were slung, these sharp hooks in some cases traversing their breasts. Thus were they foolishly shedding their blood. When the chariots with the Idols reached the spot where these wretched men were, they stopped and these men filling their hands with their cursed blood sprinkled it, as an offering, on the Idols. So great was the crowd that rushed towards the sanguinary oblation, with every kind of cloth, to catch drops of that damned blood, that it was necessary to call in cavalry and drive them back with blows to prevent the people being suffocated. This was done with difficulty, as any man who was unable to obtain a drop of what they hold to be sacred blood considered himself most unfortunate. These wretched folk most gladly gave up their lives in such martyrdom, holding that they would at once enter into eternal joys: but the joy which these unhappy men attain is nothing but the general applause with which all these heathen honour and vener-

ate them. Later on all the Raulins of the neighbouring districts arrived in procession, accompanied by a crowd of people, and took the bodies down from the poles and placed them with the other corpses which had similarly sacrificed their lives under the wheels of the chariots. They were then removed in a special triumphal car to a selected spot and there cremated on a pyre of odoriferous wood. As the bodies of the martyrs of the Devil were being consumed, many devotees threw rich rings and bracelets of gold and silver, and clothes richly embroidered in gold and silver, on to the fire in order to assist in the cost of the journey of these souls. It was all these rites which caused me much anguish and compassion when I saw and noted on the one hand the large number of followers the Devil had obtained and the great efforts they made to please him and so lose themselves while believing themselves to be great gainers, and on the other hand I thought how little we true believers were doing to save ourselves. May God in His infinite mercy give both us and them His grace so that we should not fail to reach the end for which we were created.

REVIEW QUESTIONS

1. What did Manrique dislike about this ceremony?
2. What, to you, is the most interesting feature of this ceremony?
3. If you had to find something positive to say about the Sansaporau festival, what would it be? What positive things does Manrique say?
4. What purpose do you think the Sansaporau festival served in this society?

2

South and Southwest Asia, 1500–1800

As in East Asia, merchants followed the explorers into South and Southwest Asia. Members of European mercantile companies successfully kept the missionaries out, fearing they would interfere with commerce by creating a hostility to Europeans. One good example comes from England. There, Queen Elizabeth I commissioned the East India Company on December 31, 1600, to go to India, and gradually the company gained control of that country, largely as a result of the power vacuum left by the disintegration of the Mughal Empire. Following victories in a series of conflicts in North America, Europe, and India in the eighteenth century, the British subdued French contenders and then took advantage of local political and military conflicts in Bengal to establish control. For their part, the various Indian ethnic groups considered the British not so much as outsiders but as just another party seeking a share of the spoils. Indians did not think of themselves as Indian and did not view other regional powers as Indian either, but merely as rivals. Thus the British were not perceived as a threat until it was too late. Nor did the British, at least early on, view themselves as power seekers; they were simply merchants who took military action whenever it was necessary to defend their compounds. Indeed, it was a private company that ruled British India until 1858, when the Crown took over.

Whereas early modern contact of Europeans with East Asia was largely by sea, contact with South and Southwest Asia continued to be primarily by land; geography and centuries-old travel patterns by Europeans through the Middle East and Iran into India had set an established route. There often was high adventure involved, and the men who participated in the events of the period had interests and talents as varied as their backgrounds. Ludovico di Varthema pushed his luck throughout his career: by entering Mecca as a Muslim; by being arrested, jailed, and rescued by a sultana; and by traveling to many places with people from many cultures. Through it all, he was a keen observer (perhaps a reason for his remarkable sense of survival). Evliya Efendi was a scholar, soldier, diplomat, and a breeder of extraordinary dogs for use in agriculture and in war. His reminiscences were valued in their own time and still are of interest today. Pietro della Valle's travels seem to have been rivaled in intensity only by his affairs of the heart. Niccolo Manucci was a physician (largely self-taught), soldier, speculator, and a discerning observer of politics and conscientious student of history. In his voluminous writings he expressed his opinions and views in an uncompromising and often negative manner. François Valentijn, although active in the Indian Ocean area, never visited Sri Lanka, but he did collect accounts by others and turned them into a report on the people and their customs.

This chapter also includes observations by participants in the Mughal rule of India. Babur, the first of the Mughal emperors, invaded India from Central Asia. In his short reign, he never really identified with India, in spite of the balanced observations he gives in his autobiography. His writing reveals his remarkable abilities as a leader of men and an analyst of society and culture. Abul Fazl, another commentator, was one of the closest advisors to Akbar, Babur's grandson and an emperor ranking with Asoka (third century B.C.E.) as India's greatest ruler. Fazl's summary of the harem, a major institution in Mughal India (as elsewhere), describes its role in the imperial structure.

An Italian Scoundrel Brags About His Adventures in Damascus (1503–1508)

The Travels of Ludovico di Varthema

In 1510 an Italian from Bologna, Ludovico di Varthema, published a book describing his travels and adventures in Egypt, Syria, the Arabian peninsula, India, and lands farther east. A soldier, he enlisted in a Mameluke army and became the first non-Muslim known to have entered Mecca, the holy city forbidden to all but Muslims. He kept detailed notes about the city, its commerce, and its religion. Afraid of being discovered and killed, he deserted. Further adventures found him passing himself off as a cannon maker for the Arabs (who were concerned with the Portuguese encroachment in their trade monopoly in the Indian Ocean), and a few years later he was knighted by the Portuguese governor of Goa for his services.

Varthema's adventures are the stuff movies are made of: passing as a Muslim in a Muslim army, hiding in a mosque, disguising himself, being arrested as a Christian spy, being rescued by a sultana, traveling to the west coast of India and to Ceylon (Sri Lanka), getting to Borneo, Java, and Sumatra, returning to India where he served in the Portuguese army and government, and finally returning to Europe in 1510, after eight years of travel. His traveling companions included a Persian merchant and Chinese Nestorian Christians.

THE FIRST CHAPTER CONCERNING DAMASCUS

Truly it would not be possible to describe the beauty and the excellence of this Damascus, in which I resided some months in order to learn the Moorish language, because this city is entirely inhabited by Moors and Mamelukes and many Greek Christians. Here I must give an account of the government of the lord of the said city, which lord is subject to the Great Sultan of Cairo. You must know that in the said city of Damascus there is a very beautiful and strong castle, which is said to have been built by a Flor-

entine Mameluke at his own expense, he being lord of the said city. And, moreover, in each angle of the said castle, the arms of Florence are sculptured in marble. It is surrounded by very wide fosses, and has four extremely strong towers and drawbridges, and powerful and excellent artillery are constantly mounted there. Fifty Mamelukes, in the service of the Grand Sultan, are constantly quartered with the governor of the castle. This Florentine was a Mameluke of the Grand Sultan; and it is reported that in his time the Sultan was poisoned, and could find no one who could relieve him of the said poison, when it pleased God that this Florentine should cure him. For this service he gave him the said city of Damascus, and thus he came to build the castle. Afterwards he died in Damascus; and the people held him in great veneration as a holy man, possessing great knowledge, and from that time forward the castle has always been in the possession of the Sultan. When a new Sultan succeeds to the throne, one of his lords, who are called *Amirra,* says to him: "Lord, I have been for so long a time your slave, give me Damascus, and I will give you one hundred thousand, or two hundred thousand, teraphim* of gold." Then the lord grants him this favour. But you must know, that if in the course of two years the said lord does not send him 25,000 teraphim, he seeks to kill him by force of arms, or in some other manner; but if he makes him the said present, he remains in the government. The said lord has always ten or twelve lords and barons of the said city with him, and when the Sultan wants two or three hundred thousand teraphim from the lords or merchants of the said city, who are not treated with justice, but whom they vie with each other in oppressing by robbery and assassination (for the Moors live under the Mamelukes like the lamb under the wolf), the said Sultan sends two letters to the governor of the said castle, one of which simply enjoins him to bring together in the castle such lords or merchants as he may think proper. And when they are assembled, the second letter is read, the object of which is immediately carried out, whether for good or for evil. And in this manner the said lord seeks to obtain money. Sometimes the said lord becomes so powerful that he will not go into the castle; whereat many barons and merchants, feeling themselves in danger, mount their horses and retire towards Turkey. We will say no more upon this subject, excepting that the men of the guard of the said castle, in each of the four great towers, are always on the watch. They make no cry during the night, but each has a drum, made in the shape of a half-box, upon which they beat vigorously with a stick, and

each answers the other with these said drums. He who delays answering for the space of a *pater noster,* is imprisoned for a year.

THE SECOND CHAPTER CONCERNING THE SAID DAMASCUS

Now that we have seen the customs of the Lord of Damascus, it is necessary that I should make mention of some circumstances relating to the city, which is extremely populous and very rich. It is impossible to imagine the richness and elegance of the workmanship there. Here you have a great abundance of grain and of meat, and the most prolific country for fruits that was ever seen, and especially for fresh grapes, during all seasons. I will mention the good and the bad fruits which grow there. Pomegranates and quinces, good: almonds and large olives, extremely good. The most beautiful white and red roses that were ever seen. There are also good apples and pears and peaches, but with a very bad taste, the reason of which is that Damascus abounds much in water. A stream runs through the city, and the greater number of the houses have very beautiful fountains of mosaic work. The houses are dirty externally, but within they are very beautiful, adorned with many works of marble and porphyry.

In this city there are many mosques. One, which is the principal, is as large as St. Peter's at Rome. It has no roof in the centre, but the surrounding parts are covered in. It is reported that they keep there the body of St. Zachariah the prophet, and they pay him very great honour. In the said mosque there are four principal doors of metal, and within there are many fountains. Again, we see where the canonica stood, which belonged formerly to the Christians, in which canonica there are many ancient works in mosaic. Again, I saw the place where they report that Christ said to St. Paul, "Saule, Saule, cur me persequeris?" which is without the city, about a mile from one of the gates thereof. They bury there all the Christians who die in the said city.

---

*A gold coin of varying value.

Again, there is that tower in the wall of the district where (as they say) St. Paul was imprisoned. The Moors have many times rebuilt it, but in the morning it is found broken and thrown down, as the angel broke it when he drew St. Paul out of the said tower. I also saw the house where (as they say) Cain slew Abel his brother, which is a mile without the city in the opposite direction, on the side of a hill in a large deep valley.

CHAPTER THE THIRD, CONCERNING THE MAMELUKES IN DAMASCUS

The Mamelukes are renegade Christians, who have been purchased by the said lord. Certain it is that the said Mamelukes never lose any time, but are constantly exercising themselves either in arms or in letters, in order that they may acquire excellence. And you must know that every Mameluke, great or little, has for his pay six saraphi per month, and his expenses for himself, his horse, and a family; and they have as much more when they are engaged on any warlike expedition. The said Mamelukes, when they go about the city, are always in companies of two or three, as it would be a great disgrace if they went alone. If they accidentally meet two or three ladies, they possess this privilege, or if they do not possess it they take it: they go to lay in wait for these ladies in certain places like great inns, which are called Chano, and as the said ladies pass before the door each Mameluke takes his lady by the hand, draws her in, and does what he will with her. But the lady resists being known, because they all wear the face covered, so that they know us, but we do not know them. The Mameluke says to her, that he wishes to know who she is, and she replies: "Brother, is it not enough that you do with me what you will, without desiring to know who I am?" and she entreats him so much that he lets her go. And sometimes they think that they take the daughter of the lord, when in fact they take their own wives; and this has happened while I was there. These ladies go very well clad in silk, and over it they wear certain white garments of wool, thin and bright like silk, and they all wear white buskins and red or purple shoes, and many jewels around their heads, and in their ears, and on their hands. These ladies when they are married, at their own will and pleasure, that is, when they do not wish to remain with their husbands any longer, go to the cadi of their faith and cause themselves to be talacare, that is, to be separated from their husband; and then they take another, and he takes another wife. Although they say that the Moors have five or six wives, I for my part have never seen any who had more than two or three at the most. These Moors for the greater part eat in the streets, that is, where the clothes are sold; they have their food cooked and eat it there, and there are very many horses, camels, and buffalos, and sheep and goats. There is here an abundance of good fresh cheese; and if you wish to purchase milk, there are forty or fifty goats, which go every day through the district, and which have ears more than a span in length. The master of these goats takes them up into your chamber, even if your house have three stories, and there in your presence he milks as much as you please into a handsome tin vessel. And there are many milch goats. Here, again, is sold a great quantity of truffles: sometimes twenty-five or thirty camels arrive laden with them, and in three or four days they are sold. They come from the mountains of Armenia and Turkey. The said Moors go clothed in certain long and wide garments, without girdles, made of silk or cloth, and the greater number wear breeches of wool and white shoes. When a Moor meets a Mameluke, although he may be the principal merchant of the place, he is obliged to do honour and give place to the Mameluke, and if he do not so he is bastinadoed. The Christians have there many warehouses, which contain cloths, and silk and satin, velvets, and brass, and all merchandize that is required; but they are ill treated.

REVIEW QUESTIONS

1. Although apparently not well educated, Varthema had an eye for detail. How do you see that quality reflected in this selection?
2. Did Varthema like Damascus? Why or why not?
3. How would you define Varthema's religious views?

A Turkish Historian Remembers His Travels in Turkey and Persia (mid-1600s)

EVLIYA EFENDI, *Narrative of Travels in Europe, Asia, and Africa*

Soldier, diplomat, scholar, and servant to the sultan, Evliya Efendi was born sometime between 1611 and 1614 in the capital of the Ottoman Empire, Istanbul (Constantinople). He was the son of the chief of the goldsmiths, who was himself a favorite of the sultan, Ahmed I. Indeed, his mother had been presented by the sultan to his father, a common practice for marriage arrangements.

Efendi has been dismissed as an "indifferent" historian, but his eyewitness descriptions of the many countries he visited are highly regarded. He wrote four volumes of travel accounts, but they cover only twenty of his forty-one years of travel. He died in Adrianople before finishing his reminiscences, sometime between 1678 and 1682. In his travels through Europe and western Asia, he claimed to have heard 147 different languages. The selection that follows deals first with a Turkish city and then with Persia.

Interestingly, in addition to his monumental *Narrative of Travels,* Efendi was known as an authority on two breeds of agricultural watchdogs, which were also used in combat. He described them as "large dogs, the size of asses, and fierce as lions." When trained they would "on command pull a man down from his horse, however stout he may be." These breeds exist and are still valued today.

DESCRIPTION OF THE MARKET OF BRÚSSA[*]

There are nine thousand shops. The Bezestán[†] is a large building with four iron gates secured with iron chains; its cupola is supported by strong columns. It contains three hundred shops (doláb) in each of which merchants reside, who are as rich as the kings of Egypt. The market of the goldsmiths is outside the bezestán, and separate from it; the shops are all of stone. There are also the markets of the tailors, cotton-beaters, capmakers, thread merchants, drapers, linen merchants, cable merchants, and that called the market of the bride, where essence of roses, musk, ambergris, &c. are sold. The brains of the passers

---

[*]Or Bursa (Prusa) in modern Turkey, near the Sea of Marmara (which connects the Dardanelles and the Bosporus).
[†]Bazaar or market

by are refreshed with the most delicious odours, and nobody is willing to leave it on account of the fragrance of the perfumes and the politeness of its merchants. These markets are established around the Bezestán, and the shops are arranged in rows. In each corner is a fountain supplying water out of two pipes. In the summer months the servants sprinkle the ground with water, so that the whole market resembles a serdáb or cooling place of Baghdád. The principal men of Brússa sit here during the hottest hours of the day. According to the descriptions of travellers there is no where to be found so pleasant a market place. The market of Haleb and of Alí Páshá at Adrianople are famous, but neither they, nor even those of Constantinople, are to be compared with the markets of Brússa. The saddlers, and the long market are the most crowded; and the one occupied by the sellers of roast meat near the rice khán is very elegant. None of the provisions at Brússa are sold by Infidels but all by true Moslims. The shops of the Sherbet-merchants are adorned with all sorts of cups, and in the summer-time they put flowers into the sherbet and also mix rosewater with it, which is not the custom any where else. The fruit merchants ornament their shops with branches bearing fruit. There are seventy-five coffee-houses each capable of holding a thousand persons, which are frequented by the most elegant and learned of the inhabitants; and three times a day singers and dancers execute a musical concert in them. . . . All coffee-houses, and particularly those near the great mosque, abound with men skilled in a thousand arts (Hezár-fenn) dancing and pleasure continue the whole night, and in the morning every body goes to the mosque. These coffee-houses became famous only since those of Constantinople were closed by the express command of Sultán Murád IV. There are also no less than ninety-seven Búza-houses, which are not to be equalled in the world; they are wainscoted with fayence, painted, each capable of accommodating one thousand men. In summer the Búza is cooled in ice, like sherbet; the principal men of the town are not ashamed to enter these Búza-houses, although

abundance of youths, dancers and singers, girt with Brússa girdles, here entice, their lovers to ruin. The roads are paved with large flint-stones, a kind of paving not met with elsewhere; these stones are not the least worn by age, but they are dangerous for horses, who stumble on them because they are so hard and bright. . . .

PRAISE OF THE AIR AND CLIMATE

By the mildness of the climate the inhabitants are all healthy and stout, with red cheeks and black beards, merry faces, and lips like rose-buds; the women are pretty, and conscious of the fairness of their skins are extremely proud; those advanced in age are of sweet company, so that the proverb, "the old is sweeter than the young," may well be applied to them. The inhabitants are all Shiís or Mulhad (impious), a great number are Dumbúlí, Khaljání, Turcomans, and Gokdúlák. There are two thousand Ulemás, amongst whom are excellent doctors, surgeons and oculists. There are more than seven thousand pious Sheiks, who are much esteemed in this town, the inhabitants never do any thing without consulting them, but their sect is not exactly known. Eighty-two most eloquent poets, authors of Diváns. Yárí and Shábí are the Saíb and Unfí of their time. Of the Mujazib or Santons (Saint fools) we saw Sherímí, whom no person ever saw eating, drinking, lying down, sleeping, or performing any of the natural offices of life for seventy years. The Persians are generally called Kizilbásh or red heads, because they wrap red sashes round their heads, though many of them also wear the Mohammedan white turban; but the cap is always pointed, and that of the Ulemás, which is called Táj, or crown, is more than two yards long. The great men wear sable. . . .

ARTS AND HANDICRAFTS, PROVISIONS, FRUITS, BEVERAGES, GARDENS, ETC.

Painters, architects, goldsmiths, and tailors are nowhere to be found so perfect as here. Precious stuffs manufactured here go all over the world;

the velvet is much renowned. The provisions consist of the white bread called Kerde, and Súmún, cracknels, pastry, roasts, chicken pies, forty different kinds of pilaw with spices, the Herisse and sweetmeat, Palúde. Among the abundance of delicious fruits are particularly the pears and exquisite apricots, they are not found in such perfection even at Constantinople. The beverages consist of seven sorts of Muscat wine, the common wine of the Royal grape, the pomegranate, the cherry wine, and oxymel; and for the common people búza of millet and rice.

There are some dining establishments for the poor, such as the Imáret of Sháh Yakúb, of Sultán Motevekel, of Lady Zobeide, and of Sultán Hassan, large buildings with kitchens worthy that of Keikavús, but in the hands of the Persians they have all decayed.

The principal walk is the mount Surkháb (Red-water) near Tabríz; at noon the sea of Rúmie may be distinguished from the top of it; it is at a farsang distance from Tabríz.

The number of gardens amounts to forty-seven thousand, the finest is that of Sháh Yakúb, where the Khán gave me a splendid entertainment. Eleven times in the day, seventy dancers and singers exerted themselves in the practice of their art, so that it resembled an evening party of Hossein Bikara. This garden owes its origin to Koja Ferhád Páshá, Governor of Tabríz under Sultán Murad III., who adorned it with numerous koshks, bowers and pleasure-houses; and at the time of the pillage of the town by Murad IV., this garden was preserved by the care of Osmán Aghá. The Chronostic of the koshk where we dined, alluding to the name of the builder, says that, Ferhád built this sweet (Shirín) palace. The walk of Sháh Sefí cannot be praised enough. It is the place of the Maïl; in the centre of it two immense columns lift their tops up to Heaven; on one of them every Friday a silver plate is put, which is aimed at by all the bowmen, who shoot at it, encouraged by the presence of the Khán. On New Year's day (Nevrúz) or the beginning of spring, battles are fought in this place by horses trained in the dark during forty or fifty days, by camels, buffaloes, sheep, asses, dogs, and cocks. These fights are peculiar to Persia. Every year on the tenth of the month Moharrem, being the feast of A'ashúra, all the population of the town assemble under tents in this large place, and during three days and nights cook many thousand dishes of A'ashúra (a kind of hotch-potch), in remembrance of the martyrs of Kerbela; these dishes are distributed with an abundance of sugar-sherbet, which is carried round in crystal vases, and cups of cornelian and turquoise: at the same time singing certain verses, such as "Their Lord gave them of the purest beverage." Some of the great men on this day carry cans and tankards round their necks, and go about distributing water like common porters. But the finest show is in the variegated tent of the Khán, where all the great men of Tabríz are assembled, and where a Hymn on the death of Hossein is recited, in the same manner as the Hymn on the Prophet's birthday is in the Turkish mosques. The hearers listen, sighing and lamenting, but when the reciter arrives at the passage where Hossein is killed by accursed Shabr, a curtain opens behind him, and a severed head and trunk of a body, representing that of the Imám when dead, is thrown on the ground, when there rises such an uproar of cries and lamentations that everybody loses his wits. At this moment some hundred men mingle in the crowd with razors, with which they cut the arms and breasts of all loving believers, who desire to shed their blood on this day in remembrance of the blood shed by the Imán; they make such deep incisions and scars, that the ground appears as if it was blooming with tulips. Some thousands brand the marks and names of Hassan and Hossein on their heads, arms, and breasts. They then carry Hossein's body away from the ground with much pomp, and finish the ceremony with great howlings.

The town has numerous fine walks and pleasure grounds, each of which may be compared to the gardens of Ispúze and Merám. The beautiful koshks worthy to be the seats of Sherín and Ferhád, of Wámik and Azra, are every where renowned; but I must refrain from their praise and description, as I have yet so many other things to mention. God be thanked! I remained here two months, which I spent in full pleasure and delight, and I shall now give the description of the districts and castles, which I visited in the Khán's company. Round Tabríz are seven districts, which furnish military men, whose office is to train birds and dogs for hunting.

REVIEW QUESTIONS

1. How would you describe the most important features of life in Brússa? Do you think Efendi would agree or disagree with you? Why?
2. How did Efendi view the importance of religion in the life of the people in Brússa?
3. What value does Efendi's attention to detail have in his observations on Persia?
4. How would you characterize his attitude toward the Persians?

The Mongol Conqueror of India Describes Hindustan (1526)

BABUR, *Baburnama*

Babur, whose name means "tiger," was a descendant of both Timur (Tamurlane) and, distantly, Chenghis Kahn, but he was really of Turkish or central Asian origin, and he disliked the Mongols. This is one of the ironies of history, for the dynasty he founded is known as the Mughal dynasty, a linguistic corruption of Mongol.

In 1504 Babur's holdings extended from central Asia to the region of Kabul; by 1525 he had conquered Lahore, the greatest city of northern India (perhaps other than Delhi), now in present-day Pakistan. The last of the Delhi sultans had attempted to establish authority over regional governors, including his own uncle, who ruled the Punjab. Babur was encouraged to challenge the sultan and did so at Panipat, with about 12,000 troops against the sultan's 100,000. With superior military technology and well-trained soldiers, Babur carried the day. He then swept through northern India, and a new dynasty seemed assured. However, it was left to his grandson, Akbar, to establish the Mughal Empire.

Babur was a child of the mountains; the plains of India with their proverbial "heat and dust" (which the British also later complained about) weakened him physically. He started a pattern followed by his successors: he built gardens and fountains designed to cool the evenings after the horrendous heat of the day. He grew homesick for his native highlands, and although he had respect for northern India, he never adjusted to it.

In addition to the climate, the intense series of battles took a heavy toll on Babur, who was an opium user and liked wine. At one critical juncture, he addressed his troops and promised to forego wine if they won. They did;

whether he gave up wine or not, he became ill and died less than four years after his conquest of Panipat. Allegedly, his son Humayun lay near death, and Babur made a deal with God: if his son was spared, he would forfeit his own life. Humayun recovered, and Babur died. Perhaps Babur's condition was so weakened that he fell mortally ill from whatever malady had afflicted Humayun.

Babur is one of the most underrated conquerors in history. He was intelligent, cultured, and a success on the battlefield. His autobiography, from which the following selection is taken, is a remarkable piece of observation, albeit with some understandable bias. It shows a versatile mind seldom seen in conquerors.

DESCRIPTION OF HINDUSTAN

Hindustan is a vast and populous kingdom and a productive realm. To the east and south, in fact to the west too, it ends at the ocean. To the north is a mountain range that connects the mountains of the Hindu Kush, Kafiristan, and Kashmir. To the northwest are Kabul, Ghazni, and Kandahar. The capital of all Hindustan is Delhi. After Sultan Shihabuddin Ghuri's reign until the end of Sultan Firozshah's, most of Hindustan was under the control of the Delhi sultans. Up to the time that I conquered Hindustan, five Muslim padishahs and two infidels had ruled there. Although the mountains and jungles are held by many petty rays and rajahs, the important and independent rulers were the following five.

One was the Afghans, who took the capital Delhi and held in their grasp from Bhera to Bihar. Before the Afghans, Jaunpur was held by Sultan Husayn Sharqi, and the dynasty was called Purabi. The Purabi ancestors were cupbearers for Sultan Firozshah and those sultans; after Firozshah, they gained control over the kingdom of Jaunpur. Delhi was in Sultan Alauddin's hands, and the dynasty was the Sayyids. When Temür Beg took Delhi, he gave the governorship of Delhi to their ancestors and left. Sultan Bahlul Lodi the Afghan and his son Sultan Iskandar seized Delhi and Jaunpur, and the two capitals formed one kingdom.

The second was Sultan Muzaffar in Gujarat, who passed away several days before the defeat of Sultan Ibrahim. He was a religiously observant ruler and a student of the religious sciences, he read hadith, and he always copied Korans. His dynasty was called the Tang. Their fathers also were cupbearers for Sultan Firoz and those sultans. After Firozshah, they gained control of the province of Gujarat.

Third were the Bahmanids in the Deccan, but as of this date the sultans of the Deccan have no power of their own left—the great begs have gained control of all the provinces. If the sultan needs anything, he has to ask the begs for it.

Fourth was Sultan Mahmud in the province of Malwa, which is also called Mandu. The dynasty was called the Khalji. Rana Sanga the Infidel defeated him and seized most of the province, but he had grown weak. The ancestors of this dynasty were patronized by Firozshah. Afterward they seized the province of Malwa.

Fifth was Nusrat Shah in Bengal. His father became padishah in Bengal and was a sayyid known as Sultan Alauddin.

Nusrat Shah ruled by hereditary succession. There is an amazing custom in Bengal: rule is seldom achieved by hereditary succession. Instead, there is a specific royal throne, and each of the amirs, viziers, or officeholders has an established place. It is that throne that is of importance to the people of Bengal. For every place, a group of obedient servants is established. When the ruler desires to dismiss anyone, all the obedient servants then belong to whomever he puts in that person's place. The royal throne, however, has a peculiarity: anyone who succeeds in killing the king and sitting on the throne becomes king. Amirs, viziers, soldiers, and civilians all submit to him, and he becomes the padishah and ruler like the former ruler. The people of Bengal say, "We are the legal property of the throne, and we obey anyone who is on it." For instance, before Nusrat Shah's father, Sultan Alauddin, an Abyssinian killed the king, took the throne, and reigned for a time. The Abyssinian was killed by Sultan Alauddin, who then became king. Sultan Alauddin's son has now become king by hereditary succession. Another custom in Bengal is that it is considered disgraceful for anyone who becomes king to spend the treasuries of former kings. Whoever becomes king must accumulate a new treasury, which is a source of pride for the people. In addition, the salaries and stipends of all the institutions of the rulers, treasury, military, and civilian are absolutely fixed from long ago and cannot be spent anywhere else.

The five great Muslim padishahs with vast realms and huge armies are the five who have been mentioned.

Of the infidels, the greater in domain and army is the rajah of Vijayanagar. The other is Rana Sanga, who had recently grown so great by his audacity and sword. His original province was Chitor. When the sultans of Mandu grew weak, he seized many provinces belonging to Mandu, such as Ranthambhor, Sarangpur, Bhilsan, and Chanderi. Chanderi had been in the *daru'l-harb* for some years and held by Sanga's highest-ranking officer, Medini Rao, with four or five thousand infidels, but in 934, through the grace of God, I took it by force within a ghari or two, massacred the infidels, and brought it into the bosom of Islam, as will be mentioned.

All around Hindustan are many rays and rajahs. Some are obedient to Islam, while others, because they are so far away and their places impregnable, do not render obedience to Muslim rulers.

Hindustan lies in the first, second, and third climes, with none of it in the fourth clime. It is a strange country. Compared to ours, it is another world. Its mountains, rivers, forests, and wildernesses, its villages and provinces, animals and plants, peoples and languages, even its rain and winds are altogether different. Even if the Kabul dependencies that have warm climates bear a resemblance to Hindustan in some aspects, in others they do not. Once you cross the Indus, the land, water, trees, stones, people, tribes, manners, and customs are all of the Hindustani fashion. The mountain range in the north that has been mentioned—as soon as the Indus is crossed these mountains are dependent provinces to Kashmir. Although as of this date the provinces in this range, like Pakhli and Shahmang, mostly are not obedient to Kashmir, nonetheless they used to be inside Kashmir. Once past Kashmir, there are innumerable peoples, tribes, districts, and provinces in this range. There are people continuously in these mountains all the way to Bengal, even to the ocean. This much has been ascertained and confirmed by the people of Hindustan, but of these groups no one can give any real information. All they say is that the people of the mountains are called Khas. It has occurred to me that since Hindustanis pronounce the sound *sh* as *s*, since the principal city in the mountains is Kashmir, which means "mountain of the Khasis," since *mir* means mountain and the people of this mountain are called Khasia, and since aside from Kashmir no other city has ever been heard of in these mountains, this may be why they call it Kashmir. The products of the people of the mountains are musk, yak-tails, saffron, lead, and copper. The people of India call the range Sivalik Parbat. In the language of India *sava* means a quarter, *lak* means a hundred thousand, and *parbat* means mountain—therefore Siwalik Parbat means "a quarter lac plus a hundred thousand mountains," that is, 125,000 mountains. The snow never melts on these mountains, and the snow-covered caps can be seen from some of the provinces of Hindustan, such as Lahore, Sirhind, and Sambhal. In Kabul this mountain range is called the Hindu Kush. From Kabul the range runs to the east and slightly to the south. South of it is all Hindustan. To the north of the range and the unknown tribes who are called Khas is the province of Tibet. Many large rivers rise in this range and flow through Hindustan. Six large rivers to the north of Sirhind—the Indus, the Bahat, the Chenab, the Ravi, the Beas, and the Sutlej—all join at one place in the vicinity of Multan. After they all join it is called the Indus. It flows to the west, passes through the province of Tatta, and joins the Indian Ocean. Aside from these six, there are other great rivers like the Jumna, the Ganges, the Rapti, the Gomati, the Gogra, the Sarju, the Gandak, as well as many other large ones, all of which join the Ganges. Flowing to the east, the Ganges passes through Bengal and spills into the ocean. The source of all of these is the Sivalik Range.

There are still other large rivers that rise in the mountains of Hindustan, like the Chambhal, Banas, and Betwa, but there is never any snow on these mountains. These rivers also join the Ganges.

Hindustan has other mountain ranges too. Among them is a range that runs from north to south beginning in the province of Delhi at a building made by Firozshah called the Jahannuma, which is situated on a rocky little mountain. Running from there are patches of rocky little mountains in the vicinity of Delhi. When they reach the province of Mewat, the mountains become larger. Passing through Mewat they go to the province of Bayana. The mountains of Sikri, Bari, and Dholpur are of this same range. Although it is not contiguous, Gwalior, which is also called Galior, is a spur of the range. The mountains of Ranthambhor, Chitor, Mandu, and Chanderi are also of this range. In some places there are breaks of seven or eight leagues. They are low, rugged, rocky, and forested and never have any snow on them. Some rivers in Hindustan have their sources in these mountains.

Most of the provinces of Hindustan are located on flat terrain. So many cities and so many provinces—yet there is no running water anywhere. The only running water is in the large rivers. There are still waters in some places, and even in cities that have the capability of digging channels for running water they do not do so. This may be for any one of several reasons. One is that the agriculture and orchards have absolutely no need for water. Fall crops are watered by the monsoon rains, and strangely the spring crops come even if there is no rain. For a year or two sapling trees are watered either by waterwheel or by bucket, but after that they have no need of irrigation. Some vegetables are watered. In Lahore, Dipalpur, Sirhind, and those regions a waterwheel is used. Two long pieces of rope are looped the size of the well. Wooden stakes are fastened across the two pieces of rope, and jars are fastened to the wooden stakes. The ropes to which the jars are fastened are thrown around a wheel that is over the well. Another wheel is put on the other end of the axle of this wheel. Next to this wheel yet another wheel like the first one is put. As an ox turns this wheel, the spokes enter the spokes of the second wheel and turn the wheel with the jars. A trough is put at the place where the water spills out, and by means of the trough the water is taken wherever it is needed.

In Agra, Chandwar, Bayana, and those regions they irrigate by means of the bucket. This is a laborious and filthy method. A forked stick is raised next to a well, and across the fork a pulley is fastened. A large bucket is fastened to a long rope, which is thrown over the pulley. One end of the rope is tied to an ox. It takes one person to lead the ox and another to empty the water from the bucket. Every time the ox is led out to pull up the bucket and then led back, the rope is dragged through the ox's path, which is sullied with ox urine and dung, as it falls back into the well. For some types of agriculture that need irrigation, water is carried in jars by men and women.

The cities and provinces of Hindustan are all unpleasant. All cities, all locales are alike. The gardens have no walls, and most places are flat as boards.

On the banks of some large rivers and riverbeds, due to the monsoon rains, are gullies that prevent passage. In some places in the plains are forests of thorny trees in which the people of those districts hole up and obstinately refuse to pay tribute. In Hindustan there is little running water aside from the great rivers. Occasionally in some places there are still waters. All the cities and provinces live from well or pond water, which is collected from the monsoon rains. In

Hindustan the destruction and building of villages and hamlets, even of cities, can be accomplished in an instant. Such large cities in which people have lived for years, if they are going to be abandoned, can be left in a day, even half a day, so that no sign or trace remains. If they have a mind to build a city, there is no necessity for digging irrigation canals or building dams. Their crops are all unirrigated. There is no limit to the people. A group gets together, makes a pond, or digs a well. There is no making of houses or raising of walls. They simply make huts from the plentiful straw and innumerable trees, and instantly a village or city is born.

REVIEW QUESTIONS

1. How would you characterize Babur's approach toward and observations of "Hindustan" (India)?
2. Do Babur's historical comments seem objective? Why or why not?
3. Does Babur seem to be an intelligent or knowledgeable observer? Why or why not?
4. What is your general impression of this author?

An Advisor to the Emperor Akbar Describes the Imperial Harem (c. 1600)

ABU'L FAZL, *The Ain-I Akbari*

Only Asoka, who ruled in the third century B.C.E., is as highly regarded as Akbar among India's kings and emperors. Humayun, son of the Mughal founder, Babur, and Akbar's father, was driven from India in 1540, ten years after his father's death, and did not regain his kingdom for another fifteen years. Shortly after returning, he fell down a steep stone stairway in his library and died (1556). His thirteen-year-old son was now emperor of the fledgling Mughal empire. Fortunately, Akbar's mother and an advisor to his father assumed control for Akbar. Orders were issued in his name, and he was trained to become an emperor.

Akbar had great charisma, and he became strong enough to forge an infrastructure and administrative system that supported the empire for a century and allowed his successors to pursue art and other private interests. His reign was characterized by religious and ethnic tolerance, but he exercised a firm hand over the bureaucracy and all officials, provincial and central. He may well be the only Muslim ruler of India who was not just respected but even loved by his Hindu subjects. A major key to his success was his diplomacy; he married a Rajput princess, a Hindu, strengthening his standing with Hindus and bringing erstwhile foes, the fierce Rajputs, into the political structure. He also suspended the jiziyah, a tax against non-Muslims. He was indeed "the real builder of the Mughal empire." His court was visited by numerous

Europeans, with whom Akbar was fond of discussing religious and philosophical ideas.

Abu'l Fazl, Akbar's close companion, kept conscientious accounts of Akbar's many activities, including his philosophical and religious explorations. He was meticulous in recording the details of his sovereign's practices and interests. When in 1602, three years before Akbar's death, Abu'l Fazl was killed by a favorite of Jahangir, Akbar's estranged son and successor, the emperor became despondent.

In the *Ain-I Akbari,* Abu'l Fazl recorded both personal and institutional features of Akbar's life and reign. The following section deals with the imperial harem. At Fatehpur Sikri, a royal establishment built by Akbar and then abandoned for lack of a reliable fresh water supply, a gigantic chess board was constructed. The ladies of the harem then served as the chess pieces. Akbar and royal guests would stand in a tower overlooking the court and direct the ladies where to move. Fatehpur Sikri, just outside of Agra, still exists as an important tourist attraction; so does the chess board.

THE IMPERIAL HAREM

His Majesty is a great friend of good order and propriety in business. Through order, the world becomes a meadow of truth and reality; and that which is but external, receives through it a spiritual meaning. For this reason, the large number of women—a vexatious question even for great statesmen—furnished his Majesty with an opportunity to display his wisdom, and to rise from the low level of worldly dependence to the eminence of perfect freedom. The imperial palace and household are therefore in the best order.

His Majesty forms matrimonial alliances with princes of Hindustan, and of other countries; and secures by these ties of harmony the peace of the world.

As the sovereign, by the light of his wisdom, has raised fit persons from the dust of obscurity, and appointed them to various offices, so does he also elevate faithful persons to the several ranks in the service of the seraglio. Short-sighted men think of impure gold, which will gradually turn into pure gold; but the far-sighted know that his Majesty understands how to use elixirs and chemical processes. Any kind of growth will alter the constitution of a body; copper and iron will turn to gold, and tin and lead to silver; hence it is no matter of astonishment if an excellent being changes the worthless into men. "The saying of the wise is true that the eye of the exalted is the elixir for producing goodness." Such also are the results flowing from the love of order of his Majesty, from his wisdom, insight, regard to rank, his respect for others, his activity, his patience. Even when he is angry, he does not deviate from the right path; he looks at everything with kindly feelings, weighs rumours well, and is free from all prejudice; he considers it a great blessing to have the good wishes of the people, and does not allow the intoxicating pleasures of this world to overpower his calm judgment.

His Majesty has made a large enclosure with fine buildings inside, where he reposes. Though there are more than five thousand women, he has given to each a separate apartment. He has also divided them into sections, and keeps them attentive to their duties. Several chaste women have been appointed as *dāroghas,* and superintendents over each section, and one has been selected for the duties of writer. Thus, as in the imperial offices, everything is here also in proper order. The salaries are sufficiently liberal. Not counting the presents, which his Majesty most generously bestows, the women of the highest rank receive from 1610 to 1028 Rs. *per mensem.* Some of the servants have from 51 to 20, others from 40 to 2 Rs. Attached to the private audience hall of the palace is a clever and zealous writer, who superintends the expenditure of the Harem, and keeps an account of the cash and the stores. If a woman wants anything, within the limit of her salary, she applies to one of the *Tahwīldārs* (cash-keepers) of the seraglio. The *Tahwīldār* then sends a memorandum to the writer, who checks it, when the General Treasurer makes the payment in cash, as for claims of this nature no cheques are given.

The writer also makes out an estimate of the annual expenditure, writes out summarily a receipt, which is countersigned by the ministers of the state. It is then stamped with a peculiar imperial seal, which is only used in grants connected with the Harem, when the receipt becomes payable. The money itself is paid by the cash-keeper of the General Treasury to the General *Tahwīldār,* who on the order of the writer of the Harem, hands it over to the several Sub-*Tahwīldārs* for distribution among the servants of the seraglio. All moneys are reckoned in their salaries at the current rate.

The inside of the Harem is guarded by sober and active women; the most trustworthy of them are placed about the apartments of his Majesty. Outside the enclosure the eunuchs are placed; and at a proper distance, there is a guard of faithful *Rājpūts,* beyond whom are the porters of the gates. Besides, on all four sides, there are guards of Nobles, *Ahadīs,* and other troops, according to their ranks.

Whenever *Begams,* or the wives of nobles, or other women of chaste character, desire to be presented, they first notify their wish to the servants of the seraglio, and wait for a reply. From thence they send their request to the officers of the palace, after which those who are eligible are permitted to enter the Harem. Some women of rank obtain permission to remain there for a whole month.

Notwithstanding the great number of faithful guards, his Majesty does not dispense with his own vigilance, but keeps the whole in proper order.

REVIEW QUESTIONS

1. What evidence is there that Abu'l Fazl was a careful observer?
2. What does this selection suggest about the proper role of women in this society? How does that role compare with a woman's place in your society?
3. What generalizations can you draw about the society that Akbar ruled from the information given here?
4. Why is the imperial harem an important topic for Abu'l Fazl?

An Italian Adventurer Describes Daily Life in India (1614–1626)

PIETRO DELLA VALLE, *The Indian Letters of "Il Fantastico"*

Born in Rome in 1586 to a noble family with ties to the papacy, Pietro della Valle was well educated and had a flair for poetry and romantic love. After a broken love affair, he fled Venice in June 1614 for Constantinople, where he lived for a year. Here he married a Syrian Christian who accompanied him on his travels. When she died at the end of 1621, he transported her body with him to Portuguese India (Surat and Goa) and finally home to Rome. When he finally returned to Rome in 1626, he was appointed papal chamberlain by Urban VIII. His second wife, a Georgian, accompanied him on his further travels. He died in Rome in 1652.

Pietro della Valle's travel accounts were in the form of fifty-four letters to a friend, a professor of medicine at Naples. They are noted for their detailed descriptions and acute observations, especially of people.

"DRINKING IN THE AIR"

. . . And they are so scrupulous that even among the Indians themselves one of more noble race not only neither eats nor makes use of the same clothes or vessels, nor communicates in anything with one less noble, but also endures not to be touched by him; if it happen by chance that he should be, he must purify himself from the defilement by washings and other arrogant ceremonies. It is a sight to behold the great respect which upon this account the ignoble bear to the more noble, and how, upon meeting in the street, the ignoble not only give place, but dance wildly up and down for fear of rushing against the noble and polluting them in any measure. If they did not do so, the noble, and especially the soldiers, would make them do it to the music of blows.

From this averseness to communicate with one another, particularly in the use of eating and drinking vessels, concerning which they are most strict, there springs a strange custom, which I was delighted not only to see, but also sometimes out of gallantry to imitate in conversation. It happens very often during hot weather, both in traveling and in towns, that people have need of refreshing themselves and drinking a little water; but not everyone has a drinking vessel of his own ready, and therefore, to avoid defiling or being defiled by his companion's cup, a way has been found whereby any person may drink in that, or any other whatever, without scruple or danger of any contamination. This is done by drinking in such manner that the vessel touches not the lips or mouth of him who drinks; for it is held up on high with the hand over the mouth, and he that lifts it up highest,

and holds it farthest from his mouth, shows himself most mannerly. And thus pouring the liquor out of the cup into the mouth, they drink round while there is any left, or so long as they please. So accustomed are the Indians to drink in this manner that they practice it almost continually with their own vessels for delight, without the necessity of shunning communication with others. And they are so dexterous at it that I remember having seen one of them take with both hands a vessel as big as a basin, and lifting it up a span higher than his mouth, pour a great torrent of water into his throat and drink it all off. Having been frequently present at such occasions, and in order that the Indians might not be shy of reaching me a cup of water wherever I came, I purposely set myself to learn this manner of drinking, which I call "drinking in the air," and at length have learned it; not with cups as big as basins, like the one above said, but with a handsome cruse, like those we use, or with a little bottle or drinking glass made on purpose. I do it very well; sometimes in conversation we drink healths, *all' Indiana,* after this fashion . . . and he that cannot do it right either wets himself well, or falls a coughing and yexing [hiccoughing], which gives occasion for laughter. . . .

AN INVITATION TO EAT

. . . The King was young, not above seventeen years of age, as they told me, yet his aspect showed him to be older; for he was very fat and lusty, as far as I could conjecture of him while sitting, and, besides, he had long hairs of a beard upon his face, which he suffered to grow without cutting, though they appeared to be but the first down. In complexion he was dusky, not black, as his mother is, but rather of an earthy color, as almost all the Malabaris generally are. He had a louder and bigger voice than youths of his age used to have, and in his speaking, gestures and all other things he showed judgment and manly gravity. From the girdle upward he was all naked, saving that he had a thin cloth, painted with several colors, cast across his shoulders. The hair of his head was long after their manner, and tied in a great knot, which hung on one side wrapped up in a little plain piece of linen and looked like a nightcap fallen on one side. From the girdle downward I saw not what he wore, because he never rose from his seat and the chamber was somewhat dark. Besides that a painted cloth on his shoulders hung down very low. His nephew, who sat beside him, was not naked, but clad in a wholly white garment, and his head was wrapped up in a greater fold of white cloth, like a little turban.

When I came before the King his men made me come near to the little porch in the midst of them, where standing by myself, after the first salutations, the King presently bid me cover my head. This I forthwith did without further entreaty; though with his mother being a lady, I was willing to superabound in courtesy, speaking to her all the time uncovered. But with the son I was minded to enjoy the privilege of my descent, and to receive the favor which he did me as due to my quality. At first they offered me nothing to sit upon, nor was it fitting to sit down upon the bare ground. Yet, to show some difference between myself and the bystanders, after I had put on my hat I leaned upon my sword and so talked as long as I was standing, which was not long, the King, who at first sat sidewise, turning himself directly toward me, although by so doing he turned his back to his nephew. He asked me almost all the same questions as his mother had done: Whence I came, what countries I had traveled through, what princes I had seen, whether I had left my own country upon any misfortune, and how I would have done, thus alone in strange countries, in case of sickness or other accidents. To all which

I answered as I had done to his mother; and upon my saying that I wandered thus alone, up and down, trusting in the help of God, he asked me, Who was my God? I answered him (pointing upward), "The God of Heaven, the Creator of the Universe." Whereupon certain soldiers there present (in all likelihood Moors), as if applauding me, said, "Ah! *Chodia, Chodia,*" which in the Persian tongue signifies Lord and is meant for God, inferring that I worshiped the true God, whom the Moors pretend to know, in opposition to the idols of the gentiles of the country. . . .

The King told me several times that he had very great contentment in seeing me and that no European of any quality had ever been in his country; that my person well showed of what quality I was. Nor was he mistaken herein; for what other person would ever go out of Europe into his country except some Portugal merchant, one of those who come hither for the most part to seek wood to make masts and yards for ships, these woods abounding with very goodly trees. I told him I was sorry I had nothing worthy to present to him; that in my country there wanted not gallant things for his Highness, but, it being so many years since my departure thence, and my travels extending so far, I had nothing left as I desired; yet, as a memorial of my service, I should venture to give him a small trifle from my country. Whereupon I caused my interpreter, who carried it, to offer him a little map of the world which I had brought with me out of Italy; telling him what it was, and how all the countries, lands, seas and islands of the world were exactly delineated on it, with their names set to each place in our tongue, and all that was necessary to make him understand what it was. The King was greatly pleased with it and desired to see several countries, where they lay, and how great they were, asking me sundry questions about them. But since he did not understand our letters written thereon, he satisfied himself with the sight only and with showing it to all the bystanders as a curious and ingenious work of art. Then he asked me whether I could eat in their houses, or of their meats; for he desired to give me something to eat. . . . I told him that if his intention were only to give me meat, the time was already past, nor was I disposed to eat; but if it were to see me eat, I could not eat in that place after the fashion of my country, not having the preparations necessary thereunto, so that his Highness would not see what, perhaps, he desired; and therefore I besought him to excuse me. Nevertheless he was so urgent for it that, not to appear discourteous, I consented to obey him. . . .

The meat was not long in preparing, and, it being now in order, the King called for me again to enter into the room where it stood ready; and one of the Brahmans, who spoke Portugal and was wont to accompany me, asked me whether it would not be more convenient for me to ungird my sword and put off my cassock. I answered that my cassock gave me no trouble, nor was there occasion to lay it off; but my sword might be laid aside, and, therewith ungirding it, I gave it to him to hold. Which I did the rather because, all princes being commonly suspicious, I imagined the King would not like my entering in with arms; and he that goes into another's house to visit him and do him honor ought not to disgust, but to comply with, him in all points. So I entered without a sword, but yet with shoes and stockings on, though with them it be unusual to do so; for none enter into that place but barefoot, and the King himself is so there. Nor did I scruple as to their taxing me with uncleanliness, as undoubtedly they would have done in Turkey and Persia if I had entered into their rooms with shoes or slippers on, because there all the rooms are covered with carpets, but there were no carpets here, only pavement glossed with cow dung. . . .

Entering in this manner and saluting the King as I passed, I went to sit down at the upper end of the chamber, where they had prepared a little square board of the bigness of an ordinary stool, which might serve for a single person, but raised no more than four fingers above the ground. Upon this I sat down, crossing my legs; and that little elevation helped me to keep them out from under me with such decency as I desired. Right before the seat, upon the bare floor, they had spread, instead of a dish (as their custom is, especially with us Christians, with whom they will not defile their own vessels, it not being lawful for them ever to eat again in those wherein we have eaten), a great leaf of that tree which the Arabians and Persians called *mouz,* the Portugals in India *fichi d'India,* Indian fig trees. Upon the leaf they had laid a good quantity of rice, boiled, after their manner, only with water and salt. But for sauce to it there stood on one side a little vessel made of palm leaves and full of very good butter melted. There lay also upon another leaf one of those Indian figs, clean and pared; and hard by it a quantity of a certain red herb, commonly eaten in India, and called by the Portugals *brèdo* (which is the general appellation of all sorts of herbs). In another place lay several fruits used by them, and, among the rest, slices of the bamboo, or great Indian cane, all of them preserved in no bad manner, which they call *acciaò,* besides one sort pickled with vinegar, as our olives are. Bread there was none, because they use none, but rice instead of it; which was no great defect to me, because I am now accustomed to do without it, and eat very little. The King very earnestly prayed me to eat, excusing himself often that he gave me so small an entertainment on the sudden; for if he had known my coming beforehand he would have prepared many *carils* [curries] and divers other more pleasing meats. . . .

. . . And so, to comply with him, although I had little will to eat, I tasted lightly here and there of those fruits and herbs, wherewith my hand was a little soiled, which upon occasion I wiped with my handkerchief, since they use no other table linen, nor had any laid for me. The King, seeing that I touched not the rice, spoke to me several times to eat of it, and to pour upon it some of that butter which stood by it prepared. I did not, because I would not grease myself, there being no spoon; for the Indians eat everything with the hand alone, and so do the Portugals, I know not whether as having learned so to do in India of the Indians, or whether it be their own natural custom . . . for with the same hand, if need be, they mingle together the rice, the butter, the *caril* and all other things how greasy soever, daubing themselves up to the wrist, or rather washing their hands in their meat before they eat it (a fashion indeed sufficiently coarse for people of Europe) . . . The truth is they wash their hands many times during one dinner, to wit, as often as they grease them, but they wipe them not first . . . I, being accustomed to the neatness of Italy, could not conform to slovenliness; and, let them cover this barbarous custom with what pretense they please, either of military manners, or what else they think fit, it is little trouble for a civil man to carry even in war and travels, among other necessary things, a spoon, knife and fork, wherewith to eat handsomely. The Turks themselves, barbarous as they are, yet are so much observers of this that among them there is not the meanest soldier, but who, if he has not other better convenience, at least carries his spoon tied to the belt of his sword.

In short, the King frequently urged me to eat of the rice, and I as often refused with several excuses. At last he was so importunate that I was fain to tell him I could not eat that meat in that manner because I had not my instruments. . . . So I sent my Brahman and my Christian servant with my key, and they, the King so enjoining, went and returned in a moment, for my house was directly over against the palace. They brought me a spoon, a silver fork and a clean and fine napkin, very handsomely folded in small plaits. This I spread upon my knees, which it covered down to my feet, and so I began to eat rice, pouring the butter upon it with a spoon, and the other things with the fork, after a very cleanly manner, without greasing myself, or touching anything with my hands. The King and all the rest admired these exquisite, and to them unusual, modes, crying out with wonder, *"Deuru, deuru,"* that I was a *deuru,* that is, a great man, a god, as they speak. I told the King that for eating according to my custom there needed much preparation of a table, linen, plates, dishes, cups and other things; but I was now traveling through strange countries, and treated myself *alla soldatesca,* after the soldiers' fashion, leading the life of a *gioghi* [yogi], and consequently had not with me such things as were necessary. The King answered that it sufficed him to see thus much, since thereby he easily imagined how all my other things would be, and that, in brief, he had never seen any European like me, and that it was a great contentment to him to see me.

REVIEW QUESTIONS

1. What is Pietro della Valle's main point in the section entitled "Drinking in the Air"?
2. What impressed him the most about his encounter with the king? Would you have been similarly impressed?
3. In what ways do his observations demonstrate an interest in detail?

An Italian Physician Comments on the Manners and Customs of the Hindus (late 1600s)

Niccolò Manucci, *Mogul India, 1653–1708*

When he was fourteen years old, Niccolò Manucci (c. 1639–c. 1717) ran away from his home in Venice and hid on a ship bound for Smyrna (in modern Turkey). There, he met an English aristocrat, Henry Bard, or Viscount

Bellomont, entered his service, and accompanied him to Persia (Iran) and India. After Bard's death in 1656, Manucci went to the Mughal (Mogul) court in Delhi, where he obtained an introduction to Prince Dara Shukoh, eldest son of Shah Jahan (the fifth Mughal emperor and Akbar's grandson). Manucci enlisted as an artilleryman in Dara's service and spent the rest of his life in India, serving in the army and as a physician at the Mughal court and elsewhere in the country. His medical knowledge must have been limited, but it was evidently sufficient to give him a good reputation. His practice consisted of bleeding, purging, and cautery. (He took credit for being the first to use enemas in India.) He made, and lost, a great deal of money during his lifetime, married a Portuguese widow, and traveled a great deal.

Written in Portuguese, the *History of the Mogul Empire* is divided into five parts. The first two offer a personal account of Manucci's journey from Venice to Delhi, a short history of political events from Tamurlane to Aurangzeb (1658–1700), and Manucci's personal reflections on his journeys and adventures. The third part of the book describes the Mughal court and system of government. In the final two parts of the book, according to one editor of Manucci's work, "it is hardly possible to discover any plan." Nevertheless, for the later years of Shah Jahan's reign and for that of Aurangzeb, Manucci's statements cannot be ignored. He was honest and specific about his sources, biased against Aurangzeb, the Portuguese, and the Jesuits, and, occasionally, bitter and bigoted in his remarks about Hindus and Muslims. The following selection is from Part III of Manucci's book.

OF THE MANNERS, GOVERNMENT, AND CUSTOMS OF THE HINDŪS AMONG THEMSELVES

The first error of these Hindūs is to believe that they are the only people in the world who have any polite manners; and the same is the case with cleanliness and orderliness in business. They think all other nations, and above all Europeans, are barbarous, despicable, filthy, and devoid of order.

The civilities they pay to each other are as follows, divisible into five categories. In the first they raise the hands to the head and prostrate themselves on the ground; this is the form in which they adore God, and salute their spiritual leaders, the *Sannyāsīs,* who are their monks, and they also employ it for kings, princes, and the great. Although this is practised by nearly every caste, it is not observed by the Brahmans; they prostrate themselves only before God, their teachers, who are always Brahmans, and their monks, also invariably of their own caste.

The second manner of salutation is to lift the hands to the head. It is in this fashion that they salute ordinary persons, governors, generals, and ministers of kings and princes. The third manner is to raise the hands only as high as the stomach; and this is the course adopted by equals and friends, followed by an embrace. The fourth manner is to display the two hands with the palms joined. This is done by the learned and by monks before princes and the great, when those persons make use to them of one of the three methods above described. Finally, the fifth and last mode of salutation is to display the palm of the right hand raised on high; this is how superiors act to inferiors.

Brahmans salute kings in the second manner only; and to it the latter respond in the same form. But what is delightful is to see a Brahman on a visit to another man, for without the slightest salutation he seats himself, and in the conversation the host accords him the title of lordship or excellency, and often that of highness. When he takes his leave he goes off most solemnly without being any more polite on going away than on entering.

There are also among these Hindūs some families in the east called Śūdra, the least noble of the four castes I have spoken of (and to this caste belong nowadays the kings and princes of this country), who are called Vanangamory (Vaṇangāmoṛi). These people pay no civility either to princes or kings, not even to their own false gods; they appear neither in the palaces nor the temples. If you ask them the reason why, recognising as they do the king for their lord, and confessing the idol to be their god, they do not pay them homage like other men, they tell you that the greatness of their sect consists in this; and with that answer, being content with it themselves, they imagine you ought also to be satisfied.

With respect to their fashions of dress, I may say that the great nobles wear nothing more than the following: They bind their hair with a scarf of very fine gold stuff that they call *romals* (*rūmālī*). Then they tie round their waist a piece of white cloth (as is the usual practice in India); it is about four cubits in length, and has a red border. It comes down to their knees. Above this they wear a white wrapper; but it is to be noted that the manner of putting this on varies in each caste. Some among them wear gold or silver rings on their toes. The children of these last carry from birth to seven years of age little bells on their legs, either of gold or silver, and a little chain of the same metal round the waist. As for the rest, they are no more covered than when they were brought into the world.

Some great lords wear a soft turban on their heads, and put on a gown of white cloth that they call a *cabaye (qabā)*, and underneath it very tight drawers; on their feet they have shoes of velvet or of red leather. These they remove when they enter a house or speak to a person of quality, for it is a great piece of bad manners in this country to speak to such a person with your shoes on and your head uncovered. The monks, called *Sannyāsīs*, are excepted, also ascetics, called Tavagi *(tāpasa)*, and Brahmans, and all castes up to about the age of eighteen. This last exception is because up to that age they neither allow their

hair to grow nor bind on the scarf of gold, of which I spoke above; they only leave on the middle of the head a little tail of hair.

The above is the apparel of the princes and the richest nobility. As for the soldiers, labourers, and other ordinary people, they have no more than a cloth bound round their head, and a little string round their middle, attached to which is a morsel of cloth, a span wide and a cubit in length, about the size of one of our ordinary napkins. With this cloth they cover the parts of the body that natural modesty requires to be concealed. Lastly, they have another cloth, somewhat of the same size, bound round the body, which serves in the day-time as a garment and at night as a bed, their mattress being identical with the damp earth. A stone or a piece of wood serves as bolster. Thus what would be looked on in Europe as a severe penance is in this country the ordinary habit. There are some so badly provided that they content themselves with the piece of cloth spoken of above as used to cover the private parts. In this equipment they hold themselves fully dressed and fit to talk to anyone, wherever it might be.

Having spoken of men's dress, the next thing is to say a little about that of women. It is very indifferent, and little can be said about it. From the age of twelve and upwards almost all of them allow their hair to grow long; up to that age they wear only a small tail of hair on the top of the head, like that of the little boys. They do not bind anything on, nor do they make the hair into tresses, but make it into a roll on one side of the head. All have their ears pierced, but not in the European way, for the holes are so large that the ears droop almost to the shoulders. In these holes they wear their ornaments, each according to her degree or her wealth. The custom of having the ears pierced is in this country common to men and women.

Women, when they are not widows, also wear ornaments on the neck, according to the diversity of their castes or of their wealth. Up to the age of nine or ten years they have no more clothing than, as I described above, is worn by boys up to the same age. After that time they wear a piece of white or red cotton cloth that they bind on like a petticoat. Sometimes the *pane (punjam)*—for so they call this cloth—is striped in two colours. One half of the said *pane (punjam)* is thrown over the shoulders or the head when speaking to a person of any position; but when they go to the well or a spring to fetch water, and when at work in their houses, they keep the whole *pane (punjam)* bound round the waist, and thence upwards are naked. They wear nothing on the feet, not even princesses and queens; but the latter wear on their legs jewels of great value, and any other women who are able to afford it do the same.

This is briefly the clothing of these people. Their dwellings also are very small. Excluding the temples of their false gods, some of which cost great sums, and the palaces of a few kings, princes, *et cetera,* which are built of brick and mortar, and even then have no architectural style, all other houses are constructed of earth and pieces of wood bound together with ropes, without much regard to appearances. These wooden posts serve as supporting pillars, and the roof is of thatch. In this way they build a house without using a single nail. The floors of the houses are not stone-paved, nor covered with the sort of cement they make in this country of lime, eggs, and other ingredients mixed together. The floors are of pounded earth only, spread over with a wash of cow's dung. This is the bed of the great majority of humble people in this country, who have no other mattress to lie on. However, rich people have a mat or a quilt on which they sleep; and those that possess this much believe themselves in possession of one of the greatest luxuries in the world.

The ordinary dwelling of these Hindūs being as poverty-stricken as I have described it, their mode of life is no better. For in this land there are no tables or chairs; everybody sits upon the ground. They do not use table-napkins, table-cloths, knives, spoons, or forks, salt-cellars, dishes, or plates; they eat no bread, they drink no wine, and all eat seated upon the ground.

Princes and kings eat in the following manner: They are seated on the ground on a piece of fine cloth. Then the house or the room in which they are to eat is rubbed over with a solution of cowdung. As the palaces of kings have floors made of a cement which looks like fine marble, there they do nothing more than throw down some cowdung mixed in water, and then wipe the floor with a piece of cloth. The floor then looks like a looking-glass. Without all this ceremonial of cleansing with the dung of this animal, as above described, no person of quality sits down to eat. These preparations finished, they bring a great platter of enamelled gold, which is placed on the ground in front of the diners, but without allowing it to touch the cloth on which they are seated. After this some small gold dishes are placed around, and the food is brought from the kitchen in bowls or vessels of silver, fashioned in the shape of cooking-pots. First of all, from these bowls they place rice cooked without salt or other condiment in the large dish, and on this they put some stew. If the whole cannot be contained in the large dish, they put the remainder in the small dishes round about it.

Then the rajah takes whatever pleases him, throwing it with his hand into a plate of rice, where he mixes it and rolls it into balls, which he throws into his mouth with the right hand. The left hand is not allowed to touch any food. All is swallowed without mastication. This fashion they consider very cleanly, and that there is no better way of satisfying oneself; and they say that Europeans eat rice like pigs. Then, before finishing the meal, they send as much as they think sufficient to their wives. For in this country these never eat with their husbands, even though those waiting on the king be eunuchs, children, or women.

The way of eating among the other castes who are not kings is as follows: Monks, ascetics, Brahmans, and the learned before eating wash their hands and bodies. Then they put upon their foreheads, stomach, shoulders, knees and sides a little ashes mixed in water. This ash is either of a white earth they call *naman (nāmam),* or of sandal, according to their caste or the faith they follow. Next they enter the house, finding its floors all rubbed over with cowdung, in the way I have spoken of. They bind round their body a piece of cloth, and sit down with their legs crossed, or upon a small mat of about one cubit in length. Before them is placed the large leaf of certain trees, or smaller leaves of other trees stitched together, not with needle and thread, but with rushes. Upon this leaf is put first of all a pinch of salt and two drops of butter, with which they anoint or rub the leaf. This ceremony completed, they deposit on this platter some rice cooked in water without salt, followed by a little vegetables and some green stuff. When this is eaten, they throw upon the rice left on the said leaf a little sour curds or some whey. When all this food has been swallowed, they rise from the place and move to a courtyard or garden, if there is one in the house where they live. If there is not, they go into the street, and there bathe their hands, mouth, and feet. They do not return to their dwellings till the leaves they have eaten from have been removed, and the ground has been rubbed over afresh in the way already mentioned. For they say that if they did so their bodies would be as polluted as the house.

Since neither Brahmans, ascetics, monks, nor the learned eat any meat or fish in this country (eggs, being here included under the head of meat, are also avoided), I think it as well here to state the food and manner of eating of the other castes. None of those I have hitherto spoken of ever eat cow's flesh. To do so is a very low thing, a defilement, and sinful beyond all imagination. But they eat all the other meats consumed in Europe, and, in addition thereto, rats and lizards. As for shell-fish, these also are classed among the most impure of things, and are not used except by the pariahs. However, almost all the castes eat of the other kinds of meat, and judge it to be most delicious fare.

The food of these people is usually placed on a little cooked rice, and it consists generally of a portion of dry and salted fish. For goats, sheep, chicken, rats, and lizards, are only for the nobility, and if other men eat of these, it is solely at

their festivals and at marriages. Their plate is a leaf, as described above, or a small plate of copper, out of which the whole family eats, one after the other.

Although these people hold it an abomination to eat of the cow, they believe, however, that it is a venerable thing, and one worthy of all praise, to drink that animal's urine, and to smother their faces with it. It is in pursuance of this opinion that the most noble and the most gallant among them rise betimes in the morning, and holding a cow's tail, worship the spot covered thereby. The reason they give is that this is Lakshmī, mother of their god, Vishṇu, and the goddess of prosperity. Their worship over, they hold out their two hands and receive the cow's urine, of which they take a drink. Then, turning the tail into a sort of holy-water sprinkler, they immerse it in the said liquid, and with it they daub their faces. When this ceremonial is over, they declare they have been made holy.

To obtain plenary indulgence for all their sins, they say it is necessary to obtain a beverage composed of milk, butter, cowdung and cow's urine. With this medicament not only is all sin driven away, but all infamy. In this the Brahmans intervene, for it is they alone who can secure this "jubilee." It is obligatory when marrying for the first time, when women arrive at puberty, and on any unlucky day. Even the cleverest men, those who look down on the rest of the world, have their houses rubbed with cowdung before they eat, and then, without other ceremony, have their food brought, and eat it.

There is another class of persons called Nostiguer (?Nāstika), who not only may not be looked upon when eating, but may not hear the sound of any human voice while so occupied. So far is this carried that, when eating, they cause a copper vessel to be beaten hard at their door. Men of this caste do not allow their beard to be touched, either by the razor or by scissors, but it is dragged out, hair by hair, with a small pincers. The first time that the pulling out of the hair of the head and beard is begun, if the patient betrays no sign of pain, he is accepted as a firm disciple; if, on the contrary, he weeps, cries, or makes faces, they say he is too tender, and thereby unworthy to be admitted into the confraternity.

These men are not the only ones who may not be seen eating, for other castes may not look at Brahmans who are eating. In regard to this these Hindūs have a rather amusing habit. The Brahmans, according to their view, are the noblest family of all mankind, and the one most venerated, not merely as superiors, but as gods. Other castes cannot wait on them or fetch them water, nor cook for them. They must wait upon each other for these two purposes, or do it each for himself. With all that, however, they may carry water and cook for the other castes, which appears a moral contradiction, for if it dishonours them to be served by others, how can they be servants to others?

When Brahmans cook for another caste they act as follows: after having cooked the food, they bring it in brass or copper vessels to the house where it is to be eaten—that is, of the man who has given the order. Not being a Brahman, he cannot enter the kitchen, nor inspect the pots in which the food is being cooked. The food having been brought, it is laid out upon leaves, or on copper or brass vessels made like dishes. Having helped the food, the Brahmans do the waiting until the end of the repast. Then they and the master and his guests, if any, come out, and the Brahmans throw water over the eaters' hands and feet; but they do not clear away what has not been eaten, for that would be a dishonour and a disgrace beyond repair. To remove the unused food it is necessary to have another man who is not a Brahman, and if there is none such, he who has eaten must himself remove the leavings, along with the leaf or dish from which he has eaten, and afterwards cleanse the house in the way already described.

As to their mode of eating, it is as follows: they all eat with the right hand, and may not touch anything with the left, not even the plate or leaf from which they have eaten, nor the spoon with which they sup a concoction by way of wine, which is some water boiled with pepper. But a vessel of cold water they lift with the left hand, at the same time never putting the vessel to the mouth. They hold their mouth open and raised to catch the liquid they pour into it. In fine, the greatest piece of refinement in this country is considered to be eating in a clean and orderly way, but this is carried out in no other manner than that described above. Yet, being so very different from that practised by Europeans and Mahomedans, it forms the ground for their strong contempt for these latter.

REVIEW QUESTIONS

1. Manucci has been described as having strong opinions. Is that characteristic expressed in the above selection? How? If you think not, what evidence supports your opinion?
2. How would you characterize Hindu society from this description? Do you like or dislike it? How does your opinion compare with Manucci's?
3. Why is it important to understand the concept of caste in Indian society?
4. What cultural values do all Hindus seem to share, regardless of caste, in these descriptions?

An Employee of the Dutch East India Company Reports on Sri Lankan Society (early 1700s)

François Valentijn's Description of Ceylon

François Valentijn never visited Ceylon, but he did collect accounts from contemporaries and he was familiar with the general region, having spent his career as a minister of the reformed church in the service of the Dutch East India Company in the Dutch East Indies, or Spice Islands (now Indonesia). He was born in 1666 in the Dutch city of Dordrecht to a middle-class family. He was well educated and had a flair for languages, and he secured an appointment with the Dutch East India Company at the young age of nineteen. On board the ship to the East Indies he learned Portuguese, the language of trade in the Indian Ocean, and in the Indies he learned Malay from a young company widow, Cornelia Snaats, whom he married. He was socially popular, in part for his musical abilities but also for his collection of native memorabilia—especially a collection of sea shells—and his scholarly papers. He translated the Bible into Malay and spent a lifetime fruitlessly trying to get it published. He also wrote and published, in a rather disorganized format, a multivolume series of descriptions of the Indian Ocean region, including places, such as Ceylon, which he had not visited. He died in The Hague in 1727 and was given an extravagant funeral.

Valentijn is not remembered for his ministerial career, which was marked by disputes with superiors and his refusal to give in to what he conceived as their unfairness and hypocrisy. It is, rather, his five-volume account of the cultures of the Indian Ocean that has preserved his name. However, its information was sometimes questionable or false, and it was also biased—characteristics that may well have resulted from the unavailability to corroborate his sources.

In the course of its history, the island has been ruled, all or in part, by the Sinhalese (Cingalese in the selection), Indo-Aryan Buddhists. Tamils, Hindu Dravidian speakers originally from Tamilnadu in southeast India, have been present since ancient times, and their presence was intensified in the nineteenth century when many were brought in by the British to be coolies on tea plantations in the northeast region of the island. Political and economic frictions have led to a guerilla war—which has almost become a civil war—that is two decades old and comparable to the situations in Northern Ireland and the Middle East. A tenuous truce has been developed by Norwegian peacekeepers, in part spurred by President Bush's declared war on terrorism.

As regards the Cingalese,[1] the native and oldest inhabitants of this land, they are not entirely black but brownish-yellow in colour, with long and wide ears, not large of stature, somewhat thin in the back, very weak of limbs, swift in body and very ingenious in mind, as they know how to make many beautiful things. They are very hardy by nature both in enduring many

---

[1] Sinhalese; i.e., people of Ceylon

discomforts and in subsisting on poor food and little sleep.

As regards their nature and character, they are very friendly, and very much attached to their language. But they are also very greatly conceited and very proud, to such an extent that they will eat no food prepared in a house of one of lower rank than they imagine themselves to be, nor will they ever marry with them. Lying is not a sin nor a shame among them but a natural thing and they will not blanch the slightest when caught at it.

They are very avaricious but not fighters or thugs, and not envious. On the contrary they are inclined to help all poor and serve all others. They detest robbery very much and are verbally very strongly for virtue. But they do not follow this closely in action. However they have a great esteem for upright and virtuous people.

As most Indians are superstitious, so also are the Cingalese in the utmost degree, and encountering the slightest thing as they go out is enough for them to return home or to abandon something that they have already begun. In the seriousness of their countenance, dealings and walk, they resemble very much the Portuguese. They are very swift in judgment, quick in comprehension and very sharp-witted. But they are also cunning, crafty and very clever at discovering loopholes so that one should not believe them whatever promise they may make.

It is also true that the men are not at all jealous, having no scruples about giving their daughter or even their wives to sleep for a time with their friends who are staying with them. But if a daughter comes to have dealings with someone below her rank, she may well put herself under the protection of her friends, as her father will certainly kill her, not because of a desire for virtue or out of an abhorrence of prostitution but only out of pride that she has fornicated with one less than he. Otherwise, there is no more common sin among them than whoredom to which they even lead their children. Also they will never insult each other as prostitutes, even in the utmost anger, except where a daughter has mixed with one of lower

rank. Also a wife has not much to fear from her husband if she is inclined to adultery, if only she is not caught in the act; for then he has the right to put both to death. . . .

As we have said, they will never marry with one of lesser rank, even though they could gain very much wealth by it. But as this is mostly observed for the daughter and, as a man does not worry about sleeping with one lower, he is never reproached for this if only he does not also eat and drink with her or marry her, nor is it considered a shame. For if he should marry someone lower he would be punished by the overlord with a fine or with imprisonment or both and is henceforth reckoned no higher in rank than his wife and cut off from his caste like a rotten limb.

They let their daughters marry early at 10 to 11 years because they will be assured that their brides are still virgins, though others among them pay very little heed to it. The deciding of the marriage depends completely on the parents who give the daughters some property according to their ability. But as they separate now and then as easily as they come together, in such a case that property, being a bridal dowry, must first be returned. They also do not satisfy themselves with one wife but often take many if they have the ability to feed them. The bridegroom provides the bride's clothing and if he does not have enough he may borrow them.

In their housekeeping they are reasonably neat. And just as they never eat or drink with anyone of a lower status, they will also not do so with their own women. While drinking out of a goblet, they will never put it to their mouth but hold it high up and pour the water in. . . .

The women have to serve the men while they eat and provide what is necessary. After the men have eaten the women eat what remains on their plates. Their rice and food is taken on porcelain plates or even leaves.

Their drink is water or sometimes even some *suri* or *towak*. They are silent during mealtimes and speak little to each other. While the wife serves the rice from the pot, no one may speak but they may do so after this.

They wash their hands and mouth before and

after eating. They always do this for themselves, never letting another do it for them (as happens in some cases among them), as they consider this a vile shame.

Also they are very clean in body and head as they are always accustomed to wash both very often.

The women must prepare the food, pound the rice, go to market, fetch firewood and carry it on their heads, doing nothing else other than eating arecanut the whole day and smoking tobacco or preparing this for their husbands. Moreover, no woman may sit on a stool in the presence of a man. Also they may not give any order to another in the King's name on pain of losing their tongue (this is only permitted to men). As against this is the privilege that women are free of all taxes in respect of their inherited goods which on death go to the King, as also all female animals which are also taxed.

If they go out they go well before daybreak and this gives them status, wearing jewels, and if they do not have these, they think it no shame to borrow them from another. They sleep on mats and the high status ones on quilts. But the children sleep generally without anything under the body.

Thus the men here are mostly lords and the women generally in the Indies mostly slaves of the men.

If they have children, they first consult with an astrologer whether it is born under a lucky or an unlucky star and if the latter they kill it (though seldom the first born) or give it to other people who are inclined to rear it.

Also the children when they grow older never keep the name which they received in their childhood, but receive other lofty titles to which they are very much attached.

REVIEW QUESTIONS

1. Was Valentijn a careful scholar? What evidence supports your opinion?
2. In your opinion, what is his most interesting description?
3. How would you characterize his opinion of the people of Ceylon? Based on the information given here, would you form the same opinion as Valentijn?

3

Africa, 1500–1800

Between 1500 and 1800, the lives of peoples changed irrevocably on the vast African continent. African nations that had been involved in international trade for many centuries continued to export a variety of products, but they found themselves increasingly concentrating on the commodity of slaves. The early Muslim traders to West Africa gave way to those from European nations coming by water, who began to upset the balance of trade in West Africa from Senegal to Angola. Kingdoms on the upper Niger River continued to service Arab camel caravans in the old manner, but the seaport communities gained direct access to foreign goods by trading with Europeans, such as the Portuguese.

The Portuguese took the lead in this transition, but competition from French, English, and Dutch slave traders developed very fast on both the east and west coasts. Whereas trade from Africa had always been a multiproduct market with gold and ivory the most desirable commodities, the demand for workers in the Americas by the late sixteenth century changed the commodity balance rapidly. By contrasting the native account of Leo Africanus of the early 1500s with that of the Portuguese at midcentury and of de Almada at the end of the century, the reader can observe how Portuguese slave traders in the end saw a much different world than did the North African Muslim. The native account of Olaudah Equiano from the mid-eighteenth century provides a picture of the contrasting attitudes and treatment of African traders and Europeans when the slave trade was at its height.

Competition for coastal markets in West Africa can be seen from the accounts already noted, as well as from that of Jean Barbot. The Portuguese enjoyed the privilege of papal authorization and a treaty ensuring their monopoly of the Atlantic slave trade, but as the trade grew in size and profits, Europeans from other nations entered the picture. When Portuguese pilots voyaged from São Thomé to the Mina coast in the late sixteenth century, this agreement still held sway. By the beginning of the seventeenth century, however, competition for the slave trade inspired the English and French to develop a system of licensed privateers that provided employment for ordinary sailors. By licensing a ship captain who was a pirate, England, France, and other European trading nations acquired a ship to prey only upon their enemies. This convention provided additional naval forces for poorer nations, and it gained significant wealth for both privateers and the licensing country. By the time Barbot sailed for the English to sabotage French slave trade south of Senegal in 1695, all European nations with American colonies had become engaged in the slave trade.

The four accounts of travel on the east coast of Africa present the astounding story of how a thriving Indian Ocean and South China Sea trade changed its commodity of preference, how Portuguese attempts to create monopolies affected the lives of

Africans on the coast and inland, and how other European sailors entered the East Africa trade. About a hundred years after the Portuguese drove Arab traders from the East African coast, the Dominican priest John dos Santos was sent to the Swahili port of Sofala and then six hundred miles up the Zambezi River to Christianize the Shona people in Tete and to establish trade connections. A few decades later the Franciscan friar Bernadino and shipwrecked Portuguese Francis Vaz d'Almada found evidence of weakened Portuguese control and renewed influences of Arab Muslims as well as increasing warfare against Portuguese ports by the Dutch. Finally, in 1784, the French slave trader Crassons de Medeuil found a very open commerce in East Africa and hoped that the French would be able to plant colonies on offshore islands.

Africa held an abundance of resources that were largely ignored during this era in favor of an almost exclusive reliance on the slave trade. As African peoples who traded with Christians became entrepreneurs, they captured people from rival ethnic groups; as a result, some Africans profited while others suffered from the concentration upon this one industry.

Usually only natives would travel to the interior of the continent, some on expeditions to capture slaves and some fleeing slave entrepreneurs. European travel into the continent was hampered by diseases, inhospitable geography, and ignorance about native peoples. For these reasons, most travelers wrote of coastal peoples or those who lived only a few hundred miles inland. The writers of many of these accounts use the Muslim term *kaffir* to describe the people of South and East Africa— a term for native African people that carried the sense of "heathen." Whether the term was used by a Muslim or Christian, it implied that the subject being discussed was backward, barbarian, and without religion.

A Moor from Granada Recounts His Travels in West and Central Africa (1507)

LEO AFRICANUS, *The History and Description of Africa*

Al-Hassan Ibn-Mohammed Al-Wezaz Al-Fasi was born a Moor (a North African Muslim) in 1491 in Granada, Spain, was baptized as Giovanni Leone, and became known in modern literature as Leo Africanus. When the Moorish armies were defeated in the following year, his family moved across the Straits of Gibraltar to Morocco. There they were given asylum by Sultan Abu 'Abd Allah Mohammed eth-Thâbiti. Leo's education in law and business, as well as his early travels, exposed him to political and social conflicts in the Mediterranean Basin during the early sixteenth century. In 1520, when returning from a second voyage to Constantinople, he was captured by Venetian pirates and taken to Rome as a present to Pope Leo X (Giovanni de' Medici). The pope accepted the gift, but finding that his new slave was a man of learning and a traveler to strange countries, he freed Leo and gave him a handsome pension.

The following accounts describe one of the earlier voyages that helped to create Leo Africanus's reputation and further his education. His travels into

West and Central Africa probably occurred when he was in his twenties, possibly in 1513 to 1515. He was often very unclear about the dates of his sojourns, and his writings reveal either a misunderstanding of specific geographic locations or a loss of memory between the time of his traveling and his writing of the events. In addition, some experts believe he may have included some information that he did not observe himself but learned from other merchants who had visited sites at different times. The two passages that follow describe places quite far from each other: Melli (Mali) is in West Africa on the Niger River drainage, and Cairo is at the mouth of the Nile River in Egypt.

OF THE KINGDOME OF MELLI

In this kingdome there is a large and ample village containing to the number of six thousand or mo families, and called Melli, whereof the whole kingdome is so named. And here the king hath his place of residence. The region it selfe yeeldeth great abundance of corne, flesh, and cotton. Heere are many artificers and merchants in all places: and yet the king honourably entertaineth all strangers. The inhabitants are rich, and haue plentie of wares. Heere are great store of temples, priests, and professours, which professours read their lectures onely in the temples, bicause they haue no colleges at all. The people of this region excell all other Negros in witte, ciuilitie, and industry; and were the first that embraced the law of Mahumet, at the same time when the vncle of *Ioseph* the king of Maroco was their prince, and the gouernment remained for a while vnto his posteritie: at length *Izchia* subdued the prince of this region, and made him his tributarie, and so oppressed him with greeuous exactions, that he was scarce able to maintaine his family. . . .

OF THE CITIE CALLED MECHELLAT CHAIS

The Mahumetans hauing conquered Egypt, built this citie vpon an high hill standing by the westerne banke of Nilus. The fields of this citie being high ground, are apt for to plant vines vpon, bicause the waters of Nilus cannot ouerflow them. This towne affoordeth new grapes vnto Cairo, almost for halfe the yeere long: but the inhabitants are vnciuill people, being most of them watermen and bargemen.

A DESCRIPTION OF THE HUGE AND ADMIRABLE CITIE OF CAIRO

Cairo is commonly reputed to be one of the greatest and most famous cities in al the whole world. But leauing the common reports & opinions thereof, I will exactly describe the forme and estate wherein it now standeth. And that I may begin with the Etymology or deriuation of the name, Cairo is an Arabian word, corruptly pronounced by the people of Europe: for the true Arabian worde is El Chahira, which signifieth an enforcing or imperious mistresse. This citie built in ancient times by one *Gehoar Chetib* a Dalmatian slaue (as I haue before signified in the beginning of my discourse) containeth within the wals not aboue eight thousand families, being inhabited by noblemen, gentlemen, and merchants that sell wares brought from all other places. The famous temple of Cairo commonly called Gemih Hashare, that is to say, the glorious temple, was built also by the foresaide slaue, whom we affirmed to be the founder of the citie, and whose surname was *Hashare,* that is to say, famous, being giuen him by the Mahumetan patriarke that was his prince. This city standeth vpon a most beautiful plaine, neere vnto a certaine mountaine called Mucatun, about two miles distant from Nilus, and is enuironed with stately wals, and fortified with iron gates: the principall of which gates is called Babe Nanfre, that is, the gate of victory, which standeth eastward towards the desert of the red sea; and the gate called Beb Zuaila being next vnto the old citie and to Nilus; and also Bebel Futuh, that is to say, the gate of triumph, standing towards the lake and the fieldes. And albeit Cairo aboundeth euerie where with all kinde of merchants and artificers, yet that is the princi-pall streete of the whole citie which stretcheth from the gate of Nanfre to the gate of Zuaila; for in it are builte most stately and admirable palaces and colleges, and most sumptuous tem-ples, among which is the temple of Gemith El-hechim the third schismaticall Califa of Cairo. Other temples there are of a maruellous bignes, which to describe in particular, I thinke it su-perfluous. Heere are many bathstoues also very artificially built. Next of all is the streete called Beinel Casrain, containing to the number of threescore cooks or victualers shops, furnished with vessels of tinne: there are certaine other shops also, wherein are to be solde delicate wa-ters or drinkes made of all kinds of fruits, be-ing for noblemen to drinke of, and these waters they keepe most charily in fine vessels, partly of glasse, and partly of tinne: next vnto these are shops where diuers confections of hony and sugar, vnlike vnto the confections of Europe, are to be sold: then follow the fruiterers shops, who bring outlandish fruits out of Syria, to wit, quinces, pomegranates, and other fruits which grow not in Egypt: next vnto them are the shops of such as sell egges, cheese, and pancakes fried with oile. And next of all there is a streete of the principall artificers shops. Beyond which streete standeth a college built by the Soldan called *Ghauri,* who was slaine in a battaile against *Se-lim* the great Turke. And next vnto the college are diuers rankes of drapers shops. In the first ranke there is most outlandish linnen cloth to be sold, as namely fine cloth of cotton brought from Balabach, and cloth called Mosall diuers colours, like to the windowes of some places of Europe; and their gates be artificially carued and beautified with gold and azure. Some of these palaces are for the Soldan and his familie: others

for the familie of his wife, and the residue for his concubines, his eunuches, and his garde. Likewise the Soldan had one palace to keepe publique feastes in; and another wherein to giue audience vnto forren ambassadours, and to exalt himselfe with great pompe and ceremonies: and another also for the gouernours and officials of his court. But all these are at this present abol-ished by *Selim* the great Turke.

OF THE CUSTOMES, RITES, AND FASHIONS OF THE CITIZENS OF CAIRO

The inhabitants of Cairo are people of a merrie, iocund, and cheerefull disposition, such as will promise much, but performe little. They exer-cise merchandize and mechanicall artes, and yet trauell they not out of their owne natiue soile. Many students there are of the lawes, but very few of other liberall artes and sciences. And al-beit their colleges are continually full of stu-dents, yet few of them attaine vnto perfection. The citizens in winter are clad in garments of cloth lined with cotton: in summer they weare fine shirts: ouer which shirts some put on lin-nen garments curiously wrought with silke, and others weare garments of chamblet, and vpon their heads they carrie great turbants couered with cloth of India. The women goe costly at-tired, adorning their foreheads and necks with frontlets and chaines of pearle, and on their heads they weare a sharpe and slender bonet of a span high, being very pretious and rich. Gownes they weare of woollen cloth with streite sleeues, being curiously embroidered with needle-worke, ouer which they cast certaine veiles of most excellent fine cloth of India. They couer their heads and faces with a kinde of blacke scarfe, through which beholding others they cannot be seene themselues. Vpon their feet they weare fine shooes and pantofles, somewhat after the Turkish fashion. These women are so ambitious & proud, that all of them disdaine either to spin or to play the cookes: wherfore their husbands are constrained to buie victuals ready drest at the cookes shops: for very few, except such as haue a great familie, vse to prepare and dresse their victuals in their owne houses. Also they vouchsafe great libertie vnto their wiues: for the good man being gone to the tauerne or victualling-house, his wife tricking vp her selfe in costly apparell, and being perfumed with sweet and pretious odours, walketh about the citie to solace her selfe, and parley with her kinsfolk and friendes. . . .

REVIEW QUESTIONS

1. In what ways are these two accounts similar? How do they differ?
2. Which city did Leo Africanus find to be the most attractive and with the most desirable residents? Explain.
3. To what extent do these descriptions reveal Leo to be a merchant?
4, To what extent do these descriptions reveal him to be educated?

A Portuguese Missionary Describes "Strange Customs" in Ethiopia (1590)

JOHN DOS SANTOS, *Ethiopia Oriental (Eastern Ethiopia)*

Zimbabwe is a Shona word meaning "dwelling of a chief," and the king whom dos Santos met in 1590 lived in one of many zimbabwes on the Zambesi River. The village of Tete, a place about six hundred miles inland from the Indian Ocean where this Dominican priest spent about a year, is still a town on a river in the westernmost part of Mozambique. By the end of the sixteenth century, villages such as Tete had acquired a greater role in the direct trade with Europeans because of the demise of empires such as Greater Zimbabwe. This, consequently, brought them to the attention of Portuguese missionaries and traders. The Shona people dos Santos encountered here were neighbors of the Bantu, whom we will meet in a later selection.

Dos Santos was sent from Lisbon as a missionary and was stationed at Sofala for four years before proceeding up the Zambesi River. He and his companion, Father John Madeira, recorded 1,694 baptisms at Tete. His zeal caused him to once set fire to a mosque, which in turn caused the Muslim natives of Sofala to react strongly against dos Santos and Madeira. After a year in the upcountry, he was sent back to Sofala and stayed on the coast until 1597, when he was transferred to Goa in India. As can be seen from the following text, dos Santos paid particular attention to customs that astonished him, such as the ritual killing of a deceased king's wives while his concubines became the property or responsibility of his successors.

OF KITEVE, KING OF THAT COUNTRY, WITH THE STRANGE CUSTOMS OBSERVED IN THOSE PARTS, IN COURT, CITY, AND COUNTRY

The king of these parts is of curled hair, a gentile, which worships nothing, nor hath any knowledge of God; yea, rather he carries himself as God of his countries, and so is holden and reverenced of his vassals. He is called Kiteve, a title royal and no proper name, which they exchange for this so soon as they become kings. The Kiteve hath more than one hundred women all within doors, amongst which one or two are his queens, the rest as concubines. Many of them are his own aunts, cousins, sisters, and daughters, which he no less useth, saying that his sons by them are true heirs of the kingdom without mixture of other blood. When the Kiteve dieth, his queens must die with him to do him service in the other world; who accordingly at the instant of his death take a poison (which they call *lucasse*) and die therewith. The successor succeedeth as well to the women as the state. None else but the king may, upon pain of death, marry his sister or daughter. This successor is commonly one of the eldest sons of the deceased king, and of his great women or queens; and if the eldest be not sufficient, then the next, or if none of them be fit, his brother of whole blood. The king commonly, while he liveth, maketh the choice, and trains up him to affairs of state, to whom he destines the succession. Whiles I lived there . . . the king had above thirty sons, and yet showed more respect to his brother, a wise man, than to any of them, all honoring him as apparent heir.

The same day the king dies, he is carried to a hill where all the kings are interred. And early the next morning, he whom the king had named his successor goeth to the king's house where the king's women abide in expectation, and by their consent he enters the house, and seats himself with the principal of them in a public hall, where the king was wont to sit to hear causes, in a place drawn with curtains or covered with a cloth, that none may see the king nor the women with him. And thence he sends his officers, which go through the city and proclaim festivals to the new king, who is now quietly possessed of the king's house, with the women of the king deceased, and that all should go and acknowledge him for the king: which is done by all the great men then in court, and the nobles of the city, who go to the palace now solemnly guarded, and enter into the hall by licence of the officers, where the new king abides with his women; entering some, and some creeping on the ground till they come to the middle of the hall, and thence speak to the new king, giving him due obeisance, without seeing him or his women. The king makes answer from within, and accepts their service: and after that draws the curtains, and shows himself to them; whereat all of them clap their hands, and then turn behind the curtains, and go forth creeping on the ground as they came in. And when they are gone, others enter and do in like sort. In this ceremony the greatest part of the day is spent with feasting, music, and dancing through the city. The next day the king sends his officers through the kingdom to declare this his succession, and that all should come to the court to see him break the bow. Sometimes there are many competitors and then he succeeds whom the women admit into the king's house. For none may enter by law without their leave, nor can be king without peaceable entrance—forceable entry forfeiting his right and title. By bribes, therefore, and other ways, they seek to make the women on their side.

Near the kingdom of Kiteve is another of laws and customs like thereto, where the Sedanda reigns: both of which were sometimes but one kingdom. Whiles I was in Sofala, the Sedanda being incurably sick of a leprosy, declared his successor, and poisoned himself: which also is the custom there, if any king have any deformity in his person. The named successor sought admittance of the women. But they, much distasting him, had secretly sent by night for another prince whom they better liked, as more valiant and better beloved; whom they admitted, and assembled themselves with him in the public hall, and caused proclamation to be made to the people of his succession. The other, whom they had rejected, fled for fear of his life, and, being mighty, assembled a great power, and by force entered the king's house. But this was strange to all, who therefore forsook him, and stuck to him whom the women had chosen. Whereupon the other fled and no more lifted up his head.

Before the new king begins to govern, he sends for all the chiefs in the kingdom, to come to the court and see him break the king's bow, which is all one with taking possession of the kingdom. In those courts is a custom then also to kill some of those lords or great men, saying they are necessary for the service of the deceased king; whereupon they kill those of whom they stand in fear or doubt, or whom they hate, in stead of whom they make and erect new lords. This custom causeth such as fear themselves to flee the land. Anciently the kings were wont to drink poison in any grievous disasters, as in a contagious disease, or natural impotency, lameness, the loss of their fore-teeth, or other deformity; saying that kings ought to have no defect. Which if it happened, it was honor for him to die, and go to better himself in that better life, in which he should be wholly perfect. But the Kiteve which reigned while I was there, would not follow his predecessors herein; but having lost one of his fore-teeth, sent to proclaim through his kingdom that one of his teeth were fallen out, and (that they might not be ignorant when they saw him want it) that if his predecessors were such fools, for such causes to kill themselves, he would not do so, but await his natural death, holding his life necessary to conserve his estate against his enemies, which example he would commend to posterity.

If the Kaffirs have a suit, and seek to speak with the king, they creep to the place where he is, having prostrated themselves at the entrance, and look not on him all the while they speak, but lying on one side clap their hands all the time (a rite of obsequiousness in those parts), and then, having finished, they creep out of the doors as they came in. For no Kaffir may enter on foot to speak to the king, nor eye him in speaking, except the familiars and particular friends of the king. . . .

Every September the Kiteve, at the change of the moon, goeth from Zimbabwe his city to a high hill to perform obits or obsequies to his predecessors there buried, with great troops both of the city and other parts of the kingdoms called up therefore. As soon as they are ascended, they eat and drink their *pombe,* the king beginning, till they be all drunk; continuing their eating and drinking eight days, one of which they call Pemberar of a kind of tilting exercise then used. In this feast the king and his nobles clothe themselves in their best silks and cotton clothes, which they have with many thrums, like carpet fringes, wrought therein, hanging down on the eyes and face as a horse's fore-top. They tie about the head a large ribbon, and divided into two parts, they run one against another on foot with bows and arrows in their hands, which they shoot upwards that none be hurt; and thus make a thousand careers and feats till they be tired and cannot stir. And they which hold out longest are accounted the valiantest properest men, and are therefore rewarded with the prize propounded. . . .

After this eight days' festival, they spend two days or three in mourning. And then the devil enters into one of the company, saying he is the soul of the deceased king, father of the present, to whom those obsequies are performed; and that he comes to speak to his son. The Kaffir thus possessed falls down on the ground in an ill plight and is distracted, the devil speaking by his mouth all the strange tongues of all the Kaffir nations about them, many of which some of the men present understand. After this, he begins to behave himself and to speak like the king pretended, by which signs the Kaffirs acknowledge the coming of the deceased king's soul. The king is now made acquainted herewith, and comes with his grands to the place where the demoniac is, and do him great reverence. Then all the rest go aside, and the king remains with him alone, speaking friendly as with his father departed, and inquireth if he be to make wars, whether he shall overcome his enemies, touching dearth, or troubles in his kingdom, and whatever else he desireth to know. And the devil answereth his questions, and adviseth him what to do.

The Kiteve has two or three hundred men for his guard, which are his officers and executioners, called *inficia,* and go crying, "Inhama, inhama," that is "Flesh, flesh." He hath another sort called *marombes,* jesters, which have their songs and prose in praise of the king, whom they call, Lord of the Sun and Moon, King of the Land and Rivers, Conqueror of his Enemies, in everything great, great thief, great witch, great lion; and all other names of greatness which they can invent, whether they signify good or bad, they attribute to them. When the king goeth out of doors, these *marombes* go round about him with great cries of this argument. He hath others which are musicians in his hall, and at the court gates, with divers instruments resounding his praises. Their best musical instrument is called *ambira,* much like to our organs. . . .

They use three kinds of oath in judgement most terrible, in accusations wanting just evidence. The first is called *Lucasse,* which is a vessel full of poison, which they give the suspected, with words importing his destruction and present death if he be guilty, his escape if innocent. The terror whereof makes the conscious confess the crime. But the innocent drink it confidently without harm, and thereby are acquitted of the crime. And the plaintiff is condemned to him whom he falsely had accused; his wife, children, and goods being forfeited, one moiety to the king, and the other to the defendant.

The second oath they call *xoqua,* which is made by iron heated red hot in the fire, causing the accused to lick it being so hot with his tongue, saying, that the fire shall not hurt him if he be innocent; otherwise it shall burn his tongue and mouth. . . .

The third oath they call Calano, which is a vessel of water made bitter with certain herbs which they put into it, whereof they give the accused to drink, saying that if he be innocent he shall drink it all off at one gulp without any stay, and cast it all up again at once without any harm. If guilty he shall not be able to get down one drop without gargling and choking.

The Kiteve makes some royal huntings, with three or four thousand men, in the deserts near the city: encircling all the beasts in that compass, tigers, lions, ounces, elephants, buffalos, deer, wild swine, and the rest, driving them together, and then setting on their dogs, with cries, arrows, and assegais, pursue and kill what they can. Then may they kill the lion, which at other times by the Kiteve's prohibition is a deadly offence, because he is entitled Great Lion. After this they eat in the same place with great jollity; but the most they carry home, and hang it for the king and for themselves.

Their houses are round, of unhewn timber covered with straw, like a thatched country house, which they remove at pleasure.

The Kaffirs buy of the parents their wives, for kine, clothes, or otherwise, according to their ability. And therefore they that have many daughters are rich. If any mislike his wife, he may return her to him that sold her, but with loss of the price paid; and the parent may sell her again to another husband. The wife has no liberty to forsake her husband. The ceremonies of marriage are dances and feastings of the neighbors; every invited guest bringing his present of meal, maize, inhames, fitches, or other victuals for that day's expenses. He which is able may have two wives, but few are able to maintain them, except the great men which have many, but one is principal, the rest as handmaids. Some of them live like wild beasts, and when they are near time of travail, they go to the wilderness or untilled places, and there go up and down receiving the savor of that wild place, which causeth to them quicker delivery. They, after their delivery, wash themselves and their children in a lake or river, and then return to their houses with them in their arms without swaddling them.

REVIEW QUESTIONS

1. What did dos Santos find most significant about the Shona people in Tete?
2. Did dos Santos respect the royalty and religion of the kingdom of the Kiteve? Why do you think so? Why not?
3. How would you characterize the religious practices and behaviors dos Santos described?
4. What was the role of women in Tete? What evidence exists in this account of class differences among women?

A Portuguese Trader Describes the People and Trade of Gambia (c. 1594)

ANDRÉ ÁLVARES DE ALMADA, *Brief Treatise on the Rivers of Guinea*

Beginning in the fourteenth century, the Gambia River became very important in international trade primarily because of the organization of Mandinka merchants (also spelled Mandinga, an African native cultural group) into small companies that conveyed goods from the interior to the West African coast. When the nation of Ghana split into successor states by midcentury, the Mandinka gained control of lands stretching from the upper Niger River state of Kangaba through the length of the Gambia River to the sea. Consequently, when the Portuguese began an extensive slave trade to the Americas in the mid–sixteenth century, the Mandinka nation played a key role in the enterprise by capturing and selling slaves to Europeans, thereby becoming wealthier.

Almada, a Portuguese trader operating from the Cape Verde Islands, exchanged European guns and bullets for African slaves, gold, and ivory during the 1560s and until the early 1590s. Although the English later built Fort James at the mouth of the Gambia in 1618, at the time Almada saw only the possibilities and problems of sustained Portuguese trade. The following description of the people and trade on the Gambia is from the perspective of one who was seeking a way to benefit personally.

1. The Kingdom of Gambia begins at the entrance to its very famous river, five leagues from the bar of the River of the Barbacins. The river can be entered very easily and without risk, because the entrance is like a bay. It has to the leeward Cape St. Mary—which is in Mandinga territory—and to the windward a number of islands, some swampy, some not, lying between the River of the Barbacins and the Gambia River, (all of them) covered with forests of mangrove and other trees. Some of

the islands are settled, some are not; and they are called the islands of Jubander. Between the islands lies a little river called the Rio de Lagos: it leads into the River of the Barbacins, near the palace of the King of Broçalo which is called Ganjal.

2. The Gambia River is settled throughout its length, on both banks, by Mandinga blacks. Each twenty leagues they have a king, who is subject to other rulers called *Farons,* this being a title among them which counts higher than that of king. Thus, the whole of this river is extensively settled with blacks and has many kings. The King of Broçalo . . . is the ruler of the north bank of the river for many leagues, and he has kings under him who obey him and pay tribute. It is true that sometimes they revolt when one king dies and another succeeds by forcefully imposing himself on the kingdom, but as the monarchy is powerful the king soon reduces them to subjection again. . . .

6. These blacks are very war-like, and in this land there are more weapons than in any other land in Guinea. The reason for this is that, as they have iron here which they smelt, they make spears, darts, knives and arrows in quantity. The poison used by the Mandingas is more venomous than any other (known in Guinea). (This we know from what) we saw at the port of Caçan. At nine or ten in the morning, the blacks and our men had a serious affray which left dead on each side. At vespers, when the blacks had withdrawn and our people sought to bury the dead, those who had been struck by poisoned arrows could not be carried away from where they lay dead, because the poison was so effective that already their bodies were decaying, to the extent that if they were lifted up by an arm it fell off from the body, and the same thing happened if a leg was lifted. All that could be done was to dig graves where the corpses lay and push them in. Such is (the power of) the poison used by the blacks. They are mostly a treacherous lot. All those on the south side of the river are bad: they take a delight in killing whites and seizing ships, which they have done on several occasions. One can only go there in a strong ship carrying a stout crew well-armed, and it is necessary at all times to keep a careful watch on the blacks, since they never behave other than treacherously. Along the river and its creeks are certain military fortifications which the blacks call *sãosans*. These are made of very strong wooden stakes, their pointed ends embedded (in the ground), and a rampart of earth behind. Each has its guard towers, bastions, and parades, from which they fight by shooting arrows. They also make a kind of pitch with tar which they heat up in vessels. And when the enemy attack they hurl these vessels at them to make them withdraw. As stated, they make their fortresses along the river and its creeks; (this is) because of (the supply) of water and because they have boats in which they attack other places. Hence, when they are at war, they rob those who pass by.

7. Along the river on each bank there are many villages of Fulos, who live in these parts after having left their own lands in search of the pasturage and water which they need for their animals. Hence, the district has large numbers of cattle. Along the river are very beautiful meadows, which they call *lalas,* in which many kinds of game are to be found at all times, both beasts and birds. The river has excellent fishing, and very fine plaice can sometimes be taken. It contains large crocodiles, which often seize men and cows, and carry them off to eat in their lairs. But crocodiles are so made that in the deep of the river they are unable to seize or harm any creature. (They are dangerous) only in places where they can strike their tail into the ground, for if they cannot do this they lack the power to do anything. There is no risk except along the shore, where the river has little depth. So many crocodiles live in this river and do so much damage, that the blacks in the settlements they inhabit have the practice of building within the river a fenced enclosure, which acts as a rampart. Within this, they can water their stock in safety and wash and draw water, where otherwise they would run great risk (of being seized).

8. Up this river, on one side or the other, are many kings, twenty leagues or less separating one from another; but there are other kings with large territories, and (even) emperors among them called *Farin.*

9. The clothes they wear, the arms they carry, and the oaths they take are like those of the Jalofos and Barbacins. The slaves which they own and sell are enslaved either in war, or by the courts, or else by being kidnapped, for they go about robbing one place or another, being great thieves. (As a result) they sell large numbers of slaves. (But Christians are) forbidden to buy from them black slaves which have been kidnapped. It has been known here in Guinea, (especially) in this river and in the Rio Grande, for the blacks to bring certain slaves to sell to our people, and when our people refused to buy them, because this is forbidden, the blacks who brought them and offered them for sale killed them on the spot, so that (their kidnapping of them) would not be discovered. I am not sure that it would not have been better to have bought them, since this would have meant that they received baptism and became Christians. (However) I do not meddle further in this business, for it involves points (of moral law) which I am not competent to determine. . . .

11. The imported goods which the people of this river value most are as follows: wine—they would die for it, and they call it *dolo*—, horses, white cloth from India, Indian beads as on the coast, Venetian beads, pearls large or small, small Venetian beads, red thread, red cloth, 24-weave cloth, scarlet fabric, cowries, paper, nails, copper bracelets, barber's basins, copper cauldrons weighing one or two pounds, and copper scrap. But of all the imported goods the most esteemed is cola, a fruit produced in Serra Leoa and the neighbouring district, and worth so much in this river that they would give anything in exchange for it, foodstuffs, cloth, slaves or gold. And it is so valuable that the blacks carry it as far as the Kingdom of the Grand Fulo, where it is worth a great deal, and also into the other rivers of our Guinea.

12. In this river, up-stream 120 leagues, on the north side, in the port called Jagrançura of the town called Sutuco, there is trading in gold, which is brought here in caravans by certain Mandinga merchants, who are also *bixirins* and make their prayers as others do. The gold they bring here comes mostly in the form of powder, with some in coins, and is very fine quality. The merchants are very expert with weights as they are in other points (of their trade). They carry accurate scales, the arms of which have silver inlay and the cords are of twisted silk. They carry little writing cases of unpolished leather without fasteners, and in the drawers they carry the weights, which are of brass, and are shaped like dice. The scales carry a larger brass weight of one pound, shaped like the pommel of a sword. The gold they transport in laces, in scraps of cloth, in the quills of large birds, and in the hollow bones of cats, which they hide in their clothing. They carry it this way because they go through many kingdoms and spend many days on the road, and are often robbed, despite the fact that the caravans take with them officers and guards. Depending on its worth, a caravan may have one thousand archers, or more, or less. Copper bracelets are the merchandise they chiefly buy with the gold. It seems to that (our) trading in these bracelets brings (us) no profit, or if there is any profit it cannot be much, since one pound of gold buys 1440 bracelets. (However,) there is much profit with other goods, *cano de pata*—an elongated precious stone which comes from India—, *brandil,* paper, and all the other goods mentioned earlier, except horses and wine—for these merchants do not drink wine. And also barber's basins, and small kettles of one pound in weight and more.

13. I myself took part in this trade in 1578. Because some people wondered whether the merchants had come by order of the Turk, to obtain copper to be made into guns, I carefully inquired of the gold merchants where they were going to get the gold and why the people there wanted bracelets.

14. Thus I learned with certainty that the bracelets are used only as ornaments and adornment by the people (of the gold region). They wear them on their arms and legs, and value them as much as, and even more than, we value bracelets of gold. They do not use gold because they value it little, having so much of it in their lands. Without exception, (all) this gold and the gold which comes

to Tumbocutum comes from the hills of Sofala. For when I spoke to Anhadalen, the leader of the caravan, and asked him exactly where he was going and where he was taking the bracelets, he told me it was to the Cafres (Kaffirs), using the actual term. When I asked him why they wanted them, he told me it was to wear on their arms and legs. When I asked them [*sic*] how much they gave him for each bracelet, he replied that he would not tell me that, since they were not such dull-witted merchants as to fail to make high profits on goods which they carried so far, for they spend many days on the road and pass through many lands, at great risk to their persons. And they bring the same gold to the Kingdom of Galalho, called by us Gago, and to the Grand Fulo. What makes me testify more strongly that they want the bracelets only as ornaments to wear is this. About a thousand of the bracelets I took were broken into pieces, and I asked the captain of the caravan guard if he would buy them, and he told me that they were useless. When I said that I would give him two broken ones instead of one good one, he replied that even if I gave him ten for one he would not take them, because they would be of no use, they would only take whole ones capable of being worn. Hence the suspicions I had entertained disappeared.

15. These merchants take over six months on their journey. But as they are blacks and lacking in energy it is surprising that they do not take much more time. They follow a route which fringes (the lands of) all the blacks of our Guinea, on the interior side, and they go (this way) by order of a black emperor whom all the Guinea blacks we have discussed are subject to, called Mandimansa, whom none of our people has ever seen. As soon as his name is mentioned, all the blacks who hear it immediately uncover their heads, such is his authority. The Mina people call this king the Great Elephant, and he is so well known that all the blacks respect his name for more than 300 leagues around.

16. On the occasion mentioned I had to leave the trading place (without obtaining) five quarters and eight pounds of gold which had come in the caravan, because I had no (more) goods to exchange. Today this trade is lost, because no ship has gone there for eight years; the merchants, seeing that there is no trade for them, must have joined those (trading) at Tumbocutum. Some Moors come to this trading place and bring gold, exchanging it for glazed earthenware bowls, red cloth, and a few coins, if they find any of these things there. The clothes of these merchants are the same kind as those of the Mandingas; the clothes of the guards who come with them are different, being large tunics and baggy trousers whose width continues to more than a hand-span below the knees, then they narrow like boots and cover the whole leg. They fix many feathers on their tunics, and in the caps they wear. They carry short swords like the other blacks, and two knives, one in the belt and the other attached to the upper left arm. The arrows they carry are short and the bows small. They say that they prefer these because (the arrows) are of no use to their enemies who have large bows, while the arrows of their enemies are of use to them. Although their bows are small, they shoot arrows accurately. They also carry spears and very strong shields made of poles and reeds.

REVIEW QUESTIONS

1. According to Almada, what benefits might accrue from trade with the Mandinka? What liabilities?
2. What was his impression of the level of sophistication of the Mandinka people?
3. Does this account reveal any examples of cultural diversity or exposure of the Mandinka to those of other states? Explain.

A Portuguese Clergyman Describes a Visit to East Africa (1606)

GASPAR DE SANTO BERNARDINO, *Itinerario da India*

By 1606, when Friar Gaspar de Santo Bernardino visited East Africa, the Portuguese were actively engaged in driving the Arab Muslim traders from ports they had held for centuries. In the mid-1580s, having created the Swahili trading culture on the central East African coast, the Arab traders had endeavored to protect their business from the European interlopers. The Turkish captain Amir Ali Bey came to the Zanzibar, Pemba, and Mombasa coast in 1585 to fulfill a new Ottoman strategy to create native allies against the Portuguese. He rallied the support of African Muslim traders by promising them the sultan's financial aid and by establishing a fortress at Mombasa. Despite this attempt to save the Swahili trade, the Portuguese destroyed the port of Kilwa and took military control of the ports of Zanzibar, Pemba, Pate, and Lamu, all on the central coast, during the 1590s. They exported ivory, ambergris, tortoise shell, beeswax, millet, rice, and some slaves, which were traded in India for cottons. Portuguese traders never did very well on this coast, however, especially in comparison with their thriving slave trade from their west coast ports in Angola and on the Guinea coast. Consequently, during the first half of the seventeenth century, Portuguese control slowly weakened and the ancient Arab-African trading relationships returned. By the 1640s, the queen of Zanzibar and her neighboring king on Pemba acquiesced to the return of the Swahili trade even though it resulted in the increased importance of Islam in their kingdoms.

The island of Pemba continued under Portuguese influence in the early seventeenth century, when the Franciscan friar Bernardino visited the East African coast on a trip that eventually took him to Jerusalem. He intended to disprove the fanciful accounts of earlier travelers who had written on their adventures in Africa. Such literature had become extremely popular in Portugal and Spain, especially after the discoveries in the Americas and the Pacific Ocean in the early sixteenth century. Bernardino wrote for a literate elite, but in an entertaining style, to convince his readers that other travelers had not told the absolute truth.

We remained in Pemba for five days, in which, while we have time, it will be well to speak of the islands already left behind us. Of them we will only speak in passing, since João de Barros, Damiao de Gois, Fernao Lopes de Castanheda, Diogo de Couto, Fr. Antonios de S. Romao, Pero de Mariz, and, in particular, Fr. João dos Santos in his *Etiopia Oriental* have all spoken.

Let it be sufficient to say that the chief is Quiloa, discovered by Vasco da Gama in the voyage of the first fleet that passed the Cape, on its voyage of discovery of the East. It is from eight to ten leagues in size—of the same size are the islands of Zanzibar and Mafia: between which is a detached sandbank. For this reason, it is impossible for a large vessel to pass; and we indeed feared to be grounded on it before we anchored in the island of Pemba. All the islands are low-lying but very cool. The woods are full of orange, lemon, citron, palm trees, and of a large variety of good fruit trees. The islands grow millet, rice, and have large groves of sugar-cane, but the islanders do not know what to do with it.

Cattle are abundant in these islands, and also peacocks, apes, and particularly hens, of which there is such a large quantity that they sold fifty for one *cruzado*. The truth is that the lack of money is greater here than elsewhere, and it therefore has a higher value. Marco Polo has said of the natives of Zanzibar that they are very corpulent and are large eaters; that they have great physical strength, timid eyes and long, unshapely ears; and he almost wishes to persuade us that they are of a different species or nature. I for my part state that I have not found such to be the case. We had in our party negroes born on the island, and some who had stayed there; and these stated that the natives of Zanzibar in no way differ from other negroes. While I was in Mombasa a boat arrived from Zanzibar with some slaves on board who were similar to the negroes of Mozambique and the rest of Cafraria.

The native Moors are short in stature, yellowish-brown in colour and keep the Arabic rules and ceremonies. They are very lascivious, and their women less continent than befits the honour and modesty of women. The wealthier go about perfumed with amber and musk, since these are to be had locally in abundance. They dress in the manner of Malindi. Their houses are lofty, but their streets are narrow, as is usual among the Moors.

There are Portuguese soldiers on these islands. Would to God they were fewer, since in these parts they are accustomed to live as much according to their will as against the Divine Will. Often liberty leads to licence. For this reason they are esteemed but little and are despised. . . .

A third of a league away from here upstream is the Court of the King of Malindi, who at the present time is called Sultan Mahamet, a man of middle age and of a pale brown colour, but of pleasing and agreeable countenance. Not less pleasing were his manners and conversation. On several occasions I visited him and his son the Prince, and they always received me and my companion with demonstrations of delight and affection. This same affection was found in him, in his father and grandfather, by the Portuguese from every ship which visited the port from the time when the first ship touched there to the present day. Clear proof of this may be found in all the histories of the Indies, while the subtle genius and rare gifts of our own Camoens have told of it in the Lusiads. In 1604 our Catholic Majesty, aware of the sultan's good will, rewarded it with royal and excellent gifts, which have made it possible for the sultan to be supreme over all the kings of that coast, and to be in general the most beloved and powerful among them. . . . Whenever we conversed with the king, he sat in a skilfully wrought chair of mother-of-pearl and we in chairs of scarlet velvet embroidered with fine gold thread. When our audience was over and we took our leave, he ordered bugles and trumpets, curved and of ivory, to be sounded, and the mountains and valleys repeated with their echo his pleasure and the affection with which he bade us Godspeed. We afterwards visited the city, the houses of which are lofty and raised from the ground, but are already very ancient. Their inhabitants are Moors who, although formerly rich, now live in utter poverty—their most usual occupation is that of making mats, baskets, and straw hats so perfectly finished that the Portuguese bring them out to wear on feast days.

Well towards the eastern harbour is an Augustinian monastery where not more than six fathers are housed. In the middle of the cloister is a well which is empty at high tide and full at low tide. . . .

While the report of our arrival spread through the island, the prince and the governor ordered that houses should be sought out in which we could be entertained, and each came forward to offer his own. I thanked each for his kindness, and accepted the offers of hospitality which gave us the same pleasure to receive as those who offered lodging and company felt in making their offer. As we left the ship together, all well pleased, we saw running towards us two Portuguese, who asked the Moors where the Brothers were. Our recognition of each other aroused that feeling of intence pleasure known only to those who are aware that such emotions are better described by being felt, than felt by being described. Falling at our feet and embracing them, they straightway asked us, still kneeling, for our blessing. These signs of devotion produced a similar feeling among those witnessing the scene—not least of all among the Moors, who stood staring, quite overcome by surprise, as we were by joy; for good works, though practised by few, are nevertheless envied and admired by all.

We arrived at the house of the Portuguese, accompanied by the prince to its threshold, when he courteously took leave of us. The Moors who noticed what had passed on the beach between ourselves and the Christians could hardly wait for the moment to arrive to pass on the news to the rest of the inhabitants. On the one hand they felt obliged to witness our exchange of courtesies, our customs and our manners; on the other hand they greatly desired to earn the largesse which they felt sure would be forthcoming for taking the good news to the Portuguese. Undecided as to which course to take, they lost everything.

We had already been resting for a quarter of an hour when other Portuguese arrived to see us. We were all very happy, and my companion and I told why we had come, and how we had been all but lost in Sao Lourenço. The Portuguese told us that they were merchants trading in the island, and how they hoped, if it pleased God, to return shortly to India; and they suggested that we should accompany them there. But at this point we told them of our plan to go to Ormuz, 640 leagues from Pate and to see whether it was possible to go thence to Portugal. While we were talking about this and other matters, a message arrived from the king, brought by one of his own priests. He said that His Highness welcomed our arrival; that in the city there were some eighteen Portuguese (this indeed was the number of those present), and although His Highness was himself not one, he did not deny nevertheless being a vassal of the King of Spain, and therefore a brother of the Portuguese. More-

over we could—so His Highness said—with a goodwill go to see one whose only desire was to serve us.

We all thanked the messenger, and told him that it was only lack of time which had caused us to be so remiss; but we would immediately take time to go and kneel at his feet. As three o'clock in the afternoon the king sent to tell us that he would consider it a favour if we should call on him at any time. We immediately set out, taking the Portuguese with us, all very elegantly dressed.

We found the king seated on the ground in the manner of the Moors, on costly carpets, and robed in white, as in the Moorish fashion. He was surrounded by all the principal persons of the city. He had had placed for us two cushions near him; and for the Portuguese, chairs. He made a sign for us to sit down, and immediately one of his entourage asked us about our arrival and our health. The king said that we were the first of our Order and habit to have been there, and he trusted that God would henceforward give him good fortune, such as had been his so far, and that he had never before had that good fortune which he was at the moment enjoying. He asked us if we would care to accept his hospitality during the days we spent there; and although it was a Moor who made the offer, the spirit in which it was made was Christian. We thanked him kindly, pointing out, however, that as there were so many Portuguese in the town, it was not right for us to leave them. Benegogo— this was the king's name—agreed and said no more, but merely offered us whatever was necessary for our journey back.

This king was about thirty-five years old, of gentle character which everybody praised; and with a merry expression, but serious in his conversation, and modest in his manner. In short, all that was lacking to make him appear a perfect prince was the name of true Christian. . . .

Mubana Mufama Luvale—this was the king's name—was dressed in long trailing robes, and wore on his head a striped turban of damasked silken cloth. His robe was of quilted cotton; while from his left shoulder there was slung gracefully a curved and perfectly finished Turk-ish scimitar. He was about sixty years old, and had very fine features, although he was rather dark in colour.* He had a fine judgement and in-telligence, if one may say so of one who does not know God. He accompanied us to the church door, and then retired after having taken leave of us courteously, according to his custom. He seemed to realize that, all the time he was accom-panying us, he was imitating—and was pleased to do so—the [Augustinian] Father.

We prayed, and when we had finished and gone outside, we found the Father Rector of the Church, Fr. Diogo do Spirito Santo as he was called, who, with many signs of affection, embraced us, showing that extreme kindliness which members of this Order show everywhere to members of other religious orders. We returned home, and spent nearly all the day giving an ac-count of ourselves and of our arrival. The next day, which was the Day of the Ascension, 4 May 1606, I heard confession from the Portuguese, and, as the Lord was pleased, I administered Holy Communion. Later, in order to make the occasion even more festive, we dined together. Often, among a friendly company, the friend-ship which is in the heart and soul shines forth.

Towards evening, three of us, that is, the three Brothers only, went to see the king, whose delight in seeing us at his palace was such that we could not but be pleased to see a heathen prince so attached and devoted to the Christian religion. That he was devoted was clear, since he, a Moor full of grey hairs, old age and troubles, had, at the time of the building of the church, carted and even carried on his shoulders stones and mortar for the church; and had, moreover, given a considerable sum in alms which were spent on its construction. I myself would never have believed this if the Father Rector had not told me the story in the presence of the king himself, who was ashamed because of the small contribution he had made to the task. We thanked him for his outstanding service to our Lord, and placed ourselves—for what we were

worth—at his service. He replied: "Fathers, while I had no Christian church in my city I lived in fear; now, however, I live well content and at peace because in the church I have walls which guard my city; and, in the Fathers, soldiers to defend it." Well may one raise one's voice at peace because in the church I have walls which guard my city; and, here to remind those Chris-tians who live like Moors to learn from this Moor how to be Christians. But since my inten-tion is only to describe what took place on this journey, I must not deviate.

When our talk was over, we took leave of the king, and three days later of the Father Rector. Those three days seemed, indeed, like one. Plea-sure, when it is great, does not permit one to feel the passage of time.

As the island was small and at peace, we de-cided to return to the city of Pate by land rather than by sea. On our way we entered the city of Siu where we found neither Christian nor Por-tuguese, nor anyone who knew about us, with the exception of two heathen merchants, of whom we had heard in Ampaza. These men were na-tives of the island of Diu where they had seen members of our order, whose monastery had been built with alms which they—the merchants—had given more willingly than when they had contributed to their infamous temples. These took us to the king's palace, and acted as inter-preters since they knew Portuguese very well. The king, Mubana Baccar Muncandi, treated us well, inviting us to be his guests and remain with him that day. We excused ourselves, saying that we would describe all that he was pleased to talk about; but that we only craved of him leave to see the interesting sights of the city. The mer-chants spent a long time with him telling him about the Franciscan way of living in poverty, and of begging alms from door to door, or living in a cloister where the time was spent in prais-ing God. This indeed met with the approval and excited the wonder of the Moors. We spent some three hours with the king talking of such things, at the end of which time the king ordered that some of the more highly born of his subjects should show us the whole of the city. There was

---

*This is obviously a different king.

nothing in it worthy of note, except that it was larger in circumference and more populous than the other cities of the island—so many people indeed came to their windows and on to their terraces to see us that it seemed impossible that they should be so numerous. Then we went again to the king, to thank him and to take our leave for Pate, where the Portuguese were already waiting for us, having assembled all their provisions and made all necessary preparations for the journey.

REVIEW QUESTIONS

1. What evidence do you find that Bernardino was attempting to set the record straight on Africa?
2. What was his opinion of the kings and the pageantry he found on the islands? Explain.
3. What evidence of competition between the Portuguese and native peoples do you find in this account?
4. Do you believe that Bernardino was pleased by what he found on Pemba and the islands? Why or why not?

A Portuguese Soldier Describes the Plight of Castaways on the East African Coast (1622)

FRANCIS VAZ D'ALMADA, *The Tragic History of Sea, 1529–1622*

Almost two decades after the voyage of Fray Gaspar de Santo Bernardino (see previous selection), the Portugese ship *St. John the Baptist,* en route to the Portuguese colony of Goa in India, encountered two Dutch East Indiamen in the far southwest Indian Ocean. During the ensuing nineteen-day battle, *St. John the Baptist* was badly damaged, demasted, and left rudderless. She made landfall on a rocky area of the South African coast in late September (the start of the warmer months), not far from present-day East London in South Africa. Two situations had conspired to cause this catastrophe: Dutch traders' intentions to end Portuguese control of the trade routes to India and Southeast Asia, and the 1620 alliance between England and the Dutch to form a joint fighting force, the "Fleet of Defence." *St. John the Baptist* and its crew and cargo fell victim to that fleet in 1622.

The following account was published in Lisbon in 1625. Its author, Francis Vaz d'Almada, had been a soldier on that ill-fated voyage. In addition to providing a firsthand account of the survival of the ship's crew, this excerpt provides significant information about the extent of the Bantu migration into southern Africa by the seventeenth century. Between 500 B.C.E. and about 1000 C.E., a linguistically similar and culturally well-developed group known as the Bantu people migrated from the central Congo basin into almost all of central and southern Africa, from the Atlantic to the Indian Oceans. This migration is particularly significant because of their advanced farming technology and the mining and iron smelting industry. Combining their knowledge with that of the people into whose regions they migrated greatly increased development throughout southern and central Africa. Added to this development, of course, was the increased trade with Arab Muslims from the 800s onwards, which brought wealth to nation-states such as Zimbabwe. The customs and the language of the Kaffirs described here are those of the Bantu people.

. . . The necessary provisions and weapons were landed, though with great difficulty, for it was a wild coast, so that every time the boat approached the shore to disembark something, it was necessary to anchor with a grapnel by the stern and wade ashore holding to the line in order to keep head-on to waves; so much so, that once when they did not anchor by the stern, eighteen persons were drowned in landing one boatload. This was the reason why we did not afterward try to build a boat, for this coast is so stormy that we feared that after it was made we would not be able to launch it.

On the 3rd October, while we were completing the landing of the things needed for the overland journey and building shacks to shelter us from the excessive cold of that region during the time we remained there, the men who kept watch raised the alarm that Negroes were approaching. We took up arms, and, as they drew near to us, they handed the assegais which they carried to their children until they were very close to us, when they squatted down on their haunches, clapping their hands and whistling softly, in such a way that they all kept in tune together, and many women who were with them began to dance. These Negroes are whiter than mulattoes; they are stoutly built men, and disfigure themselves with daubs of ocher, charcoal, and ashes, with which they generally paint their faces, though they are really quite good looking.

On this first meeting they brought as a present a very fine large ox and a leather bag of milk, which the king gave to Roderick Affonso de Mello, who was acting as captain at the time, Peter de Morais being still aboard the ship. The courtesy which this king did to the aforesaid captain was to stroke his beard many times. After we had given some pieces of iron hoops and *bertangils* as a return present to the king, he went to the ox and ordered it to be cut open alive at the navel, and he with most of those who were with him plunged their hands into the entrails of the ox while it was still alive and bellowing, smearing themselves with that filth. We realized that they performed all these ceremonies as a sign of good faith and friendship. They then cut up the ox into quarters and gave it to us, keeping for themselves the hide and entrails, which they placed on embers and devoured on the spot.

During the month and six days that we remained in that place we could never understand a word these people said, for their speech is not like that of mankind, and when they want to say anything they make clicks with the mouth, one at the beginning, another in the middle, and another at the end; so that it may be deduced from these people that the earth is not all one, nor all mankind alike. . . .

During this time we bartered for cows, which we ate, though they were not as many as we needed. We kept those which seemed fit for work in a stockade, accustoming them to carry pack-saddles, which were very well made out of carpets, for there were not wanting workmen in the camp who knew how to make them. . . .

Here I was involved in an incident which I have sufficient confidence in your worship to tell you about, and also because it was well known to all. While we were still on the hillside, before we came down to the river, the captain bade me go forward about a league with fifteen arquebusiers to see if we could discover a village, for we had now reached the region where the Kaffir had told us that we would find cows. Having advanced about half a league along the river that was winding through a plain, I saw a hamlet of fifteen straw huts, and in order not to alarm the Kaffirs I ordered six men to advance and see if there was any kind of food that they would sell us. But they declined to obey, on the plea that there seemed to be many people in the village and that we would be too far off to help them if they got into difficulties. This vexed me, and after arguing angrily with them I chose the four best arquebusiers present, who were John Ribeiro, Cyprian Dias, Francis Luis, and the ship's steward, with whom I descended the hill and crossed a valley which lay between us and the Negroe's kraal, in which there was a river then at high tide, and we forded it with the water to our chests.

Having reached the entrance of their enclosure, we asked them to sell us something to eat, speaking to them by signs, and putting our hands to our mouths; for by carelessness or forgetfulness we had not brought an interpreter with us to explain what we wanted, nor had we asked the captain for one, although these Kaffirs could understand the Negro slaves we had brought from India. They were amazed at seeing us white and clothed, and the women and children made a great hullabaloo, calling to the people of another kraal which was in the bush. [We retired] and their husbands who were with them followed us closely, throwing fire-hardened sticks at us. Seeing the harm which they might do us, I ordered John Ribeiro to fire at them with an arquebus, which he immediately did, but it did not go off, and the Kaffirs grew more enraged, thinking that the making of the flame was witchcraft. Seeing the danger we were in, I took careful aim with my matchlock and killed three with a single shot, for I always fired with one [ordinary] bullet and three shaped like dice. These deaths caused great consternation among them, and the survivors broke off their pursuit of us. . . .

We slept that night in a valley where the long grass stood higher than a lance. Next day we rose early in the morning and marched up a hillside through some pleasant country. On meeting some Negroes we asked them about the villages, and they replied that if we walked fast we would reach them when the sun was in the meridian. Being eager and in want, though weak, we kept on climbing, and in the afternoon we reached the top of a range from which we had the most beautiful view that our eyes could desire, for many valleys lay before us, intersected by rivers and smaller hills, in which were an infinite number of villages with herds of cattle and garden plots. At this sight we descended the hillside very joyfully, and the Kaffirs came out to meet us on our way, bringing jars of milk and cows for sale.

Next day we climbed to the top of that range, which was very high, in quest of a village where dwelt the king of that whole district. We reached it in the afternoon, and it was the largest we had yet seen. The king, who was blind, came to visit the captain, and brought him a present of a little millet in a calabash. Though old, he was a healthy looking man. It is worthy of note that, though they are savages without any knowledge of the truth, they have such a serious mien and are so respected by their subjects, that I cannot exaggerate it. They rule and punish them in such a way that they keep them quiet and obedient. They have their laws, and they punish adulterers gallantly in the following manner: if a woman is guilty of adultery toward her husband, and he can prove it by witnesses, she is ordered to be put to death, together with the adulterer if they can catch him, whose wives the aggrieved husband then marries.

When anyone wishes to marry, the king makes the match, so that no marriage can take place unless he names the bride. It is their custom when their sons are ten years old to turn them into the bush, where they clothe themselves from the waist downward with the leaves of a tree like the palm, and rub themselves with ashes till they look as if they were whitewashed. They all keep together in a body, but they do not come to the village, their mothers taking food to them in the bush. These boys have the duty of dancing at weddings and feasts which it is customary to hold, and they are paid with cows, calves, and goats where there are any. When anyone of them has got together in this way some three or four head of cattle, and has reached the age of over eighteen years, his father or mother goes to their king and tells him that they have a son of fitting age who by his own exertions has gained so many head of cattle, and the said father or mother is willing to help him by giving him something further, and they request the king to give him a wife. The king then replies: "Go to such a place, and tell so-and-so to bring his daughter here." When they come, he arranges about the dowry which the husband is obliged to pay his father-in-law, and the king's palms are always greased in making these contracts. This is the custom as far as Inhaca Manganheira, which is the river of Lourenco Marques.

All these Kaffirs wear cloaks of very well-dressed skins, which hang below their hips. The skins are those of small animals with beautiful fur, and these furs vary according to the quality of the Kaffir who wears them, and they are very punctilious about this. They wear nothing but these capes and a politer skin which covers their privy parts. I saw a grave Kaffir with a cloak of sable skins, and when I asked him where these animals were to be found, he said that there were so many of them farther inland, that nearly everyone wore them.

I also found upon the ground two assegais and a little piece of wood of the thickness of a finger and about two and a half spans long, covered from the middle upward with a monkey's tail. It is customary to carry a stick of this kind throughout almost the whole of Kaffraria as far as the river of Lourenco Marques, and they never converse without it, for they emphasize all their talk by gesticulating with this stick in their hand, and they call it their mouth, making gestures and grimaces.

REVIEW QUESTIONS

1. What immediate problems and needs did the castaways find upon landing? How did they solve these?
2. The Portuguese castaways had African slaves in their party. Do you find any evidence of prejudice or disdain by d'Almada toward the Africans he encountered? Explain.
3. What was d'Almada's response to and opinion of the Kaffirs' customs? Explain.

A French Merchant Observes Life Along the Coast of Guinea (1678–1712)

The Writings of Jean Barbot on West Africa

Born in 1655 into a large Protestant family at Saint-Martin on the Ile of Ré, Jean Barbot became part of the thriving slave trade on the Guinea coast of West Africa. In response to religious persecution by the French government after the revocation of the Edict of Nantes in 1685, he and his brother fled to England. Having grown to adulthood in a lively shipping and commercial town, he had visited England before he moved there and had many friends in the shipping business. He became a naturalized English citizen in 1696 and was married in the prestigious and conformist Huguenot church of Savoy in London.

Barbot enjoyed great success in his adopted homeland, and his writings about expeditions to the coast of West Africa brought him a certain amount of fame. As a merchant and French refugee, he was selected by an officer of the English government in 1695 for "secret service" collecting information about French naval matters. Consequently, his writings from 1678 to 1712, of which the following is an excerpt of two letters, involve information gleaned to enable the English to foil French activities in the Gulf of Guinea. The first account deals with the people of Senegal, and the "Ethiopian Gulf" to which he refers is the Gulf of Guinea. The second, contrasting excerpt describes people living in villages much further south and around the cape at Sierra Leone.

LETTER 8

The blacks (nègres) *of these lands, their character, dress, occupations, houses, food, and ceremonies. The education of their children, their wars and weapons, their oaths, etc.*

The Senegal blacks are in general tall, upright, well-built, well-proportioned and loose-limbed. They are blacker than those on the Gold Coast or at Ardres. Their noses are somewhat flattened, their lips are thick, their teeth as white as ivory and well-set, their hair either curled or long and lank, and piled up on their head in the shape of a pointed cap. Those who live on the North banks of River Senegal are more of a tawny colour. The blacks have an attractive, shiny black skin, which comes from their washing and anointing it. They are affable and polite in social intercourse, and they have a lively disposition. But they are lazy, the result of the bounty and fertility of the land they occupy, which furnishes them with all that is necessary for life, in abundance and almost by nature alone. Hence they are considered less suitable for work in America than those from the Ethiopian Gulf and from Angola. Furthermore they are sensual, knavish, fond of lying, gluttons, abusive, more luxurious than can be imagined, foul eaters, drunkards who drink spirits like water, and so unindustrious that many of them prefer to become brigands in the woods and wastes rather than undertake honest work for their keep. They commit many murders between the villages of Yaray and [blank]. . . . The wives of the Africans are well-shaped, tall and loose-limbed. They are lively and wanton, and eager to be amused. All of them have a warm temperament and enjoy sexual pleasures, European men being more pleasing to them than their own men. Few of them will refuse the final favour if offered the most trifling gift. This is what makes the black men so jealous.

Both men and women talk like turkey-cocks, stretching out their neck or shortening it according to the subject matter. They pronounce their words very quickly. Their language, Songay, is close to the language of the Arabs.

Men and women of the common sort for the most part go about naked, or if they cover themselves, it is only with a *pagne* (length of cloth) or a scrap of cloth, over the parts modesty requires them to hide. Men have merely a loincloth around the waist and some have only a little strip of leather around the loins to which they attach behind and before a strip of cloth which hides what it is not decent to name. This cloth hangs at the rear like the tail of a horse. Some of them also wear several cloths sewn together, making 2–3 ells [12–18 feet] in length, or that same length in some European material, passed around the arms and shoulders, and then hanging down to their heels, which makes it look like a long mantle. The drawings I am giving you will show more clearly the manner of this dress, and the manner of all the other most common forms of dress. Women wear a cloth around their loins and another cloth on their head, like a cap or veil.

The noble sort of either sex can be distinguished from commoners since almost all the [noble] men have a shirt of striped cotton which hangs down to the knees and has long and open sleeves, and under that another cloth shaped like drawers called a *jouba.* This style of dress is borrowed from the Arab Moors. The material is so thick and heavy that they can hardly walk at any speed. The cotton shirt is closed at the neck as a purse is. In the hot season they wear linen shirts or shirts made from old linen. They also wear little caps made of cloth or leather; and all over their body, on their head, neck, arms, waist, and legs, they have little leather pouches resembling small boxes, either elongated or square. These pieces of leather contain a number of scraps of paper covered with characters in either Moorish or Arabesque script and given them by the *lyncherins.* They call these *grigri.*

You can hardly credit, Sir, the extent to which these Africans carry their belief in the magical properties of these *grigri,* properties which operate in all sorts of contingencies. They cherish them as closely and spend as much on them as do Italian and Spanish bigots in relation to the relics of their supposed saints. The latter have relics for all contingencies, each saint having special powers: the former say that one *grigri* will save them from drowning at sea, and another from being killed in war; another again will give a woman a safe childbirth, another will prevent fires, another heal fevers, and so on. You cause an uproar if you even pretend to remove one of their *grigris* from them. I snatched one from a black at Cabo-Verdo and was quite unable to appease him until I had exercised my authority and had him given several bottles of spirits. I opened the *grigri* and found within two large pieces of paper, very worn pieces, covered all over with characters both strangely arranged and strangely shaped. I think you will not be displeased if I send you a piece of the original. I must state that I cannot understand it at all, and do not know if it is Moorish, Arabic, Syrian or Chaldaean. These characters are written on the paper by the *lyncherins* or *marabous.* But they do not oblige for nothing—far from it. As at Rome,

religion provides the chief source of gain for those who devote themselves to it, and here, just as there, they make large profits out of childish superstitions. A certain black lord carries on him *grigris* to the value of thirty slaves, that is 300 *louis* in our money. The viceroy Condy, whom I saw at Racho, carries *grigris* costing almost that sum, and the Alquaire of Rio-Fresco almost the same. *Grigris* are the chief form of conspicuous expenditure for lords and nobles and serve to distinguish them from commoners. The *grigris* worn by the poor are merely made from cloth, the two pieces of paper I mentioned above having been enclosed in cloth. Finally, nobles, and those commoners who can afford them, adorn their dress with lumps of red coral, which they intersperse among the leather pouches containing *grigris.* They also add two or three rows of India shells, of the sort we call *bouges* and in the Maldives "cowries." Their little caps, shaped in the Hungarian style, carry more of all this adornment than any other part of their dress.

Because these peoples have many Turkish and Arab customs, like the Turks and Arabs they can have as many wives as they can afford to keep. But what will doubtless amuse you greatly is that they do not marry women until they have lost their virginity. And not only that, they have to be assured, by the past experience of the women they marry, that they are fertile, and hence they will not attach themselves to women unless the women have already had children. They are free to divorce their wives at will, on the smallest excuse, and allegedly at mere whim.

Few formalities mark their weddings. The mutual consent of both parties, declared in the presence of witnesses, followed by celebrations in the local manner, constitutes what we call a wedding. The wedding feast is always held in the village to which the bride belongs, and a cow or sheep or kid, or something of that kind, depending on the standing of the persons marrying, is provided for the feast. Women always receive something from their father when they marry. The more well-to-do normally receive two or three slaves and two or three cows, the number depending on the wealth of the parents.

If a husband divorces his wife he must hand back the dowry he received when he married her. The most common reason for divorce is what often happens—the men find their wives misbehaving, either with a European or with some blacks [*sic*]. Favours shown to the latter the men are jealous about, but not about favours shown to whites. If they catch a black with their wife, they kill him if they can; but contrariwise they encourage their wives and daughters to win over Europeans with their embraces and they tell them to refuse them nothing. If there is any profit to be hoped for from these transactions, they themselves will arrange the price. This extreme laxity on the part of these wretches provides the opportunity for many Europeans to abandon themselves to excessive debauchery, and brings about their total ruin, on account of the differences in temperament between the European man and the African woman, the latter being always on heat and eager. . . .

As these African women are robust, they deliver their children easily and without much pain. The common sort have generally so much strength that after giving birth they take their baby to the river or the nearest water, to wash it. . . . These black women usually take very great care of their newly-born babies as long as they are breast-feeding them, but they use no swaddling cloths. They carry their infants about on their backs almost the whole time, both while they are undertaking household tasks and when they travel between villages. They carry them in cloths fastened around the neck and under the armpits. You cannot sufficiently admire the way in which these young creatures accept this posture, for they fall asleep on their mother's shoulders as if in a cradle, however much she moves her body or arms. At night-time, the mothers place their babies on mats alongside themselves, and the babies are often naked. When infants can move around, the mothers allow them to go wherever their fancy takes them, and they do not greatly worry about what might happen to them. In my opinion, there is nothing more pleasing than to see groups of these little black children playing together at crossroads or in the open spaces of the villages, for they scamper around on all fours like kittens. This sort of upbringing which seems hard and cruel to us is not at all like that for these young Africans. On the contrary, I think that this is what makes them strong and vigorous so quickly, despite what is said about swaddling being necessary in order to strengthen children—I am not sure that what is said on this matter is correct. The mothers of these little blacks always have plenty of milk, this being perhaps also a major reason why they become so strong and robust in so short a time.

The houses, or rather huts, in which the Africans live are almost always round in shape. They build a wall of 5–6 feet in earth tempered with clay, or else they tie reeds together, and do it so closely that nothing can pass between them. They make roofs for these houses from millet stalks, woven together with some skill. Each individual builds himself five or six of these huts, for his own use, some of the huts for one purpose and some for another, according to his various needs, and the huts are placed next to each other, arranged according to the extent of the land, just where they were built. Most Africans enclose the huts with a fence of thick reeds fixed together. The Foulles build better and more substantially than the other blacks around them. They mix ox-hair into the thick white earth they use for their buildings, and they know how to make better roofs. In sum, they are more skilled in this than their neighbours, and are better housed. They have no walled towns, only large villages and market-towns, which comprise 200–300 of these houses, all thrown together, without system or symmetry, or any other pleasing feature other than the palm-trees and banana-trees which they plant here and there in the little courtyards of their houses. Rio-Fresca is completely open. Its houses, when seen from afar, look like a military camp in the field, for almost all the houses are round, and their roof goes to a point. The villages of the Foulles are only enclosed by a fence of briars and felled branches, which is built solely in order to keep out lions and tigers, which otherwise would harass them terribly, for these animals are much more common and are fiercer among these peoples than in neighbouring countries. They would also otherwise kill their livestock.

Camalingue and Silatik, the two villages in which the kings of these names usually reside, contain about 300 of these houses, piled together. In all these towns of the blacks it is very inconvenient to pass through when it is raining, since the streets are so narrow and the roofs of the houses so low that the water from the roofs cannot be avoided. Cayore also has about 300 houses, and contains the king's palace. But do not think that this is a building like the Tuilleries, let alone Versailles. This palace, like that of every other king in Nigritia and Guinea, is only distinguished from other residences by its size and by the number of soldiers on guard who normally surround it. The residence of the king of Cayore consists of only 8–10 apartments built of boards or tree-trunks, 18–20 feet in height, with roofs supported by thick reeds and covered with straw. The door to these buildings is low and narrow.

These houses are no more well-provided within than without. The only household effects to be seen are axes, iron shovels, a number of pots, and if the individuals are fishermen, nets and the tools of their trade. There are no seats, tables or beds. They sit, eat and sleep at night on a mat. The mats are flimsy but clean enough. However, a few of them, in imitation of the Europeans, place their mats on an *estrade* or platform made of pieces of timber, four inches high, and sleep on that, without a cover or pillow.

These Africans live a poor sort of existence in a land where a people who worked harder and more persistently would be able to lead a pleasant, comfortable and well-to-do life, for the country they live in has all the qualities to provide that. But they do not care to exert themselves greatly, either in body or mind. But it must be added that some of them are livelier, and that apart from exercising themselves in war, an activity to which all abandon themselves from the moment they gain any knowledge of the world, they occupy themselves either in tilling the fields or sowing them, because this oc-

cupation is the most honoured after that of soldiering. Those who make fishing-nets, and the potters, the fishermen, the weavers and the weapon-makers, are considered mere mechanics. Elderly men employ themselves guarding the flocks in the fields, and others trade here and there, in the country or outside it. Some apply themselves to the preparation of various kinds of hides and curry them, which they do successfully. . . .

LETTER 19

Their way of building, the household management of their wives, and their feeding in general.

. . . Generally the houses are dirty, uncomfortable and for the most part stinking, particularly those which have privy-huts (*huttes de commoditez*), from which the great heat causes a very foul air to spread abroad, and this the land wind carries even to the vessels in the roadstead. These houses are located in groups at various points, and thus they form a village, intersected by small streets, very narrow and irregular, leaving a large space empty in the middle, where people hold their market and their meetings. . . . The only windows are small holes, and the doorway is so low and narrow that one must virtually bend double to enter. The doorways are closed by reeds woven together, or with a few little pieces of board, suspended by strings instead of hinge-pins, and opening either inwards or outwards, as is wished. . . . Every house has in addition two or three small huts. The houses of the rich have seven or eight, each separated from the others, and each used for some purpose—some for wives, others for children, others for kitchen use. Further, each of these [? last] huts has two small rooms, one for preparing the maize and the other as the kitchen. In addition, you see in several of these little cabins (*loges*) slight partitions of canes, reeds or other material. All of the huts are without symmetry or order and are surrounded by a fence of maize-stalks, tied very closely together. Only the main building has its exit on to the street; all the others can scarcely be seen [from outside], for the fences are made as tall as the roofs, in order that passers-by may not look into the courtyard. . . . These people are ignorant of the use of paving-stones [in their streets], although the parade-grounds of Corso and Mina have them.

These Africans hardly spend anything on furniture. They limit themselves to what is necessary, and the only things you see in their homes are a few wooden seats, a small chest, a few pots for cooking or drinking, and some weapons hung on the walls. Noblemen have tables and rush mattresses, on which they spread their mats to sleep. The mattresses are an inch thick. Others have simply mats, or a few cattle-hides and skins of other animals, and as a head-rest a small piece of wood, as I have said. The rich use a sort of pillow after their fashion, and a large copper cauldron, for washing themselves without going outside, as the common people do. The whole of this limited household equipment is always in the dwelling-place of the women; for in that of the men you find nothing but their weapons, a seat and a mat, and in that of artisans all the equipment of their profession. . . . The houses are usually built in 7–8 days, by specialists. The cost never amounts to as much as two *louis d'or*. The materials cost nothing except [the labour of] collecting them, which they do themselves or send slaves to do.

. . . As soon as it is evening, the women make sure that they have the quantity of rice and maize (in sheaves) that they judge necessary for the following day, sending slaves or their daughters to fetch it from the granaries they have outside the village. (Throughout the year they keep their grain in these granaries or even inside their houses.) At daybreak on the following day they set to work (with their people), beating and pounding the grain in wooden mortars made from a thick tree-trunk, or in holes hollowed out of a rock. They then winnow it, pound it on a stone in order to turn it into flour, and finally beat it again to make it up [with water] (in the same manner as painters make their colours). Following this, they mix it with millet and from this dough make round loaves the size of a hand, which they cook in a large earthenware pot, covered and full of boiling water. This bread is not good, being heavy. The bread they make on well-heated stones is better. . . . This manner of preparing maize is very laborious. Yet the women do it while singing, and most of them with their children on their backs—all in the blazing sun, which shines perpendicularly on their heads.

They boil fish with salt and malaguetta [pepper], and in the embers they roast yams and sweet potatoes, from which they make a good pap. They dry over the fire bananas, which can take the place of bread. They also eat pineapples, figs, roast maize, rice boiled with chicken or goat, or simply with salt and palm oil. They also use several kinds of legumes, which they cultivate and prepare fairly well. The rich often have the meat of pigs, goats, harts and cows, as well as of a large number of fowls, from which they even make [stock for] cabbage soup, and several other stews which they have learned from the whites and passed on from one to another. Malaguetta is always prevalent in all their stews. In some places the men go so far as to be seated at table and have themselves served like us, but the common people eat on the ground, with their legs crossed, or lying on their sides. You also see some who eat the flesh of elephants and buffaloes. . . . With all my heart, I am, Sir, etc.

REVIEW QUESTIONS

1. What similarities did Barbot find between these two cultures?
2. What differences did Barbot find between these two cultures?
3. What evidence of class differences among each group do you find in these readings?
4. What did Barbot believe caused the conditions and lifestyles of the Africans he encountered? What do those assumptions tell you about the society in which Barbot lived?

A Former African Slave Remembers His Life (late 1700s)

The Interesting Narrative of the Life of Olaudah Equiano

Surely the most poignant account of the slave trade by a native African is that of Olaudah Equiano, as told by himself. Equiano was born in an Ibo village in 1745 and at the age of eleven was captured by slave traders.[*] He spent ten years in Virginia and served in the British navy before he earned his freedom in 1766. Then, as a free man, he confronted challenges that would change the course of his life. While living in the Americas, Europe, and Africa he worked and wrote for the abolitionist cause until his death in 1797.

The following account from his well-written autobiography illustrates the varied conditions of the slave trade in Africa and the changes to which individuals were forced to adjust. Equiano was one of about fifty thousand Africans brought to the New World in 1756. In the Americas, the slave captain took him to Barbados to sell to sugar plantation owners. To Equiano's good fortune, he was not purchased there, probably because he was so young, for most slaves sold into Barbados during the eighteenth century died from the work. Consequently, he was sent to Virginia, where he was sold to a tobacco planter, and in 1757 he was purchased by an officer of the British navy. Serving on British warships until he was seventeen, he began to understand who he was and the world into which he had been thrust. He also learned to read and write English. This skill then gave him the opportunity to succeed when a Quaker merchant purchased him and allowed him to buy his freedom in 1766.

Thus I continued to travel, sometimes by land, sometimes by water, through different countries and various nations, till, at the end of six or seven months after I had been kidnapped, I arrived at the sea coast. It would be tedious and uninteresting to relate all the incidents which befell me during this journey, and which I have not yet forgotten; of the various hands I passed through, and the manners and customs of all the different people among whom I lived—I shall therefore only observe, that in all the places where I was, the soil was exceedingly rich; the pumpkins, eadas, plantains, yams, &c. &c., were in great abundance, and of incredible size. There were also vast quantities of different gums, though not used for any purpose, and everywhere a great deal of tobacco. The cotton even grew quite wild, and there was plenty of red-wood. I saw no mechanics whatever in all the way, except such as I have mentioned. The chief employment in all these countries was agriculture, and both the males and females, as with us, were brought up to it, and trained in the arts of war.

The first object which saluted my eyes when I arrived on the coast, was the sea, and a slave ship, which was then riding at anchor, and waiting for its cargo. These filled me with astonishment, which was soon converted into terror, when I was carried on board. I was immediately handled, and tossed up to see if I were sound, by some of the crew; and I was now persuaded that I had gotten into a world of bad spirits, and that they were going to kill me. Their complexions, too, differing so much from ours, their long hair, and the language they spoke (which was

---

[*]Recent scholarship has reexamined Equiano's life and thrown some details of his identity into question. See Vincent Carretta, "Olaudah Equiano or Gustavus Vassa? New Light on an Eighteenth-Century Question of Identity," in *Slavery and Abolition,* Vol. 20, 1999, pp. 96–105.

very different from any I had ever heard), united to confirm me in this belief. Indeed, such were the horrors of my views and fears at the moment, that, if ten thousand worlds had been my own, I would have freely parted with them all to have exchanged my condition with that of the meanest slave in my own country. When I looked round the ship too, and saw a large furnace of copper boiling, and a multitude of black people of every description chained together, every one of their countenances expressing dejection and sorrow, I no longer doubted of my fate; and, quite overpowered with horror and anguish, I fell motionless on the deck and fainted. When I recovered a little, I found some black people about me, who I believed were some of those who had brought me on board, and had been receiving their pay; they talked to me in order to cheer me, but all in vain. I asked them if we were not to be eaten by those white men with horrible looks, red faces, and long hair. They told me I was not, and one of the crew brought me a small portion of spirituous liquor in a wine glass; but being afraid of him, I would not take it out of his hand. One of the blacks therefore took it from him and gave it to me, and I took a little down my palate, which, instead of reviving me, as they thought it would, threw me into the greatest consternation at the strange feeling it produced, having never tasted any such liquor before. Soon after this, the blacks who brought me on board went off, and left me abandoned to despair.

I now saw myself deprived of all chance of returning to my native country, or even the least glimpse of hope of gaining the shore, which I now considered as friendly; and I even wished for my former slavery in preference to my present situation, which was filled with horrors of every kind, still heightened by my ignorance of what I was to undergo. I was not long suffered to indulge my grief; I was soon put down under the decks, and there I received such a salutation in my nostrils as I had never experienced in my life: so that, with the loathsomeness of the stench, and crying together, I became so sick and low that I was not able to eat, nor had I the

least desire to taste anything. I now wished for the last friend, death, to relieve me; but soon, to my grief, two of the white men offered me eatables; and, on my refusing to eat, one of them held me fast by the hands, and laid me across, I think, the windlass, and tied my feet, while the other flogged me severely. I had never experienced anything of this kind before, and, although not being used to the water, I naturally feared that element the first time I saw it, yet, nevertheless, could I have got over the nettings, I would have jumped over the side, but I could not; and besides, the crew used to watch us very closely who were not chained down to the decks, lest we should leap into the water; and I have seen some of these poor African prisoners most severely cut, for attempting to do so, and hourly whipped for not eating. This indeed was often the case with myself.

In a little time after, amongst the poor chained men, I found some of my own nation, which in some small degree gave ease to my mind. I inquired of these what was to be done with us? They gave me to understand, we were to be carried to these white people's country to work for them. I then was a little revived, and thought, if it were no worse than working, my situation was not so desperate; but still I feared I should be put to death, the white people looked and acted, as I thought, in so savage a manner; for I had never seen among any people such instances of brutal cruelty; and this not only shown towards us blacks, but also to some of the whites themselves. One white man in particular I saw, when we were permitted to be on deck, flogged so unmercifully with a large rope near the foremast, that he died in consequence of it; and they tossed him over the side as they would have done a brute. This made me fear these people the more; and I expected nothing less than to be treated in the same manner. I could not help expressing my fears and apprehensions to some of my countrymen; I asked them if these people had no country, but lived in this hollow place (the ship)? They told me they did not, but came from a distant one. "Then," said I, "how comes it in all our country we never heard of them?"

They told me because they lived so very far off. I then asked where were their women? had they any like themselves? I was told they had. "And why," said I, "do we not see them?" They answered, because they were left behind. I asked how the vessel could go? They told me they could not tell; but that there was cloth put upon the masts by the help of the ropes I saw, and then the vessel went on; and the white men had some spell or magic they put in the water when they liked, in order to stop the vessel. I was exceedingly amazed at this account, and really thought they were spirits. I therefore wished much to be from amongst them, for I expected they would sacrifice me; but my wishes were vain—for we were so quartered that it was impossible for any of us to make our escape.

While we stayed on the coast I was mostly on deck; and one day, to my great astonishment, I saw one of these vessels coming in with the sails up. As soon as the whites saw it, they gave a great shout, at which we were amazed; and the more so, as the vessel appeared larger by approaching nearer. At last, she came to an anchor in my sight, and when the anchor was let go, I and my countrymen who saw it, were lost in astonishment to observe the vessel stop—and were now convinced it was done by magic. Soon after this the other ship got her boats out, and they came on board of us, and the people of both ships seemed very glad to see each other. Several of the strangers also shook hands with us black people, and made motions with their hands, signifying I suppose, we were to go to their country, but we did not understand them.

At last, when the ship we were in, had got in all her cargo, they made ready with many fearful noises, and we were all put under deck, so that we could not see how they managed the vessel.

But this disappointment was the least of my sorrow. The stench of the hold while we were on the coast was so intolerably loathsome, that it was dangerous to remain there for any time, and some of us had been permitted to stay on the deck for the fresh air; but now that the whole ship's cargo were confined together, it became absolutely pestilential. The closeness of the place, and the heat of the climate, added to the number in the ship, which was so crowded that each had scarcely room to turn himself, almost suffocated us. This produced copious perspirations, so that the air soon became unfit for respiration, from a variety of loathsome smells, and brought on a sickness among the slaves, of which many died—thus falling victims to the improvident avarice, as I may call it, of their purchasers. This wretched situation was again aggravated by the galling of the chains, now became insupportable, and the filth of the necessary tubs, into which the children often fell, and were almost suffocated. The shrieks of the women, and the groans of the dying, rendered the whole a scene of horror almost inconceivable. Happily perhaps, for myself, I was soon reduced so low here that it was thought necessary to keep me almost always on deck; and from my extreme youth I was not put in fetters. In this situation I expected every hour to share the fate of my companions, some of whom were almost daily brought upon deck at the point of death, which I began to hope would soon put an end to my miseries. Often did I think many of the inhabitants of the deep much more happy than myself. I envied them the freedom they enjoyed, and as often wished I could change my condition for theirs. Every circumstance I met with, served only to render my state more painful, and heightened my apprehensions, and my opinion of the cruelty of the whites.

REVIEW QUESTIONS

1. Do you believe that Equiano's description of his experiences would have been much different if he had recorded a journal as they occurred rather than in an autobiography several decades later?
2. Critics have concluded that Equiano was extraordinarily fortunate and intelligent. What information in this excerpt might lead to that conclusion?

3. What conditions on the slave ship during the voyage had the greatest impact upon Equiano? What do you think would have affected you the most?
4. Do you think that Equiano's experiences on the sea voyage would have been different if he had been an adult? Why or why not?

A French Ship's Captain Describes Economic Opportunities and the Slave Trade on the East African Coast (1784–1785)

J. CRASSONS DE MEDEUIL, *The French Slave Trade in Kilwa*

The port of Kilwa changed hands frequently after 1480. At one time an important trading port along the Swahili coast that sent goods to India and the Mediterranean, Kilwa was destroyed in 1505 because its ruler refused to trade with the Portuguese. As we saw in the account by Santo Bernadino, the Portuguese power on the East African coast waned by the latter seventeenth century, and Kilwa once again became home to Swahili traders. The Portuguese continued to use the port for ships en route to India and Southeast Asia, but they shared the privilege with ships from many other European nations.

In 1784, Joseph Crassons de Medeuil captained a slaving ship on the East African coast and wrote the following account as part of his letter to the Royal Commissioner, to be included in a report to the Minister of the Navy. His primary trade was in slaves for the French sugar plantations that had been established on Mauritius Island beginning in 1714. Crassons may not have known of the growing political tensions in France as he wrote or the uncertainty the government officials he addressed might have been facing. He could not have known, also, that the French were in that very year abolishing slavery in their nation, or that their primary slave markets in Haiti would vanish when the island became independent of France within a decade. Consequently, this letter expresses the ideas and perspective of an entrepreneur who saw an opportunity for the French monarchy and himself to make a fortune.

Almost the whole of the East Coast of Africa is unknown to us. The detailed maps of Mr. D'Apris [Jean Baptist Nicolas Denis d'Après de Mannevillette] are not accurate. The mapping of the coast line seems to have been done in a haphazard manner and [a] number of islands and reefs known to certain navigators are not marked on these maps.

We only have approximate knowledge of the coast from the Cape of Good Hope to Cape Corrientes. Even in this stretch several bays are still unknown to us, in particular the Bay of Lourenço Marques. This bay merits the most careful attention.

From Cape Corrientes to Cape Natal the coast looks most inviting and attractive. It is presumably thickly populated if one can judge by the number of fires visible along it.

The coast, from Cape Corrientes to Cape Delgado and in particular as far as the Angoxa Islands, is very sparsely inhabited and little known. The Portuguese have always made a mystery of this section. We are assured that they have trading posts on all the rivers, including the Quilimani, stretching fifty miles inland.

The stretch between Mozambique and Ibo is fairly thickly populated. It is there we go in search of our blacks. We trade for them at Kerimba, Ibo and Mozambique, small islands detached from the coast and inaccurately marked on the map.

From Cape Delgado to Kilwa the coast is inhabited only by Moors and Arabs who take from it a prodigious number of blacks (*in margin:* inferior to those of Kilwa but which they bring there to sell to us), particularly from the river Mongallo, a little-known river which flows through fertile and thickly populated country stretching a long way inland.

This stretch of country is entirely unknown to us, the approach to it is very difficult and we rarely go there.

From Kilwa to Mafia, a large and lovely island which is at the moment engaged in making itself independent of the King of Kilwa, the sea, according to the map, appears to be without hazards and easily navigable. But there is a mass of islands which occupies a space of more than ten leagues and notably the island of Songo Songo, which is thickly populated. Here M. Crassons bargained for blacks and food supplies in 1754. This island is six leagues from the mainland. The channel is from twelve to fifteen cubits deep.

The Islands of Zanzibar are well known. It was among them that the vessel *St. Pierre,* carrying a rich cargo of *piastres,* and commanded by M. Maurice was lost. The vessel had been equipped in Mauritius. (*Marginal note:* There is [in Zanzibar] a fortress which belongs to the Imam of Muscat, to whom the Moors and Arabs of Mombasa, Pate and Barawa pay dues. The whole of the remaining part of this coast as far as the entrance to the Red Sea itself ought to be better known to us.) He escaped to Kilwa with the remains of his fortune. This man was a surgeon

and he rendered such valuable services that the King of Kilwa treated him with friendliness and wanted to settle him in his domains. For the sum of 4,000 *piastres* he ceded to him the northern portion of Kilwa in which is situated the ancient Portuguese citadel. It is very favourably situated as it commands the northern channel which has a depth of fifteen to twenty-two cubits. Death put an end to M. Morice's progress. He was mourned for and is still spoken of with tenderness and veneration. The original of this deed of sale was sent to Mauritius. The counterpart is in the possession of the son of the former minister Bwana Muhammad by name, leader of the religion of Kilwa and whose father was our friend.

A COMMUNICATION PRESENTED TO M. DE CURT, ROYAL COMMISSIONER, TO MAKE TO MONSEIGNEUR LE MARÉCHAL DE CASTRIES, MINISTER OF THE NAVY

Kilwa.

Let it be known that the Seigneur Joseph Crassons de Medeuil, a captain in the merchant navy, who has served in the wars of 1758 and 1778, sometimes as a pilot and sometimes as an auxiliary officer in His Majesty's ships, and who has recently come from India, feels it is his duty to report to His Excellency the Marshal on what he has seen and done during his voyages along the East Coast of Africa in his ship *La Créolle,* and particularly in the port of Kilwa situated in latitude nine degrees and a few minutes south. He went thither on two occasions to trade for blacks and found this island friendly disposed towards establishing this type of trade in a manner likely to commend itself to the Ministry, which appears to wish to engage in it, since it has had time to study and to take note of the size and safety of this port for the accommodation of a very great number of ships and even of fighting fleets. In view of the type of slaves obtainable in this area and the qualities of the piece of land adjacent to this great bay, which has been released by the king whom they call sultan, and also in view of the fact that the great majority of the natives are disposed to be friendly to us, ardently desiring as they do to be able to enjoy and share in the protection of France and to make an effective treaty of alliance with us, a letter was composed in a general assembly held for this purpose, addressed to the king, asking for his protection and for a guarantee against all foreign invasion, particularly against the Arabs and the Portuguese who are the two neighbours most likely to give them trouble; in the said address made to His Majesty they offer to hand over a part of the island on its North Coast in which is situated the fort formerly belonging to the Portuguese and from which they were driven out by the present king's [of Kilwa] father, with immediate possession of the same piece of land which was formerly purchased by M. Maurice, a Frenchman who died in the said place, with permission to build there a fortress, to plant our flag, to have sole exclusive right to the trade in negroes and in all other such materials and products as may suit us; that in the said fortress we may have as many soldiers as we find necessary and establish everywhere on the coast and in the interior the trading centres required for purposes of cultivation. They even offer to maintain 200 men and in order to do so to divide with the officer who is given command of the fort the six *piastres* which they levy on each captive. The above document, with which I have been entrusted, I put into the hands of the Governor on my arrival in Pondichéry.

FURTHERMORE

While we were busy with the King or Sultan of Kilwa drawing up the above-mentioned document, an armed corvette arrived at the said place carrying the son of the Imam of Muscat, who is a pretender to the Government of the town and to the succession of the Estates of his father, who died about three or four years ago, but this son was despoiled of his inheritance by another brother, whose faction is the more powerful; in consequence the former fled from Muscat to come and collect supporters on this coast from Zanzibar, Pate, Mombasa, Barawa, as far as the island of Socotra, which is almost entirely inhabited by Moors and Arabs who are in sympathy with his cause; and he being anxious to be able to take possession again of Muscat and seeing the zeal of the Sultan [of] Kilwa in invoking the protection of France, has joined him and made a special request on his behalf, offering and promising full satisfaction of France's commercial needs on the seas and in the ports of Arabia and the Persian Gulf and a fort and a counting house at Muscat under the [French] flag. Further he undertakes to pay and reimburse all expenses which might arise in this connexion and he is eager to come to France in person to ask for these things. He even wished to buy my ship but found it too small as he was purposing at that time to attack the fortress of Zanzibar (whose commander had been appointed by his brother) and was levying troops in Kilwa; for his enterprise I had offered him everything at my disposal, two twenty-four inch cannon, twenty guns, powder, bullets and money. He did not see fit to accept these, assuring me that he would make himself master by the force of persuasion alone and of the respect that these people generally have for their chiefs. As he had always treated me with the greatest deference and with all the marks of open friendship we parted with a desire to meet again. In consequence I promised to come in person to submit his request to the attention of the Ministry, and on his part he gave me a passport signed by himself and bearing his seal with which I can present myself at any of the Arab ports belonging to his faction with a very strong recommendation that I should be served, protected and welcomed as he would be himself, whose envoy I am. This is the sole motive of my journey to Paris, having sought in this negotiation only to procure for the king and the nation such things as might be useful, to extend the glory and importance of his protection; to extend our trade and our sea routes which are too restricted in this area and in which we could develop our trade and influence very profitably.

CONCERNING THE PORT OF KILWA

This Port is well placed particularly for doing damage in time of war to English warships on their way to India as it is situated at the Northern exit of the Mozambique Channel.

The Port is vast and safe and can hold a prodigious number of ships. The timber there is of good quality and appearance and is easily worked and plentiful. Water might be a little less plentiful because the inhabitants have only the number of wells necessary to them on the island. But it must be possible to find water in the neighbouring rivers of which there are five in as much as a ship of 200 tons could go up some of them to a distance of more than ten leagues, the sea is fifteen feet deep and I have been inland with my *pirogue* for more than eleven leagues. I found two delightful springs and there must be others, seeing that the river ends up in two charming mountains; in the two passes there is enough water for the largest vessels, it being at its shallowest fourteen fathoms deep. The country is superb and pleasing once one has extricated oneself from the forests of half submerged trees called Mangroves. Judging from the ruins of stone-built houses, which can be seen not only on the island of Kilwa but also on the southern side of the pass, it appears that this was once a very important town and that it must have had a big trade; at Kilwa one can see the whole of a big mosque built in stone whose arches are very well constructed. Within the last three years a pagoda which stood at the southern extremity, and which was very curious looking, fell. Finally, this country produces millet, indigo, superb cotton, silkier even than the cotton produced on the Ile de Bourbon, sugar cane, gums in abundance, brown cowries of the second sort which are currency at Jiddah and in Dahomey, besides elephant ivory which is very common, as are elephants, and lastly negroes—superb specimens if they are selected with care. This selection we cannot make ourselves, being at the discretion of the traders, who are now aware of our needs and who know that it is absolutely essential for us to sail at a given season in order to round the Cape of Good Hope. In addition to competition amongst ourselves the expeditions have never been properly thought out and always left to chance, and so it happens that three or four ships find themselves in the same place and crowd each other out. This would not happen if there were a properly organized body and the expeditions were planned to fit in with the seasons and the quantity of cargo and the means of using up surplus also planned, since it is not the business of seamen to concern themselves with correspondence and administration. . . .

It is clear that if this number of captives, i.e., 4,193, who were traded for at least in this period of three years, cost forty *piastres* each, this represents a sum of 167,720 *piastres,* raised for the most part from the Ile de France and from Bourbon, or from France direct. It is therefore important not only to safeguard this trade but also to find a way of spending rather fewer *piastres,* which would be quite possible if one considers that the *piastres* which we give them for their captives do not remain long in their hands and that they almost immediately give them to the Moors and Arabs who provide them with their needs which are rice, millet, lambs, tunics, shirts, carpets, needles, swords, shoes, and silk materials for dresses and linings. The Arabs obtain most of these things from Surat, and why should we not get them direct from there ourselves? We should make the profit they make, and we should employ men and ships and we should keep a good number of our *piastres* which would remain in the Ile de France and in Bourbon; more certainly still, if privately owned ships from Europe or these islands could not go to the coast of Mozambique and if ships belonging to a private company sent out from Europe could participate in this trade only by means of *piastres* taken to Kilwa, it can be estimated how much we have paid into the hands of the Portuguese at Mozambique, Kerimba and . . . [omitted: Ibo] where they make us pay fifty or sixty *piastres* each for them. This does not include presents and tiresome vexations. What need is there to give our money to the Portuguese, when we have the means to operate among ourselves and when we can use our own industry and keep our money? I have heard for a long time talk of establishing a settlement or trading post in Madagascar. Truly, seeing the number of idle hands we have and the great number of poor and needy and foundlings in our almshouses it is surprising that we have not yet considered this plan, at least as far as that part of the island which we have most visited over a long period is concerned, and also, in certain ports which are particularly well situated, trading posts could be established without straining the resources of the State.

REVIEW QUESTIONS

1. Why did Crassons believe that the French should concentrate more on trade with the East African coast?
2. What steps had Crassons taken to ensure continued trade? With whom?
3. Considering the condition of the French monarchy in the 1780s, do you think that his plans were well founded? Why or why not?
4. Do Crassons's plans for stimulating French settlements and business with Madagascar and other islands in the Indian Ocean resemble the plans of others that have been presented in this chapter? Explain.

4

The Americas and Oceania, 1500–1800

The following accounts of exploration that took place after the initial discovery of the American continent and Pacific Ocean states and societies have three principal themes: the growth of competition among European nations, the negative reactions of native peoples to the incursions of foreigners, and the inquisitiveness of individuals who wanted to understand people who were drastically different from themselves. As the British, French, and Dutch entered the race for overseas dominion in the late sixteenth century, they competed intensely with the Spanish and Portuguese. Burgomaster Witsen and Pedro Fernandez de Quiros both sought wealth in island trade against fearsome competition. The native people who inhabited these continents and islands used various techniques to defeat or subvert the interlopers. Certainly the most dramatic example of native hostility toward Europeans is the case of Hans Staden. Tupinambá cannibals in Brazil captured the German mercenary. In fact, at one point he was led into a native village and forced to announce, "Here I come, food for you." No doubt the Tupinambá were disappointed when Staden made his escape and lived to tell the tale of his captivity.

A second interested observer of Brazilian society was the French Catholic André Thevet. After a stay of approximately ten weeks in Brazil, he returned to France and claimed that on the way home his ship was blown off course and, as a result, he had the opportunity to visit various regions of North America, including Mexico, Florida, and the eastern part of modern-day Canada. Thevet's account shows the inquisitiveness of Europeans in the New World. Others with similar curiosity include Sir Walter Raleigh, Thomas Gage, and Cristoval de Acuña.

Mere curiosity, however, was not the sole motivation of European travelers in this period. Religion also played a key role. Fray Bernardino de Sahagún traveled to Mexico, learned to speak Nahuatl, and dedicated himself to rescuing the culture of the native peoples of Mesoamerica from the destruction wrought by his predecessors. In the 1520s, the conquistadors and priests who had accompanied Hernan Cortéz systematically burned native books and forced natives to dismantle their temples to build Catholic churches. Sahagún dedicated his life to recreating this great cultural loss. A second Spanish cleric, Fray Diego Durán, also learned the native language in order to record more accurately the history of the Aztecs. Other Spanish churchmen, such as Cristoval de Acuña (Peru) and Martín de Munilla (the New Hebrides), primarily sought to bring Christianity to the natives.

Given the large number of Spanish explorers and missionaries, it is not surprising that travelers from other countries would take note of Spain's growing imperialistic aspirations. The Englishman Thomas Gage reported on Spanish control of the Caribbean coasts of Honduras and Guatemala. His interest in Spain's overseas foreign policy shows the competition that had developed among European states.

A French Friar Describes Life Among the Florida Natives (1575)

ANDRÉ THEVET, *Cosmographie Universelle*

The essentially medieval outlook of André Thevet is a prominent feature in the following description of his alleged visit to Florida in the mid–sixteenth century. His strong support of the Catholic faith in France during the period of the Religious Wars also colors his account. A Franciscan, Thevet became an author of travel accounts after a journey to the Middle East in 1549 and a short visit to Brazil in 1555–1556. One might suppose that his ten-week-long exposure to the New World might limit the amount of geographical literature he could compose, but it did not. As the French king's "royal cosmographer," Thevet had the opportunity to interview sailors and sea captains, such as Jacques Cartier, who had made extended voyages along the St. Lawrence River. He also read voraciously the often obscure, published and unpublished, contemporary accounts about the travels of others. He then simply wrote his accounts as though he had been there himself.

Although criticized by his contemporaries for his blatant plagiarism, Thevet's information is generally reliable and very revealing of the European interest in and perception of the Americas in the sixteenth century. For the following description of the Timucuan natives of the Florida peninsula, Thevet said he obtained his information from René de Laudonnière, who had been the leader of a French expedition that established Fort Caroline on the northeast coast. Thevet also may have used the drawings of the Huguenot artist Jacques Le Moyne, who accompanied the Laudonnière expedition to Florida.

So I must return to our point of Florida, where the people are just like those of the flat country except that they are not so cruel and nonetheless very stupid and simple. They are of sallow complexion, of large stature and well-proportioned, and dressed in all weather in skins of animals, the men as well as the women. Most of them have their bodies painted, on the arms and thighs, with very pretty divisions [areas] which can never be removed because they are pricked into the skin. They are great deceivers and traitors, personally valiant however and fight well.

They have no other arms than bows and arrows, the cord of which they make from the gut and leather of the stag, as well made and of as many different colors as anyone could make in France. They tip their arrows with the teeth of fish and with stone which they prepare most cleverly. They exercise their young men at running and the use of the bow, and they have a prize which they give to the one who can hold his breath the longest. They also take great pleasure in hunting and fishing. The kings of the country make war on each other, warring only by surprise, and they kill all the men they can capture, then remove their heads to have the hair, which they carry off to exhibit in triumph in their houses. However, they spare the women and children, whom they support and keep permanently with them. On their return from war they assemble all their subjects and in their great joy they dance, sing, and feast for three days and nights. And they even make the old women of the country dance, holding in their hands the scalps of their enemies: and while dancing they sing the praises of the sun, attributing to him the honor of the victory.

They have no knowledge of God nor of any religion, other than that which they see like the sun and the moon. They have priests whom they call *Jarvars* to whom they lend all faith because they are great magicians, soothsayers, and invokers of the Devil, and they serve them as physicians and surgeons since they always carry with them a sack of herbs and drugs to treat the ill. They are very subject to women and girls, whom they call daughters of the sun, and most of them [are] sodomites. The kings are permitted to have two or three wives, however only the first is honored and recognized as queen and only her children inherit the property and authority of the father. The women do all the housework, and they [the men] do not cohabit with them when they are pregnant, nor eat any food they have touched while they are menstruating.

When they go to war, the king whom they name *Paracousti* (others *Paraousti*) marches at the head with a club in one hand and his bow in the other, with his quiver full of arrows, and is followed by his people also armed with their bows and arrows. [The king] before departing sits in a bower surrounded by the kings who are going to accompany him on this expedition. This done, gazing at heaven [he] begins to discourse of various things, and to urge his subjects to fight well and valiantly, picturing to them the glory and honor he will acquire if they should win a victory over their enemy, and contrariwise the shame it will be to them if they are defeated and lose the battle. Threatening with a furious look which he casts in the direction of his enemies, he gives his subjects to understand the desire he has to vanquish them [the enemy], and in the course of his speech casts often his look on high, asking the sun to give him a victory over the aforesaid adversaries. This having gone on for half an hour, he pours with his hand some of the water which is brought to him in a vessel over the heads of the *Paracousis* who surround him, and the rest he hurls as if in fury and spite on a fire which has been prepared there for this purpose. In doing this he thrice cries out the name of his enemy, which all those who follow him do after him. This ceremony from what I have been able to learn of it, signifies that he is begging the sun to grant him a victory so heroic that he will be able to shed the blood of his enemies at

will just as he has showered all this water around: also that the *Paracousis* sprinkled with some of this water will be able to return with the heads of their enemies, which is the sole and supreme symbol of their victories.

For when it is a question of fighting they utter great shouts and exclamations, and the king would not dare to budge before the battle is finished. For if he were so mad as to flee, seeing that his men were getting the worst of it, it would be all up with him and they would not fail to massacre him. And that is the way the Persians still do, and it has not been very long since the Turks did the same, and several Levantine nations. And if mayhap they obtain the victory, they take the heads of their dead enemies and cut off all the hair with a part of the scalp. This done they go home giving thanks to the sun and singing his marvels. Also, they send a messenger ahead to announce the victory to those who stayed behind to guard the houses, who begin immediately to weep. But when night comes, they have a great dance and celebration in honor of the occasion. The *Paracousi,* having returned home, has all the scalps of his enemies set before his door surrounded with laurel branches, showing with this spectacle the triumph of the victory he has obtained. Then begin the weeping and lamentations, which at nightfall are converted into dancing and pleasures.

Their weapons are bows with arrows whose tips are poisoned and in some places the wood also is poisoned. On the tips instead of iron they place bones of wild beasts or teeth of fish so sharp that I doubt if iron penetrates better than these bones, hurled by the steely hands of these barbarians. The coast-dwellers content themselves with killing their enemies without eating them, while the inhabitants of the interior (being idolatrous), eat them after having sacrificed them to their idols. The coast people, but not all of them (as I said before), adore the sun without building any altar to it or making any sacrifice to it. They are of good stature and live a long time; there are some who are 150 years old at least.

And Captain Laudonnière will be my witness to this: who in 1564 by the command of the late

King Charles [IX] made the Florida voyage for the second time. There he had the fort of the *Carolina* built, on the May river, in honor of the said King. Having then arrived in this country and exploring the lands adjacent to his fort, he arrived at a mountain of medium height, along which he set foot on ground. Having rested himself a while, [he] walked with some of his troops in the woods arriving at a reedy marsh. Finding themselves tired from the march, they went into the shade of a great laurel-tree to rest a bit and discuss some problem of their enterprise. They then discovered five barbarians of that region half-hidden in the woods who seemed somewhat afraid of our Frenchmen, who greeted them in their own language saying *Antipola Bonnasou,* so that hearing such words they would approach more confidently, which they soon did. But since they noticed that the four last ones were carrying the train of the pelts [with] which the first was clothed, they suspected that he was of higher rank than the others, plus the fact that they called him Paracousti. So some of the [French] company approached him and sweet-talking him pointed to their captain (for whom they had made a bower of laurels and palms in the fashion of the country) so that by such signs they would see and understand that the French had formerly had association with their fellows. This *Paracousti* having approached the captain, began to address to him a rather long harangue, whose effect was that he begged the Frenchmen to come see his dwelling and his family. Which having been granted him by the said Frenchmen, he gave to the said Laudonnière in token of his great friendship the very pelt with which he was clothed.

This done, [he] took him by the hand and struck off through the swamps: across which the Paracousti and the said captain with several Frenchmen were carried on the shoulders of these savages. The others who could not pass because of the mud and [under]growth went through the woods and followed a little narrow path which guided them to the dwelling of the *Paracousti*. From this [there] issued forth fifty of these savages the more honorably to receive the Frenchmen, and entertained them in their fashion. Following which they immediately presented [to] them a large earthen jar of curious style, full of clear spring water and very excellent, which they presented to each, following a certain order and ceremony as they carried it to the various persons to drink. Thirst having been quenched in this way and the Frenchmen refreshed, the *Paracousti* conducted them to the lodge of his father, one of the oldest living people on earth. The Frenchmen, respecting his age, began to gratify him by the use of the term Friend, Friend, at which the old man appeared very happy. They then questioned him about his age, to which he answered claiming to be the living ancestor of five generations. [He then showed] them another old man seated across from him, who was much older than he. Indeed it was his father, who more resembled the bark of a tree than a living man. He had the tendons, veins, arteries, bones, and other parts of his body showing under his skin so that you easily could not have counted them and told them apart from each other; and his age was so great that the good man had lost his sight and could not, without a very great effort, utter a single word.

REVIEW QUESTIONS

1. What important elements of technology did Thevet observe among the Timucuans? Was he favorably impressed? Why or why not?
2. In what way did the position of *Paracousti* resemble that of a European monarch? How was it different?
3. What was the role of elite women among the Timucuans? The role of elite men?
4. What evidence appears in this excerpt that Thevet did not hesitate to use the experiences and writings of others in his account?

A Spanish Priest Recreates the History of Meso-American People (mid-1500s)

FRAY BERNARDINO DE SAHAGÚN, *Florentine Codex: General History of the Things of New Spain*

Fray Bernardino de Sahagún's *Florentine Codex* is an attempt to recreate the history of the Native American peoples in Mesoamerica. Since European conquistadors and missionaries had burned native books to eliminate the "works of the devil," sixteenth-century European accounts such as the *Florentine Codex* are the best written descriptions of native life and societies that still exist. Sahagún's work is also important because it reflects the European mentality and priorities after the Spanish conquest of the Aztec empire. This selection focuses on the everyday life of several American ethnic groups, including their houses, clothing, occupations, religions, and relations with each other.

Sahagún came to Mexico in 1529, learned the Nahuatl language of the Aztecs, and started writing accounts of native life in that language. By the 1550s, he had become one of the first missionaries to recognize that the native conversion to Christianity was superficial and that native observances of Christian services and rituals contained many non-Christian references. In 1560, his superior, Fray Francisco de Torval, instructed Sahagún to dedicate himself to collecting the histories of native peoples. In 1571 and 1577, however, the Church in Spain censured him for his work and took his accounts of native peoples from him. Sahagún died in 1590 without seeing any of his work published. Indeed, his work was not published until the beginning of the twentieth century.

Several of Sahagún's references deserve a word of explanation. For example, the widely-used term *Chichimeca* is Nahuatl for "barbarian" and was used by various peoples to characterize their rivals in the Valley of Mexico. In this selection, Sahagún concentrates on describing the life and society of the Tolteca and Otomí peoples who inhabited the Valley of Mexico before the arrival of the Aztecs in the mid–fourteenth century. The account also refers to the Nahuatl priest, Quetzalcoatl, who is celebrated in many later accounts as being the "God who will return from the rising sun." Some natives interpreted Cortez's arrival in Mexico in 1519 as the fulfillment of the tale of Quetzalcoatl's return.

First, those named the Tolteca, so-called: these first came to live here in the land, called land of the Mexica, land of the Chichimeca. And for several four-hundreds of years they dwelt in the vicinity of Tollantzinco. Since they really lived there, they left many of their traces which they had fashioned. In that area they made what was their temple; its name was "house of beams." Today it stands; it exists, considering that it is indestructible; for it is of rock, of stone.

Then there they went—they went to live, to dwell on the banks of a river at Xicocotitlan, now called Tula. Because verily they there resided together, they there dwelt, so also many are their traces which they produced. And they left behind that which today is there, which is to be seen, which they did not finish—the so-called serpent column, the round stone pillar made into a serpent. Its head rests on the ground; its tail, its rattles are above. And the Tolteca mountain is to be seen; and the Tolteca pyramids, the mounds, and the surfacing of Tolteca [temples]. And Tolteca potsherds are there to be seen. And Tolteca bowls, Tolteca ollas are taken from the earth. And many times Tolteca jewels—arm bands, esteemed green stones, fine turquoise, emerald-green jade—are taken from the earth.

And these Tolteca were called Chichimeca. There [was] no real word for their name. Their name is taken from—it comes from—their manner of life, their works. The Tolteca were wise. Their works were all good, all perfect, all wonderful, all marvelous; their houses beautiful, tiled in mosaics, smoothed, stuccoed, vary marvelous.

Wherefore was it called a Tolteca house? It was built with consummate care, majestically designed; it was the place of worship of their priest, whose name was Quetzalcoatl; it was quite marvelous. It consisted of four [abodes]. One was facing east; this was the house of gold. For this reason was it called house of gold: that which served as the stucco was gold plate applied, joined to it. One was facing west, toward the setting sun; this was the house of green stone, the house of fine turquoise. For this reason was it called the house of green stone, the house of fine turquoise: what served as the stucco within the house was an inlay of green stones, of fine turquoise. One was facing south, toward the irrigated lands; this [was] the house of shells or of silver. That which served as the stucco, the interior of the walls, seemed as if made of these shells inlaid. One was facing north, toward the plains, toward the spear house; this [was] the red [house], red because red shells were inlaid in the interior walls, or those [stones] which were precious stones, were red.

And there was the house of feathers. That which served as the stucco within the house was a covering of feathers. It also consisted of four

[abodes. One] was facing east. Within the house, applied to the wall surface, was a covering of yellow feathers, such as parrot feathers; and all was yellow, of very yellow feathers. And [one] was facing west, toward what is called the sun's setting-place; it was called the house of precious feathers. For this reason was it called the house of quetzal feathers, the house of blue cotinga feathers: they placed—they pasted—the quetzal feathers, the blue cotinga feathers, to capes or nets [and] then hung them on the wall. Hence was it called house of quetzal feathers. And the house of white plumes was facing south, toward the irrigated lands, and it was called the white house. For this reason was it called the white house: of white feathers was the covering of the house walls, and that which was white was feathers, such as eagle feathers. And [one] was facing north, toward the plains, toward the spear house. Also red was the covering of feathers, such as the red spoonbill, the red arara, etc.

Very many were the marvelous houses which they made. The house of Quetzalcoatl, which was his place of worship, stood in the water; a large river passed by it; the river which passed by Tula. There stood that which was the bathing place of Quetzalcoatl, called "In the Waters of Green Stones" [Chalchiuapan]. Many houses stood within the earth where the Tolteca left many things buried.

And these, the traces of the Tolteca, their pyramids, their mounds, etc., not only appear there at the places called Tula [and] Xicocotitlan, but practically everywhere they rest covered; for their potsherds, their ollas, their pestles, their figurines, their arm bands appear everywhere. Their traces are everywhere, because the Tolteca were dispersed all over.

The Tolteca were skilled; it is said that they were feather workers [who] glued feathers. In ancient times they took charge of the gluing of feathers; and it was really their discovery, for in ancient times they used the shields, the devices, those called *apanecaiotl,* which were their exclusive property. When the wonderful devices were entrusted to them, they prepared, they glued the feathers; they indeed formed works of art; they performed works of skill. In truth, they invented all the wonderful, precious, marvelous things which they made.

And in this way were the Tolteca learned: they knew well, they understood well, that which pertained to herbs, to the nature of their essence; which ones were good, which esteemed, and which of them were just plants, which ones bad, evil, harmful, or really deadly.

They invented the art of medicine. The old men Oxomoco, Cipactonal, Tlaltetecui, Xochicaoaca, were Tolteca. They were the wise men who discovered, who knew of, medicine; who originated the medical art.

So learned were they [that] they were the ones who, for the first time, discovered, found, and, for the first time, used the green stones, fine turquoise, [common] turquoise, then common obsidian, the emerald-green jade—all kinds of wondrous precious stones. . . .

The following is the food of the Chichimeca: nopal, tuna, roots of the *cimatl* herb, *tziuactli* cactus, honey, maguey, yucca flowers, yucca sap, maguey sap, bee honey, wild bees, wild honey; and the roots of which they had knowledge, which were in the ground; and all the meats— rabbit, snake, deer, wild animals; and all [things] which flew.

Such was the food of these Chichimeca, that they never sickened much. They became very old; they died only at an advanced age; they went on to be white-haired, white-headed. And if sickness settled upon someone, when after two days—three days—four days—he recovered not, then the Chichimeca assembled together; they slew him. They inserted a bird arrow into his throat, whereof he died. And they likewise slew those who became very old men [or] very old women. As for their killing the sick, the aged, it was said that thus they showed him mercy; it is said [that it was] in order that he would not suffer on earth, and so they would not feel sorry for him. And when they buried him, they paid him great honor; two days, three days, they mourned; there was dancing, there was singing.

Such was their food and so limited their clothing, that they were strong, lean, hard, and very wiry, sinewy, powerful, and they ran much. As they went, as they climbed mountains, it was as if they were carried by the wind, for they were lean—they had no folds of fat—so that nothing impeded them.

These always went taking their women with them, [as] hath been said. And when the woman was already pregnant, her helpmate many times applied heat to her back; he went pouring water on her back. It was said that he told her that thereby he bathed her. And when she had been delivered, when the child was born, then the Chichimeca [man] kicked this newly delivered woman twice, thrice, in the back. It was said that this stopped the blood. Then they placed their child in a small carrying frame; the women loaded it on her back. Where night came upon them, there they slept. On the morrow, likewise; [the next day, likewise].

And if their child which was born were a girl, when she became four years old—five years old— then also they gave her to a Chichimeca boy. Then he took her; he always went carrying her.

And if [it were] a boy, when he became one year old, then they gave him a bow; then he went about practising the shooting of arrows. The Chichimeca taught him no play, only the shooting of arrows.

These Chichimeca knew, practised, administered the evil eye, the doing of ill, the blowing of evil. These Chichimeca dispensed with their hair-cut; the hair was merely worn long, parted in the middle; as the men [were], just so [were] the women. . . .

A little is mentioned here of those [who were] the Otomí and of their way of life, their qualities.

The name of the Otomitl comes from, is taken from, the name of him who first became the leader of the Otomí. They say his name was Oton. His children, his descendants, and his subjects were all called Otomí; a single one, Otomitl.

These Otomí had a civilized way of life. The men wore capes, clothed themselves, wore breech clouts, wore sandals. The women wore skirts; they wore shifts. The clothing, the capes, the sandals of the men were of good quality; the skirts, the shifts of the women were of good quality.

There were rulers who governed them; there were nobles, there were lords; there were the so-called stewards; there were leaders; there were priests, the so-called Otomí priests. There was their supreme priest by the name of Tecutlatoa. There was their wise man, whom they called, whom they named, Tlaciuhqui. That is, he performed sorcery for [the god]; he was equal to, he resembled [a god]; he addressed them as if [he were] a god. He addressed the gods; he informed them of that which they desired. The Otomí inquired of [the sorcerer], if it were necessary to go to war, whether perchance they would die in war; they inquired of him whether there would be rain during the year, or whether, perhaps, there would be no [rain]; they inquired [if] famine, if perhaps sickness might come—might spread. They asked many things of the sorcerer. They worshipped [sorcerers] as gods; hence were they very highly esteemed; they were regarded well everywhere.

These Otomí possessed gardens; they possessed maize bins; good [was] their food, good [was] their drink. The name of their god was Iocippa. Very good [was] his temple, which they had erected for him, had dedicated to him—the straw hut of trimmed and smoothed straw called the temple of Oton. All provided themselves with straw huts, grass huts; they did not greatly esteem flat-roofed houses. There in their temples lived the priests, and there the small boys were reared; there they did penance, passed the night, entered the bath; maguey spines were placed; they bled themselves, they cut themselves, they fasted. All night they played the two-toned drum on the top of their temple. It was said they held guard on top. (This they said.)

In this manner were they adorned. The hair of the still small boys was cut short leaving a little hair on the back of the head. They named it *pi-ochtli.* Then lower lips were perforated; lip plugs were provided; ear plugs were provided. And they shaved over the foreheads of the grown men, and on the backs of their heads they left much long hair. Hence were they called *piocheque.*

The lip plugs of the rulers were green stone lip plugs, or sea shell lip plugs, or gold lip plugs. And also the ear plugs of the brave men, the brave warriors, were gold ear plugs or copper ear plugs, or sea shell ear plugs, or mirror stone ear plugs, or turquoise [mosaic] ear plugs. The lip plugs of all the [other] people were of rock crystal, obsidian, or smoky stone, and their ear plugs were of obsidian or smoky stone, or those known as stalactites, green ones resembling turquoise, or ear plugs made of black beetles, or pottery ear plugs. And furthermore, at last came their ear plugs of dried maize stalks or reed ear plugs.

When the women were still young girls, they cut their hair short; but when [they were] grown, when [they were] young women, the hair covered their shoulders. However, the hair over the forehead was cut. And when one was a mature woman, when perhaps she also [had delivered] her child, the hair was bound about her head. Also they wore ear plugs, and their arms, their breasts, were painted. Their painting was well scratched, well scarified, very green, bluish, very beautiful.

This [was] their food: maize, dried maize ears, beans, chili, salt, tomatoes. Their greatest specialties or, as I have mentioned it, their great pleasures, [were] fruit tamales, cooked beans, dogs, gophers, deer.

Behold the defects, the faults of the Otomí. They were untrained, stupid. Thus was there scolding, or thus was one scolded; thus was there the scolding of one untrained. It was said: "Now thou art an Otomí. Now thou art a miserable Otomí. O Otomí, how is it that thou understandest not? Art thou perchance an Otomí? Art thou perchance a real Otomí? Not only art thou like an Otomí, thou art a real Otomí, a miserable Otomí, a green-head, a thick-head, a big tuft of hair over the back of the head, an Otomí blockhead, an Otomí. . . ."

With all this one was scolded, one was shamed. It was taken, it stemmed, from the uncouthness of the Otomí.

The Otomí were very covetous, that is, very desirous, greedy. That which was good, they bought all; they longed for all of it even though it was not really necessary.

The Otomí were very gaudy dressers—vain

people; that is to say, what there were of capes, of clothing, which were one's special privilege, they took all, they wore all, to be vain people. It was not worn in good taste; thus of them was said: "Hath it possibly been said that someone called thee an Otomí? Is it true that thou art an Otomí?"

Likewise the women, who also bought up all the skirts, [all] the shifts, did not wear the skirts well; they did not wear the shifts well. Such gaudy dressers [were] the young girls [that] they pasted their legs, their arms, with red feathers. Faces were smeared with yellow ochre, and teeth were darkened. Faces were covered a fine brown.

And as gaudy dressers, as vain as the [other] Otomí, were the old women, who still also cut the hair over the forehead; who still also cut the hair on one side, leaving the other side long; who still also darkened their teeth, still painted their faces, still pasted themselves with red feath-

ers; who still also put on the embroidered skirts, the embroidered shifts.

The Otomí were lazy, shiftless, although wiry, strong; as is said, hardened; laborers. Although great workers of the land, they did not apply themselves to gaining the necessities of life. When they had worked the land they only wandered.

Behold what they did: they went catching [game]; they went catching rabbits, spearing rabbits, snaring rabbits in nets, shooting rabbits with reed arrows, hunting rabbits with balls; they went catching quail with snares; they went catching game with snares, catching game with a throw-net, catching game with a lasso; they went shooting deer with arrows, catching deer in nets; they went setting traps; they went setting dead-falls; they went boring the maguey plant, becoming drunk; there they went whiling away their time.

REVIEW QUESTIONS

1. What were the most important common characteristics of these different groups of people?
2. What were the most important differences among these various groups?
3. What characteristics of Native American peoples or societies seemed to have been interesting or important to Sahagún?
4. What characteristics of Native American peoples or societies seem to be most interesting or important to you?

A Spanish Friar Describes the Funeral of an Aztec Warrior (c. 1575)

DIEGO DURÁN, *The History of the Indies of New Spain*

Diego Durán was born in Seville about 1537 but was brought to New Spain while still a very young child. He entered the Dominican Order in Mexico in 1556 and was ordained a deacon in 1561. Although he worked among Mixtec peoples of the Oaxaca region for a few years, he performed most of his missionary work around Mexico City among Nahuatl-speaking people. He is said to have learned the Aztec language, Nahuatl, as a child in Texcoco. He began to write *The History of the Indies of New Spain* in 1574 and completed it in 1581, only seven years before his death. Because of his very early and intense immersion into Aztec culture, Fray Durán's record of native lives and history provides unusually accurate insights. He devoted almost his entire life to chronicling ancient Mexican history—the record of which had been largely destroyed by the Spaniards who burned all Aztec codices (books) they found.

In the following excerpt, Durán describes an Aztec funeral rite for warriors killed in battle. Aztecs revered their brave warriors and believed that this world was only the first of many that the gods had created for them. This belief is clearly reflected in the following poetic songs and narrative.

The funeral rites began the following way: the Cuauhuehuetl, who were like field marshals, went to the homes of the deceased and spoke to the widows:

"O my daughter, let not sadness overwhelm you
Or end the days of your life. We have brought you the tears and sighs
Of those who were your father, mother, and strength.
We have brought them to your door. Take courage, show your love
For our sons who did not die plowing or digging in the fields,
Who did not die on the road, trading, but for the honor of our country.
They have departed, holding each other's hands, and with them went
The great lord Huitznahuatl, a close relative of our king and monarch.
All of them are now rejoicing in the shining places of the sun,
Where they walk about in his company, clothed in his light.
They will be remembered forever! Therefore, O illustrious Aztec matrons,
Weep for their memory!"

Those whose profession it was to sing for men who had died in battle came into the square. On their heads were tied black leather bands. They brought out an instrument and began to play a sad and tearful music. The lamentations began with hymns for the dead. When all of this had started the widows of the dead men appeared, carrying the cloaks of their husbands on their shoulders and their loincloths around their necks. The hair of the widows was loose and all of them, standing in a line, clapped their hands to the beating of the drum. They wept bitterly and at times they danced bowing their heads toward the earth; at other times they danced leaning backwards. The children of the dead men were present also, wearing their fathers' mantles, carrying on their backs small boxes containing the lip, ear, and nose-plugs, and other jewelry. They clapped their hands like their mothers, and the other relatives wept with them. The men stood there, dumb, holding the swords and shields of the deceased in their hands, occasionally joining the women in their lamentations. . . .

Four days after the ceremony had taken place, images of the dead were made from slivers of firewood, each one with feet, arms and head. Faces were placed upon them—eyes and mouth—and paper loincloths and mantles also. On their shoulders were put wings of hawk feathers, as it was believed that in this way they would fly before the Sun every day. The heads of these bundles were feathered and pendants for the ears, nose and lips were placed upon them. These statues were taken to a room called *tlacochcalco.* The widows then entered and each one placed in front of her statue a dish of a stew called *tlacatlacualli,* which means "food of human flesh," together with some maize cakes called *papalotlaxcalli,* which means "butterfly bread," and a little flour made of toasted maize dissolved in water as a drink. After this food had been offered the drum began to sound again and the singers began their hymns which told of mourning and of tears. The chanters came dressed in filthy stained cloaks and with dirty leather bands tied to their heads. They called this chant *tzocuicatl,* "song of dirt." Their heads were smeared with the ground bark of a tree which is used to kill lice. Each carried a gourd vessel of the white native wine and they placed it in front of each statue. These vessels were *teotecomatl,* the divine gourds. In front of the statues were also placed flowers and tobacco and thick straws for drinking. This type of straw is called "sun drinker." The chanters of the dead then took the gourds of wine in their hands and raised them twice, thrice, in front of the statues. After this they poured the wine in the four directions around the statue.

At dusk the widows offered the singers cheap mantles, loincloths and digging sticks. The elders then gathered the bundles and set them on fire. All the firewood and paper wrapped around it went up in flames, and the widows stood about the fire, weeping with great sorrow.

The old men then addressed the widows.

"O sisters, daughters, be strong, widen your
    hearts!
We have abandoned our sons, the jaguars,
    the eagles!
Do not think that we will see them again.
    Do not imagine that this is
Like the times when your husband left your
    house sulking and angry

So that he would not return for three or four
    days;
Nor when he departed for his work, soon to
    return.
Understand that they have gone forever!
This is what you must do now: you must be
    occupied in your
Womanly occupations of spinning and
    weaving, of sweeping and watering,
Of lighting the fire and remaining in the
    house,
And have recourse to the Lord of All
    Created Things, or Day and Night,
Of Fire and Water."

On hearing this, the women burst forth into tears; it was frightening and made one pity them. From this day on they went into mourning, not washing their clothes or face or head until eighty days had gone by. The dirt that lay on their cheeks was so thick that the elders sent special ministers after the eighty days to scratch the filth from their faces. They would wrap it in paper and take it to the priests, who then ordered that it be cast into a place called *Yaualiuhcan,* which means "round place." Those who went to throw the tears and sadness in this place, which was outside of the city, were given gifts of clothing by the widows. The latter went to the temple, when these rites had been completed, and prayed, offering paper, incense and sacrifice. Their weeping and mourning was over now and they returned to their homes happy and consoled as if nothing had happened. Thus they became free of weeping and sadness.

REVIEW QUESTIONS

1. How would you characterize this funeral ceremony? What seems to be the importance of each stage of the funeral?
2. How did this elaborate ceremonial sequence meet the needs of a warlike culture? Why might so many different people (Cuauhuehueti, the singers, widows, children) have been involved?
3. Were the mourners crying for the death of the warrior, or were they weeping because they were not able to follow him into the next world? Explain your reasoning.

An English Privateer Recounts His Experiences on the Orinoco River (1595)

SIR WALTER RALEIGH, *The Discovery of the Large, Rich, and Beautiful Empire of Guiana*

By the time English explorers and privateers entered the contest for control of the Americas, the majority of the two continents had officially been claimed by the Spanish and Portuguese governments. Consequently, Sir Walter Raleigh's voyage on the Amazon and Orinoco Rivers in the mid-1590s presented a physical and political assault against the Iberian kingdoms. In the same manner as Sir Francis Drake, who "explored" the Spanish colonies of Cartagena and Santo Domingo in 1586, Raleigh was under contract with the English government and was therefore qualified as a privateer, a sea captain licensed by one nation to attack and confiscate the goods of its enemy nations. In 1603, English officials found Raleigh guilty of being involved in a plot against King James I, and they jailed him until 1617. He gained his freedom by promising James that he would again travel to the Orinoco River to find a gold mine he knew must be in the region.

The following account is from Raleigh's writings of his experiences on the Orinoco River in 1595. He hoped that the promises of gold and stories of adventures would entice other English explorers and adventurers to come to the region. In addition, he realized that he needed to attract the attention of the English aristocracy. England was gaining in naval and economic power, and Raleigh's assertiveness foreshadowed the eventual English acquisition of many Caribbean Islands and the territory of Guiana. The text retains the Old English style, which you will want to read phonetically and with a bit of imagination as to what some of the words may mean. It provides an insight into the changes of the last four hundred years to the language we currently use.

At the last we determined to hang the Pilot, and if we had well knowen the way backe againe by night, he had surely gone, but our owne necessities pleaded sufficiently for his safetie: for it was as darke as pitch, and the river began so to narrow it selfe, and the trees to hang ouer from side to side, as we were driuen with arming swordes to cut a passage thorow those branches that couered the water. We were very desirous to finde this towne hoping of a feast, bicause we made but a short breakfast aboord the *Galley* in the morning, and it was now eight a clock at night, and our stomacks began to gnaw apace: but whether it was best to returne or go on, we began to doubt, suspecting treason in the Pilot more and more: but the poore olde Indian euer assured vs that it was but a little farther, and but this one turning, and that turning, and at last about one a clocke after midnight we saw a light, and rowing towards it, we heard the dogs of the village. When wee landed we found few people, for the Lord of that place was gone with diuers *Canoas* aboue 400 miles of, vpon a iourney towards the head of *Orenoque* to trade for gold, and to buy women of the *Canibals,* who afterward vnfortunatly passed by vs as we rode at an ancor in the port of *Morequito* in the dark of night, and yet came so neer vs, as his *Canoas* grated against our barges: he left one of his companie at the port of *Morequito,* by whom we vnderstood that he had brought thirty yoong woomen, diuers plates of gold, and had great store of fine peeces of cotton cloth, and cotton beds. In his house we had good store of bread, fish, hens, and Indian drinke, and so rested that night, and in the morning after we had traded with such of his people as came down, we returned towards our *Galley,* and brought with vs some quantity of bread, fish, and hens.

On both sides of this riuer, we passed the most beautifull countrie that euer mine eies beheld: and whereas all that we had seen before was nothing but woods, prickles, bushes, and thornes, heere we beheld plaines of twenty miles in length, the grasse short and greene, and in diuers parts groues of trees by themselues, as if they had been by all the art and labour in the world so made of purpose: and stil as we rowed, the Deere came downe feeding by the waters side, as if they had beene vsed to a keepers call. Vpon this riuer there were great store of fowle, and of many sorts: we saw it in diuers sorts of strange fishes, and of maruellous bignes, but for *Lagartos* it exceeded, for there were thousands of those vglie serpents[1], and the people call it for the abundance of them the riuer of *Lagartos,* in their language. I had a *Negro* a very proper yoong fellow, that leaping out of the *Galley* to swim in the mouth of this riuer, was in all our sights taken and deuoured with one of those *Lagartos.* In the mean while our companies in the *Galley* thought we had beene all lost, (for we promised to returne before night) and sent the *Lions Whelps* ships bote with Captaine *Whiddon* to follow vs vp the riuer, but the next day after we had rowed vp and downe some fower score miles, we returned,

and went on our way, vp the great riuer, and when we were euen at the last cast for want of victuals, Captaine *Gifford* being before the *Galley,* and the rest of the botes, seeking out some place to land vpon the banks to make fire, espied fower *Canoas* comming downe the riuer, and with no small ioy caused his men to trie the vttermost of their strengths, and after a while two of the 4 gaue ouer, and ran themselues ashore, euery man betaking himselfe to the fastnes of the woods, the two other lesser got away, while he landed to lay hold on these, and so turned into some by-creeke, we knew not whither: those *Canoas* that were taken were loden with bread, and were bound for *Marguerita* in the west Indies, which those Indians (called *Arwacas*) purposed to carrie thither for exchange: But in the lesser, there were three Spaniards, who hauing heard of the defeat of their gouernour in *Trinedado,* and that we purposed to enter *Guiana,* came away in those *Canoas:* one of them was a *Cauallero,* as the Captaine of the *Arwacas* after told vs, another a soldier, and the third a refiner.

In the meane time, nothing on the earth could haue been more welcome to vs next vnto gold, then the great store of very excellent bread which we found in these *Canoas,* for now our men cried, let vs go on, we care not how farre. After that Captaine *Gifford* had brought the two *Canoas* to the *Galley,* I tooke my barge, and went to the banks side with a dozen shot, where the *Canoas* first ran themselues ashore, and landed there, sending out Captaine *Gifford* and Captaine *Thyn* on one hand, and Captaine *Calfield* on the other, to follow those that were fled into the woods, and as I was creeping thorow the bushes, I saw an Indian basket hidden, which was the refiners basket, for I found in it, his quicksiluer, saltpeter, and diuers things for the triall of mettals, and also the dust of such ore as he had refined, but in those *Canoas* which escaped there was a good quantity of ore and gold. I then landed more men, and offered 500 pound to what soldier soeuer could take one of those 3 Spaniards that we thought were landed. But our labours were in vaine in that behalfe, for they put themselues into one of the small *Canoas:*

---

[1] The Alligator *(Crocodilus sclerops)* and Cayman *(Crocodilus acutus,* Cuv.) are very numerous in the Orinoco. The former seldom reaches a greater length than six or eight feet, and does not prove dangerous to man. It is however otherwise with the latter, which is said to reach sometimes twenty-five feet in length. We have seen the skeleton of a Cayman which we found lying on the banks of the Rio Negro, twenty feet long. The largest animal of that description which we measured in the river Berbice was sixteen feet. The number of Indians along the banks of the Rio Orinoco, the Rio Negro, and other rivers in Guiana, who fall annually a prey to these monsters is very considerable.

and so while the greater *Canoas* were in taking, they escaped: but seeking after the Spaniards, we found the *Arwacas* hidden in the woods which were pilots for the Spaniards, and rowed their *Canoas:* of which I kept the chiefest for a Pilot, and carried him with me to *Guiana,* by whom I vnderstood, where and in what countries the Spaniards had labored for gold, though I made not the same knowen to all: for when the springs began to breake, and the riuers to raise themselues so suddenly as by no meanes we could abide the digging of anie mine, especially for that the richest are defended with rocks of hard stone, which we call the *White spar,* and that it required both time, men, and instruments fit for such a worke, I thought it best not to houer thereabouts, least if the same had been perceiued by the company, there would haue bin by this time many barks and ships set out, and perchance other nations would also haue gotten of ours for Pilots, so as both our selues might haue been preuented, and all our care taken for good vsage of the people been vtterly lost, by those that onely respect present profit, and such violence or insolence offered, as the nations which are borderers would haue changed their desire of our loue and defence, into hatred and violence. And for any longer stay to haue brought a more quantity (which I heare hath bin often obiected) whosoeuer had seene or prooued the fury of that riuer after it began to arise, and had been a moneth and od daies as we were from hearing ought from our ships, leauing them meanly mand, aboue 400 miles off, would perchance haue turned somewhat sooner than we did, if all the mountaines had been gold, or rich stones: And to say the truth all the branches and small riuers which fell into *Orenoque* were raised with such speed, as if wee waded them ouer the shooes in the morning outward, we were couered to the shoulders homewarde the very same daie: and to stay to dig out gold with our nailes, had been *Opus laboris,* but not *Ingenij:* such a quantitie as would haue serued our turnes we could not haue had, but a discouery of the mines to our infinite disaduantage we had made, and that could haue been the best profit of farther search or stay; for those mines are not easily broken, nor opened

in haste, and I could haue returned a good quantity of gold readie cast, if I had not shot at another marke, than present profit.

This *Arwacan* Pilot with the rest, feared that we would haue eaten them, or otherwise haue put them to some cruell death, for the Spaniards to the end that none of the people in the passage towards *Guiana* or in *Guiana* it selfe might come to speech with vs, perswaded all the nations, that we were men eaters, and *Canibals:* but when the poore men and women had seen vs, and that we gaue them meate, and to euerie one some thing or other, which was rare and strange to them, they began to conceiue the deceit and purpose of the *Spaniards,* who indeed (as they confessed) tooke from them both their wiues, and daughters daily, and vsed them for the satisfying of their owne lusts, especially such as they tooke in this maner by strength. But I protest before the maiestie of the liuing God, that I neither know nor beleeue, that any of our companie one or other, by violence or otherwise, euer knew any of their women, and yet we saw many hundreds, and had many in our power, and of those very yoong, and excellently fauored which came among vs without deceit, starke naked.

Nothing got vs more loue among them then this vsage, for I suffred not anie man to take from anie of the nations so much as a *Pina,* or a *Potato* roote, without giuing them contentment, nor any man so much as to offer to touch any of their wiues or daughters: which course, so contrarie to the Spaniards (who tyrannize ouer them in all things) drew them to admire hir Maiestie, whose commandement I told them it was, and also woonderfully to honour our nation. But I confesse it was a very impatient worke to keepe the meaner sort from spoile and stealing, when we came to their houses, which bicause in all I could not preuent, I caused my Indian interpreter at euery place when we departed, to know of the losse or wrong done, and if ought were stolen or taken by violence, either the same was restored, and the party punished in their sight, or els it was paid for to their vttermost demand. They also much woondred at vs, after they heard that we had slain the Spaniards at *Trinedado,* for they were before resolued, that no nation of *Christians* durst abide their presence, and they woondred more when I had made them know of the great ouerthrow that hir Maiesties army and fleete had giuen them of late yeers in their owne countries.

REVIEW QUESTIONS

1. What were Raleigh's priorities upon his arrival at the river? How did those priorities influence his communication with native people?
2. What was the reaction of the native people to him and his crew?
3. How well did he fare in his search for gold and wealth? What would have made him think that he could possibly find gold if he returned later (in 1617)?
4. How did Raleigh's competition with Spain influence his narrative?

An English Traveler Discusses Life Among Escaped African Slaves on the Caribbean Coast (1648)

THOMAS GAGE, *Travels in the New World*

Thomas Gage was born in England in 1603—the year Queen Elizabeth I died and the Stuart king of Scotland, James VI, ascended the English throne as James I. Gage died in Jamaica in 1656, just one year after England officially acquired the island from Spain. The younger brother of an ancient but minor aristocratic family, Gage entered the priesthood and served as a Dominican friar for sixteen years before he renounced the Catholic faith, became a Protestant, and advocated Puritan ideals. His *Travels in the New World* (1648) exposed Christian and government excesses in the Americas and gave many examples of the competition between European powers as they tried to govern their colonies.

The original editor of this excerpt described Gage as cantankerous and something of a scoundrel. He most certainly was an independent thinker. Beginning in 1625, he kept an eye-witness record of daily events in the colonies he visited, from the Philippines to central Mexico, Honduras, and Guatemala. This excerpt discusses the level of Spanish control on the Caribbean coasts of Honduras and Guatemala. For the Spanish government and settlers, Honduras and Guatemala had little to offer; some gold had been discovered early, but that was quickly gone. Several Maya groups constituted the majority of the natives in the area; reluctant to work on Spanish haciendas, they preferred to move into the hill country of the middle of the region or into the eastern lowlands. The Blackamoors, or *cimarrones,* in this account are the escaped African slaves who fled their owners to establish communities of their own. Many of those "maroon" towns throughout the Americas evolved into native towns and trade centers that still exist today.

I have often heard the Spaniards jeer and laugh at the English and Hollanders, for that having come into this gulf, they have gone away without attempting anything further upon the land. Nay, while I lived there, the Hollanders set upon Trujillo, the head port of Comayagua and Honduras, and took it (though there were some resistance), the people for the most part flying to the woods, trusting more to their feet than to their hands and weapons (such cowards is all that country full of). The Hollanders might have fortified themselves there and gone into the country, or fortifying that, have come on to the gulf, which all Guatemala much feared, not being able to resist them. Instead they left Trujillo contenting themselves with a small pillage, and gave occasion to the Spaniards to rejoice and to make processions of thanksgiving for their safe deliverance out of their enemies' hands.

The way from this gulf to Guatemala is not so bad as some report and conceive, especially after Michaelmas until May, when the winter and rain is past and gone, and the winds begin to dry up the ways. For in the worst of the year mules laden with four hundred-weight at least go easily through the steepest, deepest, and most dangerous passages of the mountains that lie about this gulf. And though the ways are at that time of the year bad, yet they are so beaten with the mules, and so wide and open, that one bad step and passage may be avoided for a better; and the worst of this way continues but fifteen leagues, there being *ranchos,* or lodges, in the way, cattle and mules also among the woods and mountains, for relief and comfort to a weary traveller.

What the Spaniards most fear until they come out of these mountains are some two or three hundred Blackamoors, *cimarrones,* who for too much hard usage have fled away from Guatemala and other parts from their masters unto these woods, and there live and bring up their children and increase daily, so that all the power of Guatemala, nay, all the country about (having often attempted it), is not able to bring them

under subjection. These often come out to the roadway, and set upon the *recuas* of mules, and take of wine, iron, clothing, and weapons from them as much as they need, without doing any harm unto the people, or slaves that go with the mules. Rather, these rejoice with them, being of one color, and subject to slavery and misery which the others have shaken off. By their example and encouragement many of these also shake off their misery, and join with them to enjoy liberty, though it be but in the woods and mountains. Their weapons are bows and arrows which they use and carry about them, only to defend themselves if the Spaniards set upon them; else they use them not against the Spaniards, who travel quietly and give them part of what provision they carry. These have often said that the chief cause of their flying to those mountains is to be in a readiness to join with the English or Hollanders, if ever they land in that gulf, for they know, from them they may enjoy that liberty which the Spaniards will never grant unto them.

After the first fifteen leagues the way is better, and there are little towns and villages of Indians, who relieve with provision both man and beast. Fifteen leagues further is a great town of Indians, called Acazabastlán, standing upon a river [Motagua], which for fish is held the best of all that country. Though here are many sorts, yet above all there is one which they call *bobo,* a thick round fish as long or longer than a man's arm, with only a middle bone, as white as milk, as fat as butter, and good to boil, fry, stew, or bake. There is also from hence most of the way to Guatemala in brooks and shallow rivers, one of the best sort of fishes in the world, which the Spaniards judge to be a kind of trout, it is called the *tepemechin,* the fat whereof resembles veal more than fish.

This town of Acazabastlán is governed by a Spaniard who is called *corregidor;* his power extendeth no farther than to the gulf, and to those towns in the way. This governor hath often attempted to bring in those *cimarrones* from the mountains, but could never prevail against them. All the strength of this place may be some twenty muskets (for so many Spanish houses there may be in the town) and some few Indians that use bows and arrows, for the defence of the town against the Blackamoor *cimarrones*.

About Acazabastlán there are many *estancias* of cattle and mules, much cacao, achiote, and drugs for chocolate. There is also apothecary drugs, as *zarzaparilla,* and *cañafistula*, and in the town as much variety of fruits and gardens as in any one Indian town in the country; but above all Acazabastlán is far known, and much esteemed of in the city of Guatemala, for excellent muskmelons, some small, some bigger than a man's head, wherewith the Indians load their mules to sell all over the country.

From hence to Guatemala there are but thirty short leagues, and though some hills there be, ascents and descents, yet nothing troublesome to man or beast. Among these mountains there have been discovered some mines of metal, which the Spaniards have begun to dig, and finding that there have been some of copper, and some of iron, they have let them alone, judging them more chargeable than profitable. But greater profit have the Spaniards lost, than of iron and copper, for using the poor Indians too hardly, and that in this way, from Acazabastlán to Guatemala, especially about a place called El Agua Caliente, where is a river, out of which in some places formerly the Indians found such store of gold that they were charged by the Spaniards with a yearly tribute of gold. But the Spaniards, being like Valdivia in Chile, too

greedy after it, murdered the Indians for not discovering unto them where about this treasure lay, and so have lost both treasure and Indians also. Yet unto this day search is made about the mountains, the river, and the sands for the hidden treasure, which peradventure by God's order and appointment doth and shall lie hid, and kept for a people better knowing and honoring their God.

At this place called El Agua Caliente, or The Hot Water, liveth a Blackamoor in an *estancia* of his own, who is held to be very rich, and gives good entertainment to the travellers that pass that way. He is rich in cattle, sheep, and goats, and from his farm stores Guatemala and the people thereabout with the best cheese of all that country. But his riches are thought not so much to increase from his farm and cheeses, but from his hidden treasure, which credibly is reported to be known unto him. He hath been questioned about it in the Chancery of Guatemala but hath denied often any such treasure to be known unto him. The jealousy and suspicion of him is, for that formerly having been a slave, he bought his freedom with great sums of money, and since he hath been free, hath bought that farm and much land lying to it, and hath exceedingly increased his stock. To this he answereth, that when he was young and a slave, he had a good master, who let him get for himself what he could, and that he, playing the good husbandman, gathered as much as would buy his liberty, and at first a little house to live in, to the which God hath since given a blessing with a greater increase of stock.

REVIEW QUESTIONS

1. What was Gage's opinion of the Spanish in Guatemala? Did he respect and admire the Spanish administrators? Why or why not?
2. What was the attraction that brought the Spanish, English, and Dutch to the Caribbean? Did Gage believe that any but the English could attain their objectives?
3. How did Gage's discoveries in Guatemala compare with those of another Englishman, Walter Raleigh, in Guiana less than half a century earlier?

A German Mercenary Remembers His Captivity Among Brazilian Cannibals (mid-1500s)

HANS STADEN, *The True History of His Captivity*

Another European to make an early-sixteenth-century voyage to the New World, Hans Staden was born in the German principality of Hesse. In 1547 he sailed from Holland to Lisbon, where he found employment on a ship carrying Portuguese convicts to the colony in Brazil. He reached Pernambuco in January 1548. There, he found himself in a small colony in the middle of a war with the natives who were attempting to drive the Europeans into the Atlantic Ocean. He returned to Portugal in October 1548, but he sailed west with a fleet of three ships again in 1549. This expedition encountered bad storms in the western Atlantic, whereupon two ships landed on the coast of Guinea and the third was lost. While gathering provisions to make an attempt to travel down the coast of the Rio de la Plata, Staden and three companions were captured by the Tupinambá. They assumed he was a Portuguese, one of their mortal enemies, and took him to their settlement of Ubatuba where they intended to kill and eat him.

Staden's only hope was to convince the natives that he was French, one of their allies, and not a Portuguese. His period of captivity lasted two years, during which he learned much of the Tupi lifestyle, and ultimately convinced them that he was not only French, but that he had powerful spiritual abilities to heal. He attempted to escape when a French ship came to Ubatuba to trade, but the French refused to aid him or take him with them. Ultimately he gained his freedom when another French ship stopped; in 1555 he returned to Germany by way of London and Antwerp. Staden's account of his captivity provided exciting reading for his contemporaries in Germany when it was published in 1578. The following excerpt describes his capture and first experiences with the Tupinambá.

HOW I WAS CAPTURED BY THE SAVAGES, AND THE WAY IN WHICH THIS HAPPENED

I had a savage man, of a tribe called Carios; he was my slave, who caught game for me, and with him I also went occasionally into the forest.

Now it happened once upon a time, that a Spaniard from the island of Sancte Vincente came to me in the island of Sancte Maro, which is five miles (leagues) therefrom, and remained in the fort wherein I lived, and also a German by name Heliodorus, from Hesse, son of the late Eoban of Hesse, the same who was in the island

of Sanct Vincente at an ingenio, where sugar is made, and the ingenio belonged to a Genoese named Josepe Ornio. This Heliodorus was the clerk and manager of the merchants to whom the ingenio belonged. (Ingenio, are called houses in which sugar is made). With the said Heliodorus I had before had some acquaintance, for when I was shipwrecked with the Spaniards in that country, I found him in the island of Sancte Vincente, and he showed me friendship. He came again to me, wanting to see how I got on, for he had perhaps heard that I was sick.

Having sent my slave the day before into the wood to catch game, I purposed going the next day to fetch it, so that we might have something to eat. For in that country one has little else beyond what comes from the forests.

Now as I with this purpose walked through the woods, there arose on both sides of the path loud yells such as the savages are accustomed to make, and they came running towards me; I knew them, and found that they had all surrounded me, and levelling their bows with arrows, they shot in upon me. Then I cried, "Now God help my soul;" I had scarcely finished saying these words when they struck me to the ground and shot (arrows) and stabbed at me. So far they had not (thank God!) wounded me further than in one leg, and torn my clothes off my body; one the jerkin, the other the hat, the third the shirt and so forth. Then they began to quarrel about me, one said he was the first who came up to me, the other said that he had captured me. Meanwhile the others struck me with their bows. But at last two of them raised me from the ground where I lay naked, one took me by one arm, another by the other, and some went behind me, and others before. They ran in this manner quickly with me through the wood towards the sea, where they had their canoes. When they had taken me to the shore, I sighted their canoes which they had drawn up from the sea on to the land under a hedge, at the distance of a stone's-throw or two, and also a great number more of them who had remained with the canoes. When they, ornamented with feathers according to their custom, saw me being led along they ran towards me, and pretended to bite into their arms, and threatened as though they would eat me. And a king paraded before me with a club wherewith they despatched the prisoners. He harangued and said how they had captured me their slave from the Perot (so they call the Portuguese), and they would now thoroughly revenge on me the death of their friends. And when they brought me to the canoes, several of them struck me with their fists. Then they made haste among one another, to shove their canoes back into the water, for they feared that an alarm would be made at Brikioka, as also happened.

Now before they launched the canoes, they tied my hands together, and not being all from the same dwelling-place, those of each village were loath to go home empty-handed, and disputed with those who held me. Some said that they been just as near me as the others, and that they would also have their share of me, and they wanted to kill me at once on that very spot.

Then I stood and prayed, looking round for the blow. But at last the king, who desired to keep me, began and said they would take me living homewards, so that their wives might also see me alive, and make their feast upon me. For they purposed killing me "Kawewi Pepicke," that is, they would brew drinks and assemble together, to make a feast, and then they would eat me among them. At those words they left off disputing, and tied four ropes round my neck, and I had to get into a canoe, whilst they still stood on the shore, and bound the ends of the ropes to the boats and pushed them off into the sea, in order to sail home again. . . .

HOW MY TWO MASTERS CAME TO ME AND TOLD ME THAT THEY HAD PRESENTED ME TO ONE OF THEIR FRIENDS, WHO WAS TO KEEP ME AND KILL ME, WHEN I WAS TO BE EATEN

I knew not then their customs so well as I have since learned them, and I thought "Now they prepare to kill thee." After a little while those who had captured me, named Jeppipo (Yeppipo) Wasu, and his brother Alkindar Miri, came to me and told me how they had, from friendship, presented me to their father's brother Ipperu Wasu, who was to keep me, and also to kill me, when I was to be eaten, and thus to gain a new name with me.

For this same Ipperu Wasu had a year before also captured a slave, and had as a sign of friendship presented him to Alkindar Miri. Him he had killed and thereby he had gained a name; so that Alkindar Miri had in return promised to present Ipperu Wasu with the first whom he might capture. And I was the first.

Further the two above-mentioned who had taken me said, "Now will the women lead thee out to the Aprasse:" this word I understood not then, but it means dancing. Thus they dragged me along with the ropes, which were round my neck, from out of the huts on to an open place. Then came all the women who were in the seven huts, and seized hold of me, and the men went away. Several of the women led me along by the arms, and several by the ropes which were bound round my neck, so roughly and tightly that I could hardly breathe. In this manner they went along with me, and I knew not what they intended doing to me, upon which I remembered the sufferings of our Lord Jesus Christ, and how he suffered innocently at the hands of the vile Jews, whereby I consoled myself and became more resigned. Then they brought me before the huts of the king, who was called Vratinge Wasu, which means in German, the Great White Bird. Before his huts lay a heap of freshly dug earth, whither they led me and sat me down thereon, and some held me, when I thought nothing else but that they would dispatch me at once. I looked round for the Iwara Pemme, wherewith they club men, and asked whether they were going to kill me then, when they answered, "not yet." Upon which a woman came from out of the crowd towards me, holding a fragment of a crystal, set in a thing like a bent ring, and with this same piece of crystal shaved off my eyebrows, and would also have cut the beard from my chin, but this I would not suffer, and said, that they should kill me with my beard. Then they replied, that for the present they would not kill me, and left me my beard. But after some days they cut it off with a pair of scissors, which the Frenchmen had given them. . . .

HOW THEY TOOK ME TO THEIR CHIEF KING CALLED KONYAN BEBE, AND HOW THEY TREATED ME THERE

Several days afterwards they took me to another village, which they call Arirab, to a king named Konyan Bebe, the principal king over all of them. Many others had assembled at his place and made great rejoicings in their manner; they also wanted to see me, for he had ordered that I also should be brought there that day.

Now when I came close upon the huts, I heard a great noise of singing and blowing of horns, and in front of the huts were fixed some fifteen heads on stakes. These belonged to a tribe who are also their enemies, and are called the Markayas, whom they had eaten. As they led me past them, they told me that the heads were from the Markayas, who were also their enemies. Then terror possessed me; I thought, thus they will also do with me. Now as we were entering the huts, one of those who had me in their keeping, went before me and spoke with loud words, so that all the others heard it, "Here I bring the slave, the Portuguese." And he appeared to think it was something worth seeing, when a man had his enemy in his power. He said also many other things as is their custom, and then he led me to where the king sat and drank together with the others, and had made themselves drunk with the beverage which they make, called kawawy. He looked savagely at me, and said, "O our enemy! art thou come?" I said: "I am come, but I am not your enemy." Then they gave me also to drink. Now I had heard much of the king Konyan Bebe, how great a man he was, also a great cannibal at eating human flesh. And there was one among them who seemed to be he, and I went up to him and spake to him in the manner of their language, and said: "Art thou Konyan Bebe? livest thou still?" "Yes," said he, "I still live." "Well then," said I, "I have heard much of thee, and that thou art so fine a man." Then he arose, and strutted before me with proud conceit, and he had a large round green stone, sticking through the lips of his mouth (as their custom is). They also make white rosaries from a kind of sea-shell; such are their ornaments: of these the king had also some six fathoms length hanging round his neck. It was by his ornaments I perceived that he must be one of the noblest.

Thereupon he again sat down, and began to question me about what his enemies the Tuppin

Ikins and the Portuguese were doing. And he asked further, why I had wanted to fire at them in the district of Brikioka, for he had been informed, that I had served there against them as a gunner. Then I said that the Portuguese had stationed me there and that I was obliged so to do. Upon which he said that I also was a Portuguese, and he spoke of the Frenchman who had seen me as his son, and said, that he who had seen me had stated, that I could not speak with him, and that I was a genuine Portuguese. Then I said, "Yes it is true, I have been so long out of my country that I have forgotten my language." Thereupon he observed, that he had already helped to capture and eat five Portuguese, who had all said that they were Frenchmen, and yet had lied. So that I gave up all hopes of life and resigned myself to God's will; for I heard nothing else from all of them, but that I should die. Then he again began to ask what the Portuguese said of him, they must surely be in terrible fear of him. I said: "Yes," they know much to tell of thee, how thou art wont to wage great war against them, but now they have fortified Brikioka more strongly. "Yes," he said, and therefore he would catch them now and then in the wood as they had caught me.

I further said to him: "Yes, thy real enemies, the Tuppin Ikins, are equipping twenty-five canoes, and will soon appear and invade thy country;" as also happened.

The while he so questioned, the others stood and listened. In short he asked me much and told me much; boasting to me how he had already killed many a Portuguese, and savages besides who had been his enemies. During the time he was thus talking to me, the liquor in the huts was drunk up. Then they moved off to another hut to drink therein also, so that he ceased speaking.

After this those in the other hut began to carry on their jokes and to deride me. The said king's son having tied my legs together in three places, I was made to hop with joined feet through the huts; at this they laughed and said, "there comes our meat hopping along." Upon this I asked my master (Ipperu Wasu) who had taken me there, whether he had led me thither to be killed. He said no, it was the custom, that foreign slaves were treated in this manner, and they again untied the ropes round my legs, thereupon they walked round about me and grabbed at my flesh, one said the skin of the head belonged to him and another that he claimed the fleshy part of the leg. Then I had to sing to them, and I sang spiritual songs. These I was asked to translate to them in their language, and I said, "I have sung of my God." They said my God was filth, that is in their language, "Teuire." These words hurt me much and I thought, "O merciful God, how long-suffering Thou art!" Now on the next day when all in the village had seen me and had heaped every insult upon me, the king Konyan Bebe told those who had charge of me, that they were to watch me carefully.

Thereupon, when they again led me from out of the huts, and were going to take me to Uwattibi, where they intended killing me, they called mockingly after me that they would not fail to appear at my master's hut, to drink over me and to eat me. But my master always comforted me, saying that I was not to be killed for the present.

HOW THE TWENTY-FIVE CANOES OF THE TUPPIN IKINS, WHEREOF I HAD TOLD THE KING, ARRIVED, INTENDING TO ATTACK THE HUTS WHEREIN I WAS

Meanwhile it so happened, that the twenty-five canoes belonging to the savage tribe of whom the Portuguese are allies, and who as I also stated previous to my being captured, were desirous of proceeding thither to make war; it so happened (I say) that one morning they fell upon the village.

Now when the Tuppin Ikins were about to attack the huts, and together began shooting in upon them, those in the huts became distressed, and the women prepared for flight.

Then I said to them, "You take me for a Portuguese, your enemy; now give me a bow and arrows and let me go loose, and I will help you to defend the huts." They handed me a bow and arrows; I shouted and shot and acted as like them as I possibly could, and encouraged them to be of good heart and valorous, and that no harm would come to them. And my intention was to push through the stockade which surrounds the huts, and to run towards the others, for they knew me well, and also were aware that I was in the village. But they watched me too well. Now when the Tuppin Ikins saw that they could not succeed, they again repaired to their canoes and sailed away. When they had departed, I was imprisoned again.

REVIEW QUESTIONS

1. What evidence does this account give of the division of labor and individual responsibility by gender among Tupinambás?
2. How would you characterize the lifestyle of these native people? Did Staden find it hard to adopt their customs? Why or why not?
3. What was the significance of cannibalism within Tupinambá culture? What role did it play in their religion?
4. Do you believe that you would have reacted in the same manner as did Staden if you had been in his position? What other options might you have had?

A Spanish Jesuit Describes Life Along the Amazon (1639)

CRISTOVAL DE ACUÑA, *A New Discovery of the Great River of the Amazons*

The Society of Jesus (Jesuits) played a crucial role in the encounter between Europeans and Native Americans. Confirmed by Pope Paul III in 1540, the organization became a key instrument in the Church's Counter-Reformation, and individual Jesuit priests participated in the Inquisition in the Americas. Jesuits were obliged to minister to the Native Americans and to educate them in the Catholic religion, as well as to eradicate and prevent Protestant influences. In 1639, a Jesuit priest from Spain, Cristoval de Acuña, made his "New Discovery of the Great River of the Amazons." De Acuña held the title of "Censor of the Supreme General Inquisition," and an important goal of his mission was to search out idolatry and heresy.

De Acuña traveled from his assigned post in the Spanish province of Quito in Peru to the Amazon River. Natives described by de Acuña were the Tupinambá (Tupi), a wide-ranging and resourceful people. This term designated several different ethnic groups who lived in the forested areas of the Amazon River drainage system and spoke related languages. The land of the Amazon River drainage and the Tupi natives of this account belonged to Portugal, not Spain. Consequently, de Acuña was in enemy territory because the Spanish did not conquer Portugal until 1640.

THEIR MEANS OF COMMUNICATION ARE BY WATER, IN CANOES

All those who live on the shores of this great river are collected in large villages, and, like the Venetians and Mexicans, their means of communication are by water, in small vessels which they call canoes. These are usually of cedar wood, which the providence of God abundantly supplies, without the labour of cutting it or carrying it from the forest; sending it down with the current of the river, which, to supply their wants, tears the trees from the most distant Cordilleras of Peru, and places them at the doors of their habitations, where each Indian may choose the piece of timber which suits him best. It is worthy of remark that among such an infinity of Indians, each wanting at least one or two trees for his family, whence to make one or two canoes; it should cost no further labour than just to go out to the banks of the river, throw a lasso when the tree is floating past, and convey it to the threshold; where it remains secure until the waters have subsided; when each man, applying his industry and labour, manufactures the vessel which he requires.

THE TOOLS WHICH THEY USE

The tools which they use to make not only their canoes, but also their houses and anything else they require, are hatchets and adzes, not forged in the smithies of Biscay, but manufactured in the forges of their understanding, having, as in other things, necessity for their master.

By it they are taught to cut from the hardest part of the shell of the turtle, which covers the breast, a plate about a *palmo* long, and a little less in breadth, which, cured in smoke and sharpened with a stone, they fix into a handle. With this hatchet, though not with much rapidity, they cut what they require. Of the same material they make their adzes, to which the jaw bone of the pegebuey serves as a handle, which nature formed in a curved shape, adapted for such a purpose.

With these tools they work as perfectly, not only in the manufacture of their canoes, but also of their tables, boards, seats, and other things, as if they were the best instruments of Spain.

Amongst some of the tribes these hatchets are made of stone, which, worked by hand, are finer, and run less risk of breaking than those made of turtle shell, and cut down any tree however thick it may be. Their chisels, and gouges, for more delicate work, are made of the teeth of animals fitted into wooden handles, which do their work as well as those of fine steel. Nearly all the tribes possess cotton, some more, some less, but they do not all use it for making clothes. Most of them go about naked,—both men and women, excepting that natural modesty obliges them not to appear as if they were in a state of innocence.

OF THEIR RITES, AND OF THE GODS THEY ADORE

The rites of all these infidels are almost the same. They worship idols which they make with their own hands; attributing power over the waters to some, and, therefore, place a fish in their hands for distinction; others they choose as lords of the harvests; and others as gods of their battles. They say that these gods came down from Heaven to be their companions, and to do them good. They do not use any ceremony in worshipping them, and often leave them forgotten in a corner, until the time when they become necessary; thus when they are going to war, they carry an idol in the bows of their canoes, in which they place their hopes of victory; and when they go out fishing, they take the idol which is charged with dominion over the waters; but they do not trust in the one or the other so much as not to recognize another mightier God.

I gathered this from what happened with one of these Indians, who having heard something of the power of our God, and seen with his own eyes that our expedition went up the river, and, passing through the midst of so many warlike nations, returned without receiving any damage; judged that it was through the force and power of the God who guided us. He, therefore, came with much anxiety to beseech the captain and ourselves, that, in return for the hospitality he had shewn us, we would leave him one of our gods, who would protect him and his people in peace and safety, and assist them to procure all necessary provisions. There were not wanting those who wished to console him by leaving in his village, the standard of the cross, a thing which the Portuguese were accustomed to do among the infidels, not with so good a motive as would appear from the action itself. The sacred wood of the cross served to give colour to the greatest injustice, such as the continual slavery of the poor Indians, whom, like meek lambs, they carried in flocks to their houses, to sell some, and treat the others with cruelty. These Portuguese raise the cross, and in payment of the kind treatment of the natives when they visit their villages, they fix it in the most conspicuous place, charging the Indians always to keep it intact. By some accident, or through the lapse of time, or purposely because these infidels do not care for it, the cross falls. Presently the Portuguese pass sentence, and condemn all the inhabitants of the village to perpetual slavery, not only for their lives, but for the lives of all their descendants.

For this reason I did not consent that they should plant the holy cross; and also that it might not give the Indian, who had asked us for a god, occasion for idolatry, by attributing to the wood the power of the Deity who redeemed us.

However, I consoled him by assuring him that our God would always accompany him, that he should pray to him for what he wanted, and that some day he would be brought to a true knowledge of him. This Indian was well persuaded that the gods of his people were not the most powerful on earth, and he wished for a greater one, to obey.

AN INDIAN WOULD MAKE HIMSELF GOD

With the same understanding as the above, though with more malice, another Indian displayed his intellect. As he could not recognize any power or deity in his idols, he declared himself to be the god of that land. We had notice of this man some leagues before we reached his habitation; and, dispatching news that we brought a true and more powerful God, we asked him to wait our arrival. He did so, and our vessels had scarcely arrived at the banks, when, eager to know the new God, he came out in person to ask for him. But though it was declared to him who the true God was; because he was unable to see him with his eyes, he remained in his blindness, making himself out to be a child of the sun, whither he declared he went every night, the better to arrange for the government of the following day. Such was the malice and pride of this Indian.

Another shewed a better understanding, when asked why his companions were retiring into the forests, apprehensive of the vicinity of the Spaniards, while he alone with a few relations came out fearlessly to place himself in our power. He answered that he considered that a people who had once gone up the river through the midst of so many enemies, and returned without any hindrance, could not be less than lords of this great river, who would often return to navigate and occupy it; and as this was so, he did not want always to be attacking them under the shade of night; but to know them, and recognize them from that time as friends; while others would be forced to receive them. This was a sensible discourse, which, should God permit it, we shall some day see put into execution.

OF THEIR SORCERERS

Following the thread of our narrative, and returning to the rites of these people; it is worthy of notice that they all hold their sorcerers in very great estimation, not so much on account of the love they bear them, as for the dread in which they always live of the harm they are able to do them. These sorcerers usually have a house, where they practise their superstitious rites, and speak to the demon; and where, with a certain kind of veneration, the Indians keep all the bones of dead sorcerers, as if they were relics of saints. They suspend these bones in the same hammocks, in which the sorcerers had slept when alive.

These men are their teachers, their preachers, their councillors, and their guides. They assist them in their doubts, and the Indians resort to them in their wars, that they may receive poisonous herbs with which to take vengeance on their enemies.

Their methods of interring their dead differ among the Indian tribes. Some preserve them in their own houses, always retaining the memory of the dead in their minds. Others burn in great fires not only the body, but also all that the deceased possessed when alive. Both the one and the other celebrate the obsequies of their dead, for many days, with constant mourning, interrupted by great drinking bouts.

THESE INDIANS ARE OF MILD DISPOSITIONS

These tribes of infidels have good dispositions, with fine features, and are of a colour not so dark as those of Brazil. They have clear understandings, and rare abilities for any manual dexterity. They are meek and gentle, as was found in those who once met us, conversed with us confidently, and eat and drank with us, without ever suspecting anything. They gave us their houses to live in, while they all lived together in one or two of the largest in the village; and though they suffered much mischief from our friendly Indians, without the possibility of avoiding it, they never returned it by evil acts. All this, together with the slight inclination they display to worship their own gods, gives great hope that, if they received notice of the true Creator of heaven and earth, they would embrace His holy law with little hesitation.

REVIEW QUESTIONS

1. How did Acuña attempt to make seventeenth-century European Catholics understand what he was describing?
2. Did he pay more attention to native men or women? What was his opinion of their lives? Their beliefs?
3. Did he believe the Spanish or the Portuguese were the best guardians and guides of these natives? Why?
4. From this excerpt, what seemed to be his greatest concern about the native people he encountered?
5. What role did nature, especially the river, play in the lives of the Tupi?

A Spanish Adventurer Encounters Natives in the South Seas (1595)

The Voyages of Pedro Fernandez de Quiros

The Spanish government of Philip III wanted to expand as far as possible into the Pacific through the discovery of non-Christian lands. One of the voyages he commissioned for that purpose was captained by the noted explorer Alvaro de Mendaña de Neira. Mendaña had found a group of islands directly north of the New Hebrides and had received a royal concession to colonize them in 1595. The chief pilot for that enterprise was a young but accomplished Portuguese sailor, Pedro Fernandez de Quiros, who had married a prominent woman in Madrid and moved to Peru. It was from Peru, then, that Quiros joined Mendaña's expedition, but Quiros had some misgivings about the voyage because of the quarrelsome character of his captain. Later, in 1606, Quiros himself commanded another voyage of exploration for Spain to the South Seas.

In this account, Quiros told how his ship, the *Capitana,* was greeted by a fleet of ten small canoes from a nearby island. In an earlier paragraph (not in this excerpt), he complimented the men in these canoes as being handsome, fit, and dexterous. The encounter, however, turned unpleasant.

Five natives came in a canoe, the middle one vigorously bailing the water out of the vessel. His red hair came down to the waist. He was white as regards colour, beautifully shaped, the face aquiline and handsome, rather freckled and rosy, the eyes black and gracious, the forehead and eyebrows good, the nose, mouth, and lips well proportioned, with the teeth well ordered and white. In fine, he was sweet in his laughter and smiles, and his whole appearance was cheerful. Being rich in so many parts and graces, he would be judged to be very beautiful for a girl; but he was actually a youth of about thirteen years. This was he who at first sight stole away the hearts of all on board the ship; he was most looked at and called to, and he to whom all offered their gifts, and to whom the Captain, with great persuasion, desired to present a dress of silk, which he accepted, and put on with much grace. It was pain [plain] to the Captain that the youth could not be kept, to take as a proof of the greatness of God in those parts.

Many natives came to the launch, and, having fastened a cord to the bowsprit, they tried to drag her on to the beach. Others, diving into the water, fastened ropes to the cable and dragged for the anchor. Others took up positions to conceal their tricks. The Captain of the launch, seeing their diligence and how quickly they went to work, fired off arquebuses to frighten them. But they, ignorant of the effects, showed no fear at all, even seizing hold of naked swords with their hands, until some were hurt, when there

was a disturbance and talk among themselves, and they rowed away in their canoes at a great rate. At this time a very audacious old man came in one of their canoes to the *Capitana,* with a very long and thick lance of palm wood, well balanced; and he had on a sort of cloak or hood made of a leaf dyed crimson, and a hat they had given him from the launch. He was a tall, robust man, and very supple, and showed himself to be arrogant. Wounded in feet and legs, they trembled violently. He made fierce faces with his eyes and mouth. In a very loud voice he seemed to order us to surrender. With his lance, brandishing it menacingly, he made as many thrusts as he could. With the intention of making him quiet, two muskets were fired off. The others cried out and threw up their arms, but he made light of it. With great pride he showed more signs of his anger; and, finding he could do nothing, he quickly passed both ships and went to where the launch was, following all the other canoes.

At this time both the ships anchored, there being a land breeze, and all the natives went on shore, and showed themselves ready for war. In a short time the wind was abeam, and though light, it swung the ships so as to bring them too near the shore, and they were in great danger. The Captain ordered the cables to be slipped and sail to be made in great haste, sending the boats to recover the anchors and cables. The natives, it seemed, either for love or sorrow, on seeing how quickly we departed without carrying out our good or evil intentions, not understanding the reasons any more than we understood theirs, many of them came swimming and taking hold of the oars of one of the boats, trying with all their force to take them from those who were rowing. Such was the courage and audacity of the old man with the cloak that, only with a stick, he attacked an Ensign standing on the forecastle, who received the blow on his shield. He did not like to return it, because it was the Captain's order that no harm was to be done to the natives either in person or property. But I suspect, according to what happened afterwards, that there was less care about this order than appeared.

The launch and boats collected where the ships had been. The Captain sent for the Admiral, and told him that he had determined to send an armed party on shore next day with the boats, and the launch as an escort. The party, by good management, was to bring on board at least four boys, one of them being the youth who has already been described, and the others to be like him. It is to be noted that, the ships and crews being placed in such manifest danger in so small an island, this method or some other is necessary to get the wood and water of which we are in want, and which should be sought for to the S. and S.W. These instructions were repeated several times, and a strong desire was expressed that the Admiral himself should be the leader of the party.

We stood off and on during the night, very desirous that it should come to an end, and when the day dawned the Admiral started with the landing party. At the first place the landing was opposed by the natives, and he was obliged to go further on. Here all the men jumped into the sea, the waves dashing against them and rolling them over, and they reached the shore after much buffeting and in great danger. One boat was capsized, leaving the four rowers underneath. Another wave righted her again, and the men were saved. They were not sailors, so that the loss caused by them was serious, in jars and other things for getting water and fuel, and in a certain number of arquebuses.

On the beach there were a great number of natives, ranged in order and armed; and all with one voice gave a *pabori,* which I understand to be a kind of intoned shout or war cry, and they closed with a noise very brief but terrible. They came against us, and it was necessary to attack them with vigour owing to their being so close; and the arquebuses, which are a terror to those who do not know them but see their effects, terrified them, and they fled, carrying, as they had brought, the king or chief in a litter on their shoulders, holding palm leaves to shade him. Two or three were left behind, and set fire to the dry grass at intervals. We understood that this was either a signal of peace, or an imitation of the fire from our muskets.

The fugitives all fled to a village under a grove of palm trees, near a lake which the island has in the middle. Most of them went in canoes to the other side.

The Admiral formed his *corps de garde,* and a boy came to them, as they said, so beautiful and with such golden hair, that to see him was the same as to see a painted angel. With crossed hands he offered them his person, either as a prisoner or to do what they liked with him. The Admiral, seeing him so humble and so handsome, embraced him and dressed him in breeches and shirt of silk, which the Captain had given out of the store for barter, supplied with this object by His Majesty. The boy, to show his pleasure, climbed up some very tall palm trees with agility, and threw down cocoa-nuts for us, asking if we wanted more. Many other natives, seeing that he was well treated, came down and arrived where our people were. The Admiral, without moving, called that, the better to secure them, the capture would be much easier when they were close together. But Satan, who does not sleep at such important junctures, contrived that an ill-conditioned recruit should enter one of their houses. The owner opposed his entrance. Another of our men came up; but the native used his club so well that he would have killed one if others had not come, for he was lying senseless on the ground, while his companion ran away. The native faced our people, and an ensign named Gallardo, who came up first, fired a shot at him.

When he felt that he was wounded and saw the blood, he rushed upon Gallardo with great courage, who, to stop him, ran him through with his sword. He fell dead on the ground who, as a valiant defender of his house, did not deserve such a fate. Owing to this death, and to others which followed, the Admiral lost the opportunity he had desired and planned. And now, to follow the plan and what depended upon it, he set forward to wrestle with fortune. When the natives saw what had happened, they fled like the rest, and so our people remained with all their trouble in vain; for so great a misfortune suffices and exceeds what is wanted. One of our men said of the dead that it was of little importance that we should have sent them to the Devil to-day, as they would have to go to-morrow—a sentiment very far from all reason, and especially when they had the Faith of Christ at the doors of their souls.

The soldiers, divided into squadrons, marched into the interior. On the path taken by Gallardo and some friends a noise was heard, and the branches were seen to move. They all got ready their arms, and Gallardo cocked his piece and pointed it, moving to see what it was. Coming near, there rose up some children in haste and fear—two boys and three girls, all pretty creatures, the oldest about ten years—and with them a lady, graceful and sprightly, with neck, bosom, and waist well formed, hair very red, long and loose. She was extremely beautiful and pleasant to look upon, in colour very white; and, being so pretty, it was a great surprise to our people, more than to her; for, with quick steps and smiling face, she came forward to receive Gallardo, who gave her his new cloak, which he carried doubled under his left arm; and presently, with great love, both arms extended, she embraced him, and gave, according to their custom, the kiss of peace on the cheek. The finding of this nest did not fail to be useful to our people, as they told me afterwards, for the lady did not prove to be prudish in going with them; so that—and I say this—they left behind them a rich capture, which I shall always feel to be the great loss of six souls.

Passing onwards, they saw behind some bushes an old man concealed, who could scarcely open his eyes. Gallardo, seeing that he was so afflicted, gave him a hand, and was surprised that he could grasp with such strength, and that there should be such vigour in one who seemed so weak.

Having seen what he could of the island, the Admiral went back to the boats with his party, where he found the surf as furious as when he landed. To such an extreme did they come on the sight of it, that many wanted to remain on the island, where the sea urchins on the beach hurt their feet. They embarked with difficulty and danger, and returned to the ships. The Admiral excused himself from having an interview with the Captain, whose regret need not be mentioned, owing to his annoyance at the mismanagement.

In the houses of the natives a great quantity of soft and very fine mats were found, and others larger and coarser; also tresses of very golden hair, and delicate and finely woven bands, some black, others red and grey; fine cords, strong and soft, which seemed of better flax than ours, and many mother-o'-pearl shells, one as large as an ordinary plate. Of these and other smaller shells they make, as was seen and collected here, knives, saws, chisels, punches, gouges, gimlets, and fish-hooks. Needles to sew their clothes and sails are made of the bones of some animal, also the adzes with which they dress timber. They found many dried oysters strung together, and in some for eating there were small pearls. Certain white hairs were seen, which appeared to be those of an animal.

This island is very flat, and about 6 leagues long. In one part, which is nearly submerged, is the water which the natives drink, which seems to me to be only rain-water detained in the sand on its passage to the sea. In this same part there are some collections of huts. The land is divided among many owners, and is planted with certain roots, which must form their bread. All the rest is a large and thick palm grove, which is the chief sustenance of the natives. Of the wood and leaves they build and roof their houses, which are of four *vertientes,* curiously and cleanly worked, each with a roof, open behind, and all the floors covered and lined with mats, also made of palms; and of the more tender shoots they weave fine cloths, with which the men cover their loins, and the women their whole bodies.

Of these palms the natives also make their canoes, and some very large vessels, twenty yards in length and two wide, more or less, in which they navigate for great distances. They hold about fifty persons. Their build is strange, there being two concave boats about a fathom apart, with many battens and cords firmly securing them together. Of these palms they make masts, and all

their rigging, sails, rudders, oars, paddles, utensils for baling, their lances and clubs. On these palms grow the cocoa-nuts, which serve them for food and drink, grease for their wounds, and cups to hold their water. It may almost be said that these trees sustain the good people who are here, and will remain in the wilderness until God takes pity on them.

This island was calculated to be 1,600 leagues from Lima, in latitude 10° 20'. The port where the vessels were anchored is on the north side, very near the land, and in front of the village. It appeared well to the Captain that it should receive the name of "Peregrina."

REVIEW QUESTIONS

1. Considering that this Spanish expedition intended to start a colony on uninhabited islands, do you believe their approach to the "unexpected" natives they found seemed reasonable? Why or why not?
2. What characteristics of the native people seemed most important to Quiros? Why do you think he mentioned them in this account?
3. What were the natives' strategies for dealing with the Spaniards? Were they effective? Why or why not?
4. What strategies did Mendaña use to gain the acquiescence of the native people to the Spanish occupation?

A Spanish Cleric Relates His Dealings with Tribal Leaders in the New Hebrides (1617–1627)

The Journal of Fray Martín de Munilla

As the hunt for spice-growing islands in the South Pacific intensified, new islands were brought under European rule during the late sixteenth and early seventeenth centuries. Spain retained a prominent role in this treasure hunt when in 1606 Captain Pedro Fernandez de Quiros blundered into Tahiti and the small island group, the New Hebrides, located far east of Australia and near the Fiji Islands claimed by the English. The South Pacific and South China Sea hosted increasing numbers of English and Dutch adventurers, and Spanish captains of de Quiros's rank went to great lengths to hide what they had found from rival fortune seekers.

Subsequently, the Franciscan Missionary Plan of 1617–1627 brought the Spanish priest, Martín de Munilla, to the New Hebrides with a message of

Catholic Christianity for the native people. This plan sought to reassure the traders and soldiers left in the area that Spain had control of the islands and over their trade with Spain's European rivals. On his arrival, as the selection relates, Fray Munilla found no organization among or between the Spaniards or natives, and he had to negotiate with various tribal leaders, *caciques,* for supplies and help with necessary shelters.

Throughout this country, so it seemed, and our men had occasion to explore these parts, no organised settlement was to be seen. All the villages and dwellings were isolated, we might say, twenty dwellings here, and ten there; in one part only were fifty found. The whole country was in this way covered with settlements, the inhabitants being exceedingly numerous because, in the limited part we did see, there must have been more than two thousand huts disposed thus. On several forays made by our men, they took along the only native remaining out of the four taken from the island of Madre de Dios de Loreto. He took his bow and arrows to fight against the blacks of this bay who seemed to be enemies of his, because although left at large, he never once wanted to go with them. He had a good disposition and answered well the questions he was asked. He was shown the nutmegs found in this bay. He said that in the island whence we had brought him there were large quantities of them. Asked what use they made of them, he replied that they made a paste and from that an ink to dye the arrows and clubs and other objects which they use, afterwards discarding the nut.

He also said, on being shown some pearls, that they too could be found in his country, although they were small, but that in other islands he knew of, there were larger ones. This native appeared not to belong to that island where we captured him but to another which he said was called Chicayana, and from what we gathered he was something of a captive in the island of Nuestra Señora de Loreto, being a menial of the head *cacique.* Our men went ashore every day. Nothing happened worthy of mention. They collected yams and other fruits which they ate.

Thursday, 25th, was the Feast of Corpus Christi. Early in the morning the men went ashore. On the previous day the bower and chapel had been prepared and arranged for the procession. Four lanes, adorned with many palms and branches, had been made around it, and over each there was an arch, the ground being strewn with greenery and flowers. Under each archway there was an altar with a number of altar-pieces, well arranged and decorated, rendering this spot very peaceful and pleasant. High Mass was celebrated by our Father Commissary with the other religious assisting. Then the procession of the Most Blessed Sacrament was held with great solemnity and joy. There were two dances, one of boys and the other of men, all of them dressed in their costume of Chinese silk with many little bells attached. All contributed to the joy of the festival. The General walked accompanied by the recently created *regimiento* of the new City, and the Officers of War busied themselves arranging their men, all of whom were lining the route along the said lanes. As the procession was passing they [i.e. those nearby] fired salutes, so that until it ended there was a continuous salvo. Twelve salvoes were fired as the Blessed Sacrament was borne into the chapel above the flags and standards; [all of] which aroused great devotion. It was a thing of wonder and awe and a most powerful incentive to all of us, and even for Christians not present but who may hear of it, to give boundless thanks to God because in our days, in lands so remote and unknown, His most Holy Name is glorified. And I hold this to be a most certain sign that in times to come in this New World His most Holy Name shall be known and glorified, and the natives converted to our holy faith. All the religious who were priests said Mass and a large number of the men received Holy Communion. May God be glorified for ever.

When the solemnities were over, the General

wished to go and see a cultivated plot where many seeds had been sown, such as maize, pumpkin, cotton, and others. All the men went with them, and they saw that the seeds had now all sprouted and the maize was already well grown, a good proof of the fertility of the soil. They had been sown in order that the natives might profit from them and especially from the maize, because it is an extraordinary thing that among all these peoples no grain food-stuffs have been found such as maize, rice, wheat and the like, but only yams, fruit, pigs and poultry.

Sunday, 28th. At sunrise we set sail from the port of Vera Cruz, pursuing our discoveries. The weather in the bay was then favourable, continuing so until we reached the middle of the bay when the wind became increasingly rough. We proceeded thus as far as the mouth [of the Bay], where a very high wind from the E to E S E was blowing with very heavy seas. This night almost all the men fell suddenly sick: some had acute nausea with vomiting and gastric trouble, and others had aches in all their joints. We were in a sad plight because, out of eighty people who were on board this *capitana,* not eight could be found to work the sails. We were astounded at the suddenness of the onset, not knowing what to do for ourselves and unable to assist one another; nor did we know the cause of it. We were all making conjectures. Some wondered if it could be poison that the natives had cast into the river and others said something else, until experience showed the cause of this sickness to be our having eaten some fish called *pargos.* Sailors who had been in the Windward Islands and on the coast of the Spanish Main said that these fish were the cause, as the same thing happens in those parts to those who eat similar fish which there they call *çiguatos.* They say this sickness is due to the fish eating a certain herb called *manzanilla* which is said to be poisonous. In Cartagena de las Indias a great deal of it is found on trees which grow on the banks of some rivers and by the sea.

REVIEW QUESTIONS

1. What aspects of native culture appeared to be most favorable to Fray Munilla? To what did he object most strongly?
2. What problems did Fray Munilla encounter on this voyage? Which ones seemed to cause him the most concern?
3. How did Fray Munilla mark the observance of the Feast of Corpus Christi? What was he demonstrating to the natives with these formalities?
4. In what manner did the natural life and climate of the South Seas islands affect Fray Munilla's expedition?

A Dutch Observer Depicts Native Life in New Guinea (1678)

BURGOMASTER WITSEN, *Noord en Oost Tartarye*

During the sixteenth and seventeenth centuries, voyages of discovery by Western European nations led to strenuous competition and secrecy. Explorers wrote accounts of finding numerous lands, but they were very unclear as to the exact position of the newfound territory. Their descriptions of the physical and social characteristics of the people they encountered, however, were usually very detailed. The Dutch proved successful in locating the islands of the South Pacific during the 1600s, and they concentrated on defining and describing the peoples and the islands so they could claim undisputed international title to them. From Sumatra to Australia, the Dutch explorers used ruthless and desperate tactics to grasp trade opportunities from the English, Spanish, Portuguese, and French.

Much more than a successful merchant, the author of the following account lived an active life. Born in 1641, Witsen was a geographer, magistrate, scientist, diplomat, and friend of Czar Peter the Great. His impressive list of activities and credentials included being the burgomaster of Amsterdam thirteen times and a board member of the Dutch East India Company (VOC). He also served in the States-General and as a special envoy to England. During his active life, he amassed an extensive and famous library as well as a collection of thousands of biological specimens, including the fetus of a hippopotamus and a small child from Siam (Thailand) preserved in formaldehyde and alcohol. At his death in 1717, his wife and six children inherited an estate worth over one hundred guilders, including many books and artifacts too valuable to be priced.

In the following account, Witsen related how he participated in a Dutch East India Company (VOC) enterprise in 1678. Witsen believed that the VOC had discovered an island that was "barren and uncultivated, being in few spots either planted or fenced in." This island, however, was populated by the Ceram natives who were of a culture similar to those people on other Polynesian islands. Witsen used the Spanish designation of 'Mestizo' (as in Ceram-Mestizos) to designate those peoples who were obviously, to him, of mixed native and European heritage. These details, of course, convinced the Dutch that they had a right to the land. Without further formalities, the natives of New Guinea became subjects of the VOC.

About the north-western parts, the natives are in general lean and of the middle size, jet black, not unlike the Malabars, but the hair of the head shorter and somewhat less curly than the Caffres. In the black pupil of their eyes gleams a certain tint of red, by which may in some measure be observed that bloodthirsty nature of theirs which has at different times caused us so much grief, from the loss of several of our young men, whom they have surprised, murdered, carried into the woods, and then devoured.

They go entirely naked without the least shame, except their rajahs or petty kings, and their wives, which are not native Papoos, but mostly Ceram-Mestizoes, and are richly dressed after the manner of Ceram. Their weapons are bows of bamboo, with arrows of the same, to whose ends are fastened sharp pointed fish bones with dangerous barbs, which, when shot into the body, cannot be extracted without great difficulty. They likewise use lances, made of certain very heavy wild Penang wood; these they throw at their mark with great accuracy at a distance of six or seven fathoms. Some of them, living near the shore, use a certain kind of swords, sold to them by the people of Ceram, the hilt of which is tied to their hand by a rattan.

Of their manners and religion, nothing else can be said than that, in many respects, they are more like wild beasts than reasonable human beings. Their women are delivered in the fields, or roads, or wherever they may happen to be taken in labour. After the birth they instantly put the infant in a bag, in which they carry their provisions, made of beaten bark of a tree. The women of the better class rub their faces with bruised coals, by which they make themselves look more like devils incarnate than human creatures; though it cannot be denied that they seem to possess, by the law of nature, a knowledge of the existence of a God, which they show by pointing with folded hands towards the heavens. For when any one lands at any place frequented by these people of Ceram, they require of us to raise our hands as they do: and with a sharp bamboo they cut both their own arms and those of their visitors. The mutual sucking of the blood from these wounds constitutes their oath, and implies a promise to do each other no mischief. Amongst them are found some letters or characters, written with a sort of red chalk on a rock. On this rock, also, were still to be seen some skulls and the bust of a man, looking as if put up as an ornament, with a shield and other weapons near it, the meaning of all which may be guessed at, but not fixed with certainty.

Their food consists of roots, tree fruits, herbs, etc., but chiefly fish, caught by them at low water in holes in the bed of the river, as we, when lying at anchor thereabouts, could distinctly see by the motion of the thousands of little lights which they used. They know very little of cooking or drying their food, but generally eat it raw, except pork, which they eat when it has been a little smoked, and is less than half roasted.

In about 8° or 9° south latitude, we found a tall, terrible, and disgusting race of people, whose chiefs have the inside of the upper lip slit from the nose downwards, the two parts being kept asunder by what they call a gabbe-gabbe. The two sides of the nose, also, are bored through with sasappen, or thin awls, which gives their voices a frightful and hollow sound, as if coming out of a deep cellar. . . .

The following is an extract from a letter written to me from Amboina, as an account of New Guinea and Hollandia Nova, otherwise called the South Land.

'The inhabitants of all New Guinea are a tall, ugly, and misshapen people, not so much by nature as choice; for they cut their nostrils asunder, that you may nearly see into their throats, from which it may be conceived what fine faces those must be, after having their promontories demolished in this manner. They go mostly naked, except those who live upon the islands, who, by their intercourse with the Ceram Lauers, are becoming a little more polished. Of them they get some little clothing, with which they cover themselves, though but scantily; but on the continent they are altogether a savage barbarous people, who can on no account be trusted. They are addicted to thieving and murder, so that the Ceram Lauers cannot trade with them except at a distance. They lay their goods down upon the beach, being put up in heaps, when the most venturesome among the strange traders comes forward and makes it understood by gestures and signs how much he wants for them. Their commerce consists in Tamboxe swords, axes to cut the trees down with, bad cloths, sagoe-bread, rice, and black sugar; but the rice and black sugar must be given beforehand, to induce them to trade. No traces of government, order, or religion are discernible amongst them. They live together like beasts: those upon the islands erect houses, and a kind of villages, placing their houses commonly upon posts, raised to a considerable height above the ground. On the continent they have slight huts, covered with leaves, like hogstyes; in them lie indiscriminately men, dogs, and hogs, upon the bare sand, otherwise they lie down in any place where they can but find white sand. They mourn more for the loss of a dog or hog than for their mothers. They bury their dead hogs and dogs, but not their deceased relations, whom they lay down upon high rocks to decay under the rain and sun, till nothing remains but the white bones, which at length they bury when they think proper. Their food consists chiefly of fishes, with which their seas abound, and of yams and plantains. They have no sagoe trees, neither do they know how to prepare the bread from it if they had any. Their arms are hasagays, clumsy and long arrows, and also a weapon formed from a sort of blue stone or slate, pointed at both ends, having a hole in the middle, in which a stick is put for a handle. With this they attack one another in such a manner, that with one stroke the skull is crushed to pieces: the farther you go to the south the more savage, tall, and ugly the people are, in particular Lacca-iha to Oero-goba.

REVIEW QUESTIONS

1. What criteria did Witsen use to evaluate the people of New Guinea? What conclusions did he reach based on those criteria?
2. What opinion did Witsen hold of the foods, habits, or religion of the New Guinea natives?
3. What evidence do you find in this passage that the people of New Guinea had contact with other Europeans? With natives on other islands?

5

Europe, 1500–1800

Fundamental cultural and political changes and shifts occurred in Europe between 1500 and 1800. In 1500, a large part of Europe could still be described as medieval; by 1800 much of the continent was almost modern. In 1500, the Catholic Church still had a monopoly over religion in western and central Europe; most European nations were monarchies whose rulers were focused primarily on increasing their autocratic powers, and burgeoning new technologies were still relatively uncomplicated. By 1800, however, Protestantism was not only established and accepted but had become institutionalized, major nations like France and England had either severely regulated the powers of their kings or had done away with monarchs altogether, and the Industrial Revolution had begun to revolutionize not only manufacturing but the social and economic fabric of Europe as well.

In addition to these profound social, political, and economic shifts, there were also fundamental changes in the physical orientation of Europe. At the beginning of this time period, medieval Europe comprised two distinct regions, northern Europe and southern (or Mediterranean) Europe. These divisions were based primarily on climate and geography, which determined the general patterns of travel: overland in northern Europe and maritime in the Mediterranean south. This north-south orientation of Europe is clear in the writings of the Italian churchman Antonio de Beatis, who crossed the Alps and discovered very different customs as he traveled through France and Germany. Increasingly, however, the differences that divided Europe depended less on geography and more on economic, cultural, religious, and political factors—differences that were oriented along east-west lines. The observations of Lady Mary Wortley Montagu particularly reflect this shift: Montagu was focused on the contrasts between women's roles in Ottoman (eastern) Europe and western Europe.

One of the main themes of this period is the Protestant Reformation, begun in 1517 by Martin Luther. Many of the authors of these passages were extremely critical of different forms of Christian worship. This was particularly true of Protestant Englishmen like Fox (the servant of Henry Cavendish) and Thomas Coryat, who witnessed the Roman Catholic celebration of the Feast of Corpus Christi in Paris and did not particularly like the "popish" foolishness he observed.

Another theme is social behavior. Manners were a new focus of the educated elite—or those who wanted to join their ranks—and books on etiquette proliferated. A selection from Giovanni della Casa's *Galateo* offers an example of this trend. Nearly all European travelers in this period were concerned with manners, and they frequently used them as a basic point of departure for criticizing either the country they were visiting or, more rarely, the culture they had left at home. De Beatis, for example, was amused by the crude behavior of French noblemen and surprised to discover French manners to be less refined than German manners. Fox paid little attention to manners until he arrived in the Ottoman Empire, but from that point differences in hospitality became a focus of his writing as he traveled from Constantinople through eastern Europe on his way home to England. Montagu, on the other hand, was delighted with the behavior and manners of Ottoman court women.

There were also new motives for travel in the early modern era. Religious pilgrimage, which had been a major focus of many medieval travelers, became less and less important. Business and education also continued to motivate travelers, but traveling for pleasure emerged and increased over the three centuries covered in this chapter. For example, De Beatis's superior, Cardinal Luigi, officially justified his trip through Europe as a "diplomatic mission," but nonetheless it was essentially a pleasure trip. Similarly, Fox's employer, Harry Cavendish, accompanied a friend on a business trip to Constantinople, but his presence was not actually required—he was along for the adventure. Thomas Coryat wanted to "finish" his education by seeing "the world" and decided, after his first journey to the European continent, that travel was the sweetest of all pleasures. Likewise, as Lady Mary Montagu accompanied her husband to his new diplomatic posting in Constantinople, she viewed her experiences essentially as a tourist would have.

Despite these new motives for travel, there is an unfortunate scarcity of travel accounts from this era. Very few true outsiders traveled to Europe in the early modern period, though many Europeans themselves traveled far from their home lands, as other chapters in this volume clearly demonstrate. Most of the selections in this chapter, in fact, feature Europeans describing other Europeans: an Englishman describing France, an Italian describing Germany, and so forth. The two truly foreign observers of European behavior, Otsuki Gentaku and Hirata Atsutane, never traveled beyond the confines of their own country; instead they described Dutch, English, and Russian travelers to Japan.

This chapter includes the Ottoman Empire as one of the nations of Europe. Historically, it was one of only a few countries that straddled two continents—a sizeable portion of it was located in eastern Europe. Moreover, Ottoman influence in Europe stretched beyond the physical borders of the empire, as its attack on Vienna in 1628 shows. It is also important to remember that a great deal of Ottoman culture was built upon that of its predecessor, the Byzantine Empire, which itself was a hybrid of earlier Greek and Roman culture. Nevertheless, the differences between the Muslim parts of eastern Europe and the rest of the continent, which was predominantly Christian, were marked, especially in the eyes of English writers like Montagu, Bargrave, and Fox.

Finally, several selections feature "old" or antiquated English, with curious spellings and grammar. In the earliest cases, the original English has been modernized to facilitate reading. In later cases, which contain only occasional or minor instances of outdated language, no changes have been made.

An Italian Archbishop Prescribes Proper Dress and Table Manners (early 1550s)

GIOVANNI DELLA CASA, *Galateo*

Giovanni della Casa (1503–1556) was Archbishop of Benevento, an important church administrator, and the author of several works of prose and poetry. He wrote *Galateo* in the early 1550s, but it was not published until 1558—two years after the author's death. After Castiglione's *Courtier,* it remains the most important Italian book on etiquette, courtesy, and proper social behavior. One may measure its impact by the fact that French, German, English, Spanish, and Latin translations appeared before the end of the sixteenth century. Furthermore, it is still read today.

As the following selection reveals, *Galateo* is much more than a book of manners. Della Casa's attempt to describe and interpret the ideals and manners of sixteenth-century Italian society effectively reveals the *mentalité* of the age. In addition, the book reflects the values and experiences of the author, an important figure in his time. Two beliefs form the foundation for the advice that della Casa offers here. The first, often cited as typical of the Renaissance individual, is that people can improve themselves and instinctively desire to do so. The second belief is centered on the concept of utility: "no one will deny that knowing how to be gracious and pleasant in one's habits and manners is a very useful thing to whomever decides to live in cities and among men, rather than in desert wastes or hermit's cells." Della Casa's advice is similar in form to that given by his fellow Florentine, Niccoló Machiavelli, in *The Prince.* Both authors teach from experience, using specific examples to give the reader advice about how to succeed personally and in society.

[2]

So that you may learn this lesson more easily, you must know that it will be to your advantage to temper and adapt your manners not according to your own choices but according to the pleasure of those with whom you are dealing and act accordingly. This you must do with moderation, for when someone delights too much in favouring someone else's wishes in conversation or in behaviour he appears to be more of a buffoon or a jester, or perhaps a flatterer, rather than a well-mannered gentleman. And, on the contrary, someone who does not give a thought to another's pleasure or displeasure is boorish, unmannered, and unattractive.

Therefore, our manners are considered pleasant when we take into consideration other people's pleasures and not our own. And if we try to distinguish between the things which generally please the majority of men and those which displease them we can easily discover what manners are to be shunned and what manners are to be selected for living in society.

Let us say, then, that every act which is disgusting to the senses, unappealing to human desire, and also every act that brings to mind unpleasant matters or whatever the intellect finds disgusting, is unpleasant and ought to be avoided.

[3]

Dirty, foul, repulsive or disgusting things are not to be done in the presence of others, nor should they even be mentioned. And not only is it unpleasant to do them or recall them, but it is also very bothersome to others even to bring them to mind with any kind of behaviour.

Therefore, it is an indecent habit practised by some people who, in full view of others, place their hands on whatever part of their body it pleases them. Similarly, it is not proper for a well-mannered gentleman to prepare to relieve his physical needs in the presence of others. Or, having taken care of his needs, to rearrange his clothing in their presence. And, in my opinion, when returning from nature's summons, he should not even wash his hands in front of decent company, because the reason for his washing implies something disgusting to their imaginations.

For the same reason it is not a proper habit when, as sometimes happens, one sees something disgusting on the road to turn to one's companions and point it out to them. Even less so should one offer something unpleasant to smell, as some insist on doing, placing it even under a companion's nose saying: "Now Sir, please smell how this stinks," when instead he should be saying: "Don't smell this because it stinks."

And just as these and similar actions disturb those senses which they affect, so grinding one's teeth, or whistling, or shrieking, or rubbing together rough stones, or scraping metal is unpleasant to the ear, and a man ought to abstain as much as possible from doing such things. Not only this, but he must avoid singing, especially solo, if his voice is out of tune and unharmonious. But few refrain from doing this; in fact it seems that whoever has the least natural talent for singing is the one who sings most often.

There are also some who cough or sneeze so loudly that they deafen everybody. And some who are so indiscreet in such actions that they spray those near them in the face.

You will also find the type who, when he yawns, howls and brays like an ass; or someone who opens his mouth wide as he begins to speak or carries on with his argument, producing thus a voice, or rather a noise, that a mute makes when he attempts to speak. And these vulgar manners

are to be avoided because they are bothersome to the ear and to the eye.

Indeed, a well-mannered man ought to abstain from yawning too much because, besides the above-mentioned reasons, it seems that yawning is caused by boredom and regret, because whoever yawns would much rather be somewhere else and dislikes the company he is with, their conversation, and their activities. Certainly, even though a man is inclined to yawn at any time, it will not occur to him to do it if he is involved in some pleasure or thought; but when he is inactive and indolent he easily remembers to yawn. And so when someone else yawns in the presence of idle and carefree persons, everybody else will immediately start to yawn, as you may have seen many times, as if that person had reminded them of something which they would already have done themselves, had they thought of it first. And many times have I heard learned men say that in Latin the word for yawning is the same as that for lazy and careless. It is therefore advisable to avoid this habit which, as I have said, is unpleasant to the ear, the eyes, and the appetite, because by indulging in it we show that we are not pleased with our companions, and we also give a bad impression of ourselves, that is to say, that we have a drowsy and sleepy spirit which makes us little liked by those with whom we are dealing.

And when you have blown your nose you should not open your handkerchief and look inside, as if pearls or rubies might have descended from your brain. This is a disgusting habit which is not apt to make anyone love you, but rather, if someone loved you already, he is likely to stop there and then. The spirit in the Labyrinth, whoever he may have been, proves this: in order to cool the ardour of Messer Giovanni Boccaccio for a lady he did not know very well, he tells Boccaccio how she squats over ashes and coughs and spits up huge globs.

It is also an unsuitable habit to put one's nose over someone else's glass of wine or food to smell it. By the same token I would not want someone to smell even his own drink or food for fear that some things that men find disgusting may drop from his nose, even if it should not happen. And I would advise you not to offer your glass of wine to someone else after you have had your lips to it and tasted it, unless he were someone very close to you. And even less should you offer a pear or some other fruit into which you have bitten. Do not consider the above things to be of little importance, for even light blows can kill, if they are many. . . .

[7]

Everyone must dress well according to his status and age, because if he does otherwise it seems that he disdains other people. For this reason the people of Padua used to take offence when a Venetian gentleman would go about their city in a plain overcoat as if he thought he was in the country. Not only should clothing be of fine material, but a man must also try to adapt himself as much as he can to the sartorial style of other citizens and let custom guide him, even though it may seem to him to be less comfortable and attractive than previous fashions. If everyone in your town wears his hair short, you should not wear it long; and where other citizens wear a beard, you should not be clean shaven, for this is a way of contradicting others, and such contradictions, in your dealings with others, should be avoided unless they are necessary, as I will tell you later. This, more than any other bad habit, renders us despicable to most other persons. You should not, therefore, oppose common custom in these practices, but rather moderately adapt yourself to them, so that you will not be the only one in your neighbourhood to wear a long gown down to your feet while everyone else wears a short one, just past the belt. It is like having a very pug face, that is to say, something against the general fashion of nature, so that everybody turns around to look at it. So it is also with those who do not dress according to the prevailing style but according to their own taste, with beautiful long hair, or with a very short-cropped beard or a clean-shaven face, or who wear caps, or great big hats in the German fashion. Everyone turns around to look at them and crowds

around to see them, as one does, for example, with those people who seem ready to come to blows with everyone in their neighbourhood.

Clothes must also fit well and suit the wearer, for men who wear rich and noble clothes that are so ill-made that they do not seem made for them indicate one of two things: either they have no conception that they could please or displease others, or they have no conception of what grace and measure are. With their manners these men then make their companions suspect that they have a low opinion of them, and so are ill-received by most groups and are not well liked.

[8]

There are others who are more than suspect, for they act and behave in such a manner that it is impossible to put up with them. They always cause delay, annoyance, and discomfort for everybody; they are never ready, never orderly, never satisfied. When everybody is ready to sit down at the table, for example, and the food is ready to be served, and everyone has washed his hands, they ask for pen and paper, or for a urinal, or complain that they missed their daily exercise and say: "It's still early. Surely you can wait a while. What's the hurry this morning?" and by being concerned so much with themselves and their own needs, totally oblivious of others, they hold up the entire company. Moreover, they want to have an advantage over others in all things; they want to sleep in the best beds, in the most beautiful rooms, and sit in the most comfortable chairs and take the place of honour, and expect to be served or seated before anyone else, and never like anything unless they themselves thought it up, turning up their noses at everything else, and think that others ought to wait for them before taking a meal, going out riding, playing a game, or being entertained.

Some other people are so touchy, contrary-minded, or strange that nothing can be done to please them. They always answer with a sour face, no matter what is said to them. They never cease yelling at or scolding their servants, and keep the entire company in constant misery.

"Some fine hour you called me this morning! Look here how well you shined this shoe! And you didn't come to church with me! You ass, I don't know what's keeping me from punching you right in the snout!" All of these are unsuitable and rude manners which must be avoided like the plague.

REVIEW QUESTIONS

1. If you had to take all the specific advice that della Casa offers here and reduce it to one general principle of behavior, what would that principle be? What evidence from the reading supports your answer?
2. Why do you think that della Casa believed that table manners are important?
3. Do you think that della Casa had an accurate understanding of human nature? Why or why not?

An Italian Clergyman Compares Customs in France and Lower Germany (1517)

The Travel Journal of Antonio de Beatis

On May 9, 1517, Cardinal Luigi of Aragon left Italy on a tour of northern Europe. He was only forty-three years old and had been a cardinal for twenty-three years. He was motivated, supposedly, by his desire to meet—and to be met by—some of the great rulers of early-sixteenth-century Europe: Charles I of Spain, Francis I of France, Henry VIII of England, and the Holy Roman Emperor, Maximilian. Coincidentally, the cardinal was not on good terms with Pope Leo X, and his journey conveniently removed him from Rome for over a year. Nevertheless, the cardinal's itinerary and the luxury in which he traveled indicate that the trip was undertaken more for pleasure than for business or politics. Accompanying him was an entourage of thirty-five courtiers and servants. Wherever the cardinal and his retinue traveled, they were met with hospitality and deference, and they had access to churches, palaces, and private art collections that ordinary travelers did not. The timing of the trip was likewise fortunate: on the eve of the Protestant Reformation, Europe was experiencing a brief period of peace.

Accompanying the cardinal on this journey was his chaplain and private secretary, Antonio de Beatis. Each day he meticulously described the countryside through which the cardinal and his company traveled, the towns and cities in which they stayed, and the customs and appearance of the people who hosted them. As a result, de Beatis's journal has been called one of the "clearest impressions we have of the quality of life in north-western Europe in the Renaissance."

In the following selection, notice how carefully de Beatis compared French people and customs to those he observed in Germany and the Low Countries.

The French excelled in some areas and the Germans in others, in his opinion. At no time did he express a clear preference for one over the other, showing a restraint and cultural objectivity that was remarkable for the time period.

As we have repeatedly passed to and fro between province and province, I have not been able to offer separate descriptions of Brittany, Normandy, France, Dauphiny and Provence, as I did in the case of Upper Germany, Flanders and the small stretch of Picardy we crossed. But now that we find ourselves back in the fair, sweet, pleasant, gentle and temperate land of Italy, I feel duty-bound to say something about these provinces. I shall be as brief as possible, weary as I am both from such a long journey and from the variety and multiplicity of customs in regions and among peoples so unlike those of Italy. And since the provinces in question are similar in most respects, I shall take them all together, distinguishing between them, however, wherever it may seem necessary, and beginning with conditions in the hostelries.

Conditions are usually good in these provinces, much better than in Germany where rooms invariably contain as many beds as can be fitted in, whereas here each room has a large bed for the master and a little one (which, too, is a featherbed) for the valet, and there is a good fire. They also make good stews, pies and tarts of every sort. Yet whereas in Germany there are one or two tin chamber-pots to every bed (in Flanders they are made of brass and very clean), in France for want of any alternative one has to urinate on the fire. They do this everywhere, by night and day; and indeed, the greater the nobleman or lord, the more readily and openly will he do it. Good veal and beef are usually to be had, but the mutton (that is, wether-meat) is first-rate: there is no other meat, however much of a delicacy, that one would not leave off eating for a shoulder of roast mutton served, as is the custom all over France, with titbits. Partridges, pheasants, peacock, rabbits, capons and chickens are all cheap, abundant and well-prepared. There is game of every description and the plumpest you ever saw, it being the custom never to hunt wild animals out of season.

But of all these provinces it is France which has the best inns and, thanks to court and aristocratic society, is the most civilized. In all of them, especially France, window recesses, doorways and fireplaces are commonly decorated with plasterwork. The fireplaces in particular are richly ornate. Dress, both men's and women's, is the same everywhere, though in France, for the reason already mentioned, they dress more elegantly and in better quality cloth. The women everywhere line their skirts, usually with black or white lambswool, on account of the severe winters; and on their heads, under their velvet or woollen chaperons they wear linen coifs which tie under the chin and are very warm indeed. In rainy weather, they wear a kind of small hooded cloak of camlet which comes down to the waist. As in Flanders and Germany, they do all kinds of work and sell all sorts of merchandise. There is not an inn which does not have three or four chambermaids. The women are good-looking on the whole (though less so than in Flanders), pleasant and polite and can always be kissed as a mark of courtesy and respect. Also, in many parts of these provinces the women shave the men, and they do it very well, with great skill and delicacy. Frequent banquets are another custom, and all gentlewomen (there are always a good many present) dance with supreme grace and a perfect grasp of the music.

Although the same language is spoken everywhere, there are some differences of vocabulary from province to province, and since, as I have said, the Court resides there, France proper is more refined and politic than the rest of the country.

In general, the men are deficient in stature, and still more so in presence, except for the noblemen, who are often well-built and handsome. Most of the nobility bear arms, and those who do not nonetheless live with the Most Christian King, who pays them pensions for being in attendance at Court four months in the year.

When they have served their term, they are free to go where they choose. But most of them go and spend their periods of leave from court service at their castles or country houses, hunting in the forests, living cheaply and "saving their velvet." The nobility are exempt from all taxes or levies, while the peasants are in complete subjection, more ill-treated and oppressed than dogs or slaves. Not only noblemen but commoners, the merchants and men of every rank and station, so be they French, are devoted to feasting and jollity, and are so given to eating, drinking and lechery that I do not know how they remain capable of doing anything worthwhile. But to conclude my remarks on the nobility, let me say that, in view of all the prerogatives, privileges and favours they enjoy, all French noblemen can be more thankful to God than those of any other part of the world. For they are certain, as gentlemen-born, never to starve nor to engage in any base occupation as most noblemen do in our part of the world. Very few Italians in fact live the life of true gentlemen, even if they have the manner and style of a gentleman.

In none of the provinces in question are the towns nearly so fine or attractive as in Germany or Flanders: they lack the fine squares and streets, the imposing houses and public buildings of those countries which, above all, are extremely well fortified, with walls and wide moats usually containing deep water from a river or a marsh. But they do often have fine churches, where divine worship is well performed; and there is not a cathedral or main church anywhere which does not have figured music[1] and more than one sung mass daily, led by six or eight choirboys who are learning to sing and who serve, tonsured like little monks, in the choir, receiving free food and clothing in return. They all have cloaks of red cloth with hoods, such as canons wear in Italy. This custom is also found throughout Flanders and in many German towns.

France consists almost entirely of plain, and so too for the most part do Brittany and Normandy, which have a long ocean coast. In Picardy, Normandy and Brittany, in addition to using farm manure, they extract from their estates a kind of earth as white as chalk,[2] and spread it over the farm-lands to fertilize them. It is found, however, only at a considerable depth. In Brittany the Bishop of Nantes, Monseigneur de Laval and many other lords and gentlemen maintain that a certain species of bird similar to the shearwater is generated from the rotting firwood of the masts of ships that founder off the coasts. These are variously known as *anatifes,* bernacles or *zopponi.* They cling to the wood with their beak until they are fledged and can fly. Then they emerge from the water and live on shore; and although it goes against philosophy, which lays down that no lunged creature can live without air, vast numbers of them are to be found in those parts. Thus, in this instance, experience contradicts biological principles. These birds are the size of a large duck and most pretty creatures.[3] The Cardinal was given two by the Bishop of Nantes, but owing to negligence on the part of the carter who was transporting them in an uncovered cage they died from cold near Marseilles. The same carters came as far as Marseilles with some of our goods and a royal litter which the Cardinal had had made at Blois. There he sent them on to Rome aboard a galleon, together with upwards of two hundred and fifty dogs, which included ones of both slight and heavy build, ranging from bloodhounds to greyhounds. He had already dispatched overland to Rome twenty-eight horses—curtals, hobbies and saddle-horses—when we were at Lyons. We were also told that inside oysters caught in the ocean in the months of April and May crabs have been observed to have formed, and so they are not eaten at that time of year; and that crabs are

---

[1] "Musica figurata," i.e. written for several parts.

[2] Marl: a readily friable form of limestone.
[3] The Barnacle or Brent Goose (also formerly called the Tree Goose) became the subject of this legendary and long-lived explanation because it was not realized that they bred outside Europe, i.e., in the Arctic.

found in the long, black sea mussels, and grubs or lice in the sea crayfish which have soft exteriors and which we in the Bari region call *salepici.*

All the provinces in question are very rich in cereals and forage, and in red cows like Germany; and there are large numbers of sheep, which yield wool of the finest quality. Yet though there is no lack of woodlands, pigs are not plentiful; but those that are to be found, are, however, extremely large, especially in Savoy, and generally pink. Pig-meat is hardly ever eaten except salted. In Dauphiny they have a large breed of cows and oxen, which are black all over with a hide like fine velvet. Around Avignon there is a type of goat with a variegated hide and ears a span long; and not only there but throughout the provinces in question, wherever we saw goats their fleece was as fine as the wool of our sheep.

In the two provinces of Normandy and Brittany, they do not have a single vine owing to the cold winters, and instead of vineyards there are huge estates entirely planted with apple and pear trees. They extract the juice, keeping the two fruits separate, and drink it all the year round. They call this beverage cider. In taste it is incomparably better than beer, but it is not so wholesome. They make large quantities of it, wringing the pears and apples, when they have been well crushed, in presses, just as oil is extracted from olives. The beer is so wholesome because it is made by decoction of barley, oats and spelt in water, to which they add an infusion of hop-flowers, which are unpleasant in taste but most refreshing. The cereals undergo three decoctions, but the first is the best. The beers of Flanders are generally excellent and large quantities are produced. There they grow hops, carefully tended on stakes, in plantations just like our vineyards, and it must be said that they present a very pretty appearance. They have no other kinds of fruit apart from apples and keeping pears which grow there to perfection, especially a variety known as "Bon Chrétien." Since olives are not to be found in most parts, they use oil extracted from walnuts, which are plentiful. They also have some filbert or hazel-nut trees, and some plum and wild cherry trees. They de-

rive great advantages from the many rivers which they have, all of them navigable.

The vineyards extend southwards from France, and they produce excellent red and white wines, though the latter are less common. There are a great many varieties of the red wine which they call *clairet,* and these make a most perfect drink, as light and refreshing as any I have ever tasted elsewhere. The same holds good for Dauphiny and Savoy, and for Provence where high quality figs and olives are also plentiful thanks to the mild sea air. France produces many more kinds of fruit than Normandy and Brittany but no figs. At Avignon, however, when we were there, which was in November, we ate black figs in perfect condition and a variety of hard-fleshed black grapes, just freshly picked, which would not have been better at Naples at the most favourable time of the year.

The length of the league. The Breton league is the longest, and by my reckoning is equal to four Italian miles. In Normandy, Dauphiny and Provence, and in the small part of Savoy we passed through, it was three miles, but in France only two, the French league being the shortest of all, equivalent to a league of the best going to be found anywhere else. And although everywhere difficult going or overestimation of the distance may result in one mile, league or whatever else the units may be called being greater than the last, this does not mean that the leagues of the four provinces in question and of the Kingdom of France can all be considered without distinction theoretically equal to three Italian miles.

Throughout the French provinces they erect wayside crosses. But these are not crucifixes on the German pattern, nor are they so numerous. The nobility and wealthy apart, the dead are buried outside the churches, and what is worse, the graveyards are not enclosed, so that graves are scattered about the country towns and villages, albeit close to the churches, just as if they were the graves of Jews. Justice is rigorously dispensed everywhere: gallows are generally to be found at every turn, and they are always well supplied.

REVIEW QUESTIONS

1. What aspects of life in France did de Beatis find particularly attractive? What things did he find unattractive?
2. Note de Beatis's description of French noblemen. What was his opinion of their appearance and behavior?
3. In de Beatis's journal, how did the people and customs of France compare to those of lower Germany? In what areas did the French excel? In what areas did the Germans excel?

An English Servant Writes about Serbia, Bulgaria, Wallachia, and Moldavia (1589)

Journey of Harry Cavendish (by his servant, Fox)

Harry Cavendish (1550–1616) was an English nobleman with illustrious connections; his godmother, for example, was none other than Queen Elizabeth I. He has been described as a typical Elizabethan knight: his character was fiery, turbulent, and adventurous. He kept minstrels, loved horses, and was a member of Parliament, although not a particularly distinguished one. He also saw military service in 1578 in the Low Countries with English forces who aided the Dutch against the Spanish. His wife, Grace Talbot, was reputedly a friend of Mary Queen of Scots, who was imprisoned between 1584 and 1585 in Tutbury Castle. Next door to the castle was the former Benedictine priory of Tutbury, the home of Cavendish and his wife.

In 1589, the thirty-nine-year-old Cavendish accompanied his friend Richard Mallory to Constantinople, where Mallory apparently had business of some sort. They departed from Leigh, in Essex, on March 28 and arrived in Constantinople sometime in June, making extraordinarily good time for overland travel. Cavendish was accompanied by a number of servants, one of whom, Fox, wrote a detailed account of their journey. Fox's travel diary is only the second written account of an overland journey from England to Constantinople, the first having taken place only three years earlier, in 1586. It is also fairly clear in Fox's writings that Cavendish seems to have undertaken this journey simply for the experience and adventure.

Adventure was apparently one of Harry Cavendish's chief interests, and he frequently involved his servants. Twice before his journey to Constantinople, he and his men were involved in "homicidal affrays" that required the intervention of the authorities; several years after he returned home, he was called before the privy council to answer charges that he, "his servants and folowers" had committed "sondrie foule abuses and outrages" against a neighbor. In the 1590s and early 1600s, Cavendish and his men were involved in a plot to depose King James I. Cavendish, however, managed to evade serious charges and died of natural causes in 1616.

Unfortunately, nothing is known of Cavendish's servant, Fox, the author of the account of their travels, except what little the author himself chose to reveal in his journal. Although Fox was a man of limited education and vocabulary, his personality dominates the story. He was interested in farmland, food, and buildings, but not in art or the beauties of nature. He was a devout Protestant, with a sound sense of morality. Throughout the journey, Fox showed "dogged good-humoured patience" and was relatively impervious to the discomforts of travel.

The following selection contains a brief description of Venice and lengthy descriptions of Serbia, Bulgaria, Wallachia, and Moldavia, all regions that were part of the Ottoman Empire in 1589. Note the great differences in the standard of living that Fox encountered in each region, as well as the different religions. For the most part, Fox compared most of what he saw to his homeland, and found foreign places wanting. His views are distinctly English. No doubt he returned to England absolutely convinced that there was no better place on earth in which to live.

Upon Saturday the third day of May we came to this great city [Venice] where we stayed for the receipt of money and convenient shipping for Ragusa until Saturday the 10th of May at night. I will leave the report of this city to others that do understand the state of it better, but in my simple opinion it is a prison of much liberty and a place of all manner of abomination. The gentlemen be merchants and very rich and therefore proud. They have wives only for fashion sake, for they prefer a common courtesan before their married wives, for they constrain their wives to honesty by locking them up. If he find his wife to be too liberal of her honesty her punishment is death, not by the law, but by the bloody hand of her husband. If the friends of any gentlewoman so killed would have satisfaction they must have it by the sword. These men love this sweet sin so well that they term most virtuous what I think to be most vicious, but why should not the citizens be like the city, which is a foul stinking sink, as evil kept as the keepers be evil conditioned. They honor Saint Mark by which they hold their titles of honor. There be many places of good note such as the Rialto,* the Grand Canal, Saint Mark's Church, the Duke's palace, and the Arsenal which is the storehouse for their navigation with diverse other places. It was credibly reported unto us that there were 8,000 courtesans in this city allowed by the senate, which yielded much profit to their treasury. . . .

Cavendish and his company left Venice by ship on May 10. After stopping at several ports on the Adriatic they arrived in Ragusa eight days later, then began an overland journey to Constantinople.

Upon Whitsun† Evening we arrived at Ragusa, which is a very fine small city and very rich. In this town there is a fair church which was built by an English king,‡ but the reason why the king did build it we could not learn. At this place we hired a janissary, one of the Turk's guard, to conduct us to Constantinople and paid him for himself and his horse fifty dollars. At this town we lay at the house of one Mr. William Robinson, an Englishman, a man of many words

---

*The bridge that crosses the Grand Canal.

†White Sunday, or Pentecost, the seventh Sunday after Easter.
‡Probably Richard I, who spent two months in Ragusa in 1192. According to local tradition, he is the founder of the cathedral there.

but slow in performing, for time has so altered the man that he has become a Slavonian in nature, but a very kind fellow in his fashion.

Here we made our provision for our journey. We bought a kettle and spices with bread, butter, though not very good, parmesan rice and wine, and our bottle that we carried our wine in was a great bag made of deerskin dressed with the hair inward. And upon Whitsun Monday we with three merchants of that town and our janissary set forward toward Constantinople, but the merchants went but to Sofia. At this place we hired horses and had a man that had a commission to take the horses by the way. So with much toil and hard lodging we spent the time until the Friday following before we came to any town and that day we rode through a town called Foca, and upon Saturday we rode through one other town and upon Sunday one other. Those towns be of Dalmatia. This Sunday we came to the abbey of Saint Sabbas . . . we were showed a little chapel in this monastery wherein there was a great chest, in which chest the body of that holy patriarch lies consumed to dust. The chest was opened, and about the breast of the man there was standing a silver dish which had in it both silver and gold; for it is a shrine that the ignorant people resort unto for health and do offer gifts into it. It may be thought that this patriarch was a great taker when he was alive that takes so much being dead. They brought forth his staff upon the top whereof there is a fair crystal ball wherewith the merchants rubbed their eyes for it is esteemed very precious for the sight.

About two miles beyond this place we met with two Turks. . . . These proud Turks perceiving us to be Christians came to us and struck us with their riding whips and took away a hat and would not let us have it again without money. We complained to our janissary but patience was our remedy. Thus by small journeys we passed the way and time, and upon the 29th of this month we passed by Novibazar but went not into the town for our janissary said that it was a thievish place and that many robberies and murders had been committed there. The 29th we

passed by Nish but left the town for the like causes and when it drew towards night we left the way to seek for a convenient place to lodge in. We found a little poor house wherein there were three little mills driven by a small spring that came out of the next hill. The water was very hot but Mr. Millner would not give us entertainment, so seeking farther found a poor house where we stayed that night, some upon the ground. This day as we came by Nish we met a convoy of camels laden with merchants goods. The number was fifty. These were the first that we saw therefore I took notice of them. The next night we lay a mile wide of Pirot in a peasant's house, and the second of June we came to Sofia where we were well lodged in a stable and had good cheer of our own dressing. At this town my master put off his clothes for a merchant that came with us from Ragusa, lent him a pair of sheets and a mattress. At this town we lay three nights to get wagons to carry us to Philippopolis. The ordinary pace between Sofia and Philippopolis is two days journey but we made three days travel of it, for there was the wife of a Bassa* that traveled our way, in whose company we had leave to go by means of one Voinik† that attended upon her.

Sofia is a very bad town and the people of an evil nature, for they would stand and stare upon us and spit upon us, but they did not beat us. Upon Friday the 8th of this month we came to Philippopolis about eleven of the clock and, having found a convenient corner to set our wagons in and to give them meat, we placed ourselves very easily in a church porch that was railed in like the cage at Billingsgate.‡ So having gotten bread, a pot of good water and a few cherries, we fell to our dinner. But the malicious cleric, whether envying our ease or grudging that we should fare so well, came and turned us out and

---

*A bashaw or pasha, a man of high rank, or a Turkish government official.
†The Voiniks were Bulgarian Christians who took care of the sultan's horses. They served as grooms during wartime and as attendants for influential individuals.
‡The gate and fish market in London.

gave us ill word but struck us not. So we stood in the streets half an hour and at last our janissary got us a cooks shop where our fare was well mended, for we had meat well dressed with garlic and onions and excellent ill wine, but we forgot to drink to the cleric of the church.

Upon the Wednesday next we came to Adrianople and having sought a long hour for good lodging at last we were entertained into a smiths shop. So our chamber was the utter chamber to a common stable wherein there were horses, oxen, and asses, and they came all through our chamber. If we had store of dreg [manure] there we had but such stuff as we brought. This is a very great town but of base building all saving one church, which is a wonderful beautiful thing far beyond any that we had seen either in Italy or Germany.[1] At this town we hired wagons to Constantinople, being five days journey. Upon Monday the 15th of June we found that great city, which we had so long sought.

Constantinople, otherwise called Istanbul. It passes my understanding to say much of this great city for our time there was but short, about 14 days, but I see it evilly built and the inhabitants rude and proud and very malicious toward Christians, terming them dogs and offering them many abuses. Many of this city were so malicious to Christians that they would not sell us their wares but waved us away from them with their hand.

Cavendish and his party left Constantinople on June 29. Their return journey did not take them back the way they came; instead they headed north, overland through Bulgaria and Romania. They crossed the Danube River into Wallachia at the town of Silistria.

Wallachia is a plain country without hills, the soil good, but for want of good husbandry it bears but bad corn.* They plow their land but

once, at which time they sow their corn, and they never weed their corn. They have a great store of ground, but small store of cattle, for want whereof their fields be overgrown with weeds, wormwood and sour long grass, but the soil is good and would bear both good corn and good hay if it were well husbanded. The country yields small store of wood and very bad water, but the fairest ways for travel that we had in all our journey. The prince of this country pays tribute to the Turk and takes much of the poor peasants for their poles, for they pay no rent for their land, but pay for all their family according to their number, and that being paid they care for no more than will keep them; for if any of them should be known to be rich the prince would soon make him poor. In this country flesh is very cheap, for we bought a fat sheep for three scahies, . . . and great chickens for one asper. The asper is about the value of 3 farthings. Their bread is very coarse but cheap. They bake cakes always against dinner and supper. Upon Sunday the 29th day of this month of July we came to Yasi which is the chief town of Moldavia, and the see of the prince. My master was sent for to the court where the prince entertained him kindly, and took him by the hand and talked with him the space of half an hour by his interpreter whose name is Bernadino Barrisco. This prince presented my master the first night with a sack of barley for our horses, a basket of bread, four bottles of wine, a dish of pears and a fat sheep, and every meal something for the time we stayed at Yasi.

This Yasi is but a poor wooden town and the prince's palace is but of wood and covered with boards. This prince was an old man. He sent us his passport to the custom man of his borders for our better and safe passing. The Moldavians be better husbands than the Wallachians, for their fields be well stored with cattle, both oxen, kine and sheep, and have a good breed of horses. The country is a good fertile land, well wooded and very good water, but their building much alike, for the country houses be covered with reeds and sedges and the both be but boarded. Two days

---

[1] Probably the Mosque of Selim II.
*Fox uses the word *corn* here to mean "grain."

before we came to Yasi we heard little bells ring in their churches, which we heard not since our being at Ragusa, which is about a thousand miles. At the time of our being at Yasi there happened such a storm of wind, hail, and thunder as was never heard of in those parts by the report of the people. So upon Tuesday at night, having the prince's letters for our better passing, we left Yasi and lodged two miles out of the town, and upon the Friday following we bided at Chotin, a town upon the borders, at which town we passed the river Dniester into Podolia and lodged at Kamieniec Podolski. This Kamieniec is the first town of any strength that any Christian prince has against the Turk in those parts. This town is strong and has a fair castle and a garrison of the poorest soldiers that ever I saw. Being come to the gates of the town we prayed to enter for one night's lodging. One went presently to the captain who sent one officer to conduct us to our lodging, where the captain met us and gave us kind entertainment, but I cannot let pass but to speak of the baseness of the soldiers, for they had neither good clothes nor good furniture, but most of them were very finely drunk. At this town we rested a day and then set forward toward Lwów. . . .

Lwów is a very fine little town and of good building, near unto the manner of the building of Germany. At this town we lodged at the house of one Mr. White, an Englishman, where we had beds and our meat well dressed, which we had not in all our travel between Venice and it, saving at the agent's house at Constantinople. We stayed at this place four nights to rest ourselves and our horses. In this town there be many churches of many nations, and of sundry religions. The Poles be all papists, the Jews believe in God but not Christ; they look for their messiah who is yet to come as they believe, the Russians religion I understand not more than that they do profess a poor kind of Christianity, but neither Papist nor Lutheran. When any of them revolt and turn Polish, as many of them do, they christen them again what age so ever they be. The Greeks and they have but one church. The Jews have no images in their church. The Armenians have a very fine church, and upon the altar there stands a dog of silver, which they do great reverence unto, for they being in distress in the wilderness when the Turk drove them out of Armenia agreed among themselves that what they would acknowledge it to be their deliverer and do divine reverence unto it. So it happened that there came a dog by them which they followed and came forth in safety, since which time they have done worship unto a dog, which they have set upon the altar.[†]

———————

[†]The Armenians arrived at Lwów in the thirteenth century, and the Armenian cathedral was built between 1356 and 1363. The cathedral still exists, but the dog (a common motif in Armenian art) and the altar described by Fox did not survive an interior renovation in 1640.

REVIEW QUESTIONS

1. Which of the places Fox visited did he like best? Why?
2. Which places did he dislike most? Why?
3. Fox was an English Protestant. What were his opinions of the various other religions and religious practices he encountered on his journey? Give examples.
4. Based on their treatment of the English travelers, how do you think at least some of the Turks and Greek Orthodox Christians they met felt about Christians from western Europe?

An English Protestant Examines Roman Catholicism in Paris (1608)

THOMAS CORYAT, *Coryat's Crudities*

Thomas Coryat was a well-known Elizabethan travel writer. The son of a minister, he was born in the village of Odcombe in 1577. He studied for three years at Oxford University, where he became proficient in Greek, logic, and "humane learning." Nine years after leaving Oxford, he decided that a trip through Europe would enhance his education. Leaving England from Dover on May 14, 1608, the thirty-one-year-old Coryat spent the next five months on a walking tour of France, Italy, Switzerland, and the Netherlands. When he returned home, he wrote a book describing his travels, but he was unable to get it published. Finally, he appealed to the Prince of Wales, to whom Coryat had been introduced before setting sail for France. With the prince's influence, *Coryat's Crudities* was subsequently published in 1611. The following year, Coryat undertook a second journey, this time to Constantinople, Jerusalem, Egypt, and India. His letters home were published in 1616, just before his death in India in 1617.

Coryat's tour of Europe in 1608 was an educational pilgrimage. He deliberately sought knowledge and understanding of foreign cultures and peoples. Calling himself "Peregrine of Odcombe," he clearly thought of himself as a "cultural pilgrim." (From the Latin *peregrinus,* meaning "foreigner," the name *Peregrine* means "wanderer" or pilgrim.) When Coryat returned to England, he hung up his shoes in the village church, just as a religious pilgrim would have done. Nevertheless, his journey was primarily a pleasure trip, as were the journeys of Cardinal Luigi and his secretary, Antonio de Beatis, and Harry Cavendish and his servant Fox. These men felt compelled to explain their travels in practical terms: the cardinal had set off with the purpose of meeting various foreign heads of church and state, and Cavendish felt obliged to accompany a friend on a business trip. Coryat, in comparison, felt no need to conceal his desire to travel for pleasure. In fact, he enjoyed his experience abroad so much that he declared, "Of all the pleasures in the world, travel is, in my opinion, the sweetest and most delightful."

In the following selection, Coryat describes the celebration of the feast of Corpus Christi in Paris. An opinionated Protestant, he had much to say about what he considered to be the excesses of Catholicism: the clothing of the clergy, their "pompous shows," and their "false" relics. His tone on this topic is surprisingly serious, a departure from his usual whimsical writing style. Typically ebullient and enthusiastic in his descriptions, Coryat instead was critical and disapproving in this passage. Clearly, he approached the subject of religion with more seriousness than other topics.

Seeing I have now mentioned Corpus Christi day,[*] I will also make relation of those pompous ceremonies that were publiquely solemnized that day in the streetes of the city, according to their yearlie custome: this day the French men call Feste de Dieu, that is, the feast of God. And it was first instituted by Pope Urban the fourth, by the counsell of Thomas Aquinas, a little before the raigne of the Emperour Rodolphus Habspurgensis.[†]

About nine of the clock the same day in the morning, I went to the Cathedrall Church which is dedicated to our Lady (as I have before written) to the end to observe the strange ceremonies of that day, which for novelty sake, but not for any harty devotion (as the καρδιαγνώστης[‡] God doth know) I was contented to behold, as being the first that ever I saw of that kinde, and I hartily wish they may be the last. No sooner did I enter into the Church but a great company of Clergy men came forth singing, and so continued all the time of the procession, till they returned unto the Church againe, some by couples, and some single. They walked partly in coapes,[§] whereof some were exceeding rich, being (in my estimation) worth at the least a hundred markes a peece; and partly in surplices.[||] Also in the same traine there were many couples of little singing choristers, many of them not above eight or nine yeares old, and few above a dozen: which prety innocent punies were so egregiously deformed by those that had authority over them, that they could not choose but move great commiseration in any relenting spectator. For they had not a quarter so much haire left upon their

heads as they brought with them into the world, out of their mothers wombs, being so clean shaved away round about their whole heads that a man could perceive no more then the very rootes. A spectacle very pittifull (me thinks) to behold, though the Papists esteeme it holy. The last man of the whole traine was the Bishop of Paris, a proper and comly man as any I saw in all the city, of some five and thirty yeares old. He walked not sub dio, that is, under the open aire, as the rest did. But he had a rich cannopy carried over him, supported with many little pillers on both sides. This did the Priests carry: he himselfe was that day in his sumptuous Pontificalities, wearing religious ornaments of great price, like a second Aaron, with his Episcopall staffe in his hand, bending round at the toppe, called by us English men a Croisier, and his Miter on his head of cloth of silver, with two long labels hanging downe behind his neck. As for the streets of Paris they were more sumptuously adorned that day then any other day of the whole yeare, every street of speciall note being on both sides thereof, from the pentices of their houses to the lower end of the wall hanged with rich cloth of arras,[**] and the costliest tapistry that they could provide. The shewes of our Lady street being so hyperbolical in pomp that day, that it exceeded the rest by many degrees. And for the greater addition of ornament to this feast of God, they garnished many of their streets with as rich cupboords of plate as ever I saw in all my life. For they exposed upon their publique tables exceeding costly goblets, and what not tending to pompe, that is called by the name of plate. Upon the middest of their tables stood their golden Crucifixes, with divers other gorgeous Images. Likewise in many places of the city I observed hard by those cupboords of plate, certayne artificiall rocks, most curiously contrived by the very quintessence of arte, with fine water spowting out of the cocks, mosse growing

---

[*]The feast of Corpus Christi is the Thursday following the eighth Sunday after Easter. It is a Roman Catholic festival in honor of the eucharist.
[†]Urban IV was pope from 1261 to 1264.
[‡]"Knower of the heart" in Greek. Like many educated men of this period, Coryat was fond of showing off his knowledge by sprinkling Latin and Greek words throughout his writing.
[§]A long ecclesiastical robe, often elaborately decorated.
[||]A knee-length white ecclesiastical garment with large open sleeves.

[**]A Flemish type of tapestry usually used for wall hangings, curtains, and screens.

thereon, and little sandy stones proper unto rockes, such as we call in Latin tophi: 'Wherefore the foresaid sacred company, perambulating about some of the principall streets of Paris, especially our Lady street, were entertained with most divine honours. For wheras the Bishop carried the Sacrament, even his consecrated wafer cake, betwixt the Images of two golden Angels, whensoever he passed by any company, all the spectators prostrated themselves most humbly upon their knees, and elevated their handes with all possible reverence and religious behaviour, attributing as much divine adoration to the little wafer cake, which they call the Sacrament of the Altar, as they could doe to Jesus Christ himselfe, if he were bodily present with them. If any Godly Protestant that hateth this superstition, should happen to be amongst them when they kneele, and forbeare to worship the Sacrament as they doe, perhaps he may be presently stabbed or otherwise most shamefully abused, if there should be notice taken of him. After they had spent almost two houres in these pompous (I will not say theatricall) shewes, they returned again to our Lady Church, where was performed very long and tedious devotion, for the space of two houres, with much excellent singing, and two or three solemne Masses, acted by the Bishops owne person. With his crimson velvet gloves and costly rings upon his fingers, decked with most glittering gemmes. Moreover, the same day after dinner I saw the like shew performed by the Clergy in the holy procession in the morn-

ing. Queene Margarite the Kings divorced wife being carried by men in the open streets under a stately cannopy: and about foure of the clocke, they made a period of that solemnity, all the Priests returning with their Sacrament to our Lady Church, where they concluded that dayes ceremonies with their Vespers. . . .

They report in Paris that the thorny crowne wherewith Christ was crowned on the Crosse is kept in the Palace, which upon Corpus Christi day in the afternoone was publiquely shewed, as some told me, but it was not my chance to see it. Truely I wonder to see the contrarieties amongst the Papists, and most ridiculous vanities concerning their reliques, but especially about this of Christs thorny crowne. For whereas I was after that at the city of Vicenza in Italy, it was told me, that in the Monastery of the Dominican Fryers of that citie, this crown was kept, which St. Lewes King of France bestowed upon his brother Bartholomew Bishop of Vicenza, and before one of the Dominican Family: wherefore I went to the Dominican Monastery, and made suit to see it, but I had the repulse; for they told me that it was kept under three or four lockes, and never shewed to any, by any favour whatsoever, but only upon Corpus Christi day. If then this crowne of Paris, whereof they so much bragge, be true, that of Vincenza is false:[1] Lo the truth and certainty of Papistical reliques.

_____

[1] If that of Vincenza be true, this of Paris is false.

REVIEW QUESTIONS

1. Although he was generally critical of the Roman Catholic ceremonies he observed, some things Coryat admired. What were they? Why do you suppose he felt this way?
2. Generally, Coryat did not approve of "pompous shows" in church. What did he particularly dislike and why?
3. Both Thomas Coryat and Harry Cavendish's servant Fox were devout Protestants. Which man do you think had the least tolerant view of Catholicism? Explain your choice.

An English Merchant Describes Turkey (1647)

The Travel Diary of Robert Bargrave, Levant Merchant

Robert Bargrave was born on March 25, 1628, in Kent. Educated at Cambridge and Oxford, he probably expected to follow in the footsteps of his father Isaac, the dean of Canterbury Cathedral, by pursuing a career in the church. Bargrave, however, was in his teens during the English civil war and came of age during Oliver Cromwell's reign as lord protector. Because Bargrave's prominent family had strong royalist sympathies, government appointments were probably difficult to obtain. Instead he became a merchant, making two major journeys to Constantinople between 1647 and 1656. After the restoration of the English monarchy and the accession of Charles II in 1660, Bargrave became the secretary to the Levant Company, a significant appointment that probably would have led to further political and diplomatic service. Unfortunately, in February of 1661, he became ill and died en route to his new posting in Constantinople. He was buried in Turkey in the cemetery of Santa Veneranda, near Smyrna. His wife and three young children, who had accompanied Bargrave to Constantinople, returned to England alone.

The following selection is taken from the travel journal Bargrave kept on his first journey to "the Levant," a term used by English merchants for the territories on the far eastern shore of the Mediterranean Sea. He traveled from England to Constantinople by ship in the company of Sir Thomas Bendish, the newly appointed ambassador to "the Porte," the government of the Ottoman Empire. Bargrave was nineteen years old at the time, essentially a trainee, and the voyage was his introduction to business and trade in the eastern Mediterranean. His observations, especially of Turkey, are youthful, exuberant, and mostly free of the national bias that was so often a major feature of the writings of older travelers of this age—and that Bargrave himself later developed. His relative open-mindedness is particularly evident in his descriptions of the rituals of a bathhouse and of hunting practices on the lands of a judge at whose luxurious home Bargrave and his companions were lodged in the fall of 1647.

. . . His Lordship having now ripened [finished] his affairs in Smyrna and fitted himself for Turkish travel, we set out toward Constantinople overland, in a Caravan of about 100 English, together with their Servants. Our Harbingers [scouts] went daily before us to prepare all things for his Lordship's coming. We had little to do other than to spread his Lordship's Tent, ours being spread to our hands (the glorious Sky) and our beds ready made (the even Ground). On this Road are none but despicable Villages, nor anything of note, but there are rich manured lands and there are many handsome, pleasant Fountains for relief of thirsty Travelers. Only the City of Bursa is indeed remarkable, having formerly been an Imperial Seat, both to the Turks and Christians,[*] and is to this day a large and a Rich City.

---

[*]Bargrave is referring to Eastern Orthodox Christianity, which was practiced in the Byzantine Empire before it fell to the Turks.

On the south side there of is a high Rock, and on the top of it a great old Castle, which the Turks keep even yet in competent repair; but the Glory of this place has ever been its famous Natural Baths [hot springs] much beyond all that I have yet seen or heard of. Over them is built a Stately Fabrick [building] having within it many Stately rooms, some with large Cisterns of Stone, with fair Galleries round them, which men use to bathe by swimming, and some dry sweating Bagnios [bathhouses] handsomely paved and having diverse cocks of water running at pleasure into them, both from the hot and the Cold Springs, as also fair Seats of Stone to sit on. Every Room differs from another in its degree of heat, and here their Custom is to strip stark naked, to a Cloth of modesty alone; and then the keepers lay you down, first on your back, then on your belly, stroking and stretching the Joints, throughout the body, in many accurate [carefully positioned] postures, which feels very little pleasing, though they pretend them very cherishing [beneficial] both to Nerves and Limbs. Then having washed your body all over, and scoured and cleansed it with a Mohair glove, they put on you a Tufted drying Shirt* and bring you into a more moderate Room to dress you, and thence into a Third, much cooler yet, where you close all with a Dish of Coffee, and the payment of your money.

The Town has a gallant view to the Northward of pleasant and fruitful Plains, while the Southward mountains are always covered with Snow, from whence Constantinople is furnished the whole Summertime, the snow being packed up in hairy (Skin) Sacks and carried thither daily in boats. From there we traveled over the Plains to a small Town called Montania, about 200 miles from Smyrna, and 30 Leagues short of Constantinople. Here we embarked ourselves, our baggage and our horses, rowing about 10 miles in the River Scamander mentioned by Virgil,† and not far distant from Troy, often dyed with Greek and Trojan blood. Then entering upon the Hellespont, we rowed on to the completion of our voyage to Coinstantinople. . . .

We spent much of our time in a fair Country Palace, about 6 miles distant from the City, where we had many pleasing divertisements, and sundry Priveledges granted us by our noble Patron Mehmet Efendi,‡ Cadiliskièr (chief Judge) first of Anatolia (Asia),‖ then of Romeli[1] (Europe). The Palace we commanded as our own, with the conveniences of a Dairy of Buffalos,** Cows and Goats, and also of Gardens such as the country yields, serving the mouth more than the Eye. The house was situated on the side of a little Hill, over a pleasant narrow Dale, which was embraced by a Rivulet [small stream] in two Branches, and fenced with woods almost round it, such as afforded a various and pleasant chase of wild Boars, of wolves, of Jackals, and of wild Deer, so that we seldom wanted Venison of sundry sorts besides Pheasant, Partridge, and wild-fowl in cheap plenty. Here the great number of Nightingales invite (in the Spring) many great Persons to hear their Melody; and oftentimes came there great Families of Concubines to recreate themselves, attended only by their Eunuchs, not contented unless they saw the Franks' Chambers (by which name they call all western Christians) and there entertaining themselves and us, with Dancing, Leaping, and roaring like wild persons let out of a Prison. But above All I was in Love with the Solitude of the Place: the Fountains, Shades, the Rivulet and private Walks conferring much to the stolen Contemplation I delighted in.

Sometimes also we met, (as we rode abroad) the Grand Signor's Falconers, or Huntsmen, both of whom were clad in red Velvet, Wearing fantastic Fool's caps cut with five lolling ears.

---

*Probably made of cotton Turkish toweling, i.e., terry cloth.

†Roman poet, author of the *Aeneid*.

‡A title given to particularly wise or well-educated men who were often in service to the Ottoman government.

‖Europeans frequently referred to Asia Minor simply as "Asia" in this time period (and earlier).

[1]Rumelia, Turkey's territorial European possessions.

**A bovine animal more closely related to a wild cow (such as a water buffalo) than a familiar dairy cow.

They fly two or three Hawks at the same Covey,* and kill with their Dogs and horses what the Hawks do not catch. They carry the hawks always unhooded,† making them thus so well acquainted with each other, that being all off at once, they do not (like our Hawks) fly One at another. The Grand Signors hunting is Diverse; sometimes All Sorts of Game are caught alive and brought into some spacious Plain, where a vast Circle is made by the multitude of his Followers. The wild Beasts are let loose, and, according to their species, combat with Dogs, or with weapons, as suits each proper Chase, while the Grand Signor looks upon them from a high Seat amid an armed Guard. But the more noble Chase is when multitudes of men are put into some great woods, with numerous Trumpets, Drums, and loud brass Instruments, which together with the People's shouting, make a dreadful confused noise, which frightens all the Beasts the woods contain and drives them out, into some spacious Plain, in fair view of the Grand Signor and his Retinue, who stand all in array, fitted to encounter them, be they of what Species so ever; some with Spears, with Javelins, Darts, and Swords; others with Dogs that are kept on purpose in dark houses and in chains to heighten their Fierceness; being yet combed, washed, and clothed to make them handsome and agile.

---

*A brood of partridges.
†Europeans traditionally put leather hoods on birds used for hunting as a measure of control.

REVIEW QUESTIONS

1. Bargrave's physical description of the Turkish bath he visited indicates that he was impressed with that he saw, but how did he react to his own bath and massage? Why might a sixteenth-century Englishman have been uncomfortable with this experience?
2. For what purpose did the women of the sultan's harem visit the estate where Bargrave was lodged?
3. What was Bargrave's opinion of hunting practices in Turkey? Did he admire or dislike them? Explain.

An English Noblewoman Praises Turkish Women and Their Clothing (1717)

The Letters of Lady Mary Wortley Montagu

After leaving Vienna, Lady Mary Wortley Montagu and her husband Edward traveled to Adrianople and then to Constantinople. Her observations of life in Turkey constitute the most famous of her prodigious correspondence, known collectively as the "Turkish Embassy Letters." Two are offered in this selection. The first was written in 1717 by Montagu to an unknown correspondent, and the second to her sister, Lady Mar. Writing from Adrianople, Montagu described with delight the habits and clothing of Turkish women, which she occasionally adopted and which she found comfortable. Note, in particular, her unusual (for a European) admiration of a non-Christian people and her praise of upper-class Turkish women. She did not find their lives confining in any way, and she enjoyed their relaxed and natural behavior. Her ability to evaluate a foreign culture according to its own values and not her own was unusual for travel writers of this period.

Sadly, Montagu's life after her return to England late in 1717 was marred by ridicule and unpopularity. Disfigured by smallpox, Montagu tried to popularize the Turkish practice of inoculating against the disease and had her own children inoculated in front of witnesses. A public outcry ensued. Montagu then found herself embroiled in a financial scandal and a series of injudicious personal relationships, which further increased her notoriety. One contemporary remarked, "Her principles are as corrupt as her wit is entertaining." Among her most vitriolic critics were Horace Walpole, a famous letter-writer himself, and Alexander Pope, her erstwhile close friend. Walpole exaggerated her eccentricities into the grossest of character defects, describing her as slovenly and dirty, and Pope nicknamed her "Lewd Lesbia." Her husband, meanwhile, disappeared from the political scene and spent the rest of his life hoarding money. Lady Montagu finally fled England for life on the continent, where she lived from 1739 to 1762. Her reputation, however, pursued her, and she chose to move frequently. She did not return to London until the year of her death.

LETTER XXVII

To Lady—,[*]

Adrianople, 1 April 1717

I am now got into a new world, where everything I see appears to me a change of scene, and I write to your ladyship with some content of mind, hoping at least that you will find the charm of novelty in my letters, and no longer reproach me that I tell you nothing extraordinary. I won't trouble you with a relation of our tedious journey, but I must not omit what I saw remarkable at Sofia, one of the most beautiful towns in the Turkish empire, and famous for its hot baths, that are resorted to both for diversion and health. I stopped here one day on purpose to see them. Designing to go incognito I hired a Turkish coach. These voitures are not at all like ours, but much more convenient for the country, the heat being so great that glasses would be very troublesome. They are made a good deal in the manner of the Dutch coaches, having wooden

lattices painted and gilded, the inside being also painted with baskets and nosegays of flowers, intermixed commonly with little poetical mottos. They are covered all over with scarlet cloth, lined with silk, and very often richly embroidered and fringed. This covering entirely hides the persons in them, but may be thrown back at pleasure and ladies peep through the lattices. They hold four people very conveniently, seated on cushions, but not raised.

In one of these covered waggons, I went to the bagnio [bathing house] about ten o'clock. It was already full of women. It is built of stone in the shape of a dome, with no windows but in the roof, which gives light enough. There was five of these domes joined together, the outmost being less than the rest and serving only as a hall, where the portress stood at the door. Ladies of quality generally give this woman the value of a crown or ten shillings and I did not forget that ceremony. The next room is a very large one paved with marble, and all round it raised two sofas of marble one above another. There were four fountains of cold water in this room, falling first into marble basins, and then running on the

---
[*]The identity of the addressee is unknown.

floor in little channels made for that purpose, which carried the streams into the next room, something less than this, with the same sort of marble sofas, but so hot with steams of sulphur proceeding from the baths joining to it, 'twas impossible to stay there with one's clothes on. The two other domes were the hot baths, one of which had cocks of cold water turning into it to temper it to what degree of warmth the bathers have a mind to.

I was in my travelling habit, which is a riding dress, and certainly appeared very extraordinary to them. Yet there was not one of them that showed the least surprise or impertinent curiosity, but received me with all the obliging civility possible. I know no European court where the ladies would have behaved themselves in so polite a manner to a stranger. I believe, in the whole, there were two hundred women, and yet none of those disdainful smiles or satirical whispers that never fail in our assemblies when anybody appears that is not dressed exactly in fashion. They repeated over and over to me; "Güzelle, pek güzelle," which is nothing but "charming, very charming." The first sofas were covered with cushions and rich carpets, on which sat the ladies, and on the second their slaves behind them, but without any distinction of rank by their dress, all being in the state of nature, that is, in plain English, stark naked, without any beauty or defect concealed. Yet there was not the least wanton smile or immodest gesture amongst them. They walked and moved with the same majestic grace which Milton describes of our general mother. There were many amongst them as exactly proportioned as ever any goddess was drawn by the pencil of Guido or Titian, and most of their skins shiningly white, only adorned by their beautiful hair divided into many tresses, hanging on their shoulders, braided either with pearl or ribbon, perfectly representing the figures of the Graces.

I was here convinced of the truth of a reflection I had often made, that if it was the fashion to go naked, the face would be hardly observed. I perceived that the ladies with finest skins and most delicate shapes had the greatest share of

my admiration, though their faces were sometimes less beautiful than those of their companions. To tell the truth, I had wickedness enough to wish secretly that Mr Gervase[1] could have been there invisible. I fancy it would have very much improved his art to see so many fine women naked, in different postures, some in conversation, some working, others drinking coffee or sherbet, and many negligently lying on their cushions while their slaves (generally pretty girls of seventeen or eighteen) were employed in braiding their hair in several pretty manners. In short, 'tis the women's coffee house, where all the news of the town is told, scandal invented etc. They generally take this diversion once a week, and stay there at least four or five hours, without getting cold by immediate coming out of the hot bath into the cool room, which was very surprising to me. The lady that seemed the most considerable amongst them entreated me to sit by her and would fain have undressed me for the bath. I excused myself with some difficulty, they being however all so earnest in persuading me, I was a last forced to open my shirt, and show them my stays, which satisfied them very well, for I saw they believed I was so locked up in that machine, that it was not in my own power to open it, which contrivance they attributed to my husband. I was charmed with their civility and beauty, and should have been very glad to pass more time with them, but Mr Wortley resolving to pursue his journey the next morning early I was in haste to see the ruins of Justinian's church, which did not afford me so agreeable a prospect as I had left, being little more than a heap of stones.

Adieu, madam, I am sure I have now entertained you with an account of such a sight as you never saw in your life, and what no book of travels could inform you of, as 'tis no less than death for a man to be found in one of these places.

---

[1]Charles Jervas (?1675–1739) Irish portrait painter, disciple of Kneller; friend of Pope and well known to literary circles.

LETTER XXX

To Lady Mar,

Adrianople, 1 April 1717

I wish to God, dear sister, that you were as regular in letting me have the pleasure of knowing what passes on your side of the globe as I am careful in endeavouring to amuse you by the account of all I see that I think you care to hear of. You content yourself with telling me over and over that the town is very dull. It may possibly be dull to you when every day does not present you with something new, but for me that am in arrear at least two months news, all that seems very stale with you would be fresh and sweet here. Pray let me into more particulars. I will try to awaken your gratitude by giving you a full and true relation of the novelties of this place, none of which would surprise you more than a sight of my person, as I am now in my Turkish habit, though I believe you would be of my opinion that 'tis admirably becoming. I intend to send you my picture. In the meantime accept of it here.

The first piece of my dress is a pair of drawers, very full, that reach to my shoes, and conceal the legs more modestly than your petticoats. They are of a thin rose colour damask, brocaded with silver flowers, my shoes of white kid leather embroidered with gold. Over this hangs my smock of a fine white silk gauze, edged with embroidery. This smock has wide sleeves hanging half way down the arm and is closed at the neck with a diamond button; but the shape and colour of the bosom is very well to be distinguished through it. The *entari* is a waistcoat made close to the shape, of white and gold damask with very long sleeves falling back and fringed with deep gold fringe, and should have diamond or pearl buttons. My caftan of the same stuff with my drawers, is a robe exactly fitted to my shape and reaching to my feet, with very long straight-falling sleeves. Over this is the girdle of about four fingers broad which all that can afford have entirely of diamonds or other precious stones; those that will not be at that expense have it of exquisite embroidery on satin, but it must be fastened before with a clasp of diamonds. The cüppe is a loose robe they throw off, or put on, according to the weather, being of a rich brocade (mine is green and gold) either lined with ermine or sables. The sleeves reach very little below the shoulders. The headdress is composed of a cap, called kalpak which is in winter of fine velvet embroidered with pearls or diamonds and in summer of a light shining silver stuff. This is fixed on one side of the head, hanging a little way down with a gold tassel, and bound on either with a circle of diamonds (as I have seen several) or a rich embroidered handkerchief. On the other side of the head the hair is laid flat and here the ladies are at liberty to show their fancies, some putting flowers, others a plume of heron's feathers and, in short, what they please; but the most general fashion is a large bouquet of jewels made like natural flowers; that is, the buds of pearl, the roses of different coloured rubies, the jessamines of diamonds, the jonquils of topazes, etc, so well set and enamelled 'tis hard to imagine anything of that kind so beautiful. The hair hangs at its full length behind, divided into tresses braided with pearl or ribbon, which is always in great quantity.

I never saw in my life so many fine heads of hair. I have counted a hundred and ten of these tresses of one lady, all natural. But, it must be owned that every beauty is more common here than with us. 'Tis surprising to see a young woman that is not very handsome. They have naturally the most beautiful complexions in the world and generally large black eyes. I can assure you with great truth that the court of England, though I believe it the fairest in Christendom, cannot show so many beauties as are under our protection here. They generally shape their eyebrows and both Greeks and Turks have a custom of putting round their eyes on the inside a black tincture that, at a distance, or by candlelight, adds very much to the blackness of them. I fancy many of our ladies would be overjoyed to know this secret, but 'tis too visible by day. They dye their nails rose colour; I own I cannot enough accustom myself to this fashion to find any beauty in it.

As to their morality or good conduct, I can say, like Harlequin, that 'tis just as 'tis with you, and the Turkish ladies don't commit one sin the less for not being Christians. Now that I am a little acquainted with their ways I cannot forbear admiring either the exemplary discretion or extreme stupidity of all the writers that have given accounts of them. 'Tis very easy to see they have more liberty than we have, no woman, of what rank so ever being permitted to go in the streets without two muslins, one that covers her face all but her eyes and another that hides the whole dress of her head, and hangs half way down her back and their shapes are also wholly concealed by a thing they call a *ferace* which no woman of any sort appears without. This has straight sleeves that reaches to their fingers ends and it laps all round them, not unlike a riding hood. In winter 'tis of cloth and in summer plain stuff or silk. You may guess then how effectually this disguises them, that there is no distinguishing the great lady from her slave and 'tis impossible for the most jealous husband to know his wife when he meets her, and no man dare either touch or follow a woman in the street.

This perpetual masquerade gives them entire liberty of following their inclinations without danger of discovery. The most usual method of intrigue is to send an appointment to the lover to meet the lady at a Jew's shop, which are as notoriously convenient as our Indian houses, and yet, even those that don't make use of them do not scruple to go to buy pennyworths and tumble over rich goods, which are chiefly to be found amongst that sort of people. The great ladies seldom let their gallants know who they are, and 'tis so difficult to find it out that they can very seldom guess at her name they have corresponded with above half a year together. You may easily imagine the number of faithful wives very small in a country where they have nothing to fear from their lovers' indiscretion, since we see so many that have the courage to expose

themselves to that in this world, and all the threatened punishment of the next, which is never preached to the Turkish damsels. Neither have they much to apprehend from the resentment of their husbands, those ladies that are rich having all their money in their own hands, which they take with them upon a divorce with an addition which he is obliged to give them. Upon the whole, I look upon the Turkish women as the only free people in the empire. The very Divan pays respect to them and the Grand Signor himself, when a pasha is executed, never violates the privileges of the harem (or women's apartment) which remains unsearched entire to the widow. They are queens of their slaves, which the husband has no permission so much as to look upon, except it be an old woman or two that his lady chooses. 'Tis true, their law permits them four wives, but there is no instance of a man of quality that makes use of this liberty, or of a woman of rank that would suffer it. When a husband happens to be inconstant, as those things will happen, he keeps his mistress in a house apart and visits her as privately as he can, just as 'tis with you. Amongst all the great men here, I only know the *tefterdar* (ie treasurer) that keeps a number of she-slaves for his own use (that is, on his own side of the house, for a slave once given to serve a lady is entirely at her disposal) and he is spoke of as a libertine, or what we should call a rake, and his wife won't see him, though she continues to live in his house.

Thus you see, dear sister, the manners of mankind do not differ so widely as our voyage writers would make us believe. Perhaps it would be more entertaining to add a few surprising customs of my own invention, but nothing seems to me so agreeable as truth, and I believe nothing so acceptable to you. I conclude with repeating the great truth of my being, dear sister etc.

REVIEW QUESTIONS

1. What did Montagu admire most about Turkish women? Why?
2. How did Montagu's own clothing compare to that of the Turkish women she met?

What did Turkish women think of her European clothing? What about wearing Turkish clothing did Montagu like and why?

3. How does Montagu's description of harem women compare to Robert Bargrave's?

4. "I look upon Turkish women as the only free people in the empire," said Montagu to her sister. What prompted this observation, and what does it say about Montagu's perception of her own situation in life?

Two Japanese Views of the Dutch and the Russians

OTSUKI GENTAKU, *Introduction to Dutch Learning* (1775)
HIRATA ATSUTANE, *Summary of the Ancient Way* (1800)

Unlike many of the selections in this volume, the following two passages were not written by visitors traveling in foreign lands, but by natives describing foreign visitors. The simple explanation is that for more than two centuries, it was illegal for Japanese subjects to travel abroad and Japan permitted entry to only a very limited number of Europeans. Not surprisingly, foreigners were the subject of many rumors and much curiosity.

Europeans first made contact with Japan in 1543 when Portuguese sailors reached the islands. Over the next century, they were followed by the Spanish, Dutch, and English. At first Japanese rulers welcomed the Europeans, hoping to open new and lucrative trade with the West. The Europeans, however, immediately began quarreling among themselves, in part over the question of religion. A Jesuit priest, Francis Xavier, had begun converting some of the Japanese to Roman Catholicism after his arrival in 1549, and eventually aggressive proselytizing by Roman Catholics and Protestants alike antagonized the Japanese. Fearing that the missionaries and traders would soon bring armies, the Japanese ordered all Christian priests to leave Japan and all Japanese to give up Christianity. In 1637, government troops massacred several thousand Japanese Christians at Shimabara and then forced all Europeans to leave the islands. All contact between foreigners and Japanese was prohibited. Since the Dutch had not sponsored any Christian missionaries, a very limited and severely regulated amount of trade was allowed to them, and they were confined to a small island in Nagasaki Bay. This state of isolation continued until American ships under the command of Commodore Matthew C. Perry arrived in 1853. Given this lack of contact between Europeans and Japanese, it is not surprising that rumors abounded in Japan about the nature of the Dutch. The Russians, too, aroused much curiosity—and not a little fear—as they expanded their empire eastward across Siberia and ventured with increasing frequency into Pacific waters.

One of the first to point out the absurdity of some of these rumors was Otsuki Gentaku (1757–1827), a physician and scholar of Dutch who wrote *Introduction to Dutch Learning* in 1775. In the first selection, he systematically dismantles ridiculous rumors about the Dutch. Otsuki's self-assurance resulted from his participation in *Rangaku* (or *Dutch Learning*), the study of Western science in the Dutch language. Because of the work of a small number of interpreters and translators necessary for trade with the Dutch, the Japanese ruling class had decided that the Westerners had exceptional and valuable knowledge in many fields. Then in 1720, the ban on Western books, except for Christian religious literature, had been lifted. Otsuki and others founded a number of private Rangaku academies, which contributed significantly to the Meiji Restoration and the modernization of Japan ahead of all other Asian nations.

In contrast, a nationalist scholar named Hirata Atsutane (1776–1843) deliberately perpetuated misinformation about Europeans. Humiliated by early failures in the study of Confucianism (for which his fellow students dubbed him the "laughing stock of his village"), Hirata ran away from home while still in his teens. Several years later he was adopted by a samurai, whose patronage allowed him to devote his time to study, especially of Taoist and Shinto philosophy. Hirata, too, was interested in Western learning, but for a different reason: he felt it could help him attack Chinese Confucian and Buddhist beliefs. He once said, "The only reason to study foreign books is for the potential benefits they contain for Japan." With this attitude, Hirata's conclusions were foregone: Japan was far superior to the "Chinese, Indians, Russians, Dutch, Siamese, Cambodians, or any other people." His attitudes easily explain his perpetuation of amusing but grossly incorrect views of the Dutch and Russians, stereotypes that Otsuki Gentaku had denied twenty-five years earlier.

INTRODUCTION TO DUTCH LEARNING

There is a rumor that Dutchmen are short-lived. Is it true?

I cannot imagine where such a report originated. The length of human life is bestowed by Heaven and does not appear to differ in any way from one country to another. . . . The life-span of the Dutch, like that of the Japanese, is not the same for all. Some men live to be a hundred; others die at a mere ten or twenty years of age.

People say that the Dutch are born without heels, or that their eyes are like animals', or that they are giants. Is it true?

Where, I wonder, do such false reports originate? Is it because their eyes differ somewhat in shape from ours that the Dutch are slandered as

being animal-like? Perhaps because of the difference in continents, Europeans do differ somewhat from us Asians in appearance. But there is no difference whatever in the organs they possess or in their functions. If one goes to Nagasaki, one sees that the dark people from India [Javanese servants of the Dutch] also have eyes of a rather different shape. There are differences too among Chinese, Koreans, and Ryukyuans. Even among Japanese there are recognizable differences in the appearance of the eyes of people from different parts of the country. In each instance the eyes may differ a little in appearance, but the use made of them is always identical. If Japanese differ, how much more likely is it that people living over 20,000 miles away on a different continent should differ! Although we are all products of the same Creator, it is only to be expected that there should be regional differences in looks. As for the heels, they are the base on which the entire body rests—how could anyone get along without them? It is a subject unworthy of discussion. And as for the Dutch being giants, to judge by the height of the three men I have seen in Edo, it is the same way it is with age I mentioned—some are tall and some short. . . . Moreover, stories to the effect that when Dutchmen urinate they lift one leg like dogs, or that they have many erotic arts, or that they use all kinds of aphrodisiacs are all base canards undeserving of consideration.

SUMMARY OF THE ANCIENT WAY

As everybody knows who has seen one, the Dutch are taller than other people and have fair complexions, big noses, and white stars in their eyes. By nature they are lighthearted and often laugh. They are seldom angry, a fact that does not accord with their appearance and is a seeming sign of weakness. They shave their beards, cut their nails, and are not dirty like the Chinese. Their clothing is extremely beautiful and ornamented with gold and silver. Their eyes are really just like those of a dog. They are long from the waist downwards, and the slenderness of their legs also makes them resemble animals. When they urinate they lift one leg, the way dogs do. Moreover, apparently because the backs of their feet do not reach to the ground, they fasten wooden heels to their shoes, which makes them look all the more like dogs. This may explain also why a Dutchman's penis appears to be cut short at the end, just like a dog's. Though this may sound like a joke, it is quite true, not only of Dutchmen but of Russians. Kōdayū, a ship's captain from Shirako in Ise, who some years ago visited Russia, recorded in the account of his travels that when he saw Russians in a bathhouse, the end was cut short, just like a dog's. . . . This may be the reason the Dutch are as lascivious as dogs and spend their entire nights at erotic practices. . . . Because they are thus addicted to sexual excesses and to drink, none of them lives very long. For a Dutchman to reach fifty is as rare as for a Japanese to live to be a hundred. However, the Dutch are a nation given to a deep study of things and to fundamental investigations of every description. That is why they are certainly the most skilled people in the world in fine works of all sorts, and excel in medicine as well as in astronomy and geography.

REVIEW QUESTIONS

1. A recurring theme in Hirata Atsutane's description of Dutchmen is their resemblance to animals. What did Otsuki Gentaku have to say about this misconception and its origin?
2. How did Gentaku explain physical differences between different peoples he had seen in Nagasaki?
3. Why didn't Gentaku think differences in human physical appearance were important? What might his opinion tell you about his own religious or philosophical beliefs?

Part II

On the Eve of Modernity, 1800–1918

Part II of this volume expands upon many of the same themes as Part I. Contact among the peoples of the world increased and broadened, bringing people in relatively isolated areas into the global network of trade, tourism, and international relations. In addition, societies that had been closed or partially closed, such as Japan and China, became more accessible to outsiders. Travelers continued to be motivated by religion, commerce, and the love of adventure, but now they were inspired by the quest for knowledge and the desire merely to see and appreciate new places. Today, we call these people tourists. Many were genuinely interested in foreign cultures simply for their own sake. A heightened sympathy for subjugated and impoverished populations—one of the chief legacies of imperialism and the greater disparity of wealth brought about by the Industrial Revolution—is evident in the writings of some Westerners. For their part, eastern writers observed western civilization from a variety of perspectives. Writers from both camps exhibited the prejudice and ignorance that accompanies ethnocentricity.

Two particularly obvious changes in this period are the dramatic increase in the number of women traveling—some traveling alone—and the number of students, journalists, and social and natural scientists who traveled to expand their knowedge of the world and its peoples. Marianne North was an Englishwoman who traveled alone to Sarawak (in Indonesia) in order to observe and paint local flora. Dr. J.J. von Tschudi visited Peru to expand his rare fish collection but ended up taking a greater interest in the people he encountered than in the fish. Foreign experiences caused some authors to consider themselves citizens of the world. One good example is Lafcadio Hearn, a Greek-born reporter for American newspapers and magazines who went to Japan on assignment for *Harper's Magazine,* became a schoolteacher, married a Japanese woman, and spent the rest of his life there. Inoue Ryokichi, a Japanese student, came to the United States to take advantage of its educational system.

An increasing number of Asians traveled to other parts of the world and wrote about their experiences. These include M.K. Gandhi, who spent the first part of his career in South Africa, and Liu Hsi-hung, who traveled to London and later became the first Chinese ambassador to Germany. Asian writers also have left us valuable accounts of their own societies, such as Ch'iu Chin and Ch'en Shu-hsien, two Chinese women who decried the practice of footbinding, and the Nobel laureate Rabindranath Tagore, who described the idyllic setting of a Bengali village. Some Asian authors, such as Aizawa Seishisai and Rai San'yo, seized the opportunity to portray visiting Europeans in an extremely unflattering light in order to inculcate patriotic feeling among their reading public.

One of the salient features of this era was industrialization, which began in Britain and eventually spread through much of the world. Not only was travel made easier because of steamships and trains, but industrialization—and its impact on business and commerce—motivated individuals to seek out new markets and prospects in foreign lands. For example, Edward Tylor went to Cuba to visit sugar plantations and cigar factories. James Bryce enjoyed U.S. corporate support and investigated investment opportunities in South America. Industrialization also had its critics. Many yearned for the pleasures of the simple life, away from the hustle and bustle—and pollution—of modern industrial urban life. Mark Twain, for example, depicted the simple pleasures of life in the Hawaiian Islands. A second group of critics focused more specifically on those populations left behind by the rising tide of materialism created by the new industrial age. Jack London, for example, described the poverty in London's East End, and Emile Zola, in a gripping novel, vividly described the industrial poor in France.

Part II considers events from the Industrial Revolution to the conclusion of World War I. The former certainly changed the lives of millions of people around the world, for better or worse. It made travel faster, easier, and more comfortable. Moreover, it allowed members of the new middle class, who had not traveled a great deal in the earlier periods covered in these volumes, to see the world and record their observations. This is particularly evident in the selections written by women, scientists, journalists, and students. The terminal point for Part II, World War I, marks the beginning of a new world order that is characterized, among other things, by the retreat of Western domination of the rest of the world, the rise of the United States and the Soviet Union to superpower status, and the interdependence of the world civilizations to an unprecedented degree. Selections in Part III will address these themes.

6

East and Southeast Asia, 1800–1918

Commodore Matthew Perry's appearance off the coast of Japan in 1853 and the ensuing "opening" of Japan focused a great deal of attention on the previously "closed" nation. Indeed, Westerners became fascinated with East Asia in general. Marianne North traveled extensively, even to parts of the world not frequented by many Europeans, such as Chile and Southeast Asia. Her primary interest was botanical painting, for which she was respected and praised. Another British botanist, Robert Fortune, was to have a socioeconomic impact that must have been beyond his imagination. When he gathered tea plants from China for the British East India Company, he instituted a major imperial industry in India, rivaling perhaps the earlier introduction of noodles, then tomatoes, into the Italian cuisine.

In this time period, women traveled more, and more often on their own. Isabella Bird Bishop, like Marianne North, traveled extensively through several parts of Asia. Mary Crawford Fraser, who had a sophisticated background and upbringing, married a diplomat and thus was exposed to many enriching experiences (including, like Marianne North, time in Chile). Her account of her life in Japan was made into a play that was produced in Tokyo in the late twentieth century. Nellie Bly (née Elizabeth Jane Cochrane), a radical reporter for her day, made a whirlwind trip around the world, surpassing the record of the fictional "80 days" of Jules Verne. She spent 120 hours in Japan (publicity was such that time was reckoned in hours). Considering that the round-the-world trip took only 72 days, 5 days in Japan was an appreciable amount of time. She took remarkable notes on her travels.

Many of the selections show that travelers were often entranced by what they saw. For example, Japan was a favored place for writers like Lafcadio Hearn, Nellie Bly, and Mary Fraser. Lafcadio Hearn was one of the earliest and best interpreters of Buddhist thought and Japanese culture for Americans. A major reporter and essayist whose writings even today seem remarkably contemporary, he had a knack for expressing complex concepts clearly, of making an unfamiliar culture seem less alien. This chapter balances these favorable impressions by including thoughts on long-standing problems within Asian cultures, such as the upper-class practice of foot-binding in China and the evils of class discrimination in Japan.

An English Botanical Illustrator Describes Indonesian Town Life (1876)

MARIANNE NORTH, *Recollections of a Happy Life*

Sarawak, in the northwest part of Borneo, is the largest state in the Federation of Malaysia. The population consists of a number of ethnic groups, the largest of which are the Malays, not only in Sarawak but throughout the Federation, which includes the Malay peninsula and nearby islands. The Malays are composed of people from Yunnan in southern China and tribes from the Straits area, Thailand, India, and Arabia. Malay culture similarly contains a diversity of influences, with Indian or Hindu culture being dominant, although since the fifteenth century Malays have been principally Muslim.

Marianne North's visits to Sarawak in 1876 and 1880 were part of her travels through Southeast Asia, South Africa, and South Asia. She also traveled to California and Chile. Born into an affluent family in Hastings, England, in 1830, North began traveling with her father, a member of Parliament, as a young girl. After her father's death in 1869, she undertook longer journeys in order to paint flowers and plants in their natural setting. Without formal training in drawing or painting, North nevertheless developed a distinctive style that was admired by botanists and artists alike. She knew Charles Dickens, who encouraged her travels and work. She sometimes had difficulty reaching the settings of her subjects, but she seemed little concerned with danger.

In 1882 North gave 832 of her paintings to Kew Gardens in London and had a gallery built especially for their display. Even though the popularity of her paintings was partly due to the fact that she painted nature as she saw it, not beautifying the setting or the plants, her autobiography shows little interest in the native peoples she saw. She also identified strongly with British imperialism, which is not surprising given her background. She died in Gloucestershire in 1890.

After a fortnight at Government House, Sir William wrote me letters to the Rajah and Rani of Sarawak, and I went on board the little steamer which goes there every week from Singapore. After a couple of pleasant days with good old Captain Kirk, we steamed up the broad river to Kuching, the capital, for some four hours through low country, with nipa, areca, and cocoa-nut palms, as well as mangroves and other swampy plants bordering the water's edge. At the mouth of the river are some high rocks and apparent mountain-tops isolated above the jungle level, covered entirely by forests of large trees. The last mile of the river has higher banks. A large population lives in wooden houses raised on stilts, almost hidden in trees of the most luxuriant and exquisite forms of foliage. The water was alive with boats, and so deep in its mid-channel that a man-of-war could anchor close to the house of the Rajah even at low tide, which rose and fell thirty feet at that part. On the left bank of the river was the long street of Chinese houses with the Malay huts behind, which formed the town of Kuching, many of whose houses are ornamented richly on the outside with curious devices made in porcelain and tiles. On the right bank a flight of steps led up to the terrace and lovely garden in which the palace of the Rajah had been placed (the original hero, Sir James Brooke, had lived in what was now the cowhouse). I sent in my letter, and the Secretary soon came on board and fetched me on shore, where I was most kindly welcomed by the Rani, a very handsome English lady, and put in a most luxurious room, from which I could escape by a back staircase into the lovely garden whenever I felt in the humour or wanted flowers.

The Rajah, who had gone up one of the rivers in his gunboat yacht, did not come back for ten days, and his wife was not sorry to have the rare chance of a countrywoman to talk to. She had lost three fine children on a homeward voyage from drinking a tin of poisoned milk, but one small tyrant of eighteen months remained, who was amusing to watch at his games, and in his depotism over a small Chinese boy in a pigtail, and his pretty little Malay ayah. The Rajah was a shy quiet man, with much determination of character. He was entirely respected by all sorts of people, and his word (when it did come) was law, always just and well chosen. A fine mastiff dog he had been very fond of, bit a Malay one day. The man being a Muhammadan, thought it an unclean animal, so the Rajah had it tried and shot on the public place by soldiers with as much ceremony as if it had been a political conspirator, and never kept any more dogs. He did not wish to hurt his people's prejudices, he said, for the mere selfish pleasure of possessing a pet. . . .

The little town was full of life and civilisation, the bazaars and houses gay with colour, porcelain panels with raised flowers and griffins being let into the walls. At night the lights got so magnified in reflection that one could fancy oneself almost at Cologne or Mayence. Above and below for miles the semi-amphibious Malays had built their basket-like dwellings on stakes in the mud or on the banks above—thatched, walled, and floored with the leaf-stalks of the nipa palm, which delights in growing in brackish water, being almost drowned at high tide and almost dry at low. The Malays get wine, salt, and sugar from its juice, and oil from the nuts, which are contained in a cone as big as a cannonball. The sunsets were superb on the river. When the tide was very high we used to go up some of the small side-streams, and push our way under arches of

green tangle, which broke off bits of our boat's roofs, as well as the rotten branches over our heads. We watched troops of monkeys gambolling in the trees, chattering and disputing with one another as to who we were, and what we came for. One day we were overtaken by darkness in one of these expeditions, and made a short cut home overland, with a native to guide us by an almost invisible path through the bush, very suggestive of snakes, but we saw none. The wild jungle came close up to the garden on three sides, and none but native eyes could discover paths beyond or through it.

There were acres of pine-apples, many of them having the most exquisite pink and salmon tints, and deep blue flowers. These grew like weeds. They were merely thinned out, and the ground was never manured. They had been growing on that same patch of ground for nine years. They were wonderfully good to eat. We used to cut the top off with a knife and scoop out the fruit with a spoon, the truest way of enjoying them. The mangosteen, custard-apple, and granadilla were also in abundance. The mangosteen was one of the curious trees people told me never had a flower. But I watched and hunted day by day till I found one, afterwards seeing whole trees full of blossoms, with rich crimson bracts and yellow petals, quite as pretty as the lovely fruit. This last is purple, and about the size of an orange, with a pink skin inside, divided into segments, six or more, which look like lumps of snow, melting in the mouth like it with a grape-like sweetness. The duca was a still finer fruit of the same order, growing in bunches, with an outer skin or shell like wash-leather, and a peculiar nutty flavour in addition to its juiciness. The custard-apple was well named, for it is a union of both words. Its outside is embossed with lozenges of dark green on an almost creamy ground, and over the whole a plum-like bloom, very difficult to paint, and indescribably beautiful.

My dresses were becoming very ragged, so I sent for a bit of undyed China silk and a tailor to make it. He appeared in the morning in a most dignified and gorgeous turban and other garments, and squatted himself in the passage outside my door at his work; but when I passed him on my way to our midday breakfast, all these fine garments, even the turban, were neatly folded in a pile beside him, and he was almost in the dress nature made him. Every one peeled more or less in the middle of the day, many going regularly to bed in dark rooms. I never did, but worked on quietly till the day cooled into evening, and I could go out again. The Rani gave me entire liberty, and did not even make me go with her for her somewhat monotonous constitutional walk every afternoon, crossing the river to the one carriageable road, tramping nearly to its end and back, always dressed to perfection, and escorted by the Rajah or some of the "officers." She used to time those walks so as to take me for a row before the splendid sunsets were over, and I never minded how long I sat in the boat waiting for her, watching the wonderful colours and the life on the river.

Now and then the wives of some of the rich Malays used to come and pay her a visit, dressed in all the brightest silks of China or Japan. They wore many ornaments of gold, much worked, and coloured rose or lilac, with ill-cut diamonds and other stones set in them. They had exquisite embroidery on their jackets, but were most proud of their heads of long hair, and delighted in letting it down to show us. The Rani took me one day to return a visit of ceremony from the family of the principal shipbuilder, a member of the Rajah's council. He and his son received us at the landing-place, and we mounted a high ladder (over the stilts) to his house, and were taken into the great barn-like room, where fifty Malay ladies had been invited to meet us in their gaudiest dresses, covered with gold bangles and dangling ornaments. They all sat round against the walls of the room, on the floor; we were conducted by our elbows to some chairs round a table in the middle, on which were two wax can-

dles lighted in our honour, while coffee, with two large trays of curious cakes, was brought. At the end of the room were five big drums, some singing women, and many babies in and out of clothes. A most frightful noise began. Once our host got up, went and spoke to the orchestra, and returned to tell us he had told them "to play louder; they were not making half noise enough!" (the more noise the more honour being his maxim). Many of the women were pretty, and their manners very sweet and gentle. On our return another boat followed us with the two candles and trays of cakes as presents. The latter were made of rice-flour, gum arabic, and sugar, in different proportions, flavoured with almonds and spices. They all had a great family likeness to one another.

One night we found about fifty Sea-Dyaks all squatted round the luxuriously furnished English drawing-room when we came out from dinner. They had very little dress except tattooing, long wild hair, and coloured pocket-handkerchiefs round their necks, and sat perfectly silent, only giving a gratified grunt if the Rajah made an observation or relit his cigar, till the Rani got up to say good-night; then they also departed, apparently contented. They had come down the river in a long canoe from a great distance, to ask leave to take the heads of another tribe which had insulted them, and had been told they must not have that pleasure. They seemed to submit without a murmur to the prejudices of civilisation. Of course these people were full of superstition, and we used often to see small canoes and cocoa-nut shells full of burning oil floating down the stream with the receding tide, having been started from some house where there was fever, to scare away the malaria, and save doctors' bills. They used also to beat drums for the same purpose, which was much more disturbing to the neighbourhood.

REVIEW QUESTIONS

1. Although Marianne North elsewhere in her writings showed little interest in native people, there is a long description of a Malay community in this selection. How can you reconcile this apparent contradiction?

2. How were her botanical and artistic interests reflected in her writing? In its content? In her style?
3. How would you characterize her attitude toward rich Malay women?

A Scottish Horticulturist Travels Incognito in China (c. 1850)

ROBERT FORTUNE, *A Journey to the Tea Countries of China*

A Scottish botanist, Robert Fortune (1813–1880) was engaged by the East India Company to acquire tea plants for establishing plantations in India. His success in this endeavor had significant repercussions on the history, society, and especially the economy of British—and later independent—India. He was a perfect choice for this task. An accomplished horticulturalist, he had earlier traveled in China, where he secured plants for the Royal Horticultural Society's garden in Chiswick, England. From his travels to Taiwan, Japan, and other countries, he introduced into Europe new species of flowers and trees and a number of books. His scientific accomplishments included a description of silkworm culture and the manufacture of rice paper.

In the following selection Fortune describes an event in his travels during which he tried to appear incognito, as some sort of foreigner other than a European. The Opium War of 1839 had taken place just a few years previously, and the British in particular were not highly regarded in China. His account shows how much he relished his charade and how fascinated he was with the food and the people he encountered.

THE OPIUM SMOKER

My fellow-passengers, who were chiefly merchants and servants, were quiet and inoffensive; indeed they did little else but loll in bed and sleep, except when they were eating or smoking. One of them was a confirmed opium-smoker, and the intoxicating drug had made him a perfect slave. I have seen many opium-smokers in my travels, but this one was the most pitiable of them all; he was evidently a man of some standing in society, and had plenty of money. His bed was surrounded with silk curtains, his pillows were beautifully embroidered, and his coverlet was of the richest and softest satin. Everything about him told of luxury and sensual pleasures.

But let me take a peep inside his bed-curtains and describe what I saw on the first day of our acquaintance. The curtains were down and drawn close round, particularly on that side from which the wind came. He was clothed in the finest silks, and had lain down on his side upon a mat; his head was resting on one of the embroidered pillows. A small lamp was burning by his side, an opium-pipe was in his mouth, and he was inhaling the intoxicating fumes. After smoking for a few minutes he began to have the appearance which a drunken man presents in the first stage of intoxication; the fumes had done their work, and he was now in his "third heaven of bliss."

In a minute or two he jumped up and called for his teapot, from which he took a good draught of tea; he then walked about the boat evidently a good deal excited, and talked and joked with every one he met. After spending some time in this manner he began to smoke tobacco; he then took another draught out of his teapot and lay down to sleep; but his slumbers were not of long duration, and were evidently disturbed by strange and frightful dreams. He awoke at last, but it was only to renew the dose as before; and so on from day to day. Even in the silent night, when all around was sunk in repose, his craving for the stimulant was beyond his feeble powers of resistance. Often and often during this passage, when I happened to awake during the night, I could see his little lamp burning, and could smell the sickening fumes as they curled about the roof of the boat.

The effects which the immoderate use of opium had produced upon this man were of the most melancholy kind. His figure was thin and emaciated, his cheeks had a pale and haggard hue, and his skin had that peculiar glassy polish by which an opium-smoker is invariably known. His days were evidently numbered, and yet, strange to tell, this man tried to convince others and himself also that he was smoking medicinally, and that the use of opium was indispensable to his health.

[He arrives in the green-tea district of Hwei-chow and begins his investigation of local tea cultivation. Having collected seeds and shrubs, he returns to Hong Kong to have them transshiped to India. Then he starts north to visit the black-tea districts over the mountains of Bohea. His report of this journey is full of pleasant glimpses of peaceful scenes on road, river and plantation.]

THE INN

Although small villages and houses for refreshment extended, at short intervals, along the whole line of road, we rarely passed any town even of moderate size. About mid-day, however, we came to a place considerably larger than any we had passed—I forget its name—and before I knew where I was, I was set down at the door of a large inn. Numerous chairs were standing at the door which belonged to travellers who were either going the same road as myself, or returning from the west to Chang-shan and the other towns in the east.

The moment I got out of my chair the inn-keeper presented himself, and my chair-bearers very officiously informed him that it was my intention to dine there. I felt rather annoyed, but thought it best to put a good face on the matter, and ordered dinner accordingly. I had given Sing-Hoo strict injunctions never to stop at the inns much frequented by merchants, as I had no wish to meet men who were in the habit of seeing foreigners both at Shanghae and Canton. I had the greatest objection to meeting Canton men, who are continually travelling to and from the tea country, and who, with the same knowledge of foreigners as the Shanghae people, are much more prejudiced against us. Sing-Hoo had fallen behind, however, and was not aware of what the chair-bearers had done until it was too late. It appeared afterwards that the men had a good and substantial reason for their conduct, inasmuch as they got their own dinner free as a reward for bringing a customer to the house.

The inn was a large and commodious building extending backwards from the main street of the town. Its front was composed of a number of boards or shutters which could be removed at pleasure. The whole of these were taken down in the morning and put up again at night. The floor of the building was divided into three principal compartments, the first facing the street, the second being behind it, and the third at the furthest end. Some small rooms which were formed on each side were the bedrooms.

Coolies and chair-bearers crowded that part of the building next to the street, in which they had their meals and smoked their pipes. The second and third divisions were destined for travellers, but, as there were large doors between each which stood wide open, it was easy to see through from the front to the back part of the premises.

When I got out of my chair I followed "mine host" into the second compartment, in which I observed a table at each side of the room. One of them being unoccupied, I sat down at it, and with becoming gravity lighted my Chinese pipe and began to smoke. The host set a cup of tea before me and left me to attend upon some one else. I had now leisure to take a survey of the strange scene round me. At the opposite table sat two merchants, who a single glance told me were from the province of Canton. They were evidently eyeing me with great interest, and doubtless knew me to be a foreigner the moment I entered the room. One of them I had frequently seen at Shanghae. This person looked as if he wished me to recognise him, but in this he was disappointed, for I returned his inquiring look as if I had never seen him before. I now observed him whispering to his companion, and thought I heard the word Fan-Kwai used. In the meantime Sing-Hoo, who had just arrived, came in and began to bustle about and get in the dinner, which was soon ready. The host was a civil sort of man, but very inquisitive, and as he set down the dinner he put various questions to me. With Chinese politeness, he asked me my name, my age, where I had come from, and whither I was bound, and to all such questions he received most satisfactory answers. For example, when asked where I had come from, I replied, "From Chang-shan"; and to the question as to whither I was bound I answered, "To Fokien." These answers were perfectly true, although not very definite. The Canton merchants were all eyes and ears while this conversation was going on, and one of them quietly prompted the inn-keeper to ask for a few more questions.

These gentlemen wanted to know the starting-point of my journey, the particular part of Fokien to which I was bound, and the objects I had in view. As I could not see that answers to these questions concerned them very much, or could be of any use, I judged it better to keep them in the dark.

Several dishes being now set before me, and a cup of wine poured out by the host, I took a sip of it, and taking up my chopsticks went on with my dinner. Having had great experience in the use of the chopsticks, I could handle them now nearly as well as the Chinese themselves; and as

I had been often accustomed to all the formalities of a Chinese dinner, I went on with the most perfect confidence.

On my former journey in the interior, as well as on this, I had discarded all European habits and luxuries. Chopsticks were substituted for knives and forks, tea and light wines for stronger drinks, and a long bamboo Chinese pipe for Manilla cheroots. By these means I had arrived at a high state of civilization and politeness. In eating my dinner, such rude things as knives and forks were never thought of. The cutting up of meat and vegetables was done by servants in the kitchen, before the food was cooked or brought to table. When the various dishes, prepared in this manner, were brought to table, the chopsticks—those ancient and useful articles—answered every purpose. Talk of knives and forks indeed! One cannot eat rice with them, and how very awkward it would be to pick out all those dainty little morsels from the different dishes with a fork! In the first place, it would be necessary to push them to the bottom of the basin before the fork would take a proper hold; and in many instances we should do what the novice in the art of using chopsticks frequently does—drop the food on its way from the dish to the mouth. There is no such difficulty or danger with the chopsticks when properly used. The smallest morsel, even to a single grain of rice, can be picked up with perfect ease. In sober truth, they are most useful and sensible things, whatever people may say to the contrary; and I know of no article in use amongst ourselves which could supply their place. Excepting the fingers, nature's own invention, nothing is so convenient as the chopsticks.

When I had finished dinner, a wooden basin containing warm water and a wet cloth were placed before me, in order that I might wash my hands and face. Wringing the wet cloth, I rubbed my face, neck, and hands well over with it in Chinese style. Having finished my ablution, I returned again to the table. The dinner and dishes having in the meantime been removed, tea was again set before me.

The Canton men still remained at the opposite

table, but the greater part of the others, who, at their instigation, had been taking sly peeps at me, had gone away. I suppose, when they saw that I ate and drank just like the rest, they must have felt some little surprise, and had their original opinion strengthened, namely, that after all I was only one of themselves.

My chair-bearers having dined as well as myself, they sent a message by Sing-Hoo to say that they were ready to proceed. Making a slight bow to mine host, and a slighter one to the Canton gentlemen, in Chinese style, I got into my chair and went my way. As soon as I had left the house, Sing-Hoo, who was paying our bill, was closely questioned about me. According to his account he had completely mystified them, by informing them, as he had done others before, that I came from some far country beyond the great wall, a statement which those who knew best would not have called in question. . . .

REVIEW QUESTIONS

1. Do you think Fortune's narrative reflects an imperialistic attitude? Why or why not?
2. Do you think Fortune was a careful observer? Why or why not?
3. How did his praise of chopsticks affect his story?

An English Tourist Describes Life in Canton (1896)

ISABELLA BIRD BISHOP, *The Golden Chersonese*

Isabella Bird Bishop suffered from a spinal ailment as a young girl, for which her doctors suggested travel as a cure. It was, as Professor Anne Pringle-Harris observed in the *New York Times* (October 28, 2001), "a peculiar prescription but one that seems to have worked, because the patient spent much of the rest of her life galloping through India, Tibet and points east, taking notes for books as she went."

Bird was an inveterate traveler, loving to go where she knew there would be few if any other Europeans. Her keen observations resulted in a dozen travel books, and much of her writing is considered to be classic in the genre. It is almost as though this daughter of a strict clergyman was a refugee from Victorian England, fleeing from its values and beliefs, but at the same time not renouncing them.

CANTON: THE RIVER LIFE AND THE TARTAR DISTRICT

At some distance below Shameen there are moored tiers of large, two-storied house boats, with entrance doors seven feet high, always open, and doorways of rich wood carving, through which the interiors can be seen with their richly decorated altars, innumerable colored lamps, chairs, and settees of carved ebony with white marble let into the seats and backs, embroidered silk hangings, gilded mirrors and cornices, and all the extravagances of Chinese luxury. Many of them have gardens on their roofs. These are called "flower boats," and are of noisy and evil reputation. Then there are tiers of three-roomed, comfortable house boats to let to people who make their homes on the water in summer to avoid the heat. "Marriage boats," green and gold, with much wood carving and flags, and auspicious emblems of all kinds; river junks, with their large eyes and carved and castellated sterns lying moored in treble rows; duck boats, with their noisy inmates; florists' boats, with platforms of growing plants for sale; two-storied boats or barges, with glass sides, floating hotels, in which evening entertainments are given with much light and noise; restaurant boats, much gilded, from which proceeds an incessant beating of gongs; washing boats, market boats, floating shops, which supply the floating population with all marketable commodities; country boats of fantastic form coming down on every wind and tide; and, queerest of all, "slipper boats," looking absurdly like big shoes, which are propelled in and out among all the heavier craft by standing in the stern.

One of the most marvelous features of Canton is the city of house boats, floating and stationary, in which about a quarter of a million people live, and it may with truth be added are born and die. This population is quite distinct in race from the land population of Canton, which looks down upon it as a pariah and alien caste. These house boats, some of which have a single bamboo circular roof, others two roofs of different heights, and which include several thousand of the marvelous "slipper boats," lie in tiers along the river sides, and packed closely stem and stern along the canals, forming bustling and picturesque water streets. Many of the boats moored on the canals are floating shops, and do a brisk trade, one end of the boat being the shop, the other the dwelling-house. As the "slipper boats" are only fifteen to twenty feet long, it may be imagined, as their breadth is strictly proportionate, that the accommodation for a family is rather circumscribed, yet such a boat is not only the home of a married pair and their children, but of the eldest son with his wife and children, and not infrequently of grandparents also! The bamboo roofs slide in a sort of telescope fashion, and the whole interior space can be inclosed and divided. The bow of the boat, whether large or small, is always the family joss-house; and the water is starred at night with the dull, melancholy glimmer, fainter, though redder than a glowworm's light, of thousands of burning josssticks, making the air heavy with the odor of incense. Unlike the houses of the poor on shore, the house boats are models of cleanliness, and space is utilized and economized by adaptations more ingenious than those of a tiny yacht. These boats, which form neat rooms with matted seats by day, turn into beds at night, and the children have separate "rooms." The men go on shore during the day and do laborer's work, but the women seldom land, are devoted to "housewifely" duties, and besides are to be seen at all hours of day and night flying over the water, plying for hire at the landings, and ferrying goods and passengers, as strong as men, and clean, comely, and pleasant-looking; one at the stern and one at the bow, sending the floating home along with skilled and sturdy strokes. They are splendid boat-women, and not vociferous. These women don't bandage their feet.

. . . Very little indeed is known about them and their customs, but it is said that their morals are low, and that when infanticide was less discouraged than it is now, the river was the convenient grave of many of their newly-born female children. I spent most of one afternoon alone in one of these boats, diving into all canals and traversing water streets, hanging on to junks and "passage boats," and enjoying the variety of river life to the full.

On another day I was carried eighteen miles through Canton on a chair by four coolies, Mr. Smith and his brother walking the whole distance—a great testimony to the invigorating influences of the winter climate. As to locomotion, one must either walk or be carried. A human being is not a heavy weight for the coolies, but it is distressing to see that the shoulders of very many of them are suffering from bony tumors, arising from the pressure of the poles. We lunched in the open air upon a stone table under a banyan-tree at the "Five-storied Pagoda" which forms the north-east corner of the great wall of Canton, from which we looked down upon the singular vestiges of the nearly forgotten Tartar conquest, the walled inner city of the Tartar conquerors, containing the Tartar garrison, the Yamun (official residence) of the Tartar governor, the houses of the foreign consuls, and the unmixed Tartar population. The streets of this foreign kernel of Canton are narrow and dirty, with mean, low houses with tiled roofs nearly flat, and small courtyards, more like the houses of Western than Eastern Asia. These Tartars do not differ much in physiognomy from the Chinese. They are somewhat uglier, their stature is shorter, and the women always wear three rings in their ears. I saw more women in a single street in one day in the Tartar city than I have seen altogether in the rest of Canton.

The view from that corner of the wall (to my thinking) is beautiful, the flaming red pagoda with its many roofs; the singularly picturesque ancient gray wall, all ups and down, watchtowers, and strongholds, the Tartar city below, with the "flowery pagoda," the mosques, the bright foliage of the banyan, and the feathery grace of the bamboo; outside the wall the White-Cloud hills, and nearer ranges burrowed everywhere for the dead, their red and pink and orange hues harmonized by a thin blue veil, softening without obscuring, all lying in the glory of the tropic winter noon—light without heat, color without glare. . . .

Passing through the Tartar city and some streets of aristocratic dullness, inhabited by wealthy merchants, we spent some hours in the mercantile quarter; which is practically one vast market or bazaar, thronged with masculine humanity from morning till night. Eight feet is the width of the widest street but one, and between the passers-by, the loungers, the people standing at stalls eating, or drinking tea, and the itinerant vendors of goods, it is one long *push*. Then, as you are elbowing your feeble self

among the big men, who are made truly monstrous by their many wadded garments of silk and brocade, you are terrified by a loud yell, and being ignominiously hustled out of the way, you become aware that the crowd has yielded place to a procession, consisting of several men in red, followed by a handsome closed palanquin, borne by four, six, or eight bearers in red liveries, in which reclines a stout, magnificently dressed mandarin, utterly oblivious of his inferiors, the representative of high caste feeling all the world over, either reading or absorbed, never taking any notice of the crowds and glitter which I find so fascinating. More men in red, and then the crowd closes up again, to be again divided by a plebeian chair like mine, or by pariahs running with a coffin fifteen feet long, shaped like the trunk of a tree, or by coolies carrying burdens slung on bamboo poles, uttering deafening cries, or by a marriage procession with songs and music, or by a funeral procession with weeping and wailing, succeeding each other incessantly. All the people in the streets are shouting at the top of their voices, the chair and baggage coolies are yelling, and to complete the bewildering din the beggars at every corner are demanding charity by striking two gongs together.

Color riots in these narrow streets, with their high houses with projecting upper stories, much carved and gilded, their deeply projecting roofs or eaves tiled with shells cut into panes, which let the light softly through, while a sky of deep bright blue fills up the narrow slit between. Then in the shadow below, which is fitfully lighted by the sunbeams, hanging from all the second stories at every possible interval of height, each house having at least two, are the richly painted boards of which I wrote before, from six to ten feet long, some black, some heavily gilded, a few orange, but the majority red and perfectly plain, except for the characters several inches long down the middle of each, gold on the red and black, and black on the gold and orange— these, with banners, festoons, and the bright blue draperies which for a hundred days indicate mourning in a house, form together a spectacle of street picturesqueness such as my eyes have never before beheld. Than all the crowd is in costume, and such costume! The prevailing color for the robe is bright blue. Even the coolies put on such a one when not working, and all above the coolies wear them in rich, ribbed silk, lined with silk of a darker shade. Over this a sleeveless jacket of rich dark blue or puce brocade, plain or quilted, is worn, the trousers, of which little is seen, being of brocade or satin. The stockings are white, and the shoes, which are on thick, white, canoe-shaped soles, are of black satin. The cap, which is always worn, and quite on the back of the head, is of black satin, and the pigtail, or plait of hair and purse silk mixed, hangs down nearly to the bottom of the robe. Then the most splendid furs are worn, and any number of quilted silk and brocade garments, one above another. And these big, prosperous-looking men, who are so richly dressed, are only the shopkeepers and the lower class of merchants. The mandarins and the rich merchants seldom put their feet to the ground.

The shops just now are filled with all sorts of brilliant and enticing things in anticipation of the great festival of the New Year, which begins on the 21st. At the New Year they are all closed, and the rich merchants vie with each other in keeping them so; those whose shops are closed the longest, sometimes even for two months, gaining a great reputation for wealth thereby. Streets are given up to shops of one kind. Thus there is the "Jade-Stone Street," entirely given up to the making and sale of jade-stone jewelry, which is very costly, a single bracelet of the finest stone and workmanship costing £600. There is a whole street devoted to the sale of coffins; several in which nothing is sold but furniture, from common folding tables up to the costliest settees, bedsteads, and chairs of massive ebony carving; chinaware streets, book and engraving streets, streets of silk shops, streets of workers in brass, silver, and gold, who perform their delicate manipulations before your eyes; streets of secondhand clothing, where gorgeous embroideries in silk and gold can be bought for almost

nothing; and so on, every street blazing with colors, splendid with costume, and abounding with wealth and variety.

We went to a "dog and cat restaurant," where a number of richly dressed men were eating of savory dishes made from the flesh of these animals. There are thousands of butchers' and fishmongers' shops in Canton. At the former there are always hundreds of split and salted ducks hanging on lines, and pigs of various sizes roasted whole, or sold in joints raw; and kids and buffalo beef, and numbers of dogs and cats, which, though skinned, have the tails on to show what they are. I had some of the gelatinous "birds'-nest" soup, without knowing what it was. It is excellent; but as these nests are brought from Sumatra and are very costly, it is only a luxury of the rich. The fish shops and stalls are legion, but the fish looks sickening, as it is always cut into slices and covered with blood. The boiled chrysalis of a species of silkworm is exposed for sale as a great delicacy, and so are certain kinds of hairless, fleshy caterpillars.

In our peregrinations we came upon a Yamun, with its vestibule hung with scarlet, the marriage color as well as the official color. Within the door the "wedding garments" were hanging for the wedding guests, scarlet silk crêpe, richly embroidered. Some time later the bridal procession swept through the streets, adding a new glory to the color and movement. First marched a troop of men in scarlet, carrying scarlet banners, each one emblazoned with the literary degrees of the bride's father and grandfather. Then came ten heavily gilded, carved, and decorated pavilions, containing the marriage presents, borne on poles on the shoulders of servants; and after them the bride, carried in a locked palanquin to the bridegroom's house, completely shrouded, the palanquin one mass of decoration in gold and blue enamel, the carving fully six inches deep; and the procession was closed by a crowd of men in scarlet, carrying the bridegroom's literary degrees, with banners, and instruments of music. It is the China of a thousand years ago, unaltered by foreign contact.

REVIEW QUESTIONS

1. How would you characterize Bird's description of Canton?
2. How would you characterize her description of native women? What details seemed especially important to her?
3. What was her reaction to the foods she encountered? What does this cuisine tell you about the society she described?
4. Do you think Bird was a careful observer? Why or why not?

Two Chinese Women Oppose Footbinding (early 1900s)

Rules and Regulations on Marriage, Letter from Ch'en Shu-hsien to Ch'en Pan-hsien, and CH'IU CHIN, Address to Two Hundred Million Fellow Countrywomen

Although women have historically and traditionally been suppressed in societies east and west, footbinding seems to have been a custom restricted to the Chinese upper class, probably originating during the Song (Sung) dynasty (960–1280). A young girl's feet were bent back and wrapped so tightly that her arches would break. The result was curved, tiny feet. The rationale for this treatment was the notion that small feet were attractive and indicated genteel breeding. A girl with big feet could not expect a good marriage. Besides being a symbol of class status, there was an element of the erotic attached to tiny, bound feet.

The custom must have drawn criticism, but not until 1895 was a society established specifically to attack the practice. Not surprisingly, it was concurrent with the establishment of a girl's school in Shanghai, a port having considerable interaction with the outside world. It took, of course, many decades for the practice to finally become unpopular; finally, the movement became tied to social and political reform.

The following three selections are from the first decade of the twentieth century. The sources for the first two items are fairly self-evident: regulations for an anti–footbinding society and a letter from a girl to her older sister (later published in a magazine). The third item was written by an educated woman who lived from 1875 to 1907 and was active not only in radical social reform but in revolutionary politics as well. She was executed for her participation in the nationalist revolt.

The issue of footbinding became linked with the larger one of women's rights. Central to this was the matter of education for women, which is also emphasized in all three selections. It continues to be an issue in many parts of the world today. Indeed, a United Nations report in 2001 linked the issue of women's rights to important concerns about our planet's population growth, poverty levels, and environmental problems.

ANTI-FOOTBINDING SOCIETY OF HUNAN: RULES AND REGULATIONS ON MARRIAGE

1. The purpose of organizing this society is to provide opportunities for members to arrange marriages for their children so that girls who do not bind their feet will not become social outcasts. For this reason, society members must register the names and ages of all their children, and this information will be made available to all members in their selection of mates for their children.

2. Every member is entitled to make selections among the registered children. However, marriages with nonmembers' families are allowed if the young ladies do not have bound feet.

3. In selecting mates for their children, members must observe strict compatibility of age and generation. Furthermore, no match can be made unless both families agree to it. No member is allowed to coerce, intimidate, or use any other forms of undesirable persuasion in arranging a marriage.

4. Since society members have come from all parts of Hunan province, marriages can be arranged between families situated very far apart. The society encourages men of vision and determination to willingly send their daughters to distant places to be married.

5. A matchmaker may be engaged to arrange the marriage contract. Local customs and rituals may be followed regarding the exchange of gifts. The society suggests that frugality and simplicity be observed by all members, regardless of how wealthy they are. Furthermore the bride's family is not allowed to demand wedding gifts from the groom.

6. Similarly, in preparing the bride's dowry, the society recommends frugality and simplicity. The groom's family should still observe all the courtesies and should not vent their dissatisfaction with the dowry by ill-treatment of the bride.

7. The marriage ceremony should be discarded because ancient rituals are no longer suitable for today. However, members are allowed to follow the commonly accepted rituals and ceremonies of the Ch'ing dynasty because sometimes, for the sake of expediency, we have to do what others do.

However, the society recommends that members be guided by frugality and simplicity.

8. The clothing worn by members' daughters should conform with the accepted style. However, their footwear should conform to the style of their brothers. There should be no exceptions, because other styles of footwear may be shocking and offensive to other society members, thus injuring the girl's chances for marriage.

9. If people want to have worthy daughters, then they must promote women's education. If men want their wives to be worthy, then they must donate money to establish local women's schools. The size of the school is determined by the amount of the contribution. By helping other people's daughters learn, one also helps one's own wife because only after women's education has been popularized can the foundations of a marriage be solid.

10. The above rules have been written one by one in a very simple and lucid style so they can be easily understood by everyone. If anyone feels he cannot follow any of them, he should not join the society. Furthermore, we urge all applicants to study these rules carefully to avoid future regrets.

A LETTER FROM CH'EN SHU-HSIEN TO CH'EN PAN-HSIEN

When I received your letter of the 13th, I wanted to write back to you immediately. However, something important came up on the following day, and since then I haven't had a free moment. I feel very guilty and ashamed for putting off writing back to you, but I am sure you won't be angry at me; perhaps when I tell you the reason for this delay, you will even be happy for me.

Well, it all started when I heard Shang Yu's speech denouncing footbinding. Afterwards, Eighth Sister and I decided to unbind ours. We told Father and he said that we could do it if we wanted to, but as he saw it, large feet will not be accepted by society as a whole, even though Shang Yu supports it. Furthermore, he said that large feet really aren't very attractive anyway. At the time I thought that, bound feet or no bound feet, I would have to stay in the house all the time anyway since there was no place to go. (I was in An-ch'ing at the time and all the women there had bound feet; besides, An-ch'ing did not have a woman's publication office nor did it have women's schools or organizations to promote women's education and freedom.) So, when I heard Father say that large feet are not very attractive, Eighth Sister and I decided to put it off for a while. Later (back home) I read an article in a women's newsletter published by Miss Chi-fen in which she urged all women to stop binding their feet. At the same time I also heard a speech delivered by Miss Chang Ching-hsien telling us that footbinding is contrary to the principles of Heaven and man and harmful to our country and our people. One by one she eloquently attacked the evils of footbinding. It was such a good speech that since that day I have not bound my feet very tightly. One reason is that the pain is so hard to live with; another is that, although I wasn't able to unbind them then, I hoped to be able to do so someday.

One day sister Ch'a told me that she was going to attend a meeting at the Literary Society School with Wu Ya-nan and Wu Jo-nan and asked me to join them. At first I was reluctant because the girls at the Literary Society School are all well educated and very articulate on the subject of patriotism while I am not. Furthermore, my Mandarin is not fluent so I was afraid that I wouldn't understand anything that was said and I did not want to be embarrassed. Then it occurred to me that nowadays most educated people are passionately patriotic. If they saw that I was not a well-informed person, wouldn't they treat me sympathetically and instruct me? I decided to muster up some courage and go; if I could learn something new or gain a new insight into things, it would be very good for me indeed.

Thus, on Thursday I went with Sister Ch'a and met Jo-nan and Ya-nan and talked with them for a couple of hours. I was very impressed by them. They were most vocal and articulate against footbinding and I felt as if I had listened to a well-prepared lecture. I believe that Sister Ch'a has already written you all about that night so I need

not elaborate upon it. When I went home that night I thought to myself that all the women there are so ambitious, planning to promote women's education and publish newspapers and magazines; some even said that after two more years of study, they are going to An-ch'ing to liberate all the women in our province. This experience left me both elated and ashamed. Chinese women have never considered themselves responsible citizens, and this has made China weak. I felt happy because today women like Miss K'ang, Miss Shih, Miss Ch'a Fan, Miss Ch'ing Ch'i, Miss Chu Chun, Miss Ch'ing-yun, Miss Chin-ch'ing, and Jo-nan, Ya-nan, and you have all vowed to rescue the 200 million Chinese women. We now have our own newspaper, and women's schools are being established one after another. I believe if we all work hard together, we will get our rights and enjoy freedom and equality. However, I was also ashamed of myself because all these years I have failed to acquire any knowledge and I am powerless to educate and influence illiterate and other unfortunate women. I have decided to unbind my own feet because I would be ashamed to go to meet anyone with these ugly bound feet. I discussed this matter with Eighth Sister, and we decided to unbind our feet now and in the fall to enroll in the Literary Society School.

This is what I have decided to do and I don't know whether Heaven will allow me to do it, but I intend to give it my best. Remember you told me once, "If there is a will, there is a way." I will try not to let you down.

You wrote that there are many things you wanted to tell me but you were afraid I'd take offense. You were wrong. If not, then you don't know what is in my heart. As stupid as I am, I still should know what's right and what's good for me, shouldn't I? You told me what has been happening and that everyone should pursue an education. These things are good for me; how can I but like hearing them? You are in school with a very busy schedule but you still took the time to write me. I am very grateful. You said in your letter that if you acted against the teachers' wishes, you would get punished. When I read that I was very angry. But I guess if we are to pursue knowledge, we must swallow our pride and anger, and when we graduate, they can no longer humiliate us. After you get this letter, if you don't have any time, don't worry about writing back to me. You can wait until you find time—I don't mind, really. Although I want you to write me often, I know you are in school every day and you must also write to other people. I would feel uncomfortable and guilty if you were to neglect your school work just to write to me. I still have many things to tell you, but I'll stop here and continue another time, for it's been too long since I got your last letter and you might be worried about me if you don't hear from me soon.

Your sister, Shu-hsien
5th day, fourth month, 1903

AN ADDRESS TO TWO HUNDRED MILLION FELLOW COUNTRYWOMEN

Alas! The greatest injustice in this world must be the injustice suffered by our female population of two hundred million. If a girl is lucky enough to have a good father, then her childhood is at least tolerable. But if by chance her father is an ill-tempered and unreasonable man, he may curse her birth: "What rotten luck: another useless thing." Some men go as far as killing baby girls while most hold the opinion that "girls are eventually someone else's property" and treat them with coldness and disdain. In a few years, without thinking about whether it is right or wrong, he forcibly binds his daughter's soft, white feet with white cloth so that even in her sleep she cannot find comfort and relief until the flesh becomes rotten and the bones broken. What is all this misery for? Is it just so that on the girl's wedding day friends and neighbors will compliment him, saying, "Your daughter's feet are really small"? Is that what the pain is for?

But that is not the worst of it. When the time for marriage comes, a girl's future life is placed in the hands of a couple of shameless matchmakers and a family seeking rich and powerful in-laws. A match can be made without anyone ever inquiring whether the prospective bridegroom is honest, kind, or educated. On the day of the marriage the girl is forced into a red and green bridal sedan chair, and all this time she is not allowed to breathe one word about her future. After her marriage, if the man doesn't do her any harm, she is told that she should thank Heaven for her good fortune. But if the man is bad or he ill-treats her, she is told that her marriage is retribution for some sin committed in her previous existence. If she complains at all or tries to reason with her husband, he may get angry and beat her. When other people find out they will criticize, saying, "That woman is bad; she doesn't know how to behave like a wife." What can she do? When a man dies, his wife must mourn him for three years and never remarry. But if the woman dies, her husband only needs to tie his queue with blue thread. Some men consider this to be ugly and don't even do it. In some cases, three days after his wife's death, a man will go out for some "entertainment." Sometimes, before seven weeks have passed, a new bride has already arrived at the door. When Heaven created people it never intended such injustice because if the world is without women, how can men be born? Why is there no justice for women? We constantly hear men say, "The human mind is just and we must treat people with fairness and equality." Then why do they greet women like black slaves from Africa? How did inequality and injustice reach this state?

Dear sisters, you must know that you'll get nothing if you rely upon others. You must go out and get things for yourselves. In ancient times when decadent scholars came out with some nonsense as "men are exalted, women are lowly," "a virtuous woman is one without talent," and "the husband guides the wife," ambitious and spirited women should have organized and opposed them. When the second Ch'en ruler popularized footbinding, women should have challenged him if they had any sense of humiliation at all. . . . Men feared that if women were educated they would become superior to men, so they did not allow us to be educated. Couldn't the women have challenged the men and refused to submit? It seems clear now that it was we women who abandoned our responsibilities to ourselves and felt content to let men do everything for us. As long as we could live in comfort and leisure, we let men make all the decisions for us. When men said we were useless, we became useless; when they said we were incapable, we stopped questioning them even when our entire female sex had reached slave status. At the same time we were insecure in our good fortune and our physical comfort, so we did everything to please men. When we heard that men liked small feet, we immediately bound them just to please them, just to keep our free meal tickets. As for their forbidding us to read and write, well, that was only too good to be true. We readily agreed. Think about it, sisters, can anyone enjoy such comfort and leisure without forfeiting dearly for it? It was only natural that men, with their knowledge, wisdom, and hard work, received the right to freedom while we became their slaves. And as slaves, how can we escape repression? Whom can we blame but ourselves since we have brought this on ourselves? I feel very sad talking about this, yet I feel that there

is no need for me to elaborate since all of us are in the same situation.

I hope that we all shall put aside the past and work hard for the future. Let us all put aside our former selves and be resurrected as complete human beings. Those of you who are old, do not call yourselves old and useless. If your husbands want to open schools, don't stop them; if your good sons want to study abroad, don't hold them back. Those among us who are middle-aged, don't hold back your husbands lest they lose their ambition and spirit and fail in their work. After your sons are born, send them to schools. You must do the same for your daughters and, whatever you do, don't bind their feet. As for you young girls among us, go to school if you can. If not, read and study at home. Those of you who are rich, persuade your husbands to open schools, build factories, and contribute to charitable organizations. Those of you who are poor, work hard and help your husbands. Don't be lazy, don't eat idle rice. These are what I hope for you. You must know that when a country is near destruction, women cannot rely on the men any more because they aren't even able to protect themselves. If we don't take heart now and shape up, it will be too late when China is destroyed.

Sisters, we must follow through on these ideas!

REVIEW QUESTIONS

1. Why would a reader believe that these authors are radicals? Is there any evidence of a willingness to compromise?
2. How would you describe the tone and content of the letter from Shu-hsien to her sister?
3. What are the main points in Ch'ui Chin's address? In what ways are they relevant in today's world, and beyond China?
4. Find one sentence in each selection that you believe is most essential to its argument, and explain your choice.

A Cosmopolitan American Journalist Remembers His First Day in Japan (1889)

LAFCADIO HEARN, *Glimpses of Unfamiliar Japan*

Lafcadio Hearn, who wrote for newspapers in Cincinnati and New Orleans, was one of the most respected reporters and essayists of the late nineteenth century. When he retired to Japan in 1889 to get away from the gritty newspaper business, he started writing about Japanese culture for magazines such as *Harper's* and the *Atlantic Monthly*. Many of his lectures and articles have been collected and published as books. His essays on Buddhism are among the most insightful and yet easiest to understand ever written by a Westerner. He did not convert, but he was fascinated by Buddhist thought.

Hearn was born in 1850 on the island of Santa Maura in the Ionian Sea to an Irish surgeon stationed in Greece with the British army and a Greek woman renowned for her beauty. Weak health and poor vision plagued him throughout his life. He was educated in Europe and the United States. While he was in Ohio he had an affair (Hearn insisted it was a marriage) with a woman of mixed race, which resulted in his being fired by his newspaper, since Ohio did not recognize mixed marriages. He then moved to Japan and married a Japanese woman. He also took a Japanese name (Yakumo Koizumi) and became a Japanese citizen. In 1896 he was named professor of literature at Tokyo Imperial University. He died of heart failure in 1904 and is buried in Japan. Hearn's attachment to his adopted land was such that one publisher recently noted that "Lafcadio Hearn is almost as Japanese as haiku."

MY FIRST DAY IN THE ORIENT

"Do not fail to write down your first impressions as soon as possible," said a kind English professor whom I had the pleasure of meeting soon after my arrival in Japan: "they are evanescent, you know; they will never come to you again, once they have faded out; and yet of all the strange sensations you may receive in this country you will feel none so charming as these." I am trying now to reproduce them from the hasty notes of the time, and find that they were even more fugitive than charming; something has evaporated from all my recollections of them, —something impossible to recall. I neglected the friendly advice, in spite of all resolves to obey it: I could not, in those first weeks, resign myself to remain indoors and write, while there

was yet so much to see and hear and feel in the sun-steeped ways of the wonderful Japanese city. Still, even could I revive all the lost sensations of those first experiences, I doubt if I could express and fix them in words. The first charm of Japan is intangible and volatile as a perfume.

It began for me with my first kuruma-ride out of the European quarter of Yokohama into the Japanese town; and so much as I can recall of it is hereafter set down.

I

It is with the delicious surprise of the first journey through Japanese streets—unable to make one's kuruma-runner understand anything but gestures, frantic gestures to roll on anywhere, everywhere, since all is unspeakably pleasurable and new—that one first receives the real sensation of being in the Orient, in this Far East so much read of, so long dreamed of, yet, as the eyes bear witness, heretofore all unknown. There is a romance even in the first full consciousness of this rather commonplace fact; but for me this consciousness is transfigured inexpressibly by the divine beauty of the day. There is some charm unutterable in the morning air, cool with the coolness of Japanese spring and wind-waves from the snowy cone of Fuji; a charm perhaps due rather to softest lucidity than to any positive tone,—an atmospheric limpidity extraordinary, with only a suggestion of blue in it, through which the most distant objects appear focused with amazing sharpness. The sun is only pleasantly warm; the jinrikisha, or kuruma, is the most cosy little vehicle imaginable; and the street-vistas, as seen above the dancing white mushroom-shaped hat of my sandaled runner, have an allurement of which I fancy that I could never weary.

Elfish everything seems; for everything as well as everybody is small, and queer, and mysterious: the little houses under their blue roofs, the little shop-fronts hung with blue, and the smiling little people in their blue costumes. The illusion is only broken by the occasional passing of a tall foreigner, and by divers shop-signs bearing announcements in absurd attempts at English. Nevertheless such discords only serve to emphasize reality; they never materially lessen the fascination of the funny little streets.

'Tis at first a delightfully odd confusion only, as you look down one of them, through an interminable flutter of flags and swaying of dark blue drapery, all made beautiful and mysterious with Japanese or Chinese lettering. For there are no immediately discernible laws of construction or decoration: each building seems to have a fantastic prettiness of its own; nothing is exactly like anything else, and all is bewilderingly novel. But gradually, after an hour passed in the quarter, the eye begins to recognize in a vague way some general plan in the construction of these low, light, queerly-gabled wooden houses, mostly unpainted, with their first stories all open to the street, and thin strips of roofing sloping

above each shop-front, like awnings, back to the miniature balconies of paper-screened second stories. You begin to understand the common plan of the tiny shops, with their matted floors well raised above the street level, and the general perpendicular arrangement of sign-lettering, whether undulating on drapery or glimmering on gilded and lacquered signboards. You observe that the same rich dark blue which dominates in popular costume rules also in shop draperies, though there is a sprinkling of other tints,—bright blue and white and red (no greens or yellows). And then you note also that the dresses of the laborers are lettered with the same wonderful lettering as the shop draperies. No arabesques could produce such an effect. As modified for decorative purposes, these ideographs have a speaking symmetry which no design without a meaning could possess. As they appear on the back of a workman's frock—pure white on dark blue—and large enough to be easily read at a great distance (indicating some guild or company of which the wearer is a member or employee), they give to the poor cheap garment a factitious appearance of splendor.

And finally, while you are still puzzling over the mystery of things, there will come to you like a revelation the knowledge that most of the amazing picturesqueness of these streets is simply due to the profusion of Chinese and Japanese characters in white, black, blue, or gold, decorating everything,—even surfaces of doorposts and paper screens. Perhaps, then, for one moment, you will imagine the effect of English lettering substituted for those magical characters; and the mere idea will give to whatever aesthetic sentiment you may possess a brutal shock, and you will become, as I have become, an enemy of the Romaji-Kwai,—that society founded for the ugly utilitarian purpose of introducing the use of English letters in writing Japanese.

II

An ideograph does not make upon the Japanese brain any impression similar to that created in the Occidental brain by a letter or combination of letters,—dull, inanimate symbols of vocal sounds. To the Japanese brain an ideograph is a vivid picture: it lives; it speaks; it gesticulates. And the whole space of a Japanese street is full of such living characters,—figures that cry out to the eyes, words that smile or grimace like faces.

What such lettering is, compared with our own lifeless types, can be understood only by those who have lived in the farther East. For even the printed characters of Japanese or Chinese imported texts give no suggestion of the possible beauty of the same characters as modified for decorative inscriptions, for sculptural use, or for the commonest advertising purposes. No rigid convention fetters the fancy of the calligrapher or designer: each strives to make his characters more beautiful than any others; and generations upon generations of artists have been toiling from time immemorial with like emulation, so that through centuries and centuries of tireless effort and study, the primitive hieroglyph or ideograph has been evolved into a thing of beauty indescribable. It consists only of a certain number of brush-strokes; but in each stroke there is an undiscoverable secret art of grace, proportion, imperceptible curve, which actually makes it seem alive, and bears witness that even during the lightning-moment of its creation the artist felt with his brush for the ideal shape of the stroke *equally along its entire length,* from head to tail. But the art of the strokes is not all; the art of their combination is that which produces the enchantment, often so as to astonish the Japanese themselves. It is not surprising, indeed, considering the strangely personal, animate, esoteric aspect of Japanese lettering, that there should be wonderful legends of calligraphy, relating how words written by holy experts became incarnate, and descended from their tablets to hold converse with mankind.

III

My kurumaya calls himself "Cha." He has a white hat which looks like the top of an enormous mushroom; a short blue wide-sleeved jacket; blue drawers, close-fitting as "tights," and reaching to his ankles; and light straw sandals bound upon his bare feet with cords of palmetto-fibre. Doubt-less he typifies all the patience, endurance, and insidious coaxing powers of his class. He has already manifested his power to make me give him more than the law allows; and I have been warned against him in vain. For the first sensation of having a human being for a horse, trotting between shafts, unwearyingly bobbing up and down before you for hours, is alone enough to evoke a feeling of compassion. And when this human being, thus trotting between shafts, with all his hopes, memories, sentiments, and comprehensions, happens to have the gentlest smile, and the power to return the least favor by an apparent display of infinite gratitude, this compassion becomes sympathy, and provokes unreasoning impulses to self-sacrifice. I think the sight of the profuse perspiration has also something to do with the feeling, for it makes one think of the cost of heart-beats and muscle-contractions, likewise of chills, congestions, and pleurisy. Cha's clothing is drenched; and he mops his face with a small sky-blue towel, with figures of bamboo-sprays and sparrows in white upon it, which towel he carries wrapped about his wrist as he runs.

That, however, which attracts me in Cha—Cha considered not as a motive power at all, but as a personality—I am rapidly learning to discern in the multitudes of faces turned toward us as we roll through these miniature streets. And perhaps the supremely pleasurable impression of this morning is that produced by the singular gentleness of popular scrutiny. Everybody looks at you curiously; but there is never anything disagreeable, much less hostile in the gaze: most commonly it is accompanied by a smile or half smile. And the ultimate consequence of all these kindly curious looks and smiles is that the stranger finds himself thinking of fairy-land. Hackneyed to the degree of provocation this statement no doubt is: everybody describing the sensations of his first Japanese day talks of the land as fairy-land, and of its people as fairy-folk. Yet there is a natural reason for this unanimity in choice of terms to describe what is almost impossible to describe more accurately at the first essay. To find one's self suddenly in a world where everything is upon a smaller and daintier scale than with us,—a world of lesser and seemingly kindlier beings, all smiling at you as if to wish you well,—a world where all movement is slow and soft, and voices are hushed,—a world where land, life, and sky are unlike all that one has known elsewhere,—this is surely the realization, for imaginations nourished with English folklore, of the old dream of a World of Elves.

REVIEW QUESTIONS

1. How would you describe Hearn's style of writing?
2. What is the value of knowing that this is a report of the author's first day in Japan?
3. How do Hearn's powers of observation show?
4. Do you think a Japanese would have made the connection with Cha that Hearn achieved? Explain.

An American Reporter Spends 120 Hours in Japan (1890)

Nellie Bly's Book

Nellie Bly was the pen name of Elizabeth Jane Cochrane, who in 1864 was born into a prominent family in a small Pennsylvania town. Her father, a judge, died when Elizabeth was just six. He left no will, so his widow did not inherit his estate. She soon remarried, hoping for security for her children. Instead, her new husband was abusive, which may explain Elizabeth's hesitation to marry, her strident feminism, and her fierce sense of social justice.

When she was eighteen, Cochrane wrote a letter to the editor of a Pittsburgh newspaper objecting to an article about the "women's sphere." The letter so impressed the editor that he hired her. Since she was a woman entering what was very much a man's profession at the time, it was felt necessary to protect her with a pseudonym. The title of a popular song by Stephen Foster, "Nellie Bly," was chosen.

In 1887 Nellie Bly talked her way into the office of the editor of Joseph Pulitzer's *New York World* and landed herself a job. Pulitzer's newspaper was radically innovative for the times: it included comic strips in color, a sports page, a tabloid format, and an approach designed to appeal to the working class and immigrant population. It focused on sensationalism, but with substance: it relied on hard-hitting investigative reporting, known then as "muckraking." Bly was a perfect fit. On one occasion she got herself committed to an insane asylum to report the conditions therein. The result was a grand jury investigation into the treatment of the mentally ill. She also reported on conditions in sweatshops—again, undercover.

In 1890, Pulitzer's newspaper decided to send a reporter around the world in fewer than the 80 days of Jules Verne's famous 1873 novel. Bly bristled at the assumption that the reporter must be a man, and she threatened to go around the world for a rival newspaper if she were not selected for the assignment. Pulitzer recognized the publicity he and his newspaper would receive if he sent a woman; Bly made the trip around the globe in 72 days. During her trip she spent 120 hours in Japan. The following selection is from her account of her stay there.

In 1895 Bly married Robert Livingston Seaman, an industrialist; she was about thirty, and he was about eighty. When he died about ten years later, Bly tried unsuccessfully to run his business. Not only was she ignorant about commerce, but she tried to give her employees benefits that were far ahead of her time (a recreation center, a library, elimination of piecework). After this failure Bly wanted to escape her situation, and in 1914 found herself in England. When World War I broke out, she started reporting it, but in 1919, because of her mother's ill health, she returned home. She died in 1922.

I always have an inclination to laugh when I look at the Japanese men in their native dress. Their legs are small and their trousers are skin tight. The upper garment, with its great wide sleeves, is as loose as the lower is tight. When they finish their "get up" by placing their dishpan shaped hat upon their heads, the wonder grows how such small legs can carry it all! Stick two straws in one end of a potato, a mushroom in the other, set it up on the straws and you have a Japanese in outline. Talk about French heels! The Japanese sandal is a small board elevated on two pieces of thin wood fully five inches in height. They make the people look exactly as if they were on stilts. These queer shoes are fastened to the foot by a single strap running between toes number one and two, the wearer when walking necessarily maintaining a sliding instead of an up and down movement, in order to keep the shoe on.

On a cold day one would imagine the Japanese were a nation of armless people. They fold their arms up in their long, loose sleeves. A Japanese woman's sleeves are to her what a boy's pockets are to him. Her cards, money, combs, hair pins, ornaments and rice paper are carried in her sleeves. Her rice paper is her handkerchief, and she notes with horror and disgust that after using we return our handkerchiefs to our pockets. I think the Japanese women carry everything in their sleeves, even their hearts. Not that they are fickle—none are more true, more devoted, more loyal, more constant than Japanese women—but they are so guileless and artless that almost any one, if opportunity offers, can pick at their trusting hearts.

If I loved and married, I would say to my mate: "Come, I know where Eden is," and like Edwin Arnold, desert the land of my birth for Japan, the land of love—beauty—poetry—cleanliness. I somehow always connected Japan and its people with China and its people, believing the one no improvement on the other. I could not have made a greater mistake. Japan is beautiful. Its women are charmingly sweet. I know little about the men except that they do not go far as we judge manly beauty, being undersized, dark, and far from prepossessing. They have the reputation of being extremely clever, so I do not speak of them as a whole, only of those I came in contact with. I saw one, a giant in frame, a god in features; but he was a public wrestler.

The Japanese are the direct opposite to the Chinese. The Japanese are the cleanliest people on earth, the Chinese are the filthiest; the Japanese are always happy and cheerful, the Chinese are always grumpy and morose; the Japanese are the most graceful of people, the Chinese the most awkward; the Japanese have few vices, the Chinese have all the vices in the world; in short, the Japanese are the most delightful of people, the Chinese the most disagreeable.

The majority of the Europeans live on the

bluff in low white bungalows, with great rooms and breezy verandas, built in the hearts of Oriental gardens, where one can have an unsurpassed view of the Mississippi bay, or can play tennis or cricket, or loll in hammocks, guarded from public gaze by luxurious green hedges. The Japanese homes form a great contrast to the bungalows. They are daintily small, like play houses indeed, built of a thin shingle-like board, fine in texture. Chimneys and fire places are unknown. The first wall is set back, allowing the upper floor and side walls to extend over the lower flooring, making it a portico built in instead of on the house. Light window frames, with their minute openings covered with fine rice paper instead of glass, are the doors and windows in one. They do not swing open and shut as do our doors, nor do they move up and down like our windows, but slide like rolling doors. They form the partitions of the houses inside and can be removed at any time, throwing the floor into one room.

They have two very pretty customs in Japan. The one is decorating their houses in honor of the new year, and the other celebrating the blossoming of the cherry trees. Bamboo saplings covered with light airy foliage and pinioned so as to incline towards the middle of the street, where meeting they form an arch, make very effective decorations. Rice trimmings mixed with sea-weed, orange, lobster and ferns are hung over every door to insure a plentiful year, while as sentinels on either side are large tubs, in which are three thick bamboo stalks, with small evergreen trees for background.

In the cool of the evening we went to a house that had been specially engaged to see the dancing, or *geisha,* girls. At the door we saw all the wooden shoes of the household, and we were asked to take off our shoes before entering, a proceeding rather disliked by some of the party, who refused absolutely to do as requested. We effected a compromise, however, by putting cloth slippers over our shoes. The second floor had been converted into one room, with nothing in it except the matting covering the floor and a Japanese screen here and there. We sat upon the floor, for chairs there are none in Japan, but the exquisite matting is padded until it is as soft as velvet. It was laughable to see us trying to sit down, and yet more so to see us endeavor to find a posture of ease for our limbs. We were about as graceful as an elephant dancing. A smiling woman in a black kimono set several round and square charcoal boxes containing burning charcoal before us. These are the only Japanese stoves. Afterwards she brought a tray containing a number of long-stemmed pipes—Japanese women smoke constantly—a pot of tea and several small cups.

Impatiently I awaited the *geisha* girls. In the tiny maidens glided at last, clad in exquisite trailing angel-sleeved kimonos. The girls bow gracefully, bending down until their heads touch their knees, then kneeling before us murmur gently a greeting which sounds like *"Kombanwa!"* drawing in their breath with a long, hissing suction, which is a token of great honor. The musicians sat down on the floor and began an alarming din upon *samisens,* drums and gongs, singing meanwhile through their pretty noses. If the noses were not so pretty I am sure the music would be unbearable to one who has ever heard a chest note. The *geisha* girls stand posed with open fan in hand above their heads, ready to begin the dance. They are very short, with the slenderest of slender waists. Their soft and tender eyes are made blacker by painted lashes and brows; their midnight hair, stiffened with a gummy wash, is most wonderfully dressed in large coils and ornamented with gold and silver flowers and gilt paper pom-pons. The younger the girl the more gay is her hair. Their kimonos, of the most exquisite material, trail all around them, and are loosely held together at the waist with an obi-sash; their long flowing sleeves fall back, showing their dimpled arms and baby hands. Upon their tiny feet they wear cunning white linen socks cut with a place for the great toe. When they go out they wear wooden sandals. The Japanese are the only women I ever saw who could rouge and powder and be not repulsive, but the more charming because of it. They powder their faces and have a way of reddening their under lip just at the tip that gives them a most tempting look. The lips took like two luxurious cherries. The musicians begin a long chanting strain, and these bits of beauty begin the dance. With a grace, simply enchanting, they twirl their little fans, sway their dainty bodies in a hundred different poses, each one more intoxicating than the other, all the while looking so childish and shy, with an innocent smile lurking about their lips, dimpling their soft cheeks, and their black eyes twinkling with the pleasure of the dance. After the dance the *geisha* girls made friends with me, examining, with surprised delight, my dress, my bracelets, my rings, my boots—to them the most wonderful and extraordinary things—my hair, my gloves, indeed they missed very little, and they approved of all. They said I was very sweet, and

urged me to come again, and in honor of the custom of my land—the Japanese never kiss—they pressed their soft, pouting lips to mine in parting.

Japanese women know nothing whatever of bonnets, and may they never! On rainy days they tie white scarfs over their wonderful hairdressing, but at other times, they waddle bareheaded, with fan and umbrella, along the streets on their wooden clogs. They have absolutely no furniture. Their bed is a piece of matting, their pillows, narrow blocks of wood, probably six inches in length, two wide and six high. They rest the back of the neck on the velvet covered top, so their wonderful hair remains dressed for weeks at a time. Their tea and pipe always stand beside them, so they can partake of their comforts the last thing before sleep and the first thing after.

REVIEW QUESTIONS

1. How would you characterize Bly's descriptions of Japanese men? Japanese women? Did she favor either gender?
2. How did Bly compare the Chinese to the Japanese?
3. What response did she have to the "pretty customs" of new year decorations and cherry blossoms? What does this reveal about her values? About native values?
4. What did Bly think of the *geisha* girls? What does this reveal about her values? About native values?
5. Remembering that Bly was only in Japan for 120 hours, how would you characterize her powers of observation? What kinds of subjects seemed to interest her the most?

A British Author Describes High Society in Tokyo (c. 1890)

MARY FRASER, *Letters from Japan*

Mary Crawford was born in 1851 in Italy. Her parents were American (her father, Thomas Crawford, designed the Washington Monument), but she considered Italy as her first home. Later in life she was to describe Japan as her second home. She grew up in a highly cultured environment that included literary figures such as the Brownings, Longfellow, and Hans Christian Andersen. She was educated in England.

After Mary married Hugh Fraser, a British diplomat, in 1874, she spent much of her time writing books about the places where her husband was posted, including Beijing, Santiago, and Vienna. In 1889 the Frasers moved to Tokyo, and Mary fell in love with Japan, where, she said, "beauty thrives." Her writings on Japan were extensive and have been described as possessing "a delicate, fresh and unprejudiced view of Japan and the Japanese in Meiji times." One of her books, *A Diplomat's Wife in Japan,* has been turned into a play, *The Chrysanthemum and the Rose.* The following selection, from her *Letters from Japan,* contrasts her observations of diplomatic functions and Japanese high society with, as she put it, "the life of the streets."

Our visit to the Empress was followed by several dinners at the houses of the Ministers. One does not learn much of Japanese life at these feasts, which are, as far as their appointments go, for all the world like official dinner parties in Rome or Paris or Vienna; but it is startling to find oneself between the host and some other big official, neither of whom will admit that he can speak a word of any European language. I believe they understand a great deal more than they like to confess for fear of being called upon to speak. There is generally an interpreter within hail, and three or four times in the course of the dinner my neighbour solemnly leans forward and instructs him to address a polite remark about the weather or the flowers to me, and I answer in the same three-cornered fashion, and then subside into silence once more. But the silence does not bore me. The new faces, the old historical names, the remembered biography of some hero who perhaps sits opposite to me in gold-laced uniform calmly enjoying the *foies-gras* and champagne as if there were never a blood-stained page in his country's history—all this appeals strongly to one's dramatic appreciations.

The women are really attractive with their pretty shy ways and their broken confidences about the terror of getting into European clothes. Some of them look wonderfully pretty even in these uncongenial garments. There is Countess Kuroda, for instance, the wife of the Prime Minister, who has lovely diamonds, and always appears in white satin with snowy plumes set in her dark hair. She can talk a little English, and is intensely polite about everything European, as all the little ladies are; but I fancy in their hearts they put us down as big clumsy creatures with loud voices and no manners. The very smart people here affect the most impassive countenance and a low voice in speaking; and all the change of tone and play of expression which we consider so attractive is condemned in Japan as only fit for the lower classes, who, by the way, are the most picturesque and amusing lower classes that Heaven has yet created. My daily drives in Tokyo are as full of fun and interest as was my first jinriksha ride in Nagasaki. The distances are enormous, and it often happens that I make a journey of three or four miles between one visit and another; but every step of the way brings me to some new picture or new question, reveals some unimagined poetry or bit of fresh fun in daily life. There are parties of little acrobats, children in charge of an older boy, who come tumbling after the carriage in contortions which would be terrible to see did one not feel convinced that Japanese limbs are made of India-rubber. Then there are the pedlars; the old-clothes sellers; the pipe-menders, who solemnly clean a pipe for one rin as they sit on the door-step; the umbrella-makers, who fill a whole street with enormous yellow parasols drying in the sun. Here a juggler is swallowing a sword, to the delight and amazement of a group of children; there the seller of *tofu,* or bean-curd, cuts great slabs of the cheesy substance, and wraps it in green leaves for his customers to carry away. I love watching the life of the streets, its fulness and variety, its inconvenient candour and its inexplicable reticences. I am always sorry to come in, even to our lovely home with its green lawns and gardens in flower. It is like leaving a theatre before the piece is over, and one wonders if one will ever see it again.

I went to a garden party the other day, given by Count Ito on the occasion of his daughter's marriage with a rising politician, Mr. Kenchio Suyematsu. The wedding had, however, taken place some days before. The Count's villa at Takanawa is close to the sea, or as much of the sea as comes into the almost land-locked Tokyo Bay. The house stands on high ground, which overlooks Shinagawa and the Hama Rikyu Palace, the Empress's summer house, built half in the sea like poor Maximilian's villa at Mira-mar near Trieste. Count Ito's garden slopes down to the sea-level, clothed in a dark-green mantle of lordly pines with red-gold branches, lighted here and there by a cloud of rosy fruit blossom, ethereal as mist shone through by the sun. The views over sea and land are lovely, and we had plenty of time to wander from one point to another, taking it all in. There were crowds of people in brightly tinted dresses; but I saw hardly any Japanese costumes, even Countess Ito's

youngest daughter being in European dress. No one seems to talk much at these gatherings; there is a tremendous feast, where we are all placed strictly according to precedence, and are expected to eat and drink as if it were eight o'clock in the evening instead of four in the afternoon! Count Ito has the cleverest face I have ever seen; it is not noble or elevated in any way, which is not strange, perhaps, since he did not originally belong to the higher class of Japanese, but for sheer intelligence and power I have seen few to beat it. Countess Ito is a very attractive woman, with a fine delicate face, and of course charming manners.

I am slowly learning to know one person from another in this big new circle. I heard a Japanese say that all foreigners looked alike to him, and I confess that for the first two weeks of my stay here I felt like a colley with a new flock of sheep. Now that the personalities are revealing themselves to me, I find my way about them fairly well.

REVIEW QUESTIONS

1. Which did Fraser seem to prefer, high society or street life? How can you tell?
2. How would you describe the tone and content of her letters? Is it obvious that she loves Japan? Why or why not?
3. What did she mean by the statement that initially she "felt like a colley with a new flock of sheep"?

A Japanese Novelist Portrays a Son's Reaction to His Father's Death and Funeral (1906)

SHIMAZAKI TOSON, *Hakai (The Broken Commandment)*

The influences that shaped Shimazaki Toson (1872–1943) and his writing were both Japanese and European. In addition to following the Japanese poetic diary tradition, he paid close attention to the development of European realism. In his fiction, individuals react both to their own internal emotions and to the worlds of nature and human society. Shimazaki's first major work, from which the following selection is taken, was the novel *Hakai* (*The Broken Commandment,* 1906), in which a young man has to deal with his relationship to society in terms of his moral and spiritual values. The author had been reading Leo Tolstoy, and the novel reflects that influence.

The central figure of the novel is a member of the *eta,* or pariah class of Japan, a group whose situation is comparable to that of the untouchables in India. In 1871 discrimination and even the use of the word *eta* was outlawed. The novel is set twenty years later, with subtle—and sometimes not so subtle—discrimination still continuing, as it does to varying degrees even today. The twenty-three-year old hero has been commanded by his father never, under any circumstances, to reveal that he is an *eta.* As a result, he is able to achieve modest success in life, but his sympathy for the plight of the individual *eta* results in his renunciation of the vow he made to his late father. The novel was an instant success, in part because of increasing interest in social problems among the Japanese.

He would never forget the loneliness of that trip. He had been home two summers before, but this time, as he followed the river toward Nezu, it was as though he had become a different person. A little over two years, not a long time when he thought of it; but in those years violent changes had begun in his life. Some people may move naturally and gradually away from the world, not knowing when exactly the change came; but for Ushimatsu the spiritual upheaval was violent and profound.

There was no need here to hold himself in. He could breathe the dry air freely, he could give himself up to sorrow at his ill-starred birth and to astonishment at the changes in his life. The water, stirred to a yellow-green, flowing noiselessly toward the distant sea, the leafless willow branches seemed to cower over the bank—ah, the mountain river was just as it had always been.

Now and then he passed a party of mountain travelers. Some had the faces of the ruined and slunk by like famished dogs. Others, barefoot with dirty kimonos pulled about them, might have been looking for work. A sunburned father and son, bells in hand and voices raised in a sad canticle, had chosen the rigors of the pilgrim's way. A group of wandering performers in battered sunshades—they too seemed to be fleeing the world—would play a love tune as the mood took them and beg a penny along the way. Ushi-

matsu stared at them all, comparing them with himself. How he envied even them, free to wander as they would.

But presently he began to feel as though he too were moving into a freer world. Warmed by the brilliant sunlight, he walked the ash-colored earth of the old north country road, now up a hill, now past a mulberry patch, now and again through a town with its houses lining the road. He was sweating heavily, his throat was dry, his feet and ankles were gray with dust; and yet, strangely, he felt his spirits reviving. The branches of the persimmons bent low under their loads of yellow jewels, burrs hung from the chestnut trees, beans were swelling in their pods, and here and there the sprouting winter barely showed through the stubble in the fields. Songs of farmers near and far, birds—it was the "little June," the Indian summer of the mountains. Peaks towered clear in the distance, and volcanic smoke rose blue from the deep-shadowed valleys between. . . .

The mountains in the dying light of the evening changed from red to purple, purple to brown, and as the hills and the moors grew dark the shadows crept up from valley to valley, and the last sunlight shone from the peaks. In a corner of the sky wavered a brown cloud tinged with gold, the smoke from Mt. Asama it must have been.

His happiness, if such it was, did not last. He came to the edge of a wild valley, and there, strung out over the face of the mountain beyond, white walls and earthen walls in the evening sun, dark spots, possibly persimmons, between the roofs of the mountain houses—ah, it was Nezu. Even the songs of the farmers on their way home from work added to his agitation. As he thought of his father's life, how he had left the hamlet of outcasts at Komoro and come to this obscure mountain village to live out his days, the twilight scenery quite lost its charm. It was dark when he reached Nezu.

His father had died, not there but at the herdsman's hut in the West Mouth pasture. While Ushimatsu rested by the fire, his uncle, in that genial, unassertive way of his, talked of the dead man. The fire in the hearth was strong. Ushimatsu's aunt sniffled as she listened again to the story. His father had died from an accident at his post, so to speak, and not from illness or old age. It had not seemed possible that so experienced a herdsman could make a mistake with cattle. Life is unpredictable, however, and an unfortunate chain of circumstances had begun when a bull was unexpectedly added to the herd. The freedom of the wide pasture and the calls of the cows had set the animal wild, and in the end it had lost all traces of domestication and disappeared into the mountains. Three days, four days passed. Ushimatsu's father began searching through the tall grass, but found no trace of it.

He had set out again the day before. He always took along his lunch when he planned to go far, but this time for some reason he left without it. He did not come back when he should have. The young herdsman who helped him climbed to the corral to put out salt, and in with the herd gathered happily around was the bull, quite as though it had never been away. Its horns were stained with blood. The shocked herdsman called some passers-by to help tie the animal up—and perhaps because it was already exhausted, it offered little resistance. After a long search he found Ushimatsu's father moaning in a growth of dwarf bamboo and carried him back to the hut. The wound was beyond treating, but Ushi-matsu's father was still fully conscious when the uncle arrived at the hut. He lived until ten that evening. The wake was to be tonight. Mourners were gathered at the hut now, waiting for Ushimatsu.

"And that is how it was." His uncle paused and looked at Ushimatsu. "I asked him if he had anything to say. He was in pain but his mind was clear. 'I'm a herdsman,' he said, 'and it's right I should die working with cattle. There's nothing much else to say. Ushimatsu, though—everything I've done has been for him. I made him give me a promise once. When he comes back tell him not to forget.'"

Ushimatsu listened with bowed head to his father's last message. His uncle went on. "'And I want to be buried here in the pasture. Don't have the funeral in Nezu. Have it here if you can. And don't tell them at Komoro that I'm dead. Please.' I nodded and said I understood. He lay there smiling up at me, and after a while there were tears in his eyes. He didn't say anything more."

Ushimatsu was deeply moved. The desire to be buried in the pasture, the instructions against having the funeral in Nezu and sending word to Komoro, proved that to the end his father had been thinking of him. To the end he had shown the extreme caution that had governed his life, and the intense determination that had kept him from abandoning what he had once set out upon. His sternness with Ushimatsu had gone to the point of cruelty. Indeed Ushimatsu was afraid of his father, even now that he was dead.

Presently Ushimatsu and his uncle set out for the West Mouth pasture. The funeral arrangements were all made. The autopsy was over, the coffin had been bought, and an old priest from a temple in Nezu had already gone up for the wake. Ushimatsu had only to be present. It was a mile and a half over a lonely mountain road to the pasture. The darkness seemed to clutch at their faces, it was impossible to see even their feet. Ushimatsu went ahead, guiding his uncle by the light of a lantern. The path grew narrower as they walked out from the village, dwindling in the end to a faint line of footsteps through the fallen leaves. It was a path

Ushimatsu as a boy had often traveled with his father.

The little hut was crowded with people. Light leaked through cracks in the walls, and the priest's wooden drum, echoing on the mountain air, blended with the murmuring of the brook to make the quiet seem yet more intense. The hut was no more than a shelter to keep off the rain and the dew. Except for travelers who went over the mountain to the hot springs beyond, there were few visitors here from outside. This was the harsh world of the forest ranger, the charcoal-maker, and the herdsman.

Ushimatsu put out the lantern and went into the hut with his uncle. The old priest, the village guildsmen who had come to help, and the farm men and women who had been friends of the dead man greeted Ushimatsu with appropriate words of consolation. Altar candles lighted the night through clouds of incense. The little room seemed cluttered, confused. The rough wooden coffin was draped in a white cloth, and before it stood a newly inscribed memorial tablet, offerings of water and sweets, and bunches of chrysanthemums and anise leaves. A pause came in the prayers. On a signal from the priest the mourners, tears streaming down their faces, went up in turn to take leave of the old herdsman. Ushimatsu, following his uncle, bowed slightly to look down at his father for the last time. In the dim candlelight the face seemed to say that the lonely herdsman's life was over and there remained but to lie deep in the earth of the pasture. Ushimatsu's uncle, faithful to the old way of doing things, had provided for the journey to the next world a sunshade and a pair of straw sandals. A knife to ward off devils lay on the lid of the coffin. The praying and the beating of the drum began again, and talk of the dead man, punctuated by artless laughter and the clatter of dishes, was sad and at the same time lively.

So the night passed. There had been those last instructions not to send word to Komoro, and it was seventeen years since the dead man had left the town. No message was sent, no one came

from that hamlet of outcasts. Ushimatsu's uncle was on tenterhooks, even so, lest word somehow reach Komoro that the old "chief" was dead, and an embarrassing mission arrive for the funeral. Ushimatsu's father had long thought of being buried in the pasture, his uncle said. It might be that a temple funeral would be allowed to pass like any other farm funeral, but there was always a possibility that the body would be turned away. By custom members of the pariah class could not be buried in ordinary cemeteries. For Ushimatsu's sake his father had endured the privations of life in the mountains, and for Ushimatsu's sake he had chosen to rest here in the pasture.

The following afternoon the mourners gathered in and around the hut. The owner of the pasture, the dairyman who kept his cattle there, everyone who had heard of the death, came to pay respects. The grave had been dug under a small pine tree atop a hill in the pasture. Presently the time came to commit the body, and the old herdsman was carried from the hut he had known so well. The priest followed the coffin with a pair of mischievous-looking acolytes behind him. Ushimatsu wore straw sandals like his uncle. The women all had white cloths around their heads. There were as many fashions of dress as there were mourners. Some wore formal cloaks, some homespun. The lack of display seemed in keeping with the rough life of the herdsman. There was no order to the procession, no ceremony. There was only the valedictory of honest hearts as the group moved quietly over the pasture.

The service at the hut, too, had been simple, and yet the plain rhythm of drum and bell and the mechanical chanting of the requiem had been a moving elegy to one caught up in memories.

The last of the late-blooming daisies had been trampled to the ground by the gravediggers. When each of the mourners had thrown down a handful of earth, making a little heap, it was shoveled roughly into the grave. It struck the lid of the coffin with a rumble as of an avalanche, sending out a pungent smell to call up thoughts almost unbearable. The grave filled, a mound grew up over it. Ushimatsu watched, sunk in thought, to the end. His uncle too was silent. Do not forget, his father had commanded with his dying words; and now his father was deep under the earth of the pasture.

Somehow they had come through safely. Leaving the owner of the pasture to look after the grave, and the young herdsman to take care of the hut, the mourners started back for the village. Ushimatsu thought of taking along the black cat his father had kept at the hut, but it was cold to his overtures. When he offered food, it refused to eat; when he called, it refused to come. They could hear it mewing forlornly under the veranda. Beast though it was, it seemed to miss its dead master. How would it live, they wondered, what would it find to eat when snow began to fall in the mountains? "Maybe the poor thing will go wild," said Ushimatsu's uncle.

One by one they started back. The young herdsman went along, carrying salt for the cattle, to see them as far as the corral. A wan November sun made the West Mouth pasture seem lonelier than ever. Low pines grew here and there along the way. In the spring the hills were blanketed with white mountain azalea, which the cattle refused to eat, but now there was only the withered grass. Everything brought memories to Ushimatsu of his father. He remembered how toward the end of May two years before he had visited his father in this pasture. He remembered that it had been the season when the horns of the cattle were itching and these withered azaleas were blooming in a wild profusion of reds and yellows. He remembered the children gathering spring herbs. He remembered the calls of the mountain doves. He remembered the pleasant breeze that had blown over the lilies of the valley and brought the scent of early summer. He remembered how his father had pointed to the new green on the hills and described the advantages of the West Mouth for grazing. He remembered the stories his father had told, of like animals that herded together, of jousts with horns when a new animal entered

the herd, of the sanctions cattle apply to each other, of queens that had ruled the herd.

Ushimatsu's father had retired to the obscurity of the mountains, but all his life he had burned with a desire for fame and position. Quite unlike his genial brother, he had nursed a smoldering anger: his birth kept him from working his way ahead in the world; very well, he would withdraw to the mountains. And if he could not have the things he wanted for himself, he would have them for his children and his children's children. Even on the day the sun began coming up in the west that determination at least must not change. Go, fight, make your way in the world—his father's spirit lived in those words. As Ushimatsu thought over that lonely life, he felt more and more deeply the passion and the hope in the message his father had left behind. Death is mute, and yet it spoke now with the force of a thousand and ten thousand words to make Ushimatsu meditate on his life and destiny.

From the corral he could look back at the work his father had left. Cattle were scattered among the low pines, and in the corral itself were a number of still hornless calves. The young herdsman, mindful of his duties as host, started a fire from dead grass and went about gathering fuel. The mourners who were left had been up all the night before, and their labors today had been strenuous. Several of them half-dozed with the smell of burning leaves in their nostrils.

Ushimatsu's uncle put out little heaps of salt for the cattle, and Ushimatsu watched with a certain tenderness as he thought how near his father had been to the animals. The herd circled at a distance with quivering noses. A black cow flicked its tail, a white-faced red shook its ears, a brindle calf mooed. Two or three edged a little closer. They would as soon have their salt, but what of this uninvited audience? Ushimatsu's uncle laughed, Ushimatsu laughed too. With such entertaining companions it might be possible to live in these remote mountains.

Presently they took their leave of the ground where Ushimatsu's father would rest forever. The high mountains fell away behind them. As they passed the Fuji Shrine Ushimatsu turned back to look again at his father's grave, but even the corral was out of sight. He could see, beyond that lonely pasture it would be, only a column of smoke trailing off into the sky.

REVIEW QUESTIONS

1. Even in dying, the father protects his son. Why? How?
2. What is the symbolic significance of the burial in the pasture?
3. How would you describe the relationship between father and son?
4. What is the significance of the father's nearness to animals and his intentional distancing from society?
5. Does the image of Japanese society presented in this novel contradict or reinforce the image of Japan that you have formed from the travelers' accounts in this chapter?

7

South and Southwest Asia, 1800–1918

When the Portuguese sent Vasco da Gama around the southern tip of Africa to India in 1498, they hoped that his journey would eliminate, or at least reduce, the role that Muslim traders played in Asian commerce. His journey was reinforced by a second aspiration, to convert Asians to Christianity. Da Gama could not have reached India without the benefit of Portuguese expertise in shipbuilding, navigation, and weaponry, especially as those fields developed under the direction of Prince Henry the Navigator. Europe's technological superiority over Asia continued from the "Age of Exploration" through the "Age of Imperialism," which reached its apex in the decades prior to World War I. Europeans also continued to buttress their technological advantages with ideology. During this period, Social Darwinism gained prominence in Europe, fostering the belief that white people were superior to others, as were their civilization and religion; thus, the political conquest and exploitation of "inferior" peoples was beneficial for both the rulers and the ruled. One famous expression of the Europeans' belief in their superiority over others, and indeed their moral obligation to enlighten inferiors, came from the English writer and Nobel Laureate Rudyard Kipling, who characterized Europe's colonial subjects as "half-devil and half-child" and called for Americans to exercise the "white man's burden" in the Philippines (as had the British in India): that is, to assume the responsibilities of imperialism by governing a non-Western society.

European contact with Indian cultures followed this pattern. To the great English historian, member of Parliament, and antislavery crusader Thomas Babington Macaulay, Indian culture was nothing more than "false history, false astronomy, false metaphysics, and false religion." He wrote the famous "Minute on Education" in 1835, which mandated English-style education in British India, rather than that based on Sanskrit and Persian. His purpose was to "civilize India." As a result, Western education made rapid progress among the upper-class elite. The irony was that Macaulay's dictum made possible, perhaps even inevitable, the education of future independence leaders, like Mohandas K. Gandhi and Jawaharlal Nehru, in Western liberalism, nationalism, and parliamentary democracy.

However, any chapter on travelers' views of South and Southwest Asia would distort the historical record if it were confined merely to descriptions of Western arrogance and attitudes of superiority. Although this attitude did predominate (as some selections in this chapter illustrate), there were Westerners who had empathy with and respect for the peoples and cultures they encountered. John Lloyd Stephens, for example, had an appreciation of the culture and history of the Jews in Jerusalem. Much like his countryman Stephens, Mark Twain had an open mind and an honest interest in other cultures. Perhaps not many of Twain's contemporaries would have possessed his sensitivity or powers of observation in regard to such an unfamiliar custom as the Parsis' disposal of their dead. Rabbi d'Beth Hillel had an insider's interest in the Jewish communities of India. His writing, too, revealed a sympathetic feeling for cultural differences: Jewish communities, while sharing Judaism, were far from being alike.

In addition to these three men, this chapter includes observations about Indian society written by two Englishwomen. Emma Roberts expressed genuine interest in India, but she was reserved in her views and activities, perhaps because of personal circumstances. Helen Douglas Mackenzie was less approving of India than Roberts. She sometimes appeared to be dispassionate—even cold—toward her subject.

The chapter also includes letters by India's only Nobel Laureate in literature, Rabindranath Tagore, scion of one of the most important Bengali families in commerce and culture during the period of British rule. Bengali arts and literature had an ancient and rich tradition, and since Calcutta (Kolkata) was the capital of British India, a cultural fusion was to be expected. The result was the Bengali Renaissance. Tagore, who considered himself a cosmopolitan rather than a nationalist, combined an appreciation of western culture with an almost romantic outlook in regard to rural Bengal and its people. Although he was a resident of Calcutta, in the selection herein we see a deep-seated awareness of and attachment to rural Bengal.

An American Archaeologist Observes Jews in Jerusalem (1835–1836)

JOHN LLOYD STEPHENS, *Incidents of Travel in Egypt, Arabia Petraea, and the Holy Land*

John Lloyd Stephens (1805–1852) was a lawyer, diplomat, and archaeologist who published several books about his travels and explorations. While traveling in the Middle East from 1835 to 1836, he became interested in the archaeology of the region, which resulted in two two-volume books, supplemented with drawings by the English archaeologist Frederick Catherwood. A few years later the two collaborated on two books describing the Maya ruins of Central America. Stephens had heard of the ruins while on a diplomatic mission to the area. Intrigued, he and Catherwood searched for them in the jungle. Their discovery resulted in another two books, and Stevens was praised for having "generated the archeology of Middle America."

Stephens, however, had interests that went beyond ruins and archaeology: he was fascinated by contemporary cultures and places as well. His observations of them have been described as "refreshing" for their sensitivity on the one hand, and their blunt objectivity on the other; he would express genuine sympathy for a people, then use derogatory terms to describe their holy site. At the same time, he put distance between himself and the events and circumstances that he neither appreciated nor approved.

In the following selection Stephens shows appreciation for hospitality, awareness of bias and cruelty toward Jews, and respect for what Jews experienced "under the Assyrian, the Roman, the Arab, and the Turk." He also expresses admiration for the cultural "law" that holds the community together.

THE JEWS OF JERUSALEM

The reader may remember the kindness with which I had been received by the chief rabbi at Hebron. His kindness did not end there; a few days after my arrival, the chief rabbi of Jerusalem, the high-priest of the Jews in the city of their ancient kings, called upon me, accompanied by a Gibraltar Jew who spoke English, and who told me that they had come at the request of my friend in Hebron, to receive and welcome me in the city of their fathers. I had already seen a great deal of the Jews. I had seen them in the cities of Italy, everywhere more or less oppressed; at Rome, shut up every night in their miserable quarters as if they were noxious beasts; in Turkey, persecuted and oppressed; along the shores of the Black Sea and in the heart of Russia, looked down upon by the serfs of the great empire of vassalage; and, for the climax of misery, I had seen them condemned and spit upon even by the ignorant and enslaved boors of Poland. I had seen them scattered abroad among all nations, as it had been foretold they would be, everywhere a separate and peculiar people; and everywhere, under all poverty, wretchedness, and oppression, waiting for, and anxiously expecting, the coming of a Messiah, to call together their scattered tribes, and restore them to the kingdom of their fathers; and all this the better fitted me for the more interesting spectacle of the Jews in the holy city. In all changes and revolutions, from the day when the kingdom of Solomon passed into the hands of strangers, under the Assyrian, the Roman, the Arab, and the Turk, a remnant of that once-favoured people has always hovered around the holy city; and now, as in the days of David, old men may be seen at the foot of Mount Zion, teaching their children to read from that mysterious book on which they have ever fondly built their hopes of a temporal and eternal kingdom.

The friends made for me by the rabbi at Hebron were the very friends above all others whom I would have selected for myself. While the Christians were preparing for the religious ceremonies of Easter, the Jews were making ready for the great feast of the Passover; and one of the first offers of kindness they made me was an invitation to wait and partake of it with them. The rabbi was an old man, nearly seventy, with a long white beard, and Aaron himself need not have been ashamed of such a representative. I would have preferred to attach myself particularly to him; but, as I could speak neither Arabic nor Hebrew, and the English Jew was not willing to play second, and serve merely as interpreter, I had but little benefit of the old man's society.

The Jews are the best topographers in Jerusalem, although their authority ends where the great interest of the city begins; for, as their fathers did before them, they deny the name of Christ, and know nothing of the holy places so anxiously sought for by the Christians. The same morning they took me to what they call a part of the wall of Solomon's temple. It forms part of the southern wall of the mosque of Omar, and is evidently older than the rest, the stones being much larger, measuring nine or ten feet long; and I saw that day, as other travellers may still see every Friday in the year, all the Jews in Jerusalem clothed in their best raiment, winding through the narrow streets of their quarter; and under this hallowed wall, with the sacred volume in their hands, singing, in the language in which they were written, the Songs of Solomon and the Psalms of David. White-bearded old men and smooth-cheeked boys were leaning over the same book; and Jewish maidens, in their long white robes, were standing with their faces against the wall and praying through cracks and crevices. . . .

About nine o'clock the next morning I was with him [the English Jew] and in a few moments we were sitting in the highest seats in the synagogue, at the foot of Mount Zion. My old friend the rabbi was in the desk, reading to a small remnant of the Israelites the same law which had been read to their fathers on the same spot ever since they came up out of the land of Egypt. And there they sat, where their fathers had sat before them, with high, black, square-topped caps, with shawls wound around, crossed in front, and laid very neatly; long gowns fastened with a sash, and long beards, the feeble remnant of a mighty people; there was sternness in their faces, but in their hearts a spirit of patient endurance, and a firm and settled resolution to die and be buried under the shadow of their fallen temple.

By the Jewish law the men and women sit apart in the synagogues; and, as I could not understand the words of exhortation which fell from the lips of the preacher, it was not altogether unnatural that I should turn from the rough-bearded sons of Abraham to the smooth faces of their wives and daughters. Since I left Europe, I had not been in an apartment where the women sat with their faces uncovered; and, under these circumstances, it is not surprising that I saw many a dark-eyed Jewess who appeared well worthy of my gaze; and it is not a vain boast to say, that while singing the songs of Solomon, many a Hebrew maiden turned her bright black orbs upon me; for, in the first place, on entering we had disturbed more than a hundred sitting on the steps; secondly, my original dress, half Turk, half Frank, attracted the eyes even of the men; and, thirdly, the alleged universal failing of the sex is not wanting among the daughters of Judah.

The service over, we stopped a moment to look at the synagogue, which was a new building, with nothing about it that was peculiar or interesting. It had no gold or silver ornaments; and the sacred scroll, the table of the law, contained in the holy of holies, was all that the pride of the Jew could show. My friend, however, did not put his own light under a bushel; for, telling me the amount he had himself contributed to the building, he conducted me to a room built at his own expense for a schoolroom, with a stone in the front wall recording his name and generosity.

We then returned to his house; and, being about to sit down to dinner with him, I ought to introduce him more particularly to the reader. He was a man about fifty-five, born in Gibraltar to the same abject poverty which is the lot of most of his nation. In his youth he had been fortunate in his dealings, and had been what we

call an enterprising man; for he had twice made a voyage to England, and was so successful, and liked the country so much, that he always called himself an Englishman. Having accumulated a little property, or, as he expressed it, having become very rich, he gratified the darling wish of his heart by coming to Jerusalem, to die and be buried with his fathers in the Valley of Jehoshaphat. But this holy purpose in regard to his death and burial did not make him undervalue the importance of life, and the advantages of being a great man now. He told me that he was rich, very rich; that he was the richest, and in fact, the only rich Jew in Jerusalem. He took me through his house, and showed me his gold and silver ornaments, and talked of his money and the uses he made of it; that he lent to the Latin Convent on *interest,* without any security, whenever they wanted; but as for the Greeks—he laughed, laid his finger on his nose, and said he had in pledge jewels belonging to them of the value of more than twenty thousand dollars. He had had his losses too; and while we were enjoying the luxuries of his table, the leaven of his nature broke out, and he endeavoured to sell me a note for fifteen hundred pounds of the Lady Esther Stanhope [the eccentric Englishwoman who had established herself on Mount Lebanon], which he offered at a discount of fifty per cent; a bargain which I declined, as being out of the line of my business. . . . I have never regretted not having shaved the note of the Queen of the East, in the hands of the richest Jew in Jerusalem.

It was Saturday, the Jewish Sabbath. The command to do no work on the Sabbath day is observed by every Jew, as strictly as when the commandment was given to his fathers; and to such an extent was it obeyed in the house of my friend, that it was not considered allowable to extinguish a lamp which had been lighted the night before, and was now burning in broad daylight over our table . . . I must not forget the Jew's family, which consisted of a second wife, about sixteen, already the mother of two children, and his son and son's wife, the husband twelve, and the wife ten years old. The little gentleman was at the table, and behaved very well, except that his father had to check him in eating sweetmeats. The lady was playing on the floor with other children, and I did with her what I could not have done with a bigger man's wife— I took her on my knee and kissed her. Among the Jews, matches are made by the parents; and, immediately upon the marriage, the wife is brought into the household of the husband. A young gentleman was tumbling about the floor who was engaged to the daughter of the chief rabbi. I did not ask the age of the lady, of course; but the gentleman bore the heavy burden of three years. He had not yet learned to whisper the story of his love to his blushing mistress, for, in fact, he could not talk at all; he was a great bawling boy, and cared much more for his bread and butter than a wife; but his prudent father had already provided him.

REVIEW QUESTIONS

1. How does Stephens show sensitivity toward the customs of the Jews of Jerusalem?
2. How does he show an awareness of the history of Jews in Europe?
3. In what ways does he emphasize individualism, as opposed to group stereotypes?

A Lithuanian Rabbi Examines Jewish Life in India (1824–1832)

RABBI DAVID D'BETH HILLEL, *Unknown Jews in Unknown Lands*

From at least the time of the Romans, Jews and others from the eastern Mediterranean acted as commercial agents along the central and southwestern coast of India. Although scholars do not know how long Judaism had existed in southwest India, it can be inferred that Jews have lived there at least since the first century C.E. To Hindus, Jews were just another element in the diverse mix, especially in the area that stretched from Kerala (the state in southwest India) to Bombay.

Jews in Bombay have been able to trace their ancestry back for many centuries. Congregations in Kerala likewise have a long history. Yet such continuity should not be mistaken for uniformity or cultural isolation. Rabbi d'Beth Hillel was well aware of the divisions within Judaism in India. His acceptance of Judaism within the Indian religious milieu is also impressive, especially when compared with the Western tendency to dismiss native Indian religions as "pagan."

The rabbi traveled in India from October 1828 to August 1832 as part of a journey through several lands. He left his native Lithuania in 1824, traveling through eastern Europe, the Middle East, and then to India. It appears he became a British subject while in India. Later he visited India twice again, probably in 1837 and 1845, and he died in Calcutta in 1846. His motives for extensive travel seemed to be personal rather than religious. When asked his purpose, he told an Indian raja that it was "merely to see the world." Of course, he may have wished not to get into a prolonged discussion about motives with a Hindu ruler, for his writings reveal a great deal of curiosity about Jewish communities. His inquiries are of a scholarly and comparative nature, involving culture, ethnicity, and sectarian practices.

THE JEWS IN COCHIN AND THEIR DIVISION

There were here about 200 families of White Jews when I was there. They have a very fine synagogue paved with porcelain from China. It is so fine that it does not perhaps exist in any parts of Europe and Turkey which I have traveled hither. The Dutch presented the synagogue with an excellent clock for which a separate tower is built. It is richly endowed with garden lands. On festival days there is a grand display of gold and silver ornaments, some of which are placed upon the manuscripts as they are carried from the Holy Ark to the pulpit where the law is read and occasionally explained.

In the time of the Dutch the *White Jews* were great and wealthy merchants, but they have since that time sunk weak and are even in a miserable state, living chiefly by the sale of trinkets and furnitures purchased in more fortunate days.

They are too proud to work for their livelihood, but spend their time chiefly in making visits. Even the reading of the Holy Scriptures is not usual with them. But some families still retain their landed property in value from about two thousand to ten thousand rupees. Their marriages, like those of the Hindus, are attended with considerable expense as to deter many young men from marrying. They double the number of days of matrimonial feasting, customary among the Jews according to Genesis, ch. xxix, v. 27.

One of the privileges granted to them in their ancient charter is the royal distinction of bridegrooms wearing a golden chain, and the firing of guns during the fourteen days of the wedding festivity. This charter is engraved in copper in the Malayalam language and characters. It was granted by the five contemporary kings whose signatures are affixed, and from whom they are allowed by this charter to make converts. Another privilege is the holding of their paternal lands from the crown at half the annual acknowledged value which would be due from the same lands. If any other Jew or foreign White Jew may purchase these lands they retain the privilege which would be lost if the property should pass to another class of people.

I do not know the date of this copper charter, but have reason to suppose that the White Jews arrived there some little time before the Portuguese, for I have met in parts of Europe with persons of the same family names as those in Cochin, as for instance the Rothenburgs, Sarfathis, Ashkenazis, and Sargons, etc. They have no manuscripts more than two or three centuries old.

The *Black Jews* in Cochin and the surrounding villages, viz., *Ernakulam, Chennamangalam* (Shenoth), and *Mala,* consist of about 1,500 families. They have six synagogues, two in Cochin, two in Ernakulam, and one in Chennamangalam and one in Mala. These are neat buildings. The ornaments for the manuscript are few but handsome. The Black Jews are good people, and most of them are engaged in mechanical employments. There are no agriculturists among them. Even their garden grounds are cultivated by the Hindus; many are in easy circumstances, and scarcely a poor man is to be found among them. Yasoni, a ship builder, is reputed to be very rich and is in every point a respectable man.

The Black Jews are much more respectable for moral character and conduct than the White Jews. They are in general well acquainted with the Hebrew scriptures, which they readily translate into Malayalam and as far as circumstances allow they walk according to the law. They have not among them a single priest or a Levite. The White Jews say of them that they are descendants of numerous slaves who were purchased and converted to Judaism, set free, and carefully instructed by a White Jew some centuries ago; at his cost they say were all their old synagogues erected. The Black Jews believe themselves to be the descendants of the Israelites of the first captivity who were brought to India and did not return with the Israelites who built the Second Temple. This account I am inclined to believe correct; though called Black Jews they are of somewhat darker complexion than the White Jews, yet they are not of the colour of the natives of the country or of persons descended from Indian slaves.

Besides the White Jews are two other classes, one called in Hebrew *Meshuhrarim,* the other *Avadim.* Both classes were formerly slaves, the Meshuhrarim are those who have been emancipated; when one of the Avadim obtains his freedom from his master a written document in testimony thereof is granted to him under the seal of the synagogue, for which the master or the emancipated person pays forty-one rupees. I have remonstrated against the existence of slavery in a place under the British government which has declared slavery to be unlawful, and the precept regarding the articles of property is according to the Jewish Talmud: *Dina d'malchuta dina,* meaning, "The law of the state is law." My remonstrance however excited only displeasure. I was asked, "Why do you wish to deprive us of our property?" Persons of one class have not intermarried with families of the other three classes, although fornications are by no means uncommon. . . .

A Cochin White Jew, by name Judah Ashkenazi (a German family name), told me that many years ago a Cochin Black Jew, whom he as a child had seen, went to China, and when there accompanied some of the inhabitants to a fair held without the walls of a large town. The people of this town came outside for the purpose of traffic but would not suffer any of the strangers to enter into their gates. On seeing the Jew and learning from him who he was, they professed that they also were Jews to whom the whole of the country on that side of the river belongs. They would not permit him to go within the gate, but brought out food for him, and among other things flesh boiled in milk. Of this he refused to partake. He asked them how they if

Jews could use food which is not customary for the Jews in India and other parts of the world to eat. They replied that Moses only forbids the seething of a kid in mother's milk; this flesh was not boiled in the mother's milk and therefore not unlawful to eat. He said according to the rules of the Talmud, flesh must not be eaten with milk of any kind. They replied, "Who is greater, Moses or the Talmudists?" He then ate what was set before him; and ever since afterwards used similar food, saying in reply to every remonstrance, "Who is greater, Moses or the Talmudists?"

THE ARABIAN JEWS [IN BOMBAY]

There are about 20 families of Jews collected from Arabia who have hired a small house from a Parsee for divine service. These Jews from Arabia are dominated over by Solomon Yakob, a rich man and the first Arabian Jew who established himself in Bombay. He is a man of a bad disposition and notorious character, and having no means to injure those who disapprove his evil practices. On this account the Jews who speak their mind freely enough of him in his absence are careful to assent to all his saying; he is extravagant and is conciliated by flatterers even of the grossest kind. I had not been accustomed to such dishonorable subterfuges and I am a man who worships only my Creator. For this cause and on account of my refusing to conform to their unlawful usages which they have learnt from the Arabs and Hindus, and concerning which there is a prohibition in Leviticus, ch. xviii, v. 3: "In their statutes," etc. I was the object of his persecution.

I stayed there very discontentedly, owing to the Arabian Jews and Arabs, for on exhibiting myself with a beard and English dress, they thought I was an Arab who had been proselytized to Christianity, and I was in consequence many times badly treated by them in the streets, and in my own dwelling.

I tried two or three times to go and complain of this matter to Mr. Gray, who was then the Police-Master at Barcot, but I could not get access to his presence, owing to his head writer being a Hindu, who wanted a bribe, and most of his peons are Mahometans, all of whose work is done by bribery, and this I say not of opinion but by proof, as they had charged me. Once I complained to Mr. Dewytry who was the magistrate in the fort when I was there. The offenders were brought before him, but I did not receive full justice, because they do not trouble themselves to sit long and enquire into the cause properly. I said that I could prove all these things by witnesses but they would not attend to it, as it would take a long time; but since then, I was not importuned by them so much.

THE BENE ISRAEL

There are native Jews who call themselves *"Bene Israel,"* about 600 families who are separated from all the nations in their manners and customs, and will not take even water from another caste. They are circumcised and sanctify the day of atonement, but no other customs belonging to the Mosaic law. They were formerly very ignorant of the Hebrew language, having not a single book, but they were well acquainted with the Marathi books and language; but since the Arabian Jews came to Bombay, they commenced to learn some of the Hebrew language and purchased some of the Hebrew books.

About five or six years ago the "Madras Jewish Society" established a school among them for the purpose of training up their children in the Hebrew language. They had no synagogue before, but some years ago a fine synagogue was built by one of them named Samuel, who was a captain on the Honorable Company's Army. He was a very rich man and childless; therefore he caused this synagogue to be built with many

houses around it, the rent of which is to be appropriated for the sundry expenses of the synagogue. It is denominated in the native language "Masjad Bene Israel," and it is situated at Barcot, not far from the custom-house; there are no manuscripts. They are accustomed to marry their children when very young from three years and upward, to marry two or three children at once. Some of them are very rich, and many of them are in the Honorable Company's army; most of them are artificers; scarcely a poor man is to be found among them.

In the Marathi countries around Bombay are about 8,000 families of them; no one Levite or priest among the whole of them. I tried very much to make out from whence they came there, but it was not possible to trace it properly, because they have no chronicle, but only some traditions; even these are not written, it is merely oral. Some of them say that after the destruction of Jerusalem by Titus, seven vessels full of Israelites arrived on the Marathi Coast, which is very near to Bombay, and when the vessels were lying at anchor, a storm arose and all the vessels were lost; and from all of them were only saved seven families, of whom they sprung out. Some say only one family, but I cannot incline to this, as it is not mentioned in any of our histories that in the time of Titus, Jews proceeded to India. But I conjecture that they are from those which are related in the book entitled "Kuzri Rishon," which gives a history of one Jew who about eight or nine hundred years ago, having come to King Kuzari, had a great argument about religion; after that the king himself and all his subjects were converted to Judaism and very likely these are their descendants.

REVIEW QUESTIONS

1. Rabbi d'Beth Hillel was fully aware of the language of Kerala, Malayalam. What does this say about his approach to Indian culture?
2. In what ways does he show an awareness of diversity within the Jewish community?
3. What topics concerning Indian Jews seemed to have interested Rabbi d'Beth Hillel the most? Why do you think this was so?

An English Newspaper Editor Describes Crowds in Delhi (1837)

EMMA ROBERTS, *Scenes and Characteristics of Hindostan*

Born into a military family in 1794 near Leeds, England, Emma Roberts showed an interest in India, but she was reserved about venturing into the country. From her mother she inherited a love of writing, and her prose has been described by one critic as comparable to photography, capturing "facsimiles" and dealing with "the surface of things." She took an interest in people and became involved in trying to improve the education of Indian women.

In 1828, upon the death of her mother, with whom she had been living, Roberts joined her sister and brother-in-law in India. He was an officer in the Bengal Infantry, and she found her dependency upon him debilitating or, as she herself put it, "wretched." The situation was especially problematic because he was frequently sent to different locations. After her sister's death she took the job of editor of an English newspaper in Calcutta. In 1832, exhausted from overwork, she went back to England, only to return to India again in 1839. She quickly became ill again (in 1840) and was taken to Poona (Pune) because of its favorable climate. Roberts died there in September 1840.

During her time in Calcutta and in England, Roberts pursued her own writing interests: poetry and accounts of her travels and observations. In 1839 she published a practical book of travel advice. Her writings were little appreciated by her contemporaries but were nevertheless recognized for their astute observations.

PICTURESQUE CROWDS

The crowd of an Indian city, always picturesque, is here [in Delhi] particularly rich in showy figures of men and animals; elephants, camels, and horses, gaily caparisoned, parade through the streets, jingling their silver ornaments, and the many-coloured tufts and fringes with which they are adorned: the *suwarree* of a great personage sweeping along the highways, little scrupulous of the damage it may effect in its progress, forms a striking spectacle viewed from some safe corner, or from the back of a tall elephant. The *coup-d' oeil* is magnificent; but to enter into details might destroy the illusion; for, mingled with mounted retainers, richly clothed, and armed with glittering helmets, polished spears, and shields knobbed with silver, crowds of wild-looking half-clad wretches on foot are to be seen, increasing the tumult and the dust, but adding nothing to the splendour of the cavalcade. No great man—and Delhi is full of personages of pretension—ever passes along in state without having his titles shouted out by the stentorian lungs of some of his followers. The discordant songs of itinerant musicians, screamed out to the accompaniment of the tom-tom, with an occasional bass volunteered by a *chetah,* grumbling out in a sharp roar his annoyance at being hawked about the streets for sale, with the shrill distressful cry of the camel, the trumpetings of the elephants, the neighing of horses, and the rumbling of cart-wheels, are sounds which assail the ear from sunrise until sunset in the streets of Delhi. The multitude of equipages is exceedingly great, and more diversified, perhaps, than those of any other city in the world. English carriages, altered and improved to suit the climate and the peculiar taste of the possessor, are mingled with the palanquins and bullock-carts open and covered, chairs, and cage-like and lanthorn-like conveyances, of native construction. Prince Baber, the second surviving son of the reigning monarch, drives about in an English chariot drawn by eight horses, in which he frequently appears attired in the full-dress uniform of a British general officer, rendered still more striking by having each breast adorned with the grand cross of the Bath. Mirza Sale, another of the princes of the imperial family, escorts a favourite wife in a carriage of the same description; the lady is said to be very beautiful but the blinds are too closely shut to allow the anxious crowd a glimpse of her charms. Regular English coaches, drawn by four horses, and driven by postillions, the property of rich natives, appear on the public drives and at reviews; and occasionally a buggy or cabriolet of a very splendid description may be seen, having the hood of black velvet, embroidered with gold. The *chetahs* and hunting leopards, before-mentioned, are led hooded through the streets; birds in cages, Persian cats, and Persian greyhounds, are also exposed in the streets for sale, under the superintendence of some of those fine, tall, splendid-looking men, who bring all sorts of merchandize from Cashmere, Persia, and Thibet, to the cities of Hindostan—an almost gigantic race, bearing a noble aspect in spite of the squalidness of their attire, and having dark, clear complexions, without a tinge of swarthiness. Beggars in plenty infest the streets; and, in addition to the multitudes brought together by business, there are idle groups of loungers—Mussulmans of lazy,

dissipated, depraved habits, gaudily decked out in flaunting colours, with their hair frizzled in a bush from under a glittering skullcap, stuck rakishly at the side of the head.

Such are a few of the distinguishing features of Chandeny Chowke [Chandni Chowk], which abounds in hardware, cloth, *paan,* and pastry-cooks' shops, the business, as usual, carried on in the open air, with all the chaffering, haggling, and noise common to Asiatic dealings. How anything of the kind is managed, amidst the bustle and confusion of the streets, the throng of bullock-carts, the strings of loaded camels, the squadrons of wild horses, the trains of elephants, and the insolent retainers of great men, only intent upon displaying their own and their master's consequence, by increasing the uproar, seems astonishing. The natives of India form an extraordinary compound of apathy and vivacity. In the midst of noises and tumult which would stun or distract the most iron-nerved European in the world, they will maintain an imperturbable calmness; while in ordinary matters, where there appears to be nothing to disturb their equanimity, they will vociferate and gesticulate as if noise and commotion were absolutely essential to their happiness.

By a very little attention to order and comfort, the Chandeny Chowke might be rendered one of the most delightful promenades in the world; the famous canal of Delhi, shaded by fine trees, runs down the centre, and nothing could be more easy than to allay the clouds of dust, at present so intolerable, by keeping the avenues on either side well watered.

REVIEW QUESTIONS

1. How do you see the quality of "photography" reflected in this selection?
2. How did Roberts go beyond this quality of "photography" to reveal her sensitivity?
3. Do the English conveyances detract or add to the Indian scenes described by Roberts? Explain your opinion.

A Scottish Woman Observes a Wedding Procession in Delhi (1847)

HELEN DOUGLAS MACKENZIE, *Life in the Mission, the Camp, and the Zenana; or, Six Years in India*

Helen Mackenzie, who signed herself as Mrs. Colin Mackenzie, was a member of a Scottish clan renowned for writing and for service to the "Raj," or the British Empire in India. The following account, of an event in 1847, is fairly straightforward, even though elsewhere she expressed disapproval of all things Indian, lamenting that Indians—men, women, and children—did not have "the least sense of decency." She viewed India as a corrupt influence on Englishmen and stated that Indian boys should be "instructed *exactly* as Christian boys would be." This opinion was by no means unusual for Britons in nineteenth-century India. Despite this attitude, Mackenzie was capable of observing a great deal.

At the end of the selection is a reference to Matthew 35:10 (actually 25:10). This passage reads, "And while they went to buy, the bridesgroom came; they that were ready went in with him to the marriage: and the door was shut."

A MARRIAGE PROCESSION

[To see the procession, at] about five o'clock we drove to a house in the Chandi Chouk, belonging to one of the native sub-collectors, a Mussalman, who had prepared seats for us, whence we could see everything. The Chandi Chouk is a double street, and divided down the middle by a stone watercourse, the edges of which were crowded with people. The procession was passing down the side furthest from us, and turning at the top of this immense street, it paraded before the bride's house, which was a little way above us, and then came close under our windows. It was more than a mile long! The balconies and flat roofs of the houses, which are generally low, were covered with people; here was a variegated group of men and children, there a bevy of shrouded Muhammadan women, the first I have seen, and the appearance of the crowd was that of a bed of tulips.

Just as we had seated ourselves numbers of empty palkis were passing, then a crowd of Ton-jons, some empty, some with one or two children in them. Many of these were gorgeously dressed in brocade or velvet with Greek caps of gold and silver, and some of them were borne by four men in scarlet, and attended by a man on each side, with Chouries of the tail of the Yak or Thibet Ox, to keep the flies off. All the friends of the bridegroom's family do him as much honour as they can, by sending their led-horses, elephants, vehicles of every description, and their children richly dressed, to form part of the procession. The ladies of the King's harem were there in bullock carts, with scarlet hangings, to see the show. His Majesty had also sent his guards, and his camels carried small swivel cannon, which were fired at intervals. The led-horses formed a very picturesque feature in the procession; some of them were painted; a white one had his legs and tail dyed red with henna, and splashes of the same on his body, as if a bloody hand had been repeatedly laid on his side. Then came a whole body of men clothed like soldiers, at the Rajah's expense, with a band that was executing a Scotch melody. Then appeared a whole tribe of magnificent elephants, their faces elaborately painted in curious patterns, and gaily caparisoned in scarlet, green, and other bright colours.

On a small baby-elephant, most richly adorned, sat a little boy, with an aigrette of jewels, in front of his turban. His dress was a robe of lilac gauze, edged with gold, reaching to his feet, and most carefully spread out, fan-wise, on each side, as he sat astride on his elephant. Then came the little bridegroom, who was a mass of gold. He sat alone in his howdah, with a careful servant behind him; his turban was covered with a veil of gold tissue, which he held up with both hands, that he might see all that was going on. Bearers of peacock fans, and others with gold pillars, walked by him, while his elephant was as splendid as he could be. A few other elephants closed the procession, the beginning of which now passed under our window on its return. It consisted of huge trays filled with artificial flowers, the effect of which, as we looked down the street, was extremely pretty, like a parterre of the gayest colours. Then there were moving pavilions, with beds of flowers in front of them, peacocks on the top, and bands of musicians inside. Such music! fancy flutes in hysterics, drums in a rage, violins screaming with passion, and penny trumpets distracted with pain, and you may have some idea of it. A crowd of women and boys of the poorest of the people, then appeared, carrying little flags.

Eastern processions are like Eastern life, they comprise the greatest contrasts of poverty and magnificence. They seem to think everything, no matter what, helps to make a show. After, and among the moving flower-beds, came trays of huge dolls, and others of little puppets, one set of which represented a party of European officers at dinner, with their Khitmadgars waiting behind them. Another was a little regiment of soldiers such as children play with at home. Suddenly the mob rushed in upon the bearers, and down went the trays; one snatched a great doll, which, in the struggle had a leg pulled off; he seized the dissevered limb, whirled it round his head like a shillelah, and valiantly defended the rest of his prize with it. The trays were seen swaying about till they were torn in pieces, and the fortunate ones rejoiced in having got a bunch of flowers, or perchance a doll's limb. I believe they are stuffed with some kind of sweetmeat, and the people think it lucky to get any fragment of these trays, which are always given up to be scrambled for, after they have passed the house of the bride. It was the first time I had seen the natives in a state of excitement, and I certainly thought they managed the scramble with much good humour, and nothing like the angry fighting that would have taken place in England on a similar occasion.

After this appeared several nauch girls, splendidly dressed in red and gold, their muslin petticoats full of gathers, and very wide, and their long hair hanging down their backs, each carried on a canopied platform, by men. One of them was very handsome, but they stood in theatrical attitudes, beckoning, smiling, and joking with the populace, and had a boldness of manner most unpleasing in a woman. By this time it was dusk, and the blaze of torches opposite the bride's house was very pretty, as seen through the trees, of which there are a good many in the middle of the street. We returned to the carriage, and drove to a spot opposite the house; the bridegroom soon arrived, and looked most brilliant by the glare of the torches. We watched him slowly entering the gateway, and which was immediately shut, reminding us strongly of Mat. xxxv. 10. It was very interesting to *see* it. (1847)

REVIEW QUESTIONS

1. Do you think Mackenzie was a careful observer? Why or why not?
2. How would you compare this selection with the previous one by Emma Roberts?

An Indian Nobel Laureate Describes a Bengali Village (1891)

RABINDRANATH TAGORE, *Glimpses of Bengal*

Rabindranath Tagore (1861–1941) was the grandson of the founder of modern Bengal's most prominent family. His grandfather was Dwarkanath Tagore (1794–1846), entrepreneur and industrialist, who helped make possible the cultural explosion known as the Hindu Renaissance and the Bengal Renaissance, which was led to a considerable extent by his son Debendranath Tagore (1817–1905).

Rabindranath was awarded the Nobel Prize for literature in 1913 and was knighted by the British in 1915, which honor he renounced in 1919 after the massacre of Indian civilians at Amritsar. His abilities as a novelist, poet, dramatist, and essayist were matched by his talents in painting and music. Two nations (India and Bangladesh) have taken his music and poetry as their national anthems. Throughout his work—literature, music, and painting—runs a mystical streak and deep-rooted love for traditional village society. The latter characteristic can be seen in the following selection, as can his ability to observe individual behavior.

A characteristic often noted about this giant of twentieth-century literature and art is his internationalism: his drama reflects a knowledge of Western theater, Sanskrit classical drama, and Bengali folk opera. Even more remarkable is his ability to express the basics of life; he once said, "Every child comes with the news that God is not yet discouraged with mankind."

Nearing Shazadpur, January 1891.

We left the little river of Kaligram, sluggish as the circulation in a dying man, and dropped down the current of a briskly flowing stream which led to a region where land and water seemed to merge in each other, river and bank without distinction of garb, like brother and sister in infancy.

The river lost its coating of sliminess, scattered its current in many directions, and spread out, finally, into a *beel* (marsh), with here a patch of grassy land and there a stretch of transparent water, reminding me of the youth of this globe when through the limitless waters land had just begun to raise its head, the separate provinces of solid and fluid as yet undefined.

Round about where we have moored, the bamboo poles of fishermen are planted. Kites hover ready to snatch up fish from the nets. On the ooze at the water's edge stand the saintly-looking paddy birds in meditation. All kinds of waterfowl abound. Patches of weeds float on the water. Here and there rice-fields, untilled, untended, rise from the moist, clay soil. Mosquitoes swarm over the still waters. . . .

We start again at dawn this morning and pass through Kachikata, where the waters of the *beel* find an outlet in a winding channel only six or seven yards wide, through which they rush swiftly. To get our unwieldly house-boat through is indeed an adventure. The current hurries it along at lightning speed, keeping the crew busy using their oars as poles to prevent the boat being dashed against the banks. We thus come out again into the open river.

The sky had been heavily clouded, a damp wind blowing, with occasional showers of rain. The crew were all shivering with cold. Such wet and gloomy days in the cold weather are eminently disagreeable, and I have spent a wretched lifeless morning. At two in the afternoon the sun came out, and since then it has been delightful. The banks are now high and covered with peaceful groves and the dwellings of men, secluded and full of beauty.

The river winds in and out, an unknown little stream in the inmost *zenana* of Bengal, neither lazy nor fussy; lavishing the wealth of her affection on both sides, she prattles about common joys and sorrows and the household news of the village girls, who come for water, and sit by her side, assiduously rubbing their bodies to a glowing freshness with their moistened towels.

This evening we have moored our boat in a lonely bend. The sky is clear. The moon is at its full. Not another boat is to be seen. The moonlight glimmers on the ripples. Solitude reigns on the banks. The distant village sleeps, nestling within a thick fringe of trees. The shrill, sustained chirp of the cicadas is the only sound.

Shazadpur,
February 1891.

Just in front of my window, on the other side of the stream, a band of gypsies have ensconced themselves, putting up bamboo frameworks covered over with split-bamboo mats and pieces of cloth. There are only three of these little structures, so low that you cannot stand upright inside. Their life is lived in the open, and they only creep under these shelters at night, to sleep huddled together.

That is always the gypsies' way: no home anywhere, no landlord to pay rent to, wandering about as it pleases them with their children, their pigs, and a dog or two; and on them the police keep a vigilant eye.

I frequently watch the doings of the family nearest me. They are dark but good-looking, with fine, strongly-built bodies, like north-west country folk. Their women are handsome, and have tall, slim, well-knit figures; and with their free and easy movements, and natural independent airs, they look to me like swarthy Englishwomen.

The man has just put the cooking-pot on the fire, and is now splitting bamboos and weaving baskets. The woman first holds up a little mirror to her face, then puts a deal of pains into wiping and rubbing it, over and over again, with a moist piece of cloth; and then, the folds of her upper garment adjusted and tidied, she goes, all spick and span, up to her man and sits beside him, helping him now and then in his work.

These are truly children of the soil, born on it somewhere, bred by the wayside, here, there, and everywhere, dying anywhere. Night and day under the open sky, in the open air, on the bare ground, they lead a unique kind of life; and yet work, love, children, and household duties—everything is there.

They are not idle for a moment, but always doing something. Her own particular task over, one woman plumps herself down behind another, unties the knot of her hair and cleans and arranges it for her; and whether at the same time they fall to talking over the domestic affairs of the three little mat-covered households I cannot say for certain from this distance, but shrewdly suspect it.

This morning a great disturbance invaded the peaceful gypsy settlement. It was about half-past eight or nine. They were spreading out over the mat roofs tattered quilts and sundry other rags, which serve them for beds, in order to sun and air them. The pigs with their litters, lying in a hollow all of a heap and looking like a dab of mud, had been routed out by the two canine members of the family, who fell upon them and sent them roaming in search of their breakfasts, squealing their annoyance at being interrupted in enjoyment of the sun after the cold night. I was writing my letter and absently looking out now and then when the hubbub suddenly commenced.

I rose and went to the window, and found a crowd gathered round the gypsy hermitage. A superior-looking personage was flourishing a stick and indulging in the strongest language. The headman of the gypsies, cowed and nervous, was apparently trying to offer explanations. I gathered that some suspicious happenings in the locality had led to this visitation by a police officer.

The woman, so far, had remained sitting, busily scraping lengths of split bamboo as serenely as if she had been alone and no sort of row going on. Suddenly, however, she sprang to her feet, advanced on the police officer, gesticulated violently with her arms right in his face, and gave him, in strident tones, a piece of her mind. In the twinkling of an eye three-quarters of the officer's excitement had subsided; he tried to put in a word or two of mild protest but did not get a chance, and so departed crestfallen, a different man.

After he had retreated to a safe distance, he turned and shouted back: "All I say is, you'll have to clear out from here!"

I thought my neighbours opposite would forthwith pack up their mats and bamboos and move away with their bundles, pigs, and children. But there is no sign of it yet. They are still nonchalantly engaged in splitting bamboos, cooking food, or completing a toilet.

Shazadpur,
February 1891.

The post office is in a part of our estate office building,—this is very convenient, for we get our letters as soon as they arrive. Some evenings the postmaster comes up to have a chat with me. I enjoy listening to his yarns. He talks of the most impossible things in the gravest possible manner.

Yesterday he was telling me in what great reverence people of this locality hold the sacred river Ganges. If one of their relatives dies, he said, and they have not the means of taking the ashes to the Ganges, they powder a piece of bone from his funeral pyre and keep it till they come across some one who, some time or other, has drunk of the Ganges. To him they administer some of this powder, hidden in the usual offering of *pán*,[1] and thus are content to imagine that a portion of the remains of their deceased relative has gained purifying contact with the sacred water.

I smiled as I remarked: "This surely must be an invention."

He pondered deeply before he admitted after a pause: "Yes, it may be."

On the Way,
February 1891.

We have got past the big rivers and just turned into a little one.

The village women are standing in the water, bathing or washing clothes; and some, in their dripping *saris,* with veils pulled well over their faces, move homeward with their water vessels filled and clasped against the left flank, the right arm swinging free. Children, covered all over with clay, are sporting boisterously, splashing water on each other, while one of them shouts a song, regardless of the tune.

Over the high banks, the cottage roofs and the tops of the bamboo clumps are visible. The sky has cleared and the sun is shining. Remnants of clouds cling to the horizon like fluffs of cotton wool. The breeze is warmer.

There are not many boats in this little river; only a few dinghies, laden with dry branches and twigs, are moving leisurely along to the tired plash! plash! of their oars. At the river's edge the fishermen's nets are hung out to dry between bamboo poles. And work everywhere seems to be over for the day.

Chuhali,
June 1891.

I had been sitting out on the deck for more than a quarter of an hour when heavy clouds rose in the west. They came up, black, tumbled, and tattered, with streaks of lurid light showing through here and there. The little boats scurried off into the smaller arm of the river and clung with their anchors safely to its banks. The reapers took up the cut sheaves on their heads and hied homewards; the cows followed, and behind them frisked the calves waving their tails.

Then came an angry roar. Torn-off scraps of cloud hurried up from the west, like panting messengers of evil tidings. Finally, lightning and thunder, rain and storm, came on altogether and

---

[1] Spices wrapped in betel leaf.

executed a mad dervish dance. The bamboo clumps seemed to howl as the raging wind swept the ground with them, now to the east, now to the west. Over all, the storm droned like a giant snake-charmer's pipe, and to its rhythm swayed hundreds and thousands of crested waves, like so many hooded snakes. The thunder was incessant, as though a whole world was being pounded to pieces away there behind the clouds.

With my chin resting on the ledge of an open window facing away from the wind, I allowed my thoughts to take part in this terrible revelry; they leapt into the open like a pack of school-boys suddenly set free. When, however, I got a thorough drenching from the spray of the rain, I had to shut up the window and my poetising, and retire quietly into the darkness inside, like a caged bird.

Shazadpur,
June 1891.

From the bank to which the boat is tied a kind of scent rises out of the grass, and the heat of the ground, given off in gasps, actually touches my body. I feel that the warm, living Earth is breathing upon me, and that she, also, must feel my breath.

The young shoots of rice are waving in the breeze, and the ducks are in turn thrusting their heads beneath the water and preening their feathers. There is no sound save the faint, mournful creaking of the gangway against the boat, as she imperceptibly swings to and fro in the current.

Not far off there is a ferry. A motley crowd has assembled under the banyan tree awaiting the boat's return; and as soon as it arrives, they eagerly scramble in. I enjoy watching this for hours together. It is market-day in the village on the other bank; that is why the ferry is so busy. Some carry bundles of hay, some baskets, some sacs; some are going to the market, others coming from it. Thus, in this silent noonday, the stream of human activity slowly flows across the river between two villages.

I sat wondering: Why is there always this deep shade of melancholy over the fields and river banks, the sky and the sunshine of our country? And I came to the conclusion that it is because with us Nature is obviously the more important thing. The sky is free, the fields limitless; and the sun merges them into one blazing whole. In the midst of this, man seems so trivial. He comes and goes, like the ferry-boat, from this shore to the other; the babbling hum of his talk, the fitful echo of his song, is heard; the slight movement of his pursuit of his own petty desires is seen in the world's market-places: but how feeble, how temporary, how tragically meaningless it all seems amidst the immense aloofness of the Universe!

The contrast between the beautiful, broad, unalloyed peace of Nature—calm, passive, silent, unfathomable,—and our own everyday worries—paltry, sorrow-laden, strife-tormented, puts me beside myself as I keep staring at the hazy, distant, blue line of trees which fringe the fields across the river.

Where Nature is ever hidden, and cowers under mist and cloud, snow and darkness, there man feels himself master; he regards his desires, his works, as permanent; he wants to perpetuate them, he looks towards posterity, he raises monuments, he writes biographies; he even goes the length of erecting tombstones over the dead. So busy is he that he has not time to consider how many monuments crumble, how often names are forgotten!

Shazadpur,
June 1891.

There was a great, big mast lying on the river bank, and some little village urchins, with never a scrap of clothing, decided, after a long consultation, that if it could be rolled along to the accompaniment of a sufficient amount of vociferous clamour, it would be a new and altogether satisfactory kind of game. The decision was no sooner come to than acted upon, with a *"Shabash,* brothers! All together! Heave ho!" And at every turn it rolled, there was uproarious laughter.

The demeanour of one girl in the party was very different. She was playing with the boys for want of other companions, but she clearly viewed with disfavour these loud and strenuous games. At last she stepped up to the mast and, without a word, deliberately sat on it.

So rare a game to come to so abrupt a stop! Some of the players seemed to resign themselves to giving it up as a bad job; and retiring a little way off, they sulkily glared at the girl in her impassive gravity. One made as if he would push her off, but even this did not disturb the careless ease of her pose. The eldest lad came up to her and pointed to other equally suitable places for taking a rest; at which she energetically shook her head, and putting her hands in her lap, steadied herself down still more firmly on her seat. Then at last they had recourse to physical argument and were completely successful.

Once again joyful shouts rent the skies, and the mast rolled along so gloriously that even the girl had to cast aside her pride and her dignified exclusiveness and make a pretense of joining in the unmeaning excitement. But one could see all the time that she was sure boys never know how to play properly, and are always so childish! If only she had the regulation yellow earthen doll handy, with its big, black top-knot, would she ever have deigned to join in this silly game with these foolish boys?

All of a sudden the idea of another splendid pastime occurred to the boys. Two of them got hold of a third by the arms and legs and began to swing him. This must have been great fun, for they all waxed enthusiastic over it. But it was more than the girl could stand, so she disdainfully left the playground and marched off home.

Then there was an accident. The boy who was being swung was let fall. He left his companions in a pet, and went and lay down on the grass with his arms crossed under his head, desiring to convey thereby that never again would he have anything to do with this bad, hard world, but would forever lie, alone by himself, with his arms under his head, and count the stars and watch the play of the clouds.

The eldest boy, unable to bear the idea of such untimely world-renunciation, ran up to the disconsolate one and taking his head on his own knees repentantly coaxed him. "Come, my little brother! Do get up, little brother! Have we hurt you, little brother?" And before long I found them playing, like two pups, at catching and snatching away each other's hands! Two minutes had hardly passed before the little fellow was swinging again.

REVIEW QUESTIONS

1. What characteristic is most interesting about Tagore's observation of the village? Why?
2. How would you describe his view of the gypsies?
3. How are his talents in poetry and painting reflected in this selection?

A Celebrated American Author Describes the Towers of Silence in Bombay (1896)

MARK TWAIN, *Following the Equator*

Mark Twain (1835–1910) represents the heart of American literature and the heartland of American culture. But there was more to him than Hannibal,

Missouri, Tom Sawyer white-washing Aunt Polly's fence, and Huckleberry Finn rafting on the Mississippi with Jim—important as these are. Samuel Clemens, a sophisticated international traveler, kept and exercised a balanced if sardonic view of life, including respect for and suspicion of all cultures, including his own.

A typical nineteenth-century American must have found the Parsi (Parsee) Towers of Silence incomprehensible. The towers are the result of the Zoroastrian belief that fire, earth, and water are sacred and must not be defiled by death. Hence, bodies are exposed in towers, where vultures pick the flesh from the bones, and those bones are eventually swept down into the depths below the towers. The sensitivity over this issue has been poignantly expressed by the poet Keki Daruwalla in "Fire-Hymn":

The burning ghat erupted phosphorescence:
And wandering "ghost-lights" frightened passers-by
as moonlight scuttled among the bones.
Once strolling at dawn past river-bank and ghat
we saw embers losing their cruel redness
to the grey ash that swallows all. Half-cooked limbs
bore witness to the fire's debauchery.
My father said, "You see those half-burnt fingers
and bone-stubs? The fire at times forgets its dead!"
A Zoroastrian I, my child-fingers clenched
into a little knot of pain
I swore to save fire
from the sin of forgetfulness.

It never forgot, and twenty years since
as I consigned my first-born to the flames
—the nearest Tower of Silence was a thousand miles—
The fire-hymn said to me, "you stand forgiven."
Broken, yet rebellious, I swore this time
to save it from the sin of forgiving.

Mark Twain observed these towers with a sensitivity, knowledge, and understanding that is, frankly, lacking in most Westerners today. Twain said, "The Parsees are a remarkable community." Largely concentrated in and around Bombay (Mumbai), they are descendants of eighth-century Zoroastrian refugees from Persia (Iran; hence "Parsi") who were fleeing an Arab invasion and conversion of the country to Islam. Today a small minority, Parsis are financial leaders (Tata Industries) and cultural leaders (Zubin Mehta, Persis Kambhatta), and were involved in the independence movement (Minoo Masani). Perhaps no minority, especially such a tiny minority, has had such an impact upon such a huge society as have the Parsis on India. The writer Zareer Masani refers to them as "India's smallest and most westernized minority."

On lofty ground, in the midst of a paradise of tropical foliage and flowers, remote from the world and its turmoil and noise, they stood— the Towers of Silence; and away below were spread the wide groves of cocoa-palms, then the city, mile on mile, then the ocean with its fleets of creeping ships—all steeped in a stillness as deep as the hush that hallowed this high place of the dead. The vultures were there. They stood close together in a great circle all around the rim of a massive low tower—waiting; stood as motionless as sculptured ornaments, and indeed almost deceived one into the belief that that was what they were. Presently there was a slight stir among the score of persons present, and all moved reverently out of the path and ceased from talking. A funeral procession entered the great gate, marching two and two, and moved silently by, toward the Tower. The corpse lay in a shallow shell, and was under cover of a white cloth, but was otherwise naked. The bearers of the body were separated by an interval of thirty feet from the mourners. They, and also the mourners, were draped all in pure white, and each couple of mourners was figuratively bound together by a piece of white rope or a handkerchief—though they merely held the ends of it in their hands. Behind the procession followed a dog, which was led in a leash. When the mourners had reached the neighborhood of the Tower—neither they nor any other human being but the bearers of the dead must approach within thirty feet of it—they turned and went back to one of the prayer-houses within the gates, to pray for the spirit of their dead. The bearers unlocked the Tower's sole door and disappeared from view within. In a little while they came out bringing the bier and the white covering-cloth, and locked the door again. Then the ring of vultures rose, flapping their wings, and swooped down into the Tower to devour the body. Nothing was left of it but a clean-picked skeleton when they flocked out again a few minutes afterward.

The principle which underlies and orders everything connected with a Parsee funeral is Purity. By the tenets of the Zoroastrian religion,

the elements, Earth, Fire, and Water, are sacred, and must not be contaminated by contact with a dead body. Hence corpses must not be burned, neither must they be buried. None may touch the dead or enter the Towers where they repose except certain men who are officially appointed for that purpose. They receive high pay, but theirs is a dismal life, for they must live apart from their species, because their commerce with the dead defiles them, and any who should associate with them would share their defilement. When they come out of the Tower the clothes they are wearing are exchanged for others, in a building within the grounds, and the ones which they have taken off are left behind, for they are contaminated, and must never be used again or suffered to go outside the grounds. These bearers come to every funeral in new garments. So far as is known, no human being, other than an official corpse-bearer—save one—has ever entered a Tower of Silence after its consecration. Just a hundred years ago a European rushed in behind the bearers and fed his brutal curiosity with a glimpse of the forbidden mysteries of the place. This shabby savage's name is not given; his quality is also concealed. These two details, taken in connection with the fact that for his extraordinary offense the only punishment he got from the East India Company's Government was a solemn official "reprimand"—suggest the suspicion that he was a European of consequence. The same public document which contained the reprimand gave warning that future offenders of his sort, if in the company's service, would be dismissed; and if merchants, suffer revocation of license and exile to England.

The Towers are not tall, but are low in proportion to their circumference, like a gasometer. If you should fill a gasometer half-way up with solid granite masonry, then drive a wide and deep well down through the center of this mass of masonry, you would have the idea of a Tower of Silence. On the masonry surrounding the well the bodies lie, in shallow trenches which radiate like wheel-spokes from the well. The trenches slant toward the well and carry into it the rainfall. Underground drains, with charcoal filters in them, carry off this water from the bottom of the well.

When a skeleton has lain in the Tower exposed to the rain and the flaming sun a month it is perfectly dry and clean. Then the same bearers that brought it there come gloved and take it up with tongs and throw it into the well. There it turns to dust. It is never seen again, never touched again, in the world. Other peoples separate their dead, and preserve and continue social distinctions in the grave—the skeletons of kings and statesmen and generals in temples and pantheons proper to skeletons of their degree, and the skeletons of the commonplace and the poor in places suited to their meaner estate; but the Parsees hold that all men rank alike in death—all are humble, all poor, all destitute. In sign of their poverty they are sent to their grave naked, in sign of their equality the bones of the rich, the poor, the illustrious, and the obscure are flung into the common well together. At a Parsee funeral there are no vehicles; all concerned must walk, both rich and poor, howsoever great the distance to be traversed may be. In the wells of the Five Towers of Silence is mingled the dust of all the Parsee men and women and children who have died in Bombay and its vicinity during the two centuries which have elapsed since the Mohammedan conquerors drove the Parsees out of Persia, and into that region of India. The earliest of the five towers was built by the Modi family something more than two hundred years ago, and it is now reserved to the heirs of that house; none but the dead of that blood are carried thither.

The origin of at least one of the details of a Parsee funeral is not now known—the presence of the dog. Before a corpse is borne from the house of mourning it must be uncovered and exposed to the gaze of a dog; a dog must also be led in the rear of the funeral. Mr. Nusserwanjee Byramjee, Secretary to the Parsee Punchayet, said that these formalities had once had a meaning and a reason for their institution, but that they were survivals whose origin none could now account for. Custom and tradition continue them in force, antiquity hallows them. It is

thought that in ancient times in Persia the dog was a sacred animal and could guide souls to heaven; also that his eye had the power of purifying objects which had been contaminated by the touch of the dead; and that hence his presence with the funeral cortège provides an ever-applicable remedy in the case of need.

The Parsees claim that their method of disposing of the dead is an effective protection of the living; that it disseminates no corruption, no impurities of any sort, no disease-germs; that no wrap, no garment which has touched the dead is allowed to touch the living afterward; that from the Towers of Silence nothing proceeds which can carry harm to the outside world. These are just claims, I think. As a sanitary measure, their system seems to be about the equivalent of cremation, and as sure. We are drifting slowly—but hopefully—toward cremation in these days. It could not be expected that this progress should be swift, but if it be steady and continuous, even if slow, that will suffice. When cremation becomes the rule we shall cease to shudder at it; we should shudder at burial if we allowed ourselves to think what goes on in the grave.

The dog was an impressive figure to me, representing as he did a mystery whose key is lost. He was humble, and apparently depressed; and he let his head droop pensively, and looked as if he might be trying to call back to his mind what it was that he had used to symbolize ages ago when he began his function. There was another impressive thing close at hand, but I was not privileged to see it. That was the sacred fire—a fire which is supposed to have been burning without interruption for more than two centuries; and so, living by the same heat that was imparted to it so long ago.

The Parsees are a remarkable community. There are only about sixty thousand in Bombay, and only about half as many as that in the rest of India; but they make up in importance what they lack in numbers. They are highly educated, energetic, enterprising, progressive, rich, and the Jew himself is not more lavish or catholic in his charities and benevolences. The Parsees build and endow hospitals, for both men and animals; and they and their womenkind keep an open purse for all great and good objects. They are a political force, and a valued support to the government. They have a pure and lofty religion, and they preserve it in its integrity and order their lives by it.

We took a final sweep of the wonderful view of plain and city and ocean, and so ended our visit to the garden and the Towers of Silence; and the last thing I noticed was another symbol—a voluntary symbol this one; it was a vulture standing on the sawed-off top of a tall and slender and branchless palm in an open space in the ground; he was perfectly motionless, and looked like a piece of sculpture on a pillar. And he had a mortuary look, too, which was in keeping with the place.

REVIEW QUESTIONS

1. How would you characterize Twain's approach to his subject?
2. What are the advantages and disadvantages of the Parsi method of disposal of the dead?
3. What is the most important thing you learned from this selection? Explain.

8

Africa, 1800–1918

In this chapter, as in several others, sources are severely restricted by what has been translated into English. Nineteenth-century Europeans were very much interested in travels to Africa; consequently, much that has been written in and translated into English are accounts of European and United States travelers—explorers, traders, missionaries, and scientists. The following selections represent a broad section from that literature, with only one contribution from a traveler from another part of the world.

Often the travelers represented in this chapter were motivated by dual purposes. Missionaries were often explorers, if not by their own definition, certainly by their actions, as in the case of David Livingstone. His fascination for African geography, animals, and peoples dominates the accounts of his missionary travels. Expeditions such as those of Mungo Park were ostensibly for exploration, but they also carried the overtones of European rights to imperial possession. The accounts of P. Dallons and John Duncan reveal the continuing existence and impact of the slave trade into the nineteenth century in Africa, which may have been the primary purpose of their visits.

After the mid–nineteenth century, however, the nature of passages into the African continent changed dramatically, reflecting the impact of the Second Great Awakening of Protestantism. Although imperial goals and trade considerations remained important, the missionaries now came without other primary priorities. Likewise, scientists saw African peoples as subjects for intense study to prove already existing conclusions about evolution and the course of human development. They abandoned most pretexts of exploration. Unlike the dual-purposes of David Livingstone, Agnes McAllister saw only the need to improve the lives of Africans by bringing them Christianity.

Finally, the account of M.K. Gandhi from India brings a totally different perspective on African travels. Partly as a result of existing scientific theory, Gandhi entered a South Africa where anyone of color was seen as automatically inferior and a potential threat to the white establishment. Perhaps like other travelers from Asia whose writings have not been translated to English, Gandhi came as an educated Hindu into the strongly Protestant nation of South Africa. The treatment he received during this visit would have been the same for anyone from an Asian nation.

A Scottish Surgeon Describes Life Along the Niger River (1795–1797)

MUNGO PARK, *Travels in the Interior Districts of Africa*

In 1788 Europeans continued to believe that a "great river" flowed across central Africa, and the young Scottish surgeon Mungo Park was one of those sent by Great Britain to investigate. Although the dates of this writing might place it with an earlier chapter on Africa in this volume, the material in this selection places Park's experience within the nineteenth-century European mania to "discover Africa." This expedition "funded by Great Britain" mirrored many others launched by fledgling imperialist European countries in the late eighteenth century. The common beliefs about the geography and peoples of the African continent revealed an amazing lack of factual knowledge. Maps from both centuries depict the African continent with a range of mountains running from the Gulf of Guinea in the west to just north of the horn of Somalia in the east. The lands of Africans living north of these "Mountains of the Moon" were fairly well understood, but south of the line much of the interior of Africa was labeled "Ethiopia: Unexplored Region." It was commonly believed that the source of the Nile River was located somewhere in those mountains.

Mungo Park had served as a ship's surgeon on an East Indiaman but lacked the experience he would need for his assignment to locate the great river. In 1795, the expedition commenced at the mouth of the Gambia River with little equipment and only two days' food because Park and his party intended to buy what they needed from the natives. They were soon captured by the Muslim king of Ludamar, and Park was held for four months before escaping. He finally reached the Niger River and followed it north and east for about three hundred miles. Caught in the beginning of the rainy season and destitute of food and clothing, the party admitted defeat and began the trek back to the Gambia River. Park was in very poor health and was suffering greatly from hunger when a Muslim native slave trader rescued him, nursed him back to health, and invited him to join his caravan going west. The following extracts relate Park's observations during his detention in Ludamar by the Moorish King, Ali.

PRISONER OF A MOORISH CHIEFTAIN

. . . We reached at length the king's tent, where we found a great number of people, men and women, assembled. Ali was sitting upon a black leather cushion, clipping a few hairs from his upper lip; a female attendant holding up a looking glass before him. He appeared to be an old man, of the Arab cast, with a long white beard, and he had a sullen and indignant aspect. He surveyed me with attention, and inquired of the Moors if I could speak Arabic; being answered in the negative, he appeared much surprised, and continued silent. The surrounding attendants, and especially the ladies, were abundantly more inquisitive; they asked a thousand questions, inspected every part of my apparel, searched my pockets, and obliged me to unbutton my waistcoat and display the whiteness of my skin; they even counted my toes and fingers, as if they doubted whether I was in truth a human being. In a little time the priest announced evening prayers; but before the people departed, the Moor who had acted as interpreter informed me that Ali was about to present me with something to eat; and looking round, I observed some boys bringing a wild hog, which they tied to one of the tent strings, and Ali made signs to me to kill and dress it for supper. Though I was very hungry, I did not think it prudent to eat any part of an animal so much detested by the Moors, and therefore told him that I never ate such food. They then untied the hog, in hopes that it would run immediately at me; for they believe that a great enmity subsists between hogs and Christians; but in this they were disappointed; for the animal no sooner regained his liberty than he began to attack indiscriminately every person that came in his way and at last took shelter under the couch upon which the king was sitting. . . .

At sunrise, Ali, with a few attendants, came on horseback to visit me, and signified that he had provided a hut for me, where I would be sheltered from the sun. I was accordingly conducted thither, and found the hut comparatively cool and pleasant. It was constructed of corn stalks set up on end, in the form of a square with a flat roof of the same materials, supported by forked sticks; to one of which was tied the wild hog before mentioned. . . .

I observed that, in the night, the Moors kept regular watch, and frequently looked into the hut, to see if I was asleep, and if it was quite dark, they would light a wisp of grass. About two o'clock in the morning a Moor entered the hut, probably with a view to steal something, or perhaps to murder me; and groping about he laid his hand upon my shoulder. As night visitors were at best but suspicious characters, I sprang up the moment he laid his hand upon me; and the Moor in his haste to get off stumbled over my boy and fell with his face upon

the wild hog, which returned the attack by biting the Moor's arm. The screams of this man alarmed the people in the king's tent, who immediately conjectured that I had made my escape, and a number of them mounted their horses and prepared to pursue me. I observed upon this occasion that Ali did not sleep in his own tent, but came galloping upon a white horse from a small tent at a considerable distance; indeed, the tyrannical and cruel behaviour of this man made him so jealous of every person around him that even his own slaves and domestics knew not where he slept. When the Moors had explained to him the cause of this outcry, they all went away, and I was permitted to sleep quietly until morning.

MARCH 13TH.—With the returning day commenced the same round of insult and irritation; the boys assembled to beat the hog, and the men and women to plague the Christian. It is impossible for me to describe the behaviour of a people who study mischief as a science and exult in the miseries and misfortunes of their fellow-creatures. It is sufficient to observe that the rudeness, ferocity, and fanaticism which distinguish the Moors from the rest of mankind found here a proper subject whereon to exercise their propensities. I was a *stranger,* I was *unprotected,* and I was a *Christian;* each of these circumstances is sufficient to drive every spark of humanity from the heart of a Moor; but when all of them, as in my case, were combined in the same person, and a suspicion prevailed withal that I had come as a *spy* into the country, the reader will easily imagine that in such a situation I had every thing to fear. . . .

During his captivity, Park felt very vulnerable to the abuses of the common folk, but he had the opportunity to witness a wedding among the Hottentots that seemed to combine their native religious beliefs with Islam.

A great number of people of both sexes assembled, but without that mirth and hilarity which take place at a Negro wedding; here was neither singing, nor dancing; nor any other amusement that I could perceive. A woman was beating the drum, and the other women joining at times, like a chorus, by setting up a shrill scream; and at the same time moving their tongues from one side of the mouth to the other with great celerity. I was soon tired, and had returned into my hut, where I was sitting almost asleep, when an old woman entered with a wooden bowl in her hand and signified she had brought me a present from the bride. Before I could recover from the surprise which this message created, the woman discharged the contents of the bowl full in my face. Finding that it was the same sort of holy water, with which, among the Hottentots, the priest is said to sprinkle a new married couple, I began to suspect that the old lady was actuated by mischief or malice; but she gave me seriously to understand that it was a nuptial benediction from the bride's own person; and which, on such occasions, is always received by young unmarried Moors as a mark of distinguished favour. This being the case, I wiped my face, and sent my acknowledgements to the lady. . . .

One whole month had now elapsed since I was led into captivity; during which time, each returning day brought me fresh distresses. I watched the lingering course of the sun with anxiety, and blessed his evening beams as they shed a yellow lustre along the sandy floor of my hut; for it was then that my oppressors left me, and allowed me to pass the sultry night in solitude and reflection.

About midnight, a bowl of kouskous with some salt and water was brought for me and my two attendants; this was our common fare, and it was all that was allowed us to allay the cravings of hunger and support nature for the whole of the following day. For it is to be observed that this was the Mahomedan Lent; and as the Moors keep the fast with a religious strictness, they thought it proper to compel me, though a Christian, to a similar observance. Time, however, somewhat reconciled me to my situation: I found that I could bear hunger and thirst better

than I expected; and at length I endeavoured to beguile the tedious hours by learning to write Arabic. The people who came to see me soon made me acquainted with the characters; and I discovered that by engaging their attention in this way they were not so troublesome as otherwise they would have been. Indeed, when I observed any person whose countenance I thought bore malice towards me, I made it a rule to ask him either to write in the sand himself or to decipher what I had already written; and the pride of showing his superior attainments generally induced him to comply with my request.

A WOMAN SLAVE

April 24th

Before day break the Bushreens said their morning prayers, and most of the free people drank a little *moening* (a sort of gruel), part of which was likewise given to such of the slaves as appeared least able to sustain the fatigues of the day. One of Karfa's female slaves was very sulky, and when some gruel was offered to her she refused to drink it. As soon as day dawned we set out, and travelled the whole morning over a wild and rocky country, by which my feet were much bruised, and I was sadly apprehensive, that I should not be able to keep up with the coffle during the day; but I was in a great measure relieved from this anxiety, when I observed that others were more exhausted than myself. In particular, the woman slave who had refused victuals in the morning began now to lag behind and complain dreadfully of pains in her legs. Her load was taken from her and given to another slave, and she was ordered to keep in the front of the coffle. About eleven o'clock, as we were resting by a small rivulet, some of the people discovered a hive of bees in a hollow tree, and they were proceeding to obtain the honey, when the largest swarm I ever beheld flew out, and attacking the people of the coffle, made us fly in all directions. I took the alarm first, and I believe was the only person who escaped with impunity. When our enemies thought fit to desist from pursuing us, and every person was employed in picking out the stings he had received, it was discovered that the poor woman above mentioned, whose name was Nealee, was not come up; and as many of the slaves in their retreat had left their bundles behind them, it became necessary for some persons to return and bring them. In order to do this with safety, fire was set to the grass a considerable way to the eastward of the hive, and the wind driving the fire furiously along, the party pushed through the smoke and recovered the bundles. They likewise brought with them poor Nealee, whom they found lying by the rivulet. She was very much exhausted, and had crept to the stream in hopes to defend herself from the bees by throwing water over her body, but this proved ineffectual, for she was stung in the most dreadful manner.

When the Slatees had picked out the stings as far as they could, she was washed with water and then rubbed with bruised leaves; but the wretched woman obstinately refused to proceed any further, declaring that she would rather die than walk another step. As entreaties and threats were used in vain, the whip was at length applied, and after bearing patiently a few strokes, she started up and walked with tolerable expedition for four or five hours longer, when she made an attempt to run away from the coffle, but was so very weak that she fell down in the grass. Though she was unable to rise, the whip was a second time applied, but without effect; upon which Karfa desired two of the Slatees to place her upon the ass which carried our dry provisions; but she could not sit erect, and the ass being very refractory, it was found impossible to carry her forward in that manner. The Slatees however were unwilling to abandon her, the day's journey being nearly ended; they therefore made a sort of litter of bamboo canes, upon which she was placed and tied on it with slips of bark; this litter was carried upon the heads of two slaves, one walking before the other, and they were followed by two others who relieved them occasionally. In this manner the woman

was carried forward until it was dark, when we reached a steam of water at the foot of a high hill, called Gankaran-Kooro, and here we stopped for the night and set about preparing our supper. As we had only eaten one handful of meal since the preceding night, and travelled all day in a hot sun, many of the slaves who had loads upon their heads were very much fatigued, and some of them snapped their fingers, which among the Negroes is a sure sign of desperation. The Slatees immediately put them all in irons, and such of them as had evinced signs of great despondency were kept apart from the rest and had their hands tied. In the morning they were found greatly recovered.

April 25th

At daybreak poor Nealee was awakened, but her limbs were now become so stiff and painful that she could neither walk nor stand; she was therefore lifted like a corpse upon the back of the ass, and the Slatees endeavoured to secure her in that situation by fastening her hands together under the ass's neck, and her feet under the belly, with long slips of bark; but the ass was so very unruly that no sort of treatment could induce him to proceed with his load, and as Nealee made no exertion to prevent herself from falling, she was quickly thrown off and had one of her legs much bruised. Every attempt to carry her forward being thus found ineffectual, the general cry of the coffle was, *Kang-tegi, kang-tegi,* "Cut her throat, cut her throat," an operation I did not wish to see performed, and therefore marched onwards with the foremost of the coffle. I had not walked above a mile, when one of Karfa's domestic slaves came up to me with poor Nealee's garment upon the end of his bow and exclaimed *Nealee affilita* (Nealee is lost). I asked him whether the Slatees had given him the garment as a reward for cutting her throat; he replied that Karfa and the schoolmaster would not consent to that measure, but had left her on the road; where undoubtedly she soon perished and was probably devoured by wild beasts.

REVIEW QUESTIONS

1. How did the wedding Park witnessed differ from what he expected of African weddings? What does this observation tell you about him?
2. How was Park treated during his captivity? How did he respond to that treatment?
3. What about Park's behavior reveals his knowledge of the people with whom he was living?
4. Do you believe Park's behavior while a prisoner exhibited intelligence? Why or why not?

A French Slaving Captain Describes the East Coast of Africa (1804)

P. DALLONS, *Manuscript from the Mauritius Archives*

Not much can be said of P. Dallons except that he was an experienced French slaving captain who knew a great deal about the east coast of Africa. The following excerpt is from his account of a voyage to Kilwa and Zanzibar in 1804—the same year that the English outlawed the trade of slaves on the high seas. If he knew of this pronouncement, Dallons shows no sign of giving it much notice. The report he made to his captain-general was found in the archives on the island of Mauritius east of Madagascar, which was owned by the French.

I have the honour to submit to the Captain-General some reflections on our commerce with the various Arab establishments on the coast of Africa; the manner of trading there; the difficulties one encounters; the vices of the government; the authorizations which have become necessary as a result of the prejudiced self-interest of the people of these islands; their disregard of our Colours; and the absence of protection which the Sultan of Muscat, to whom these islands are subject, should give us, and which we have not had up to now because of the feebleness of our last government.

The island of Zanzibar is fifteen leagues long by eight broad. It is six leagues from the African mainland, in Latitude of 6° South, Longitude 38° East. Provisions are plentiful [and include] rice, maize, millet, coconuts, cattle, goats, and chickens, all at the cheapest possible price, even though it receives a great quantity of provisions from the mainland. However friendly the island might be to our Government, this could only be prejudicial [to us], for it would only awaken the vigilance of our enemies.

Zanzibar is governed by the Prince of Muscat. It suffers constant changes because of the fear the Sultan has of a governor becoming too well established and taking the lordship from him. This has happened at Pemba, Mombasa and Pate. The choice of commanders becomes daily more difficult, and nowadays he only appoints eunuchs, and even divides [the civil and military] powers between them. The armed forces are under a man of this kind; the civil power and the customs are under a Banyan or an Arab whose rich estates in Muscat guarantee his fidelity to the Prince. He has farmed out the mainland to a third person who has similar sureties to give him. (One calls the mainland all the coast near the island which bears the same name.)

All the revenues and dues within the Government of Zanzibar . . . [words omitted] . . . [? are sent to Muscat] amounting to 40,000 *piastres* a year. They are paid at the end of the North-East Monsoon, which occurs in the months of March and April. At this time the new Governor arrives, and ordinarily he commits atrocious and revolting extortions, always sheltering himself under the veil of the Prince's interests. He is often supported by Arabs of high standing who live in this island and are called al-Harthi; they always take part in the violent actions of the government.

When we were going to trade in this island, we at first promised ourselves a good and advantageous treaty, but we were soon disappointed of our hopes. On our arrival the government gave us an interpreter who is no doubt devoted to it, and on whom, under the appearance of the greatest liberty, we had entirely to depend. We brought them trade goods, such as cloves, sugar, iron, and so on. The government only asked from us a first option at the same price [as others], and made us an immediate offer, but without telling us that it had forbidden the people of the country to trade with us concurrently. By their use of such means, the French are always made to submit to the price fixed by the government, and, by a payment of the Governor, to suffer a further loss of thirty per cent. by his atrocious underhandedness.

Before engaging in trade the French are made to give very costly presents to the government and to the interpreter, a subtle and pliant man on whom all success depends. If his eager cupidity is not satisfied, he finds every means to deflect them from their object.

Black slaves are sold by auction amid the shouts of public auctioneers. It is between these and the interpreter that takes place the commercial arrangements which ruin the French. They put up the price of the blacks at will, and end by making us fear that we shall not obtain them at any price, because their religion, as they say, forbids them in such a case to sell to white men. If one complains to the Arab government, it gives every appearance of hastening one's business; but matters none the less remain in their original state, until, at length, driven by one difficulty and another, we reach the conclusion of our trading. It is then that the Governor comes on board ship to count the blacks, and makes us pay dues of eleven *piastres* a head. Once the dues are paid the Governor overwhelms the French with offers of his services, which may be reduced to that at least no further present will be demanded.

The inhabitants of the country trade in blacks as follows: they transport them to different markets, to Muscat, the Red Sea, and the Persian Gulf; and, although for this reason they can hardly fear our joining in the trade, above all because they pay only one *piastre* a head, they do all they can to keep us away from the island. Both the interests and the policy of the Prince of Muscat call us to it, and for certain the governors carry out neither the one nor the other.

Although the Sultan of Muscat is much feared at close quarters, his authority is only feeble so far away. During my last stay in Zanzibar I saw Frenchmen arrive with an order to the government of the island to let them trade freely. The outcome was not happy because of the contrariness they were shown, and everything proved to me that the orders of the Prince as regards ourselves will not be carried out until our government protects our commerce in this area in an imposing manner.

Kilwa, another Arab station on the African coast, lies in 8° South. It is under a governor who transmits to the Prince 6,000 *piastres* a year. He levies customs dues as he likes, and makes the French pay twelve *piastres* a head on slaves.

In 1788 the French government ordered M. de Roussillon, the commander of a frigate, to visit all the trading ports in Africa, and then to go to Muscat to fix with the Sultan what dues the French should pay. They were fixed at five *piastres* a head except for trade goods. This treaty did not last long. In spite of it, on my first voyage to Zanzibar and Kilwa in 1799, I was made to pay a duty of eight *piastres* a head, and it has constantly risen since: the Arabs, certain that they can act with impunity, have ended by being most vexatious and making the most exaggerated claims.

I give the Captain-General my reflections which are dictated by the experience of all my voyages on this coast, and must assure him that we shall be most happy in our trade and of more importance if he will protect us with his power.

In these days an Arab vessel is leaving for Zanzibar. The island is governed at this moment by Bahadur, the Military Commandant, and by a eunuch named Yaqut who is Chief of Customs. It is he with whom the French have to deal direct. There is no one who has not many complaints to make about him in every way; and a strong letter from the Captain-General to this man would be of the greatest usefulness to us, warning him that a ship has been sent to Muscat to take letters from the Captain-General to make known his intentions to the Sultan. It is this Yaqut who has always prevented the French making contact with the continent of Africa. I am the only man who has obtained this favour, yet I was surrounded by a numerous company which was given me, in appearance to guarantee my safety, but in reality to prevent me from seeing what they wished to hide from me.

These details may appear trivial to the Captain-General, but it is important for him to be given to know them. Constant experience has proved to us that trade cannot be happy except with government protection, and one must dare to tell the Captain-General, without fear of displeasing him, all that can make for our prosperity and development.

It would be of the greatest advantage to us if the Captain-General would have the kindness to let the Sultan of Muscat know what [ill] treatment, bad faith and annoyance French subjects have suffered in their trade with the Arab ports; to regulate the dues payable by the French; to establish treaty rights for the ships of the Republic on voyages for reasons of state; and to place at Zanzibar a French Resident with power to trade freely as such, submitting only to dues defined by treaty and having a direct connexion with the Sultan of Muscat alone.

The dispatches of the Captain-General [have] been delivered to a ship now sailing to Muscat. The Sultan's reply will come by way of Zanzibar in February.

I submit, Captain-General, herewith a translation of the letter from the Governor of Zanzibar. I particularly wish to accomplish your aim, and pray you to believe in my most sincere and respectful devotion.

(Signed) P. Dallons.

Port Nord Quest,
Isle de France,
5 Fructidor an 12,
1804.

REVIEW QUESTIONS

1. Considering the competition for islands near the east coast of Africa represented in Chapter 3 of this volume, what group seemed to have the upper hand in the East African trade by the early nineteenth century?
2. What problems did the French traders have at Zanzibar that Dallons seemed unable to resolve?
3. Where were the East African slaves destined to be sold?
4. Why did Dallons believe that his trade would be more profitable if the French captain-general would provide protection? From whom did he need protection?

A French Sailor Depicts Life Along the Gambia and Senegal Rivers (1816)

G. MOLLIEN, *Travels in Africa*

Following the famous trek of Mungo Park in 1795 to the source of the Niger River, or the *Dialli-Bá* as it was known by the natives, several Europeans attempted expeditions from the West African coast toward the core of the continent. Representing France, Mollien was one of those who intended to prevent British interlopers from obtaining a foothold on or knowledge about the Gambia and Senegal Rivers. In 1816 he sailed on the frigate *Medusa.* The ship was wrecked on the coast of Africa, and he and some of his shipmates used a boat to come ashore, landing south of Cape Blanco, over a hundred miles north of the mouth of the Senegal. He was quite amazed when he found an "extensive space with all the marks of sterility" instead of the cities and farms described by Leo Africanus and Park. In 1817 he returned to Paris for approval of his plans for exploration; frustrated by not being received by the proper authorities, he proceeded to Senegal without the approval he sought. In the second decade of the nineteenth century, only a narrow strip of land south of the Senegal River was claimed by France, and much of the area in which Mollien traveled was open savannah neither claimed nor controlled by any European nation. Consequently, he encountered many different ethnic groups, who professed Muslim, Christian, native animistic, or any combination of these beliefs.

In the course of the year 1817, I returned to France, to solicit permission to execute my original project. Unable to procure a definitive answer from the Minister, I embarked again for Senegal, in the expectation of meeting with a patron in M. de Fleuriau, the new Governor of the Colony. This officer entered, with uncommon ardour, into all my views; my plans were approved of, and he ordered all the preparations necessary for such an enterprise. In vain, he represented the dangers I might be exposed to; my resolution was not to be shaken. Dispatch was requisite, as the rainy season was coming on, and secrecy was no less so, to prevent the jealous suspicions of the Moors.

With a pretended hunting party, I repaired to Gandiolle, a village in the kingdom of Cayor, about four leagues to the S. E. of St. Louis, and opposite the mouth of the Senegal. The Damel or king was then in the village, which was full of

his troops. As I needed his protection, I took with me an interpreter, who carried presents of brandy, tobacco, and beads.

In our way, we had to cross an uncultivated plain, replenished, here and there, with ponds of salt water; these, when evaporated by the sun, leave a whitish dust that dazzles the eye. We soon arrived at the village of Gandiolle, which was then a scene of pillage and plunder. Most of the huts were destroyed; the Damel had exacted a contribution of 83 slaves, which he could only enforce by violence, and many of the inhabitants had removed to Babagua, to avoid the vengeance that was impending.

In passing through the streets, a number of *griots* or public singers, were in the train of the princes and horsemen, chanting their praises. After scaling a sand hill, we discovered some princes and warriors ranged round a hut. All was gloomy silence, for the tyrant's orders were very often so many death warrants. On my interpreter announcing that two white men requested to see the Damel, we had to wait a full half hour, when I signified to the chamberlain, that white men never waited, and we departed, but we were almost instantly recalled; a porter received us at the first door, and we next entered a court, where the horses of the Damel were kept. These are thorough bred Arabians, the price of one being as high as 15 captives. We were desired to sit down on a bed, in a hut, which was full of guards. As white men, we retained our arms, those of every one else being deposited elsewhere, previous to an audience of the king.

After passing through several courts, we arrived at the royal hut, of an oval form, and with a door so low, that we must crawl on hands and knees. With our hats on our heads, and musquets in our hands, we advanced, and reported the object of our visit. The Damel made us a sign of protection, and assumed a mild demeanor. He is very corpulent, about 26 years of age, with an insinuating voice, but a look rather turbid and wild. His fingers were studded with silver rings; his dress was like that of the negroes; he had a blue cotton cap on his head, and he was seated on a mat, cross legged. The Moors beside him appeared to great advantage, and they very often obtain the favour of the princes, from their superior talents and address.

The palace and huts of a negro king and his subjects are similar in their construction. The wall and the roof are of straw and reeds; the ground floor is the only one, and a great number of amulets hung about the walls, are an exclusive indication of a royal residence.

Some bottles of Bourdeaux wine were ranged before the Damel, to which he frequently applied to, and there were calabashes filled with palm wine, for the courtiers and attendants. When my presents were brought, he distributed the tobacco among those who were around him, the beads he reserved for his wives, and the brandy was laid aside, for the use of some particular favourites.

Our interpreter paid his majesty some compliments, which he listened to, with complacency, and he then dismissed us. In retracing our steps, we passed by several negro princes, that were either waiting for an audience, or for orders to commence some predatory expedition. A certain degree of consideration was the result of our introduction to the sovereign, and from that moment we enjoyed the title of his friends. After this, we were secure from all insult, throughout his country. As before intended, I now purchased an excellent horse, at the price of 12 guineas, and we then repaired again to our boat, without the slightest molestation or insult from the unruly soldiers that crowded the streets of Gandiolle.

At St. Louis, I made every preparation for my departure, and was authorized by M. Fleuriau, to take from the government stores, whatever might be helpful to the undertaking. I calculated on providing for the wants of fifteen months, and the following was what I received from the government store-houses:—Two double-barrelled guns, ten pounds of gun-powder, fifty gun flints; fifty musket balls, three pounds and a half of coral, two pounds and two ounces of unwrought yellow amber; eighteen packets of beads, fourteen pounds of tobacco, one hatchet, and one-third of a yard of scarlet cloth.

I also took care to provide myself with a blanket, two leathern bottles for water, a powder-horn, and a portmanteau. I had two daggers by my side, and three pocket compasses, to ascertain the direction of the routes I might proceed in. An ass also was purchased to carry my baggage. I had instructions from M. Fleuriau, but they were mostly a repetition of the particulars which had entered into the plan of my own projection.

A Marabout, named Diai Boukari, a native of the Foota country, was to serve as my interpreter, at a salary of one hundred and eighty francs per month. This man evinced a cordial attachment to Europeans, and was in repute for his integrity. He spoke the Arabic, Poola, and Joloff languages; his age was about thirty-six; he was a negro in colour, but his features seemed cast in a European mould. He brought with him his son, aged fifteen, and a slave, named Messember, of the same age, both of whom I was afterwards obliged to send back to St. Louis.

Diai Boukari having emphatically announced the 28th of January, as a lucky day, and that we must depart before sun-set, at two in the afternoon, I sent my horse, ass, and baggage, to the main land, and without the knowledge of my friends, I set out at five in the evening. Before he embarked, my Marabout traced several Arabic characters on the sand, as if to presage the event of our journey; the answer being favourable, he gathered up a handful of sand into a little bag, esteeming it the palladium of his life and safety.

Accompanied by my friend, M. Mille, I entered a boat which had been previously conveyed to a retired place. The prayers addressed by my Marabout, to the Supreme Governor of the universe, and the affecting farewell which he took of his mother and wife, detained us a few minutes. At ten o'clock, we arrived at Diedde, a village in the country of Cayor, situated on the channel between the islands of Saur and Babagué.

Having sent back our boats, we began to load our beasts. I gave my European clothes to my friend, and put on the Moorish dress, but it did not sufficiently cover me against the musquitoes. My horse, tormented by these insects, ran off into the country, and my Marabout had trouble enough to overtake him. My friend and I separated, and we took the route to Leibar, after having passed Toubé. Being in the dark, and fatigued, we returned to Toubé. All the inhabitants were in bed, nor could we obtain hospitality from the chief of the village. My Moorish costume, which he perceived through the reeds that formed his door, suggested that I might be a partisan of the Damel. We took up our quarters in the open air, which was so sharp and cold, that I had no sleep, especially as I thought myself obliged to watch for the preservation of my baggage, in a place open on all sides. When daylight appeared, the master of the hut, near which we had halted, enquired who we were, with excuses for having suffered us to pass the night, in such a situation; "but," said he, "I took you for a troop of Moors."

We departed, without loss of time, and we took the road to Gue; the soil all along consisted of a reddish sand, wholly destitute of culture. Our progress was tedious, till we came to Kelkom, where we arrived at noon, and found the Damel had been plundering the village. Some mutilated negroes that remained, reported the miseries endured by their families. Several of their relatives had fallen in the act of resisting the sanguinary orders of their king, but the greater number were in chains. Others, tranquil in their huts, and suspecting no danger, had been sold, without their knowledge, by this rapacious tyrant. The inhabitants of this village possessed a degree of industry; they cultivated indigo with care, and made use of its colouring matter, which they knew how to extract, in dying cotton stuffs.

Bidienne, the next place we passed through, expected to be ravaged by the Damel's men, and I did not think it a proper place to halt in. Near each negro village, the inhabitants have wells; that of Bidienne was eleven fathoms in depth, being much higher than the river, from which it was about four leagues distant. We proceeded till six in the evening. Unaccustomed to travel in so hot a climate, and exposed by my Moorish dress to the scorching rays of the sun, I felt somewhat discouraged. The terror struck by the Damel, had caused most of the inhabitants of Niakra, where I arrived at sun-set, to desert their habitations. We unloaded the beasts at the door of the chief, expecting he would furnish us with lodgings.

My dress had not prevented me from being every where recognized as a European; it proved of no service, and the negroes surveyed me with a malignant air. The hatred which they bear against the Moors, made them turn away with horror from one who had assumed their apparel. Of course, I sent away Boukari's slave to St. Louis, to procure some European apparel.

Fali Loum was the name of the chief; he invited us to enter his hut, and, indeed, gave it up to our use. This old man pitying the fatigues that I had undergone, asked my Marabout what dishes I liked best. When supper was ready, we all three seated ourselves before a wooden bowl filled with boiled millet, here called couscous. The daughter of Fali Loum brought us water for our ablutions, and presented it to me on her knees, a kind of homage paid to the whites, which made me prognosticate a successful issue to my African travels.

In twenty-four hours, what a change! No rare dishes now, no highly seasoned ragouts, no expensive wines; milk, couscous, and water, were our only sustenance. The guests raised the food to their mouths, with the right hand alone. I was busy in thought, when Fali Loum remarking my want of appetite, ejaculated: "Thou dost not find here the good cheer of white men; how wilt thou accustom thyself to our mode of life?" A mat spread on the ground served me for a bed. From fatigue, I felt no difference from that which I had quitted.

While waiting the return of my messenger, from St. Louis, for two days, I was overwhelmed with visits. The negroes came in crowds to see a white man, who was an entirely new object to most of them. Some brought me provisions for my tobacco, and I lived, in fact, much better than Fali Loum, his rank of chief not permitting him to taste the provisions of a traveller. So I had no want of fowls and fresh eggs, while my host contented himself with his couscous. As to eggs, the Negroes never touch them.

My host led a very regular life. Fali Loum rose with the sun: a rigid observer of the Koran, and strongly tinctured with devotion, his first words were addressed to the Supreme Governor of the universe. After this duty, held sacred by all mankind, he came to enquire how we had passed the night, and stirred our fire. He then received visits from the negroes, who never failed to come daily and pay him their respects. The conversation turned on the cruel character of the Damel, and the wretched condition of his subjects. We often heard them swear never to receive any of his envoys. Some related that they had seen men crouching in the grass near their village, who were watching for an opportunity to carry off the women or children on their way to the spring. They durst not, however, revenge these

atrocious intrusions, for they well knew the miseries which a neighbouring village had endured from the vengeance of the Damel, for killing one of his slaves. Fali Loum, to allay their fears, insisted that the main body of the Damel's army was far distant; that they must cherish a military spirit, and instead of selling their gunpowder for poultry and tobacco, they should carefully preserve it for their defence.

Fali Loum, occasionally seated himself under a great tamarind tree, near his hut. He was teaching his sons to write, and he would reproach them frequently for their inattention. In fact, when the father turned his back, they threw aside the board on which they were writing, and ran off in pursuit of guinea-fowls, which they brought to me for sale. I gave them tobacco in exchange, with which they bought milk.

At noon, Fali Loum came to invite us to his table. His wife and children, at such times, retired, not being permitted to eat, till their father has finished; and in token of humility, they even turn away their faces, that they may not see him eat. After his repast, he mounted his horse, on a visit to the neighbouring chiefs, to concert measures for opposing the sudden invasions of the Damel. His eldest son never quitted him. In the evening, he returned to render devout thanks to the Almighty, for his blessings, and to intreat he would keep away the Damel. He had slaves, but it was the children who took care of his horse, drove home his goats into the fold, and cut the grass for his beasts.

One slight service I could render to Fali Loum, and that was, at his request, armed with my gun, to accompany his wife to the fountain; this I did several times, to protect her from wild beasts and the people of the Damel.

At eight o'clock, supper was ready. When finished, sleep soon overtook these people, prepossessed with the notion of fatality, that if their village was not destined to be pillaged, the Damel would never have power to accomplish his rapacious wishes.

The description of the interior of this hut, and the manner of living adopted by this chieftain, may be considered as similar to that of the other free negroes. The same order, the same uniformity, are every where visible in other villages.

February 4th

News from all quarters, that the Damel and his emissaries seized or destroyed every thing that came in their way. On this, I felt apprehensive that my messenger had been arrested by these banditti. My agitation made me awake Boukari, in the night, and I told him we must go and meet his slave. Fali Loum lent his horse to my Marabout, and we were soon on the march. My horse, however, frightened by the scent or appearance of some wild beast, started, fell, and I fell with him. Some negroes passing by, afforded us assistance, and we reached a village. I presently awoke one of the inhabitants, to enquire if he had seen a slave, called Messember, whom we were seeking. "He is in the next hut," answered this negro. I hastened to the place, and there I found Messember. He had brought the bundle of European clothes for which I sent him, but the excuses which he made to justify his delay, far from proving satisfactory, made me determine to discharge him at the first opportunity. We then returned to Niakra. It was three o'clock in the morning, but the schools were already open, and the children round a large fire, were repeating their lessons aloud. While the Marabouts addressed their [prayers] to God, the women were busily employed in pounding millet. At this early hour, all was bustle in the African villages, while stilness and repose shed their influence over those of Europe. The extreme difference in the temperature, creates a difference in the hours of relaxation and business. The coolness of night here invites to labour, the heat of day becomes a signal for rest.

I next put on my European dress, and found that my hat and shoes secured me a degree of respect of which my Moorish habit had deprived me, among a people who so detest the Moors. "Now," said Fali Loum to me, when he saw my changed exterior, "this is really a white man." I had some reason to be satisfied, not only as these clothes made me appear more estimable in the opinion of the negroes, but because I could henceforth travel without the dread of thorns or muskitoes. My Marabout did not fail to observe the admiration excited by his white companion; according to him, the price of a camel would not pay for my wardrobe, though it only consisted of four pair of shoes, two pair of pantaloons, two woollen waistcoats, two handkerchiefs, and a hat.

When about to depart, I enquired of my host what recompence we should make him for his kindness, to which he generously replied, that he would only intreat one favour of us, which was to call at his house on our return. Such an answer surprised me from a negro, not so much for the benevolence it evinced, as for the delicate manner in which it was expressed. I pressed Fali Loum, to inform me what would please him, but on his hesitating, I was lucky enough to perceive, that he wished for some musket balls, to defend himself and friends, from the attacks of the Damel. With pleasure, I gave him six balls, six flints, and four heads of tobacco, with a few coral beads for his wife. On this, the thanks of Fali Loum were unlimited, manifesting an uncommon warmth of gratitude, combined with goodness of heart. He launched out in my praises, with expressions of regret at having given me a reception so inadequate to my presents. He moreover accompanied us, as our guide, for a quarter of a league. At the moment of parting, alighting from his horse, he raised his hands to heaven, and with impressive fervour, implored the divine protection on our expedition.

Scarcely had we quitted Fali Loum, when sentinels on the surrounding heights began to examine who we were, fearing lest we might belong to the Damel, and be sent to surprise the neighbouring villages. Our answer proved satisfactory, and we continued our march.

Our course this day turned towards the south, and after an hour's march, we stopped at Moslache, a large village inhabited by Poulas, and negroes. The night was dark, but Boukari conducted us, safely, to the hut of his aunt, who was a Poula woman. She threw some branches of trees on the ground, over which she spread the hide of an ox; my saddle, on this occasion, became a pillow, and recumbent about a good fire, we awaited the hour of supper.

The manner in which hospitality is practised in Africa, is truly commendable. While taking some rest on my mat, my Moslache host ran to procure grass for my beasts, his wife, at the same time, dividing with me the supper of her family.

REVIEW QUESTIONS

1. Although England had outlawed the trade of slaves on the world's oceans, what evidence do you find in this account to indicate that the trade in humans continued as a regular part of commerce?
2. What contrasts of wealth between different groups of people did Mollien encounter? How did he respond to those changing circumstances?
3. In what way do you believe this excursion by Mollien helped the French to claim the Gambia River?
4. Compare this account with that of Mungo Park. What are the similarities and differences?

An English Missionary Describes Life Along the Zambezi River (1840–1856)

DAVID LIVINGSTONE, *Missionary Travels and Researches in South Africa*

David Livingstone found traveling in Africa much easier than writing about it. The famed Scottish missionary, however, composed an extraordinarily detailed account of his 1840–1856 excursions across the southernmost parts of the continent. His writings reveal that Dutch settlers, Afrikaners, had a tremendous impact upon native culture as they advanced into the Transvaal region and demanded native labor on their large estates. As Livingstone discussed this phenomenon, he carefully distinguished between people whose customs had been changed by such contact with the Dutch and native ethnic groups who had not been so exposed, such as the Balonda. As a missionary, Livingstone was intent upon converting natives to Christianity, but his writings also reveal an intense interest in the customs and courtesies of the African people, whom he truly admired.

On the 6th of January, we reached the village of another female chief, named Nyamoána, who is said to be the mother of Manenko, and sister of Shinté or Kabómpo, the greatest Balonda chief in this part of the country. Her people had but recently come to the present locality, and had erected only twenty huts. Her husband, Samoána, was clothed in a kilt of green and red baize, and was armed with a spear, and a broad-sword of antique form, about eighteen inches long and three broad. The chief and her husband, were sitting on skins, placed in the middle of a circle, thirty paces in diameter, a little raised above the ordinary level of the ground, and having a trench round it. Outside the trench sat about a hundred persons of all ages and both sexes: the men were well armed with bows, arrows, spears, and broad-swords. Beside the husband sat a rather aged woman, having a bad outward squint in the left eye. We put down our arms about forty yards off, and I walked up to the centre of the circular bench, and saluted him in the usual way, by clapping the hands together in their fashion. He pointed to his wife, as much as to say, the honour belongs to her. I saluted her in the same way, and, a mat having been brought, I squatted down in front of them.

The talker was then called, and I was asked who was my spokesman. Having pointed to Kolimbota, who knew their dialect best, the palaver began in due form. I explained the real objects I had in view, without any attempt to mystify or appear in any other character than my own, for I have always been satisfied that, even though there were no other considerations, the truthful way of dealing with the uncivilised is unquestionably the best. Kolimbota repeated to Nyamoana's talker what I had said to him. He delivered it all verbatim to her husband, who repeated it again to her. It was thus all rehearsed four times over, in a tone loud enough to be heard by the whole party of auditors. The response came back by the same roundabout route, beginning at the lady to her husband, &c.

After explanations and re-explanations, I perceived that our new friends were mixing up my message of peace and friendship with Makololo affairs, and stated, that it was not delivered on the authority of any one less than that of their Creator, and that, if the Makololo did again break His laws and attack the Balonda, the guilt would rest with the Makololo and not with me. The palaver then came to a close.

By way of gaining their confidence, I showed them my hair, which is considered a curiosity in all this region. They said, "Is that hair? It is the mane of a lion, and not hair at all." Some thought that I had made a wig of lion's mane, as they sometimes do with the fibres of the "ife," and dye it black, and twist it, so as to resemble a mass of their own wool. I could not return the joke, by telling them that theirs was not hair but the wool of sheep, for they have none of these in the country; and even though they had, as Herodotus remarked, "the African sheep are clothed with hair, and men's heads with wool." So I had to be content with asserting, that mine was the real original hair, such as theirs would have been, had it not been scorched and frizzled by the sun. In proof of what the sun could do, I compared my own bronzed face and hands, then about the same in complexion as the lighter-coloured Makololo, with the white skin of my chest. They readily believed that, as they go nearly naked and fully exposed to that influence, we might be of common origin after all. Here, as everywhere when heat and moisture are combined, the people are very dark, but not quite black. There is always a shade of brown in the most deeply coloured. I showed my watch and pocket compass, which are considered great curiosities; but, though the lady was called on by her husband to look, she would not be persuaded to approach near enough.

These people are more superstitious than any we had yet encountered; though still only building their village, they had found time to erect two little sheds at the chief dwelling in it, in which were placed two pots having charms in them. When asked what medicine they contained, they replied, "Medicine for the Barimo"; but when I rose and looked into them, they said they were medicine for the game. Here we saw the first evidence of the existence of idolatry, in the remains of an old idol at a deserted village. It was simply a human head carved on a block of wood. Certain charms mixed with red ochre and white pipe-clay are dotted over them, when they are in use; and a crooked stick is used in the same way for an idol, when they have no professional carver.

As the Leeba seemed still to come from the

direction in which we wished to go, I was desirous of proceeding farther up with the canoes; but Nyamoana was anxious that we should allow her people to conduct us to her brother Shinte; and when I explained the advantage of water-carriage, she represented that her brother did not live near the river, and, moreover, there was a cataract in front, over which it would be difficult to convey the canoes. She was afraid, too, that the Balobále, whose country lies to the west of the river, not knowing the objects for which we had come, would kill us. To my reply, that I had been so often threatened with death if I visited a new tribe, that I was now more afraid of killing any one than of being killed, she rejoined, that the Balobale would not kill me, but the Makololo would all be sacrificed as their enemies. This produced considerable effect on my companions, and inclined them to the plan of Nyamoana, of going to the town of her brother, rather than ascending the Leeba. The arrival of Manenko herself on the scene, threw so much weight into the scale on their side, that I was forced to yield the point.

Manenko was a tall strapping woman about twenty, distinguished by a profusion of ornaments and medicines hung round her person; the latter are supposed to act as charms. Her body was smeared all over with a mixture of fat and red ochre, as a protection against the weather; a necessary precaution, for, like most of the Balonda ladies, she was otherwise in a state of frightful nudity. This was not from want of clothing, for, being a chief, she might have been as well clad as any of her subjects, but from her peculiar ideas of elegance in dress. When she arrived with her husband, Sambánza, they listened for some time to the statements I was making to the people of Nyamoana, after which the husband, acting as spokesman, commenced an oration, stating the reasons for their coming, and, during every two or three seconds of the delivery, he picked up a little sand, and rubbed it on the upper part of his arms and chest. This is a common mode of salutation in Londa; and when they wish to be excessively polite, they bring a quantity of ashes or pipe-clay in a piece of skin, and, taking up handfuls, rub it on the chest and upper front part of each arm; others, in saluting, drum their ribs with their elbows; while others still, touch the ground with one cheek after the other, and clap their hands. The chiefs go through the manœuvre of rubbing the sand on the arms, but only make a feint at picking up some. When Sambanza had finished his oration, he rose up, and showed his ankles ornamented with a bundle of copper rings; had they been very heavy, they would have made him adopt a straggling walk. Some chiefs have really so many, as to be forced, by the weight and size, to keep one foot apart from the other; the weight being a serious inconvenience in walking. The gentlemen like Sambanza, who wish to imitate their betters, do so in their walk; so you see men, with only a few ounces of ornament on their legs, strutting along as if they had double the number of pounds. When I smiled at Sambanza's walk, the people remarked, "That is the way in which they show off their lordship in these parts."

REVIEW QUESTIONS

1. What type of ceremony did Livingstone witness on January 6? Explain.
2. What role did physical characteristics play in the relationship between Livingstone and the native people with whom he visited?
3. What was the role of women in this society? Did they appear subservient to the men? Explain.

A British Observer Investigates a Muslim Town in Dahomey (1845–1846)

JOHN DUNCAN, *Travels in Western Africa in 1845 and 1846*

Given the disastrous nature of his first expedition to Africa, it is surprising that John Duncan returned a second time, but his love of adventure seems to have overcome any reservations he might have had. Born in 1805 in Kirkcudbright, Scotland, Duncan was drawn to the military from an early age and enlisted in the First Regiment of Life Guards at the age of seventeen. Following his retirement after sixteen years of "meritorious service," the thirty-three-year-old artist and mechanic obtained an appointment as master-at-arms in an expedition to the Niger River. Not long after it reached Africa, however, the venture had to be aborted, since an unknown fever struck down both members of the expedition and the Africans who were aiding them. Duncan reported that only five of the original three hundred members survived, and he thereafter always referred to himself as a member of the "Late Expedition to the Niger." He himself, though stricken by the fever and suffering an attack of gangrene in an old leg wound, healed sufficiently to return to England, where he made an almost complete recuperation (although he admitted that his leg, which he described as "entirely denuded above the ankle bone," never entirely regained its former strength). Duncan modestly credited his astonishing recovery to his own "robust consitution" and "athletic frame" (to which he referred rather frequently).

Duncan's second expedition to Africa began in 1845 under the auspices of the Royal Geographical Society. Its mission was to penetrate and explore the interior between the coast and the "Kong Mountains" (the hilly highlands of Lower Guinea). Although Europeans had been trading along the Gulf of Guinea (especially the Gold Coast and the Ivory Coast) for more than three hundred years, the region investigated by Duncan's group had not yet been fully explored by whites. The people whom they encountered were far different from others elsewhere in Africa. Many, such as the Dahomey, were tremendously wealthy, especially from the sale of slaves. Others, such as the Whydah and the Oyo, were impoverished victims of African, European, and Islamic slave traders.

Although Duncan's descriptions of the slave trade are only incidental sections in his account of the expedition, *Travels in West Africa* was published during the peak period of antislavery efforts by British and American abolitionists. At the time of its publication in 1847, slavery had already been outlawed in British colonies (1840), and the French were about to follow suit (1848). Slavery was not abolished in the United States until 1865, however. In Spanish colonies it lasted until 1886, and in Brazil until 1888. It still persists in some parts of Africa and the Caribbean.

The Spaniards and Portuguese treat their slaves in every respect better than the African slave-merchants; and I know, from personal inquiry, that none of M. de Suza's slaves would accept their liberty from choice. I have found by calculation, that the expense of maintaining slaves for domestic purposes is much greater than the hire of them to perform any labour would be. The only advantage in holding slaves is, that you always have them in the house or premises, and in fact they are always considered as part of the master's family, and their services readily procured, which is not the case in regard to hired slaves; for, so long as the African can procure food by theft or otherwise (at least it is so along the coast), they can never be induced to work. This is the great drawback upon all enterprise and improvement, either in agriculture or manufacture. The greatest suffering which the slaves undergo is in shipping; but owing to the vigilance of the English men-of-war cruisers, few opportunities for shipping them offer. When these do occur, large numbers are put on board, which frequently causes a loss in the number before reaching their place of destination.

Since my arrival on this coast, I have often considered whether better and more humane measures might not be adapted in regard to the Slave Trade; first, by making it a law in all colonies to which slaves are transported, that they shall be free in a certain number of years—say ten years, if they be transported before sixteen years of age, and seven years, if after the age of eighteen years; and that the free transportation of slaves from the coast of Africa should be allowed. This system might in the end be attended with more beneficial results to Africa, and the slave in general, than the present system.

The price of slaves (owing to the suppression of the Slave Trade) is very high, consequently the kings and chiefs in the interior go annually on a two or three months' slave-hunt, which they call a war. The result of this hunt is, of course, the capture of a number of slaves. These slaves (with the exception of those detained as wives or slaves, *for they are the same, or both,*) are sold at a high price to the white men, which is conse-

quently an encouragement to the kings in the interior to follow up these annual hunts. If the trade were open, the markets would be soon supplied, and the kidnapping trade would not be worth following. And if agents were appointed in all our colonies, to which slaves are transported from this coast, to make entry of all the slaves employed, so as to insure their freedom after a limited period, with opportunities of returning to their native country, these slaves would only be serving an apprenticeship to their calling, whatever it might be. They would then return to their native country with a full knowledge of the system of agriculture, of which at present they are entirely ignorant. This would prove, in my humble opinion, the most effectual way to civilize and cultivate Africa. Missionaries are very useful, where the people whom they come to instruct are even partially prepared to receive them; but where the natives are not raised either in knowledge or habit above the brute, I am of opinion that schoolmasters and schools of industry ought to precede the labours of the missionaries. After paving the way for them, no doubt their services would be highly beneficial.

If the plan I have ventured to suggest were adopted, the condition of slaves on their transportation would be much improved, as not more than one-fourth of the number at present put on board of one ship would be sent. Suffocation is well known often to be the result of the crowded state of the slave-ships; in fact, many slave vessels have been run on shore, with full cargoes of slaves on board, of whom two-thirds have perished! Then let us think of the enormous expense of keeping so many English cruisers on this coast, and of the sacrifice of life amongst our seamen. And, again, what must be the result of the numerous captures of slaves, who have been taken to Sierra Leone! I fear these poor creatures will not (in the event of their being sent to the West Indies) *much* improve their condition, more than if they were compelled to serve for the same period in the Brazils. . . .

There are several other markets of minor importance in Whydah, all subject to the same scale of duties, which are collected by the Avoga's officer. All goods sent out of the country pay a very heavy duty, such as palm-oil or ivory; in fact, the native duty here on ivory is so great, that very little is now bought. It is always levied on the sellers, who, of course, are subjects of the King of Dahomey. Any hesitation in paying would cost the individual his head. All persons who possess any regular income are taxed accordingly. Some idea may be formed of the enormous revenue exacted by the King, when even one of M. Ke Suza's slaves pays annually a tax of head-money alone to the amount of two thousand five hundred dollars, and another one thousand five hundred; these two sums are head-money alone, which is always paid according to rank, reputation, and income, independently of duties paid for trade in articles either exposed for sale, or passed from one part of the kingdom to another, or to any other country not under the control of the King of Dahomey. The duty on slaves is very high, and is charged upon the number shipped on board, which is upon the declaration of the Avoga, which is always made by his own head. When more than one party ships slaves, one of the party pays the Avoga generally in rum or tobacco, and then settles with the others, according to the number shipped by each party. All head-money is paid in cowries. Every native of Dahomey is a slave, and pays a duty of so much head-money to the King, consequently many are very glad to leave their country, preferring a foreign bondage where less severity is exercised. . . .

The country ten or twelve miles round Whydah is very interesting, the soil good, land level, and in many places well cultivated by people returned from the Brazils, as I before stated. Since my last mention of these people I learn that many of them were driven away from Brazil on account of their being concerned in an attempted revolution amongst the slaves there, who turned against their owners. These people are generally from the Foolah and Eya countries. Many, it appears, were taken away at the age of twenty or twenty-four years, consequently they can give a full account of their route to Badagry, where they were shipped. They are by far the most industrious people I have found. Several very fine farms, about six or seven miles from Whydah, are in a high state of cultivation. The houses are clean and comfortable, and are situated in some of the most beautiful spots that imagination can picture. It is truly gratifying to find unexpectedly a house where you are welcomed in European fashion, and asked to take refreshment. I invariably found upon inquiry that all these people had been slaves. This would seem to prove that to this country slavery is not without its good as well as bad effects.

There is another class of colonists, emancipated slaves from Sierra Leone, who emigrated to Whydah, with the intention of farming; but they are inferior in that science to the former class. Though most of them can read, and write a little, unfortunately the male portion of them appear nearly as indolent as the uncivilized native; notwithstanding that the King of Dahomey has afforded them every encouragement, by making them gratuitous grants of land on which they have built a small town. Immediately adjoining, is their cultivated land, which is little more than sufficient to meet their own consumption; but this is chiefly owing to the jealousy of the great slave-merchants, who use their combined influence to keep their produce out of the market. There is consequently little stimulus to exertion in agriculture. Through some means these colonists had been informed that I had come to Whydah for the purpose of establishing a model farm; and I was consequently waited upon by their headman, accompanied by several of his people, at the English Fort. They offered to give up to me all the cultivated land belonging to their settlement, upon condition of my affording them employment on the farm when labour was required, as they said that their united efforts, under a proper leader, would be worthy the attention of some of the European merchants trading on that coast. They all seemed much disappointed when I told them that I was not in a position to accept their proposal. They derive support chiefly from the females, who are during the season employed in the bush collecting palm-nuts for making oil, for which a market can always be found. Several are also engaged in washing, which they obtain from European slave-agents, who are numerous here. I had during my residence in this place a servant as interpreter, one of these colonists, who had himself been a slave, but had been captured by a British cruiser while on passage to Brazil, and carried to Sierra Leone, and there educated. He afterwards emigrated to Understone or Abbakuta—that saintly place of so many converts—and commenced slave-dealing. While on his passage, on board a slaver, he was again captured with several slaves in his possession. The slaves were carried to Sierra Leone; but he himself was with the crew of the slaver put on shore at Whydah, where he is now a resident in the above settlement of liberated Africans from Sierra Leone. . . .

26th.—

An American brig from Portland, Captain Goodriche, master, was sold by the captain for six thousand dollars to the slave merchants. The crew then turned mutinous and refused to work after the slaves were put on board. The vessel was then manned by Spaniards, who had been put on shore from prizes taken by English men-of-war. Sending vessels nearly valueless to the coast with general cargo, and after having been visited by an English man-of-war several times, discharging their cargoes, and selling them to slave dealers, seems now to be a favourite plan with the Yankees. When the vessel sails she is not suspected, from her apparent unfitness for that trade. This vessel took on board six hundred slaves in a few hours, and though the swell was so heavy that none of the vessels in the roads could discharge their cargo, not one of the slaves was drowned.

Knowing that a shipment of slaves was to take place, I stationed myself on the road where I knew they would have to pass. The first party consisted of about seventy very strong athletic men, apparently from twenty to twenty-five years of age. These were followed by a number more, carrying pails or buckets for their food on the passage. About forty were children, varying from seven to ten years of age. These were not in chains; but marched with two slight grass cords, knotted at intervals of a yard. The two cords are put, one on each side of the neck, and another knot is made in front of the neck, leaving sufficient room, but so tight as to prevent the head from being slipped through. The others were all in chains; sometimes eighty on one chain. At intervals of a yard are large circular links, which open to receive the neck, and which are secured by a padlock. I was surprised to see with what cheerfulness they all bustled along as if going to a fair. The returned or liberated slaves were all out to witness the procession, which seemed to give them great satisfaction; for they declared they had spent their happiest days in Bahia. I asked several their reason for leaving such a pleasant bondage; they assured me that it was owing to the revolt amongst some of the slaves in Bahia, who had been the means of ruining many slave-holders and large sugar manufacturers, who were unable to keep or employ them any longer. But, in all probability, these men were of the mutinous party, and had been sent out of the country.

I have just learned that two more American vessels are in Whydah roads at present for the same purpose, and one has lately sailed from Popoe with a cargo of slaves: in fact, the American government seems to wink at the trade. Whoever heard of an American man-of-war capturing a slaver, though there are three American men-of-war on the coast at present? I forgot to mention the circumstance of a Spaniard who was employed as a hand on board the *Medora* schooner, from London. Upon perceiving the slaves put on board the American brig, anchored at a short distance, he jumped overboard to swim to her, but had only been in the water a few seconds, before a large shark approached him. The poor fellow kicked with his feet towards the shark, endeavouring to keep it off, but the shark darted on him, and tore away his arm. A boat was immediately lowered, but before it reached him the shark made a second attack, and the poor fellow, who was swimming with one hand, was again seized on the back of the shoulders, and dragged under water, the tail of the shark remaining in sight. When the boat reached the spot, the shark appeared on the surface, still holding the man. One of the men in the boat struck the shark's head with a boat-hook, when he relinquished his hold; but the poor fellow's flesh was completely torn from the bone. A small rope was fastened round his back, and he was got into the boat, and after being taken on board the *Medora* died in half an hour.

This coast abounds with sharks; and if a man is so unfortunate as to fall overboard he is sure to be caught by one of them.

REVIEW QUESTIONS

1. Do you believe Duncan's mission was "scientific"? If so, why? If not, how would you characterize it, and why?
2. Did Duncan approve or disapprove of slavery and the slave trade? How can you tell?
3. How does Duncan's description of slavery compare to accounts written in the 1700s, particularly those by Olaudah Equiano and Crassons de Medeuil?
4. How did this exploration of West Africa differ from others, especially that of Mungo Park?

A Methodist Missionary Recounts Her Observations on the Kroo Coast of West Africa (1890s)

AGNES MCALLISTER, *A Lone Woman in Africa*

A Methodist missionary who came to the Garaway Mission Station on the west African coast in the 1890s, Agnes McAllister published an autobiography of her "call to the work" in 1896. McAllister represents the hundreds of Christian missionaries who came to Africa in the wake of the Berlin Conference of 1884, which formally allotted African lands to European nations. By the turn of the century, the activity of missionaries, merchants, and explorers had increased dramatically. Africans in secluded villages, however, often had no idea they were the focus of such widespread interest.

McAllister's description of the people to whom she ministered and her representation of their daily customs are largely ethnographic and focus on the entire community rather than upon individuals. Although her tone does not tend toward condescension, she quite innocently describes her subjects according to the Christian preconceptions she brought to share with them.

THE AFRICAN WOMAN

When a child is born in Liberia some member of the family is sent at once to the devil-doctor to inquire who it is and what its name shall be.

The devil-doctor's deeds are all done in the dark. He goes up into the housetop, which is a small windowless attic used as a storeroom and rice granary. He takes with him the cowhorn. This he blows to call the devil; and the devil is supposed to tell who it is that has come back to this world. For the people believe that every newborn child is some deceased member of the family who has returned to life among them. It sometimes receives the same name it had before, and sometimes the name is changed.

When the devil-doctor has blown his horn long enough to call the devil and receive an answer he begins to tell whose child it is by describing the parents. Sometimes he has already heard of the birth and knows the family; but it sometimes happens that he has had to guess, in which case he often makes serious mistakes. The people do not always believe in him; but it is their custom to consult him, and it is hard to break it up.

After finding out who the parents are, and whether the child is a boy or a girl, the devil-doctor goes on to describe it. The inquirer must come prepared to pay for the information with plates, cloth, and tobacco. The devil-doctor may say, for example, that the child is (or was) the mother of a certain man named Scere. In that case she will be called *Scere-day,* or Scere's mother, *day* meaning "mother." If the child is a boy it will, perhaps, be declared to be some great man who has died; and if so the babe will be much respected.

When a son was born to Kalenky—one of our chief men—the father sent to the devil-doctor to inquire who it was that had returned to the earth. The doctor said it was a great warrior named Wear, and that they must train him for war, as he had come to protect them.

When this was told to the father he brought a gun, a powder case, a shot bag, a war dress, and a fringe for the waist made from palm leaf, charms for the head, neck, arms, waist, knees, and ankles, and another peculiar charm in the shape of a cake of soap. This last, moistened with a little water, was to be rubbed with the hands on the infant's skin. They say it toughens the skin so that no shot can pierce it; and a soldier that has this charm need not fear the enemy. All these things were brought and laid on a mat by the side of an infant but a few hours old.

I have sometimes seen infants without any-

thing on their bodies, not even the string of beads which they think so necessary. A child usually wears one of these about its neck, several around its waist, and others on its wrists and ankles. When it is a few days old its ears are pierced, and small rings are put in, or, if the rings cannot be had, a piece of fine wire or a cotton thread.

The child is washed three and four times a day in hot water, and rubbed with a white mixture like paint. Every morning when it is washed several of the older women are called in. Some of them are very competent, and they take charge of the babe. A young mother is never left with the care of her child. These nurses may be seen any morning sitting on one of their common "chairs," which is no more than a stick of stove wood—outdoors if it is warm, otherwise in the house—with a pepper board by their side. They will rub one of their fingers in the pepper on the board, then thrust it as far down the child's throat as possible, and rub and stretch the throat thoroughly until the poor child is almost strangled and throws up all that is in its stomach. This looks like unmerciful treatment; but they believe it necessary to the child's health and strength. The child is then given an injection of some herb, and laid down to sleep on its little mat on the floor by the fire. Many infants die very young, and I fear that this severe treatment is sometimes to blame.

When the child gets to be nine or ten months old small bells are tied to its person, at its wrists, waist, and ankles. These are intended to coax it to walk. When it moves the bells will tinkle. Pleased by the sound, it will be induced to make another movement, and so will learn to go alone. The mother at this time will take her child to the devil-doctor, and he will make a charm for it which will be tied around the waist.

When the child begins to walk they put on its ankles the native "gless"—a kind of anklet made with several small bells in each ring. From six to ten of these are put on each ankle. No child is supposed to learn to walk without these assistants.

But to return to the children one sometimes

sees not dressed in the usual way. I have inquired the reason of the mother when I have seen one of these babies looking so uncared for. I have been told that the child is supposed to be some one who has come from the spirit world only to find articles to carry back, and that if they should dress it or give it anything it would not stay, but would take the things and be gone. Therefore they do not give it anything to wear; and so, since it has nothing to take with it, it is obliged to stay here and grow up. They hope that thus it will change its mind and consent to live with its people.

When a girl is from six to ten years of age she wears on her forearm brass rods, sometimes simply twisted in a spiral, and sometimes bent into separate rings. These are put on halfway up to the elbow—put on with a hammer to stay. They are worn night and day until the flesh becomes sore. Then they may be taken off, for the scars will always be there to prove that she wore jewelry when she was young.

If a woman grows up without these marks on her arms it is a lasting source of annoyance to her; for if her neighbors become vexed with her and wish to insult her, they cast it up to her that her mother was a poor woman and could not afford to put jewelry upon her children. This is a great reproach to a woman, as they all aspire to be reputed wealthy.

The little girls, as soon as they are able to follow their mothers to the farm and the bush, go along to help them; and when they are quite small, not able even to walk all the way, the little daughters may be seen coming home from the farm with their mothers. After having carried one on her back most of the way, the mother will put her down to walk and give her a stick of wood to carry on her head, although she is too small to carry a wood rack, or "banna."

The mother always keeps on hand a small waterpot for her little daughter to learn to carry; and the child may often be seen coming along the road before or behind her mother, with the water splashing over her from the pot, in her first attempts to imitate her mother.

The father will make a little wood rack for her, and she will have a small fanner for fanning rice. Her highest ambitions are to beat her mother's rice, carry a big load of wood on her head, and have her own farm. Then she is considered by all to be a smart girl and fitted to make a smart wife for some man.

A girl is often betrothed at the age of seven, and sometimes while she is yet an infant in her mother's arms. She is sold to be the wife of whatever man may choose to purchase her.

At about the age of ten or twelve years she is taken to live with her betrothed's people, where she will be associated with him and learn "his fashion." She is supposed to study his wishes and live to please him. Some of the men make slaves of their wives, and do not consider that any of their wishes are to be consulted; while others are not so, but treat their wives with a great deal of respect and try to please them, so that they live very happily together.

The girls in Africa reach mature womanhood much earlier than in America. At the age of fourteen or fifteen they are married. The marriage ceremony is very simple. When a man takes his betrothed to be his wife he has a fowl killed and some rice cooked. They both partake of these, and it is understood by all that the pair are henceforth man and wife. They really have no marriage ceremony at all.

A man generally has one favorite wife, or head wife. A man may choose his own wife; but his family—which is the whole family connection—pays for her. Upon his death his women, who are family property, are divided up among the other members. The head wife has charge of all the rest, unless they refuse to submit to her, in which case they live entirely independent of her, while doing their part toward caring for the husband.

A man has from three to twelve wives, according to his wealth and importance. If a man has the reputation of being a good husband, he often gets wives without paying for them. They run away from other tribes and come to him, hoping to better their condition. But if their lot turns out to be no better than with their former husbands they often go back to them again.

A man in going off to his work in the morning is never sure that he will find his wife at home when he returns in the evening. It is a common thing for wives to run away; and she is considered a queer woman who at some time has not run away from her husband or for some reason been separated from him. . . .

The last months of the year are spent in house building. As the native houses begin to decay in about five years much time is spent in making repairs. It is a good house, and one that has been well cared for, that will last fourteen years. The thatch used for roofing often has to be brought a long distance, and always on the head; for the people have no wagons or carts, not even a wheelbarrow, and no roads except narrow footpaths.

The men go out to the bush, cut the leaves, and start home with them, and their wives meet them on the road and carry the burden the rest of the way. The timbers of the house frame may also need to be carried a long distance, and a good wife is often seen following her husband in the road, with as heavy a load of building poles on her head as he bears on his.

When the house is up and the woodwork pretty well finished the women begin to plaster. The walls are made of narrow pieces of native plank set on end, and need a great deal of plastering on account of the numerous holes. A woman seldom plasters her house alone, but she will invite her neighbor's wife in to help her, and in turn will assist her neighbor when she may be in need. In this way the work is lightened.

The floor is the last thing to be put into a house. The women bring the mud or clay for the floor. The men often help to beat it; but it has to be washed over with a substance which they call "bleen," and this the women always do.

The women can hardly be called fishermen, as the men consider that their work. But there are many shellfish that the women gather, and a very small fish called "necklies," which they catch with a cloth. Four women go together to fish in

this way. They wade out into the river until they see a school of these fish. Then they arrange the cloth in the water, two of them holding it, while the other two surround the fish and drive them into the cloth, which is then gathered up like a net, and the fish emptied out into a brass kettle or a bucket brought for the purpose. Then the cloth is let down for another draught. When they are through they divide the fish and return home. These are the smallest fish I ever saw them take for food, being not over three quarters of an inch long.

They also set traps to catch a fish resembling the eel. In time of high water they set these traps in swamps or marshy places. Crabs are often caught along with the fish, and these are generally dried and put away for the dry season, when fish are not so easily taken.

In time of war the women are the messengers, as the warriors—every man is a warrior—are not allowed to go to the enemy's town. A man's life would not be safe; but the women can go in safety, and, as a rule, they are allowed to return. Sometimes they are imprisoned; but if it is known that they have been sent by the other tribe with a message of peace they are generally well received and allowed to return to their homes in peace.

When a woman becomes old and not able to earn more than her own living the husband's attention is generally devoted to his new and younger wives, and his first wife, now being neglected, seeks a better home among her children, generally with one of her sons.

I remember one of these neglected wives, an old woman, who had lived for several years with her daughter. The daughter died, and the old woman's husband, seeing that his first wife's child had died and that she was now homeless, felt it his duty to take her back. He built a little home for her near his own, and supported her in her feeble old age.

When a woman dies all the women turn out to dance, for it is a great honor to the dead to have a good dance at the funeral. Since they all want to be buried with honors they try to be present at every dance, so that when they die themselves everybody will make an effort to be present and dance for them.

When an old person dies the natives never say that some one has witched them, but that their time is finished and God has taken them.

The women exert great influence over the men. In their palavers they do not generally call on the women to say anything unless they have a serious question to settle, when they call upon the women to help them decide.

In case of war, if all the soldiers wished to go and fight, and the women rose up and said, "No, we are not willing, you must not do so," they would all be afraid to go, fearing defeat; for they say, "Woman got witch past man," and they are afraid to displease them for fear of being witched, and so defeated or killed.

Every town has its head woman, and when any person has done what the women think deserves punishment, the men keep silence and do not interfere. I have scarcely found a single man that had courage enough to face the women at such a time and say, "This thing that you are doing is wrong; it shall not be done." I have sometimes asked why it is that the men are afraid to oppose the women, and been told, "Well, woman is the mother of man, and we ought to listen to her."

Some of the women are remarkably good speakers. Not every woman would attempt to rise in a meeting of the people to give her reasons why certain things ought or ought not to be done. But they have certain women who are recognized as public speakers.

The woman in our tribe who was considered the best speaker was called "Queede." I have seen her standing in the midst of a crowd of people seated on the ground—kings, chiefs, soldiers, and women—and talking to them with just as much earnestness and decision, and receiving as much attention, as any man I ever saw.

If the women have anything to say they meet by themselves and then appoint one or more of their best talkers to speak for them in the general council.

Woman is not the downtrodden creature in Liberia that she is in India and many other heathen lands. Yet it is harder to reach the women than the men. They do not seem to have the same desire to rise out of heathenism and receive Jesus. This may be from the fact that they have been more confined to their homes and have not seen so much of the world, and do not realize the benefits of civilization. But some of the women are coming out, and they make good workers when they are saved.

REVIEW QUESTIONS

1. How did the native belief in reincarnation affect the relationship of child and mother? Explain.
2. To what extent did native religious beliefs influence the treatment of children and the conditions in which they grew and developed?
3. How dictatorial did native life and custom appear to be? What were the prerogatives of men? Of women?
4. What was the nature of education for children?

An Indian Icon Remembers His Experiences in South Africa (1893)

MOHANDAS K. GANDHI, *An Autobiography: The Story of My Experiments with Truth*

After returning from law school in England, Gandhi began a law practice in India. He had difficulty being accepted into the profession, however, and was unable to find a position with an established firm. Fortunately, his brother helped him establish his own small law office in Bombay and steered many clients to Gandhi. One of these early clients provided Gandhi with a commission to represent a firm that had a large claim in a South African court. In April 1893, Gandhi left for Pretoria, South Africa. The following excerpts from his account of that passage from Bombay to Pretoria foreshadow the racist insults that Gandhi faced for the rest of his life. He found the intolerable situation of racial persecution and ethnic harassment in Africa impossible to solve.

I soon came in contact with the Christian Indians living in Durban. The Court Interpreter, Mr. Paul, was a Roman Catholic. I made his acquaintance, as also that of the late Mr. Subhan Godfrey, then a teacher under the Protestant Mission, and father of Mr. James Godfrey, who, as a member of the South African Deputation, visited India in 1924. I likewise met the late Parsi Rustomji and the late Adamji Miyakhan about the same time. All these friends, who up to then had never met one another except on business, came ultimately into close contact, as we shall see later.

Whilst I was thus widening the circle of my acquaintance, the firm received a letter from their lawyer saying that preparations should be made for the case, and that Abdulla Sheth should go to Pretoria himself or send a representative.

Abdulla Sheth gave me this letter to read, and asked me if I would go to Pretoria. 'I can only say after I have understood the case from you,' said I. 'At present I am at a loss to know what I have to do there.' He thereupon asked his clerks to explain the case to me.

As I began to study the case, I felt as though I ought to begin from the A B C of the subject. During the few days I had had at Zanzibar, I had been to the court to see the work there. A Parsi lawyer was examining a witness and asking him questions regarding credit and debit entries in account books. It was all Greek to me. Book-keeping I had learnt neither at school nor during my stay in England. And the case for which I had come to South Africa was mainly about accounts. Only one who knew accounts could understand and explain it. The clerk went on talking about this debited and that credited, and I felt more and more confused. I did not know what a P. Note meant. I failed to find the word in the dictionary. I revealed my ignorance to the clerk, and learnt from him that a P. Note meant a promisory note. I purchased a book on book-keeping and studied it. That gave me some confidence. I understood the case. I saw that Abdulla Sheth, who did not know how to keep accounts, had so much practical knowledge that he could quickly solve intricacies of book-keeping. I told him that I was prepared to go to Pretoria.

'Where will you put up?' asked the Sheth.

'Wherever you want me to,' said I.

'Then I shall write to our lawyer. He will arrange for your lodgings. I shall also write to my Meman friends there, but I would not advise you to stay with them. The other party has great influence in Pretoria. Should any one of them manage to read our private correspondence, it might do us much harm. The more you avoid familiarity with them, the better for us.'

'I shall stay where your lawyer puts me up, or I shall find out independent lodgings. Pray don't worry. Not a soul shall know anything that is confidential between us. But I do intend cultivating the acquaintance of the other party. I should like to be friends with them. I would try, if possible, to settle the case out of court. After all Tyeb Sheth is a relative of yours.'

Sheth Tyeb Haji Khan Muhammad was a near relative of Abdulla Sheth.

The mention of a probable settlement somewhat startled the Sheth, I could see. But I had already been six or seven days in Durban, and we now knew and understood each other. I was no longer a 'white elephant'. So he said:

'Y . . . es, I see. There would be nothing better than a settlement out of court. But we are all relatives and know one another very well indeed. Tyeb Sheth is not a man to consent to a settlement easily. With the slightest unwariness on our part, he would screw all sorts of things out of us, and do us down in the end. So please think twice before you do anything.'

'Don't be anxious about that,' said I. 'I need not talk to Tyeb Sheth, or for that matter to anyone else, about the case. I would only suggest to him to come to an understanding, and so save a lot of unnecessary litigation.'

On the seventh or eighth day after my arrival, I left Durban. A first class seat was booked for me. It was usual there to pay five shillings extra, if one needed a bedding. Abdulla Sheth insisted that I should book one bedding but, out of obstinacy and pride and with a view to saving five shillings, I declined. Abdulla Sheth warned me. 'Look, now,' said he, 'this is a different country from India. Thank God, we have enough and to spare. Please do not stint yourself in anything that you may need.'

I thanked him and asked him not to be anxious.

The train reached Maritzburg, the capital of Natal, at about 9 p.m. Beddings used to be provided at this station. A railway servant came and asked me if I wanted one. 'No,' said I, 'I have one with me.' He went away. But a passenger came next, and looked me up and down. He saw that I was a 'coloured' man. This disturbed him. Out he went and came in again with one or two officials. They all kept quiet, when another official came to me and said, 'Come along, you must go to the van compartment.'

'But I have a first class ticket,' said I.

'That doesn't matter,' rejoined the other. 'I tell you, you must go to the van compartment.'

'I tell you, I was permitted to travel in this compartment at Durban, and I insist on going on in it.'

'No, you won't,' said the official. 'You must leave this compartment, or else I shall have to call a police constable to push you out.'

'Yes, you may. I refuse to get out voluntarily.'

The constable came. He took me by the hand and pushed me out. My luggage was also taken out. I refused to go to the other compartment and the train steamed away. I went and sat in the waiting room, keeping my hand-bag with me, and leaving the other luggage where it was. The railway authorities had taken charge of it.

It was winter, and winter in the higher regions of South Africa is severely cold. Maritzburg being at a high altitude, the cold was extremely bitter. My over-coat was in my luggage, but I did not dare to ask for it lest I should be insulted again, so I sat and shivered. There was no light in the room. A passenger came in at about midnight and possibly wanted to talk to me. But I was in no mood to talk.

I began to think of my duty. Should I fight for my rights or go back to India, or should I go on to Pretoria without minding the insults, and return to India after finishing the case? It would be cowardice to run back to India without fulfilling my obligation. The hardship to which I was subjected was superficial—only a symptom of the deep disease of colour prejudice. I should try, if possible, to root out the disease and suffer hardships in the process. Redress for wrongs I should seek only to the extent that would be necessary for the removal of the colour prejudice.

So I decided to take the next available train to Pretoria.

The following morning I sent a long telegram to the General Manager of the Railway and also informed Abdulla Sheth, who immediately met the General Manager. The Manager justified the conduct of the railway authorities, but informed him that he had already instructed the Station Master to see that I reached my destination safely. Abdulla Sheth wired to the Indian merchants in Maritzburg and to friends in other places to meet me and look after me. The merchants came to see me at the station and tried to comfort me by narrating their own hardships and explaining that what had happened to me was nothing unusual. They also said that Indians travelling first or second class had to expect trouble from railway officials and white passengers. The day was thus spent in listening to these tales of woe. The evening train arrived. There was a reserved berth for me. I now purchased at Maritzburg the bedding ticket I had refused to book at Durban.

The train took me to Charlestown.

MORE HARDSHIPS

The train reached Charlestown in the morning. There was no railway, in those days, between Charlestown and Johannesburg, but only a stage-coach, which halted at Standerton for the night *en route*. I possessed a ticket for the coach, which was not cancelled by the break of the journey at Maritzburg for a day; besides, Abdulla Sheth had sent a wire to the coach agent at Charlestown.

But the agent only needed a pretext for putting me off, and so, when he discovered me to be a stranger, he said, 'Your ticket is cancelled.' I gave him the proper reply. The reason at the back of his mind was not want of accommodation, but quite another. Passengers had to be accommodated inside the coach, but as I was regarded as a 'coolie' and looked a stranger, it would be proper, thought the 'leader', as the white man in charge of the coach was called, not to seat me with the white passengers. There were seats on either side of the coachbox. The leader sat on one of these as a rule. Today he sat inside and gave me his seat. I knew it was sheer injustice and an insult, but I thought it better to pocket it. I could not have forced myself inside, and if I had raised a protest, the coach would have gone off without me. This would have meant the loss of another day, and Heaven only knows what would have happened the next day. So, much as I fretted within myself, I prudently sat next the coachman.

At about three o'clock the coach reached Pardekoph. Now the leader desired to sit where I was seated, as he wanted to smoke and possibly to have some fresh air. So he took a piece of dirty sack-cloth from the driver, spread it on the footboard and, addressing me said, '*Sami,* you sit on this, I want to sit near the driver.' The insult was more than I could bear. In fear and trembling I said to him, 'It was you who seated me here, though I should have been accommodated inside. I put up with the insult. Now that you want to sit outside and smoke, you would have me sit at your feet. I will not do so, but I am prepared to sit inside.'

As I was struggling through these sentences, the man came down upon me and began heavily to box my ears. He seized me by the arm and tried to drag me down. I clung to the brass rails of the coachbox and was determined to keep my hold even at the risk of breaking my wristbones. The passengers were witnessing the scene—the man swearing at me, dragging and belabouring me, and I remaining still. He was strong and I was weak. Some of the passengers were moved to pity and exclaimed: 'Man, let him alone. Don't beat him. He is not to blame. He is right. If he can't stay there, let him come and sit with us.' 'No fear,' cried the man, but he seemed somewhat crestfallen and stopped beating me. He let go my arm, swore at me a little more, and asking the Hottentot servant who was sitting on the other side of the coachbox to sit on the footboard, took the seat so vacated.

The passengers took their seats and, the

whistle given, the coach rattled away. My heart was beating fast within my breast, and I was wondering whether I should ever reach my destination alive. The man cast an angry look at me now and then and, pointing his finger at me, growled: 'Take care, let me once get to Standerton and I shall show you what I do.' I sat speechless and prayed to God to help me.

After dark we reached Standerton and I heaved a sigh of relief on seeing some Indian faces. As soon as I got down, these friends said: 'We are here to receive you and take you to Isa Sheth's shop. We have had a telegram from Dada Abdulla.' I was very glad, and we went to Sheth Isa Haji Sumar's shop. The Sheth and his clerks gathered round me. I told them all that I had gone through. They were very sorry to hear it and comforted me by relating to me their own bitter experiences.

I wanted to inform the agent of the Coach Company of the whole affair. So I wrote him a letter, narrating everything that had happened, and drawing his attention to the threat his man had held out. I also asked for an assurance that he would accommodate me with the other passengers inside the coach when we started the next morning. To which the agent replied to this effect: 'From Standerton we have a bigger coach with different men in charge. The man complained of will not be there tomorrow, and you will have a seat with the other passengers.' This somewhat relieved me. I had, of course, no intention of proceeding against the man who had assaulted me, and so the chapter of the assault closed there.

In the morning Isa Sheth's man took me to the coach, I got a good seat and reached Johannesburg quite safely that night.

Standerton is a small village and Johannesburg a big city. Abdulla Sheth had wired to Johannesburg also, and given me the name and address of Muhammad Kasam Kamruddin's firm there. Their man had come to receive me at the stage, but neither did I see him nor did he recognize me. So I decided to go to a hotel. I knew the names of several. Taking a cab I asked to be driven to the Grand National Hotel. I saw the

Manager and asked for a room. He eyed me for a moment, and politely saying, 'I am very sorry, we are full up', bade me good-bye. So I asked the cabman to drive to Muhammad Kasam Kamruddin's shop. Here I found Abdul Gani Sheth expecting me, and he gave me a cordial greeting. He had a hearty laugh over the story of my experience at the hotel. 'How ever did you expect to be admitted to a hotel?' he said.

'Why not?' I asked.

'You will come to know after you have stayed here a few days,' said he. 'Only *we* can live in a land like this, because, for making money, we do not mind pocketing insults, and here we are.' With this he narrated to me the story of the hardships of Indians in South Africa.

Of Sheth Abdul Gani we shall know more as we proceed.

He said: 'This country is not for men like you. Look now, you have to go to Pretoria tomorrow. You will *have* to travel third class. Conditions in the Transvaal are worse than in Natal. First and second class tickets are never issued to Indians.'

'You cannot have made persistent efforts in this direction.'

'We have sent representations, but I confess our own men too do not want as a rule to travel first or second.'

I sent for the railway regulations and read them. There was a loophole. The language of the old Transvaal enactments was not very exact or precise; that of the railway regulations was even less so.

I said to the Sheth: 'I wish to go first class, and if I cannot, I shall prefer to take a cab to Pretoria, a matter of only thirty-seven miles.'

Sheth Abdul Gani drew my attention to the extra time and money this would mean, but agreed to my proposal to travel first, and accordingly we sent a note to the Station Master. I mentioned in my note that I was a barrister and that I always travelled first. I also stated in the letter that I needed to reach Pretoria as early as possible, that as there was no time to await his reply I would receive it in person at the station, and that I should expect to get a first class ticket. There was of course a purpose behind asking for the reply in person. I thought that if the Station Master gave a written reply, he would certainly say 'no', especially because he would have his own notion of a 'coolie' barrister. I would therefore appear before him in faultless English dress, talk to him and possibly persuade him to issue a first class ticket. So I went to the station in a frock-coat and necktie, placed a sovereign for my fare on the counter and asked for a first class ticket.

'You sent me that note?' he asked.

'That is so. I shall be much obliged if you will give me a ticket. I must reach Pretoria today.'

He smiled and, moved to pity, said: 'I am not a Transvaaler. I am a Hollander. I appreciate your feelings, and you have my sympathy. I do want to give you a ticket—on one condition, however, that, if the guard should ask you to shift to the third class, you will not involve me in the affair, by which I mean that you should not proceed against the Railway Company. I wish you a safe journey. I can see you are a gentleman.'

With these words he booked the ticket. I thanked him and gave him the necessary assurance.

Sheth Abdul Gani had come to see me off at the station. The incident gave him an agreeable surprise, but he warned me saying: 'I shall be thankful if you reach Pretoria all right. I am afraid the guard will not leave you in peace in the first class and even if he does, the passengers will not.'

I took my seat in a first class compartment and the train started. At Germiston the guard came to examine the tickets. He was angry to find me there, and signalled to me with his finger to go to the third class. I showed him my first class ticket. 'That doesn't matter,' said he, 'remove to the third class.'

There was only one English passenger in the compartment. He took the guard to task. 'What do you mean by troubling the gentleman?' he said. 'Don't you see he has a first class ticket? I do not mind in the least his travelling with me.' Addressing me, he said, 'You should make yourself comfortable where you are.'

The guard muttered: 'If you want to travel with a coolie, what do I care?' and went away.

At about eight o'clock in the evening the train reached Pretoria.

REVIEW QUESTIONS

1. What was Gandhi's attitude toward himself and his position as an attorney? What special considerations did he believe he should receive?
2. How did Gandhi respond to the insults given to him? Do you believe you would have responded in the same way?
3. Did he have any alternatives to the behavior he exhibited? What do you think he could have done?

9

The Americas and Oceania, 1800–1918

The developments and trends that began in the early 1500s continued into the early twentieth century, during which time the passage of peoples to the Americas increased greatly and helped stimulate the development of a global society. The primary force behind this expansion was the Industrial Revolution, which greatly increased the demand for cheap raw materials. The technology and scientific discoveries of the pre-1750 era also stimulated physical and intellectual exploration in the Americas. The new modes of transportation, including steam-powered trains and ships, enabled people to travel much more easily, and a new middle class of wealthier people appeared who could satisfy their curiosity about life in other nations and continents by traveling. Simultaneously, the educational systems of the new industrial countries became magnets for young men of elite families from other continents. The extraordinary account of the young Japanese student Inoue Ryokichi represents the views of hundreds of such men sent to Europe and the United States to learn. The fashion of visiting the frontier of any country, combined with an increased emphasis upon personal education, brought many to the Western Hemisphere and the Pacific. Another observer was Harriet Martineau, a single lady from England who came to the United States in the nineteenth century to investigate the conditions of women and children. Pavel N. Golovin of Russia traveled to San Francisco at a time when California had been part of the United States for only twelve years. Although their accounts of American society are shaded by their anticipation of what they would find, these commentators on the American scene attempted to document what they actually saw.

In the late nineteenth century, travelers continued to explore new lands and new peoples around the world. The lure of the unknown, the desire for new trading ports, and the rush to add new information to the scientific pool of knowledge brought many to glory, and some to unfortunate ends. The pseudo-anthropologist Edward Tylor stopped in Cuba on his way from the United States to Mexico and presented a fascinating account of the relationship between Cuba and the United States about forty years before the island became independent of Spain. Equally interesting are the observations of John L. Stephens in the Yucatan, which reveal much about this little-documented area of Mexico. Finally, the German scholar Tschudi visited Peru to find new varieties of fish, and left a very interesting account of the multiracial and multicultural life he found in a fishing village.

The reverence for scientific thought and innovation often produced unfortunate biases among these travelers. Sometimes such prejudices could be traced to the writings of Social Darwinists. However, they were just as often the result of the economic ideas of Herbert Spencer and Adam Smith, which convinced authors and businessmen from the United States and England to travel to Latin American nations in the nineteenth century to investigate the possibilities for business expansion. Tylor visited sugar plantations and cigar makers while writing about the utility of Chinese and African-Cuban workers in Cuba. The account of James Bryce, however, is the strongest example in this chapter of entrepreneurial motivations.

The impact of rampant industrialization in the United States and Europe in the nineteenth century can also be seen in these accounts. Socialist priorities are evident in John Kenneth Turner's description of the Mestizo and Indian workers in Mexico; this reading reflects the international reaction against the social and physical conditions created by industrialization and the application of capitalist principles. An opposite viewpoint is shown by the businessman James Bryce, who came to Argentina to ascertain its appropriateness as a site for industrial development by the W. R. Grace Company of New York.

Finally, this chapter contains two nineteenth-century accounts by U.S. citizens who traveled to explore parts of their own nation. Early in the century, President Thomas Jefferson sent Meriwether Lewis and William Clark to determine the nature and extent of the recently acquired Louisiana Territory. While technically never leaving the United States, they recorded encounters with native peoples of many nations. In a slightly similar expedition at the end of the century, a noted journalist and author, Mark Twain, traveled to the Pacific territory of the Hawaiian Islands. With his trademark tongue-in-cheek humor, Twain described the native peoples and the "civilization" that transported Americans were making for themselves.

An American Explorer Recounts His Exchanges with Native Americans at the Continental Divide (1805)

Meriwether Lewis, *The Journals of Lewis and Clark*

While still quite a young and poor country, the United States in 1802 purchased the Louisiana Territory from France for a very reasonable price. Since he knew nothing about the nature of this enormous acquisition, President Thomas Jefferson commissioned Meriwether Lewis, Captain of the First Regiment of Infantry, to reconnoitre and map the territory. Although it is not stated specifically in his instructions of June 20, 1803, Jefferson implied that one of Lewis's goals was to find the Northwest Passage through the continent. The president, who apparently knew nothing of world geography, advised Lewis that the U.S. consuls in Batavia on Java, "the isles of France," and the Cape of Good Hope would be able to supply his needs if he were unable to return via the same route he had taken. The party that left St. Louis in the summer of 1804 included Second Lieutenant William Clark as the second in command and an assortment of experienced interpreters, boatmen, sergeants, and privates. The military rank of private was given to individuals like John Colter, an experienced mountain man who had spent years trapping beaver in the Rocky Mountains.

As part of a scientific expedition, the explorers were charged with collecting data and recording specific details of the flora and fauna and the geology of the region, as well as of the Native American nations they visited. The information they were to obtain included all aspects of native culture and customs, as well as native relations with other nations. Lewis and Clark embarked from St. Louis on the afternoon of May 14, 1804, and used the Missouri River as their main conduit west. Between September 1804 and April 1805, they camped in the villages of the Mandan nation. On April 7 they departed from the Mandan camp and again followed the Missouri River west to the Three Forks. They then followed the Jefferson River south, crossing the Continental Divide and proceeding through Lemhi Pass. The selections from Lewis's journal from the summer of 1805 give the reader a vivid portrayal of the daily concerns and experiences of this expedition.

Tuesday August 13th 1805.

at the distance of five miles the road after leading us down a long decending valley for 2 Ms. brought us to a large cheek about 10 yds. wide; this we passed and on rising the hill beyond it had a view of a handsome little valley to our left of about a mile in width through which from the appearance of the timber I conjectured that a river passed. we had proceeded about four miles through a wavy plain parallel to the valley or river bottom when at the distance of about a mile we saw two women, a man and some dogs on an eminence immediately before us. they appeared to v[i]ew us with attention and two of them after a few minutes set down as if to wait our arrival   we continued our usual pace towards them. when we had arrived within half a mile of them I directed the party to halt and leaving my pack and rifle I took the flag which I unfurled and a[d]vanced singly towards them   the women soon disappeared behind the hill, the man continued untill I arrived within a hundred yards of him and then likewise absconded. tho' I frequently repeated the word *tab-ba-bone* sufficiently loud for him to have heard it.

I now haistened to the top of the hill where they had stood but could see nothing of them. the dogs were less shye than their masters they came about me pretty close   I therefore thought of tying a handkerchief about one of their necks with some beads and other trinkets and then let them loose to surch their fugitive owners thinking by this means to convince them of our pacific disposition towards them but the dogs would not suffer me to take

hold of them; they also soon disappeared. I now made a signal fror the men to come on, they joined me and we pursued the the back track of these Indians which lead us along the same road which we had been traveling. the road was dusty and appeared to have been much traveled lately both by men and horses.

we had not continued our rout more than a mile when we were so fortunate as to meet with three female savages. the short and steep ravines which we passed concealed us from each other untill we arrived within 30 paces. a young woman immediately took to flight, an Elderly woman and a girl of about 12 years old remained. I instantly laid by my gun and advanced towards them. they appeared much allarmed but saw that we were to near for them to escape by flight

they therefore seated themselves on the ground, holding down their heads as if reconciled to die which the[y] expected no doubt would be their fate;   I took the elderly woman by the hand and raised her up repeated the word *tab-ba-bone* and strip[ped] up my shirt sleve to s[h]ew her my skin; to prove to her the truth of the ascertion that I was a white man for my face and ha[n]ds which have been constantly exposed to the sun were quite as dark as their own. they appeared instantly reconciled, and the men coming up I gave these women some beads a few mockerson awls some pewter looking-glasses and a little paint.

I directed Drewyer to request the old woman to recall the young woman who had run off to some distance by this time fearing she might allarm the camp before we approached and might so exasperate the natives that they would perhaps attack us without enquiring who we were.[1] the old woman did as she was requested and the fugitive soon returned almost out of breath. I bestoed an equ[i]volent portion of trinket on her with the others. I now painted their tawny cheeks with some vermillion which with this nation is emblematic of peace. after they had become composed I enformed them by signs that I wished them to conduct us to their camp that we wer anxious to become acquainted with the chiefs and warriors of their nation. they readily obeyed and we set out, still pursuing the road down the river. we had marched about 2 miles when we met a party of about 60 warriors mounted on excellent horses who came in nearly full speed,   when they arrived I advanced towards them with the flag leaving my gun with the party about 50 paces behi[n]d me. the chief and two others who were a little in advance of the main body spoke to the women, and they informed them who we were and exultingly shewed the presents which had been given them

these men then advanced and embraced me very affectionately in their way which is by puting their left arm over you[r] wright sholder clasping your back, while they apply their left cheek to yours and frequently vociforate the word *âh-hi-e, âh-hi-e* that is, I am much pleased, I am much rejoiced. bothe parties now advanced and we wer all carresed and besmeared with their grease and paint till I was heartily tired of the national hug. I now had the pipe lit and gave them smoke; they seated themselves in a circle around us and pulled of[f] their mockersons before they would receive or smoke the pipe. this is a custom among them as I afterwards learned indicative of a sacred obligation of sincerity in their profession of friendship given by the act of receiving and smoking the pipe of a stranger. or which is as much as to say that they wish they may always go bearfoot if they are not sincere; a pretty heavy penalty if they are to march through the plains of their country.

after smoking a few pipes with them I distributed some trifles among them, with which they seemed much pleased particularly with the blue beads and vermillion. I now informed the chief that the object of our visit was a friendly one, that after we should reach his camp I would undertake to explain to him fully those objects, who we wer, from whence we had come and w[h]ither we were going; that in the mean time I did not care how soon we were in motion, as the sun was very warm and no water at hand. they now put on their mockersons, and the principal chief Ca-me-âh-wait made a short speach to the warriors. I gave him the flag which I informed him was an emblem of peace among whitemen and now that it had been received by him it was to be respected as the bond of union between us. I desired him to march on, which [he] did and we followed him; the dragoons moved on in squadron in our rear. after we had marched about a mile in this order he halted them and gave a second harang; after which six or eight of the young men road forward to their encampment and no further regularity was observed in the order of march. I afterwards understood that the Indians we had first seen this morning had returned and allarmed the camp; these men had come out armed cap a pe for action expecting to meet with their enimies the Minnetares of Fort de Prarie whome they Call Pâh´-kees. they were armed with b[o]ws arrow and Shields except three whom I observed with small pieces such as the N.W. Company furnish the natives with which they had obtained from the Rocky Mountain Indians on the Yellow stone river with whom they are at peace. on our arrival at their encampmen[t] on the river in a handsome level and fertile bottom at the distance of 4 Ms. from where we had first met them they introduced us to a londge made of willow brush and an old leather lodge which had been prepared for our reception by the young men which the chief had dispatched for that purpose.

Here we were seated on green boughs and the skins of Antelopes. one of the warriors then pulled up the grass in the enter of the lodge forming a smal[l] circle of about 2 feet in

[1]Drewyer is, of course, addressing the old woman in sign language, the Esperanto of the Plains tribes.

diameter   the chief next produced his pipe and native tobacco and began a long cerimony of the pipe when we were requested to take of[f] our mockersons, the Chief having previously taken off his as well as all the warriors present. this we complyed with; the Chief then lit his pipe at the fire kindled in this little magic circle, and standing on the oposite side of the circle uttered a speach of several minutes in length at the conclusion of which he pointed the stem to the four cardinal points of the heavens first begining at the East and ending with the North. he now presented the pipe to me as if desirous that I should smoke, but when I reached my hand to receive it, he drew it back and repeated the same c[e]remony three times, after which he pointed the stem first to the heavens then to the center of the magic circle smoked himself with three whifs and held the pipe untill I took as many as I thought proper; he then held it to each of the white persons and then gave it to be consumed by his warriors.

I now explained to them the objects of our journey &c.   all the women and children of the camp were shortly collected about the lodge to indulge themselves with looking at us, we being the first white persons they had ever seen. after the cerimony of the pipe was over I distributed the remainder of the small articles I had brought with me among the women and children. by this time it was late in the evening and we had not taisted any food since the evening before. the Chief informed us that they had nothing but berries to eat and gave us some cakes of serviceberries and Choke cherries which had been dryed in the sun; of these I made a hearty meal, and then walked to the river, which I found about 40 yards wide very rapid clear and about 3 feet deep. Cameahwait informed me that this stream discharged itself into another doubly as large at the distance of half a days march which came from the S.W.   but he added on further enquiry that there was but little more timber below the junction of those rivers than I saw here, and that the river was confined between inaccessable mountains, was

very rapid and rocky insomuch that it was impossible for us to pass either by land or water down this river to the great lake where the white men lived as he had been informed. this was unwelcome information but I still hoped that this account had been exagerated with a view to detain us among them. as to timber I could discover not any that would answer the purpose of constructing canoes or in short more than was bearly necessary for fuel.

these people had been attacked by the Minetares of Fort de prarie this spring and about 20 of them killed and taken prisoners. on this occasion they lost a great part of their horses and all their lodges except that which they had erected for our accomodation; they were now living in lodges of a conic figure made of willow brush. I still observe a great number of horses feeding in every direction around their camp and therefore entertain but little doubt but we shall be enable[d] to furnish ourselves with an adiquate number to transport our stores even if we are compelled to travel by land over these mountains. on my return to my lodge an indian called me in to his bower and gave me a small morsel of the flesh of an antelope boiled and a piece of a fresh salmon roasted; both which I eat with a very good relish. this was the first salmon I had seen and perfectly convinced me that we were on the waters of the Pacific Ocean.

This evening the Indians entertained us with their dancing nearly all night. at 12 O'Ck. I grew sleepy and retired to rest leaving the men to amuse themselves with the Indians. I observe no essential difference between the music and manner of dancing among this nation and those of the Missouri. I was several times awoke in the course of the night by their yells but was too much fortiegued to be deprived of a tolerable sound night's repose.

Wednesday August 14th

In order to give Capt. Clark time to reach the forks of Jefferson's river I concluded to spend this day at the Shoshone Camp and obtain what information I could with rispect to the country. as we had nothing but a little flour and parched meal to eat except the berries with which the Indians furnished us I directed Drewyer and Shields to hunt a few hours and try to kill something,   the Indians furnished them with horses and most of their young men also turned out to hunt. I was very much entertained with a view of this indian chase; it was after a herd of about 10 Antelope and about 20 hunters. it lasted about 2 hours and considerable part of the chase in view from my tent. about 1.A.M. the hunters returned had not killed a single Antelope, and their horses foaming with sweat. my hunters returned soon after and had been equally unsuccessfull. I now directed McNeal to make me a little paist with the flour and added some berries to it which I found very pallatable.

The means I had of communicating with these people was by way of Drewyer who understood perfectly the common language of jesticulation or signs which seems to be universally understood by all the Nations we have yet seen. it is true that this language is imperfect and liable to error but is much less so than would be expected. the strong parts of the ideas are seldom mistaken.

I now told Cameahwait that I wished him to speak to his people and engage them to go with me tomorrow to the forks of Jeffersons river where our baggage was by this time arrived with another Chief and a large party of white-men who would wait my return at that place. that I wish them to take with them about 30 spare horses to transport our baggage to this place where we would then remain sometime among them and trade with them for horses, and finally concert our future plans for getting on to the ocean and of the traid which would be extended to them after our return to our homes. he complyed with my request and made a lengthey harrangue to his village. he returned in about an hour and a half and informed me that they would be ready to accompany me in the morning. I promised to reward them for their trouble. Drewyer who had had a good view of their horses estimated them at 400. most of them are fine horses. indeed many of them would make a figure on the South side of James River or the land of fine horses. I saw several with spanish brands on them, and some mules which they informed me that they had also obtained from the Spaniards. I also saw a bridle bit of spanish manufactary, and sundry other articles which I have no doubt were obtained from the same source. notwithstanding the extreem poverty of those poor people they are very merry they danced again this evening untill midnight. each warrior keep[s] one or more horses tyed by a cord to a stake near his lodge both day and night and are always prepared for action at a moments warning. they fight on horseback altogether. I observe that the large flies are extreemly troublesome to the horses as well as ourselves.

REVIEW QUESTIONS

1. How would you characterize the relationship between the native peoples and the members of the expedition? Explain the reasons for your interpretation.
2. In what ways did the needs and expectations of the U.S. soldiers differ from those of the native peoples? How were they the same?
3. Specifically, how did expedition personnel communicate with the native peoples? What reasons did each group have to talk to the other group?
4. To what extent did the natives and the U.S. soldiers trust each other? Explain.

An American Author Visits Hawaii (1866)

Mark Twain, *Roughing It in the Sandwich Islands*

In the eighteenth century Captain James Cook was sailing for the British when he found a group of islands in the middle of the Pacific that he named the Sandwich Islands (later renamed the Hawaiian Islands). The British managed these very distant islands rather loosely during the latter 1700s and 1800s, and entrepreneurs from many nations came to the three principal islands to begin large agricultural plantations. Sugar and cattle became the most successful early endeavors, but by the time Samuel Langhorne Clemens (Mark Twain) visited in 1866, various fruit crops, such as pineapple, were also becoming profitable. As settlers from the United States began coming to the islands after the Civil War, they started to import laborers from the Caribbean Islands and Asia to serve as indentured servants on these plantations.

At the time of Twain's visit, the Sandwich Islands were still officially British territory. Official title to the islands did not change until 1898 when they were annexed by the United States with Britain's approval. In 1866 and until his death in 1910, Twain led a heated national debate on the issue of imperialism. European nations had expanded far into Asia and Africa, carving sizeable colonial holdings from them. Twain wrote newspaper editorials and delivered scathing lectures against U.S. expansion into lands not part of its continental holdings. During this trip to Hawaii, he observed much that would become part of his argument against U.S. imperialism, especially its effect upon the native peoples of the islands, whom he saw as living successful and satisfying lives without U.S. help.

The native canoe is an irresponsible looking contrivance. I cannot think of anything to liken it to but a boy's sled runner hollowed out, and that does not quite convey the correct idea. It is about fifteen feet long, high and pointed at both ends, is a foot and a half or two feet deep, and so narrow that if you wedged a fat man into it you might not get him out again. It sits on top of the water like a duck, but it has an outrigger and does not upset easily, if you keep still. This outrigger is formed of two long bent sticks like plow handles, which project from one side, and to their outer ends is bound a curved beam composed of an extremely light wood, which skims along the surface of the water and thus saves you from an upset on that side, while the outrigger's weight is not so easily lifted as to make an upset on the other side a thing to be greatly feared.

Still, until one gets used to sitting perched upon this knife-blade, he is apt to reason within himself that it would be more comfortable if there were just an outrigger or so on the other side also.

I had the bow seat, and Billings sat amidships and faced the Kanaka, who occupied the stem of the craft and did the paddling. With the first stroke the trim shell of a thing shot out from the shore like an arrow. There was not much to see. While we were on the shallow water of the reef, it was pastime to look down into the limpid depths at the large bunches of branching coral—the unique shrubbery of the sea. We lost that, though, when we got out into the dead blue water of the deep. But we had the picture of the surf, then, dashing angrily against the crag-bound shore and sending a foaming spray high into the air. There was interest in this beetling border, too, for it was honey-combed with quaint eaves and arches and tunnels, and had a rude semblance of the dilapidated architecture of ruined keeps and castles rising out of the restless sea. When this novelty ceased to be a novelty, we turned our eyes shoreward and gazed at the long mountain with its rich green forests stretching up into the curtaining clouds, and at the specks of houses in the rearward distance and the diminished schooner riding sleepily at anchor. And when these grew tiresome we dashed boldly into the midst of a school of huge, beastly porpoises engaged at their eternal game of arching over a wave and disappearing, and then doing it over again and keeping it up—always circling over, in that way, like so many well-submerged wheels. But the porpoises wheeled themselves away, and then we were thrown upon our own resources. It did not take many minutes to discover that the sun was blazing like a bonfire, and that the weather was of a melting temperature. It had a drowsing effect, too.

In one place we came upon a large company of naked natives, of both sexes and all ages, amusing themselves with the national pastime of surf-bathing. Each heathen would paddle three or four hundred yards out to sea, (taking a short board with him), then face the shore and wait for a particularly prodigious billow to come along; at the right moment he would fling his board upon its foamy crest and himself upon the board, and here he would come whizzing by like a bomb-shell! It did not seem that a lightning express train could shoot along at a more hair-lifting speed. I tried surf-bathing once, subsequently, but made a failure of it. I got the board placed right, and at the right moment, too; but missed the connection myself.—The board struck the shore in three quarters of a second, without any cargo, and I struck the bottom about the same time, with a couple of barrels of water in me. None but natives ever master the art of surf-bathing thoroughly.

At the end of an hour, we had made the four miles, and landed on a level point of land, upon which was a wide extent of old ruins, with many a tall cocoanut tree growing among them. Here

was the ancient City of Refuge—a vast inclosure, whose stone walls were twenty feet thick at the base, and fifteen feet high; an oblong square, a thousand and forty feet one way and a fraction under seven hundred the other. Within this inclosure, in early times, has been three rude temples; each two hundred and ten feet long by one hundred wide, and thirteen high.

In those days, if a man killed another anywhere on the island the relatives were privileged to take the murderers life; and then a chase for life and liberty began—the outlawed criminal flying through pathless forests and over mountain and plain, with his hopes fixed upon the protecting walls of the City of Refuge, and the avenger of blood following hotly after him! Sometimes the race was kept up to the very gates of the temple, and the panting pair sped through long files of excited natives, who watched the contest with flashing eye and dilated nostril, encouraging the hunted refugee with sharp, inspiriting ejaculations, and sending up a ringing shout of exultation when the saving gates closed upon him and the cheated pursuer sank exhausted at the threshold. But sometimes the flying criminal fell under the hand of the avenger at the very door, when one more brave stride, one more brief second of time would have brought his feet upon the sacred ground and barred him against all harm. Where did these isolated pagans get this idea of a City of Refuge—this ancient Oriental custom? This old sanctuary was sacred to all—even to rebels in arms and invading armies. Once within its walls, and confession made to the priest and absolution obtained, the wretch with a price upon his head could go forth without fear and without danger—he was *tabu,* and to harm him was death. The routed rebels in the lost battle for idolatry fled to this place to claim sanctuary, and many were thus saved.

Close to the corner of the great inclosure is a round structure of stone, some six or eight feet high, with a level top about ten or twelve in diameter. This was the place of execution. A high palisade of cocoanut piles shut out the cruel scenes from the vulgar multitude. Here criminals were killed, the flesh stripped from the bones and burned, and the bones secreted in holes in the body of the structure. If the man had been guilty of a high crime, the entire corpse was burned.

The walls of the temple are a study. The same food for speculation that is offered the visitor to the Pyramids of Egypt he will find here—the mystery of how they were constructed by a people unacquainted with science and mechanics. The natives have no invention of their own for hoisting heavy weights, they had no beasts of burden, and they have never even shown any knowledge of the properties of the lever. Yet some of the lava blocks quarried out, brought over rough, broken ground, and built into this wall, six or seven feet from the ground, are of prodigious size and would weigh tons. How did they transport and how raise them?

Both the inner and outer surfaces of the walls present a smooth front and are very creditable specimens of masonry. The blocks are of all manner of shapes and sizes, but yet are fitted together with the neatest exactness. The gradual narrowing of the wall from the base upward is accurately preserved.

No cement was used, but the edifice is firm and compact and is capable of resisting storm and decay for centuries. Who built this temple, and how was it built, and when, are mysteries that may never be unraveled.

Outside of these ancient walls lies a sort of coffin-shaped stone eleven feet four inches long and three feet square at the small end (it would weigh a few thousand pounds), which the high chief who held sway over this district many centuries ago brought thither on his shoulder one day to use as a lounge! This circumstance is established by the most reliable traditions. He used to lie down on it, in his indolent way, and keep all eye on his subjects at work for him and see that there was no "soldiering" done. And no doubt there was not any done to speak of, because he was a man of that sort of build that incites to attention to business on the part of an employee. He was fourteen or fifteen feet high. When he stretched himself at full length on his lounge, his legs hung down over the end, and when he snored he woke the dead. These facts are all attested by irrefragable tradition.

On the other side of the temple is a monstrous seven-ton rock, eleven feet long, seven feet wide and three feet thick. It is raised a foot or a foot and a half above the ground, and rests upon half a dozen little stony pedestals. The same old fourteen-footer brought it down from the mountain, merely for fun (he had his own notions about fun), and propped it up as we find it now and as others may find it a century hence, for it would take a score of horses to budge it from its position. They say that fifty or sixty years ago the proud Queen Kaahumanu used to fly to this rock for safety, whenever she had been making trouble with her fierce husband, and hide under it until his wrath was appeased. But these Kanakas will lie, and this statement is one of their ablest efforts—for Kaahumanu was six feet high—she was bulky—she was built like an ox and she could no more have squeezed herself under that rock than she could have passed between the cylinders of a sugar mill. What could she gain by it, even if she succeeded? To be chased and abased by a savage husband could not be otherwise than humiliating to her high spirit, yet it could never make her feel so flat as an hour's repose under the rock would.

We walked a mile over a raised macadamized road of uniform width; a road paved with flat stones and exhibiting in its every detail a considerable degree of engineering skill. Some say that that wise old pagan, Kamehameha I. planned and built it, but others say it was built so long before his time that the knowledge of who constructed it has passed out of the traditions. In either case, however, as the handiwork of an untaught and degraded race it is a thing of pleasing interest. The stones are worn and smooth, and pushed apart in places, so that the road has the exact appearance of those ancient paved highways leading out of Rome which one sees in pictures.

The object of our tramp was to visit a great natural curiosity at the base of the foothills—a congealed cascade of lava. Some old forgotten volcanic eruption sent its broad river of fire down the mountain side here, and it poured down in a great torrent from an overhanging bluff some fifty feet high to the ground below. The flaming torrent cooled in the winds from the sea, and remains there to-day, all seamed, and frothed and rippled a petrified Niagara. It is very picturesque, and withal so natural that one might almost imagine it still flowed. A smaller stream trickled over the cliff and built up an isolated pyramid about thirty feet high, which has the semblance of a mass of large gnarled and knotted vines and roots and stems intricately twisted and woven together.

We passed in behind the cascade and the pyramid, and found the bluff pierced by several cavernous tunnels, whose crooked courses we followed a long distance.

Two of these winding tunnels stand as proof of Nature's mining abilities. Their floors are level, they are seven feet wide, and their roofs are gently arched. Their height is not uniform, however. We passed through one a hundred feet long, which leads through a spur of the hill and opens out well up in the sheer wall of a precipice whose foot rests in the waves of the sea. It is a commodious tunnel, except that there are occasional places in it where one must stoop to pass under. The roof is lava, of course, and is thickly studded with little lava-pointed icicles an inch long, which hardened as they dripped. They project as closely together as the iron teeth of a corn-sheller, mid if one will stand up straight and walk any distance there, he can get his hair combed free of charge.

REVIEW QUESTIONS

1. How did Twain compare Hawaiian civilization to civilizations in other parts of the world?
2. What examples of Twain's famous humor do you find in this excerpt?
3. This excerpt describes the native ceremonial center on the island of Hawaii (the Big Island). How does Twain's characterization of the people who built and used the structures reveal their priorities?

An American Businessman Describes Life in Buenos Aires (1911)

JAMES BRYCE, *South America: Observations and Impressions*

The tone and content of the preface and introduction (not included here) with which James Bryce opens the account of his 1911 travels to South America reveal much that is relevant to understanding this excerpt. First, in his preface, Bryce thanks the officials of several railway companies and the W. R. Grace Company, a U.S. corporation then investing heavily in South American construction projects. Second, his introduction lists seven points of interest to Europeans and Americans in the South American nations, including "the economic resources of the several countries," "the prospects for the development of industry and commerce," and perhaps most importantly, "the conditions of political life in the several republics." Clearly, James Bryce's book, with such descriptions as the following one of Buenos Aires, would have appealed to any young European or American entrepreneur who might have been considering an investment in South America.

Buenos Aires is something between Paris and New York. It has the business rush and the luxury of the one, the gaiety and pleasure-loving aspect of the other. Everybody seems to have money, and to like spending it, and to like letting everybody else know that it is being spent. Betting on horses is the favourite amusement, and the races the greatest occasion for social display. An immense concourse gathers at the racing enclosure and fills the grand-stand. The highest officials of state and city are there, as well as the world of wealth and fashion. The ladies are decked out with all the Parisian finery and jewels that money can buy; and although nature has given to many of them good features and to most of them fine eyes, custom seems to prescribe that nature shall not be left to herself. On fine afternoons, there is a wonderful turnout of carriages drawn by handsome horses, and still more of costly motor cars, in the principal avenues of the Park; they press so thick that vehicles are often jammed together for fifteen or twenty minutes, unable to move on. Nowhere in the world does one get a stronger impression of exuberant wealth and extravagance. The Park itself, called Palermo, lies on the edge of the city towards the river, and is approached by a well-designed and well-planted avenue. It suffers from the absolute flatness of the ground in which there is no point high enough to give a good view over the estuary, and also from the newness of the trees, for all this region was till lately a bare pampa. But what with its great extent and the money and skill that are being expended on it, this park will in thirty years be a glory to the city. The Botanical Garden, though all too small, is extremely well arranged and of the highest interest to a naturalist, who finds in it an excellent collection of South American trees and shrubs.

As the Opera-house and the races and the Park shew one side of the activities of this sanguine community, so the docks and port shew another. Twenty years ago sea-going vessels had to lie two or three miles off Buenos Aires, discharging their cargo by lighters and their passengers partly by small launches and partly by high-wheeled carts which carried people from the launches ashore through the shallow water. Now a long, deep channel has been dug, and is kept open by dredging, up which large steamers find their way to the very edge of the city. Docks many miles in length have been constructed to receive the shipping, and large stretches of land reclaimed, and huge warehouses erected and railway lines laid down alongside the wharves. Not Glasgow when she deepened her river to admit the largest ships, nor Manchester when she made her ship canal, hardly even Chicago when she planned a new park and lagoons in the lake that washes her front, shewed greater enterprise and bolder conceptions than did the men of Buenos Aires when on this exposed and shallow coast they made alongside their city a great ocean harbour. They are a type of our time, in their equal devotion to business and pleasure, the two and only deities of this latest phase of humanity.

If the best parts of Buenos Aires are as tasteful as those of Paris, there is plenty of ugliness in the worst suburbs. On its land side, the city dies out into a waste of scattered shanties, or "shacks" (as they are called in the United States), dirty and squalid, with corrugated iron roofs, their wooden boards gaping like rents in tattered clothes. These are inhabited by the newest and poorest of the immigrants from southern Italy and southern Spain, a large and not very desirable element among whom anarchism is rife. This district which, if it can hardly be called city, can still less be called country, stretches far out over the Pampa. Thus, although the central parts are built closely, these suburbs are built so sparsely that the town as a whole covers an immense space of ground. Further out and after passing for some miles between market gardens and fields divided by wire fences, with never a hedge, one reaches real country, an outer zone in which some of the wealthy landowners have laid out their estates and erected pleasant country houses. We were invited to one such, and admired the art with which the ground had been planted, various kinds of trees having been selected with so much taste that even on this unpromising level picturesqueness and beauty had been attained. Everything that does not need much moisture grows luxuriantly. We saw rosebushes forty feet high, pouring down a cataract of blossoms. The hospitable owner had spent, as rich *estancieros* often do, large sums upon his live stock, purchasing in Great Britain valuable pedigree bulls and cows, and by crossing the best European breeds with the Argentine stock (originally Spanish) had succeeded in getting together a herd comparable to the best in England. To have first-rate animals is here a matter of pride, even more than a matter of business. It is the only interest that competes with horse-racing. Our friend had a number of Gauchos as stockmen, and they shewed us feats of riding and lassoing which recalled the old days of the open Pampas, before high stock-breeding was dreamt of, when the Gaucho horsemen disputed the control of these regions with the now vanished Indian.

Though Buenos Aires is often described as a cosmopolitan place, its population has far fewer elements than would be found in any of the great cities of the United States. There are English and German colonies, both composed almost wholly of business and railway men, and each keeping, for social purposes, pretty closely to itself. There is a French colony, its upper section including men of intellectual mark, while the humbler members serve pleasure rather than business. From the United States not many persons have come to settle as merchants or ranch owners, but the great meat companies are already at work. Of the so-called "Latin" element in the inhabitants, half or a little more is Argentine born, less than a quarter Spanish or Basque, more than a quarter Italian, largely from Sicily and Calabria. Those Slavonic parts of central and eastern Europe which have recently flooded the United States with immigrants have sent very few to South America. Thus the mass of the population in Buenos Aires is entirely Spanish or Italian in speech, and the two languages are so similar that the Italians easily learn Spanish while also modifying it by their own words and idioms. A mixed, not to say corrupt, Spanish is the result. That there should be an endless diversity of types of face is not surprising, when one remembers how great are the diversities as well in Spain as in Italy among the natives of the various provinces in both those kingdoms.

REVIEW QUESTIONS

1. What was Bryce's opinion of life in Buenos Aires?
2. In Bryce's opinion, how did Buenos Aires compare with Paris? What points seem most important in his evaluation?
3. Did Bryce believe Buenos Aires lived up to its reputation as the most cosmopolitan city in South America? What is his argument? Do you agree?

A German Scholar Describes the People of Peru (1838–1842)

J. J. VON TSCHUDI, *Travels in Peru During the Years 1838–1842*

A German scholar, Tschudi sailed from La Havre, France, on February 27, 1838, with the ultimate goal to see the mountains and primeval forests of the Andes. He sailed through the Strait of Magellan at the southern tip of South America and arrived in Lima in 1841. After visiting the sites of the Peruvian capital, he took a steamer north about 20 miles to the port of Huacho. During this period of Peru's early independence, small coastal towns such as this had begun to prosper by supplying the needs of such cities as Lima.

Tschudi's primary interest in Huacho was scientific in that he wanted to expand his ichthyological (fish) collection, and this was a thriving fishing village. Ironically, he found the people of Peru more interesting than the fish he came to study. Since villages such as this were often the haven for escaped slaves during the colonial era, Tschudi found a culture of peoples from Native and African descent. As a scientist, he was also amazed by such unusual finds as the "enormous ounce" (a type of lynx, sometimes referred to as a snow leopard).

Huacho is a little village, which, since the war of Independence, has received the title of "city." It has more than 5000 inhabitants, of whom four-fifths are Indians and the rest mestizes. Very few whites have settled here. Among them I met an old lame Spaniard, "Don Simon," who, at the beginning of the present century, accompanied the celebrated Alexander von Humboldt to the beds of salt situated a few miles to the south. In relating, with enthusiastic pleasure, his recollections of the youthful and indefatigable traveller, he told me that, some years ago, he had read through the book which Humboldt wrote on America, and he added, with great simplicity, *"pero, Señor, ahi he perdido los estribos."*[1]

The natives employ themselves in fishing, agriculture, and the breeding of poultry. Most of the poultry brought to market in Lima comes from Huacho. Every Friday large caravan-like processions of Indian women repair to the capital with fowls, ducks, and turkeys. Fifteen or twenty are tied together by the feet, and make a sort of bunch; and two of such bunches are hung at the pommel of the saddle, so that one hangs down on either side of the horse. The chola[2] sits in the middle. Under this burthen the poor animal has to travel two days and a half. Only when the caravan halts does he enjoy the relief of being unsaddled and fed. Some of the Indians of Huacho work in the salt-pits. The women plait coarse straw hats, and a kind of mats called *petates,* which they carry to Lima for sale.

The Huachanos cannot be ranked among the best classes of the Indians. They are malicious, revengeful, and knavish. Their character has evidently deteriorated amidst the numerous revolutions which preceded the establishment of the Republic, and the frequent passage of troops through the town. The Padre Requena sketched to me a terrible picture of his *Indios brutos;* but truly, under the guidance of such a shepherd, it

---

[1]Literally—"But there, sir, I lost the stirrups." Meaning that he did not understand it. The Spanish phrase, *perder los estribos,* signifies to get confused or embarrassed.

[2]*Chola* is the common designation for an Indian female. The masculine is *Cholo.*

were unreasonable to expect the flock to be very good. This venerable Cura was a fair type of the Peruvian priesthood. He was passionately fond of hunting, and for the enjoyment of that recreation he kept a number of excellent horses, and several packs of hounds, particularly *galgos* (greyhounds), for some of which he paid 150 or 200 dollars. In the most shameless way he violated the ecclesiastical vow of celibacy, and he was usually surrounded by several of his own children, who called him *uncle,* addressing him by the appellation of *tio,* the term usually employed in Peru to express that sort of relationship. The Padre used to boast of his alleged friendship with Lord Cochrane, in which he affected to pride himself very greatly. He died in a few weeks after his return to Huacho. He refused so long to make his confession, that the Indians, uttering furious menaces, assembled in crowds about his house. Some even compelled a priest to go in to him, to represent the awful consequences of his obstinacy. On the approach of death, he declared that the thought which most occupied him was his separation from his hounds, and when his hands were becoming cold he called to his negro to fetch a pair of buckskin hunting gloves, and desired to have them drawn on.

In Peru the clergy have no fixed stipend. Their emoluments are derived from the fees and perquisites which their ecclesiastical functions bring in. For baptisms, marriages, and masses, fixed sums are established; but it is not so with burials, for which the priest receives a present proportional to the circumstances of the deceased. The interment of a poor person (*entierro baxo*) costs at least from eight to ten dollars, which sum is extorted from the survivors with the most unrelenting rigor. For the burial of a rich person (*entierro alto*) the sum of two hundred dollars is frequently paid. If a wealthy man should express in his will his desire for an *entierro baxo,* the priest sets this clause aside, and proceeds with the costly ceremonies, the payment for which is insured by the pious feelings of the family. Hence some of the richer *comunerias,* of which Huacho is one, yield to the priest

annually from 12,000 to 14,000 dollars. When a priest dies, the clergy of the neighboring villages meet and bury him with great pomp, free of any payment except a good banquet.

A rich Indian of Huacho made a bargain with his countrymen that, on their paying him weekly a medio (the sixteenth part of a dollar), he would defray the expenses of their funerals. By this agreement he realized a considerable sum of money. The Cholos made it a condition that they should be buried in coffins, which is not common with the lower classes in Peru. The Indian complied with this condition. When a Cholo died, a coffin was sent to his residence. If too short, the corpse was bent and forced into it. The interment then took place according to the ritual of the Church. On the following night the Indian who had contracted for the burials repaired with a confidential servant to the churchyard, dug up the coffin, threw the body back into the grave, and carried off the coffin, with the *mortaja* (the funeral garment), which served for the next customer. The contractor made each coffin last as long as the boards would hold together. This system, at all events, secured the Cholos against the danger of being buried alive.

The churchyard of Huacho presents a revolting spectacle. A low wall surrounds a space of sandy ground, which is strewed with skulls, bones, fragments of burial clothes, and mutilated human bodies. The coffin plunderer, on replacing the corpse in the grave, merely throws some loose sand over it, and the consequence is that the remains of the dead frequently become the prey of dogs, foxes, and other carrion feeders. When the family of a deceased person can contribute nothing to defray the funeral expenses, the body is conveyed privately during the night to the churchyard. In the morning it is found half consumed.

The environs of Huacho abound in fine fruit gardens, and productive Indian farms. The climate is healthful, though very hot. The vicinity of the sea and the convenience of good bathing would render it an agreeable place of residence, were it not infested with vermin. Fleas propagate in the sand in almost incredible multitudes, especially in the neighborhood of the Indian huts, and any person entering them is in a moment covered with hundreds of those tormentors. Bugs, too, swarm in the lime walls; though that description of vermin is less numerous in Huacho than in some of the more northern towns.

In a fine valley, about two short leagues from Huacho, the little town of Huaura is situated on the bank of a river of the same name. This Rio de Huaura is formed by the union of two rivers. The larger of the two rises in the Cordillera de Paria, and flows through the wild ravine of Chuichin: the smaller river, called the Rio Chico de Sayan, rises from a lake of considerable size in the Altos de Huaquimarci. Both unite below the village of Sayan. In the vicinity of Huaura the river forms several marshes, in which malaria is generated. In very few places have I seen the stratum of malaria so distinctly separated from the atmosphere as here. It lies at an average about two, or two and a half feet above the marsh, and is carried over it by strong atmospheric currents. It is distinguished by a peculiar kind of opalization, and on certain changes of light it exhibits a yellowish tint. This is particularly perceptible in the morning, on coming down from the high grounds. The marshy plain then appears overhung with a thick color-changing sheet of malaria. Malignant intermittent fever and diseases of the skin are frequent in Huaura. The town is thinly peopled; the number of inhabitants being not more than 2000.

A great sugar plantation, called El Ingenio, is situated at about a quarter of a league from Huaura. It formerly belonged to the Jesuits, but is now the property of a rich Lima family. The *trapiche,* or sugar-mill, is worked by a water-wheel, the first ever established in Peru, a circumstance of which the owner proudly boasts.

The valley which opens here is magnificent, and to ride through it easterly eleven leagues towards Sayan is one of the finest excursions which can be made in Peru. Over this beautiful district are scattered many rich plantations. The one next in importance to El Ingenio is Acaray, which, though not very large, is most carefully cultivated: another, called Huillcahuaura, has a splendid building erected on it. In the middle of the valley is the extensive sugar plantation of Luhmayo. Near this place I saw, in a negro's hut, an ounce of immense size, which had been killed a few weeks previously. More than fifty Negroes and Indians had been engaged in subduing this ferocious animal, which was not killed until after a conflict of two days, in the course of which several negroes were dangerously wounded. This gigantic specimen measured, from the snout to the tip of the tail, eight feet three inches; the tail itself measuring two feet eight inches.

REVIEW QUESTIONS

1. From this description, do you sense any particular benefits or limitations of Huacho village life? Explain.
2. How would you describe the various relationships that exist in this village?
3. Would you like to live in a village such as this? Why or why not?

An American Archeologist Examines Mayan Society (mid-1800s)

JOHN L. STEPHENS, *Incidents of Travel in Yucatan*

When the American archaeologist John Stephens came to Mexico in the 1830s and 1840s, the Yucatan Peninsula was a state only loosely connected, politically and economically, to the rest of Mexico. The "gigantic memorials of a mysterious people" lured him to the region to examine and chart the pyramids and residences that had been overgrown by the jungle.

This excerpt from the journal of his travels near the regional capital of Mérida describes the Catholic festival of Todos Santos (All Saints) at the beginning of November. Throughout Mexico and most of Latin America, the last day of October and the first three days of November had always been celebrated as the Día de los Muertos (Day of the Dead). Because of their similar timing and themes, these two religious observations resulted in an easy synthesis of cultures. The exact ceremonies and practices differed by region and nation, but the details described by Stephens are easily recognizable to natives throughout Latin America.

One fiesta was hardly ended when another began. On Monday was the great fête of Todos Santos. Grand mass was said in all the churches, and in every family prayers were offered up for the souls of the dead; and, besides the usual ceremonies of the Catholic Church throughout the world, there is one peculiar to Yucatan, derived from the customs of the Indians, and called Mukbipoyo. On this day every Indian, according to his means, purchases and burns a certain number of consecrated candles, in honour of his deceased relatives, and in memory of each member of his family who has died within the year. Besides this, they bake in the earth a pie consisting of a paste of Indian corn, stuffed with pork and fowls, and seasoned with chili, and during the day every good Yucateco eats nothing but this. In the interior, where the Indians are less civilized, they religiously place a portion of this composition out of doors, under a tree, or in some retired place, for their deceased friends to eat, and they say that the portion thus set apart is always eaten, which induces the belief that the dead may be enticed back by appealing to the same appetites which govern when living; but this is sometimes accounted for by malicious and skeptical persons, who say that in every neighborhood there are other Indians, poorer than those who can afford to regale their deceased relatives, and these consider it no sin, in a matter of this kind, to step between the living and the dead.

We have reason to remember this fête from one untoward circumstance. A friendly neighbour, who, besides visiting us frequently with his wife and daughter, was in the habit of sending us fruit and dulces more than we could eat, this day, on the top of a large, undisposed-of present, sent us a huge piece of mukbipoyo. It was as hard as an oak plank, and as thick as six of them; and having already overtasked ourselves to reduce the pile on the table, when this came, in a fit of desperation we took it out into the courtyard and buried it. There it would have remained till this day but for a malicious dog which accompanied them on their next visit; he passed into the courtyard, rooted it up, and, while we were pointing to the empty platters as our acknowledgment of their kindness, this villainous dog sneaked through the sala and out at the front door with the pie in his mouth, apparently grown bigger since it was buried.

The fêtes were now ended, and we were not sorry, for now, for the first time, we had a prospect of having our clothes washed. Ever since our arrival, our linen, &c., accumulated during the voyage, had stood in gaping bundles, imploring us to do something for them, but during the continuance of the fiestas not a lavandera in Merida could be found to take in washing.

REVIEW QUESTIONS

1. What elements of synthesis between pre-Colombian traditions and Catholic beliefs seem evident in this account?
2. Did Stephens see different social classes among the Maya he describes? Explain.
3. What was Stephens's opinion of the rituals? Give details to support your answer.

An English Author Comments on Floridians in Cuba (1856)

EDWARD B. TYLOR, *Anahuac: Or, Mexico and the Mexicans, Ancient and Modern*

An English author of pseudo-scientific books such as the *Early History of Mankind* and *Primitive Culture,* Edward Tylor came to the Americas in the mid–nineteenth century to investigate evolution—the current rage in biology. After spending almost a year in the United States, he arrived in Havana, Cuba, in the spring of 1856. As he had in Louisiana, Tylor spent his time visiting sugar plantations and "botanizing" in the tropical jungles. In Cuba, however, he also inspected the operation of copper mines and coffee estates.

Tylor's publication on Cuba reveals much about the conditions in Havana. The city was already becoming a haven for disaffected "Americanos" who had fled the United States for social or financial reasons, as he found in the colony of Floridians. In the United States, tensions were building toward what would be the Civil War of 1860–1865. Tylor's comments on the Cuban *ménage* (household) are consistent with the European thought of his era. His observations about the imported Chinese workers, however, reflect this attitude without recognizing the negative effects of the British opium trade in China. As increasing numbers of Chinese in port cities, such as Hong Kong and Shanghai, became victims of the social and economic ravages of the illegal trade, the British arranged for Chinese men to be taken to the Caribbean islands, such as Cuba, as laborers.

Whether any social condition can be better for the black inhabitants of the West Indies, than that of these settlers, I very much doubt. They are not a hard-working people, it is true; but hard work in the climate of the tropics is unnatural, and can only be brought about by unnatural means. That they are not sunk in utter laziness one can see by their neat cottages and trim gardens. Their state does not correspond with the idea of prosperity of the political economist, who would have them work hard to produce sugar, rum, and tobacco, that they might earn money to spend in crockery and Manchester goods; but it is suited to the race and to the climate. If we measure prosperity by the enjoyment of life, their condition is an enviable one.

I think no unprejudiced observer can visit the West Indies without seeing the absurdity of expecting the free blacks to work like slaves, as though any inducement but the strongest necessity would ever bring it about. There are only two causes which can possibly make the blacks industrious, in our sense of the word—slavery, or a population so crowded as to make labour necessary to supply their wants.

In one house in the Floridan colony we found a ménage which was surprising to me, after my experience of the United States. The father of the family was a white man, a Spaniard, and his wife a black woman. They received us with the greatest hospitality, and we sat in the porch for a long time, talking to the family. One or two of the mulatto daughters were very handsome; and there were some visitors, young white men from the neighbouring village, who were apparently come to pay their devoirs to the young ladies. Such marriages are not uncommon in Cuba; and the climate of the island is not unfavourable for the mixed negro and European race, while to the pure whites it is deadly. The creoles of the country are a poor degenerate race, and die out in the fourth generation. It is only by intermarriage with Europeans, and continual supplies of emigrants from Europe, that the white population is kept up. . . .

The history of these Chinese emigrants is a curious one. Agents in China persuade them to come out, and they sign a contract to work for eight years, receiving from three to five dollars a month, with their food and clothing. The sum seems a fortune to them; but, when they come to Cuba, they find to their cost that the value of money must be estimated by what it will buy. They find that the value of a black labourer is thirty dollars a month, and they have practically sold themselves for slaves; for there is no one to prevent the masters who have bought the contract for their work from treating them in all respects as slaves. The value of such a contract— that is, of the Chinaman himself, was from £30 to £40 when we were in the island. Fortunately for them, they cannot bear the severe plantation-work. Some die after a few days of such labour and exposure, and many more kill themselves; and the utter indifference with which they commit suicide, as soon as life seems not worth having, contributes to moderate the exactions of their masters. A friend of ours in Cuba had a Chinese servant who was impertinent one day, and his master turned him out of the room, dismissing him with a kick. The other servants woke their master early next morning, with the intelligence that the Chinese had killed himself in the night, to expiate the insult he had received.

Of African slaves brought into the island, the yearly number is about 15,000. All the details of the trade are matter of general notoriety, even to the exact sum paid to each official as hush-money. It costs a hundred dollars for each negro, they say, of which a gold ounce (about £3 16s.) is the share of the Captain-general. To this must be added the cost of the slave in Africa, and the expense of the voyage; but when the slave is once fairly on a plantation he is worth eight hundred dollars; so it may be understood how profitable the trade still is, if only one slaver out of three gets through.

The island itself with its creeks and mangrove-trees is most favourable for their landing, if they can once make the shore; and the Spanish cruisers will not catch them if they can help it. If a British cruiser captures them, the negroes are made emancipados in the way I have already explained.

Hardly any country in the world is so thoroughly in a false position as England in her endeavours to keep down the Cuban slave-trade, with the nominal concurrence of the Spanish government, and the real vigorous opposition of every Spaniard on the island, from the Captain-General downwards. Even the most superficial observer who lands for an hour or two in Havana, while his steamer is taking in coals, can have evidence of the slave-trade brought before his eyes in the tattooed faces of native Africans, young and middle-aged, in the streets and markets; just as he can guess, from the scored backs of the negroes, what sort of discipline is kept up among them.

We slept on board the steamboat off the pier of Batabano, and the railway took us back to Havana next morning.

REVIEW QUESTIONS

1. Why did Tylor believe that life was good for the black inhabitants of Cuba? From this and other material you may have read on this topic, do you agree?
2. Who were the Floridians, and why were they in Cuba? Did Tylor find their presence strange or unusual?
3. What type of racial mix did Tylor find in Cuba? What was his perspective or opinion on the state of slavery in Cuba?

An American Muckraking Socialist Comments on Mexico During the Revolution (1910)

JOHN KENNETH TURNER, *Barbarous Mexico*

Born in Portland, Oregon, in 1879, John Kenneth Turner had earned a reputation as a "muckraking socialist" before he ventured into Mexico in 1907 to investigate stories about conditions of the working people under the dictatorship of Porfirio Díaz. The very affluent Los Angeles Socialist party member Elizabeth Darling Trowbridge financed his trip. Unable to speak Spanish, Turner enlisted the aid of Lázaro Gutiérrez de Lara, who had come to Los Angeles from Sonora in 1906 and was a member of the Liberal party in Mexico. In 1905 political dissidents from Mexico came to the United States to organize the Liberal party, which eventually would participate in the revolution of 1910. Turner published numerous articles from the material gathered in Mexico plus information gleaned from political articles and government publications in the United States. He returned to Mexico City in January 1909 with his wife and worked for an American-language newspaper, the *Mexican Herald,* while collecting information on Díaz's political machine. *Barbarous Mexico* is the product of both those visits and Turner's fact-finding efforts.

At the time of Turner's second trip to Mexico, the nation was already fracturing into competing groups intent upon assuming Díaz's position as soon as possible. Díaz himself had announced his approaching retirement by 1909 but had reconsidered at the urging of his supporters. The Díaz system of government had always consisted of a loosely coordinated group of local governors who received favors from Díaz in exchange for their loyalty and cooperation. By 1910 that cooperation had worn very thin, and support had swung to regional military leaders. The following excerpt from Turner's works presents some indication of why Mexico's political organization was failing and what regional organizers may have offered the natives and Mestizos to obtain their following.

The face of the old patriarch told a story of burdens and of a patient, ox-like bearing of them such as no words could possibly suggest. He had a ragged, grizzled beard and moustache, but his head was still covered with dark brown hair. He was probably seventy, but was evidently still an active worker. His clothing consisted of American jumper and overalls of ordinary denim washed and patched and washed and patched—a one-dollar suit patched until it was nothing but patches!

Beside the patriarch sat the old lady, his wife, with head bowed and a facial expression so like that of her husband that it might have been a copy by a great painter. Yes, the expression differed in one detail. The old woman's upper lip was compressed tight against her teeth, giving her an effect of perpetually biting her lip to keep back the tears. Perhaps her original stock of courage had not been equal to that of the man and it had been necessary to fortify it by an everlasting compression of the mouth.

Then there was a young couple half the age of the two. The man sat with head nodding and granulated lids blinking slowly, now and then turning his eyes to stare with far distant interest upon the merrymakers around him. His wife, a flat-breasted drooping woman, sat always in one position with her head bent forward and her right hand fingering her face about the bridge of the nose.

Finally, there were two boys, one of eighteen, second son of the old man, and one of sixteen, son of the second couple. In all that night's journey the only smile I saw from any of the six was a smile of the youngest boy. A passing news-agent offered the boy a book for seventy-five *centavos*. With slightly widening eyes of momentary interest the boy looked upon the gaily decorated paper cover, then turned toward his uncle and smiled a half startled smile. To think that anyone might imagine that *he* could afford to purchase one of those magical things, a book!

"We are from Chihuahua," the old man told us, when we had gained his confidence. "We work in the fields—all of us. All our lives we have been farm laborers in the corn and the beans and the melons of Chihuahua. But now we are running away from it. If the bosses would pay us the money they agree to pay, we could get along, but they never pay all—never. This time the boss paid us only two-thirds the agreed price, yet I am very thankful for that much, for he might have given us only one-third, as others have done in the past. What can I do? Nothing. I cannot hire a lawyer, for the lawyer would steal the other two-thirds, and the boss would put me in jail besides. Many times I and my sons have gone to jail for asking the boss to pay us the full amount of our agreement. My sons become angry more and more and sometimes I fear one may strike the boss or kill him. That would be the end of us.

"No, the best thing to do, I decided at last, was to get away. So we put our wages together and used our last dollar to pay for tickets to Torreon, where we hope to find work in the cotton fields. I hear we can get one *peso* a day in busy times. Is it so? Or will it be the same story over again there? Perhaps it will. But what else can I do but try? Work! work! work! That's all there is for us—and nothing in return for the work! We do not drink; we are not lazy; every day we pray to God. Yet debt is always following us, begging to be taken in. Many times I have wanted to borrow just a little from my boss, but my wife has always pleaded with me. 'No,' she would say, 'better die than to owe, for owing once means owing forever—and slavery.'

"But sometimes," continued the old man, "I think it might be better to owe, better to fall in debt, better to give up our liberty than to go on like this to the end. True, I am getting old and I would love to die free, but it is hard—too hard!"

The three-quarters of a million of chattel slaves and the five million peons do not monopolize the economic misery of Mexico. It extends to every class of men that toils. There are 150,000 mine and smelter workers who receive less money for a week's labor than an American miner of the same class gets for a day's wages. There are 30,000 cotton mill operatives whose wages average less than thirty cents a day in American money. There are a quarter of a million domestic servants whose wages range from one to five dollars a month. There are 40,000 impressed soldiers who get less than two dollars a month above the scantiest rations. The common policemen of Mexico City, 2,000 of them, are paid but fifty cents a day in our money. Fifty cents a day is a high average for street-car conductors in the metropolis, where wages are higher than in any other section of the country except close to the American border. And this proportion is constant throughout the industries. An offer of fifty cents a day without food, would, without the slightest doubt, bring in Mexico City an army of 50,000 able-bodied laborers inside of twenty-four hours.

From such miserable wages it must not be guessed that the cost of the necessities of life are less than they are here, as in the case of other low wage countries, such as India and China. On the contrary, the cost of corn and beans, upon which the mass of the Mexican people eke out their existence, is actually higher, as a rule, than it is in the United States. At this writing it costs nearly twice as much money to buy a hundred pounds of corn in Mexico City as it does in Chicago, and that in the same money, American gold or Mexican silver, take it as you like it. And this is the cheapest staple that the poverty-stricken Mexican is able to lay his hands upon.

As to clothing and shelter, the common Mexican has about as little of either as can be imagined. The tenements of New York City are palatial homes compared to the tenements of Mexico City. A quarter of a mile in almost any direction off Diaz's grand Paseo de la Reforma, the magnificent driveway over which tourists are always taken and by which they usually judge Mexico, will carry the investigator into conditions that are not seen in any city worthy

the name of civilized. If in all Mexico there exists a city with a really modern sewer system I am ignorant of its name.

Travelers who have stopped at the best hotels of the metropolis may raise their eyebrows at this last statement, but a little investigation will show that not more than one-fifth of the houses within the limits of that metropolis are regularly supplied with water with which to flush the sewers, while there are many densely populated blocks which have no public water whatsoever, neither for sewer flushing nor for drinking.

It will take a few minutes' reflection to realize what this really means. As a result of such unsanitary conditions the death rate in that city ranges always between 5 and 6 per cent, usually nearer the latter figure, which places that percentage at more than double the death rate of well-regulated cities of Europe, the United States and even of South America. Which proves that half the people who die in Diaz's metropolis die of causes which modern cities have abolished.

A life-long resident once estimated to me that 200,000 people of the country's metropolis, or two-fifths the entire population, spend every night on the stones. "On the stones" means not on the streets, for sleeping is not permitted on the streets or in the parks, but on the floors of cheap tenements or lodging houses.

Possible this is an exaggeration. From my own observations, however, I know that 100,000 would be a very conservative estimate. And at least 25,000 pass the nights in *mesones*—the name commonly applied to the cheapest class of transient lodging houses.

A *meson* is a pit of such misery as is surpassed only by the *galeras,* the sleeping jails, of the contract slaves of the hot lands—and the dormitories of the Mexican prisons. The chief difference between the *mesones* and the *galeras* is that into the latter the slaves are driven, tottering from overwork, semi-starvation and fever—driven with whips and locked in when they are there; while to the *mesones* the ragged, ill-nourished wretches from the city's streets come to buy with three precious copper *centavos* a brief and scanty shelter—a bare spot to lie down in, a grass mat, company with the vermin that squalor breeds, rest in a sickening room with hundreds of others—snoring, tossing, groaning brothers and sisters in woe.

During my most recent visit to Mexico—in the winter and spring of 1909—I visited many of these *mesones* and took a number of flashlight photos of the inmates. The conditions in all I found to be the same. The buildings are ancient ones—often hundreds of years old—which have been abandoned as unfit for any other purposes than as sleeping places for the country's poor. For three *centavos* the pilgrim gets a grass mat and the privilege of hunting for a bare spot large enough to lie down in. On cold nights the floor and yards are so thick with bodies that it is very difficult to find footing between the sleepers. In one room I have counted as high as two hundred.

Poor women and girls must sleep, as well as poor men and boys, and if they cannot afford more than three cents for a bed they must go to the *mesones* with the men. In not one of the *mesones* that I visited was there a separate room for the women and girls, though there were many women and girls among the inmates. Like a man, a girl pays her three cents and gets a grass mat. She may come early and find a comparatively secluded nook in which to rest her weary body. But there is nothing to prevent a man from coming along, lying down beside her and annoying her throughout the night.

And this thing is done. More than once, in my visits to *mesones,* I saw a young and unprotected girl awakened from her sleep and solicited by a strange man whose roving eye had lighted upon her as he came into the place. The *mesones* breed immorality as appallingly as they breed vermin. Homeless girls do not go to *mesones* because they are bad, but because they are poor. These places are licensed by the authorities and it would be a simple matter to require the proprietors to set apart a portion of the space exclusively for women. But this the authorities have not the decency to do.

REVIEW QUESTIONS

1. According to Turner, what are the most pressing problems faced by the poor in Mexico? If you were assessing this situation, might you draw different conclusions about their plight? Why or why not?
2. Turner was a Socialist. Do his prejudices seem to color his descriptions of the Mexican Mestizo or Indian worker?
3. Turner states that the "economic misery of Mexico . . . extends to every class of men that toils." Does he prove this statement to your satisfaction? Why or why not?

A Russian Naval Officer Observes Life in San Francisco (1860–1861)

PAVEL N. GOLOVIN, *Civil and Savage Encounters*

The author of this account, Pavel N. Golovin, was a nineteenth-century member of a famous and elite Russian family that had received the honored title of Count from the Holy Roman Emperor in 1701. Born in 1822, Golovin was raised in St. Petersburg but often lived on family estates in Estonia. He became a naval cadet in 1837 and a midshipman a year later. In March 1853 Golovin was promoted to captain-lieutenant and given commands that took him far from his homeland in the Baltic Sea to ports in the Mediterranean and the North Atlantic Ocean.

On leaving St. Petersburg in July 1860 Golovin was under orders to stop in Washington, D.C., to confer with the Russian ambassador to President James Buchanan. From there he traveled to Panama, crossed to the Pacific, and proceeded to the ports of Acapulco in Mexico, San Francisco in the new state of California, and Sitka in Russian-owned Alaska. He then returned to St. Petersburg via the Kamchatka Peninsula and Siberia. His letters home contain valuable perspectives on life in the places he visited. As the following selection details, Golovin witnessed vigilante justice in the boom-town atmosphere in San Francisco.

24 October/5 November 1860

When gold was discovered in California, naturally a great mass of humanity swarmed here from all the corners of the world, all hoping to get rich quick. And of course most of these people were adventure seekers. With all of this you can imagine how these people inundated California. The madness for gold seized everyone. They all tried to get it any way possible—and this led to murder, armed robbery, et cetera. Authorities, even elected officials, took part in the pillage and connived with swindlers. But in the meantime law-abiding people gradually began to come in too. The city spread out and was built up, but there was neither order nor security. With a bribe of money a known murderer could be freed from justice and could escape to the Atlantic states or to some other land where there was no possibility of pursuit. People complained, but affairs went on the same way.

Then suddenly a man came who resolved to publish the details of all these abuses. This was the literary figure Williams King [James King of William]. He published a newspaper [*Evening Bulletin*] in which he mercilessly branded all the culprits, named them, presented the facts in support of his accusations. In a short time he acquired a great following among loyal people, but at the same time he infuriated the authorities and a whole group of scoundrels, who tried in every way they could to buy him off. They

even tried to frighten him, but he carried on, neither succumbing to bribes nor being frightened by threats. Finally the scoundrels decided to kill him. One day he was on his way home from his office to have breakfast, and as he was crossing one of the main streets, a man ran up to him, saying, "Defend yourself!" and shot him with a revolver. Williams fell, mortally wounded. The people rushed up to the killer and took him to the police. More than 30 men testified as to what had happened. Williams died, and the trial of the killer, [James] Casey, dragged on. Rumors spread throughout the city that Casey's lover, a very rich woman, had paid money to get him out of San Francisco.

The people were incited to the point of rebellion. One day more than 6,000 men gathered at a meeting and elected representatives whom they called the Committee for Vigilance. They immediately armed themselves and moved on to the police station, arrested the police, and seized Casey and several other murderers who were in prison, and brought them to a building where they posted a citizens' guard. Then patrols of these same citizens went all through the city to maintain order, and the Committee immediately tried Casey and the other murderers by legal means. The evidence was all too clear. Casey and one other man [a murderer named Cora] were sentenced to death.

On the day of the journalist Williams' funeral, the supporters of the Committee, consisting of 6,000 armed citizens, lined up on one of the squares and placed their cannon in such a way that by firing they could stop any movement among the people who were gathering in crowds around the square and in nearby streets and buildings. They fastened two horizontal beams on the roof on a building, and the ends of the beams protruded from the roof so as to hang over the windows of the upper floor. They fastened a block and ropes there, and erected a small platform from the two windows that were below the beams. When Williams' coffin was put on the hearse, Casey and the other man condemned to death were brought out to the platform through the window. Nooses were placed around their necks. When the funeral procession started, the supports were knocked out from under their feet, and the murderers spun in the air. They say the effect was a sensation.

The Committee did not stop with this. Patrols constantly went through the city picking up suspects. Many scoundrels were arrested and sentenced; three or four were hanged and the Committee sent the rest, at its own expense, by ship to Australia, the Sandwich Islands, or to the Atlantic states, and warned them not to return to California under threat of death. In this manner order was gradually restored, and the Committee discontinued its activity when new authorities elected by the people took office. Thanks to these measures, one no longer hears about robberies here, and at night one can walk safely along all the streets where it was previously impossible to go unarmed, even in daytime. However, the Committee did not completely disband. It still exists, and at any hint of trouble may again take over. Of course murders are still being committed as a result of fights, quarrels, et cetera but the Committee is not concerned with such matters. A murderer is arrested, tried,

hanged, and that is the end of it. Sometimes there are abuses, but this is a result of misuse of the law, and where are there no abuses? Let me tell you about one such case.

A man named [David C.] Broderick, a California senator, aroused the dissatisfaction of the opposition party. Hostility grew greater and greater. Several times Broderick was insulted in various ways, but did not pay any attention. But finally a man named [David S.] Terry insulted him publicly, in such a way that Broderick had to challenge Terry to a duel. At the appointed time the opponents met, and Broderick was killed. Then rumors spread that the duel had been improperly carried out, that Broderick's pistol had been loaded with cotton wadding, and that Terry had actually killed him like a dog. Witnesses were found, and Terry was arrested. When the matter came to court, Terry declared that he wanted to be judged not in San Francisco but in the little town of San Antonio, because the court in San Francisco might be prejudiced. The law was on Terry's side, and the trial was moved to San Antonio. A jury was selected and a day set for the trial. Witnesses were to come from San Francisco to testify against Terry. The court was to open for business at 10:00 AM. The witnesses actually did gather on time for the ship, and left for San Antonio. But the ship's captain had been bribed, as well as the judge and the jury, so the witnesses did not reach San Antonio until 11:00, and the court had begun promptly at 10:00. Since there were no witnesses, the jury declared Terry not guilty, and he was released. When the ship arrived, the matter was over, and the witnesses came just in time to see Terry celebrate his freedom. This happened some time before our arrival. These are just some small examples of California happenings for you.

REVIEW QUESTIONS

1. From the tone of Golovin's description, do you believe he approved or disapproved of the legal system in San Francisco? On what information do you base your opinion?
2. What is the source of this conflict in the city? How does it reflect conditions in a frontier society?

3. To what extent did the U.S. judicial system succeed in imposing law? What extenuating conditions seem to have existed relative to the trial?
4. Do you believe vigilante action was appropriate here, according to Golovin's description? Why or why not?

A Japanese Student Experiences Life in Boston (1872)

INOUE RYOKICHI, *A Japanese Student's Views of the United States*

Following the resumption of trade with Western nations in the mid–nineteenth century, the Meiji government of Japan began sending promising young men to Europe and the United States for college educations. These young people entered universities to study Western science and technology, as well as to learn all they could about the nations in which they studied. A brilliant young man who suffered from poor health most of his life, Inoue Ryokichi, also known as Inoue Rokusaburo (1852–1879), came to the Worcester Military Academy in Boston in 1867. Following the successful completion of his studies there, he decided to study law under Oliver Wendell Holmes and received the first degree ever bestowed upon an Asian by Harvard Law School.

Having completed his American education and able to fulfill the role prescribed him by his government, he returned to Japan in 1875. Ryokichi immediately received an appointment as a professor of law at the new Tokyo national university. Three years later, he committed suicide by jumping into a well. The reader might speculate, from the following excerpt of his description of American culture, whether his success also brought conflicting emotions and depression.

THE PRACTICAL AMERICANS

Is it a disgrace to the Americans that they are a practical people?

Before entering into the discussion which the theme demands, let me define the position from which I am obliged to look at this delicate question. Japan, before the late revolution, was undoubtedly the most aristocratic nation in the world. As is usually the case under such circumstances, the downtrodden mass of the people strikingly manifest that characteristic which is the subject of my present essay—namely, an acquaintance only with those ways of life which relate to the supply of the actual wants and necessities of mankind. This is because, the greater portion of the nation's wealth being in the hands of the ruling class, the lower classes have to make the most of everything within their reach. I, like any other thoughtless born-aristocrat, despised this tendency of the commons. I acknowledge now that this was very unjust, but still something of this spirit will no doubt influence me in the decision of the great question now before us, and I request my kind readers constantly to bear in mind this circumstance.

The Americans, who unmistakably inherited the virtues as well as the vices of their ancestors, are a nervously energetic, enterprising people. When they threw off the British yoke, what remained was to develop the hidden resources of the country; and how well they have performed this the present prosperity of the country sufficiently attests. In the course of this stupendous undertaking they were being continually brought into contact with new difficulties, and they have always proved themselves equal to any emergency.

The world is indebted to the Americans for the steamboat, telegraph, and many other very useful inventions. It may be broadly asserted that whatever had a practical application was studied and improved by them. A glance at its educational system enables one to form some idea of the people. The cities have their business colleges, while agricultural colleges dot the face of the country. Then there are schools of engineering, architecture, medicine, and other departments of the useful arts, and these are faithfully attended to, while the general education of the youths is designed to make practical men. The fine arts, which refine, ennoble, and delight mankind, are sadly neglected. The fact is, an American does not want to be a painter, sculptor, poet, or rhetorician, but a rich man. Wealth is the sole object of ambition of the people at large. I must say now that I am entering on very serious grounds. I am not so presumptuous as to attempt to trespass on theology, but I must confess I shall go very near the frontiers of it. The Americans who point the fingers of scorn against the rest of Christendom as lukewarm in the cause of religion, and freely condemn without fair trial the rest of mankind as ignorant of the duties of man, seem to think that money-making is the most important business of life; and, taking this as a standard, I shall finish the rest of my essay accordingly. It is not possible that the Americans should be such enthusiastic champions of Christianity, and yet reject its teachings in their ordinary life.

But Christianity teaches them that their souls live after their bodies, and therefore they must better the condition of their minds by the cultivation of virtues in this world. The money-loving Americans are doing just the opposite of this. So-called business men, who constitute a large portion of "the life and the blood" of American society, seemingly have no souls, for they are exposed for sale, if not already exchanged, for hard cash. When their souls are disposed of they receive the millions of money they desire; but what is to be done with it? . . .

If money-making is the source of enjoyment to them, as drunkenness and gluttony are to some men, I have only to say that their taste is a corrupted one. It is but just to say that the riches of these men are gained by hard, patient labor; hence they are more to be pitied than condemned, for the question again returns, "What is to be done with these riches, and what have they made themselves by the operation?"

Another set of men, thinking this a rather unprofitable way of making money, adopt a system which combines both theft and perjury, and insures to those men a life of misery, which they richly deserve. I refer to those who seek fortune by a lucky marriage—an excellent mode of self-selling! A man who is so degraded as to go through a formal loving of an innocent, confiding woman for the sake of her money, shows a disposition which, if an opportunity presented, would sell country, religion, anything and everything which mankind so sacredly prizes. All these things arise from that intense love of money which is so deeply ingrafted in the hearts of the Americans. If they should pay more attention to philosophy and the fine arts, they would be far more intellectual as a people; but as long as they are admirers of wealth, no matter how gained, they are merely practical and inconsistent people. Inconsistent, because priding themselves on their republican simplicity, they are the most willing slaves of fashion; or pretending to be true republicans, they are never so happy as when they have an opportunity of paying respect to a prince or a duke. Where is the trouble? The answer is plain. They are too practical.

When Franklin, than whom there cannot be a more practical American, with all the simplicity of Cincinnatus[1] presented himself before the court of Versailles, even the ultra-royalists could not withhold the veneration due the man for true dignity, and he commanded the respect of even the bitterest enemies. Compared with this glorious spectacle, the idea of the Americans of the present day, with much money, trying to imitate the manners of other countries whose teachers they might well become, and making bad blunders, is really disgraceful. In their eagerness to educate all the young persons to be practical, they almost neglect their moral training. Man is both an intellectual and moral being. He must be so educated as to develop both these capacities. If his intellect is trained more than his moral nature, he will be a dangerous man, for his power for evil is increased beyond measure.

In this connection I may again observe a strange inconsistency of the Americans. Though they thus neglect their moral training at home, they send missionaries to teach the wretched heathen to be good, and at the same time send a company of practical men who show their practicability by extracting the riches in every way, and when they could, by cheating those men whom their fellow-countrymen undertake to teach—to be what?—to be good!

So I might go on, but I think I have said enough to make you acknowledge, at least to yourself, that it is a disgrace to the Americans that they are a practical people.

THE STRENGTH AND THE WEAKNESS OF REPUBLICS

The republican form of government is now generally conceded to be "theoretically the best,"

but its claim to be also the strongest is still disputed, or at least not yet firmly established. The Declaration of Independence by the American Colonies, the French Revolution, and various important subsequent events, until the present time, all unite in proclaiming to the nations of the world the right of a people to govern itself, and by so doing demonstrated clearly the absurdity of the divine rights of the kings to rule.

The whole political heaven is, as it were, being charged with republican electricity. The explosion will come sooner or later. Meanwhile, the diffusion of intelligence among the people makes them more enlightened and more jealous of their rights than ever before; despots tremble on their thrones, and as they make concessions most reluctantly, most readily do the people call for more. Judging from such circumstances, it would appear that all the nations of the world, as if by common consent, are converging rapidly toward that point where Republicanism reigns supreme.

It is then a matter of the utmost importance to us to endeavor to discover in what lie the strength and the weakness of republics.

In a republic, every citizen is interested in any measure before the government, and it would be safe to set this down as one of the great elements of strength.

The government is influenced, to a great extent, not by the opinions of a king, or, what is worse, those of a few ambitious politicians, but by the mighty voice of an almost infallible people. It is evident that the government thus situated will be more faithful in the execution of its duties than in monarchical countries, where the character of the government depends a good deal on the disposition of the sovereign. Another strong point in a republic, is the bicameral feature of its government. One body acts as a check on another, and, if their characters are different, for instance, the first radical, and the second conservative, the course of legislation will be neither too progressive, with which the people cannot keep pace, nor so conservative as to interfere with the enterprises of the country.

---

[1]Lucius Quinctius Cincinnatus (b. 519 B.C.), a general who, according to legend, led Romans to victory over the Aequi in a single day, then returned to his work as a farmer.

The right to struggle for fame, for learning, and wealth, is the grandest heritage of humanity, and this right is most scrupulously respected in almost all the republican countries of the present day; hence, the poorest and humblest can have fair play to become superior in position to any other.

This state of things keeps the people ever in activity.

. . . If we go back a few years in the history of the world, we shall find the true strength of republicanism displayed in the American [Revolutionary] war. We do not purpose to look at that memorable contest in all its bearings, but will content ourselves with an observation illustrating one of the secrets of the success of the Americans. Every historian has dwelt with enthusiasm on the retreat of Washington through New Jersey with a few thousand of the barefooted and famishing soldiers. Was it the devotion to their illustrious commander which enabled those brave men to encounter so cheerfully the manifold dangers of that disastrous campaign?

No, noble Washington did much, but the real strength of the army lay in the fact that every soldier was also a citizen, imbued with a hatred of the tyrant, and conscious of fighting in the cause of freedom and humanity.

When we see so much dignity in common soldiers, we shall not be dazzled by the sublime spectacle of the Revolutionary Congress defying the power of the strongest nation in the world, often fleeing before the victorious foe, yet firm and unyielding, and, at last, after a long struggle, giving the country a glorious peace, and placing her by the side of the proudest nations of the world!

Thus far, we have looked at the strong sides of the republic. Now we shall investigate some of the causes of its weakness. "When you assemble a number of men to have the advantage of their joint wisdom, you inevitably assemble with those men all their prejudices, their passions, their errors of opinion, their local interests and selfish views." The history of every republic too clearly illustrates the above remarks of Franklin. Grant that all the legislators chosen are conscientious men; they determine to be true to their sacred trust. But alas! they do not, nay, cannot, agree as to the best method of promoting the interests of their constituents, for nothing is dearer to a man than his theory; and especially is this true of such upright men as we suppose them to be. And then, a particular member, in pleading the cause of his constituents, may badly interfere with carrying out of a measure which will be beneficial to the whole people as a nation. It may be contended that the majority will rule; but, if our supposed member happen to be also an influential man, he may so exert his powers as to cause the very majority to enter into his views.

. . . It will be admitted that the officers of a republic are not always the best and ablest men of the land, but that they sometimes are the most cunning, perhaps the most unprincipled.

By the most unprincipled, we refer to that class of politicians called demagogues. These persons rarely succeed in securing the confidence of the respectable portion of the people, and when they do so, they cannot retain it long.

To the mere outsiders, they would seem to be wholly incapable of doing any serious injury to the state. But when we study the effect of their proceedings, we shall be very likely to change our opinion. Too often have the glories of the state been tarnished by the disgraceful conduct of these men, too often their impudence, vulgarity, and recklessness have so prevented an enlightened statesman from carrying out his plans, that they deserve to be set down as at once worse than traitors. . . .

. . . In a republic, a constant change of officers exerts a very baneful influence, and is the cause of bitter political and party strife. Thus there can be no stability in the government. And the stability, it must be remembered, is an important element of the strength.

Beholding a republic with her weakness and strength before us, and a monarchy with hers in the same position, we shall fear the latter as our enemy, for she is strong, but the former we shall love as we love the truth; we shall encourage as we would an inexperienced youth, for her strength is not yet as fully developed as that of her elder sister, monarchy!

REVIEW QUESTIONS

1. What conflicts does Ryokichi find between U.S. customs and his Japanese beliefs?
2. On the whole, is he favorably impressed by the U.S. citizens and their behavior? Explain.
3. Do you believe Ryokichi would describe American life and values differently today than he did 150 years ago? Why or why not?
4. To what political strife does Ryokichi refer in the next to last paragraph of this excerpt?

An English Educator Discusses Society in the United States (1834)

HARRIET MARTINEAU, *Society in America*

Many Europeans visited the United States before the 1860s to investigate the social and political experiment of a democratic nation. In 1834 England's abolition of slavery stimulated much interest in and condemnation of the continuation of slavery in a country with such high ideals as the United States. The standards of England's thriving women's movement can also be seen in Harriet Martineau's interest in suffrage for women in the United States.

By the time Martineau came to the United States in 1834, she had won a reputation as a scholar of political economics. An educator in England, Martineau belonged to the Unitarian Church, had published widely on many social topics, and was an avowed abolitionist. She supported herself with her own earnings, including proceeds from the sale of her nine-volume work *Illustrations of Political Economy* and a single-volume discourse entitled *Illustrations of Taxation.*

Martineau never married, traveled extensively, and saw her visit to the United States as both a vacation and a research trip. In spite of her statement that she was "as nearly as possible unprejudiced about America," she already had very strong opinions about Americans based upon their reputations in Europe. During her two years in the United States, her particular interest in women and children occasioned many comparisons with those of England. The following passage reveals her ideas on the education of American youth.

Nothing less than an entire work would be required for the discussion of the subject of education in any country. I can only indicate here two or three peculiarities which strike the stranger in the discipline of American children; of those whose lot is cast in the northern States; for it needs no further showing, that those who are reared among slaves have not the ordinary chances of wisdom and peace.

The Americans, particularly those of New England, look with a just complacency on the apparatus of education furnished to their entire population. There are schools provided for the training of every individual, from the earliest age; colleges to receive the élite of the schools; and lyceums, and other such institutions, for the subsequent instruction of working men. The provision of schools is so adequate, that any citizen who sees a child at play during school-hours, may ask "why are you not at school?" and, unless a good reason be given, may take him to the school-house of the district. Some, who do not penetrate to the principle of this, exclaim upon the tyranny practised upon the parents. The principle is, that, in a democracy, where life and society are equally open to all, and where all have agreed to require of each other a certain amount of intellectual and moral competency, the means being provided, it becomes the duty of all to see that the means are used. Their use is an indispensable condition of the privileges of citizenship. No control is exercised as to how and where the child shall be educated. It rests with the parent to send him to a public or private school, or have him taught at home: but in case of his being found in a neglected state as to education, it is in the power of any citizen to bring him to the advantage provided for him by society.

The instruction furnished is not good enough for the youth of such a country, with such a responsibility and such a destiny awaiting them as the working out the first democratic organisation that the world has witnessed in practice. The information provided is both meagre and superficial. There is not even any systematic instruction given on political morals: an enormous deficiency in a republic. But it must be remembered how young the society is; how far it has already gone beyond most other countries; and how great is the certainty that the majority, always ultimately in the right, will gradually exalt the character of the instruction which it has been already wise enough to provide. It must be remembered too, how much farther the same kind and degree of instruction goes in a democracy than elsewhere. The alphabet itself is of little or no value to a slave, while it is an inestimable treasure to a conscious young republican. One needs but go from a charity-school in an English county to a free-school in Massachusetts, to see how different the bare acquisition of reading and writing is to children who, if they look forward at all, do it languidly, and into a life of mechanical labour merely, and to young citizens who are aware that they have their share of the work of self-government to achieve. Elderly gentlemen in the country may smile, and foreigners of all ages may scoff at the self-confidence and complacency of young men who have just exercised the suffrage for the first time: but the being secure of the dignity, the certainty of being fully and efficaciously represented, the probability of sooner or later filling some responsible political office, are a stimulus which goes far to supply the deficiencies of the instruction imparted. It is much to be wished that this stimulus were as strong and as virtuous in one or two colleges whose inmates are on the very verge of the exercise of their political rights, as in some of even the primary schools. The aristocratic atmosphere of Harvard University, for instance, would be much purified by a few breezes of such democratic inspiration as issue from the school-houses of some of the country districts.

Some persons plead that there is less occasion for school instruction in the principles of politics, than for an improved teaching of some other things; because children are instructed in politics every day of their lives by what they hear at home, and wherever they go. But they hear all too little of principles. What they hear is argumentation about particular men, and immediate measures. The more sure they are of learning details elsewhere, the more necessary it is that they should here be exercised in those principles by which the details are to be judged and made available as knowledge. They come to school with their heads crammed with prejudices, and their memories with words, which it should be part of the work of school to reduce to truth and clearness, by substituting principles for the one, and annexing ideas to the other.

A Sunday-school teacher asked a child, "Who killed Abel?" "General Jackson."—Another inquired of a scholar, "In what state were mankind left after the fall?"—"In the State of Vermont."

REVIEW QUESTIONS

1. According to Martineau, what are the problems with education of the young in the United States?
2. Does she find the universities and schools of higher learning adequate, superior to, or inferior to England's? Explain.
3. Are there any characteristics or priorities of the U.S. educational system that she seems to misunderstand? Explain.

10

Europe, 1800–1918

Selections in this chapter expand upon ideas introduced in Chapter 5, but they also introduce several new ones. Contact between peoples of the world continued to increase, as more Asians and particularly Americans visited Europe, the latter as what can only be described as tourists. Those who remained at home, for various reasons, were able to enjoy the travels of others vicariously through a plethora of travel literature with which publishers bombarded the curious public. Several themes can be discerned in this new type of literature, including the industrialization and modernization of previously underdeveloped parts of Europe, and the lifestyles of the "rich and famous," as well as of the "poor and unknown."

Until the nineteenth century, accounts of Europe by non-Europeans are rare. Europeans constituted the vast majority of world travelers and travel writers before the transportation revolution of the late eighteenth century. After 1800, steam power enabled more people everywhere to travel—and to travel more widely—for profit, politics, and pleasure. As a result, Europeans quickly lost their near-monopoly of foreign travel, while Asians and, to a greater extent, Americans joined the ranks of travelers to Europe in their own version of the "grand tour." Originally a British custom designed to put the finishing touches on an upper-class university education, by the late nineteenth century the "grand tour" became a social requirement for wealthy or successful Americans of all ages who sought to find perspective and meaning in their mostly European roots. These were the heirs of the Englishman Thomas Coryat (see Chapter 5), a "cultural pilgrim" who journeyed through Europe to supplement his formal education and to enjoy the opportunities afforded by the great cultural centers of Europe.

Catharine Maria Sedgwick, a prominent American novelist, went on her own "grand tour" from 1839 to 1840. She spent a good deal of her time hobnobbing with Europe's cultural and literary elite. Her contacts gave her the opportunity to study Europeans, both as individuals and as representative types illuminating national characteristics. Another American novelist, Theodore Dreiser, also traveled throughout Europe searching for his roots. In this case, Dreiser, the son of a German immigrant, was particularly interested in German society. Americans also journeyed from their homelands for more prosaic reasons. Yet another famous novelist from the United States, Jack London, was motivated more by politics and the lure of adventure than by a desire to experience the high society and cultural attractions that Europe had to offer. Therefore, when he went to London in 1902, he did his sightseeing in the East End, observing the squalor of what he called "the underworld." A century earlier, the famous Mexican author and revolutionary Fray Servando Teresa de Mier traveled to and within Europe primarily to escape persecution and imprisonment by religious and political authorities back home.

As already noted, this period witnessed an explosion of travel literature. So much was written that it almost seems as though every tourist who visited Europe felt compelled to record his or her experiences, recollections, and judgments. Books, letters to relatives, and newspaper stories were published for the almost insatiable appetites of the reading public at home. Some writers, in fact, were sent abroad for the express purpose of describing and analyzing foreign countries, conditions, and customs. One such author was Henry de Windt, who undertook a visit to the Balkans as special correspondent of the *Westminster Gazette.* Of the other works mentioned so far, only Meir's journal was an unintended result of his adventures as a fugitive. London, Sedgwick, and Dreiser were all professional writers who intended to publish accounts of their travels from the outset.

The works included in this chapter highlight several important themes and topics. The impact of industrialization, for example, motivated London's depiction of the poor. He presents portraits of those left behind by the rising tide of material well-being. Many authors, however, chose to focus on the middle and upper classes. For example, Edwin Pears—a British lawyer, historian, and social critic—turned his attention to family life among a relatively prosperous segment of the Turkish population. Liu Hsi-hung, a Chinese diplomat, included in his journal a description of social life at the very highest levels of British society.

Liu's diplomatic mission to London, and later Berlin, underscores the rising importance of nation-states and modern diplomacy in the nineteenth century. His firsthand experiences and observations in London broadened his perspectives and allowed him to accept Western values and behaviors at face value. As Liu's experience demonstrated, knowledge of foreign places and peoples usually led to greater understanding and acceptance. Often such was not the case with writers who did not benefit from direct experience in foreign lands or with foreign peoples. Two Japanese authors who never left Japan, Rai San'yo and Aizawa Seishisai, expressed very negative views of Europeans. They found European values and beliefs to be repugnant, and they used criticism of European behavior as a way to indirectly argue for the supremacy of their own traditions.

Clearly, the issues presented in this chapter reveal that the world during this period was becoming more complex and complicated. Authors came from more varied backgrounds than before and addressed a wider range of topics. Despite the new awareness of social and economic class disparity, however, it is evident that travel and firsthand observation of other societies and peoples did not necessarily lead to tolerance for others and for other points of view. This difficulty will become more evident in Chapter 15.

A Mexican Friar Describes Life in Paris (1801)

Fray Servando Teresa de Mier, *Memoirs*

In 1794, the Dominican friar Servando Teresa de Mier (1763–1827) suggested that the image of the Virgin of Guadalupe was brought to Mexico by the Apostle Thomas—obviously well before 1531, the date at which the Virgin was generally believed to have appeared before the Indian Juan Diego.

Church authorities, antagonized and threatened by this bold revision of such a significant event in Mexican religious history, defrocked the friar and sentenced him to ten years in prison in Spain. For the next thirty years he faced persecution by the Inquisition. The true story of his numerous arrests, imprisonments, and escapes is almost theatrical. So too is the account of his corpse. Fifteen years after his death, in 1842, his body was exhumed and preserved in the ossuary of the Monastery of Santo Domingo in Mexico. In 1861 his mummy was sold to don Bernabé de la Barra, owner of a circus, who wanted to exhibit it in Brussels and Buenos Aires. Indeed, in 1882 Mier's mummy was said to have been exhibited in Brussels as that of a victim of the Inquisition. The whereabouts of these remains today is unknown.

While Mier's political writings (i.e., *Historia de la revolucíon de Nueva España*) have guaranteed his place in the history of the Mexican independence movement, his *Memoirs* are just as important in the field of travel literature. They tell the story of his adventures as a fugitive and as an eyewitness to European events. Moreover, Mier's narrative turns the image of the world recorded in the European travel literature of the era upside down. The "others" are the Europeans, whose societies, cities, and habits are described as if they were features of some primitive society under investigation by an amateur anthropologist.

Something quite noteworthy in Paris, because it is the most popular meeting place, is what is called the *Palais Royal,* built around the former garden of the palace of the Duke of Orléans. It is a square lined with galleries, with apartments above the splendid facade, and trees in the middle, forming a promenade and a little flower garden; it is so large that it takes a quarter of an hour to go all the way round it, and has two walkways through it bordered by fashionable shops. All the notices about various works, novelties and so on are posted on the columns of it, and in its shops, which are below the galleries, whatever objects are the most refined of their sort, including books, are for sale. There is no one in Paris who is not seen there at one time or another, and the prettiest and most gallant courtesans also stroll about there as though in their houses, and pay a special tax to the Government in order to do so. Without ever leaving the confines of the *Palais Royal* one can come by everything necessary for one's sustenance, luxury and diversion. In it there were eleven kitchens, fourteen cafés, two large theaters and three small ones and even scribes or public clerks with their *bureau* or money-changer's table, and men in wigs

who supplied little napkins with which to tidy oneself up, and lavender water, or *alhucema* as we call it, so as to come out with one's behind nicely perfumed.

In the cafés one finds all the Paris daily papers, which are many in number, as well as the official gazette, which is called *Le Moniteur.* And foreign newspapers as well. One can read everything without having to pay, and every café is a refuge against the cold for poor decent folk, because one doesn't feel the cold inside them, on account of the stoves. Since the war with Spain people tend to drink chocolate rather than coffee, except after a meal. And almanacs, some in prose and some in verse, listing women of ill repute by their names, addresses, talents and endowments, are also sold there.

In the Café Borel there was a ventriloquist, a man who spoke through his belly, something that, if it were not an art, one would take for a magic trick. He barely opens his mouth and projects his voice wherever he wishes, far away, up close, in the roof beams, on the wall, as he chooses, and a person would swear with all his senses and all his soul's verities that someone is speaking there in the place where he projects his voice. He varies the tone of it in a thousand ways, and it is enough to drive a person mad. So, a person who took a newcomer to the Café Borel would secretly apprise the ventriloquist of the name and homeland of the latter, and as he was about to drink his coffee, the ventriloquist would enter, ask what his name was and then immediately project his voice into a tall window and call him by his name to come get a letter for him from such and such a place in the country that he was from. The man thus summoned would go upstairs at once, search all about the hallways and find no one. But the minute he returned to his seat, he was again called by name, by a voice telling him: "Come here, I'm here." The newcomer would go back, and the entire café would be amused.

There were other cafés with two rooms, and in one music was played and women sang, while in the other some little play or short comedy was put on, and performances were given in turn in the two rooms, till eleven at night. There was also the spectacle called a phantasmagoria, or the art of the Gentile priests whereby they made the gods and the shades or manes of the dead appear and do things and even go so far as to fling themselves on top of a person. Galvanism or animal electricity had also been recently discovered, whereby the nerves of a dead animal, if touched by two metals at the same time, would make it leap about and jerk its limbs. A dead man's eyes open, and I have seen one move his arms and lie there pulling out his innards, because his body was slit open. I am unable to describe the luxury of the theaters, of which there were thirty. The largest theater, or Theater of the Arts, was very expensive, and was always full; yet even so it was necessary for the Republic to grant it a subsidy of a million pesos each year. It took a thousand young girls to perform the dances alone, and the sum spent on the decor and stage costumes of the opera based on the mysteries of Isis amounted to seven hundred thousand francs, the equivalent of seven hundred thousand columnarias. A Spanish columnaria is what we would call two reals, because the Spanish peseta is worth one Spanish real less than ours. In Spain, there are twenty reals to a peso, which they call a duro, and there are four of these reals to each of its pesetas. So that one Spanish real is worth less than one medio of ours, since it is worth ten and a half cuartos, and a Spanish real de vellón is worth eight and a half cuartos.

It may seem surprising that I leave Paris without saying anything about the city in general, about its population or about France. Such a subject belongs under the head of statistics or geography, and there are books in which to study it. Moreover it varies endlessly, and Napoleon's wars have devastated the population of Europe. Spain once had a population of 10 million; I would be surprised if it has even 8 million today. Madrid was calculated to have 140,000 inhabitants; I doubt whether it has more than 60,000 today. France had a population of more than 30 million at the time of the Republic; I do not believe that it has today even the 24 million it had at the time of Louis XVI, because the annual military conscription led all the young men of France to the slaughter. Paris was calculated to have 700,000 inhabitants in 1801; it was my impression, when I returned there in 1814, that it had less than 400,000, including foreigners. Italy once had a population of 18 million; today I doubt that it has 12 million. Rome numbered 166,000 souls, including 26,000 Jews. I was still there at the time of the first invasion of the French, when 30,000 souls disappeared. Today it has 70,000 to 80,000 at most. Naples, at the time of the Republic, was estimated to have 500,000, and the entire kingdom 5 million. Today it probably has 4 million at most, and the city no more than 200,000 souls. Portugal, including the islands, had 3 million, and Lisbon, its capital, 300,000 in 1807, when I was there. What with the war and the emigration that followed upon that of the king, the kingdom probably has a population of no more than 2 million, and the capital no more than 150,000.

As for the cities, there are none in Europe that can compare to those of our America or of the United States. All of the former appear to have been founded by a people inimical to straight lines. They are all nothing but streets and alleyways that are blind ends, labyrinths with no order and no ostentation. All the houses are made of stone, brick and wood, and the walls are as burning hot as the roofs. The latter are made of tiles, and are not flat, as ours are. In Spain some small measure of regularity and beauty has been introduced in such ports as Cádiz, Puerto de Santa María, Bilbao, Barceloneta that carry on trade with America, by following our example. Churches in Europe are Gothic, except in Rome. In conclusion: in each kingdom little road guides are sold, showing their distances and listing places and things worth seeing along each one. In the large cities a map of them is sold, in the form of a small book, to guide foreigners, along with a list of everything to be found in them. Only in Spain is there no such thing. And such a guide would be useless, because in the small towns and villages only the parish priest and the sacristan know how to read. Everyone journeys like a barbarian through a land of barbarians, trembling at the highwaymen who sally forth to rob travelers, and a carriage is escorted only by troupes of beggars and children, clamoring for alms at the top of their lungs.

What there is not such a great lack of, at least in the capital of Spain, is libraries, for there is the Royal Library and that of San Isidro, where people go to study. In Paris there is the Royal Library, or that of Cardinal Richelieu, whose books number in the millions, and one is given all the books to read that one asks for in the two hours that it is open in the morning. The library of the Institute is very good, and there are others, such as the one at the Collège Mazarin, etc. There are also reading rooms, very neatly arranged and sheltered from the cold, where for a mere nothing one can read not only all the periodicals, but also everything new that has come out. One can also ask for portable books, that is to say, small-sized ones. And if one is not a regular customer, for four sols a day one can go there morning, noon and night, and sit at his own little table, with his own fire and inkwell. And there are also circulating libraries, in which a person can sit down to read and for a paltry sum per month take home as many books as he needs. None of this exists in Spain either. But enough of Paris.

REVIEW QUESTIONS

1. What did Mier dislike about Paris? What did he like?
2. What features of Paris seemed most important to Mier? Do you think you would emphasize the same features if you were writing down your impressions of the city?
3. Why did Mier like American cities better than European ones?
4. Why did Mier bother to give so many population figures in this selection? What was his point? What was his point of view?

Two Japanese Views of Europeans

RAI SAN'YO, *Dutch Ship* (1818)
AIZAWA SEISHISAI, *Shinron (New Theses)* (1825)

Like earlier Japanese writers, Rai San'yo (1781–1832) and Aizawa Seishisai (1782–1863) did not travel outside of Japan to observe foreign cultures; instead they described visitors to their homeland. Both were Japanese nationalist thinkers, and in many ways they echoed the convictions of their predecessor, Hirata Atsutane (see Chapter 5), especially in their belief in Japanese supremacy. Like Atsutane, they attacked foreign "barbarians," although from a different perspective. Rai San'yo's poem, written in 1818 in Nagasaki, bemoaned the arrival of Western ships that had begun to appear off the Japanese coast in increasing numbers. Writing in 1825, Aizawa Seishisai vehemently argued that Western foreigners were untrustworthy and their every action threatening. Eventually he advocated the need to study Westerners so that their tactics could be understood, their technology learned, and their aggression resisted.

Both men were Confucian scholars and supporters of the imperialist loyalist cause. Aizawa, in fact, was a leading figure in the Mito school, an ultranationalist form of Confucianism. He was also virulently anti-Christian, believing that Japanese supremacy resulted from the imperial family's direct descent from the sun goddess Amaterasu. Loyalty to the emperor, he felt, was the basis for morality. The views of these two writers contributed substantially to the overthrow of the Tokugawa shogunate and the restoration of the emperor to power in 1868.

DUTCH SHIP

In Nagasaki Bay, southwest where sky and
    water meet,
suddenly at heaven's edge a tiny dot appears.
The cannon of the lookout tower gives one roar
and in twenty-five watch stations bows are
    bared.
Through the streets on four sides the cry breaks
    forth:
"The redhaired Westerners are coming!"
Launches set out to meet them, we hear the
    drum echo,
in the distance signal flags are raised to stay
    alarm.
The ship enters the harbor like a ponderous
    turtle,
so huge that in the shallows it seems certain to
    ground.
Our little launches, so many strings of pearls,
tow it forward amid a clamorous din.
The barbarian hull rises a hundred feet from
    the surface,

sea winds sighing, flapping its pennants of felt.
Three sails stretched among ten thousand lines,
fixed to engines moving up and down like
    wellsweeps.
Blackskinned slaves nimble as monkeys
scale the masts, haul the lines, keeping them
    from tangling.
The anchor drops with shouts from the crew,
giant cannon bellow forth roar after roar.
Barbarian hearts are hard to fathom; the
    Throne ponders,
aware that defenses are far from complete.
Ah, the wretches, why do they come to vex our
    eyes,
pursuing ten thousand miles their greed for
    gain,
their ships pitiful leaves upon the monstrous
    waves,
drawn like giant ants to rancid meat?
Do we not bear ox-knives to kill a mere
    chicken,
trade our most precious jewels for thorns?

SHINRON (NEW THESES)

The Barbarians' Nature

For close to three hundred years now the Western barbarians have rampaged on the high seas. Why are they able to enlarge their territories and fulfill their every desire? Does their wisdom and courage exceed that of ordinary men? Is their government so benevolent that they win popular support? Are their rites, music, laws, and political institutions superb in all respects? Do they possess some superhuman, divine powers? Hardly. Christianity is the sole key to their success. It is a truly evil and base religion, barely worth discussing. But its main doctrines are simple to grasp and well-contrived; they can easily deceive stupid commoners with it. Using clever words and subtle phrases, they would have commoners believe that to deceive Heaven is to revere it, and that to destroy the Way is needed for ethical understanding.

They win a reputation for benevolence by performing small acts of kindness temporarily to peoples they seek to conquer. After they capture a people's hearts and minds, they propagate their doctrines. Their gross falsehoods and misrepresentations deceive many, particularly those who yearn for things foreign. Such dupes, with their smattering of secondhand Western knowledge, write books with an air of scholarly authority; so even daimyo or high-ranking officials at times cannot escape infection from barbarian ways. Once beguiled by Christianity, they cannot be brought back to their senses. Herein lies the secret of the barbarians' success.

Whenever they seek to take over a country, they employ the same method. By trading with that nation, they learn about its geography and defenses. If these be weak, they dispatch troops to invade the nation; if strong, they propagate Christianity to subvert it from within. Once our people's hearts and minds are captivated by Christianity, they will greet the barbarian host with open arms, and we would be powerless to stop them. Our people would consider it an honor and a privilege to die for this foreign god, and this willingness to die, this fearlessness, would make them fit for battle. Our people would gladly cast their riches into the sacrificial coffers of this foreign god, and those riches would finance barbarian campaigns. The barbarians believe it their god's will that they seduce other peoples into subverting their respective homelands; they borrow the slogan "universal love" to achieve their desired ends. Barbarian armies seek only plunder, but do so in the name of their god. They employ this tactic in all lands they annex or conquer. . . .

. . . Russia has expanded tremendously of late. It utilized Christianity to seduce the Ezo tribes* into submission and to capture island after island [to our north]. Now Russia has turned its predatory eyes on Japan proper. The English also appear at frequent intervals, furtively trying to beguile our commoners and peoples in outlying areas. . . .

The peoples of Europe happen to be at war with each other now. But they all revere the same god. When the opportunity for a quick kill presents itself, they combine forces, and [after attaining victory,] divide the spoils. On the other hand, when they encounter difficulties, each withdraws to its own territory. This explains why we enjoy peace here in the east whenever there is strife in the west, and why there is peace in Europe whenever they venture to the east seeking plunder and territory. Russia, after subduing the lesser barbarians to the west, has turned its attention to the east. It has captured Siberia, and wants to infiltrate the Amur River area. But the Ch'ing empire, as strong as ever, is frustrating Russian designs there. As a countermove, Russia now is invading our Ezo territories. . . .

First, the Russians confined themselves to drawing sketches and maps of our terrain and coastline and to studying our moves and countermoves. Then they began to seduce our commoners into their fold and politely requested permission to trade. But when we denied this

———
*Another word for the Ainu, an indigenous people of Japan.

request, they ravaged Ezo, seized our weapons, and set fire to our outposts there. Then they requested permission to trade once more. In other words, after slowly and methodically reconnoitering our position, they make their requests, sometimes under the cloak of politeness and correct protocol, sometimes accompanied by armed violence. They use every conceivable technique to achieve their ulterior motives, ulterior motives that are clear to any thinking man.

But our temporizing, gloss-it-over officials say, "They only come for provisions of rice; there is no cause for alarm." What simpletons! Unlike us, the barbarians eat flesh, not rice: A lack of rice should not bother them. . . .

But the Russians have been strangely quiet of late, and in their place, the English have suddenly appeared. First they perpetrated violence in Nagasaki. Then they forced their way into Edo Bay.* In short, the Russians, who have harbored designs on us for over one hundred years, suddenly disappear without a trace, and the English, who have rarely ventured to our coasts, just as suddenly zoom in to reconnoiter and probe. Can this be mere coincidence? Vicious birds of prey always pounce on their victims from dark shadows: The Russians are now hiding in wait for the kill. To facilitate their sly stratagem, they have English underlings do their reconnaissance work. . . .

The bakufu† once made it plain to Russia that Japanese law requires us to destroy on sight any barbarian ship approaching our coasts. But now the English regularly appear and anchor off our shores, and we do not lift a finger to drive them away. [Quite the contrary], . . . when they have the gall to land, we go out of our way to provide for their needs and send them merrily along. Will the barbarians have any respect for our laws after they hear about this? The English come and go as they please, draw maps and sketch our terrain, disrupt our inter-island transport sys-

tem, and win over our commoners with their occult religion and the lure of profit. If smuggling increases and we fail to stop commoners from aiding and abetting the barbarians, who knows what future conspiracies may hatch?

But our temporizing, gloss-it-over officials reply, "The foreigners are just fishermen and merchants doing nothing out of the ordinary; there is no cause for alarm." What simpletons! The barbarians live ten thousand miles across the sea; when they set off on foreign conquests, "they must procure supplies and provisions from the enemy." That is why they trade and fish. Their men-of-war are self-sufficient away from home. If their only motive for harpooning whales was to obtain whale meat, they could do so in their own waters. Why should they risk long, difficult voyages just to harpoon whales in eastern seas? . . .

. . . The English barbarians come and anchor off our shores whenever they please; they learn all about convenient approaches to our islands, about the location of bays and inlets along our coastline, and about our climate and our people's spiritual make-up. Should we let them occupy the small islands off to our southeast, . . . and establish bases on Hachijōjima, Yaskushima, and Tanegashima,[1] they would be in a perfect strategic position to invade our Middle Kingdom. This would be another case of two birds with one stone. It is easy to see why the English conspire with the Russians and spy on our coastal fortifications: They are eager to combine forces and obtain spoils.

But those ignorant of the bakufu's astute reasoning and farsightedness argue, "If we treat the barbarians with kindness, they will comply docilely; to intimidate them only invites reprisals." Such men cling to out-dated, erroneous views with unbelievable tenacity. They would have the bakufu issue injunctions when in fact the barbarians understand nothing but force.

For hundreds of years the barbarians have desired and resolved to subvert enemy nations

---

*Edo was the original name of the modern city of Tokyo, and Edo Bay the name of Tokyo Bay.
†Literally "tented headquarters," a term for the government of the shoguns.

---

[1]Islands off the coast of Japan.

through their occult religion and thus conquer the whole world. They will not be deterred by occasional acts of kindness or displays of force. When they wreak vengeance against us, they intimidate us into backing down; when they submit meekly before us, they lull us into a false sense of security. They employ these two tactics "to probe for strengths and weaknesses." Those spied on can never fully fathom the thoughts and feelings of the spies: The barbarians "assume different guises and employ a variety of feints." This forces us to commit ourselves one way or the other on each occasion and throws us off balance; so we often commit blunders in spite of ourselves. This should explain the acuity and astuteness behind the policy of armed expulsion. . . .

Again the dimwits argue, "The barbarians' religion is a set of shallow, base doctrines. They may deceive stupid commoners with it, but they will never beguile our superior men (*chūn tzu*). There is no cause for alarm." But the great majority of people in the realm are stupid commoners; superior men are very few in number. Once the hearts and minds of the stupid commoners have been captivated, we will lose control of the realm. The ancient sage kings enforced harsh penalties for seditious and subversive activities . . . ; such was their hatred for those who incited stupid commoners to rebel. The barbarians' religion infiltrated Kyūshū once before, and spread like the plague among stupid commoners. Within less than a hundred years, two hundred eighty thousand converts were discovered and brought to justice. This indicates how fast the contagion can spread. . . . It is of no avail for a few superior men to remain untouched by the pollution spreading around them. The immunity of superior men to Christianity does not permit complacence.

REVIEW QUESTIONS

1. Explain what Rai San'yo might have meant when he said that the "redhaired Westerners" were "drawn like giant ants to rancid meat."
2. Why did Aizawa Seishisai feel that Christianity was the greatest tool of the "barbarians" and therefore the greatest threat to the Japanese?
3. Which author seemed to harbor the most hostility toward Europeans? Explain your choice.

An American Novelist Analyzes the German Character (1839–1840)

CATHARINE MARIA SEDGWICK, *Letters from Abroad to Kindred at Home*

Catharine Maria Sedgwick (1789–1867) grew up in New England and maintained a strong affinity for this region throughout her life. She published more than two dozen books in her career. One of them, *Hope Leslie; or Early Times in Massachusetts* (1827) was the first American novel based on Puritan New England. It, and others such as *Live and Let Live; or Domestic Service*

Illustrated (1837), and *Married or Single?* (1857), emphasized the importance of the American home and established Sedgwick as the most popular female writer in the country during the 1820s and 1830s. Harriet Martineau, whose own work appears elsewhere in this volume, recommended her works as accurate portrayals of American life. Several of Sedgwick's books were translated into foreign languages.

For fifteen months in 1839–1840 Sedgwick traveled to Britain, France, Italy, Switzerland, Germany, and Belgium. She published her travel letters in two volumes under the title *Letters from Abroad to Kindred at Home* (1841). As an accomplished author, she normally associated with members of Europe's cultural elite. In the following selection, taken from a letter written from Wiesbaden, Germany, Sedgwick offers her opinions about the character of the Germans and compares it with that of other groups she has encountered, especially the English.

We have now been here more than a month, and I may venture to speak to you of what has been a constant subject of admiration to us all, the manners of the Germans. The English race, root and branch, are, what with their natural shyness, their conventional reserves, and their radical uncourteousness, cold and repelling. The politeness of the French is conventional. It seems in part the result of their sense of personal grace, and in part of a selfish calculation of making the most of what costs nothing; and partly, no doubt, it is the spontaneous effect of a vivacious nature. There is a deep-seated humanity in the courtesy of the Germans. They always seem to be feeling a gentle pressure from the cord that interlaces them with their species. They do not wait, as Schiller* says, till you "freely invite" to "friendlily stretch you a hand," but the hand is instinctively stretched out and the kind deed ready to follow it.

This suavity is not limited to any rank or condition. It extends all the way down from the prince to the poorest peasant. Some of our party driving out in a hackney-coach yesterday, met some German ladies in a coach with four horses, postillions, footmen in livery, and other marks of rank and wealth. What would Americans have

done in a similar position? Probably looked away and seemed unconscious. And English ladies would have done the same, or, as I have seen them in Hyde Park, have leaned back in their carriages, and stared with an air of mingled indifference and insolence through their eyeglasses, as if their inferiors in condition could bear to be stared at. The German ladies bowed most courteously to the humble strangers in the hackney-coach.

Yesterday, at the table d'hôte, I observed a perpendicular old gentleman, who looked as if he had been born before any profane dreams of levelling down the steeps of aristocracy had entered the mind of man, and whose servant, in rich livery, as stiff as himself, was in waiting behind him, bow to the persons opposite to him as he took his seat, and to those on his right hand and his left. Soon after our landlord came to speak to him, and familiarly and quite acceptably, as it appeared, laid his hand on the nobleman's shoulder while addressing him.

Soon after we came here, a gentleman with whom we passed a few hours in a Rhine steamer met us at the table d'hôte. "Had I not," he said, "the pleasure of coming from Bonn to Cologne with you? I see one of your party is absent. She is, I hope, well," &c. To appreciate as they deserve these wayside courtesies, you should see the relentless English we come in contact with, who, like ghosts, *never* "speak till they are spoken to."

A few days since, as we were issuing from our

---

*Sedgwick probably is referring to Friedrick von Schiller (1759–1805), the German playwright. For more than a century after his death, Schiller remained Germany's favorite playwright.

lodgings, a very gentlemanly German stopped us, begging our pardons, and saying, "English, I believe?" and then added, that as we appeared to be strangers in quest of lodgings, as he had just been, he would take the liberty to give us the addresses of two or three that had been recommended to him. This was truly a Samaritan—a *German* kindness. The hotel-keepers, that important class to travellers, often blend with the accurate performance of the duties of "mine host" the kindness of a friend. Their civility, freedom, and gentlemanliness remind me of my friend Cozzens and others, the best specimens of their fraternity at home. The landlord often sits at the table with his guests, and, with his own country people, converses on terms of apparent equality.[1]

The same self-respect blends with the civility of the shopkeeper. He is very happy to serve

and suit you, but, if he cannot, he is ready to direct you elsewhere. Shopmen have repeatedly, unasked, sent a person to guide us through the intricate Continental streets to another shop.

The domestics are prompt, faithful, and cheerful in their services. There is freedom, but no presumption in their manners, and nothing of that unhappy uncertainty as to their exact position, so uncomfortable in our people. In all these subordinate classes you see nothing of the cringing servility that marks them in England, and to which they are exposed by their direct dependance on their employers.

Our English friend, Miss ——, who has been repeatedly in Germany, and is a good observer, acquiesces in the truth of my observations, and says this general freedom of deportment comes from people of all ranks freely mingling together. If so, this surely is a healthy influence, a natural and beneficent effect from an obedience to that Divine precept, "honour all men." Wo to those who set the brethren of one family off into *castes,* and build up walls between them so that they cannot freely grasp hands and exchange smiles!

[1]This opinion may appear to have been formed on a very slight acquaintance with the country. It was afterward amply confirmed in Germany and Switzerland, where the manners are essentially the same.

REVIEW QUESTIONS

1. What did Sedgwick like about German behavior?
2. Did Sedgwick emphasize similarities or differences when she compared Germans to the English? Which group did she like better? Why?
3. Did Sedgwick distinguish among Germans by class or gender? What evidence supports your opinion?
4. Does Sedgwick strike you as a biased observer? Why or why not?

A Chinese Ambassador Describes the British Upper Classes (1876–1877)

Liu Hsi-hung, *Journal of a Voyage to England*

When Liu Hsi-hung went on a diplomatic mission to England in 1876, he had to overcome three significant obstacles. First, the European practice of using resident ambassadors ran counter to the political and social system of imperial

China. In fact, the Chinese government had difficulty finding men who would willingly suffer the humiliation of being sent abroad. Since the Chinese thought that all foreigners were inferior, to be posted to a foreign locale was considered an insult and disgrace. Second, in the third quarter of the nineteenth century there was still much ignorance and confusion in China about the West. Only a few decades earlier, for example, a Chinese description of Europe claimed that England was another name for Holland, that Switzerland and Sweden were identical, and that America was a small island off the coast of England. Finally, Kuo Sung-t'ao, the leader of the mission to England, protested vigorously against Liu's proposed appointment, arguing that he knew nothing about foreign affairs, lacked patience and objectivity, and had a reputation for being stubborn and ignorant.

Kuo protested in vain. When the embassy sailed from Shanghai in December 1876, Liu was on board the ship. From the beginning of the mission he kept a diary, later entitled *Journal of a Voyage to England,* in which he recorded his impressions (all Chinese envoys were ordered to record everything of interest that they saw). The diary demonstrates that, at first, Liu certainly did distrust foreigners. It also shows that, over time, he modified his position about the West. There is no doubt that he opposed the Westernization of China, but he was fair-minded when it came to appraising the achievements of Europeans in their own countries. He also had a flexibility of mind that allowed him to see things in perspective. For example, in his account of a society ball, included in the following selection, he comments rather objectively about how fashionable English women mingle with men. At the time, no Chinese woman would have appeared at a social function or spoken to a strange man.

In November 1877, Liu was transferred to Berlin and became the first Chinese ambassador to Germany.

{Undated}

At balls, the man and the woman face each other and hold on to each other. The man holds on to the waist of the woman with one hand, while the woman holds on to the man's shoulder with one hand. They dance this way in the middle of the hall. Usually there are four or five pairs who dance at the same time, going several times around the hall before stopping. The women expose much of their bodies while the men are neatly dressed. But in this country, the men wear formal suits with pants of flesh colour, tightly fitted to their legs, so that, when looked at from afar, they seem to expose the lower parts of their bodies, which is not at all nice to see. They say that this custom has come down from

very ancient times, and that the whole Western world follows it. In various Ministries of this country, there are always ballrooms for solemn gatherings, as if they consider dancing an essential part of their official business. Since the fourth [lunar] month, more than ten English families have invited us over to attend such balls. On account of my illness, I have not gone to any of them. On the evening of 22 June, the Queen invited us to a tea-party, so I went to attend it at Buckingham Palace. That night, the ambassadors from various countries all gathered there; high-ranking men and women were all assembled together. Music was played in the front of the hall to accompany the dancing. Even the Crown Prince and his wife took part in the dance. The Prince took another woman as his partner while his wife danced with another man, for husbands and wives are not supposed to be each other's partners.

During the last two months, we have been receiving several invitations every day to go to tea-parties. At each tea-party there are long tables provided with tea, wine, fruit, and cakes for the guests to take and drink, and the whole room as well as the doors are delightfully decorated with fresh, fragrant flowers. . . .

At parties at night many lamps and candles burn. Men and women mingle together, rubbing elbows and shoulders. Sometimes actors and singers are called in to perform plays, to sing and to play music to amuse the guests. (Some people sing and play themselves. European ladies play the piano to amuse the guests. No one finds this strange.) Each party costs over £100. When there are five or six hundred guests at a party all stand round the tables to drink. However, the host personally offered the Chinese envoys tea and wine with his own hands. The English are very hospitable and quite used to spending money. Furthermore, when they know some tricks, they always perform these in public to show their abilities. When they have collections of precious objects, tapestries and the like, they exhibit everything in the room, showing every piece to the guest, fearing only that he has not seen everything. The Chinese prefer to hide their abilities and their wealth and never let them be seen; the English like to show everything to the outside world, without hiding a fraction of an inch. When we Chinese see talented people and wealth often, we get used to such things and are heedless of their attractions. But when an Englishman suddenly possesses talents and wealth, he finds it very unusual and keeps boasting about them to others. When we consider these attitudes, we realize it is difficult to urge people to change their pettifogging manners. Every year, the tea-party season lasts from the third [lunar] month to the middle of the sixth [lunar] month. . . .

{August 6–8 1877}

Men and women here all select their own partners in marriage. When a woman likes a man, she invites him to her house to entertain him. (It seems to me that women here are encouraged to be unchaste, while men are not. When a woman likes a man, she often asks whether he already has a wife. If not, she brazenly arranges a rendezvous. The man does not dare to make the first move.) They often talk intimately together, away from others, and go out together. Their parents do not forbid them. After a long period of acquaintance, if the two like each other, they tell their parents. Then they investigate each other's financial situation. If they are unequally matched, they do not marry. (When incorrect reports are made and someone is cheated, then even after marriage, the woman still does not consider the man as her husband, nor does the man consider the woman as his wife. Instead, one will treat the other as no more than a servant.) If they are well matched financially, then they are informed of this and allowed to decide whether or not to marry. After their engagement (a ring is used for engagement to control the other party, so that he or she will not look for someone else), they have even greater freedom to go out together. At marriage (men marry at thirty) the family of the bride go to a Christian Church and ask a clergyman to chant prayers. Many guests are assembled. A crucifix is placed on the table. The bride and groom enter and kneel in front of it. The bridesmaids also kneel. (Their number is not fixed. The Mayor's daughter had sixteen of them.) The clergyman also kneels down, and then gets up to perform the marriage ceremony for the bride and groom, after which he blesses them, and conducts them to a room at the rear, where they write their names in the registry. Then they go together to the official registry of that district where they write down all their particulars. Later, they often travel several hundred leagues to consummate the marriage in an hotel. Those who see them would at first not know they were newly-weds. The bride wears white, with a white veil on the head. (When going out, women often wear a black or white veil to cover their heads, in order to avoid the dust. This is not unique to the bride.) The groom wears everyday clothes. Often when people marry off their daughters, they give them as dowry good thick clothes, useful articles, and all kinds of other necessities. The groom's family and friends also contribute to the bride's dowry, but give nothing towards the groom's wedding expenses. On 8 August, I went to the house of the Mayor of London to see this ceremony for myself.

According to English customs, the daughter-in-law does not live with the father and mother-in-law. Even old people of seventy or eighty are often without children to serve them food and drink, and do their laundry. How to behave as a daughter-in-law should, and understand the virtue of feminine obedience is not known here at all. According to Hillier, after her engage-

ment, the woman often visits the house of her future parents-in-law. But no other formalities are observed as part of the wedding ceremony. As Tai Sheng remarked, when the difference between man and woman is observed, the affection between father and son is established; when the father and son have mutual affection, then comes righteousness; when there is righteousness, there will be ritual propriety; when there is ritual propriety, all things will be in harmony. These few words clearly express all there is to say about the propriety and order that govern heaven and earth. It is very clear and very deep. Westerners do not understand what it means to have parents. Some say that the religion of Jesus considers Heaven as Ancestor, and does away with everything else. When their sons grow up, they each seek their own livelihood, without asking their parents. Some who serve as officials leave their parents for more than ten years, and do not even go to visit them on their return to their home town.

REVIEW QUESTIONS

1. In addition to the example mentioned in the introduction, what other evidence shows that Liu was objective, or at least tolerant of what he saw in London? Is there evidence that he was intolerant of England in any way?
2. What aspects of English life seem to have interested Liu the most? What does this tell us about his own values or the purpose of the diplomatic mission?
3. Did Liu like England and the English? Cite evidence for your opinion.
4. Nineteenth-century Chinese are often described as having a strong belief in the superiority of their own civilization. Is there any hint of that conviction in this selection? What evidence supports your answer?

An American Novelist Describes Poverty in London's East End (1902)

JACK LONDON, *The People of the Abyss*

Jack London (1876–1916) spent his youth working at various odd jobs, first in San Francisco and then in Oakland. He delivered newspapers, worked on an ice wagon, set up pins in a bowling alley, and worked in a cannery. For recreation, he went to the public library and read romances, adventure stories, and travel narratives. Growing up on the Oakland waterfront, London formed a lifelong passion for the sea. At fifteen he bought a boat, made a living robbing oyster beds, and won the title "Prince of the Oyster Pirates." After several more years of sailing (including a trip to Japan), experiencing life as a tramp, and attending the University of California for a brief time, London joined the gold rush to the Klondike (1897–1898). Upon his return to the bay area, he began to write about his experiences. When the *Atlantic Monthly* accepted "An Odyssey of the North" in 1899 and Houghton Mifflin took *The Son of the Wolf* in the following year, his career took off. During the five-year period 1899–1903 he published eight volumes, including two novels. The second of these, *The Call of the Wild* (1903), brought him fame. During his lifetime, he wrote more than fifty books. Several of these are autobiographical, including *John Barleycorn* (1913), an autobiographical account of London's battle with alcoholism; *The Road* (1907), about his experiences as a tramp; *The Cruise of the Snark* (1911), about his voyage across the Pacific; and *Martin Eden* (1909), about the beginnings of his career as a writer.

In the mid-1890s London became interested in sociology, read Herbert Spencer, and became a socialist. He made soap-box speeches, was arrested, and gained some notoriety. In the summer of 1902 he went to London and spent several weeks in the slums of the East End. As he wrote in the preface to *The People of the Abyss* (1903), from which the following selection is taken, "I went down into the under-world of London with an attitude of mind which I may best liken to that of the explorer. I was open to be convinced by the evidence of my eyes, rather than by the teachings of those who had not seen, or by the words of those who had seen and gone before. Further, I took with me certain simple criteria with which to measure the life of the under-world. That which made for more life, for physical and spiritual health, was good; that which made for less life, which hurt, and dwarfed, and distorted life, was bad." The description that follows is from his account of that exploration. It exemplifies the author's interest in social conditions and displays his vivid style of writing.

My first impression of East London was naturally a general one. Later the details began to appear, and here and there in the chaos of misery I found little spots where a fair measure of happiness reigned,—sometimes whole rows of houses in little out-of-the-way streets, where artisans dwell and where a rude sort of family life obtains. In the evenings the men can be seen at the doors, pipes in their mouths and children on their knees, wives gossiping, and laughter and fun going on. The content of these people is manifestly great, for, relative to the wretchedness that encompasses them, they are well off.

But at the best, it is a dull, animal happiness, the content of the full belly. The dominant note of their lives is materialistic. They are stupid and heavy, without imagination. The Abyss seems to exude a stupefying atmosphere of torpor, which wraps about them and deadens them. Religion passes them by. The Unseen holds for them neither terror nor delight. They are unaware of the Unseen; and the full belly and the evening pipe, with their regular 'arf an' arf,' is all they demand, or dream of demanding from existence.

This would not be so bad if it were all; but it is not all. The satisfied torpor in which they are sunk is the deadly inertia that precedes dissolution. There is no progress, and with them not to progress is to fall back and into the Abyss. In their own lives they may only start to fall, leaving the fall to be completed by their children and their children's children. Man always gets less than he demands from life; and so little do they demand, that the less than little they get cannot save them.

At the best, city life is an unnatural life for the human; but the city life of London is so utterly unnatural that the average workman or workwoman cannot stand it. Mind and body are sapped by the undermining influences ceaselessly at work. Moral and physical stamina are broken, and the good workman, fresh from the soil, becomes in the first city generation a poor workman; and by the second city generation, devoid of push and go and initiative, and actually unable physically to perform the labor his father did, he is well on the way to the shambles at the bottom of the Abyss.

If nothing else, the air he breathes, and from which he never escapes, is sufficient to weaken him mentally and physically, so that he becomes unable to compete with the fresh virile life from the country hastening on to London Town to destroy and be destroyed.

Leaving out the disease germs that fill the air of the East End, consider but the one item of smoke. Sir William Thistleton-Dyer, curator of Kew Gardens, has been studying smoke deposits on vegetation, and, according to his calculations, no less than six tons of solid matter, consisting of soot and tarry hydrocarbons, are deposited every week on every quarter of a square mile in and about London. This is equivalent to twenty-four tons per week to the square mile, or 1248 tons per year to the square mile. From the cornice below the dome of St. Paul's Cathedral was recently taken a solid deposit of crystallized sulphate of lime. This deposit had been formed by the action of the sulphuric acid in the atmosphere upon the carbonate of lime in the stone. And this sulphuric acid in the atmosphere is constantly being breathed by the Lon-

don workmen through all the days and nights of their lives.

It is incontrovertible that the children grow up into rotten adults, without virility or stamina, a weak-kneed, narrow-chested, listless breed, that crumples up and goes down in the brute struggle for life with the invading hordes from the country. The railway men, carriers, omnibus drivers, corn and timber porters, and all those who require physical stamina, are largely drawn from the country; while in the Metropolitan Police there are, roughly, 12,000 country-born as against 3000 London-born.

So one is forced to conclude that the Abyss is literally a huge man-killing machine, and when I pass along the little out-of-the-way streets with the full-bellied artisans at the doors, I am aware of a greater sorrow for them than for the 450,000 lost and hopeless wretches dying at the bottom of the pit. They, at least, are dying, that is the point; while these have yet to go through the slow and preliminary pangs extending through two and even three generations.

And yet the quality of the life is good. All human potentialities are in it. Given proper conditions, it could live through the centuries, and great men, heroes and masters, spring from it and make the world better by having lived.

I talked with a woman who was representative of that type which has been jerked out of its little out-of-the-way streets and has started on the fatal fall to the bottom. Her husband was a fitter and a member of the Engineers' Union. That he was a poor engineer was evidenced by his inability to get regular employment. He did not have the energy and enterprise necessary to obtain or hold a steady position.

The pair had two daughters, and the four of them lived in a couple of holes, called "rooms" by courtesy, for which they paid seven shillings per week. They possessed no stove, managing their cooking on a single gas-ring in the fireplace. Not being persons of property, they were unable to obtain an unlimited supply of gas; but a clever machine had been installed for their benefit. By dropping a penny in the slot, the gas was forthcoming, and when a penny's worth had forthcome the supply was automatically shut off. "A penny gawn in no time," she explained, "an' the cookin' not arf done!"

Incipient starvation had been their portion for years. Month in and month out, they had arisen from the table able and willing to eat more. And when once on the downward slope, chronic innutrition is an important factor in sapping vitality and hastening the descent.

Yet this woman was a hard worker. From 4:30 in the morning till the last light at night, she said, she had toiled at making cloth dress-skirts, lined up and with two flounces, for seven shillings a dozen. Cloth dress-skirts, mark you, lined up and with two flounces, for seven shillings a dozen! This is equal to $1.75 per dozen, or 14¾ cents per skirt.

The husband, in order to obtain employment, had to belong to the union, which collected one shilling and sixpence from him each week. Also, when strikes were afoot and he chanced to be working, he had at times been compelled to pay as high as seventeen shillings into the union's coffers for the relief fund.

One daughter, the elder, had worked as green hand for a dressmaker, for one shilling and sixpence per week—37½ cents per week, or a fraction over 5 cents per day. However, when the slack season came she was discharged, though she had been taken on at such low pay with the understanding that she was to learn the trade and work up. After that she had been employed in a bicycle store for three years, for which she received five shillings per week, walking two miles to her work, and two back, and being fined for tardiness.

As far as the man and woman were concerned, the game was played. They had lost handhold and foothold, and were falling into the pit. But what of the daughters? Living like swine, enfeebled by chronic innutrition, being sapped mentally, morally, and physically, what chance have they to crawl up and out of the Abyss into which they were born falling?

REVIEW QUESTIONS

1. What evidence in this selection supports the idea that London was interested in sociology?
2. What evidence is there that London was a socialist?
3. For London, what are the most pressing problems for the poor?
4. Did London have any optimism about the future for these slum dwellers? Why or why not?

An English Newspaper Correspondent Reports on the Balkans (1906)

HARRY DE WINDT, *Through Savage Europe*

All we know about Harry de Windt (1856–1933) is that he was an English newspaper correspondent who obviously liked to travel and to write about it. His books include *Siberia As It Is* (1892), *The New Siberia* (1896), *Through the Gold-Fields of Alaska to the Bering Straits* (1898), *Finland As It Is* (1910), and

Russia As I Know It (1917). The following selection is taken from *Through Savage Europe* (1907), which carries the subtitle "Being the narrative of a journey (undertaken as special correspondent of the 'Westminster Gazette'), throughout the Balkan states and European Russia." De Windt justifies his use of the term *savage* at the beginning of the first chapter: "The term accurately describes the wild and lawless countries between the Adriatic and Black Seas. . . . The remoter districts are, as of yore, hotbeds of outlawry and brigandage, where you must travel with a revolver in each pocket and your life in your hand. . . ."

In 1907, when de Windt published the first edition of *Through Savage Europe,* the Balkans were entering a period of crisis and violence. Russia, suffering from its recent defeat by the Japanese in 1904, now wished to replace Turkey and Austria-Hungary as the dominant power in the Balkans. To achieve this objective, Russia encouraged Balkan nationalists who wanted to destroy the Austro-Hungarian empire. Russia's policy, the reactions to it by Austria and Germany, and the responses of France and Great Britain prepared the way for the "Bosnian crisis" of 1908, the First Balkan War (1912–1913), the Second Balkan War (1913), and, ultimately, World War I.

A lively remembrance of old Belgrade and its primitive methods made it a pleasant surprise on this occasion to enter a palatial railway station instead of being dumped down on a mudbank from the deck of a grimy steamer. There was one advantage in those days, however, for travellers were not subjected to the vexatious police regulations which now exist, and which are chiefly due to the unsettled condition of political affairs since the assassination of Alexander I.[*] This time it was quite as bad as entering the Russian Empire, perhaps worse, for there, at least, the Custom House officials are not (or used not to be) exacting. But at Belgrade, in these days, everything in the shape of baggage is turned upside down and closely examined, and the passport examination often occupies half a day—a very obnoxious proceeding to those who, like ourselves, had fasted for twenty-four hours. Mackenzie[†] was especially indignant, the more so when recalled, as we were on the point of leav-

ing, by an inquisitive police official. "Your name Mackenzie—yes?" inquired the latter. "Your fader live Belgrade—no? Very good man, give plenty money—yes?" "What on earth has my father got to do with you?" returned the irate Aberdonian; "and as for money, you won't get any more out of me. Here, drive on!" and the carriage dashed away, leaving the man of passports open-mouthed and apparently as puzzled as I was at this brief and mysterious colloquy. And it was only some time afterwards that we learnt that a canny Scotsman, one Mackenzie, who many years ago left the land of cakes to settle down here, had, after a prosperous career, proved such a philanthropist that he has been handed down to posterity as a public benefactor. "More fool he!" remarked my friend, quite unimpressed by the fact that a fashionable quarter of Belgrade now bears the name (with variations) of his late illustrious kinsman.

Rip Van Winkle, after his long sleep in the Katskills, can scarcely have been more astonished at the altered appearance of his native village than I was at the marvellous improvements which less than thirty years have worked in Belgrade. In 1876 a dilapidated Turkish fortress frowned down upon a maze of buildings little better than mud-huts and unpaved, filthy streets.

---

[*]Alexander I ruled Serbia from 1889 to 1903. He was murdered, together with his wife and about twenty members of his court, by a group of military men on June 10, 1903.
[†]De Windt never gives us the first name of his traveling companion, "Mr. Mackenzie." He was a Scot from Aberdeen and a "bioscope artist." A bioscope was an early form of a motion picture camera.

I had to splash my way from the river to the town through an ocean of mud carrying my own luggage, for no porters were procurable, and the half-dozen rough country-carts at the landing-place were quickly pounced upon by local magnates. Having reached the so-called "hotel" I found that it provided only black bread, a kind of peppery stew called "Paprika," and nothing else in the way of food—although all kinds of villainous wines and spirits were to be had at outrageous prices, having been laid down by a cunning landlord to meet the requirements of a thirsty Russian Legion. There was no privacy by day or night, and I was compelled to share a small, dark den with several Cossacks, a Polish Jew, and numerous other inmates which shall be nameless. To-day it seemed like a dream to be whirled away from the railway station in a neat *fiacre,** along spacious boulevards, with well-dressed crowds and electric cars, to a luxurious hotel. Here were gold-laced porters, lifts, and even a Winter Garden, where a delicious *déjeuner* [lunch] (cooked by a Frenchman) awaited me. Everything is now up to date in this city of murder and mystery, for only two landmarks are left of the old city—the cathedral and citadel, over which now floats the tricolour of Servia. Of course ancient portions of the place still exist, with low-eaved, vine-trellised houses, cobbled streets, and quiet squares, recalling some sleepy provincial town in France; but these are now mere suburbs, peopled by the poorer classes, along the banks which form the junction of the Danube and Save. Modern Belgrade is bisected by the Teratsia, a boulevard, over a mile in length, of fine buildings, overtopped, about midway, by the golden domes of the new Palace. This is the chief thoroughfare, and here are the principal hotels, private residences, and shops, which latter, towards evening, blaze with electric light. The Teratsia then becomes a fashionable promenade, and smart carriages, brilliant uniforms, and Vienna *toilettes* add to the gaiety of the scene. Servia is lavish in uniforms, most of them more suggestive of *opera-bouffe* than modern warfare. From dawn till midnight the streets and *cafés* swarm with officers, who apparently have little to do but show themselves to a rather unappreciative public. On the other hand, I seldom saw a private soldier, except those on sentry outside public buildings and in barracks, and there is, no doubt, good reason for keeping the garrison on the alert for any emergency which may arise from the present disturbed condition of affairs. This I shall refer to in another chapter, and the reader will then probably agree that "Scarlet" would be a more suitable adjective than "White" for a city which has witnessed such infamous deeds, committed under the name of "patriotism." Yet, outwardly, "White" is a sufficiently descriptive term, for the snowy buildings, cheerful streets, and luxuriant greenery undoubtedly render this the most attractive capital throughout the Balkan States. A distinguished English traveller has described Belgrade as "a smaller but neater version of Budapest." Personally I see no similarity whatever between the two cities, although in early summer, when trees and flowers are in full bloom, the open-air and exhilarating climate render the place almost worthy of the name of "Petit Paris," which was given to it, in his palmier days, by that erratic potentate, the late King Milan.† And amongst the novel and civilised objects which here met my astonished gaze was—a motor car! of the very latest Parisian build and finish. I should add, however, that this *rara avis*‡ belonged to a Frenchman who had travelled here from Vienna *en route* to Ragusa and Montenegro. And a pleasanter trip could not be imagined at this time of year, for the high-roads through the Austrian Balkans could give points to many even in France.

Strange as it may seem, there is a great similarity between the Servian and French people, which is one of the most curious characteristics of this little-known nation. This is, perhaps,

---

*A particular kind of horse-drawn coach, named after the Hotel de St. Fiacre, where they were first offered for hire.

†King Milan ruled Serbia from 1882 to 1889.

‡Literally, a rare bird. De Windt is using the phrase to mean "a wonderful thing."

explained by the fact that, ever since the attainment of Servian independence, the so-called upper classes have sent their children to France to complete their education which, in the towns at least, is of a very high standard. Nearly every Servian I met in Belgrade spoke at least three languages (one of them invariably French); although in the provinces a stranger unacquainted with the Servian tongue fares badly. When travelling through the wilder parts of the country my knowledge of Russian stood me in good stead, and enabled me to converse, although imperfectly, with the natives. This was also the case in Bulgaria, but in remoter parts of Rumania I was again as helpless with regard to language as I had been in Bosnia and Montenegro. But any way, Servians of all classes are the politest people in the world, who will always go out of their way to assist a stranger. I once inquired my way of a policeman, and he accompanied me for at least a quarter of a mile to put me on the right road.

Belgrade is now essentially a modern city, and the traveller is therefore apt to find it outwardly dull and prosaic after the towns he has visited on his way up from the Adriatic. This is partly due to an absence of colour. In Bosnia and Bulgaria bright and picturesque native costumes are continually met with (in Montenegro you rarely see anything else), but the people of Belgrade, with their tailor-made gowns and stove-pipe hats, might have walked straight out of Regent Street.* For the first day or two Mackenzie and I wore light-coloured tweeds which, however, so scandalised the fashionable strollers on the Ter-

atsia that we retreated hastily to the hotel and donned soberer suits of dark blue serge. And here, as in Russia, morning calls of an official nature must be made in thin dress clothes—an attire hardly adapted to a drive in an open sleigh in something unpleasant below zero. . . .

During the spring-time a man need never feel dull for a moment in Belgrade, especially if he can present, as I did, letters of introduction to pleasant people who will tell him what to do and how to do it. For there is no lack of amusement at any time or season amongst these careless, easy-going folk, most of whom, like the Parisians, make a business of pleasure and leave work to look after itself. I strolled into the "Kalemegdan," or public gardens one Sunday afternoon, and the family groups sitting under the trees or sipping "Bocks" at an open-air *café,* the kiosk with its military band, the nurses, soldiers, and goat-carriages, looked as though a bit of the Tuileries or Park Monceau† had dropped out of the blue sky into the Balkans! Come here at sunset and you will be repaid by a view which I have seldom seen surpassed; but it must be in summer-time, when the eye can range over leagues of forest, flood, and field, extending from the broad and sullen river at your feet to an horizon formed by the boundless prairies of Hungary. But in early spring-time the Danube overflows its banks and these steppes become a waste of water, a vast grey sea, with desolate islets formed by the higher ground, and you search in vain for the kaleidoscopic effects cast by cloud and sunshine over the fertile summer plains.

---

*An important shopping street in London.

†Gardens in Paris.

REVIEW QUESTIONS

1. De Windt's reference to "Savage Europe" in his title sounds derogatory. Are the descriptions presented here derogatory? Why or why not?
2. De Windt visited Belgrade in 1876 and again in 1906. How did he compare life in the city in these two periods? Did he see any improvements?
3. What did de Windt like about the Serbian people? What did he dislike?
4. How did de Windt support his comparison of the Serbian and French peoples? What do you think he had in mind?

An American Author Describes Life in Berlin (1911)

THEODORE DREISER, *A Traveler at Forty*

Published in 1925, *An American Tragedy* brought fame to its author, Theodore Dreiser (1871–1945). He started his career as a newspaper reporter, first for the *Chicago Daily Globe* and later for the *St. Louis Globe Democrat* and *St. Louis Republic.* After the publisher of his first novel, *Sister Carrie* (1900), withdrew it from public sale because of its candid depiction of sexual problems, Dreiser became managing editor of *Broadway Magazine* and editor-in-chief of Butterick publications. His second novel, *Jennie Gerhardt* (1911), attracted influential supporters such as H. G. Wells and launched his literary career. In addition to *An American Tragedy,* his other popular works include *The Financier* (1912), *The Titan* (1914), and *The "Genius"* (1915).

Dreiser's early life was hard. His father was often out of work, his mother took in boarders and washing, and the ten children learned to pick up coal along railroad tracks and were sometimes sent home from school because they had no shoes. There can be no doubt that his experience of poverty remained a powerful memory and a force that shaped his adult life. Indeed, Dreiser's works routinely aroused controversy because of his unflattering portrayal of American capitalist society. Readers of these books would not be surprised to learn that he joined the U.S. Communist Party, visited the Soviet Union and offered an appreciative appraisal of it in *Dreiser Looks at Russia* (1928), or had as speakers at his funeral in 1945 the Hollywood actor John Howard Lawson, who would soon be blacklisted for Communist affiliations, and Charlie Chaplin, who would soon be driven from the United States for the same reason.

The following selection is from Dreiser's *A Traveler at Forty* (1913), an account of the author's trip to Germany that contains his description of Berlin. For Dreiser, the first major American writer who was not Protestant, Anglo-Saxon, or middle class, this was the "old country." His father, John Paul Dreiser, had been a German Catholic immigrant to America, and his mother, Sarah Maria Schänäb, was of Pennsylvania German descent. Dreiser never rejected his German background. In fact, he often celebrated it with H. L. Mencken, with whom he shared beer and food at Lüchow's famous German restaurant in New York City.

The Germans are amazingly like the Americans. Sometimes I think that we get the better portion of our progressive, constructive characteristics from them. Only, the Germans, I am convinced, are so much more thorough. They go us one better in economy, energy, endurance, and thoroughness. The American already is beginning to want to play too much. The Germans have not reached that stage.

The railway stations I found were excellent, with great switching-yards and enormous sheds arched with glass and steel, where the trains waited. In Berlin I admired the suburban train service as much as I did that of London, if not more. That in Paris was atrocious. Here the trains offered a choice of first, second, and third class, with the vast majority using the second and third. I saw little difference in the crowds occupying either class. The second-class compartments were upholstered in a greyish-brown corduroy. The third-class seats were of plain wood, varnished and scrupulously clean. I tried all three classes and finally fixed on the third as good enough for me.

I wish all Americans who at present suffer the indignities of the American street-railway and steam-railway suburban service could go to Berlin and see what that city has to teach them in this respect. Berlin is much larger than Chicago. It is certain soon to be a city of five or six millions of people—very soon. The plans for handling this mass of people comfortably and courteously are already in operation. The German public service is obviously not left to supposedly kindly minded business gentlemen—"Christian gentlemen,"—as Mr. Baer of the Reading once chose to put it, "in partnership with God." The populace may be underlings to an imperial Kaiser, subject to conscription and eternal inspection, but at least the money-making "Christian gentlemen" with their hearts and souls centered on their private purses and working, as Mr. Croker once said of himself, "for their own pockets all the time," are not allowed to "take it out of" the rank and file.

No doubt the German street-railways and steam-railways are making a reasonable sum of money and are eager to make more. I haven't the least doubt but that heavy, self-opinionated, vainglorious German directors of great wealth gather around mahogany tables in chambers devoted to meetings of directors and listen to ways and means of cutting down expenses and "improving" the service. Beyond the shadow of a doubt there are hard, hired managers, eager to win the confidence and support of their superiors and ready to feather their own nests at the expense of the masses, who would gladly cut down the service, "pack 'em in," introduce the "cutting out" system of car service and see that the "car ahead" idea was worked to the last maddening

extreme; but in Germany, for some strange, amazing reason, they don't get a chance. What is the matter with Germany, anyhow? I should like to know. Really I would. Why isn't the "Christian gentleman" theory of business introduced there? The population of Germany, acre for acre and mile for mile, is much larger than that of America. They have sixty-five million people crowded into an area as big as Texas. Why don't they "pack 'em in"? Why don't they introduce the American "sardine" subway service? You don't find it anywhere in Germany, for some strange reason. Why? They have a subway service in Berlin. It serves vast masses of people, just as the subway does in New York; its platforms are crowded with people. But you can get a seat just the same. There is no vociferated "step lively" there. Overcrowding isn't a joke over there as it is here—something to be endured with a feeble smile until you are spiritually comparable to a door mat. There must be "Christian gentlemen" of wealth and refinement in Germany and Berlin. Why don't they "get on the job"? The thought arouses strange uncertain feelings in me.

Take, for instance, the simple matter of starting and stopping street-railway cars in the Berlin business heart. In so far as I could see, that area, mornings and evenings, was as crowded as any similar area in Paris, London, or New York. Street-cars have to be run through it, started, stopped; passengers let on and off—a vast tide carried in and out of the city. Now the way this matter is worked in New York is quite ingenious. We operate what might be described as a daily guessing contest intended to develop the wits, muscles, lungs, and tempers of the people. The scheme, in so far as the street railway companies are concerned, is (after running the roads as economically as possible) to see how thoroughly the people can be fooled in their efforts to discover when and where a car will stop. In Berlin, however, they have, for some reason, an entirely different idea. There the idea is not to fool the people at all but to get them in and out of the city as quickly as possible. So, as in Paris, London, Rome, and elsewhere, a plan of fixed stopping-places has been arranged. Signs actually indicate where the cars stop and there—marvel of marvels—they all stop even in the so-called rush hours. No traffic policeman, apparently, can order them to go ahead without

stopping. They must stop. And so the people do not run for the cars, the motorman has no joy in outwitting anybody. Perhaps that is why the Germans are neither so agile, quick-witted, or subtle as the Americans.

REVIEW QUESTIONS

1. How would you characterize Dreiser's view of Germans?
2. What qualities made Berlin an attractive place to live in Dreiser's opinion?
3. Dreiser said that "Germans are amazingly like Americans." What similarities do you see? What differences?
4. What did Dreiser like about Berlin's transportation system?

An Englishman Describes Turkish Family Life (1911)

SIR EDWIN PEARS, *Turkey and Its People*

As a young man, Edwin Pears (1835–1919) worked too hard and had a dinner conversation that changed his life. After graduating with distinction in Roman law from London University, Pears began to practice law in London in 1870. In addition to his legal practice, however, he served as private secretary to the bishop of Exeter and general secretary of the Social Science Association (1868–1872) and the International Prison Congress (1872). In 1872 Pears edited the congress's transactions, which were published as *Prisons and Reformatories at Home and Abroad.* In the same year he also edited *Law Magazine.* Forty-four years later, in 1916, Pears looked back on these labors in his memoir, *Forty Years in Constantinople,* and wrote, "I was working too hard and felt that my health was giving way." Fortunately for Pears, he learned of an opening for a lawyer in Constantinople while attending a dinner in London in 1873. This information changed his life. He decided to take the position temporarily. "I had never been to Constantinople, but the prospect of a change of climate and scene for two or three years appealed to me and my wife. I felt that I could not continue to work at the high pressure of the past year, and thought that by my work in editing, writing, and revising, I was drifting away from my legal professional work which I liked."

Pears arrived in Constantinople in March 1873. Once there, he became a permanent resident and eventually occupied important positions in the European legal community in Constantinople (the right of Europeans to impose their own law on their own citizens in Turkey dates back at least to the sixteenth century). He also continued to write, making a reputation as a newspaper correspondent and historian. Among his works were two histories, *The Fall of Constantinople* (1885), about the Fourth Crusade, and *The Decline of the Greek Empire* (1903), about the Muslim conquest of Constantinople in 1453. In addition, he wrote a biography of the reigning sultan, *Life of Abdul Hamid* (1917). Although Pears became one of the leaders of the British colony, he retained an independent perspective on local affairs and the "eastern question" (who would benefit from the disintegration of the Ottoman Empire?). In 1876, as a correspondent of the *Daily News,* he exposed Turkish atrocities in Bulgaria. In recognition of his long years of service to the British crown, Pears was knighted in 1909. He remained in Constantinople after the outbreak of World War I but was forced to leave Turkey in December 1914, several weeks after Turkey declared war on Great Britain. In 1919 Pears returned to Turkey, but he died in the same year from an accident at sea near Malta.

At the beginning of his *Turkey and Its People* (1911), Pears declared his interest in giving "an account of the present position of the various races which form the population of Turkey; to show how they have arrived at that position; and to indicate, as far as I can, what are the circumstances and influences which are likely to modify their development." The following selection is taken from the fourth chapter of this work, "Family Life and the Position of Turkish Women."

The foundation of family life is marriage. A Turkish marriage is arranged, and is usually the result of negotiation between the relations or representatives of the bride and bridegroom. It is supposed to be among the democratic privileges possessed by Turks that any mother with a son whom she wishes to see married has a right to enter into negotiations with the family of the girl whom she wishes him to marry and to interview the girl herself. Even if she is unknown and poor, she may present herself at the house of the girl and claim the right to see her. It is in this way that negotiations for marriage often begin. The mistress or *hanum* of the house notifies the girl, who then comes into the room where the mother or other female representative of the young man is present. The mistress retires and the girl then offers coffee and other civilities. After what may be called an interview of inspection, the representative retires to report the impression the girl has made. If the overtures are looked on with favour, a photograph of the girl may be carried away. Then negotiations begin

between the two families. Etiquette and Turkish proprieties require that these negotiations should not be mentioned in presence of the girl, but should be left to her relations. Very often the intermediary between the two sets of relations is an old slave woman, or perhaps two such women, one for each side. When they are agreed, a civil ceremony of engagement takes place before the Kadi and witnesses, the most important part of which consists in asking outside the closed door of the girl's room whether she will marry Hamid or whatever the intended bridegroom's name is. A like question has already been asked of the intending husband. If all goes right, the marriage takes place when the trousseau and house are ready. The ceremony begins by conducting the bride with considerable pomp to the house of the bridegroom.

As men are not permitted to be present, I have requested a lady who has not only lived long in Turkey, speaking Turkish well, but has an intimate knowledge of Turkish manners and customs, to take up my narrative and tell the story of an ordinary Turkish marriage among well-to-do Turks.

A Turkish wedding is celebrated in two places—the bridegroom entertains his friends in his own house. The bride's celebration is much more elaborate, and lasts for three days. During one portion of the ceremony the groom appears for a few moments. One of the most typical Turkish weddings I ever attended was in the house of an old-fashioned Pasha, whose daughter was the bride, and whose acquaintance with all the old Turkish families of the neighbourhood made the circle of guests a very large one. When we arrived at the house we were shown through the great paved court and up the wide uncarpeted stairs, through bare unpainted halls with many windows, into the specially furnished rooms of the harem. The furniture, as usual in a large Turkish house, was principally divans, chairs and chandeliers. The divans and chairs were nearly filled with ladies, listening to the weird monotonous strains of Turkish music. The musicians, with their bagpipes and lutes, were concealed by a curtain—as they were mere men. Graceful salaams were exchanged as each new guest came in. Occasionally groups of two or three ladies made a tour of the rooms, stopping a little to say a word to and gaze at the bride as she sat in the end of one long room in solemn state. She was dressed in white satin, with showers of tinsel all entwined in her long black hair, and falling over her dress, and wore quantities of diamonds and jewellery of all kinds. These jewels are often borrowed for the occasion, as it is considered very necessary to have a great display at the wedding. The bride must sit still all day at the real old-fashioned wedding, rarely speaks, and does not come to the dinner. Something is given her to eat, probably.

At some hour during this first day of the festivities, usually about noon, comes a short ceremony. The guests veil their faces but crowd around to see, as the bridegroom comes into the house and is led up to meet his bride, whom he is supposed not to have seen before. He goes into a room with her alone for a few minutes, then comes out and scatters pieces of money—small silver coins—among the guests, who scramble eagerly for them, as they are regarded as lucky coins. At the wedding of which I am speaking, the father of the bride also threw handfuls of money down into the court, and the servants and town hangers-on rushed about gathering up the shining pieces.

Then we were invited to dinner. Tables had been arranged in one large room, which would accommodate about forty-five ladies, and we all gathered and sat down, as we came in no special order. The costumes, as is always true of a Turkish gathering, were various and incongruous. Directly opposite me at the table sat a royal beauty, the daughter of a pasha in Stamboul. On her golden hair was a diamond coronet; her white satin gown was beautifully made, and cut very low, showing the most dazzling white neck and arms. Her looks and her manners would have graced any court in Europe. Next her sat a veritable old hag, dressed in a cotton-wadded jacket and skirt, shapeless and not even very clean, with no pretence of a collar. The old lady speared pieces of bread and fruit with her fork and drew them toward herself, or handed them to the haughty beauty next to her, and chattered volubly about the food and the other guests. I saw many others in the same sort of easy negligée-cotton gowns—while scattered among them were dresses that might have been Worth creations from Paris, and jewels worth a king's ransom. My companion and I were the only persons present who were not Turkish. The waitresses were as casual as the guests in their costumes. Some of them were dressed in blue satin gowns and coquettish blue satin caps on the sides of their heads, with elaborate coiffures. Others had trailing cotton wrappers, and unkempt hair, and heel-less shoes that flapped and flopped on the bare floor as they walked about. The courses of food were many and most delicious, Turkish cooking being especially excellent and savoury. Sweets and meat courses came in a haphazard sequence. But as always at a Turkish wedding, the last dish was rice, covered with a thick saffron sauce. After that the people left the tables and walked through the rooms again, listened to more weird minor music, talked or sat still, and then were free to go home. But the bride must still sit in solemn state for hours, for people came and went all the afternoon. Anyone, whether invited or not, can go to a Turkish wedding after the dinner is over—any complete stranger or passer-by—and so, curious crowds come in, and stare, and sit and drink coffee, and go out, while the weary bride sits still on her throne to be looked at and talked about for the whole of the three days, if the old custom is followed. It is now, however, becoming more usual to have only one day of this open hospitality, and after this the bride either goes to her husband's house or the newly-married couple settle down in the bride's home.

The Turkish wife resides in a separate part of her husband's house specially set aside for women and called the harem. The other part for the men is the salemlik. The haremlik intended for the seclusion of women is religiously reserved for their use. As a rule no male visitors are admitted. The practice varies to some extent. An old doctor of medicine tells me that in his younger days when called in to attend a woman patient he was never allowed to see her. A hand would be pushed between the curtains and he could feel the pulse, but this was the extent of his diagnosis. It is, however, now becoming recognized that the doctor may be admitted into the harem.

The seclusion of women is fatal to family life. A woman must not unveil except before her husband, her father, or brothers. The education which comes to European women from being present in the company of her husband and his friends, from mixing in society, attendance at receptions, lectures, and church services is all denied to Turkish women. The typical large Turkish harem is one where a number of usually good-looking women live together without any intellectual pleasure or pursuits whatever. European ladies who have lived in such harems even among those belonging to the great favourites of the Sultan are impressed with the inanity, the full-grown childishness, and most of all with the disorder, which exists. The rooms may be furnished with the latest fashions of Paris furniture; everything may be costly, rich and gorgeous; the taste usually much too loud for Englishmen or Frenchmen. Gilding, white marble, rich velvets, tapestry, abundance of mirrors, all proclaim wealth and an exuberance of display. But amid it all are specimens of barbaric taste and a survival of Circassian and other Asiatic instincts. Those who have lived in such houses speak of dinners served to various ladies separately, and at any time between five o'clock and midnight, of the dinner things left in corners of the beautiful drawing-rooms till they are wanted again for service, of the quarrelling going on between the wives and among the servants, and of other incidents which show that the women of these large harems are on a lower level of civilization than their lord. He mixes with Europeans and with other Turks who know what are the habits of civilized life. His wives see few other women, and unless they are able to read French or English novels, or happen to know foreign ladies, are ignorant of European manners.

An English lady of title who, after a life of varied and quite unique experience, ended as the wife of an Arab sheik, and had had an exceptional experience in Turkish and Arab harems, described to me many years ago harem women in general as children with the vices of women. They had at times, said she, all the charm of children, were gay and careless, but were liable to lose their tempers, and then quarrelled with the violence of children who had been allowed to run wild. As for their conversation she added, "the less I tell you about it the better." It requires, however, little knowledge of Turkish to learn from the expressions of vexation uttered in the streets even by well-dressed Turkish women that there is amongst many of them an absence of refinement and delicacy of speech.

REVIEW QUESTIONS

1. At the beginning of this chapter, Pears wrote, "The absence of family life among the Turks is the most serious hindrance to their advancement in civilization." What evidence from this selection supports that statement?

2. How would you characterize Pears's opinion about the position of Turkish women in society? Is his tone positive or negative? Do you agree or disagree with his assessment? Why or why not?

3. How are Turkish marriages arranged? What are the pros and cons of this approach?

4. Assuming that the details of the wedding celebration given here are accurate, would you like to attend such a wedding? Why or why not?

5. As noted in the introduction, Pears had a reputation as an independent and critical observer of the Turkish scene. Do you think this selection supports that view? Why or why not?

Part III

Toward the Contemporary World, 1918 to the Present

The selections in Part III reflect and illuminate some of the most significant changes in world politics and culture since the end of the First World War. Perhaps the most significant of these changes is the recognition of diversity. This is the case with both the authors themselves and the topics and subjects about which they wrote. In earlier periods, most of the authors were members of a political or economic elite. Now, the travelers come from a myriad of classes and socioeconomic groups. In perhaps the most obvious case, many of them are students. Some traveled to further their formal educations, while others sought to broaden their personal and intellectual horizons in a more informal manner. Dervla Murphy, whose formal education was cut short so she could nurse her invalid mother, began her career as a world traveler on a bicycle trip from Ireland to India after her mother's death. Some authors were reluctant to leave their families—instead they took them along. Murphy, for example took her young daughter to the Cameroons on a horse named Egbert. Before Elizabeth Marshall Thomas was married, she and the rest of her family spent nearly three years in the Kalahari, where her wealthy father liked to play amateur anthropologist.

A second notable theme is the increasing emancipation of women. This is evident both in the number of women authors and in the topics included in this section. One-third of the authors presented here are female, and almost two-thirds of the readings focus either entirely or in part on women's lives and issues. The list of women authors includes, but is by no means limited to, Ella Maillart, Colette Modiano, and Poranee Natadecha-Sponsel. Not all women wrote about women, and not all men wrote about men. Morris Deutsch, an American soldier in Europe during World War II, appears to have been very interested in French and German women and was not shy about offering his opinions of their behaviors and activities.

A particular feature of women's lives that interested a number of these authors was sex. The most obvious case is Cleo Odzer's observations of the impact of Thailand's sex industry upon the lives of one woman, her family, and friends. One traveler with sex on his mind—but only for investigative purposes—was the Italian newspaperman Guido Piovene, who went to Sweden to learn more about the "sexual revolution" that he associated with that country. Much to his surprise, he discovered that Swedish attitudes toward sex had historically been open and accepting: there had been no revolution. In contrast, Elizabeth Warnock Fernea not did even mention sex when she described domestic life among the wealthy (and somewhat spoiled) Iraqi women in a shiek's harem.

Another dominant theme in Part III is the political and cultural movements of the post–World War I era. Virtually all societies were affected, either directly or indirectly, by the instability that plagued most of the twentieth century: the Bolshevik Revolution, World War II, the partition of the Indian subcontinent, ongoing tensions in the Middle East, the superpower rivalry between the United States and the Soviet Union, the Cultural Revolution in China, and the retreat of imperialism. Although the selections in Part III do not address these issues directly, the authors could not help but be affected by the state of the world at the time they were writing. Two selections in Chapter 15, for example, address living and working conditions that were the result of political experimentation by the new Bolshevik government. Three other selections provide a good understanding of the importance of World War II. Philip Gibbs depicts attitudes in Berlin before the war, while John F. Kennedy observes life in the German capital just as the war in Europe was ending. Morris Deutsch's letter home, on the other hand, gives us a sense of the wartime experience of "an average G.I." Ellura Winters lived in East Pakistan (later Bangladesh) during the period of intense political and ethnic tension that forshadowed the eventual fracture of Pakistan into two separate nations. Winters gives us an appreciation of the violence that accompanied the birth of Bangladesh. After World War II, while the Indian subcontinent was splitting into first two and then three separate political nations, Vietnam was becoming one. Nguyen Long describes difficulties of life in Ho Chi Minh City after the end of the Vietnam War, and Anchee Min remembers the chaotic upheavals she experienced as a child at the beginning of the Cultural Revolution in China.

The legacy of imperialism is clearly the dominant theme in Chapter 13. The authors deal with such varied issues as race relations, the subjugation of women, and the struggle for political and especially economic independence. Often the movement toward self-determination was accompanied by increasing modernization. Chapter 13 begins with a portrait of a Kikuyu market, which was part of the British colonial system, and it concludes with descriptions of train travel and modern popular culture in independent Cameroon and Ethiopia. Modernization, of course, was not limited to technological advances; it also included complex changes in social behavior. In some cases, such as Indira Gandhi's wedding, there were deliberate attempts to include the traditional together with the modern.

In addition to modernization, another legacy of imperialism was the aggravation of existing racial tensions. This is particularly evident in George Orwell's "Essay on Marrakech" and Naboth Mokgatle's autobiographical account of his experiences under South African apartheid, but the issue was not limited to Africa by any means. John Clytus, a black American, hoped to escape the racism of American society by relocating to Cuba, only to find that the problem was not confined to the United States. Emmanuel John Hevi, an African student, likewise notes the presence of racism in China. Others were oppressed by class and gender rather than race. Mahadevi Varma describes the plight of her young, destitute female servant who was mistreated and betrayed by her husband.

This final section of *Global Passages* addresses complex themes. Technological changes in travel and communication have linked the peoples of the world more closely together than ever before. Travelers and foreigners often have an accurate and positive appreciation of their host societies. But this is not always the case. Students in the United States might be particularly interested in the critiques of their own society offered by Poranee Natadecha-Sponsel. What does she say about the nature of intercultural interaction and individual judgment in the contemporary world?

⫸ 11 ⫸

East and Southeast Asia, 1918 to the Present

The end of World War I in 1918 marked a dramatic change for Europe and the United States. In the East changes were coming, but they became more dramatic in the aftermath of World War II. Among the events in that aftermath were the end of imperialism in Africa and Asia (including Japan's imperial dream, which had led to the great Pacific war). Among the countries covered in this chapter, the only one directly under the control of an imperialist power was Vietnam; Thailand, China, and Japan remained politically independent, yet each experienced the power politics of European imperialist nations. Both world wars were the defining events of the twentieth century; all other wars—the Korean War, Vietnam, the oil wars of Presidents Reagan and Bush (the elder)—were attachments and extensions.

One of the legacies of war is described by Cleo Odzer, who records the Thai institutionalized whoredom of the R&R (rest and rehabilitation) resulting from the American military presence during the Vietnam War. The Thai society and government viewed the inhabitants of the Bangkok sex industry with apparent disdain and considerable hypocrisy, yet they were nevertheless willing to collect tourist *bahts* (dollars). The women involved were—and are—dismissed by proper society but not by their villages and their families. Almost next door, in Communist Vietnam, hypocrisy also prevailed, as Nguyen Long's return to his native city shows. It is almost a revisit of totalitarian Communist terror reminiscent of Stalin's Russia or Mao's China. Something of the same sort of terror is seen in Emmanuel John Hevi's experience as an African student in Mao's China, which records the millennia-old Chinese xenophobia, now reinforced by the frenzy of Maoist ideology and paranoia.

Tradition of a more positive nature is described in Jan Myrdal's meticulous and sensitive account of a wedding in a Chinese village. On the village level, it seems, some traditions endured. But Anchee Min as a young girl experienced the cruelty and ravages of urban upheaval during the Cultural Revolution, which sought to completely unhinge basic human unions and to subjugate people to a destructive state ideology. Havoc and dehumanization were the result. Although not represented in these selections, so it was to be in Cambodia for decades.

Japan lost a horrendous war, yet it held onto its cultural bases. Nikos Kazantzakis's account of a Japanese garden shows the strength of a tradition that later was to go astray because of war and imperialism but that quickly returned to its roots. After the Japanese surrender in 1945, the Allied Occupation (mostly by American military) under General Douglas MacArthur ran the country. Although there must have been antipathy, for the most part, in spite of strong cultural differences, the transition was smooth. As a result both cultures were affected, as is evident in the film *Sayonara* and in Beat writers such as Jack Kerouac and the Pulitzer Prize poet Gary Snyder. Zen had a great impact upon American society, especially on the West Coast, influencing writers, artists, and students to protest against American governmental policies—from domestic racism to the Vietnam War—in the fifties, sixties, and seventies. Perhaps next to the brilliant decision of General MacArthur to issue orders through the Emperor, the wisest decision during the Occupation was to allow families of the American soldiers to accompany them into occupied Japan. As a result, Margery Finn Brown was able to write a remarkable account of the cultural contact between Japan and the United States. Her description of a geisha can be compared to Odzer's account of a Thai prostitute—both are sympathetic portraits.

An African Student Discusses Life in China (1960–1962)

EMMANUEL JOHN HEVI, *An African Student in China*

The post–World War II emancipation of European colonies in Africa, such as Ghana, occasioned the education of many young adults from these new nations. After 1945, both capitalist and communist countries involved in the Cold War opened their arms to the young scholars and eagerly greeted them, intending to use them to foster economic, political, and social alliances. The goal was to build strong sympathetic leadership in the African nations—an objective that did not always succeed.

The author of this selection, Hevi, accepted a scholarship from the People's Republic of China and arrived in Kunming on November 27, 1960, and then continued to Beijing the next day. From the beginning he was not impressed by the people of China, most of whom he saw as "pitiful dogs cringing in fear." After the episode presented here, he left China in 1962, very dissatisfied and disgusted with what he had found.

Now to the final episode in this history of the African Students' Union in China: the events in late March 1962. I was at that time the sole African student in Peking Medical College, and I used to while away my more lonely moments in telephone conversations with African friends at the Language Institute. One Wednesday morning, in the course of such a conversation with a member of our Central Committee, I was told there had been a brawl in the city involving one of the Zanzibari students. I was not made to understand that it was anything serious. The following day I got all the details, from which it appeared it was very serious indeed.

A young Zanzibari called Ali had gone with a Mongol friend to the Peace Hotel. While there, Ali went to the counter to buy some cigarettes, but was refused by the man at the counter. As they stood arguing, two hotel stewards came out

and laid hands on Ali. They did not turn him out of the hotel, as is usually done with people who, rightly or wrongly, are regarded as nuisances; no, they hauled him off to an adjoining room and started to beat him up. Ali fought back manfully but more Chinese stewards rushed in and pitched into him, dragging him into the yard outside.

At that time there were two other Zanzibaris present in the hotel, a man and his wife, both working at Radio Peking. The woman was seven months' pregnant. Hearing the row that was being kicked up, they went, out of curiosity, to see what it was all about. As soon as they showed their faces, the Chinese fell on them also. Ever since the assault on Ali began, this mob of toughs had been yelling: *"Fei chou ren bu hao"*—Africans are not good. Since Ali had done or said something which, to their mind, merited a beating, they considered it logical to deal out similar treatment to every African in sight. *All* Africans were "not good." They weren't content with using their fists. The spittoon-covers in Chinese hotels are large disks with longish handles. When wielded as a club, these covers can be as effective as a Zulu warrior's knob-kerrie. The African woman was beaten with them till she sustained injuries on the breast and other parts of the body. Ali fainted and dropped to the floor, where his body was a target for anyone's boot.

There was a burly black-bearded West Indian staying at the hotel called John Holmes. He had been in Peking for about eighteen months and had been friendly with the African students. He had helped the Union's officers to patch up the split which developed when the Somalis wanted to carry anti-Ethiopian posters in the demonstration. Hearing the hullabaloo, Mr Holmes came down from the eighth floor, sized up the situation, and carried Ali's limp form up to his own apartment and gave him first aid.

But when he tried to convey Ali and the injured pregnant woman to hospital, the hotel lift suddenly decided to go out of order and no taxis were to be got for love or money in all Peking. You can't just go to the curb and hail a taxi in Peking; you have to telephone to the taxi-office and then sit and wait for one to arrive; sometimes it takes a whole hour, if you are lucky! If the caller happens not to be in the good books of the authorities, he can wait till he is blue in the face, but no taxi will arrive. Nor did it arrive in this case. The Chinese were clearly not satisfied with merely giving three "niggers" a good beating. There was to be no transport to take them to hospital. It was not until about four o'clock in the morning, that is *eight* hours after the assault, that the injured were finally taken away for treatment. And this was only due to the fact that their Zanzibari friends found transport for them.

Mr Holmes was disgusted and said he would "quit this bloody country" if justice were not done to the injured Africans. He belonged, so he told me, to the Committee of African Organisations in London. Some people said he was a communist. If this is so, then I take my hat off to him, for he would then be that very rare speci-

men, a communist who puts justice above the Party. Because he spoke out in indignation and demanded "justice to the injured or I quit," he was promptly accused of inciting the Africans to action. The Chinese told him he would be held responsible for any retaliatory action we students took as a result of the Ali Affair. A few days before I left China I heard that he was also packing up to leave.

The African woman involved in this appalling incident was, as I have said, employed by Radio Peking. She was an announcer on the Swahili language program. Not long before the incident, it had been part of her job to tell East Africans the story of a pregnant woman in South Korea who had been beaten up by an American sailor. The story was broadcast to show American brutality to less favoured peoples. And now she who told the story was being assaulted, not by one drunken man, but by a whole crowd of sober ruffians, beaten up by Chinese merely because she was African.

No wonder the Chinese tried to persuade us African students to keep quiet about the affair! What price Sino-African friendship now?

When the Africans at the Language Institute heard about the affair, they exploded. I found them seething with rage and demanding that the matter be placed forthwith on the agenda of the Union's meeting scheduled for Sunday, March 25. They demanded a strike—a one-week hunger strike: everyone was to down tools and go without food for a week. In these circumstances, the general meeting was bound to be stormy. Accordingly, I consulted with Mr Kassim, our President (a Zanzibari), and we agreed it was advisable to call a meeting of the Central Committee on Saturday, March 24. In the less turbulent atmosphere of the committee meeting, it might be possible to make some constructive proposals to calm down our fellow students and at the same time deal with the Chinese.

The Committee meeting started at four in the afternoon. Business had just started when a number of dignitaries turned up. These were the ambassadors of the Republic of Guinea with another diplomatist from that embassy, the ambassador of the Republic of Mali with an embassy counsellor, and the *chargé d'affaires* of the Ghanaian embassy. This was the first time we had received such an impressive delegation, but I must confess that we were less enthusiastic than we would ordinarily have been. We were too conscious of what our fellow students would do by way of direct action if they failed to be satisfied with the measures proposed by the Central Committee. The two ambassadors went aside to speak to individual students, mainly the Camerounians with whom they could speak French. The other three diplomatists came over to confer with the Central Committee, trying hard to persuade us to cancel the meeting of the whole Union fixed for the following day. They feared this meeting would lead to the students' taking action which might bring further trouble. But they made an unfortunate, and very undiplomatic, mistake: they started by telling us we were in the wrong. When a group of hotheads have risen up in holy anger and are on the warpath, no one can start off like that without raising more hell. Things were made worse when we discovered that they had heard the Chinese story, ready cooked for consumption, without bothering to get from Ali his version of the case. (I should make it clear that the ambassadors themselves did not take part in these direct discussions with the Committee. Things might have taken a different turn if they had.) Ali might well have been in the wrong, but should this be assumed automatically, and should he be condemned without a hearing? The fact is, these diplomatists came at the instance of the Chinese Foreign Ministry; they had not come to arbitrate in the dispute with the Chinese, but to get us to do what the Chinese wanted. The upshot was that we told them we could not agree there and then to their request to cancel the meeting next day, but would consider it during our deliberations on the whole affair. They left at about seven o'clock.

After a break, the Committee met again from ten o'clock to three in the morning. We considered the advice given by the diplomatists and in the end decided to ignore it for the following reasons:

1. The advice came, not from them, but from the Chinese since the diplomatists were simply acting as emissaries of the Chinese.

2. The diplomatists were not objective, showing partiality in all respects to the Chinese case.

3. We were at loggerheads with the Chinese in a local matter. There was no cause to raise it to the status of an international dispute, as was implicit in the intervention of three embassies.

4. The general meeting of the Union had been fixed two weeks earlier to deal with matters of internal discipline. We didn't intend to change our plans just to please the Chinese who had provoked trouble by beating up our friends.

5. Collective opinion in the Union was firmly against cancelling the Sunday meeting. If the Central Committee could not retain members' confidence, the students might well break loose from all control.

6. Union officers believed that, somehow or other, they could keep effective control of the situation. But to do so, they had to meet the whole body of students. The officers would be abdicating responsibility if they cancelled the meeting.

The strength of feeling among the students can be judged by the reaction of some of the Camerounian girls when I jokingly said, before going into the second session of the Committee meeting, that the general meeting was to be postponed on Chinese advice. Four or five of them flew at me in fury and it would have gone ill with me if I hadn't quickly told them I was pulling their legs.

So in the early hours of the morning it was decided that the general meeting should still take place.

That same Saturday night two other events occurred which deserve mention. There was a group amongst us which did not appear to have definite ideas of their own. These were the "drifters." On several occasions the Chinese had used these to put rifts among us. With a view to breaking student solidarity over the Ali case, the Chinese invited all the Somali students and a large section of the Camerounians to two different parties that evening. The Zanzibaris, Ghanaians and the intractable group among the Camerounians were not invited. At Sino-African Friendship House, the Chinese spent four hours trying to persuade the Somalis to dissociate themselves from any action proposed by the Union. But the sweet talk and all the wines and delicacies did not make any impression on the Somalis. On the contrary, they poured out to the Chinese all their grievances and reported back to the Central Committee. At a similar party on the premises of the Afro-Asian Solidarity Committee, the Chinese had no better luck with the Camerounians, who told them quite bluntly how miserable their lives were being made in China. No one had instructed these two groups how to behave towards the Chinese; despite all differences in the past, they rallied to the viewpoint of the majority of their fellow Africans. Chinese efforts to split us only resulted in a greater unity amongst the African students, a solidarity which overcame the petty jealousies and differences which had earlier afflicted the Union.

REVIEW QUESTIONS

1. What aspects of the Ali Affair could have been a result of cultural differences and misunderstandings? Explain.
2. Why do you believe that the African governments' officials were involved in the affair so quickly? What effect did they have?
3. Do you find the organization of the African students in China to be unusual or peculiar? How did they intend to make their organization effective?
4. What was the strategy used by the university and Chinese officials to end the affair and solve the students' problems?

A Swedish Travel Writer and Scholar Describes Wedding Customs in a Chinese Village (1962)

JAN MYRDAL, *Report from a Chinese Village*

Jan Myrdal, born in Sweden in 1927, is one of the twentieth century's most prolific travel writers. Together with his wife, photographer Gun Kessle, he has traveled to and produced books on numerous areas, including China, Cambodia, Central Asia, India, Mexico, and areas of the former Soviet Union. He had the stated aim of trying to change Eurocentric perceptions of Asia. To an amazing extent he has been successful, perhaps partly because of historical developments within his lifetime, but also to no small degree because of his powerful observations and descriptions. Myrdal is often critical of what he sees, but fairly so. At one time some of his writing was banned in the Soviet Union for noting discrimination in regard to minority peoples. His books are not mere travelogues, but deep analyses. Often considered radical when they first appeared, they have largely been vindicated by time. In the following selection he simply reports what he has learned about wedding customs in a Chinese village where he and his wife lived in 1962.

Myrdal is also a scholar of noted Swedish playwright August Strindberg (1849–1912), and he delivered the opening address at the 1990 International Strindberg Conference. He is an art historian and commentator as well. He has written in both Swedish and English and is the author of about sixty books. Of particular note are his writings about his childhood. It was an unhappy one because he had a cold relationship with his parents, both of whom were Nobel Prize winners, his mother Alva (1902–1986) for peace and his father Gunnar (1898–1987) for economics. He often stayed with his grandparents, and those times were enriching for him.

There are three principal ways of arranging marriages:

(1) The boy and the girl live in the same village. They work together in the fields and they talk together. He likes her and she admires him. They fall in love and, as they know each other, they tell each other and they marry, if their parents agree. They marry of their own free will.

(2) They live in the same village and see each other occasionally. The boy likes the girl and the girl likes the boy, but they dare not tell each other; so each asks some older person to act as go-between and tell the other: "So-and-so is in love with you." That's what Lo Han-hong and Li Chin-wa did. He had a job and she was studying. They could not talk to each other and so could only gaze at each other. She noticed that he came out of his cave-office every time she walked past on her way home from Liu Ling school, and he had noticed that she walked by, whenever he was looking for her. Then Lo Han-hong asked Li Kuei-ying to talk to Li Chin-wa, and afterwards Li Chin-wa asked Li Yang-ching to talk to Lo Han-hong, and in that way they learned that they loved each other. Then they met and went into Lo Han-hong's cave and talked together, and after that they became betrothed. It's mostly boys who get an older person to speak for them.

(3) A person with a son over twenty and not yet married grows anxious lest his son become an older bachelor. He happens to have a relative in another village, who has a neighbour with a daughter who is not yet engaged, so the man takes his son and they go together to visit this relative. The boy and the girl cannot meet otherwise. Things are arranged so that the two can see each other, and afterwards they are asked: "Did you like him?" "Did you fall in love with her?" After that, the two young people meet again and perhaps they do fall in love, become engaged and get married. When Chang Chung-liang's younger brother, Chang Chung-wen, was twenty-two and still unmarried, he went to Chi-tan hsien, where he had an uncle, and his uncle introduced him to a very young girl. They got married and she now has a child of four, though she herself is only twenty-one.

When a girl considers the boys with an eye to choosing one to marry, she looks for one who is strong and healthy and able to work well. Girls attach great importance to behaviour: the boy they choose must be even- not quick-tempered. Appearance is less important. As the girls say: "We have a long life to live together. He may look handsome now, but his looks will soon go. But if he is faithful and kind and hard-working, we can have a good life together." Boys who are known to be lazy seldom get married.

When a boy considers a girl, the first thing he asks himself is: "Can she look after a home?" Next in importance is that she should be even-tempered. Appearance plays a certain part, but not a great one. In Liu Ling no one will say that a girl is ugly or plain, just that she "looks well enough in her way."

"In the towns the girls will tell you the same as those in the villages, but they will only do that because it is the thing to say. In reality, town girls want smart, dashing-looking boys."

The person with the most say in the matter of a girl's marriage is her grandmother, then her grandfather, then her mother; what her father thinks is of least importance. What they all want for the girl they are marrying off—and what the boy's parents are also looking for—is a "good marriage" to someone who is "rich," strong and able to work well.

Once they are engaged, the boy and the girl meet often. Li Chin-wa and Lo Han-hong spent hours sitting together in his cave. They were always alone then and no one would disturb them. "We aren't so feudal in Liu Ling that we won't leave them alone together." But when Lo Han-hong goes to see Li Chin-wa, he has to sit with the whole family. Sometimes the two would go to the cinema in the town together.

There is no intercourse prior to marriage. That is held to be immoral. "No girl in Liu Ling has ever had a baby before she was married. That happens very seldom up here with us in northern Shensi." The age at which girls normally marry is such that there is no large group of sexually mature but unmarried women.

Later on, when they are to marry, the two young people go to the authorities and register. They have to say how old they are and they are asked: "Do you love each other? Do you want to marry? Are you doing this of your own free will?" Only after that are they given a marriage licence. Having got that, they are legally married, but it has never yet happened that a couple have begun living together as man and wife after just this legal marriage. There has to be a ceremony as well, and for various reasons there can be an interval of anything up to six months between the legal marriage and the wedding.

A bride's trousseau usually consists of three or four changes of clothes, two new coverlets, one mirror, one or two chests, one cup, one soft cushion, one pillow, and one wash-hand basin, and the bridegroom should have furnished the bridal chamber with one mattress and one thick coverlet. The thicker this coverlet is, the richer and happier the bride's life will be, or so they say.

The wedding is in the bridegroom's home and it will be well attended. There can be more than a hundred guests. All relations, neighbours and friends are invited. There will be wheaten bread, buckwheat noodles and cakes of "sticky millet" to eat. Altogether there ought to be eight courses; four is the minimum. There should be meat and wine and spirits, and everyone will eat and drink and sing and joke. At the start of the ceremony the guests are seated, gathered round the couple, who stand in front of the table, the bride on the right, the bridegroom on the left. There should be wine and a dish of sweetmeats and melon seeds and cigarettes and a looking-glass on the table; and there should be a picture of Chairman Mao hanging on the wall in front of the couple. The bride takes some flour and puts it in a porcelain bowl. Bride and bridegroom bow low to the portrait of Chairman Mao; then they turn to their parents and bow to them, then they bow to the elders and lastly to their guests.

Then the guests ask them to tell how they fell in love with each other, to tell "the story of their love," and they both become very embarrassed and look at each other and urge each other to do the telling. And the people call out: "Quickly! Quickly!" Then the bridegroom will mumble something in a low voice. Some just say a word or two like: "We met and so we married." Then all the guests ask lots of questions. They pretend that they have seen the two together and say things like: "We saw you! You were walking very close together down by the river." Everyone jokes and tries to make them blush as much as possible. Both bride and bridegroom wear big red paper flowers, which they exchange, and after that they drink wine. Then the guests ask the bride to sing. The couple eat a few sweetmeats from the dish, then they sit down and everyone starts eating and drinking.

Now the bride and bridegroom are congratulated and everyone drinks. After that, good friends conduct the couple to the bridal chamber. There the bride has to wait on the bridegroom and all their friends. She must light their cigarettes and fill up their cups with wine. Bride and bridegroom sing and everyone drinks wine. About midnight the couple are left alone in the bridal chamber and the guests depart.

On the third day, the couple go to the bride's family with gifts. They take cakes and sweet-meats, dried noodles, handkerchiefs and stock-ings. Then the bride's mother invites some of her good friends and relations to a dinner with meat and wine and all sorts of good things. After that the couple go back to the bridegroom's family. "This is our way of celebrating a wedding. Everyone's wedding has been like that for many years now. But the old people say that it was done differently in the old days."

The old women say that in the old days you were not allowed to choose whom you married. A young couple were not allowed to meet before the wedding. When a girl was sixteen or seventeen, the marriage-broker would come and say: "I have seen a young man in such-and-such a place and he does this or that and he is healthy and strong and of good family, and he is rich and even-tempered." If the girl's mother was interested in the offer, a day would be fixed for the young man to be presented. On the day appointed, the marriage-broker and the suitor would arrive with presents of wine and meat and other good things, as well as cloth for the girl. The girl's mother would take the meat and cook it and warm the wine, and then they would eat and drink. Meanwhile the girl would be kept hidden. She was not meant to meet her suitor. If the mother was satisfied with the suitor after she had seen him, she would say: "It is well," and then they would settle the financial arrangements.

That done, a propitious day for the wedding would be decided on with the assistance of a wise man. This had to be at least one month away in order to allow the girl time to get her trousseau ready. She had to have four baskets of embroidered shoes, quilted trousers, pieces of cloth, socks, needle and thread, and foot-bindings for her girl-children. All her relations would have to help her get the things ready in time. After this the suitor and marriage-broker would bring the girl's mother all the things the suitor had

agreed to give for the girl: money and cloth and meat and wine. The mother would cook the meat and warm the wine and accept the suitor's bride-ransom.

A girl had to weep properly on her wedding day. To begin with, she has decked out with lots of red flowers and ornaments, and then her pig-tails were unplaited. Next, she was placed in a palanquin carried by two or four men and taken to the bridegroom's home, her brother going with her. When they reached the bridegroom's home, the bride's brother gave her away. Bride and bridegroom then knelt in the big room in front of a table. The room had to be decorated with flowers and ribbons, and there had to be two red candles on the table and also fruit and sweet-meats. The couple then bowed first to heaven and earth, then to the bridegroom's parents and then to the bride's brother and the marriage-broker and all the relations. After that everyone ate and drank.

In the old days, the main dish used to be wheat-flour noodles, and throughout the ceremony some men sat by the door to see that no widows, cats or dogs got into the room, because in those days these always brought bad luck, especially at a wedding. After everyone had eaten, the curtain before the bridal chamber was pulled aside. At that moment the bride had to look desperate, otherwise people said: "Look how avid she is!"

The first three days after the bridal night, the bride had to spend sitting on the kang all the time. She was given no more to eat and drink than was necessary for survival, and if she wanted to relieve nature she could do so only at night, creeping out when everyone else was asleep, because if anyone discovered her going out she would be jeered at. During the day she had to hold it in however much it hurt. On the third day the couple went to the bride's mother with gifts. The bride's mother would have invited some close relatives and they would eat meat and drink wine, and afterwards the young couple would return to the bridegroom's home. For the first three years of her marriage a bride was not supposed to go beyond the gate. Some of the old women said that they were allowed to go a little way beyond, but they must not go far and only when it was necessary. "Well, that was the old way of marrying. It is not practised any longer. It hasn't been employed for many years and it's a long time since anyone bowed to heaven and earth."

Nowadays, when people marry, they are usually very loving for the first year. Not that they show it in front of others, we don't do that, but you can see it by the way their clothes are better and their shoes whole, and they look happy. But otherwise brides behave in the same way as before. People don't consider a bride properly married until she has had a baby. Until then she is still a girl, even though she is married. She won't dare talk and joke with the others; but everyone will joke with her and her husband. People will stop her on the road and ask: "Well, are you in love with your husband?" And if the bridegroom is coming back from the town, he will be stopped and asked: "What have you bought your bride?" They will blush, but they won't joke back till the bride has had her first child. Of course, she will be less bashful than she was before her marriage, but she isn't yet one of the married women. If they don't have any children, people usually adopt a son. That is what Tein Kuei-hua did. Her husband is a ganbu at the coal mines in Yenan. He was deputy party secretary of Liu Ling's People's Commune up to 1961, then he was moved. When they did not have any children, they adopted one. People would rather adopt the child of some close relative with lots of sons, than let their family die out. The adopted son has to be treated well, because he is the family's future. Such adoptions are quite common.

Nowadays divorce is very rare. There having been no free choice of partner under the old system, there was a sudden rush of divorces when the new order began. But that is a thing of the past. If there are children, people think it immoral and wicked to leave them. Even if the marriage is childless, people still consider divorce immoral, because now that people can choose whom they marry, they will have chosen each other and should put up with the consequences. One can always adopt a child. If, in spite of all this, they still want a divorce, the various organizations, the party, the League of Youth, the women's group, try to instruct them and explain what is the decent thing to do and the one consistent with socialist morality. If they persist, the matter is taken up by the mediation committee of the people's commune, which goes into it thoroughly with them and explains to them why they ought not to divorce, but should live together and agree. If, after all this, they refuse to give in and still want a divorce, they are, of course, entitled to go to the court in Yenan and start proceedings for a divorce; but that has not yet happened in Liu Ling, nor have any divorces been heard of in the neighbouring villages for many years, for it is a long time now since women have been granted equality and marriages have been entered into voluntarily.

Brawling and fighting were said to be unknown in Liu Ling, nor had anyone heard of anyone suffering from jealousy. Infidelity was unheard of in the village, and they had not had any great dramas of passion, let alone *crimes passionnels.* "It is all due to the fact that we in northern Shensi are different to people from Hopeh and Canton and Shantung and Kiangsu and Fukien. We aren't like they are. Down there, those sorts of things do happen; but not with us."

REVIEW QUESTIONS

1. The term *arranged marriage* is usually greeted with distaste, and sometimes outright hostility, in the West. Does the flexibility described here make the institution seem more palatable?
2. Villages are noted for stability. How does this selection reflect that condition?
3. How would you characterize Myrdal's description? Explain.

A Chinese Novelist Remembers the Cultural Revolution (1966–1976)

ANCHEE MIN, *Red Azalea*

Described both as a memoir and as an autobiographical novel, Anchee Min's *Red Azalea* is a harrowing account of the effect of the Cultural Revolution (1966–1976) on a family's life, particularly that of the eldest daughter. It is a straightforward account, even to the point of being self-critical; the passion shines through, but without histrionics. The style is simple—the author herself has termed it naive, but the very nature of the subject generates a passionate response. When asked in an interview what was most difficult in writing the book, Min replied: "To live the time over again. It was painful."

Much has been written about the horror of the Cultural Revolution under Mao Zedong (Mao Tse-tung) and Madame Mao (Jiang Ching). But just as Anne Frank's diary has more emotional force than do mere statistics, this personal account has a strong impact on the reader. Min has written two other novels about the effects of the Cultural Revolution, *Katherine* and *Becoming Madame Mao.* About the latter, Min has stated that the subject is not so much Madame Mao but rather "the process of how she, a beautiful woman who once possessed tremendous innocence, turned into a monster." Yet, Min was surprised to discover the "human side . . . as a lover, a wife, and a mother."

Anchee Min fled China in 1983 amidst the turmoil that followed Mao's death and Madame Mao's execution. She arrived in the United States knowing no English. She has since visited China, where she was well received and used as an example of what women can accomplish. Although her works have not been "officially" translated into Chinese, Min suspects that there may be some underground translations. The selection presented here is the opening portion of *Red Azalea.*

I was raised on the teachings of Mao and on the operas of Madam Mao, Comrade Jiang Ching. I became a leader of the Little Red Guards in elementary school. This was during the Great Proletarian Cultural Revolution when red was my color. My parents lived like—as the neighbors described them—a pair of chopsticks: always in harmony. My father was an instructor of industrial technique drawing at Shanghai Textile Institute, although his true love was astronomy. My mother was a teacher at a Shanghai middle school. She taught whatever the Party asked, one semester in Chinese and the next in Russian. My parents both believed in Mao and the Communist Party, just like everybody else in the neighborhood. They had four children, each one a year apart. I was born in 1957. We lived in the city, on South Luxuriant Road in a small two-story townhouse occupied by two families. The house was left by my grandfather, who had died of tuberculosis right before I was born.

I was an adult since the age of five. That was nothing unusual. The kids I played with all carried their family's little ones on their backs, tied with a piece of cloth. The little ones played with their own snot while we played hide-and-seek. I was put in charge of managing the family because my parents were in their working units all day, just like everyone else's parents.

I called my sisters and brother my children

because I had to pick each one of them up from kindergarten and nursery school while I myself was only a kindergartner. I was six when my sister Blooming was five, my second sister Coral was four and my brother Space Conqueror was three. My parents made careful choices in the names they gave us. They were considered eccentric because the neighbors named their children Guard of Red, Big Leap, Long March, Red Star, Liberation, Revolution, New China, Road of Russia, Resist U.S., Patriotic Forerunner, Matchless Red Soldier, etc. My parents had their own ideas. First they called me Lin-Shuan—Rising Sun at a Mountain. They dropped it because Mao was considered the only sun. After further contemplation, they named me Anchee—Jade of Peace. Also, it sounded like the Chinese pronunciation of the English word "angel." They registered me with it. Blooming and Coral were named after the sound of chee (jade). There were two reasons why my parents named my brother Space Conqueror: one was that my father loved astronomy; the second was to respond to Mao's call that China would soon build its own spaceship.

As I understood it, my parents were doing work that was saving the world. Every evening I would pick up the children and fight with the kids on the block all the way home. It was like eating a regular meal that I got a purple cheek or a bloody nose. It did not bother me too much. Although I was scared of crossing at traffic lights and dark alleys, I learned to not show my fear, because I had to be a model for the children, to show them what bravery meant. After I arranged for the children to play by themselves in the living room, I went to set up the stove to cook dinner. It always took me a long time to light the stove, because I did not understand that wood and coals needed air to burn. I stuffed the stove as I sang songs of Mao quotations. One time, when I tried many times and the stove would not light, I lost my patience. I went out to play, thinking that the stove was not burning. Then a kid came and told me that there was smoke coming out of our house window. This happened three times.

I tried to put the children to sleep while the sky was still bright. The children's little feet kicked the cotton blankets and made new holes over the old. The blankets soon became rags. When the room quieted down, I would lean on the windowsill staring at the entrance to the lane, waiting for my parents to appear. I watched the sky turn deep blue, Venus rising, and I would fall asleep by the window.

In 1967, when I was ten years old, we moved. It was because our downstairs neighbor accused us of having a bigger space than they had. They said, How can a family of six occupy four rooms while a family of eleven has only one? The revolution is about fairness. They came up with chamber pots and poured shit on our blankets. There were no police. The police station was called a revisionist mechanism and had been shut down by the revolutionaries. The Red Guards had begun looting houses. No one answered our call for help. The neighbors just watched.

The downstairs neighbor kept bothering us. We cleaned the shit night after night, swallowed insults in meek submission. The downstairs family became uncontrollable. They threatened to harm us children when our parents were not at home. They said their second daughter had a history of mental illness. Therefore, they could not be responsible for what she was going to do. The second daughter came up and showed me an ax that she had just sharpened. She said she could chop my head in two like chopping a watermelon. She asked me if I would like her to do it. I said, You wait here and I'll tell you whether I would like it or not later. I grabbed my sisters and brother and we ran and squeezed ourselves in a closet all day.

One day when my mother stepped into the door after work, the second daughter jumped on her. I saw them wrestle into the stairwell. Mother was pushed, crushed on the floor, and was slashed with the scissors. I was in shock. I stood right next to my mother and saw blood pouring down her face and wrists. I wanted to scream but I had no voice. The second daughter went downstairs and cut her own wrists with the scissors. She then rushed to a curious crowd outside the door, bloody hands raised high in the air. She shouted, Look at me. I am a worker who was attacked by a bourgeois intellectual. Comrades, this is a political murder. Her family members came out. They shouted, A debt of blood must be paid by blood.

My father said we must move. We must escape. He wrote little notes describing our house and what he would like in exchange. He stuck the notes on the tree trunks by the streets. The next day a truck arrived by our door loaded full with furniture. Five men got out of the truck and said they came to exchange their house with ours. My father said we hadn't looked around for our choice yet. The men said, Our house is a perfect one for you and it's ready for you to move in. My father said we didn't know what it looked like. The men said, Go and take a look at it now, you will like it. My father asked how many rooms. They said three, very nice, Shanghai standard. My mother said, Do you know that our downstairs neighbor's second daughter is mentally ill? The men said it would not be a problem. They said that they had just beaten the second daughter, and she confessed that she was normal and that her family just wanted to have more rooms. She had promised to cause no trouble in the future. The men said they were a father and sons, all workers at a Shanghai steel factory. The sons needed rooms to get married. They wanted the rooms in a hurry. My father said, Please let us think about it. The men said, We'll wait outside your door while you make up your mind. My father said, You can't do that. The men said, No problem. My parents decided to take a look at the men's house on Shanxi Road.

I was asked to guard the house while my parents were gone. I was doing my homework when I saw the men start to unload their furniture. After that they began to move our furniture. I went up to them and said, My parents aren't back yet. The men said they would like to help us while they still had the truck. There's nowhere you can borrow such a truck by the time you think you're ready to move, they said.

Are you going to move all this stuff with your bare little hands?

When my parents got back, most of our furniture was packed on their truck. My mother said, This is not what I want, you can't force us to move. The men said, We're workers, we don't play mind games. You advertised, we came with a good offer. It's Sunday, our only day off. We don't like to be fooled. We beat the second daughter downstairs because she fooled us.

My father took my mother and the children aside. He said, We must get away. Let's move, forget about fairness. So we did. We moved to Shanxi Road in the Xu-Hui district. It was a row of townhouses. Our floor was a two-room apartment shared by three families. The apartment was owned by the government. The three families had to share one toilet. We occupied the front of the floor. Besides a drawing room, we had a porch and a kitchen. The family who occupied the back of the floor had five members. They lived in one room and their stove was right next to the toilet. I did not like it because it often happened that when I took a shit they would be cooking. The third family on the floor lived in a back-porch-converted space. They were very quiet people.

My father said, Let's settle down. Think of it this way, things could be worse, we could have been killed. At least it's safe here. We all agreed and felt better. Upstairs was a big family with six children. Their third daughter was my age. Her official name was Sun Flower but she was called Little Coffin at home, because she was as thin as a skeleton. She came down and asked me if I would like to join her family's Mao study seminar every evening after dinner. I said I had to ask my father. My father said no. He said he did not want to have a revolution at home. It surprised me. I spent a night thinking whether my father was a hidden counterrevolutionary and whether or not I should report him.

Little Coffin was disappointed when she heard that I would not attend their family's Mao study seminar. She went back upstairs and I heard her family begin singing "Red in the East rises the sun. China has brought forth a Mao Tse-tung . . ."

I admired her family. I wished we could do the same thing.

We girls were arranged to sleep on the porch while my brother slept in the kitchen. My mother missed our old house terribly. She missed having a toilet of our own.

The morning after we had moved, Monday, I remember, I was waked by a loud electric bell. I leaned out the window and looked down. Our downstairs apartment was a cable and wire hardware workshop. When the loud electric bell rang at seven-thirty, a crowd of women would rush in. Heads were moving like bees crowding into a nest. There were about two hundred women working downstairs and in the back lane under a roof shed that covered one-third of the back lane. The women used to be housewives. They had no education but were good at working with their hands. Here they wired and welded all day. They brought their own lunches and ate them in the yard. From my window I could see what they ate, mostly preserved salty fish and tofu. Some of them were given milk coupons because the wires they were welding carried poisonous chemicals. The smell of these chemicals came upstairs when they laid the wires out in the yard.

REVIEW QUESTIONS

1. Mao's China has been described as a place "where the soul was secondary to the state." How do you see that condition expressed in this selection?
2. What does the central character mean by her observation "I was an adult since the age of five"?
3. How would you describe the society depicted in this selection?

A Cretan Novelist Considers the Meaning of a Japanese Garden (1935)

NIKOS KAZANTZAKIS, *Japan, China*

Nikos Kazantzakis (1885–1957) was born in Crete and educated at the University of Athens. After graduating with a degree in law, he studied philosophy with Henri Bergson at the Collège de France from 1907 to 1909. Later, in the 1930s, Kazantzakis traveled in Europe, Asia, and Africa. Like his most famous literary creation, Zorba the Greek, Kazantzakis developed an unflagging love for all that life had to offer. Among his best-known works are *The Odyssey: A Modern Sequel* (1938), *Zorba the Greek* (1943), *The Greek Passion* (1948), *The Last Temptation of Christ* (1951), and *The Poor Man of God* (1953). An autobiography, *Report to Greco* (1965), and a biography, *Nikos Kazantzakis* (1968), written by his second wife, appeared posthumously. Nominated several times for a Nobel Prize, he never received that recognition.

In the prologue of *Japan, China* (1963), from which the following selection was taken, Kazantzakis tells the following story. "A rabbi was once asked the following question: 'When you say that the Jews should return to Palestine, you mean, surely, the heavenly, the immaterial, the spiritual Palestine, our true homeland?' The rabbi jabbed his staff into the ground in wrath and shouted, 'No! I want the Palestine down here, the one you can touch with your hands, with its stones, its thorns and its mud!'" Following this story, Kazantzakis offers this assessment of his own approach, "Neither am I nourished by fleshless, abstract memories. . . . When I close my eyes in order to enjoy a country again, my five senses, the five mouth-filled tentacles of my body, pounce upon it and bring it to me. Colors, fruits, women."

Without doubt, the description of the Japanese garden that follows certainly bears witness to Kazantzakis's ability to describe a real place. Nevertheless, his description is suffused with a profound sense of the spiritual. Kazantzakis's work, especially the first four books, focuses on the relationship between the physical and spiritual realms. In this case, his subject, an original art form that has become a significant feature of Japanese culture, gives Kazantzakis the opportunity to address the same issue. The Japanese garden, of course, is composed of rocks, plants, and other tangible objects. Nevertheless, its design illustrates and portrays an appreciation for abstract representations of the world derived from several religious and philosophical systems, especially Buddhism.

A great dancer lived in Japan two centuries ago. One time he ascended the steps of a monastery tower, famous for its view from the top; from there you could see an exquisite garden. When, however, he reached the highest step, a sense of uneasiness appeared on his face. He turned to his students who followed him and said:

"Strange! Something is missing here. A step. I beg one of you to go and call the abbot."

The abbot came. The dancer asked him whether a step was missing. "I have been the abbot for thirty years," replied the monk. "When I came to the monastery, the steps were the same. Nothing changed."

"A step is missing!" insisted the dancer. "I beg you, give an order to dig up the foundation of the stairs!"

The abbot ordered two workers to start digging. And indeed the step was found. It had been covered over by time.

"I was certain," said the dancer. "When I reached the highest step, I felt that something was missing for perfect harmony. One more step was necessary for perfect harmony between the height of the stairs and the view of the garden."

I stand at the little garden of the monastery. Honganzi, in the center of Kyoto, and the finesse of that dancer disturbs and grieves my heart. If only one could develop such sensitivity as his touch! I look at the little garden: two rough rocks thrown as if by chance and at random, a small artery of running water, two low curved stone bridges, a few dry shrubs give you the impression of an endless desert.

"The great artist Simano-Ske-Asagiri designed it three hundred years ago," points out the fat, shaven monk, guardian of the garden. "Do you understand the meaning of this garden?"

"I understand," I replied, "as much as a thick-skinned Westerner can understand."

The monk laughed, pleased. He began to talk and I listened to him, enchanted:

"Our old artists," he said, "made a garden as we compose a song. A great, difficult, complicated work of art. At the beginning our great gardeners were Buddhist monks who had brought this art from China. Later, the art was passed to the great teachers of the tea ceremony, to the poets and painters, and finally to the specialist gardeners.

"Every garden must have its meaning and project an abstract concept: tranquillity, purity, wilderness, or pride and heroic grandeur. And this concept must correspond not only to the soul of the owner, but also to the soul of his family or his race. What is the value of the individual? It is something ephemeral, while the garden, as every work of art, must have elements of eternity.

"A monk imprinted on a tiny garden the omnipotence of God. How? By placing rocks with profound sensitivity, leaning them here and there, irregularly. This thought was suggested to him by a Buddhist tradition. Monk Daiti once ascended a hill and began to preach the teaching of Buddha, and the stones, as the tradition goes, were gradually covered by yellow moss and bent their peaks as if in worship.

"We have famous gardens made up only of rocks without a single tree or flower. Rocks and dried-out streams, and waterfalls without water, but sand. These rock gardens project grandeur, wilderness, inaccessible deity. And thus, the monk instead of withdrawing to the wilderness, comes to such a garden in the middle of the city and finds there all the desert that his soul needs for its meditation and salvation.

"Other gardens are adorned with trees, waters, and greenery. Those gardens are not for the hermits but for people of the world who enjoy the sweetness of life. But the most famous of all the Japanese gardens are the *chaniwa,* the tea gardens; they lead to a small room which is used for the tea ceremony. The sentiment they want to project is isolation, meditation, deliverance from the roaring of the world. Going to this sacred little house, you feel as if you were far away from the world, at a deserted shore, in an autumn twilight. In order to project the concept of loneliness, they cultivated in these gardens the moss on rocks and around trunks of trees.

"Our greatest artist of tea ceremonies was

Rikyu, in the sixteenth century. He had also been a great artist of the garden. When he was still an apprentice, his teacher ordered him to sweep the garden well so that he could serve tea. Rikyu swept it very carefully and did not leave even a tiny piece of rubbish or dried leaf on the ground; he stood back to admire it, but suddenly he felt something missing. He went to a tree and shook it, and the autumn leaves fell to the ground. Rikyu left them. The teacher came and saw the lane covered with leaves and understood; deeply moved, he put his hand on the head of his student and said to him: 'I am no longer necessary; you are my superior.'"

The monk stopped and hastily went to place a stone that had been moved that day by the crowds of worshipers in its original position. "Did you see?" he asked me, "how unbecoming this stone looked placed that way? It blocked the other two stones in front of it and diminished the view."

"Yes . . ." I murmured, and my heart was sad because I had not understood anything.

The art of the gardener in the Far East is a wonder, indeed a wonder of love and patience. The day before yesterday I had seen a pine tree in the yard of a monastery. The trunk stood erect, but all the branches bent down toward one side of the trunk. And all the foliage looked like the dense, curled, green tail of a peacock.

"How has this pine tree become like that?" I asked with admiration.

"With patience and love," a monk replied to me. "Every morning when its branches were still soft and flexible, we caressed and pressed and bent them to take on the design we wanted."

And today when I listened to the monk talk to me about the gardens, I thought that there was another art of gardening there, equally admirable, a continuation of the original: the making of your tiny heart into a vast garden and giving it the meaning which best becomes you: joy, loneliness, austerity, sensuality, tranquillity, whatever your substance may be.

I said it to the monk, and he shook his head.

"What you say is more difficult. Let's begin

from the outside gardens. They come first; the garden of the heart comes afterward. And then comes the most difficult, the most mystical, the supreme garden which is neither trees nor stones nor ideas."

"Only air?"

"Not even air."

"And what is the garden called?"

"Buddha."

REVIEW QUESTIONS

1. What features of this garden does Kazantzakis find most impressive? Are they physical or spiritual? What evidence supports your opinion?
2. Why do you think Kazantzakis uses a dialogue to describe the garden? How does that format strengthen his observations and opinions? Does it weaken them in any way?
3. Why is the Japanese garden called a work of art?
4. What social or public purposes might Japanese gardens serve? What private or individual ones?
5. What does the story of the "missing step" tell you about the values of Japanese culture? Why do you think Kazantzakis chose to begin his description with this episode?

An American Author Examines the Lives of Geishas in Postwar Japan (1946–1948)

MARGERY FINN BROWN, *Over a Bamboo Fence*

An earlier selection in this reader involved Mary Fraser as a diplomat's wife in Japan; the current selection is that of an American soldier's wife—with her children—during the American occupation just after World War II. The dust jacket for the book of her recollections describes her situation: "Mrs. Brown went to Japan with her four little girls, fourteen bags, eight steamer trunks and 5500 pounds of household belongings because her husband was to be there for two years."

It was a different era, and certainly a different Japan than that visited by Mary Fraser, Nellie Bly, and Lafcadio Hearn (see Chapter 6). Japan had waged and lost a major war; now Americans, the victors, were to "occupy" the country in an attempt to swing the nation from militarism to democracy. It was a difficult task but hugely successful, in part because of an almost mutual attraction between Americans and the Japanese people. Brown was a keen observer, and she made her experiences in Japan into a book (*Over a Bamboo Fence,* 1951). She continued writing, and in 1971 her short story "In the Forests of Riga the Beasts Are Very Wild Indeed" (*McCall's,* July 1970) won the prestigious Edgar Award.

While in Japan, even with a family to take care of, Brown found a job with a Japanese newspaper and came "to know the people of Japan as she would like to know the people at home" (dust jacket). She got to know "countesses and concubines, politicians and farmers, Buddhist priests and soldiers," who responded to her cordially. In her introduction she cautions, "If the reader is looking for a scholarly, comprehensive study of occupied Japan, this is not the place to get it." Nonetheless, her insightful study generates a feeling of sympathy and even empathy seldom achieved by Westerners. Students might well compare her observations with the previous reports in this volume by Westerners in Japan.

What *is* a geisha?

"The personification of the sheer joy of living," Lafcadio Hearn writes; a veritable "maiden of paradise making life much sweeter than it ever could be." Other visitors to the Exotic Orient have compared her to the hetaera of Greece and the temple girls of India. In modern times, she combines some of the features of a crack Powers model, café society chanteuse, front row chorine, and expensive lady of easy virtue. Yet she's none of these for she has no counterpart in any other society.

In the broadest sense of the word, a geisha is a girl who's been trained to dance, sing, wait on table, chatter with men at a party, providing the light, gay atmosphere many Japanese homes seem to lack. Nobody knows when the geisha system first began; perhaps in the old courts of Kyoto and Nara, where love flourished without constancy or sin. Then in the seventeenth century, a great number of earthquakes and fires caused thousands of homeless girls to storm tea houses, looking for jobs as waitresses. Naturally those who were the most attractive got the jobs. To take care of the overflow, *machiai* [waiting houses] began to appear for the first time in large cities.

Agents for these houses scoured the countryside looking for likely girls. Farm areas stricken with drought or famine were an especially fertile field. In 1915, a ten-year-old girl could be bought for fifteen dollars. The system, a form of slavery, had been abolished in 1895, but there were ways to evade the law. One was to have the *machiai* owner adopt the girl into his family; another was to call the fifteen dollars an advance against her future earnings, not a purchase price. After she'd repaid the debt, little Ukey, or

O-Kiku, would be as free as a bird. Actually it worked out quite differently. The cost of her wardrobe, her training and lodgings were chalked against her. She aged fast. At thirty she was passé. The only way for Ukey to terminate her contract was to be bought out by a wealthy protector [Danna-san]. He seldom married her. When his attentions wandered elsewhere he might leave her a little nest egg with which she'd open a house of her own.

The training of a geisha was varied. She learned to play the *samisen,* a stringed instrument that produces a nasal whimpering twang; to convey emotion in the dance with a twist of a kimono sleeve; to tie the intricate knots of the *obi;* to sing in a hoarse falsetto. She learned to walk with the knock-kneed, pigeon-toed glide without which a kimono gaps in ugly fashion. (This was accomplished, I was told, by making her walk with a calling card gripped between her knees.)

She also learned the more intimate arts of pleasing men. Although she was *not* a prostitute, she was naturally of more value to the house if her morals weren't too rigorous. (The same informant said that instructions in this matter were imperative because unmarried Japanese men are apt to be pretty ignorant. Although they know all about the birds, bees and flowers from the time they're children, they rarely receive practical sex information from either parent.)

At the age of fourteen or fifteen, the *maiko,* or fledging geisha, made her initial appearance. She gave every indication of being a lady but was never mistaken for one. From that time on, she cast a glittering shadow on Japanese society of the middle and upper class. No banquet of any size or dedication of a temple was considered complete without her. Japanese writers and artists extolled her grace and charms. (Oddly enough, the system was never strong in rural Japan: the poverty that caused a farmer to sell his daughter also prevented him from enjoying the luxuries of a geisha house.)

When the present Emperor excluded geishas from attending his coronation ceremony, *machiai* suffered. It was considered daring for a wealthy man to take his office secretary to the movies, a much less expensive and infinitely more novel evening. But the novelty soon wore off and the geisha business boomed again, despite the government's "austerity" drive during the war with China.

In 1940 the whole system was outlawed once more. (The price then was forty dollars for a ten-year-old girl.) *Machiai* owners were ordered to close and geishas couldn't be held for debt by law. But the system still continues in connivance with wealthy Japanese men, corrupt officials and curious Occupation personnel.

It takes a lot of money to give a geisha party today. Food for a party of five cost upwards of two hundred dollars. Another hundred to bribe the police and pay the kitchen help; fifty dollars for the *machiai* owner to find a well-secluded spot. You need two geisha, and a third to play the *samisen;* the price varies from six to fifteen dollars an hour, per geisha.

The geisha gets less than half of the thirty to seventy-five dollars she earns a night; the house owner gets the rest. Out of her share, she's expected to buy her own kimono (priced from $300 to $750), her brocade sashes and countless pairs of white foot socks. She pays for her lodging, food, and hairdresser bills which may run up into quite a sum. (It's necessary to have her hair set three times a week; between visits, she sleeps with her neck on a porcelain block to keep her coiffure intact.)

Living these days is hard for geishas. Patrons are scarce. Few Japanese can afford expensive geisha parties, and the great influx of Americans has presented another problem. Somehow they seem to have received the wrong impression of a geisha's moral standards. The U.S. health authorities ordered all geisha in Tokyo to have a monthly physical examination. The Saké and Samisen Circle was up in arms.

Mama Furashahi, oldest geisha in town, told reporters the order was an insult. "We take great pride in our profession. We're not prostitutes. We shouldn't be treated as such. Some of us may have lovers but I say that's true of women all over the world. We geisha in Tokyo will defend to our last breath"—here the type setter went amok—"the right to liye."

The right of a geisha "to liye" drives Japanese men to heights of impassioned oratory. "Pure as the first snow of winter!" . . . "The epitome of chaste refinement!" But a friend of mine, a middle-aged man whose judgment I valued, said it was all a tempest in a teapot. He'd been to a hundred or more geisha parties in his life, and always one or more of the male guests spent the night. For a fat fee, of course.

Old-style geisha were almost obsolete now, he said wistfully. They were dignified, beautiful creatures moving noiselessly as they brought course after course. They were clever conversationalists, witty, better informed than any other class of Japanese women. *Giri* [duty] obliged them to be faithful to one—only one patron.

Today's geisha were pretty gross. "Danjuro-dolls," he called them (referring to a weighted doll named for the actor Danjuro). Pushovers! Very common in Tokyo. *Giri* meant nothing to them. Three or four patrons at a time! They "yappity-yap-yap-ed all night long, drank from the guests' cups, danced like oxen and wore wigs."

But here in Kyoto—he was a Kyoto man himself—the Gion geisha were better dressed, incomparably more fastidious. For further proof, he escorted me to the Gion—a section of narrow streets with signs ordering Allied personnel to keep out. Close by is the temple consecrated to Susanoo, the "Impetuous Male" of Japanese mythology who annoyed the Sun Goddess with his mischievous tricks so much that she retired to a cave, and had to be enticed forth with bawdy dances and songs.

The Gion, itself, is thoroughly respectable in appearance. In the late afternoon light, the modest little houses looked very somber. Every now and then, a geisha passed by dressed for an evening's party. The men moved quietly as if they were on their way to the office. Only the sound of a *samisen* behind shuttered windows suggested that this was the gay quarter of Kyoto.

Waiting for us at one of the *machiai* was the owner, a pleasant-looking man; two geisha, Little Hanging Sleeves and Honorable Essence of the Bamboo; and Hisa-san, a retired geisha in her fifties, a plump knowing woman with a bun of dyed black hair worn flat on the top of her head.

In a deep grating voice—the result of years of singing—she said she was happy to meet an American woman. To the best of her knowledge I was the first to visit the Gion quarter. Was I not afraid of the Military Police?

I showed her the pass I had obtained—a very official-looking document which seemed to amuse her as much as it had me.

Hisa-san was the recently elected president of the *San-ko-kai,* the first labor union of its kind in Japan. She said the aim of the union was, first of all, "polite, virtuous and feminine" conduct; free medical care for the geisha, prostitutes and taxi dancers that belonged to the union; and better treatment from capitalists (this with a withering glance at the house owner).

Little Hanging Sleeves and Honorable Essence of the Bamboo said they were proud to be second generation Gion geisha, and charter members of the *San-ko-kai.* Their mothers had come from Nigata prefecture where the women were greatly admired for their light skins and slender bodies. They thought the life of a geisha was greatly to be preferred to the drudgery of a farm. The exercise of the dance, however, was most arduous.

I asked how many hours a week they practiced.

Sometimes as much as twelve hours a week, the house owner answered. An intense twelve hours! They went to work right after they rose in the morning. After dancing school and lunch, they had a long bath and visited the hairdressers. By six o'clock they were dressed, ready to go to the dinner appointments he had previously arranged. Little Hanging Sleeves and Honorable Essence of the Bamboo were two of the most sought-after geisha in town. They were dated up weeks in advance.

I asked the two girls if they would like their own daughters to be geisha.

Without getting a cue from the house owner, they said no. Emphatically no. The future was grim. The only people with enough money these days were new-yen rich, Koreans, and foreigners who didn't have much appreciation for the intricacies of the dance. In addition, a new type of Japanese girl was being extolled—an unfeminine, selfish breed that was the very antithesis of a geisha.

Women could vote and still be feminine, Hisa-san conceded dubiously, but manners were becoming too informal between the sexes. This very morning she'd seen a small boy carrying a girl's books home from school. And she was shocked to read in the paper about the teen-age girls who'd been caught visiting a tea house with a pair of boys.

"They said they only wanted to talk and have a cup of tea. But it's not *shukan,*" she said. "Japanese girls aren't prepared for this type of freedom. Japanese men, although they say they don't approve, will surely take advantage of the new trend. Trouble is bound to follow," she said lifting her eyebrows in a world-weary manner. "This has always been a man's world."

REVIEW QUESTIONS

1. Compare Margery Finn Brown's remarks on geishas to those of Nellie Bly (see the Chapter 6 on East and Southeast Asia, 1800–1918). Having done so, what conclusions do you reach about geishas?
2. To what extent did Brown approve of geishas? Why? To what extent did she disapprove of them? Why?
3. How did modernization after World War II influence the lives of Japanese women?

A Vietnamese Antiwar Activist Returns to Ho Chi Minh City (c. 1975)

NGUYEN LONG, *After Saigon Fell: Daily Life Under the Vietnamese Communists*

During the nineteenth and twentieth centuries, Vietnam's long occupation by French and United States military forces resulted in changes to political and social conditions within Vietnam that are complex and therefore difficult to understand. The following account of Nguyen Long helps to explain the differences between political ideologies and nationalist sentiments. It also conveys the horror that non-Communist nationalists, like Long, endured when the victorious northern forces united the country.

Educated in the United States, Long returned to his homeland and became a strong Buddhist activist supporting the antiwar movement. He knew some Viet Cong adherents but found there was no room within the Communist order for someone with his Western training and international perspective. As did many Vietnamese after the war—both those who supported the Communist government and those who did not—Long learned that vast chasms existed between the ideology and the practice of communism. Corruption on a massive scale revealed faults similar to those of the regime of Nho Dinh Diem during the early 1960s.

In mid-1976 a young Northern soldier came to my house in the conduct of a military census. He entered the front door without knocking, went through the living room and into the dining room. My nine-year-old daughter, playing at the foot of the stairs, called out that someone was there. As I went down the stairs, I saw him already sitting at the dining table as casually as though he were in his own home. I was startled, but this young man's conduct brought me face to face with habits that have developed from many years of life under a collectivist regime, which condemns individualism and cares nothing for privacy. A short digression on privacy may be permitted here. In North Vietnam, to overcome serious housing shortages (and to put collectivism into practice) the regime forced several families to live in the same house, sharing a common entrance, the same kitchen, bath, and other facilities. In such a situation entering a house without knocking could not be viewed as a violation of privacy. The Communist cadres

liked to brag that people in the North did not use locks because there were no thieves in a socialist nation. They always cited Russia as an example, saying the Russians never needed to lock their homes. Communist soldiers considered themselves the "people's children," and maintained that children entering their parents' home did not have to knock at the door.

My wife's Northern relatives came visiting from time to time. Instead of waiting for me in the living room, they would go to my bedroom, which I also used as my office, and there they would sit on my bed or a chair by my desk and make conversation. If invited to go to the living room, they would usually say, "Oh, this is quite all right here."

A knock at the door is a forewarning to the householder that an outsider wants to enter, but Communist security cadres, charged with keeping watch over the people's daily activities and attitudes, wish to avoid such forewarnings. Forcing people to live collectively, in effect, uses them to control each other, particularly under conditions of scarcity. If one person is fortunate enough to obtain a bit of good food such as chicken or pork, he has to eat it furtively. If caught, secret agents would question him as where he got it and cause no end of trouble. Southerners, once used to privacy and abundance, have lost both. Most had had no new clothing since the Communists took over. Now, they were learning how to prolong the life of their worn clothing and eat occasional bits of good food on the sly.

Under the Communist regime violations of privacy extend even to love relations and marriage. During a session of the so-called Political Study Seminar for university professors held in Saigon in late 1975, a "university education cadre" from the North spoke with pride about an instance in which a Party member had been forbidden to fall in love with a land-owner's daughter because such a relationship would violate the concept of class struggle. My arguments that the girl had not chosen to be born into the "exploiting class" and that the young man by marrying her would set an example against "class discrimination" were lost on this "education cadre."

After the military-census interrogator had made himself at home in my dining room, he asked questions concerning my personal life but was particularly interested in my education and why I did not serve as an officer in the "false armed forces" (Army of the Republic of Viet Nam).

The fact that I had studied in the United States was generally known in the ward, if not to this young Northern soldier, therefore I did not invite trouble by trying to hide it. Yet he looked at me with surprise when I informed him I had received a Ph.D. from the University of California in Berkeley, and his surprise grew when I added that it was in political science. He found it difficult to believe that a Vietnamese could obtain such a degree from a university of the "leading imperialist country." The soldier's surprise was evidence of the Northern Communists' initial belief that there were few univer-

sity graduates in South Vietnam. When, after several education censuses, they found the opposite to be true, they realized that their own society was inferior to the South in one of the three key elements of a socialist society, i.e., "socialist intellectuals," the other two being workers and peasants. To remedy that situation they conferred bachelor's degrees on a large number of engineering, educational, medical, and other cadres who had only completed high school and many who had not even achieved this level of education. Some in more responsible positions were given the title "deputy Ph.D." Thus, they hoped to show that the socialist North was superior and, at the same time, make the task of the Northern cadres in the South easier. Even so, few cadres with "deputy" degrees dared presume to possess an honest Ph.D. I talked with a number of these socialist intellectuals and found their level of competence in their particular fields inferior, and limited only to Communist experience. Still, one of my wife's Northern cousins, a high-school graduate with an instant "bachelor's" degree is now a professor at Hue University in Central Vietnam.

"Why," my interviewer asked, "with your education, did you not render your services as an officer in the 'false armed forces'?"

I replied that I was an educator; that I was given nine weeks' military training and allowed to return to my university to teach; that I had no further relations to the South Vietnamese Army. In fact, however, following my nine weeks' military training, I was still counted on the list as the Republic's effective strength. When the Republic's armed forces were disbanded after the "revolution" I tore up my military ID card. But this I kept to myself.

After this investigation I was no longer under any military obligation, except the general provision that tacitly assigned all men ages 18 to 45 and all women 18 to 35 to the combat forces of the Communist Defense Ministry. All others were declared to be in the reserve and supply forces, including old men who were designated "white-haired soldiers." . . .

SON

My next-door neighbors in Saigon from April 1975 until late 1978 were four students of Ho Chi Minh City University (formerly Saigon University). One was the house owner's nephew who later married a girl named Mai; the other three were sons of a South Vietnamese National Liberation Front (NLF) official, who did not live at the house. The following account concerns 21-year-old Son (pronounced Saun), one of the brothers, who had difficulty with his university education and frequently wandered around the streets or visited friends instead of attending classes.

Education declined rapidly after the Communist takeover of South Vietnam. Adults and children worried much more about how to obtain enough food and clothing than about learning. Son, plagued with mundane problems, sold small items from his house to neighbors, including me, for daily expenses. He even sold imitation gold.

With the establishment of socialism in South Vietnam, robbery, petty thievery, and fraud spread rapidly through the Saigon-Cholon-Giadinh metropolitan district. Bicycles, clothing, household utensils, motorcycles, repair tools, and similar items of daily use were stolen and peddled on the streets. My double-lock motorcycle was stolen on Tran Hung Dao Avenue while I was in a bookstore for two minutes. In my cluster, several persons were arrested while stealing bicycles. A domestic woman helper who had lived with my family for ten years until 1976 walked off with my wife's jewelry, clothes, and sundry household articles. Our cluster chief came to me for help in establishing a burglar-alarm system, consisting of hand-sounded bells, connected from his house at the end of the cul de sac to mine at the beginning. In each cluster and ward residents were compelled to take turns standing watch, particularly during the Tet lunar new year festival or whenever disturbances threatened because of political maneuvers by ward or district Party committees.

But while we were continually troubled with robberies, Northern cadres assigned to work in the South maintained such crimes were nonexistent in the socialist North. Robbery, prostitution, and suicide, they said, were the natural, unavoidable remnants of the Southern capitalist regime, which must be endured during the transition to socialism.

One night in 1977 a burglar entered the house of a tailor who lived next to me. The owner discovered the intruder and cried out. Security cadres, self-defense youths, ward-squad soldiers, and neighbors came out in an effort to apprehend the man. Armed security personnel leaped from roof to roof looking for him, while their comrades searched the alley. But the culprit disappeared.

Three nights later, at 3 A.M., the robber paid a second visit to the tailor's house and was again discovered. Once more the tailor cried out and once more security guards, waving their guns, raced to the rooftops to catch the villain while cluster inhabitants armed with sticks encircled the area. Again the intruder disappeared.

The security office, bewildered and angry at being shown incapable of maintaining security and having their no-crime-under-socialism propaganda exposed, initiated an extensive secret investigation. They theorized that because the thief disappeared so quickly he must live in one of the houses of our cluster.

A month after the burglary, an area security cadre came to my house and asked whether I was suspicious of Son, since I, too, had been robbed once. I replied that I had been robbed by my domestic helper, and suspected neither Son nor anyone else. The cadre asked me to show him the flat roof of my house. There, after an inspection of the walls of the duplex, he found a small window high on the back wall of Son's house. The cadre thought he had found the answer, but I conjectured that if the thief had gone through that high small window he would have to leave marks on the white-washed wall. There was no trace of dirt or footprints.

The security office, however, conducted several interrogations of Son, his brothers, and the house owner's nephew; but no one in my cluster learned the results. A short time later, Son went to work for the security office as a secret reporter.

It was apparent to me that Son's new assignment was involuntary. Even if he was not guilty of the burglaries—and I am convinced of his innocence—the security cadres had found some other charges which forced him into their service: not attending school, selling household items in the open market, selling imitation gold, and not working at any institution. These alone were sufficient reasons to send Son to a labor camp.

In late 1978 while I was preparing my third escape attempt I became aware that local security cadres were watching my daily activities, but I did not know to what extent. About this time I had started transferring daily-use items from my house to the houses of my father-in-law, cousins, and friends. These items were to be sold later to finance a fourth or even a fifth attempt, if the third or fourth were unsuccessful. These secondary plans were essential because of the high potential for failure of my primary plans. Departure times were never known in advance. Escape planners had to be ready to leave at a moment's notice. Some were alerted by their helpers that the moment was propitious, just as they sat down to dinner; they left their food on the table, locked the doors, and hurried to their appointed place. If the trip was canceled for one reason or another and the security cadres learned about it in time, they would expropriate and seal up the houses leaving the frustrated escapees homeless. Hence, dispersing one's possessions in advance of departure was a necessary insurance.

I had made every effort to conceal my intentions by moving items out one by one early in the morning or at evening meal times, but I did not know whether this activity had been reported to the security office. Early one morning, I had in fact seen Son watching me as I left home with some household goods. Even though I greeted him with a cheery good morning he avoided eye contact and did not respond. At the moment I attributed this to his usually sullen nature and thought no more of it.

One melancholy evening—there were many of those in Ho Chi Minh City—I went to the flat roof top to watch the sunset which is still beautiful in Vietnam despite socialism. There I encountered Mai, the young wife of the house owner's nephew. These two young people, now married a year, had a new-born child, and my wife had given them children's clothing which we no longer needed. Speaking softly, Mai informed me that the area security cadre that morning had asked her, "When will Mr. Long take to the sea?"

I pretended to be amused at Mai's news. "I don't even have enough money to buy food for my family," I said. "How could I ever get together sufficient taels of gold to pay for a sea trip? If I had that much money I would stay home and enjoy a happy life in Vietnam rather than risking my life on such a foolish enterprise."

In numerous public meetings everyone had heard the security cadres recite the dreadful tales, real and imaginary, about refugees who had died of starvation and thirst at sea, about those who had been raped and killed by Thai pirates, of those who had drowned, or of those who had been seized trying to escape and lost all their property. But, in addition, we had also heard factual accounts by listening clandestinely to the Voice of America and the British Broadcasting Corporation. We were well aware of the dangers and the risks.

After Mai's disclosure, I ceased moving objects out of my house and reduced contacts with my friends, especially at my house. I also passed out hints destined for the security cadres' ears that I had sold my housewares on the open market.

The security web, operating through the people's intelligence system, had caught Son in its net and had very nearly caught me too. It became obvious that Vietnam could never be freed from Communist slavery so long as this fear-based security system continued to operate.

REVIEW QUESTIONS

1. What aspects of the new social order did Long find most insulting? Which did he accept because of necessity?

2. What strategy for controlling society did the Communist government use most effectively? Which did Long find most intrusive?
3. What would have bothered you most about the situation of Long's life, as described here? Explain.

An American Anthropologist Observes the Life of a Thai Sex Worker (1988–1990)

CLEO ODZER, *Patpong Sisters: An American Woman's View of the Bangkok Sex World*

Raised in New York City, Cleo Odzer experienced the "hippie" days in Goa (India) in the late seventies, then returned to New York, where she obtained a Ph.D. in anthropology. Her dissertation was based on three years of observations in the red-light culture of Bangkok, and it resulted in the book from which the following selection is taken (*Patpong Sisters*). Her concerns included not only the women working in the Patpong district, but also the low status in which Thai women in general are held and the government's—and society's—hypocrisy in regard to the sex industry, which is a significant tourist attraction.

Many of these women—often merely young girls—are from the poorer rural areas, such as Isan in the northeast, and are the financial support for their families back home. Isan has an ancient culture but is incapable of producing subsistence agriculture. Its people are proud, but they have the lowest per capita income in Thailand. An authority on Isan, Ron Myers of San Diego State University, has described them as "a forgotten people inhabiting a forgotten land." Odzer became friends with Hoi, a Patpong entertainer, and traveled with her to her village in Isan for a visit. It was an amazing friendship between two remarkable women.

One evening a few days later, Hoi and I boarded the train for the nine-and-a-half-hour ride to Ubon in the Northeast.

I felt exhilarated to be venturing into Isan, the home of many Patpong people. Patpong, Pattaya, and other tourist areas liked to hire Isan women because of their dark skin, which Thais believed *farang* men preferred. Thai and Chinese brothels mostly hired girls from the North, where skin color was lightest. To Thai and Chinese, the lighter the better. This was also true for the brothels and massage parlors of Southern Thailand, where big business came from across the Malaysian border. Outside *farang* areas, Isan women did not make as good a living from prostitution.

Hoi and I had a couple of hours to wait before the porter would make our beds, giving us a chunk of time to get acquainted. After leaving Bangkok, the blackness of country night sealed us intimately into the soothing rumble and clack of the wheels. I wasn't sure how much Alex had told Hoi about my research. She knew I was interested in Patpong, but I didn't know if she knew I was interested in her. In any case, I didn't feel comfortable taking notes. I wanted to be with her as a friend. If I grabbed a pen every time she confided something, she might be put off.

"So your family lives in Ubon?" I asked her as I rested my feet on her seat, facing me. She already had her feet on my seat.

"Father mother come from Khon Kaen but move to Ubon to find work when mother pregnant with me. When I baby, mother die. She step on land mine. Before this my family rich, but then father drink. We sell everything."

"A land mine! That must have been during the Vietnam War, right? You're nineteen, so that was 1969?" I said before realizing that mentioning the war might put me, an American, in an unfavorable light to Thai people, especially to one whose mother had died in a related incident. I changed the subject. "How many brothers and sisters do you have?"

"Sister sixteen year older than me. When I twelve, father bring us to Bangkok. Father work build house. I work shoe factory. From sixteen to seventeen year old, I have boyfriend. Thai boy. Then I find out he see other girl. Thai man no good. Too butterfly. I very angry. I go work Patpong. Now father no work. He wait I give money to him. I work Patpong two and a half year."

"Is Rififi a good bar?" I asked. She nodded. "Then why did you switch to the Zoo?"

"One time I stay with boyfriend. No work. If I go back Rififi, I must pay bar for time away. So cannot go back. But I telephone every week, speak to my friend."

"I don't know the Zoo. Is that on the ground floor with girls dancing in bikinis?"

"Yes, but I no wear bikini. No dance. I wear dress. Very sexy."

"Did you make good money on Patpong?"

"Salary 3,000 *baht*. I make all together 15,000 *baht* one month."

Six hundred dollars. I'd read that the earnings from Patpong could equal the salary of a high Thai government official. "How much did you make the first time you went with a man?"

"First time, I get 1,500 *baht*. I go with man from all country. I meet whole world. One man pay apartment for me, 7,000 *baht* one month."

"What do you think of Patpong men?"

"They like money too much," she answered. "I had boyfriend, disk jockey from Rififi. Very

handsome. Long hair. He always want money from me. I have to finish with him."

"I thought in Thailand the man always paid for the woman."

"He want I give him money, then when we go out, he pay."

"What do you wish for your future?"

"My dream is to buy house in Ubon." She leaned over and took hold of my hair, then felt her hair. "Not same," she said. "Your white skin beautiful. Before, I cry because have black skin. Ugly." Hoi was, in fact, a light sun-tanned shade, but to color-conscious Thais—many of whose city people were part Chinese—she was considered black.

Around 10 p.m., the conductor fixed our beds and I retreated behind the curtain to write. Since Hoi wasn't a go-go girl, she was in a class different from Pong, Nok, or Dang. A hierarchy of jobs existed on Patpong. Working in a blow job bar, like Dang, or performing in Fucking Shows was at the bottom. Next came dancing nude and performing trick shows in ripoff bars, like Pong; then dancing nude and trick shows in nonripoff bars, like Nok. Bikini dancing in ground-floor establishments was high status, but working in evening clothes without having to dance, like Hoi, was higher. A distinction existed, however, between pretty women in dresses, who were bought out often, and less ravishing, perhaps fat, older women who served as hostesses only. Hostess-only types were pitied. Attractiveness and sex appeal were major elements of Patpong prestige. Being bought by young handsome men counted more than pudgy older ones. At the top of the status hierarchy were the beauties who didn't work for a bar at all but came and went on their own time. Some of the larger establishments allowed these women to mix with their clientele. If a girl found a customer there, the man paid the bar to buy her out. If she didn't find a customer, she paid the bar herself for the privilege of sitting in it. The high cost for these girls, 2,000 *baht* a night minimum (a month's salary for an office worker), insured against the occasional loss.

Loud voices disturbed my concentration. Peeping from the curtain, I spied Hoi laughing with the porters. Now that the passengers had settled in their bunks, the train crew was eating dinner. Hoi too had ordered a meal. The men seemed enthralled by Hoi's outgoingness. From the lessons at A.U.A., I knew that mingling with strange men was considered improper behavior for young Thai women. Nonprostitute Thai women had little personal freedom.

One of my Thai teachers—a twenty-two-year-old woman from a middle-class Bangkok family—had told me she couldn't ride the train to visit friends or relatives unless someone accompanied her. I remembered the passion in her voice as she recounted how she hated the bar girls who lived in her apartment building because she was jealous of seeing them do nothing all day. To the teacher who left daily to work, the prostitutes lived a life of leisure. She also related, in sad confusion, how men preferred those types of women to her. If she and a prostitute walked down the street together, no man would look at her. She noted that many of her handsome *farang* students were in love with bar girls and none had ever shown an interest in her. While her brother went out nights with his friends, she rarely went anywhere. Off work, she spent her time caring for her younger siblings. She feared her family would arrange a marriage for her with the neighbor's son, an unpleasant man destined to take over his father's dry cleaning store. When the teacher spoke of the despised bar girls, she seemed full of resentment for the things she couldn't have, such as freedom of movement, boyfriends, and spontaneity.

I fell asleep to the lively murmur around Hoi and her occasional bursts of laughter. . . .

Hoi's village was actually two hours east of Ubon, only a few miles from the Laotian border. We arrived in Ubon early in the morning and boarded a *song-tow,* a truck with two rows of seats, to a smaller town fifty minutes away. From there, we climbed into another crowded *song-tow* for the next fifty-minute ride. Then we walked along a paved, carless road. The splendid road, with its perfectly spaced lines, reflected the government's attempt to incorporate Isan into the growing economy. The absence of four-wheeled vehicles attested to the government's failure.

Swiveling around, looking for faces to greet, Hoi seemed to glow from being in her homeland. People on the side of the road waved. A school friend bicycled by and stopped short when he saw her. They exchanged hellos excitedly. A boy on a motorbike took our bags, and the school friend insisted on lending us his bicycle.

"We ride," Hoi said to me as she leapt aboard and motioned for me to sit on the back wheel frame. She pedalled and I clung, not sure how to hold my legs so that my skirt didn't catch in the wheels.

Thai-style houses were up on stilts and made of wood. Turning off the road, she bumped us down a pebbly path to our destination, a run-down old house whose thatched roof had bald spots. The motorcycle putt-putted there, waiting for us to collect our gear. A rickety ladder with wide-spaced, irregular rungs led to a porch that surrounded three sides of the house. Following Thai custom, we took off our shoes. . . .

"Is this your house?" I asked Hoi . . .

"No have house. Belong to woman who sell balloon in city."

Before I could orient myself about whose house we were in and why, a mob descended on us. News of our arrival had circulated. Four older women and two men arrived first, followed by a horde of children. One dashed up the ladder to relieve me of my luggage, and I clambered to the porch on hands and knees. The wooden slats of the floor sagged and wobbled. A woman covered a corner area with tattered straw mats. . . .

We sat around all day, Hoi receiving visitors like a queen. She ate an enormous amount of food. Meals appeared frequently at her command.

"Chicken, you want chicken?" she would ask me, or "Egg, you want egg?" I knew chicken and eggs and the other dishes Hoi ordered were rare feasts for the people of Isan. Bangkokians smirked over what Isan considered edible: beetles, lizards, and assorted worms.

Hoi handed out money and sent people running repeatedly to the store for food. She'd dispatch someone to cook a huge amount of it. When it came, she'd put some on a plate for me. Country Thais usually ate from a communal dish, but Hoi knew about *farang* customs. Only Hoi and I, plus one or two of the nearest children, would eat first.

"*Arroy* (delicious)," Hoi would declare to the others who watched every biteful as it entered her mouth. Finished, she'd regally hand out the remainder to the entourage.

Throughout the afternoon, Hoi acted like a superstar with the neighbors at her service. Everyone ran to fetch things for her, especially her niece Ah. The villagers spoke to each other in Lao, occasionally addressing me in Thai. Mostly they ignored me in their fascination with Hoi. One woman pulled a piece of straw from the roof and used it to clean her ears. I wondered how long a roof lasted if people pulled at it whenever they needed a utensil.

Hoi pointed to the group of scruffy people and said in English, "Before, I look like that too." She wrinkled her nose. She did look different, sophisticated, "mannered," more self-confident, cleaner and neater.

"What do they think of Patpong?" I asked.

"They don't like. They don't like me because I work there."

I hadn't seen evidence of the villagers' disapproval. On the contrary, they seemed to idolize her. . . .

That night, Hoi's father arrived with a group of men, including the village headman, a sturdy man with big lips and wide ears. . . .

From the thatched roof, a neighbor hung one lightbulb that was connected to an extension cord brought over from the house next door. Hoi bought liquor for everyone. Her father sat next to her and looked at his beautiful daughter with pride in his eyes. Hoi told me, "You see father's gold watch? Is present from Alex." Hoi doted on her father and made sure he had a fresh bottle of beer whenever he finished one off. He, in turn, acted as host, making sure everyone else had a drink and a cigarette and whatever other goodies his daughter bought. I couldn't understand what the headman's wife said, but the haughty looks she threw me weren't friendly. She was courteous to Hoi, though.

Hoi called my attention to five young men and said, "They no can have girlfriend because all village girl are in Patpong." . . .

Everyone drank until inebriated. Food came again, this time as a formal meal of chicken and soup. . . .

They went through eighteen bottles of beer and five bottles of *Lao Kaow*. Hoi bought marijuana, and they all had a smoke. Fumes of alcohol breath, mosquito repellent, and stinky mats with ground-in food set my nerves on edge. Where was the fresh country air I was supposed to breathe here? I couldn't inhale deeply because I wanted to avoid the marijuana cloud hovering over my head. I hadn't done that since my old hippy days. The uncontrolled hilarity of the drunken mob spooked me. . . . Fortunately, when I told Hoi I felt tired, she shooed away the crowd. Slowly they tramped off, bashing into bushes and singing.

The thump and stomp of people moving about woke me at dawn. Hoi had dressed in a sexy negligee the night before, and she kept it on all morning while receiving guests. All of yesterday's people returned, and new ones came. At one point Hoi learned to drive using someone's motorbike; the nightie flapped in the breeze behind her. A knot of neighbors gathered to watch her progress. They seemed fascinated, though they must have seen bike drivers every day. . . .

The next morning, Hoi was the last to awaken. She, her father, and I were supposed to visit his family in Khon Kaen, two hours by train from Ubon. He wanted us to stay overnight, but we were due to return that evening to Bangkok.

When her father was ready to go, I had to hunt for Hoi. I found her at the house next door, talking to a man. They sat close on a log, and Hoi didn't seem happy to see me approach.

In mock surprise, she said, "You don't really want to go to Khon Kaen, do you?" Obviously she no longer wanted to.

"Yes, I do. So does your father."

With frown lines in Hoi's forehead, we left. Nobody said goodbye or thanked us for anything. Goodbyes and thank-yous weren't Isan customs.

During the ride to Ubon, Hoi told me about the man next door. "He very rich. He like me too much. Can you see? He have big car. He make good money. Do you think he handsome?"

Opposite us in the *song-tow,* a well-dressed Thai woman conversed with Hoi's father.

"She teacher," Hoi's father informed us. Teachers were highly honored in Thailand. The job, though, was mostly restricted to the elite who had the money and influence necessary for education. In Thailand, jobs were not acquired so much by capability as by connections. For this reason, it was almost impossible for poor people to move across class lines.

Hoi put her hands together and *wai*ed the woman respectfully.

The woman asked Hoi, "Do you live in Pattaya?" which meant she assumed Hoi worked as a prostitute. Hoi didn't answer, only shook her head with a defensive hunch to her shoulders.

Even without their fashionable clothes and healthy bodies, Thai prostitutes could be immediately recognized. Long after a woman stopped working in a bar, she was labelled a bar girl, almost on sight. Having often jumped to this conclusion myself, I tried to isolate the characteristics that were so identifiable. It seemed to involve the way they interacted with others—more forthright and confident, more demanding and outgoing. Thai culture viewed these as marks of dishonor for a woman, symptoms of prostitution. A proper woman was supposed to be shy and reserved, nonassertive and pliant.

Halfway to Ubon, as we changed *song-tows,* Hoi bought herself balls of meat on a stick and discussed the folly of voyaging to Khon Kaen for only a few hours' stay. Since I knew Hoi's mind was overrun with fantasies of the man next door, her arguments didn't convince me. They convinced her, though, and by the time we arrived in Ubon, she decided not to go to Khon Kaen or even to Bangkok. She announced she was returning to the house. She offered the excuses that she would "help sister sell" and "check out hotel to be tourist guide for Alex," both of which I was positive she had no intention of doing.

Hoi boarded the first *song-tow* back. Without her as a buffer, I didn't want to face the family in Khon Kaen. Her father waited the nine hours with me in Ubon for my train to Bangkok. I bought him a bottle of *Lao Kaow* and took him to a theater, where he slept through four hours of movies, one Thai and one Chinese.

At last on the train, in a bunk with curtain drawn, I savored the feeling of not having a crowd underfoot. Upset at Hoi's abandoning me, I nonetheless relished the freedom to turn off my brain. How wonderful to be alone. Thais didn't understand the luxury of this, probably because they never had the chance to experience it. Growing up in large families, they ate and slept in packs. Their religion, too, fashioned them into teamlike family units. Even after a parent's death, children had to "make merit" in the parent's name. The amount of accumulated merit decided what one's fate would be in the next incarnation. The more children to make merit, the better one's next life. Thais needed large families for economic reasons also. Without Social Security or welfare, old folks depended on relatives to care for them. Children were mandatory for one's old age. They were, in fact, expected to support their parents as soon as they were able. Thai culture decreed that Hoi support her father. That she did it by prostitution was less important than that she did it. It was the same for Jek, who supported his mother by pimping.

REVIEW QUESTIONS

1. Why would a young village girl like Hoi get involved in the Bangkok sex world? How could everyone in her home village behave as though it was not really a big deal?
2. How would you characterize Cleo Odzer's role and attitude toward her subject?
3. What are the two or three most significant cultural differences between the worlds of Hoi and Cleo?

12

South and Southwest Asia, 1918 to the Present

The selections in this chapter are all observations of people, sometimes in groups, sometimes as single individuals, in South and Southwest Asia. While such observations extend across cultures, they reflect an uneasy accommodation to change, in varying degrees. They reveal the impending cessation of Western political power but not a corresponding decrease in Western cultural influence. These nine selections also portray a spectrum of societies that range from quasi-medieval to fully modern.

For one selection, Colette Modiano sat in a café in modern Israel and watched Hassidic men on their way to the Wailing Wall. She describes the appearance of the men and boys of this devout sect, the wall itself, and the spiritual electricity of the event. Elizabeth Warnock Fernea relates her afternoon with the ladies of an Iraqi sheik's harem, almost as if she is attending a midwestern ladies' bridge club. The women are distinct individuals, especially the favorite, Selma. Ella Maillart's observations in rural northwestern Afghanistan seem almost understated, but her experience was clearly uncomfortable.

In India, one of the first of the Western spiritual seekers, Lewis Thompson, found meaning and poetry in travel and people. Mark Tully's experience was even more intense than that of Thompson when he observed the overwhelming press of millions at the world's largest religious festival, the Kumbh Mela. This chapter also includes an essay by one of India's greatest twentieth-century poets, Mahadevi Varma, describing an oppressed woman. Nayantara Sahgal, of the famed Nehru family, describes the wedding of her cousin Indira, the future prime minister of India. In so doing, she illustrates what was almost an amalgamation of Western and traditional culture. In Pakistan, in the former British Raj, Anthony Weller describes a political hot spot on the Grand Trunk Road, Peshawar, that he did not find as hot as he had thought it would be. Finally, Ellura Winters in Chittagong records riotous events resulting from the same sort of tensions as in Weller's Peshawar.

A French Travel Writer Observes Israeli Jews in Jerusalem (1967)

COLETTE MODIANO, *Turkish Coffee and the Fertile Crescent*

Colette Modiano, a French writer who reports her travels with detachment and sensitivity, was fascinated by people and places. In addition to the Middle East and China, she traveled in Japan, Southeast Asia, India, Afghanistan, Kenya, and Mexico. She has written about her travels in China in the sardonic *Chairman Mao and My Millionaires; or, Through China with Twenty Snobs,*

1970. **For a number of years she and a colleague ran a travel service under the auspices of a French art magazine that enabled her to visit these diverse places.**

Modiano's account is important because it was written at a critical time in the history of West Asia. She visited Israel shortly after the end of the Six-Day War, during which the Jewish nation expanded through the acquisition of territory at the expense of its Arab neighbors. She first toured the region in 1967 and returned many times, remaining unbiased: "Seeking whatever truth is hidden among the tangled passions and hatreds, prejudices and traditions, I have stifled my opinions and set aside preconceptions." As a result, "the rewards are always worthwhile, often great."

By four o'clock, the Via Dolorosa was deserted and overlaid with shadows. Women do not sit in cafés, still less alone, and my neighbour's disapproval bordered on contempt. Unbuttoned and collarless, with a filthy black beret and a barbarous beard, he puffed ever more noisily at a hubble-bubble. I was relieved to be rescued by Father D. and Father S., Dominican priests with a sense of humour quite equal to their humanity and culture. One habitually wore an Australian bush-hat and was more pro-Jewish than Ben Gurion. The other was inclined to sympathize with the Arabs. "You and your Jews," he would say affectionately to his friends who would lead his pilgrim-tourists in a fervent "Our Father" at Yad-Vachem, the black marble sanctuary dedicated to Jewish victims of Nazi persecution.

The streets are never quiet for long here, and soon there were Orthodox priests with black beards and tubular head-dresses, American girls with maxi-thighs and mini-skirts, hippies showing their navels or sweating in embroidered goatskin gear, tourists and more tourists, and Israeli soldiers walking with a child or a girl-friend. A young man and two Jewish girls in trousers greeted a young Arab sitting near me.

Suddenly it seemed that the tourists gave way to the Orthodox Jews on their way to the Wailing Wall to offer prayers at the beginning of the Sabbath. They came hurrying in compact groups from Mea-Shearim where they worked and traded in workshops and salesrooms aglitter with seven-branched candelabra, ceremonial skull-caps of embroidered satin, *tallithim* or large white prayer-shawls. They were Hassidim members of the strictest, most devout of Jewish sects. The men wore frock-coats and black hats or, since today was a feast day, frock-coats of brocaded satin, and huge, flat hats of brown fur called *shtremmels*. The men, young or old, had long ringlets one on each side of the face. The younger men had unbuttoned their frock-coats, and the skirts flapped in time with their steps. They looked just like crows with their offspring held by the wingtip, sweet offspring in long shorts and short trousers, all unimpeachably black, with round hats pushed back, framing their fresh, cheery faces. Many were fair, and a few had red hair. One splendid man had a deep russet beard, and with his frock-coat and fur hat one could imagine him to be an Amsterdam diamond-merchant painted by Rembrandt.

An opulent trio in satin frock-coats flapped past me. One looked like Dirk Bogarde, the second like Christ, and the third like Gregory Peck. Alas, they were the exception. Most of them had the wan look of lettuces grown under glass; their eyes were fixed on the distant hills of Judea. They had round shoulders and sagging paunches. They were, no doubt, the pride and joy of their ladies whose heads were shaven as the Law demands but whose faces were sometimes softened by fringes of false hair just visible under their turban. They were not much to look at though one was about twenty, with a jade-green suit the colour of her eyes, and a skirt showing a daring glimpse of knee. Her pudding-face of a husband looked sulky and put-out.

I joined the current sweeping towards the Wall. The street sloped gently up-hill, shrinking in the shade of the high arched walls, past a delightful stone fountain. There was a smell of urine and refuse. Lively, grinning Arab children skipped and shouted, "Wailing Wall! Wailing Wall!" The crowd veered left, up a dozen steps into a dark alley like the tube at rush hour. I could see only the broad black back of the Hassid ahead. The pressure eased, and we were in a vast square where a Jewish soldier searched my handbag. A grenade had exploded the week before, wounding eight people. At the far side of the square stood the Wailing Wall of tall stones, all that remained of the temple Herod built on the ruins of Solomon's temple.

A chain hangs between two slender iron pillars, and only the men are allowed through, one by one. Their heads covered with small black caps, they take prayer books and, facing the Wall, they intone their prayers, punctuating them with shuffling. It was like a sea moving in rhythm with the chant, swelling and behind them others came and went: fathers with their small sons, overawed tourists, soldiers, civilians, local residents, visitors from abroad, each here in devotion, but devotion nothing like that of conventional church attendances. Here was an electric, emotional excitement. The Jews had only had access to the Wall since the Six-Day War. Before that it was just one side of a narrow street which the Jordanians used as a rubbish-dump. Now, the Jews had razed the hideous slum behind the narrow street and opened up this uncluttered approach to the Wall, where it stands out clearly as a monument restored to the full dignity of a sanctuary.

Edging my way along the chain between the spectators and worshippers, I reached the third of the Wall reserved for women. The shorn, turbaned ladies were performing the same shuffle as they prayed, but their movements were more restrained. I stepped forward, declining one of the Hebrew prayer books, but obeying a firm finger pointing at the collection box. I earned a smile.

Now I was able to see the Wall at close range. I am not a particularly reverent person by nature, but it stirred me. Its rich golden stones are covered with little holes, like old skin long-exposed to the sun; small rolls of paper are tucked in the crevices, and they spell out countless prayers and petitions. I touched the old thing; it was cool and smooth.

A few yards farther on, a barrier seals off the dig which was begun to uncover the foundations of Solomon's earlier temple. The success of the enterprise was assured, and two stones from the great temple were already lying in the earth far below.

It is possible to love Jerusalem like a person, delicately and excitedly, passionately. One is then spellbound, touched, fatigued, thrilled, tired, beguiled, offended, and love is willingly given. It is love with its drawbacks; its impulses, its anxious hearts and its extended hands.

REVIEW QUESTIONS

1. How does Modiano respond to and describe the women she sees in Jerusalem?
2. Is Modiano as unbiased as she thinks she is? What evidence supports your opinion?
3. Do you find it strange that one Dominican would be partial to the Israelis, and the other to the Arabs? Why or why not?
4. How would you compare the religious lives of men and women in Israel?
5. What feature of Modiano's description of the men on their way to the Wailing Wall strikes you as most important?

An American Educator Visits an Iraqi Harem (1956)

ELIZABETH WARNOCK FERNEA, *Guests of the Sheik*

On a rainy January night in 1956 a young American bride joined her husband at an Iraqi village, where he was doing research in social anthropology for his doctorate. They were to remain there for two years. One of her first experiences was accepting an invitation to visit the wives of the local sheik.

This was only the beginning of the Middle East adventures of Elizabeth Warnock Fernea. She also lived in Cairo (while her husband taught at the American University) from 1959 to 1965, where two of her three children were born. She has written of her experiences, most notably in *Guests of the Sheik* (which has been republished twice), from which this selection is taken, and, with her husband, in *The Arab World: Forty Years of Change* (also updated and republished). She recently retired from teaching on the Middle East, particularly on Middle Eastern women. *Al-Ahram Weekly On-line* (29 March–4 April 2001) observed in an interview with her that "the outcome of her observation was never judgmental."

Fernea's interests and expertise have resulted in several film documentaries for European and American audiences, including one for PBS.

Ali led me all the way around the fortress to a narrow opening and motioned me through. I was standing alone in a large open courtyard, the hard-packed earth of which had been carefully swept just that morning, for I could see the marks of the broom in wide swathing arcs on the ground. The only visible object was a central water tap with a small brick wall around its base. To my right, to my left, and in front of me stood low, square houses built out into the courtyard from the shelter of the compound's high mud-brick walls. These, I was to discover later, were the apartments where each of the sheik's wives lived separately with her children. Through the entry-ways of these flat-roofed apartments, arched and plastered with mud, I could see daylight in other, small inner courts.

Where was everyone? The entire compound seemed empty. I turned back, but Ali was gone and I faced the courtyard alone, where now, from doors all around the court, women and children began to emerge. Little girls in long-sleeved print dresses and boys in candy-striped dish-dashas ran and leaped toward me, then ran away giggling only to turn in a wider circle and come forward once more. The women—it seemed like hundreds of them—advanced more slowly, in their flowing black abayahs, their heads coifed and bound in black, all smiling and repeating, *"Ahlan wusahlan* [welcome]. *Ahlan, ahlan. Ahlan wusahlan."* Most of them came at a dignified pace, but the younger women could not contain their excitement, it seemed, for they would caper a bit, look at each other, choke with laughter and then cover their faces with their abayahs as the woman with the dung cakes had done. I stood still, not certain whether I should advance, until an old woman came close and put a motherly hand on my shoulder. She looked into my face and smiled broadly, which warmed her deeply wrinkled face with a kind and friendly expression despite the fact that many of her front teeth were missing. She had three blue dots, tattoo marks, in the cleft of her sun-tanned chin. She nodded and, still with her hand on my shoulder, steered me across the court.

We went in procession, the women closing ranks around me, the children still jumping and leaping on the outskirts of the group, past the water tap, to a shorter mud wall. Here, at an open doorway, a lovely, quite fleshy young woman awaited us; she was a startling contrast to the women about me, for she wore no abayah, only a dress of sky-blue satin patterned with crescents and stars. She had tied a black fringed scarf around her head like a cap, leaving her long black curly hair free to fall loosely around her shoulders.

"Ahlan wusahlan," she said and shook hands with me, laughing in a pleased way, to show perfect teeth. Her dark eyes were outlined heavily with kohl.

"Selma, Selma," called the children, "let us come in too."

"Away with you," she said good-naturedly, but made no attempt to back up her words as she led the way, through her small inner court, to a screen door where I was ushered into what seemed to be a big bedroom.

"Go on. Out! Out!" she said to the children, but they crowded in anyway after the women. There was only one chair in the room and Selma motioned me to it. I sat down and found myself face to face with a roomful of women and children, squatting opposite me on the mat-covered floor and staring up at me intently.

Selma had taken my abayah and hung it on a peg near the door. "You won't need it here," she said, pointing to herself, although she was the only woman there without it. She sat down at my feet. I felt uncomfortable sitting in a chair while everyone else sat on the floor, so I got up and sat down on the floor with them.

Selma looked upset and leaped to her feet.

"No, no, the chair is for you," she said and took my hand to pull me back up. "You are the guest."

I sat down in the overstuffed chair once more. There was a brief pause.

"Ahlan wusahlan," said Selma in the silence.

"Ahlan, ahlan wusahlan," chorused the roomful of women.

I cleared my throat. "You are Selma?"

"Yes," she said, laughing again in that pleased and very attractive way. "How did you know?"

"Everyone knows because you are the favorite wife of the sheik," replied an admiring young girl, and tweaked at Selma's blue satin skirt. She was a bit embarrassed, but pleasantly so, and swiped mildly at the girl, who ducked successfully and then giggled.

"And what is your name?" Selma asked me politely.

"Elizabeth."

"Alith-a-bess," she stumbled over the unfamiliar combinations of syllables, and several others tried out the word and failed.

Selma laughed. "That is a difficult name. We can't say it."

"I have another name," I offered, knowing that diminutive names were often used here. "It's B.J."

She picked that up as "Beeja." "She is called Beeja," she said, and so I was named.

I asked the name of the girl sitting closest to me.

"Basima," she answered and pointed to her neighbor. "Fadhila. Hathaya. Fatima. Rajat. Samira. Nejla. Sabiha. Bassoul. Sahura. Sheddir. Laila. Bahiga." How would I ever remember who they were? They looked that day so remarkably alike in their identical black head scarves, black chin scarves, and black abayahs. It was months later that I began to notice the subtle differences that the women managed to introduce into the costume: Fadhila always wore a fringed scarf, Laila's abayahs were edged with black satin braid; Samira's chin scarf was fastened on top of her head with a tiny gold pin in the shape of a lotus blossom.

But the dominant presence in the room, watched by every eye including mine, was the dazzling Selma, of ample but well-defined proportions, her air of authority softened by laughter. Mohammed had told me that Selma had five children. From her face, I guessed she could not yet be thirty, but childbearing had already blurred the lines of what once must have been a remarkable and voluptuous figure. The blue satin dress was cut Western style, but longer and looser; it moved in several directions when she moved, for Selma apparently felt that corsets were unnecessary. Her feet were bare (she had left her clogs at the door), but each slim, bare ankle bore a heavy gold bracelet. Gold bracelets were on both arms, several heavy gold necklaces swung against the blue satin dress, and long dangling gold filigree earrings caught the light when she moved. In her gold jewelry and blue satin and black silk head scarf, her eyes gay and almost black in her white face (whiter than that of any other woman in the room), she was attractive by anyone's standard and must once have been startlingly beautiful. I felt quite dowdy in my skirt and sweater and short-cut hair, and was only glad I had put on fake pearls and gold earrings.

Selma offered me a long thin cigarette, which I refused; she pressed me again, but I said I did not smoke.

"It is better not to smoke," said the old woman who had guided me to Selma's door. "Haji Hamid does not like women who smoke."

Selma looked at the old woman. "Kulthum," she said, "Haji Hamid is my husband as well as yours," and then deliberately lit cigarettes for herself and several others. In a few minutes the room was full of sweetish smoke, unlike any cigarette smoke I had smelled before. Kulthum said nothing, but I noticed she did not smoke.

I looked around me at the scrupulously clean room. Its mud-brick walls were newly whitewashed. I pointed upward, trying to indicate that the beams here were the same as the ones in my house. This was a fairly complex idea to get across, for at first the women thought I had seen something lodged in the beams and everyone peered and whispered. One woman stood up to get a better look. When they finally realized what I was struggling to communicate, they laughed, no doubt at the simplemindedness of the conversational tidbit I had contributed. Later I found that every house in the village was built in exactly the same manner, so obviously my house had beams like this one!

"Haji Hamid's bed, the sheik's," said a girl, pointing to the large double bed.

"And Selma's," said one of the girls, snickering. She showed me in mime how they lay together in a close embrace. Everyone laughed and Selma blushed with pleasure. I glanced at Kulthum, but her wrinkled face showed nothing.

REVIEW QUESTIONS

1. How would you describe the general atmosphere of the harem?
2. How would you describe the life of the children in the harem?
3. How do expectations of feminine beauty differ for the author and the women in the harem?

A Swiss Travel Writer and Photographer Encounters Afghan Officials (1935)

ELLA K. MAILLART, *The Cruel Way*

Ella Maillart, who died in her native Switzerland in 1997 at the age of ninety-four, lived an amazingly full and adventuresome life. Primarily a travel writer and photographer, she was described in her obituary as one "who defied convention." She was an athlete (Olympic sailor, competitive skier, field hockey star), movie actress and stunt woman, model, secretary, teacher, and saleswoman. Most of all, she was an inveterate traveler, crossing central Asia during the 1930s when there was little stability in the region. *Forbidden Journey* chronicles her 1935 journey to Sinkiang, a closed city in Chinese Turkestan; a renowned photographer, her photographs of this journey were featured in a 1993 Paris exhibition. At the age of 87 she traveled to Tibet. Reflecting on her travels, she told an interviewer in 1993 that her wanderlust resulted from her loathing of the excesses of World War I. "I wanted to leave Europe, go as far as possible." She spent most of World War II in India.

Two interesting anecdotes attest to the strength of character and indomitable spirit of this author. In the first, the commander of the British Mediterranean fleet was officially reprimanded for causing the fleet to miss lights out when he was entertaining four yachtswomen, one of whom was Maillart. Another involves the trip across Turkestan, which she made with Peter Fleming (younger brother of the James Bond series author, Ian Fleming), a reporter with the *Times of London.* In his account he states that Maillart put up the tent, did the cooking in all kinds of weather, as well as the sewing, washed his clothes as well as her own, and could walk fourteen miles on an empty stomach.

The following selection is from *The Cruel Way: Two Women and a Ford in Afghanistan,* which is about a trek made with a friend addicted to morphine. In part the trip was for adventure, in part to provide a change of environment for her friend. In the account she recalls, in vivid detail and without remorse or self-pity, the difficulties facing two women travelers in an area of rough terrain and political instability.

At noon we stopped near the hamlet of Dareh Boum where a delegation of worthies was waiting for us. The Elders kissed the hand of the governor who, meanwhile, looked charmingly unconcerned. We rode saddled horses as far as the white tents that had been rigged for us. After drinking some *doukh* (buttermilk, the most cooling drink of Asia) flavoured with mint, the three of us sat down cross-legged to a great repast eaten with our right hand—succulent kababs, pilau studded with nuts and spices, deep wooden dishes of creamy curds spooned up with a piece of flat bread. And as a finale, bowls of green or red tea at will. Ewer and towels were passed round for washing hands.

Some of the villagers who waited on us had carrot-coloured beards, the result of applying henna to white hair. According to an advice of the Prophet, to "bind" henna, to clean the teeth, to take wife and to use perfume are four things

every believer should do. "The benefits are many that come from the use of henna. It drives out shifting pains through the ears, restores sight when weakened, keeps nose membranes soft, imparts sweet odour to mouth and strength to the roots of teeth, removes body odours as well as temptation from Satan, gladdens angels, rejoices believers, enrages infidels, is an ornament to the user and diminishes trials in the grave."[1] Far from enraging, these flaming beards always gladden me when I see them brightening a bazaar crowd.

The hottest hours of the day were spent in the tents. When we returned to the cars we found their bonnets hidden under rugs—as a defence against the fierce heat.

In its windy valley, the great Murghau pushed its tumultuous grey waters against the piles of the sunken bridge. The German construction

---

[1]B. Donaldson: *The Wild Rue.*

was thrown down by an exceptional rise of the river, but it is an engineer's job to account for such possibilities, the governor said.

The river irrigates Merv in Soviet Turkmenistan, and ever since the Anglo-Russian convention of 1907 the Russians were annoyed by that border-line. Sometimes they accused the Afghans of using too much of "their" water and the Amir had to prove to them that the snowfalls and not his subjects were responsible for such irregularities. Nowadays there is a great model village on the river, just on the Russian side of the border.

We found no real road. In ankle-deep dust we followed a track that much too boldly attacked round-topped hills. Just where climbing cars begin to fight, choke and gasp, men were embedding rough cobbles in that powdered clay. Twelve or fifteen workmen followed us from hillock to hillock, pushing the helpless cars or spreading rush mats before the wheels. By then the governor was impatient: he wanted to arrive before the time for the sunset prayers.

We were relieved to sight the new bridge, the square walls of a citadel and thin trees quivering above walled gardens.

Our great courtyard was filled with the usual sunken flowerbeds. We spent the night on the terraced roof before our room on the first floor. There between earth and sky, the rustling of the poplar leaves lulled us to sleep before we had had time to feel drowned among the surging stars of a fathomless dark sea.

We spent a day at Bala Murghau, the governor having promised us two horses for visiting a camping tribe. But they never appeared. And so it happened that, having time to tidy our rucksack, we found a few onions from Trieste: the governor planted them at once, keen to see if they would do well in his province.

We had come down to an altitude of fifteen hundred feet and from now on a notion of heat was continually to occupy some part of our consciousness. During the hot hours, the governor took refuge in his *sardab* or cold-water room, a kind of cellar crossed by a rivulet. Joining him there from the oven-like upper world, I used to shiver, so great was the change of temperature.

Though a telephone had announced our arrival and though a disembowelled Ford adorned a corner of the garden, I felt as if plunged into the Middle Ages. Smoothly flowing, life seemed changeless. The bazaar was peaceful, even somnolent. Believers said their prayers kneeling on the platform of their booths. Subjects kissed the hand of their master. The dusty braying of asses filled the air. At the cross-road a dishevelled fakir held a beggar bowl.

It amused us to chat with the governor; and it was important to rest so that Christina should not get over-tired. Noticing that she was a great smoker, our host gave her many boxes of Russian cigarettes with cardboard mouthpieces. This was bad luck: I had just convinced Christina— or thought I had—that before attempting to master the weakness that caused her such remorse, she must train her will and gain confidence in herself through small victories like, for instance, controlling her daily smoking. And she agreed, partly no doubt because her provision had greatly dwindled!

The governor spoke about oil: "the world's best" had been struck in his province and the same quality was found as far south as Farrah. In 1936 the Inland Exploration Company of New York obtained a concession over more than two hundred thousand square miles of Western Afghanistan; the same "interests" had also secured a concession on Persian soil, thus insuring that no rival could tap their underground naphtha from across the border. But could the boring machines be brought so far and the oil be piped to Chahbar on the Indian Ocean across more than a thousand miles of desert? A five-year contract had promised twenty per cent of the benefits to the Afghans; but two years later the company had suddenly given up its claim. Some people say that the Americans were frightened by the oil-expropriation that took place in Mexico.

Shadows were lengthening across the garden. Conversation became personal.

The governor was puzzled. How could we live so long and so far away from our husbands and friends, how could we travel without them in foreign countries where everything, no doubt, seemed hostile to us or at least unusual? Once, when it had been his duty to go on tour, after two sleepless nights he had found that he could not bear to be separated from his wife: he went back to fetch her.

The following night, Christina's couch and mine were again side by side under the dazzling stars of Central Asia. Before dawn we heard quite near us the voice of our host calling "Madame!" (we knew he was camping in our wing of the house, for he had offered his apartment to a visiting official.) Tacitly, we postponed answering him till the sun rose. And then we told him how heavily we usually slept in a sheltered place,

whereas in our tent even rustling leaves disturbed us.

The governor apologised for waking us. But the night was so long. He had not slept and would have liked to talk to us. Framed in the doorway, he stood in his European dressing-gown of dark-blue silk, his attitude at the same time shy and wilful. Then, with charm and simplicity, looking beyond both of us, he said: "I would have liked to breathe the flowery fragrance of your face!"

I decided that the remark was not for me, my face having been so far likened only to horse, ship's bow or wild grass.

REVIEW QUESTIONS

1. Ella Maillart was a lifelong traveler and photographer. How are these qualities reflected in this selection?
2. Maillart was very independent, self-sufficient, and unusually observant. How are these characteristics reflected in her account?
3. What is your impression of the area of Afghanistan through which she traveled?
4. What is your impression of the Afghanis whom she met?
5. What is the attitude of the officials encountered by these two women?

An American Writer and Foreign Correspondent Travels to Peshawar (1990s)

ANTHONY WELLER, *Days and Nights on the Grand Trunk Road*

Anthony Weller, an American novelist and foreign correspondent, journeyed the fabled Grand Trunk Road, a 3,500-year-old link from the Khyber Pass to Calcutta. His motivation was that of an author: to record his travels across several cultures and also through history, for this was the route traversed by conquerors, by the Buddha, and by Rudyard Kipling's Kim. Today the Grand Trunk Road is filled with diverse peoples, animals, and vehicles of all sorts. It is a kaleidoscope of the past and the present.

The following selection is set in Peshawar, once part of British India and now in Pakistan, but perhaps having more in common with central Asia and Afghanistan. It became a haven and a crossroad for rebels, fundamentalists, and drug smugglers (not necessarily mutually exclusive categories). Although

it still has a bit of the Kiplingesque aura, new forces—the Taliban, the American intervention in Afghanistan, and the Pakistani government's crackdown on terrorism—have changed Peshawar since Weller's visit.

Peshawar has an almost stately grace and calm in the morning, which is a wonderful surprise since its reputation is for howling tribesmen just over the frontier waiting either to disembowel you or sell you a hundred kilos of opium. There are really three Peshawars: The Old City of bazaars, the British cantonment of spacious green avenues, and the modern University Town of spies, diplomats, and relief agencies. There is also the Peshawar of Afghan refugees, who live by the hundred of thousands in so-called camps that resemble moderately prosperous Indian mud villages but are far more dense, organized, and closed-off.

All coexist in a businesslike hubbub wherein you can, given savvy and a good deal of patience with complications, readily buy carpets, guns of all sizes, hard drugs, Herat bracelets, local information, unsafe passage beyond the Khyber Pass, and the odd Gandharan Buddha that will rival nearly anything in the museum. Even though Peshawar is a city, it feels like a town; you have the delight of being in a complex place it's possible to get to know, and after a few days here people start to recognize you. There weren't many places along the Grand Trunk Road that made me immediately want to return—the traveler's overnight nostalgia before he has even departed—but Peshawar, despite Kipling's calling it "the city of evil countenances," was one of them.

Dean's is one of those venerated hotels whose best qualities are age and calm in the face of a local melee. It wasn't alluring or particularly comfortable, but for over a century nearly every foreigner had stayed here, since it was practically the only white man's hotel in Peshawar. You could learn more here in the lobby than by reading the morning's *Frontier Mail*. The hotel was a cluster of low, tile-roofed, many-gabled white stucco buildings with cypress trees and a lawn with chairs for tea. The boxlike rooms, every one a suite with a little veranda, were in

a couple of ranks like attached bungalows. A clock at the front desk was permanently set at check-out time (one minute before noon). Over it hung a painting of tribesmen on horseback charging across a khaki landscape. There were slipcovered chairs, ceiling fans, harem-style hanging lamps, and a bedraggled carpet; a portrait of Jinnah, the country's founder, with warm eyes and a cocked cap, surveyed guests from over the carved-wood fireplace. In the dining room stood a decayed Bechstein upright that must be the worst example in the world of that august piano: the keyboard looked as if a tractor had dragged it through a field.

Nevertheless, Dean's was recognizable as the place where Robert Byron in 1934 had sat "drinking gin fizzes in the marble lounge" at the end of his road to Oxiana, on the way out of Persia and Afghanistan. Likewise Paul Theroux in 1973, who wrote affectionately about kicking back on a veranda, sipping a beer, and getting the blood circulating in one of those chairs with a swing-out extension while watching the sunset. Clearly, if you were coming from Meshed and Kabul, it was like reaching Paris.

I had three personal missions to accomplish in Peshawar. First, to enjoy myself in a place I'd heard and read wild tales about since I was a kid. Next, to see Darra Adam Khel, a nearby village where the Afridi tribesmen, practically while you wait, will make you working copies of any armaments from nineteenth-century British rifles to Stinger missile parts. And finally, to get through the Khyber Pass, where the Grand Trunk Road at some mystical (or arbitrary) point ceases to be the road across the subcontinent, the road to India, and becomes instead a different road, the way out, to Afghanistan, to Kabul.

That would be the end of the Grand Trunk Road—of my road, anyway. After all these miles, despite the dangerous name, I did not see any difficulties with the Khyber Pass.

At least until, after a lazy breakfast, I ambled

past an immobile watchman who sat sipping tea to the small tourist office near the hotel grounds' entry, and read a handwritten sign:

NOTICE
*All Tribal Areas are closed
to foreigners including Khyber
Pass and Darra Adam Khel.*

I read it over several times, even though there was only one sentence. Maybe it was an old sign.

The bearded, swathed man on duty within, Mr. Salhuddin, was eloquent on the impossibility of my going to either place. Darra, he implied, the village of arms makers, was much too dangerous for foreigners—I did not remotely believe this—and the famous Khyber Pass, he asserted, was quite dull. "Anyway, nothing to see there," Mr. Salhuddin insisted. "Wastage of time. Don't worry. You are not missing a thing." He looked genuinely gloomy on my behalf, then brightened. "Have you been to the museum?"

He was not unfriendly or unhelpful. He was simply stating the iron policy of the Khyber arm of the North-West Frontier Province government, which applied to everyone. How could I not have found this out before? The restrictions had been in force for a long time; all my guidebooks, which spoke of daily tours to the Khyber, were from years ago. Those tours had been scrapped. Wasn't there anyone I could talk to about special permission? No, the situation was too dicey, the tribesmen too busy. That meant guns and drugs. Who could even remember when the last foreigner had been given permission to go through the Khyber? *Impossible. Nothing to see. Wastage of time.* It was almost a mantra.

So I took Mr. Salhuddin's maps and brochures and went for a walk. This was not like being shut out of one more Hindu temple: at that moment it seemed to render the entire journey futile. I could not think what door to hammer on.

At least I was in Peshawar. It did not seem a very wild and woolly place. Outside Dean's there was a gaggle of shoe shiners, both boys and men sitting on their little unrolled patches of cloth in the shade. After fifteen minutes of the ministrations of the eldest, my feet shone as they hadn't since Delhi. Behind them, the wall of Dean's compound hid the hotel's bungalows and led along one of the town's principal streets. Here were enormous carpet emporiums for the European tour groups who descend on the town for a day or two during the autumn and spring. By now the tourists, such as they were, wouldn't be back for months and the only customers were Pakistani women in couples, Mama and daughter up from Pindi for a better deal on a big Afghan carpet. Or else the rare foreigner, usually a man trying to look like a mercenary or a foreign correspondent.

Two of them were the only foreign guests at Dean's: they came and went during my week, and at first I thought my memory was playing tricks on me, so similar were their outfits. This was the standard garb of the macho traveler, usually American, usually a man, who desperately wants to be mistaken for a war correspondent. Part of the outfit involves wearing clothes too hot for the climate, to imply that heat doesn't bother you as it does normal people. Long-sleeved shirts with lots of pockets for all those *laissez-passers* and *baksheesh* money; clodhopper boots for scrambling up mountain passes; the ubiquitous camera even at breakfast; aviator sunglasses but no hat; a two-day growth of beard and a kerchief knotted around the neck to soak up sweat (this was on mild, ideally balmy days); the trousers always a dull brown or gray-green, baggy, rumpled, and very dusty.

The most conspicuous and necessary part of the outfit—and Peshawar merchants may be excused for thinking that all Americans wear this as a national uniform—was the reporter's jacket. It was always thick, bulky, sleeveless, with a hint it might stop a few bullets if necessary. It boasted a vaguely military aspect and made anyone look burly and battle-hardened; it had subsidiary pockets and main pockets and extra pockets all over and loops for rolls of film or to attach binoculars to and one special pocket for your passport in case you had to slip over the border. It was a jacket you could drink in and dodge bullets in and sleep in and it looked ridiculous on anyone who was not a war correspondent. There were virtually none here anymore, now that the Afghan-Russian war was long over and Peshawar no longer a reporters' base, to relax in and file stories from.

I wondered if I was being overly critical of my fellow man until a party of French tourists came through for a day, on their way up to Swat, and they were all dressed normally, comfortably, enjoying fine Peshawar weather. Meanwhile the Yanks playing at journalist left urgently—decamped, rather, in full kit—on different days, carrying several carpets each.

In this I could concur, because it was an ideal town for Christmas shopping. Even my old guidebook spoke of the "great transit trade from Kabul and Bokhara and Central Asia" and recommended the bazaars, "both for the objects they contain—many of them not seen in Central India—and for the fierce-looking and picturesquely-dressed tribesmen." Peshawar was still the capital of old Asia, not the Asia of Hong Kong and Singapore and international stock markets, but the Asia of goods traveling overland, silk and spices and camels and semiprecious stones and opium and gold bracelets and automatic rifles and people on the move carrying their family carpets. Alexander and Marco Polo and Babur and everyone else had passed through here; the ruin of the largest Buddhist stupa on the subcontinent was on the outskirts. It was still the ultimate crossroads, whose role had not changed for millennia, dictated by mountains and tribal geography. The town was like a doorman with radar instincts and many hidden pockets. Peshawar was on the way to everywhere, and no missile systems or airplanes would ever render it obsolete.

It had more secondhand wristwatches than even Istanbul. This was farther down Saddar Road, past a succession of antique shops selling the spoils of people fleeing Afghanistan: a lot of old Bokhara porcelain, damaged Russian military equipment, and rugs which sometimes showed helicopters attacking horsemen wielding automatic rifles. After a few tea-stalls, cloth-ing shops, and a sunglasses vendor, suddenly there'd be three men competing against one another with cubicles selling about a dozen new clocks and, on a large sunken table as if they were shellfish being rinsed, a thousand old watches. They came from all over the world and were apparently priced by whim or the shopkeeper's aesthetic judgment, which sometimes placed a souvenir watch from an Arab economic conference above a fine Bulova. Many were Russian army surplus, and I imagined some Afghan mujahidin delicately removing the watch along with the wrist. It is amazing how much useful bric-a-brac gets left behind when an invading army next door gives up and goes home.

GHULAN MOHAMMAD DOSSUL & CO.
DEALERS IN ARMS, AMMUNITION, STABILIZER
& ELECTRONIC ITEMS
EST. 1843

The Pathan features are distinctive: skin that looks seared by the sun; a grave fastidiousness in the facial gestures, as of an actor who has been studiously preparing for a part; a slightly sour, recalcitrant, or at least highly doubtful regard for what's going on around him; likewise a masculine flair in the beard, a swagger in the headgear and turban, and an extremely relaxed and loose-limbed gait that has no hurry about it. The old men walk as if pacing off the extent of their terrain, the young ones as if hoping the fellow at the other end of the street will draw first. And though you can't always tell, Pathan men almost all carry guns. They wear arms the way a nineteenth-century Londoner wore a pocket-watch, or a necktie, as part of the normal apparel. Some men, of course, openly sport weapons slung over their shoulders.

This is not be to be confused with the Sikhs and their swords, or the Yemenis and their curved daggers. Pathans use their guns.

The men invariably wear the long pajama smocks with trousers that usually match, in some dull color—off-white, or gray, or light brown. Sometimes they wear a vest over this outfit, or even a Western-style jacket, and some men are swaddled in robes on top of the whole get-up. Their headgear identifies them by tribe—little skull caps, or turbans, or double-layered flat hats that resemble two *naan* breads squashed together. Most men have mustaches, and many bear the severe, naturally intense features one expects from the violent Pathan history. They seemed surprisingly ready to smile.

This part of downtown leading to the old British cantonment area was full of eateries, and travel agencies, and the odd hotel—Green's, for example, ripped apart by a bomb a couple of years ago and back in business now. A gaudy cinema from another era was showing an American thriller about husband-and-wife spies. With certain scenes cut for moral reasons the action

yarn must've made little sense, but there'd be enough explosions and mayhem to keep this audience happy. A couple of bookshops were remarkably vast and well stocked, with a broader selection of titles on the history of the subcontinent than I'd seen in any shop in Delhi. Many volumes were Indian publications, imported somehow, which showed an open mind and confirmed my impression of the discursive and free press in the daily papers. What the bookstores weren't free to carry was anything to do with sex or female flesh—Pathans are notoriously touchy on this subject—though the shelves held the complete works of Harold Robbins and quite a few foreign fashion magazines. Here they looked downright lascivious.

REVIEW QUESTIONS

1. Find Peshawar on a map of South Asia (one that includes Afghanistan): What does this tell you about its importance?
2. Does Peshawar seem to be suspended between two worlds? Why or why not?
3. Weller labeled Peshawar as "the Piccadilly of Central Asia." What did he mean?
4. What word or phrase would you use to characterize the author's attitude to Peshawar? Explain.

An American Wife and Mother Describes Events in Chittagong (1953–1954)

ELLURA WINTERS, *Letters from Chittagong*

In 1947, when British India obtained independence, it was split into two nations. India, primarily Hindu, was constitutionally a secular democracy, although it was composed of many different ethnic identities. Pakistan, constitutionally an Islamic nation, was also composed of several ethnic identities and was geographically split into West Pakistan and East Pakistan (composed of Bengalis), separated by 1,500 miles of north India.

There was a major difference between the east and the west wings: the Bengalis strongly associated with Bengali culture and language (there are more native speakers of Bengali than there are of German or French). In this sense they were different in every way, other than religion, from the West

Pakistanis. It had been on the sole criterion of religion that the British created a Pakistan. The artificial unity lasted only until 1971, when the East Pakistanis, after a bloody struggle, became the nation of Bangladesh. Chittagong, from which Ellura Winters wrote her letters, was transformed from a sleepy little village to the bustling port city of Bangladesh.

When the Winterses were in Chittagong in 1953–1954, it was in what was then East Pakistan (and was sometimes referred to as East Bengal, in distinction from West Bengal, which was and is a state in India). Ethnic tensions were strong even then, as indicated by the riot described in this selection, which was written on April 15, 1954. The tension rose between Bengalis and Hyderabadis, or people from Hyderabad, a city in West Pakistan.

Bob Winters was a forestry expert involved in an aid program sponsored by the U.S. Forest Service. Such programs were prevalent during the immediate postcolonial period; there are references in the selection to Italian and Swedish engineers as well. Ellura wrote a series of letters home. These were the days before CNN and jumbo jets, and traveling was an exotic (and at times uncomfortable) adventure for a midwestern, middle-class family. The adjustments were difficult, but they were handled with grace.

April 15, 1954

Yesterday morning I was at a coffee party given by Roma Agha. She had among her guests Mrs. Johannson, who had been at Chandraghona for ten months. Her husband was one of the Swedish engineers who had been helping to start the paper mill. For awhile she had been helping in the ordering of food for the head staff dining room, so she had been a part of the executive picture, and also had had some dealings with the workers. She told us much about the riot at the mill. Bob wants me to write down what I can remember. It will not mean much to you folks, except to show how deep are the hatreds and how volatile are the emotions of these people, and how quickly trouble can arise out here. But these bits and pieces will mean something to us along with what we have known.

For months, the officials had known that something was going to explode, but they did not know when. There were terrible tensions between the 1500 workers who were from East Pakistan, mostly Bengalis and some hill tribesmen, and the technicians who were mostly Hyderabadis from West Pakistan. It is true that more of the leaders for everything come from West Pak. because they are better trained, but

the Bengalis hate to admit it, and feel jealous and inferior. Mr. Kershid Ali, the head director, was a Hyderabadi, and so were most of the top people, or else Europeans. But more fundamental than that hatred between the two parts of Pakistan was the fact that the mill workers were getting such low wages. Then to make matters worse, those hiring the workers, insisted on a certain amount being paid back to them as baksheesh for giving them the jobs. Then the mill doctor decided he wanted to import a Burmese woman, and in order to have the money to get her, he forced all the sweepers who are the lowest paid group to each pay him 8–20 rupees each. That sort of thing is very common out here. When the sweepers began to complain, Mr. Ali did raise their wages a bit. But it was true that there was a different pay scale for the Bengalis. Many of the Europeans felt that the low wages were the basic cause; because with most of these people, if they have enough to eat and a place to live, they don't care about anything else.

On Sunday, the day before the riot, at the race track, where the first races of the season were being held, the workers in groups began marching around shouting insults about Kershid Ali. The workers were getting quite stirred up, and Mr.

Ali was warned by several of his executives to leave at once, since he was planning to go away in 10 days any way. But he said he had faced mobs before, and was not going to let his workers get the best of him.

Apparently the riot was a planned affair, led by a chemist who had been sent to Central America for special training in paper industry. Apparently he had learned more about organizing revolutions than about paper. Many of the household servants seemed to know on Monday morning that something was going to happen; because they said to several of the Europeans, "Don't go to office or mill, stay in bungalow." But of course they all went because they didn't want the natives to think they were afraid. At exactly 10 a.m. the riot started. When Mr. Ali was going through the mill, he found this chemist not doing the work Mr. Ali had told him to do, and the chemist refused to do it because he said he had been hired for a special job and wouldn't do anything else. So Mr. Ali fired him on the spot, and that was the signal. The workers started beating up on Mr. Ali; he was wounded on the head. His assistant and driver managed to get him into a jeep and started to the hospital with him. Workers surrounded the jeep and stopped it. A brick was thrown at the driver hitting him in the heart and he fainted, and both men were dragged out of the jeep. Many of the guards came to their help and there was a horrible fight, with eyes gouged out, ears cut off, bodies put in sacks and thrown in the river while the men were half alive, etc. Thirteen were killed in the riot.

The telephone wires were cut, so there was no way to call police. Mr. Stevens, an engineer, and another European, as soon as trouble started, tore down the curtains, draped themselves as natives and took a jeep the back road to Rangamati to get the police from there and call Chittagong and Dacca. I asked Mrs. Johannson why police had not been stationed up there since these tensions had been mounting for so long. She said that the police, being Bengalis, had said that they would not try to stop a strike if

the workers started one. Of course when killings started then they had to restore order, and the army came, too.

Mrs. Johannson said that the Europeans locked their doors and windows; and most the men had by devious ways reached their homes while the main riot was going on at the mill, because the offices are across the road from the mill. They all started packing, but expected any minute to have their homes broken into. The natives were simply like animals when they got the first smell of blood, and they chanted, jumped wildly into the air and went simply wild. About 50 of them started toward the European bungalows, but only shouted and threw stones. There was no harm done to either the mill machinery or to any Europeans, because apparently it was a family feud between Bengalis and Hyderabadis. One guest of two days was killed just because he came from West Pakistan! The chemist who was the leader in the plot apparently had not realized that this was not a gov't. revolution where he would gain some sort of power, and was not expecting to be arrested for murder. About 173 workers were arrested at the time, but many feel that even the leaders will never receive much of a sentence because they will be tried in Bengal courts.

The Europeans were all brought by public steamer to Chittagong on the second day. The paper company boats had been put out of commission when the riot started. They were questioned here by police.

The mill was closed for a week but is now running again and all European technicians have returned but have left their families here. Mr. Ispahani, the power of East Bengal, who is chairman of the board of Pakistan Industrial Development Company, the group that financed the mill, has flown to England to bring an English paper expert out to run the mill, if he can find one to come.

This pattern of riots over anything as is seen in Calcutta all the time, is of long standing. It started when the natives would do it against the British. Now they do it against their own leaders and government. Many feel that with such hatred between parts of Pakistan and greater hatred between India and Pakistan, these people may break out in civil war, and of course the Communists like to jump in wherever they can and stir up as much trouble inside these countries as possible.

So life over here can sometimes be quite exciting.

Easter week-end and tomorrow, Good Friday, is a national holiday. There will be an 11 o'clock service at our church.

Much love from us to you all,
Ellura

REVIEW QUESTIONS

1. How do you view Ellura's observations? Was she a good observer?
2. What ethnic and political tensions do you sense in this selection?
3. Toward the end of the letter Ellura notes that servants had warned their European employers to stay home. She states, "But of course they all went because they didn't want the natives to think they were afraid." Do you think there are other reasons they behaved this way? Explain.

A Hindi Poet Portrays the Married Life of an Oppressed Woman in India (1935)

MAHADEVI VARMA, *Sketches from My Past: Encounters with India's Oppressed*

Hindi is the third largest language in the world, surpassed only by English and Chinese. Mahadevi Varma (1907–1987) is one of the leading twentieth-century Hindi literary figures. In the words of her biographer Karine Schomer, "She is the only woman to have become a major figure in modern Hindi letters." Primarily known as one of the founders of Chhayavad ("voices from the shadow") poetry, a fusion of romantic style and Marxist ideals, she is also noted for her prose and paintings.

Varma came from a cultured middle-class background. Her father encouraged both her education and her independent nature; his positive and considerate attitude toward his wife and daughters was in sharp contrast to much that Mahadevi noticed outside her home. Her poetry reflects not only the socioeconomic condition of twentieth-century India, but Hindu mystical tradition as well. Her insight into the human condition, especially in regard to the individual poor (whom she never stereotypes), perhaps can best be expressed as "pensive, soulful."

The following selection is from a collection of sketches written in the 1930s, memoirs subtitled "encounters with India's oppressed." These verbal portraits reveal Varma's sympathetic feminism and a recognition of the dignity of the poor and exploited; they express not only the desperate situation, but the self-dignity of "wounded and mauled lives."

As a name, Sabiya is an abbreviation of neither Shabnam nor Shabrat. It is, in fact, a derivative of the Hindu Savitri, the mythological heroine whose piousness and unflinching devotion to her husband enabled her to convince Yama, the Lord of Death, to bring her husband back to life. To be honest, it is hard to say whether it was really our benevolent Aryan tradition that was merciful enough to allow this lowest of the low-caste Harijan to gain respectability through the use of this name. More likely, Sabiya's parents, who could conventionally be said to have departed to heaven but were actually hell-bound, stole this name like a clever pickpocket. And later, to claim it as their own, they chopped and modified the name so much that it is now difficult for anyone to establish an exclusive claim to it.

As if to defy my rule never to fire or change servants, my old sweeper, without seeking my permission, proceeded on that grand journey from which it is impossible to recall anyone. Only then did Sabiya appear. Holding a ball of flesh wrapped in a dirty rag that could perhaps qualify as a month-old infant, she materialized one day; with her other hand she led her five-year-old daughter, whose nakedness was covered only by her filth. Sabiya's face appeared to be moulded from oily, black clay, but in every line there was the same structural grace and harmony as one often finds in statues made out of plaster of paris. Round rather than elliptical, her eyes had the frightened, puzzled look of a child lost at a crowded fair. Around her hands and feet the thick bracelets and anklets crafted from dull, lusterless nickel made her look like a chained prisoner. Decorating her narrow forehead, above her linked eyebrows, was a small, round disc made of yellow-colored glass, suggestive of the yellow flower blooming on the furze shrub over a rubbish heap. Draped in a faded sari that must have once been red in color but now resembled the shade of a rusty water pot, Sabiya looked like a statue laboriously carved out of clay by an amateur sculptor: although all its ephemeral color had faded, bonded to the statue's graceful contours, the clay beneath was still visible.

I learned that Sabiya's husband had simply taken off without her knowledge. At that time she was confined to the lying-in chamber, having just given birth. Shattered at her husband's departure, she fell sick and was replaced in the bungalow where she worked by another sweeper. She told me that if I could give her a job, she would then be able to raise her children. Ignoring her assurance that she would put body and soul into serving me, I cast a suspicious glance at the tiny bundle and asked, "How are you going to be able to work dragging this infant along?" Patting her filthy, skinny daughter's back, Sabiya shook her head confidently. When she began to elaborate on her daughter's uncommon skill in looking after her baby brother, giving actual examples, I was able neither to laugh nor to stop myself from smiling. Frankly, having observed the darkness that spread across little Bachiya's glowworm-like eyes, it seemed brutal to burst out laughing and uncharitable to keep mum.

After explaining what work was expected of her, I had barely made it back to my room from the veranda when, crashing through the barrier of awe in which she held me, my old maid Bhaktin's curiosity erupted into countless questions. Bhaktin was an untiring gossip: to know everything about everyone was the principal aim in her life. It seemed as though God, who is Himself the supreme storyteller, had blessed Bhaktin's tongue with the narrating talent of the legendary Yojnabahu. From the thousands of questions strung together like a rosary for Sabiya, some scattered words forced their way to me. And the touching quality of the responses alone made it impossible for me to be indifferent to them.

I was really not able to hear clearly the question that Bhaktin asked Sabiya about her husband, but from the response—"No, ma'am, he couldn't have done anything untoward; he was, after all, a married man"—it was clear that Sabiya was close to tears. In response to Bhaktin's "That woman must have cast quite a spell!" Sabiya said defensively and in a feeble voice, "Ma'am, it's all one's fate." I tried then with considerable effort to concentrate on my writing, and at that point I lost track of the rest of Sabiya's story. By and by, I learned that not only was Sabiya's husband in no way an approximation of the noble Satyavan, the legendary Savitri's husband, but worse, he had been unable to live up to even the meaninglessness of his obscure name, Maiku. Evidently, one day, without giving any inkling of where he was headed, he ran off with someone else's new bride. That was shocking enough, considering that the bridegroom was someone from his own community and more like a caste brother. To make matters worse, Maiku left just when Sabiya was tending a three-day-old baby. From then on, she gave up all hope of his ever returning, and there was no further news of him. Partly to avenge himself and partly out of a desire to rehabilitate his deserted household, the spurned bridegroom invited Sabiya to move in with him, but she turned him down. Finally, recognizing the wisdom of the old saying, "One who has been scalded by hot milk blows on even buttermilk, waiting for it to cool down," that wretched fellow opted to marry his elderly, widowed sister-in-law and breathed a sigh of relief.

In view of what had happened, it is hardly surprising that everyone began to refer to Sabiya as an eccentric, although personally I was unable to detect any trace of eccentricity in her other than her mania for work. Every morning at the crack of dawn, spreading a torn, soiled cloth on the rocky ground under the margosa tree, she would lay down her infant. Partly to look after the baby and partly to wave away the flies, she would leave Bachiya to sit with him. Tying her waist tightly with a tattered rag, she would grab the broom. Then, on one end of the yard, accompanied by the swishing sound of the broom, Sabiya's dance would commence. She seemed to simply float through the air! And at the other end of the yard, Bachiya would begin her antics. Sometimes adopting an austere posture and at other times a heroic one, Bachiya would shoo away the flies with her tiny hands. Adding to her theatrics, she would skip on one foot or jump on both feet to scare away the crows. Bachiya's mother had a slender body that was agile like a green twig rather than rigidly inflexible like a dry stick, which indicated life instead of lifelessness. In contrast, the sapless body of the girl showed not the agility of a new leaf but the helpless movement of the soft petals of a closed bud that is covered with frost and unable to blossom—a state more indicative of inertia than of growth.

The area beneath the margosa tree outside my window was Bachiya's stage, and important spectators, such as my dog and the hostel's cat, were certainly welcome there. But there was also nothing wanting in the hospitality extended to stranger crows, unknown birds, and squirrels living in the margosa tree. Yet judging from Bachiya's keen vigilance, it appeared as though everyone, from the dog to the birds and from the squirrel to the flies, was eager to kidnap and abscond with her darling brother. To scare off those disguised bandits, she would resort to speaking in a variety of languages—ranging from a cat's meow to a bird's chirp to heaven knows what else. At the end of it all, she would blow through a kazoo whistle that could have cost no more than a nickel, as though she were announcing a truce by sounding a conch shell.

Piercing through the fortress of her dedication to duty, when pangs of hunger would rattle her insides, Bachiya would open the knotted edge of that same dirty rag on which the baby was resting, and taking out a small piece of bread, she would come to terms with the hidden enemy. But admittedly it was impossible to carry out that task in the presence of so many spectators. Once, imitating a rooster, she tried to scare a crow away, but the insurgent crow snatched her only weapon against hunger and flew away with it. Finally, by sending her some cookies and a corn-flour doughnut, I was able to perform the noble task of replacing a wooden dagger with a machine gun in her battle against hunger. From then on Bachiya used the sound "cock-a-doodle-do" to call me to her rescue; whatever foodstuffs I sent in response carried traces of grudging acrimony from my maid Bhaktin, who did not relish the thought of being asked to wait on Bachiya.

By ten o'clock, having finished all of her tasks, Sabiya would fold up her act like a conjurer and go for her bath. By the time she returned to pick up her food with her shiny, brass plate she had scrubbed to a sparkle, the leisurely dining activity in the hostel would be over. I had given strict instructions that the leftovers from the plates in the hostel's canteen should be fed to the bullocks plying the school's carts instead of being dumped on sweepers or other low-caste people. My unconventional command that Sabiya be served fresh rice and lentils from the kitchen rather than the leftovers most certainly caused enough resentment among both the cook and the dishwasher to add a caustic flavor to what was dished out to Sabiya. Of course, Sabiya herself was too hesitant to complain about anyone, fearing that by doing so, her mouth would become covered with burning blisters.

REVIEW QUESTIONS

1. What does this selection say about the condition of the poor? Is such poverty cultural, social, economic, or a fusion of all three? Explain.
2. How would you characterize the relationship between Bhaktin and Sabiya? What does it reveal about the values of this society?
3. What does this selection reveal about the role of children in society? How was your childhood similar? Different?

An English Poet Describes a Train Ride in India (1941)

LEWIS THOMPSON, *Unpublished Manuscript*

Lewis Thompson, 1909–1949, was an Englishman who lived the last sixteen years of his life in India, dying suddenly of sunstroke in Varanasi (Banaras). He kept voluminous journals, which he carried around with him, and he spent most of his time traveling. The archives of his manuscripts, journals, and letters total four linear feet.

Thompson was interested in the spirituality, landscape, and people of India. He was primarily a poet, and reacted as such. His writings (only his poems and aphorisms have been published) reveal a rare sensitivity and a troubled personality. He was an eye-witness to the Indian freedom struggle and Gandhi's great experiment in nationalist revolution by nonviolent means, yet Thompson seemed decidedly uninterested in politics. His papers reveal a strong sense of introspection of a spiritual and philosophical nature. Ella Maillart in the 1987 reissue of *The Cruel Way* acknowledged Thompson's editorial help and expressed her respect for his "amazing intuition." **Perhaps most amazing about him, he traveled about colonial India not in European garb, but wearing native clothing, which was most unusual for a Westerner, particularly an Englishman in British India. In the following excerpt he describes a train ride.**

October, 1941

In the new train at Dhond, five fifteen in the morning, October 28th., no Inter. Class available. I'm thus in third class since I'm not sure that I've got enough to pay for second. Everybody filthy. Prodigious mountains of baggage, little packages tied up in cloth, these knots always seem to suggest the touch of graceful fingers. One of the boys in the group to which this baggage belongs has strangely beautiful hands, a deep dusky brown, the nails tinted with henna. A little girl sings to herself : "La la patti laiya." The blueish dawn light comes in, the morning breeze stirs. A sweet and delicate tenderness suffuses the heart and vanishes like a perfume. The train sways. Slowly, after a night of tedium, people start talking. One rests on the knee of another a peaceful hand. How beautiful all these human lives.

At sunrise an old man offers *namaskaram* to Him and prays.

When I try to switch off the fan every hand is stretched to help me.

Blind beggars with castanets climb in on the wrong side of the train; people here seem to be less generous or perhaps they are poorer than the Tamil. The houses such as one glimpses are mean hovels: stone with sheet-iron roofs. Almost everyone wears clothes which are dirty and often tattered.

Great India Peninsula Railway
NOTICE

Warning is given that it is a common practice for Railway thieves to pretend to go to sleep on the floor of a carriage and when passengers are asleep or inattentive to open and extract articles from bundles and boxes placed under the seat.

In order that they may not be the victims of professional criminals, such as poisoners, swindlers, thieves or pickpockets, passengers are warned not to accept food or tobacco from strangers . . .

Frenetic chanting, comic, impassioned, to the rhythmical clink of little cymbals. He too, the third in half an hour, is blind.

There are plenty of Hindus here as they are imagined in Europe—just like gipsies. More cunning, less peaceful than people in the South. Not so deep, either, I would guess. Less self-contained. When I offer him a cigarette my neighbour gives me, in return, some areca-nut. A Tamil would find that indelicate, too commercial, or—too obvious, too artless. All the eyes here seem to be more brilliant, more focussed. The women are half veiled with their saris. Big pearl rings pass through their nostrils. Colours are more gay than rich.

Ratlam, October 29th.

Spent the night in second class. Everything more sordid than in the South. Flies. Clothes always dirty. Tea but no milk. Fruit very expensive. Even brighter colours: acid crimson with brilliant yellow; lime-green; turbans like multi-coloured nougat. Ganja is smoked. Waistcoats of patterned quilt or with sequins and embroidery.

When I approached Hindu cafes I was taken for a Muslim. When, at Khandwa, I asked for milk they said there was none and when I pointed to some that was being boiled they said it was no good : "Achcha nahin."

A charming and simple police officer—a big baby—came and told me he had coughed all night long, supposing that I might be a doctor. His voice croaked and I could see that his throat was inflamed. I told him he must see a doctor as soon as possible and, meanwhile, take a spoonful of honey every fifteen minutes. They say honey is easily obtainable here. The interpreter in this exchange gave me the address of a Shastri and yogi with many disciples who lives near Ajmer.

In a third class coach again with small compartments hung everywhere with colourful garments.

Since the morning, the landscape as I had always imagined it—completely flat right to the horizon.

At Neemuch I obtained chapattis, quite good although without ghee. A small boy who saw that I did not like the highly salted curry ran to get me some mango pickle. With fruit this was sufficient for me.

A surrealist woman veiled in a yellow sari, its border worked in metallic silver piped in blue; heavy manacles and fetters of elaborate silverwork; her pale hands, cruelly made up with henna, dark brown, appear soaked in the long-since dried blood of crime. All the small children, eyes heavily outlined with khol, have the air of perverse intelligence. It must be this implacable sun which intensifies everything. It weighs down, it stifles. In resisting it one becomes passionately perverse. Intense love of Apollo who created shade.

A supercilious camel, thoroughly ill-tempered. Houses of undressed stone, half-ruined; tiled roofs. Crops of maize. Small grey-green trees powdered with flowers of dusty yellow. Thorntrees, grass burnt dry.

The women are sad, patient, fatalistic.

A hill fort; flags which flap languidly in the breeze.

Young man with a silver pommel to his sword. A prisoner escorted by two policemen. They sell roasted maize here. Terribly hot: for the first time on this trip I perspire visibly.

I can see the strength to continue thus for months will make me become a famous author. Truly too hot to read, to think, to sleep. From a milky blue sky it suddenly rains.

REVIEW QUESTIONS

1. How does the account of the train ride show Thompson's fascination with the Indian people?
2. Why do you think Thompson was taken as a Muslim in the café?
3. Thompson was primarily a poet. How does his poetic bent show in this selection?

A Prominent Indian Novelist Attends the Wedding of Her Cousin, Indira Nehru Gandhi (1942)

NAYANTARA SAHGAL, *Prison and Chocolate Cake*

Nayantara Sahgal (born 1927) is one of the most prominent Indian novelists writing in English. The following selection, describing the wedding of her cousin Indira ("Indi"), is from her reminiscences of the independence movement, *Prison and Chocolate Cake* (1954). Her hero worship for her older cousin, just returned from England, can be sensed in the selection. Later in life, when Indira was prime minister, the two were to become severely estranged (as Indira became with much of her family and old family friends).

As Nayantara Sahgal notes, Indian weddings are generally sumptuous affairs, although in a 1973 filmed BBC interview Indira expressed the opinion that hers was not so grand as Indian weddings go. In part that may have been due to the stressful atmosphere of the times (imprisonments by the British were common for her family), and in part because Indira was marrying outside the faith, although the Nehru family was not religious in the strict sense. Her groom, Feroze Gandhi (no relation to Mahatma Gandhi) was Parsi, not Hindu. Indira's wedding sari was made by her father during one of his many imprisonments by the British (he spent over ten years incarcerated).

WEDDING STORY

1942 began auspiciously with our cousin Indira's wedding. She had returned from a long stay in Europe not many months earlier and Rita and I, awkward and gangly, followed her round the house admiringly, imitating her in every way we could. Hers was to be the first traditional wedding at Anand Bhawan,* because Mummie had been married at Swaraj Bhawan, and Masi's wedding had been a brief registration without any of the customary pageantry.

The traditional Hindu wedding is a sumptuous affair of which the ceremony itself is only the grand finale. To begin with, the wedding day is selected with care by the parents of the young couple after consultation with pandits.[1] This is not an unusual procedure and not one confined to weddings alone. No orthodox Indian will embark on any important venture haphazardly, whether it be moving into a new house, setting out on a long journey or getting married. He will first inquire from a pandit on which day the stars are auspicious so that his enterprise will have every possible chance of success. The Indian temperament is averse from haste, for it has been bred on the ideal that all decisions should be approached with a studied serenity. The more significant the decision in question, the calmer should be the approach to it. So an Indian would not think of waking up one morning and casually announcing that he was getting married the next day or week or even a month later. Such a matter rests with the pandit, who chooses an auspicious day. Ours was by no means an orthodox family but it was a family deeply rooted in the country's cultural traditions so, with the help of a pandit, a favourable day in March was found for the wedding.

The celebrations usually begin when the bridegroom, his relations and friends arrive in the bride's town a day or two before the wedding. From the moment of their arrival, when they are greeted at the station with garlands of flowers, they are the honoured guests of the bride's family. It is unnecessary to say "honoured guests," for in India a guest is automatically an honoured person. Whoever he may be, if he enters your house with good will, you must accord him your most gracious hospitality. This is true of a guest on any occasion and more especially on the occasion of a wedding. A house is taken for the bridegroom and his party where the bride's relations fete them and servants of a bride's family wait on them. This is the normal pattern of a wedding but at Indi's wedding the need for a house to accommodate the bridegroom's party did not arise, for Feroze Gandhi's family lived in Allahabad.

Music is part of the wedding scene. It lingers in the background and forms a continuous

---

*Anand Bhawan ("abode of bliss") is the name of the Nehru family home—almost a mansion—in Allahabad. It now belongs to the nation.

[1]pandit: A Brahman, a learned man versed in the scriptures.

accompaniment to the proceedings before the ceremony. In North India it is usually provided by the shahanai,[2] whose beautiful, rather mournful strains introduce the only melancholy note in the gaiety. Often expert musicians are invited to play at a wedding, even though this may mean their coming from distant parts of the country. This again was not the case at Indi's marriage, for at a time and in a house of important political conferences it was impossible to have a continuous programme of music. So Indi's wedding was to be a blend of the traditional with the necessary restrictions imposed by circumstances.

This had not been the case at Mummie's wedding. She was married in 1921, a year of changes for the Nehru family, but although Gandhiji's[*] influence already guided the family of Swaraj Bhawan, the wedding made no concession to Gandhian simplicity except for the fact that Mummie wore a khadi[†] sari during the ceremony itself. In every other respect it followed the conventional pattern with its hours-long marriage service and its lavish feasting of hundreds of guests who must have given full scope to Nanuji's fabled extravagance.

Mummie, the darling of her father, received a glittering trousseau of a hundred and one[3] exquisite saris with matching accessories from blouses to dainty satin slippers to go with each sari. Her jewellery was fit for a princess, for, in addition to the usual sets of necklaces, earrings and bracelets which a bride is given, Mummie was also given a gold belt such as Indian women used to wear round their waists, gold armlets and gold anklets. Normally anklets are made of silver, for no ornament made of gold is supposed to be worn below the waist except by royalty and the goddesses of Indian mythology. But Nanuji was a man of royal tastes who scorned

such distinctions. Besides this elaborate personal trousseau, Mummie was given linen, furniture and silver articles for her new home, a car and, not least, a horse. She had been taught to ride as a child and had inherited her father's love of horses. It was a trousseau which far exceeded what is ordinarily given to a girl by her parents.

Her wedding photograph, taken after the ceremony, when Mummie had changed into traditional bridal attire, is proof of the sumptuousness of the occasion. It shows a doll-like bride seated demurely on a carpet at the feet of her parents. She is dressed in a sari of heavy gold tissue encrusted with jewelled embroidery. Her palla[4] covers her head but not enough to conceal the threaded pearls which line her centre parting and extend across her forehead. Her long hair, Mummie told us, had been braided with gold cord and coiled above her neck with jewelled pins. Sitting beside her in the picture, Papu looks like a fairy-tale prince in a brocade achkan[5] and churidar-pyjama[6] with a gauzy Benaras safa[7] wound jauntily round his head.

To those who had attended Mummie's wedding, Masi's in 1933 must have presented the greatest possible contrast. Nanuji had died three years earlier, and Nanima, never in robust health, was a frail shadow of herself. 1933 had been a year of political austerity. In October Mamu was out of prison but there was no knowing when he would be arrested again. All these reasons combined to make the wedding a short and simple affair. It consisted of a brief registration in the drawing-room with Masi attired in pale pink khadi.

To us, seated gravely on one side of the room, it was not like a wedding at all, for it bore no resemblance to the gay and glamorous Kashmiri weddings which took place in Allahabad. Added

---

[2]shahanai: A musical instrument resembling a bagpipe.
[*]Gandhiji: The suffix -*ji* denotes respect and affection.
[†]khadi: The coarse cloth from the spinning wheel, made into clothing by Indians to replace the boycotted manufactured cloth from England. It became more than a symbol, almost a uniform worn by rich as well as poor as a statement against imperial rule.
[3]When making a gift of any kind in India, the odd number is always considered more auspicious than the even.

[4]palla: The portion of the sari which falls over the left shoulder.
[5]achkan: A knee-length coat with a high (Russian type) collar, buttoned all the way down.
[6]churidar-pyjama: Trousers which are close-fitting to the knees and loose above.
[7]safa: A headgear made of a length of material wound around the head at an angle. It does not fit the head squarely like the Indian turban.

to this disappointment was the thought that Masi would be going to live in far-off Bombay with a tall, quiet stranger named Raja Huthee-singh, and her room upstairs, where she had so often dressed us up in bits of finery from an old clothes' box and taught us to sing and dance, would be empty. It was altogether a forlorn occasion for us, and the sight of Nanima lying pale and quiet on a sofa across the room, her small white hands looking almost transparent against her white sari, was a sobering one to everyone assembled. Sir Tej Bahadur Sapru, who had been a dear friend of Nanuji's, echoed our bewilderment when, after the registration was completed, he asked, "But when is the wedding going to take place?" He could not believe that tradition had been side-stepped to so great an extent as to dispense with all ritual.

Now, talk of Indi's wedding sent a wave of interest through India and presents began to arrive from all over the country. Her room became a cloud of rustling tissue paper and satin ribbon from which emerged gifts of silver and crystal, lovely saris, and occasionally a velvet-lined casket containing a jewelled ornament. Most of these presents had to be carefully re-wrapped and returned to the senders, for in many cases they were from people whom the family did not know.

How seldom one realizes the significance of a solemn occasion! As children we had attended several weddings and were familiar with the ritual but because the priest chanted verses from the Sanskrit scriptures we had never understood their meaning. Now that there was to be a wedding at Anand Bhawan we wanted to understand every detail of it and asked Papu about its significance. Marriage, to us, was the height of romantic achievement, and we told him so in a burst of enthusiasm.

"Yes," said Papu, "it is that all right, but here in India we consider it something more than the concern of the two people who marry each other. It is, in a sense, their dedication to the community as well. Our marriage service emphasizes this point. I don't know of any other marriage service which does."

"Is the entire orthodox ceremony going to take place?" we asked, well knowing that a Hindu service could last all night.

"No," said Papu; "Mamu is in favour of a simplified version, so we shall have only the essential ceremony which is really all that is necessary and meaningful. It should not last longer than an hour and a half."

The ceremony was to take place on the open, circular veranda outside the room which had been my grandmother's. Facing the veranda and a few yards away from it were the apartments which had once been occupied by Bibima. Anand Bhawan on this occasion was not the full and happy house it had once been, for the years had left a widening gap. The biggest gap had been left by Indi's own mother, our Mami[8] who, for many years an invalid, had died in Europe in 1936 after a prolonged illness. Ordinarily the bride's parents sit on mats facing her and the groom during the ceremony. But instead of only Mamu's mat being placed for the service, another was placed where Mami would have sat. There was a poignancy about that small, unoccupied mat, reviving the memory of Indi's courageous young mother whose health had been sacrificed to a cause which she had considered more worthwhile.

Indi came down from her room in a shell-pink khadi sari made from yarn spun by her father and edged with delicate silver embroidery. She sat down near her father for, until the Kanya Dan took place, she was still a member of her father's house. The Kanya Dan, Papu had explained to us, was the giving away of a daughter by her father, much the same as in a Christian wedding. In India it is considered the most exalted form of gift a man can make, for there is no more precious possession than a daughter. Sometimes a man who had no daughter of his own adopted one solely for the purpose of partaking in such a ceremony and achieving the merit of Kanya Dan. After the priest had chanted the appropriate verses, Indi took her place beside Feroze and sat facing her father.

The veranda had been decorated with greenery

---

[8]Mami: A Mamu's wife is known as Mami.—Author's note

and in the centre a depression had been made to accommodate the fire, the symbol of purity. A couple married according to Hindu law require no marriage certificate, for the fire is witness to the ceremony. Guests were seated on a carpet on the veranda as well as on chairs arranged below its steps, but such was the attraction of a wedding at Anand Bhawan that hundreds of citizens had poured in uninvited and nobody had been able to stop them. They had gathered round to watch the proceedings and the more agile among them had even climbed trees to get a better view. In the middle of the enchanted scene a photographer from an American fashion magazine struggled with his equipment, beads of perspiration trickling down his temples and glistening on his upper lip. In the warm March morning the subtle fragrance of incense drifted through the air, the priest's chant rose and fell, and the fire sizzled as he dripped clarified butter into it from a silver spoon. Grouped round the glowing orange flame, the soft rich colours of silk saris shimmered in the sunshine.

Mummie, standing near one of the grey stone pillars of the veranda, was watching the ceremony, her eyes filled with tears. I wondered what was making her cry, and cry in front of all those people, a thing she had never done before. Was it the thought of Indi's mother who was no longer there, or of her own mother and father and aunt; or, looking across the garden wall at Swaraj Bhawan, a deserted giant shell of a house which had once resounded with life and laughter, was she thinking perhaps of her own wedding in that very house and the unpredictable changes that had come over her family since then? Long ago she had shed the gorgeous clothes of her trousseau. Some of her most priceless possessions had been taken away by the police on raids during civil disobedience movements. Little had she dreamed, that sheltered, flowerlike little bride of 1921, what future of hardship lay ahead of her. And now another young and beautiful bride took her vows in another Anand Bhawan twenty-one years later. How soon would she be called upon

to transform that verbal dedication into a living reality? Mummie's prayer must have been a silent one that this bride, too, might emerge from any future trials blessed with the same inner fulfilment that she herself had received.

After the Kanya Dan was completed, Mamu's role in the ceremony was over and he rose and stood on one side. The young couple, too, stood up hand in hand to perform the Sapt Padi, the seven steps round the fire during which they took their vows to each other, repeating the sanskrit words after the priest in turn. Back in their places they repeated the phrases by which they dedicated themselves to their community and the world. After this came the portion of the ceremony in which all the friends and relatives of the bride participate. Leaving our places we went up to Indi and, showering her with flowerpetals, we sang verses invoking her to uphold with dignity the honourable traditions of Indian womanhood through the ages. The verses quoted the examples of India's most revered religious heroines, and it was these simple and lovely lines which brought home to us more than any other part of the ceremony the Hindu ideal of marriage. Marriage, Papu had said, was more than love and companionship between two people, for they were not merely two individuals. They represented the link between past and future generations. Marriage was the climate for the flowering of a new generation. Ultimately, it was the continuing fulfilment of a cosmic design, so that the grand ideals of Hindu antiquity continued to have meaning for a modern Indian bride. To us it was just another indication that India's culture was a vital, breathing one expressed in her daily life, not one buried and forgotten to ancient books and monuments.

Indi and Feroze moved into a little house down the road from Anand Bhawan to spend a few happy months before an uncertain future might claim them. In September that year they were both to be imprisoned, for the law against non-co-operators was no respecter of young people who had just started life together.

REVIEW QUESTIONS

1. What does Nayantara's father mean by stating that an Indian wedding is more than a matter for two people, that "it is, in a sense, their dedication to the community as well"?
2. Why the attention to astrology in selecting the date, especially since the family members were in no way orthodox?
3. Explain the conflict between the traditional way of life and the demands of the independence struggle evident in the wedding ceremony of Nayantara's mother.

A Correspondent for the BBC Observes an Indian Religious Festival (1989)

MARK TULLY, *No Full Stops in India*

The Kumbh Mela, which takes place every twelve years at Allahabad in northern India, is probably the largest religious festival in the world. The BBC referred to the 2001 festival as "probably the largest human gathering in history." Mark Tully, a long-time BBC correspondent (who resigned rather than be transferred out of India), later the Delhi-based correspondent for *The Scotsman,* brings a sense of wonder to his report on the 1989 festival.

Little is known about this event outside of India, and much of that is misunderstood or reported as exotic aberration. One American newspaper reported the 2001 event as occurring in Delhi, the capital of India, hundreds of miles from Allahabad. Originally the festival (*mela*) seems to have been a fertility rite held at various places along rivers, where pots (*kumbh*) of grain were dipped into the river before being sown with other grain. Rivers are sacred, and the Ganges is the most sacred of all. Allahabad is sited at the confluence of the Ganges, its major tributary the Jamuna (or Yamuna), and a mythical third river. Pilgrimages are a major feature in Hinduism, and this place of confluence became the most auspicious of all the sites.

The Kumbh Mela is billed as the biggest religious festival in the world, but no one knows exactly how big it is. Perhaps the gods keep records of the devotees who wash away their sins in the rivers Ganges and Jamuna at Allahabad during the festival. As far as mortals are concerned, satellite photographs, computers and the other paraphernalia of modern technology might give a reasonably accurate estimate, but they have not so far been used for this purpose. So all one can say is that the official guesstimate was that about 10 million people bathed on the most sacred day of the 1977 Kumbh Mela. There was every reason to believe that even more would come in 1989. As the official description of the preparations for the Kumbh Mela said, "Due to increase in the population and also due to increasing interest towards religion it is expected that on the main bathing day about 15 million people will take bath near the Sangam." The Sangam is the point where the Jamuna and the Ganges meet. A third river, the Saraswati, is also said to have flowed into the Sangam, but there is no sign of it today, nor is there any record of when or how it disappeared.

The pandits said that 1989 would be the most important Kumbh Mela for 144 years, because of the particularly auspicious position of the stars and planets. I had read the pandits' predictions and the official report on the preparations for the Mela, so I was very surprised when I arrived in Allahabad a week before the big bathe to find administrators, journalists, religious leaders and the local clergy all worried that the millions might not turn out this time.

The history of the Kumbh Mela—like the history of all things Hindu—is not entirely clear and is therefore fiercely debated by historians and theologians. Indians are said to be recent converts to the study of history, so it is perhaps not surprising that the first known reference to the festival appears to have been made by a Chinese. The renowned seventh-century traveller Hiuen Tsiang found that half a million people had gathered at Prayag, the old name for Allahabad, to bathe in the rivers and to attend on the Emperor Harshvardhan who was taking part in the Kumbh Mela. The emperor distributed his wealth among his vassals. They paid for their gifts and returned them to him. He thus raised taxes from his vassals and everyone gained merit from the giving and receiving of gifts. A similar practice continues to this day. Brahmins keep calves tethered to their stalls for pilgrims to buy. The pilgrims then return them, and the calves are sold and resold many times. "Godan" or the gift of a cow is one of the most meritorious acts for devout Hindus.

The word "kumbh" means an urn, and "mela" a fair. The festival celebrates one of the creation myths of Hinduism. Brahma, the creator, was floating on the primeval ocean in a trance. When he awoke, he started to create the universe. The gods and the demons decided to speed up the process by churning the ocean. They used a mountain as the churn and a giant snake as the rope to rotate it. As the ocean frothed, miraculous gifts appeared. The most valuable was an urn of a nectar which made anyone who drank it immortal. The demons grabbed the urn, but the son of Indra, who ruled the heavens, managed to spirit it away from them. Disguising himself as a rook, he flew over the earth, chased by the demons. Some say that during his flight to the abode of the gods he rested in four places, one of which was Prayag, or Allahabad. Others say that drops of nectar fell on those four places during the flight. The son of Indra took twelve days to fly to paradise, so as one day in the life of the gods is the equivalent of a year in the life of mere mortals, Kumbh Melas are held in all four places once every twelve years. Allahabad is regarded as the king of the bathing-places, and the Allahabad Mela is the most important festival.

I was staying in Allahabad with one of my political gurus, Sant Bax Singh—a former member of parliament. After being elected the first undergraduate president of the Allahabad University Students Union, he went on to Oxford and then read for the bar at Lincoln's Inn. When he returned to India, he joined the multinational Lever Brothers, where he soon emerged as the most promising Indian executive. Sant Bax Singh's father was a raja, so ruling came more naturally to his son than managing. He rejected the prosperous life that Lever's offered him and came back to Allahabad to become the member of parliament for one of the nearby constituencies. Sant Bax Singh fell out with Indira Gandhi because he openly challenged her practice of nominating the officials of the Congress Parliamentary Party instead of allowing MPs to elect them. To spite him, she promoted the career of his younger brother, Vishwanath Pratap Singh. At the time of the Mela, Sant Bax's political career was in the doldrums while V.P. Singh, after quarrelling with Rajiv Gandhi, had emerged as the opposition candidate for the premiership. But Sant Bax Singh was not overshadowed by his younger brother and was still able to summon the leading citizens of Allahabad to meet me. . . .

A sadhu was distributing ceremonial flywhisks to the disciples who were standing behind the scholars' thrones. A naked sadhu was running hither and thither trying to find a marigold garland. The finishing touches were being put to a richly caparisoned horse which was covered with a deep-red blanket embroidered with silver and mirrorwork depicting two giant peacocks. Last-minute instructions were given to the kotwals, or policemen, of the akhara. They were wrapped in scarlet shawls and carried silver staves. Their orders were not to allow any strangers into the akhara and to ensure that nothing was stolen from the sadhus' tents when the procession moved out. The gold image of Subramaniam, the six-headed son of Shiva who was the akhara's deity, was carried out of the temple on a palanquin. He was followed by a palanquin carrying the Sun God, the deity of the Niranjani's sister akhara. Mahant Rama Krishna was striding up and down the procession moving everyone into line and sorting out disputes about orders of precedence. An elderly sadhu, apparently unmoved by all the excitement, was warming his hands over a fire and mumbling mantras. Eventually the police officer in charge of our procession received clearance on his walkie-talkie for us to move out, and we started on the march to the Sangam with the sadhus and the lay supporters of the Niranjani akhara chanting "Hara Hara Mahadev," names of Shiva.

I kept close to Mahant Rama Krishna, in case the naked nagas objected to me. He was the sergeant-major of this parade of the saints, ensuring that it moved on at a brisk pace. A party of laymen dressed in white robes were marching in two neat lines; Rama Krishna ordered them to bunch up. The disciples pulling one of the raths were told to move at the double. Rama Krishna was very proud of his procession. He said, "You've only seen half of it. There's a lot still inside the akhara."

Suddenly the procession came to a halt. Rama Krishna ran up to the front to find naked sadhus arguing with the police. Even the police horses had been unable to hold back the crowds who had burst through the barriers on to the procession route. The sadhus shouted, "Get the public out of the way." A young robed ascetic turned on a photographer and asked, "Who told you to join our procession?" The photographer replied insolently, "No one." The young ascetic shouted, "Break his camera! Break his camera!" An older colleague restrained him—"No. Let him go. Don't let's have any bad blood." Fortunately the photographer managed to duck under the crowd-control barriers before the naked sadhus could vent their wrath on him. Police reinforcements were brought up and managed to clear the route. An elderly sadhu carrying two flags like a railway guard waved the green one and the procession moved off again. A naked sadhu mounted on a pony, beating a frenetic tattoo on kettledrums led the akhara to the Ganges. Two other naked sadhus danced with abandon, twirling wooden staves like demented drum majors. The trumpets, trombones, euphoniums and sousaphones of the bands blared martial music. It should have been "When the Saints Go Marching in," but it wasn't. The crowds folded their hands and bowed their heads as the raths of the mahamandaleshwars rolled past. Bengali pilgrims welcomed the saints with their own special ululations; others shouted "Victory to the eternal dharma, long live the sadhus!"

When the road started to slope down towards the Ganges, the naked nagas broke ranks and ran shrieking with joy into the Sangam. They splashed each other like children playing and rubbed the sacred water into their bodies, but they didn't stay in long. Their robed colleagues followed, many of them wearing just the shorts which serve as underpants. The crowds again broke through the barriers, and it was soon impossible to see who were sadhus and who were not. One of the naked drum majors danced ferociously—it was a miracle that no one was hit by his stave. A young sadhu forced his way through the crowd, leading my 89-year-old friend Mahant Brij Kumar. This venerable old man stood up to his waist in the muddy river and poured water over his chest, smiling beatifically. A man and his wife pleaded with my police sergeant to look after their son so that they could bathe. "He's ill, he's ill," they implored. "We want to take a bathe to make him better." But the sergeant refused to take charge of the boy. In that crowd there was no knowing when or where the parents would emerge, and the sergeant could well have been landed with responsibility for taking their son to the Congress Party's lost-and-found bureau.

By this stage we were having the greatest difficulty in keeping out of the water, so the sergeant suggested we beat a retreat to the police watch-tower to get a safer view of the bathing.

The watch-tower was surrounded by pilgrims trying to hand in notices about their lost relatives, to be broadcast over the loudspeaker. We pushed through them only to find our way blocked by a police lady sitting firmly on the middle of the ladder leading to the first platform of the two-tiered tower. "It's dangerous," she said. "There are too many people up there already. You can't come up." My sergeant insisted, and she let us edge past her. The tower shook ominously as we scrambled on to the lower platform.

Across the Ganges, the sun had just risen. It was shrouded by the morning mist rising from the rivers and the dust thrown up by millions of pilgrims who had spread like a black cloud covering all the banks of the rivers. It was impossible even to guess how many millions there were. An armada of small craft was ferrying the more privileged pilgrims to bathe from the boats anchored in the middle of the Sangam. Below, the police were still struggling to clear the area reserved for the akharas. The last of the Niranjanis were making their way back to reform their procession. The police horses were called in again, and the crowds were forced to give way.

Sweepers cleaned the ghat in preparation for the Juna akhara, whose naked nagas were already approaching. When the nagas saw the cameramen on the watch-tower, they stopped, brandishing their weapons and roared, "No photographs!"

All the cameras were lowered with alacrity—none of the press fancied withstanding an attack by those ferocious holy men. Some nagas ran straight into the Ganges; others crouched to ease themselves before entering the sacred water. There must have been at least 500 of them. Their bodies were smeared with ash, their long hair was matted and their beards were unkempt. One elderly naga's beard came down to his ankles. They were followed by the initiates, with their skimpy loincloths and shaven heads. Then came the mahamandaleshwars, sitting under their gold-embroidered parasols. They descended from their raths, solemnly disrobed and went down to the river with their disciples. This time the police managed to keep the crowds behind the barriers. The nagas ran back from the Sangam whooping with joy and cartwheeling on the hard sand. The initiates came back shivering—they had not yet mastered the yogic skills to keep themselves warm. The mahamandaleshwars returned to their raths, and the procession moved off again. Some disciples struggled to pull their master's rath up the hill. The police allowed the crowd to break through to help them on their way.

The Juna akhara should have been followed by the Vaishnavites, but I heard over the police radio that they would not be coming. Apparently the deputy inspector general of police had failed to resolve their electoral dispute and so they could not agree who was to be given pride of place in their procession.

I made my way back to the press camp with the pilgrims who had bathed and were on their way home. I had never been in such a peaceful crowd. There was no frenzy, just the calm certainty of faith: the knowledge that what had to be done had been done.

The vast majority of the pilgrims were villagers. Their faith gave them the courage to ignore the ugly rumours and the fortitude to travel in overcrowded trains and buses, to walk for many miles and to sleep in the open. Yet the villagers are being told that their faith, which means so much to them, is superstition, and that they must be secular. The élite for the most part ignored the Kumbh Mela, but those who did come travelled in cars and slept in tents.

Two days later I went back to the commissioner's tent. He told me that 27 million people had bathed during the previous three days. I was not entirely convinced that the methods he had used to count the pilgrims were scientific, but even the querulous local press said that millions had eventually turned up. The commissioner admitted that he had been worried at one stage. Looking back on the Mela, he said, "The press and some politicians were on at me about overspending, and the Mela did seem to be rather empty when you arrived. I should have realized that there was an unusually long gap between the first two bathing-days and the big one, so the momentum was bound to die down."

"What about the BBC, then?" I asked.

The commissioner smiled. "Perhaps your coming stopped that. Actually, I now think it was just part of the campaign to discredit me."

There was only one serious accident within the Mela during the bathe and that was caused by the family of one of Rajiv Gandhi's ministers, Mrs Rajendra Kumari Bajpai, who, with her son Ashok, controlled the Congress Party in Alla-habad. The police had arranged separate embarkation and disembarkation jetties for the pilgrims who were allowed to travel by boat to the Sangam. They knew that if boats returned full to the embarkation jetties they would be swamped by waiting pilgrims. The Bajpai family, however, insisted on returning to the jetty they had set out from, and the very accident the police had feared occurred. One of their boats was swamped by pilgrims and capsized. Two of their servants were drowned.

No other country in the world could provide a spectacle like the Kumbh Mela. It was a triumph for the much maligned Indian administrators, but it was a greater triumph for the people of India. And how did the English-language press react to this triumph? Inevitably, with scorn. The *Times of India,* the country's most influential paper, published a long article replete with phrases like "Obscurantism ruled the roost in Kumbh," "Religious dogma overwhelmed reason at the Kumbh," and "The Kumbh after all remained a mere spectacle with its million hues but little substance." The *Times of India* criticized the Vishwa Hindu Parishad's politics, but made no attempt to analyse or even to describe the piety of the millions who bathed at the Sangam.

REVIEW QUESTIONS

1. Tully refers to the Kumbh Mela as "a spectacle," and in so doing reflects the view of the Indian press. Why this skepticism?
2. Tully has great affection for Indian people. How does that show in this selection?
3. How would you describe Tully's reporting on this event?
4. In what ways is the Kumbh Mela different from festivals in the West?

13

Africa, 1918 to the Present

The paired themes of colonization and decolonization so dominate twentieth-century African history that it is virtually impossible to discuss any topic related to Africa without including European political and economic domination and subsequent native African independence movements. The result of the nineteenth-century "scramble for Africa" was the division of nearly the entire continent among Great Britain, France, Italy, Germany, Spain, Portugal, and Belgium. By 1914 only Ethiopia and Liberia had managed to remain independent. Once the Europeans' claims had been made and recognized by each other—a process that was disrupted by World War I (1914–1918)—the colonial nations that had been victorious in the war moved to consolidate actual power in the territories they controlled. This often entailed putting down wars of resistance, which the Europeans usually labeled "rebellions," and it sometimes involved conflicts between groups of white settlers fighting each other for territories in the name of their homelands.

By the 1920s, Africa was firmly under European control, although the native desire for self-government never completely disappeared, nor did the European craving for further territory in Africa (exemplified by Italy's invasion of Ethiopia in 1935). After World War II (1939–1945), the native desire for self-government became a mass movement. The already war-torn European nations had to choose between fighting costly wars in Africa to maintain control of their colonies there or granting them independence. Thus, many European powers began to prepare their colonies for self-rule—a much less expensive proposition than warfare. Most granted independence to their colonies in the late 1950s and 1960s, beginning with Ghana in 1957, although France and Portugal fought strenuously—and unsuccessfully—to retain control of Algeria, Angola, Mozambique, and Portuguese Guinea (now Guinea-Bissan). Today only a few small territories and islands in Africa remain under European administration: Réunion and Mayotte (French islands off the eastern coast of Africa, near Madagascar), and Melilla and Ceuta (Spanish enclaves in Morocco). Despite decolonization, however, the effects of more than a century of European colonial policies—based on racism and prejudice—still linger in most places.

Colonial domination differed in the various regions of Africa. In southern Africa, for example, European settlers controlled the best lands and confined roughly 60 percent of native peoples to crowded and inferior lands called "native reserves." The vast majority of Europeans found nothing wrong with this system, but when Julian Huxley visited a market in the Kikuyu Reserve in Kenya in 1929, he expressed surprise that the Kikuyu did not treat him with hostility. In the Union of South Africa, whites not only implemented the reserve system, but they created an industrialized society that barred native Africans from all but the most menial of jobs and paid them less than one-fifth, on average, of what whites earned. Naboth Mokgatle, a black political activist and labor leader, wrote an autobiography that describes his life under this system: Apartheid. In western and northern Africa, however, Europeans often ruled with the help of African officials and chiefs. The result of years of white domination can be gauged by reading George Orwell's "Essay on Marrakech," a description and disparagement of the typical indifference with which most Europeans viewed the various African peoples who suffered under their rule.

Despite heavy European presence in Africa, Westernization did not penetrate all areas. However, the variety of native African cultures under European colonialism was accessible to travelers and visitors who were willing to go beyond the usual tourist or business destinations. For example, Elisabeth Marshall Thomas and her family spent the better part of three years in the early 1950s living with groups of San peoples in the Kalahari, where she observed customs and traditions that had not changed significantly in hundreds of years. Even as late as 1966, Flora Nwapa was able to draw on personal experiences and observations to recreate Nigerian village life in her novel, *Efuru.*

Most visitors to Africa in the twentieth century, however, were struck by the clash of native and European values and customs. Orwell saw this firsthand in Marrakech in 1939; and it was still a predominant theme of Irish writer Dervla Murphy and British businessman Peter Biddlecombe in Cameroon in the late 1980s and early 1990s. But perhaps nowhere in this chapter is the dichotomy between old and new, African and European, more obvious than in Pico Iyer's description of Ethiopia in 1995. Near the ancient Christian rock-cut church of Lalibela, Iyer notes that he felt like he was passing "through an illuminated Bible of the thirteenth century, except that all the figures moved." Nevertheless, he had arrived at Lalibela in a Land Cruiser, and he left by plane.

The experiences of African women also reflect this contrast between old and new. Much of Elizabeth Marshall Thomas's description of San in the Kalahari focuses on the traditional roles of the Gikwe women that she encountered. In Marrakech, George Orwell saw long lines of impoverished elderly women stooped under heavy loads of firewood. The first chapter of Flora Nwapa's *Efuru* revolves entirely around the traditional lives and customs of Nigerian women. Finally, Dervla Murphy's conversation with prostitutes in Cameroon focuses on women who have made modern choices based on traditional values and may end up paying a terrible personal price for their decisions.

Modernization and decolonization have not solved Africa's many problems—political inexperience, ethnic violence, European economic domination, overpopulation, famine, disease, and gender inequalities—most of which are the legacy of colonization and decolonization. At the beginning of the twenty-first century, Africa sits at a crossroads. On the one hand, it can remain "adrift in the wake of history," allowing the problems of the twentieth century to continue. On the other hand, it can opt to emphasize respect for human rights and strive to resolve disputes peacefully.

A British Biologist Visits a Kikuyu Market (1929)

JULIAN HUXLEY, *Africa View*

Sir Julian Huxley (1887–1975), a well-known British biologist and a prolific writer, sought to relate science to contemporary social issues. He is credited with helping to shape the direction of modern biology. His education at Eton and Oxford was followed by a noteworthy career in academia and international humanitarianism. Huxley taught at Rice Institute in Houston, Oxford University, and King's College at the University of London; he collaborated with H. G. Wells on *The Science of Life* and wrote dozens of his own books. After World War II Huxley helped found UNESCO (the United Nations Educational, Scientific and Cultural Organization), becoming its first director-general in 1946. In the last part of his life he was deeply concerned with the world's problems of overpopulation, poverty, ignorance, and the conservation of wildlife and wilderness. He also traveled extensively outside of Great Britain on behalf of various educational and government agencies.

In 1929, the British Colonial Office's Committee on Education asked Huxley to visit East and Central Africa. His report was revised and published several years later as *Africa View,* from which the following selection was taken. At the time of his visit, Kenya was a British colony, and the Kikuyu (Gikuyu) were the largest of over forty ethnic groups within its borders. In the 1920s and 1930s, they were at the forefront of what Huxley referred to as the "native problem."

In 1887, the rising wealth and land-consciousness of the Kikuyu had come to an abrupt end with the arrival of the British East Africa Company. In 1904, the British government moved in and began actively recruiting white settlers for vast tracts of land appropriated by force or threat of force. Most of the Kikuyu were displaced to higher, inferior lands, but large numbers also became low-paid laborers on the new European farms. The white settlers eventually devised an exploitative system in which "resident laborers" (often called "squatters") farmed small plots of two or three acres in exchange for their labor. The Kikuyu, not surprisingly, resented and resisted this process, but there was little actual violence: spears and arrows were no match for guns. After Kenya became an official British colony in 1920, the British settled large numbers of World War I veterans on the remaining lands of the Kikuyu, and the majority of Kenya's indigenous peoples were herded into "native reserves," the largest of which was located near Murang'a. Many individuals, particularly members of the highly adaptive Kikuyu, managed to receive a colonial education and converted to Christianity. This Westernization, however, had unforeseen results: the Kikuyu organized very quickly and became the leaders of nationalistic movements that demanded the return of expropriated lands, the elimination of racial discrimination, and eventually, independence. The first resistance groups, in fact, were formed as early as 1923.

Not surprisingly, Huxley, who was doubtless familiar with the activities of the British in Kenya, was somewhat wary of visiting the Kikuyu Reserve. As a British citizen and as a white man, he expected to be treated with hostility—or at the very least, suspicion—and was amazed when he was not. Despite his scientific training and interests in human rights, his general attitude toward native Africans was one of paternalism and condescension.

One of the peculiarities for which the Kikuyus have always been noted is their markets. Whether this be due to their bargaining temperament which makes them enjoy haggling and chaffering for its own sake, or to a love of change and company, the results are remarkable. In quite a number of places in the Reserve, markets are held once or even twice a week, and are attended by crowds of natives: it is not at all uncommon for over a thousand Kikuyu to be crowded together on such a market-ground. I was lucky enough to strike three market-days in my short trip, and brought away a very vivid impression of the activity and orderliness of these African trading centres.

The market-place is merely an open space set aside for such use, sometimes out in the open country, sometimes on a sort of village green close to a little settlement, bordered by the tin stores and ramshackle shops of Indian traders. There are no booths or tables; the goods are exposed on the bare ground, or in certain cases slung on a string between two posts. Most of the market is naturally taken up with agricultural produce; the variety of this is extraordinary, and completely contradicts the idea that the African is always content with a monotonous diet. There is millet (of at least two kinds), maize, and various other grains I did not know; beans and several kinds of peas; sweet potatoes and taro and sugar-cane; and many other kinds of produce. The vendors squat by their wares, all close together; the buyers pick their way deviously through the dense crowd and over the varied foodstuffs.

Each main category of goods has its own section of the market-ground. Over in one corner is the firewood. This is a very precious commodity, since the deforestation which the Kikuyus themselves began by constantly cutting down new areas of forest for their shifting cultivation, their goats have perpetuated by preventing the new growth of seedling trees; and their Reserve, which was once all richly wooded, is now bare of trees, save for a few sacred groves on hill summits, and patches of gum and wattle which the Government have at last persuaded them to begin planting. Anyhow, bundles of kindling cost more in Kikuyuland than they would in London.

In another place is the salt department. For some reason the vendors of this in one market I saw were all young lads. The "salt" is largely soda, with admixture of other salts, and is a very necessary ingredient of the natives' diet. It comes long distances from the salt-lakes in various parts of the colony. Here, again, is the snuff and tobacco section; the instrument used to measure out the snuff is always a cent piece attached to the end of a stick—a unit of measurement invented by the natives and rigorously adhered to by them. On the outskirts of one market was the goat department; this was for some reason rather less crowded than the rest.

Another activity of the outskirts is the sale of produce to Indian traders. You see the old shop-keeper towering above the little Kikuyu women, bowed down with their heavy sacks, weighing the produce and paying over the shillings and cents. Perhaps you are struck with amazement for a moment at the ramifications of the world's economic system, invented by man and yet seemingly now out of man's control, which sends its tentacles into these remote equatorial villages, and dislodges Indians from their proper home to come and help thrust change upon an African tribe; then the impression fades, and the actuality of the scene takes you again.

Perhaps the most intriguing parts of the market are where personal adornment is bought and sold. Kikuyu women wear an abundance of bead rings (pinkish is the fashionable colour just now) suspended in clusters on either side of their heads. These you may see, of all sizes, dangling from a string between two posts, with women dawdling along and eyeing them. Then there are elaborate beadwork belts and forehead straps, adornments for the lobe of the ear, brass neck-rings. There may be two or three "jewellers'" stands in one market; and I was interested to find by questioning them that the prices were identical in all.

Then there are the coils of wire which the women wear around their legs. These, it seems, cannot be put on by unskilled hands any more than a permanent wave can be self-administered; and on one fringe of the market is an expert who will ring a girl in style for a fee (so I elicited through my companion's interpretation) of one shilling per leg. The expert's wife and family will be engaged in preparing the wire: it is pegged down at one end, and then pulled and rubbed to make it straight and give it a polish. The expert himself was an oldish man who, seated on a nice little olive-wood stool, attended to the real business of twisting the wire in even coils round the leg. For some parts of the operation his clients can stand, but for others they have to sit on the ground, and, balancing themselves with their hands, hold up a leg. The process takes time. At the beginning one girl whom I saw being thus adorned was still there, I am almost certain, and holding up the same leg still when I left the market nearly an hour later.

What strikes one most at a Kikuyu market is its wonderful orderliness. The market-place is as active as an ant-hill; it seethes with humanity, coffee-coloured human beings talking, laughing, bargaining, picking their way through squatting forms and over heaps of grain and vegetables; there were no Europeans about, and I could not see any native policemen; and yet there was no quarrelling, not even a squabble or an unseemly raising of voices, in any of the three markets I saw.

In the markets well inside the Reserve you see very few Kikuyus wearing European dress. The women especially cling tenaciously to the tra-

ditional costume of heavy skins, greasy and dirty, no doubt, but warm and rain-resistant, the bright metal round arms and legs, the pinky-mauve bead circles bunched below the ears. There are no fashions—only Fashion, uniform and very slow-changing. The only variation is that a few women—a bride, or a guest going to a wedding or a dance—will have on their best clothes instead of their workaday ones. This means that they will be wearing a specially good skin, clean and untorn, and glistening a rich yellowy-brown from the application of a mixture of grease and ochreous earth; their hair will be shiny with the same mixture, and dressed with especial care; and they will be wearing all their bead ornaments.

The men go in a good deal for variously-coloured European blankets. Some of the dandies carry knobbed sticks or put a feather in their hair; it is a charming sight to see two such young fellows strolling through the crowd, hand in hand, a David and Jonathan couple. Many of the older men and women as they grow wizened acquire a strange look of ancient wisdom or distinction; many of all ages have the queer gnome-like look which I mentioned before as of creatures essentially incomprehensible to us alien whites; but there are many interesting faces, many merry and intelligent ones among the boys, many pretty ones among the girls, though the prettiness is not according to our ordinary European standards.

The impression you get is of an industrious, sociable people, not in the least more brutalized or less intelligent than uneducated peasantry of whatever colour or country. They, like you or me, are tied up with the destinies of England and the British Empire. Over and over again one wonders what will be the effect of the change that is inevitably creeping in upon them, through the suppression of their tribal wars and feuds, their gradual Christianizing and education, their adoption of better methods of agriculture and higher standards of comfort. The existence of a hut-tax enforces periodical migrations upon almost all able-bodied males, migrations to and from white men's estates and white men's cities where they may work for wages as labourers or house-boys.

One hopes that as time goes on more and more of them will be able to remain at home and build up a real peasant civilization of their own, comparable to the peasant civilization of Europe before the industrial revolution. A central island of Kenya may be a white man's country; but even now there are two hundred natives to every one European, and clearly our policy should be to encourage native production as it has been encouraged in West Africa. Once the natives reach a certain degree of prosperity, they will begin asking for the things we make, and a flow of native-produced exports from Kenya to Britain will mean a flow of British-produced goods—clothing materials and cutlery, agricultural implements and clocks, bicycles and trinkets—in the return direction.

This ideal is often supposed to be incompatible with the welfare of the white settlers, who demand a constant supply of native labour for their farms. But the two aims are not really opposed. As the efforts of the Medical Service begin to bear fruit, and better housing and higher standards of health and infant welfare become prevalent, the native population, which of late years has been more or less stationary or even decreasing, will turn and go up; and if this happens, there will be ample man-power to supply both the outside labour market and the development of a true native civilization. Increased native prosperity is the only permanent way to increased all-round prosperity in a country like Kenya.

REVIEW QUESTIONS

1. Why was Huxley surprised by the orderliness of the market?
2. How were the Kikuyu markets visited by Huxley an integral part of the world's economic system?
3. What of Huxley's personal biases are evident in this selection? Give examples.

A Black Labor Leader Recounts His Life Under Apartheid (1925–1926)

NABOTH MOKGATLE, *The Autobiography of an Unknown South African*

Naboth Monyadioe Moreleba Mokgatle (1911–1985) was a political activist, labor leader, and writer who spent the last twenty-one years of his life living in exile in London. His early life during the formative years of Apartheid and his experiences fighting for its abolition are the subject of *The Autobiography of an Unknown South African.* Before he was forced to leave the country, he founded and led first the Dairy Workers Union and then the African General Workers Union. Mokgatle clashed frequently with the government and was arrested and imprisoned countless times. His home and offices were often searched, his property confiscated, his mail intercepted. In the end, he was denied a South African passport to prevent him from attending the 1954

Conference of the World Federation of Trade Unions in Rumania. He wrote his own—a typed affadavit—and left the country anyway. He had no luggage, no papers, and 3 schillings and 3 pence in his pocket. South Africa refused to allow him back, capping a life of injustice and discrimination with one final outrage.

The eighth and youngest child of a family descended from chieftains, Mokgatle ran away from home at age twelve to avoid working for his uncle. Calling himself Johannes, for two years he worked for a Dutch farmer, Herman Lange. Mokgatle's parents discovered almost immediately where their son was, but they allowed him to continue working on the Lange farm in part because the payment for each year of his labor would be a female calf. Although he had no formal schooling, he was a quick learner. He spent the first year doing manual agricultural labor, but after the birth of the couple's second child, Hendrik, Mokgatle was promoted to running errands for Mrs. Lange and looking after the children. His arrival on the farm, his eventual departure, and some of his observations of race relations in rural Kroondal constitute the following selection.

Ironically, South Africa was one of the earliest of the European colonies in Africa to receive its independence. It became a British dominion in 1910 and a fully independent member of the Commonwealth of Nations in 1931. At its creation it was an artifical union of several former British colonies and two defeated Boer republics, and factionalism (especially between English- and Dutch-speaking whites) was a serious problem. The depression, however, united whites against black Africans, as farmers of both races were forced into the cities to compete for scarce though unskilled jobs. To protect whites, the government began taking steps to restrict blacks, or "coloureds," as they were designated by law. Through the 1930s and 1940s, these laws increased in severity, ultimately leading to the official adoption of Apartheid in 1948. Legal limits were placed on the number of black workers whom companies could hire. Black labor unions, multiracial political parties, and interracial marriages were all outlawed. Blacks were forbidden by law to own property in urban areas, and they were restricted to separate, vastly inferior residential areas in cities. Movement of blacks to the cities was severely limited, and "pass books" were required for all travel within South Africa and for work in urban areas. Eventually, approximately 60 percent were relegated to living on ten artificial African "homelands," similar to reserves or reservations in other nations. In the 1930s, therefore, Mokgatle's struggle against unfair and restrictive labor practices was all but futile. Although he did witness some progress in the early 1980s, he died in 1985—nine years before the government of Nelson Mandela finally put an end to Apartheid in 1994.

My first year with the Langes was a mixture of duties. At times I worked in the fields leading a team of oxen pulling the plough, cultivating the fields or pulling the farm rake levelling the earth the plough had turned upside down or inside out. On other occasions I went out with the cattle for grazing, leaving in the morning and returning shortly before sunset. All Kroondal farmers were using ox teams to cultivate their fields. All of them had large numbers of cattle from which they got milk and butter. I think that five or six weeks after I had hired myself to the Langes, one afternoon while I was leading a team of oxen driven by a man named Hendrik, I was called back to the house.

When I got to the house, I found my mother and sister Majone waiting to see me. Instead of greeting them with pleasure and a smiling face, I greeted them with tears rolling down my cheeks. I was appealing to them not to take me back with them to my uncle whom I was no longer inclined to work with. Mother, moved by my distress, waited until I had stopped weeping. After I had stopped, as though my head had no more tears to release, mother greeted me with motherly love and said, "We are here sent by your father only to find out where you are, but not to take you away. Your father says that taking you away would be useless, because you would run away again and perhaps go farther than you have gone." My employer Mr. Herman Lange, and his wife Ida, were listening all the time. Mother thanked them for having looked after me until she came and said further that my appearance convinced her that they were looking after me well and would continue to do so.

Mother then told them that my name was not Johannes, but Naboth. Mr. Lange replied that since it was easy for them to call me Johannes, they would continue to call me by that name. Afterwards, mother and my sister left, saying that since the day was far spent they would spend the night at Bethlehem Location in Rustenburg with friends of my family. I stayed behind, relieved, knowing that I had permission from my parents to work for the Langes for a female calf to be given to me at the end of twelve months.

The hiring of myself to the Langes in Kroondal showed me two things which I did not know existed. The European way of life as practised in South Africa, and Segregation, Apartheid. At first, though I did not ask, I wondered why we, the black people who worked for the Langes, slept in a tobacco shed and wheat store which was next to the horse stable. There were no chairs for us to sit down on or tables in the place where we slept. I was an innocent tribal boy beginning to live in a different world from the one I was born into and knew. One evening, it was a warm evening, still light, but stars were beginning to appear in the sky, and Mr. Herman Lange called his older men together to give them orders about the next day's work and to get reports from others as to how they performed the tasks he had set them in the morning. They all sat on the ground.

While Mr. Herman Lange's workmen sat on the ground, he sat on a bench alone giving the instructions about the next day's work in the fields and talking to others whom he had not found time to visit in the fields where they worked that day. Innocently, I joined them and went straight to the bench and sat next to Mr. Lange. All the older men and others who were already accustomed to the European way of life in South Africa became breathless. They had not seen anything like that before. An old man who drove the team of oxen I led that day tried to take me away from the bench, but Mr. Lange spoke to him in Dutch, saying, "Leave him, he is still stupid. Talk to him afterwards; make him understand."

Later, when the meeting was over, the old man, whose name was Hendrik, took me aside and said, "Boy, you mustn't sit where a white man sits; you can't sit on the chairs they use, drink from the cups they use, eat from their plates, or sleep in the same house with them. Don't do it again," he said. "Didn't you see us all sitting on the ground? You are lucky," Hendrik continued, "he didn't push you off or beat you to teach you that you can't sit on the same bench as a white man." I did not ask why, or say anything. I only listened to what Hendrik told me. That was the day on which I came into contact with colour segregation. I was twelve years old. At first, when I began to work for the Langes, I wondered why we were not sharing the house with them, or why there was no house built for us to sleep in. Hendrik explained all to me in a short time. I learned and never repeated my mistake.

As time went by I noticed that we at the Langes were not the only ones who slept in the shed or in buildings which were not built for people to sleep in. It was the same throughout Kroondal. Only female servants slept in rooms built specially for them very close to the masters' houses, so that a watch could be kept over them. Kroondal farmers and their wives were very strict with their female servants. I cannot recall a single case of a girl who worked for them and returned to her parents pregnant. I am sure that the reason Mr. Lange did not push me off the bench was that he was not a rough, violent man. During the two years I spent with him I did not once hear him swear or beat anyone, although he was strict.

Herman Lange and his wife Ida, though they practised segregation like other farmers of Kroondal and the rest of the Europeans in South Africa, were good and kind people. Like the rest of the Kroondal farmers, they cared very much for their workmen and women. Farmers' wives baked and cooked for all of us. Everyone who worked for them had enough to eat. They grew peas, potatoes, wheat, maize, fruits of many varieties, but not oranges. They were not for the market but for domestic use. Only tobacco was grown for the market. The maize porridge which was eaten by African workmen was cooked by female servants, who were found in every Kroondal home.

There was plenty of meat, mostly pork. Every winter season, pigs were reared, fed well three times a day, and by the time the next winter set in they were fat and some could hardly move. Then the slaughtering of the pigs began, providing everybody with fresh pork to enjoy. In every Kroondal home at that time, everybody ate and enjoyed tasty home-made pork sausages, and some polonies made of pigs' blood mixed with small pieces of pork. Milk, too, was produced for domestic use, though work people had to wait for it a day or so until the cream for butter-making had been taken from it. Pigs too enjoyed a good deal of it. No one who was at Kroondal at the time could complain of want of food.

Breakfast consisted of a large slice of white or brown bread baked by the farmer's wife and a large mug of coffee. The mug was made out of a jam tin by a Scotch plumber and black-smith who lived in Kroondal mending farmers' ploughs, pots and everything requiring mend-

ing. The Scotch plumber was not married and lived alone in one room behind his workshop. He was a short man with bushy eyebrows. He may have understood everything spoken in German, but I doubt whether he spoke the language, because he was spoken to only in his own language. I saw him on two occasions playing his pipes at a wedding. On the whole he seemed a lonely man, because on Sundays, when he was free from his hammers and fires, he was always sitting alone by his workshop or taking long walks enjoying the weather and fresh air. Kroondal was a lovely place, especially when crops and plants in the farmlands were green. The farms were well worked and well irrigated. As a Christian community, Kroondal farmers ceased work on Sundays and so did their work people.

On my arrival at the Langes I found them with only one child, a daughter Elizabeth who was eighteen months old. There were no other children of her age nearby, so Elizabeth had no one to play with and spent most of the time with her mother. Although Kroondal farmers as I have already said, spoke Sesotho perhaps better than I could do in my young days, in addition they spoke Dutch—known today in South Africa as Afrikaans. I do not know how well they spoke English. But they saw to it that they spoke to their children in German and encouraged them to feel that they were Germans.

There were in other Kroondal homes children of both sexes who were born there and never lived in African tribal villages as had their parents, who spoke very fluent Sesotho: these were children of families like the Penzhorns, the Benholdts, the Millers, the Bakebergs and the family of Hendrik Jorde. Parents of those families were born in African tribal villages and their children were born in Kroondal, but the children spoke Sesotho as fluently as their parents. I still do not know how they acquired the language, because all the time I was there their parents spoke to them only in German.

When they spoke Sesotho, one would never have imagined that they spoke German as well. I think that speaking the same language draws

people together. The white children of Kroondal of my age were very fond of the people who
worked for their parents. In school holidays or
on Saturdays, when they were free from school,
the boys wanted to go out with us into the grazing fields with their fathers' cattle and to be
there the whole day playing games with us.
Their parents were dead against their going out
with the cattle, but some boys used to run away
from home to join us. On many occasions we
were found with them swimming naked in the
dams. Only when they were at school did their
parents know that they were not with African
boys in the grazing fields. I had no such boy at
the Langes. Some boys told me that their boss's
sons stole things for them that they thought
their parents were not giving them. . . .

At the end of two years and three months I
left the Langes and Kroondal, accompanied by
another tribal boy from Phokeng called Chi-
anyana Rathebe. He had joined me at the Langes
at the beginning of my second year. We had
three cows between us which Mr. Herman Lange
bought us at Rustenburg cattle market. Chi-
anyana was two years older than I was and we
were born in the same street in the part of Phokeng called Saron. It was in the middle of July
nineteen-twenty-five when we said good-bye to
Kroondal. Many months before my departure
Mrs. Ida Lange did her utmost to persuade me
to stay another year, because she liked me and
their son Hendrik was so used to me looking after him. I was so homesick that, though I had no
complaint against the Langes' treatment of me,
Ida's appeals got into my right ear and got out
through the left ear.

It was because of homesickness that I left, and
my father's call that I should return to Phokeng
because he wanted me to go to school. I was
fourteen years of age and my father was worried
that if he allowed me to stay away much longer,
I would never go to school and would die a man
who could not read or write. He had not gone to
school himself, but since my four sisters had
been to school, I, his only living son and the one
who would perpetuate his name, should also go
to school. Ida suspected that it was not because
I was homesick that I wanted to leave. She complained that I was hiding from her that I felt un-
justly treated. On more than one occasion she
begged me to be frank with her and tell her the
real truth why I was leaving. When I mentioned
homesickness and my father's call she offered to
ask my father to allow me to stay another year,
and for the cure of homesickness, she said they
could let me go back to Phokeng for three weeks.
But, as I have already said, a third year was too
much for me.

I noticed that Mr. Herman Lange did not co-
operate with his wife in urging me to stay.
Though I did not tell Ida, there was also inside
me a suspicion that her husband was not keen to
keep me on because he could not use me as he
did the other boys. What discouraged me was
that one day one of the men said I was leaving
because I wanted to go to school, and when Mr.
Lange heard this he laughed and asked, "What
would a monkey do with education?" His remark went deep into my feelings. I did not re-
sent what he said about education or school, but
the fact that he compared me to a monkey.

REVIEW QUESTIONS

1. What did Mokgatle like and dislike about working for Herman and Ida Lange? Why?
2. Were the Lange family typical of other farm families in Kroondal? Explain.
3. Later in his life, Mokgatle's labor activities were fueled by a passionate desire to end
   racial injustice. Can you detect his later sense of outrage in this selection? Cite examples from the reading.

An English Novelist Discusses Race Relations in Morocco (1939)

GEORGE ORWELL, *"Essay on Marrakech"*

George Orwell was the pen name of Eric Arthur Blair (1903–1950), an English novelist and social critic most famous as the author of *Animal Farm* and *1984.* He was born in Bengal, India, where his father was a minor civil servant. The Blair family had more than a century-old tradition of employment with either the Church of England or the Colonial Civil Service, and Orwell later joked that his family's social standing was "lower-upper-middle class"— it affected all the pretensions of the well-educated bourgeoisie but lacked the finances to match.

Before beginning his career as a professional writer, Orwell studied at Eton for three years (without earning a degree), then spent six years in Burma (Myanmar) with the Indian Imperial Police. He returned to Europe early in 1928 to investigate the lives of the urban poor in Paris and London and spent the next three years deliberately experiencing their grinding poverty firsthand. The result was *Down and Out in Paris and London* (1933), which recounted—and apparently exaggerated—his observations. Its unequivocal socialist outlook also prompted him to begin using his famous pen name. The book was soon followed by *Burmese Days,* a caustic portrayal of British colonial decadence. In all, Orwell wrote nine books and a wealth of essays. His writing frequently drew on personal experience and always reflected his political sentiments. He was particularly concerned with poverty and social injustice, and he delighted in exposing the hypocrisies of the middle and upper classes. He also liked nothing better than to shock his readers.

In 1938, Orwell became ill with pulmonary tuberculosis, which plagued him for the rest of his life. He spent part of the next year in a series of convalescent homes, then traveled to Marrakech, the capital of French Morocco, hoping to benefit from the dry climate. There, on the eve of World War II, fear of the Nazis had temporarily halted a burgeoning independence movement (which eventually succeeded in 1956). The colonial policies of the French—based on racism and exploitation—were thus in full force.

In this selection, Orwell focuses on Europeans' oblivion to the lower classes in Marrakech: Jews, Senegalese blacks, the poor, the elderly, and women. In 1939, Marrakech had a population of approximately 200,000, of which he estimates at least 10 percent owned "literally nothing except the rags they stand up in." Yet no one took notice, he observes:

> When you see how the people live, and still more easily they die, it is always difficult to believe that you are walking among human beings. All colonial empires are in reality founded upon that fact. The people all have brown faces—besides, there are so many of them! Are they really the same flesh as yourself? Do they even have names? Or are they merely a kind of undifferentiated brown stuff, about as individual as bees or coral insects? They rise

out of the earth, they sweat and starve for a few years, and then they sink back into the nameless mounds of the graveyard and nobody notices that they are gone. And even the graves themselves soon fade back into the soil. Sometimes, out for a walk, as you break your way through the prickly pear, you notice that it is rather bumpy underfoot, and only a certain regularity in the bumps tells you that you are walking over skeletons."

Speculating that Europeans ignored natives because their skin was brown, Orwell tries to explain why this was so:

> In a tropical landscape, one's eye takes in everything except human beings. It takes in the dried-up soil, the prickly pear, the palm tree, and the distant mountain, but it always misses the peasant hoeing at his patch. He is the same colour as the earth, and a great deal less interesting to look at. . . . What does Morocco mean to a Frenchman? An orange-grove or a job in Government service. Or to an Englishman? Camels, castles, . . . brass trays, and bandits.

One could probably live in Morocco for years, he laments, "without noticing that for nine-tenths of the people the reality of life is an endless, back-breaking struggle to wring a little food out of an eroded soil."

When you go through the Jewish quarters you gather some idea of what the medieval ghettoes were probably like. Under their Moorish rulers the Jews were only allowed to own land in certain restricted areas, and after centuries of this kind of treatment they have ceased to bother about overcrowding. Many of the streets are a good deal less than six feet wide, the houses are completely windowless, and sore-eyed children cluster everywhere in unbelievable numbers, like clouds of flies. Down the centre of the street there is generally running a little river of urine.

In the bazaar huge families of Jews, all dressed in the long black robe and little black skull-cap, are working in dark fly-infested booths that look like caves. A carpenter sits cross-legged at a prehistoric lathe, turning chair-legs at lightning speed. He works the lathe with a bow in his right hand and guides the chisel with his left foot, and thanks to a lifetime of sitting in this position his left leg is warped out of shape. At his side his grandson, aged six, is already starting on the simpler parts of the job.

I was just passing the coppersmiths' booths when somebody noticed that I was lighting a cigarette. Instantly, from the dark holes all round, there was a frenzied rush of Jews, many of them old grandfathers with flowing grey beards, all clamouring for a cigarette. Even a blind man somewhere at the back of one of the booths heard a rumour of cigarettes and came crawling out, groping in the air with his hand. In about a minute I had used up the whole packet. None of these people, I suppose, works less than twelve hours a day, and every one of them looks on a cigarette as a more or less impossible luxury.

As the Jews live in self-contained communities they follow the same trades as the Arabs, except for agriculture. Fruit-sellers, potters, silver-smiths, blacksmiths, butchers, leather-workers, tailors, water-carriers, beggars, porters—whichever way you look you see nothing but Jews. As a matter of fact there are thirteen thousand of them all living in the space of a few acres. A good job Hitler wasn't here. Perhaps he was on his way, however. You hear the usual dark rumours about the Jews, not only from the Arabs but from the poorer Europeans.

"Yes, *mon vieux,* they took my job away from me and gave it to a Jew. The Jews! They're the real rulers of this country, you know. They've got all the money. They control the banks, finance—everything."

"But," I said, "isn't it a fact that the average Jew is a labourer working for about a penny an hour?"

"Ah, that's only for show! They're all money-lenders really. They're cunning, the Jews." . . .

Every afternoon a file of very old women passes down the road outside my house, each carrying a load of firewood. All of them are mummified with age and the sun, and all of them are tiny. It seems to be generally the case in primitive communities that the women, when they get beyond a certain age, shrink to the size of children. One day a poor old creature who could not have been more than four feet tall crept past me under a vast load of wood. I stopped her and put a five-sou piece (a little more than a farthing), into her hand. She answered with a shrill wail, almost a scream, which was partly gratitude but mainly surprise. I suppose that from her point of view, by taking any notice of her, I seemed almost to be violating a law of nature. She accepted her status as an old woman, that is to say, as a beast of burden. When a family is travelling it is quite usual to see a father and a grown-up son riding ahead on donkeys, and an old woman following on foot, carrying the baggage.

But what is strange about these people is their invisibility. For several weeks, always at about the same time of day, the file of old women had hobbled past the house with their firewood, and though they had registered themselves on my eyeballs I cannot truly say that I had seen them. Firewood was passing—that was how I saw it. It was only that one day I happened to be walking behind them, and the curious up-and-down motion of a load of wood drew my attention to the human being beneath it. Then for the first time I noticed the poor old earth-coloured bodies, bodies reduced to bones and leathery skin, bent double under the crushing weight. Yet I suppose I had not been five minutes on Moroccan soil before I noticed the overloading of the donkeys and was infuriated by it. There is no question that the donkeys are

damnably treated. The Moroccan donkey is hardly bigger than a St. Bernard dog, it carries a load which in the British Army would be considered too much for a fifteen-hands mule, and very often its pack-saddle is not taken off its back for weeks together. But what is peculiarly pitiful is that it is the most willing creature on earth, it follows its master like a dog and does not need either bridle or halter. After a dozen years of devoted work it suddenly drops dead, whereupon its master tips it into the ditch and the village dogs have torn its guts out before it is cold.

This kind of thing makes one's blood boil, whereas—on the whole—the plight of the human beings does not. I am not commenting, merely pointing to a fact. People with brown skins are next door to invisible. Anyone can be sorry for the donkey with its galled back, but it is generally owing to some kind of accident if one even notices the old woman under her load of sticks.

As the storks flew northward the Negroes were marching southward—long, dusty columns, infantry, screwgun batteries, and then more infantry, four or five thousand men in all, winding up the road with a clumping of boots and a clatter of iron wheels.

They were Senegalese, the blackest Negroes in Africa, so black that sometimes it is difficult to see whereabouts on their necks the hair begins. Their splendid bodies were hidden in reach-me-down khaki uniforms, their feet squashed into boots that looked like blocks of wood, and every tin hat seemed to be a couple of sizes too small. It was very hot and the men had marched a long way. They slumped under the weight of their packs and the curiously sensitive black faces were glistening with sweat.

As they went past a tall, very young Negro turned and caught my eye. But the look he gave me was not in the least the kind of look you might expect. Not hostile, not contemptuous, not sullen, not even inquisitive. It was the shy, wide-eyed Negro look, which actually is a look of profound respect. I saw how it was. This wretched boy, who is a French citizen and has therefore been dragged from the forest to scrub floors and catch syphilis in garrison towns, actually has feelings of reverence before a white skin. He has been taught that the white race are his masters, and he still believes it.

But there is one thought which every white man (and in this connection it doesn't matter twopence if he calls himself a socialist) thinks when he sees a black army marching past. "How much longer can we go on kidding these people? How long before they turn their guns in the other direction?"

It was curious, really. Every white man there had this thought stowed somewhere or other in his mind. I had it, so had the other onlookers, so had the officers on their sweating chargers and the white N.C.Os. marching in the ranks. It was a kind of secret which we all knew and were too clever to tell; only the Negroes didn't know it. And really it was like watching a flock of cattle to see the long column, a mile or two miles of armed men, flowing peacefully up the road, while the great white birds drifted over them in the opposite direction, glittering like scraps of paper.

REVIEW QUESTIONS

1. How does Orwell's description of the Jewish quarter in Marrakech contradict the way the city's Arab and poorer Europeans viewed the Jews?
2. Orwell notes that visitors to Marrakech, including himself, were generally more outraged by the mistreatment of animals than the mistreatment of human beings. How does he explain this?
3. A look of respect from "a tall, very young Negro" prompted Orwell to speculate about the future of race relations in Africa. What in particular concerned him? Why?

An American College Student Observes Women of the San (1955)

ELIZABETH MARSHALL THOMAS, *The Shy People of the Kalahari*

The Kalahari Desert is a dry wasteland that covers about 200,000 square miles in southwest Africa. Vegetation is sparse and water is scarce. It is not a true desert, however, and it is home to a surprising variety of living things that have been able to adapt to its seemingly harsh environment. In some places grow scrubby trees and tufts of grass; there are also a small number of wild desert plants that produce berries, melons, nuts, roots, and seeds. At the edge of the desert infrequent rain waters collect in a few shallow ponds. This generally inhospitable region is inhabited by the San, a number of nomadic groups who live much as their prehistoric ancestors did. Once called "Bushmen" or "Kalahari Bushmen," relatively little about these people was known until the publication of Elizabeth Marshall Thomas's *The Harmless People* in 1955.

Thomas, now a noted expert on dogs and the author of the best-selling *The Hidden Life of Dogs* (1993), traveled to the Kalahari for the first time in 1951. Only twenty years old, she temporarily left college to accompany her parents and younger brother John on an expedition sponsored in part by the Peabody Museum at Harvard University. Surprisingly, Thomas's parents were not professional anthropologists. Her father, Laurence Marshall, was a retired industrialist whose company, Raytheon, made the first microwave ovens and produced magnetron tubes for shipboard radar during World War II. Her mother, Lorna Marshall, taught English literature at Mt. Holyoke before her marriage. Wanting to reconnect with his wife and children after World War II, Marshall decided to take his family to Africa on an adventure—to look for the "Kalahari Bushmen." Accompanied by linguists, interpreters, and scientists, the family made three trips, the last in 1954. Thus, *The Harmless People* is not primarily a scholarly work—although it contains a great deal of ethnological information. Instead, it is the work of a young and gifted observer with a scientist's powers of observation and "a poet's power to capture mood and atmosphere."

In the Kalahari between 1951 and 1955, the Marshalls were able to make contact with a number of San groups, two of whom they lived with for extended periods: the Kung and the Gikwe. Expedition personnel also had contact with several other groups, such as the Naron and Ko. Each had its own distinct territory, which included a water supply. Within this territory a group would move from place to place, staying only one night in one spot or many weeks in another. The San lived mostly in the open, living beside fires. Sometimes they built small shelters of branches and grass.

This excerpt focuses on the Gikwe, to whom the Marshalls were introduced by Gai, a young hunter, and Ukwane, an elderly man. Extremely shy, the Gikwe shunned contact with outsiders and lived in "deep fear" of the Bantus and the European farmers of the surrounding region. The Gikwe survived primarily by hiding, subsisting on desert plants and whatever animals they could manage to shoot with arrows dipped in a poison made from beetle larvae. They owned almost no property, and what they did own was shared communally. Like other San peoples, the Gikwe averaged about five feet in height and spoke a Khoisan dialect (a language group characterized by clicking sounds).

Other than the depressions, except for a small pile of brown, twisted bean shells, no sign would show that people lived there. Later we saw another scooped pit and a stick thrust upright in the ground beside it, right at our feet, which was Gai's place; the stick was to mark the spot, although Gai could have found his shallow pit at any time of the day or night.

Nobody was there; everyone had run away. We sat down and waited while Gai put his hands to his mouth and shouted, trying to summon the people back again. When nobody came or even answered him, he flung his pipe to the ground and marched off to find them among the bushes, alternately shouting to his hidden relatives and muttering to himself, for they might be far away and the day was getting warm.

We sat in the middle ground between the depressions so that we wouldn't risk stepping on or crushing anybody's hidden things, for, without knowing it, a European can in a moment trample through a Bushman's cache, breaking the delicate bone or wooden objects, bending the reed arrows, or crushing eggshell beads. Also, among certain groups of Bushmen, every fire has a man's side and a woman's side, determined by the position of the fire as you face the doorway of the scherm [a tiny hut], the man's side being on the right, the woman's on the left. If a man sits on the woman's side, or where a woman has been sitting, he will become impotent and will also lose his power to hunt, and if a woman sits where a man has been sitting, she will get a disease in her vagina. Something intangible, invisible, but dangerously powerful, remains on the ground. We did not know which side was which of this werf's [the camp area] fires, or even for sure where the fires were; we did not even know that the Gikwe had this custom, for we had learned it from Kung Bushmen, but we knew that if they did they would not welcome our contaminating their ground. We would have liked to look around, but the best thing we could do was to keep our big boots and our bodies away from their delicate, fragile, almost invisible community.

In a short time we heard a rustle in the veld, and a young woman who seemed to be in her early twenties stepped from the bushes. She was, Ukwane said, Gai's wife, and on her hip she carried a baby, a naked three-year-old who looked at us from his wide eyes fearlessly, then, realizing that we were strangers, buried his face in his mother's arm. His mother stroked him calmly and came toward us smiling and nodding her head graciously, although a little pulse was hammering in the V of her throat. We learned later that she had been sitting in the bushes very near us, and when she had seen her husband go by she had assumed that everything was all right and had come to greet us, not bothering to answer his cries.

She was a short, sturdy woman with round arms, long thighs, and short calves. She had a rather large belly and square, strong shoulders, and she wore a very tattered cape or kaross over her back, with a small leather apron around her hips. She had no ornaments except a row of blue scars over her eyes, a decoration, and she had al-

lowed her hair to become disheveled, long, and a little tangled, hanging down over her ears in tight spirals, instead of having shaved it off as most Bushman women do. All this gave her a very matter-of-fact air, which was not deceiving, for she saw in a glance that we were harmless and, looking us over, sat down at once beside me.

Her baby pulled, twisted, and tugged at her, and from the way he behaved I judged that he kept her too busy to be forever cutting her hair or making bead ornaments. Besides, she told us later, if she wore ornaments, the baby pulled them off. She had her row of scars, though, delicate and arching over her brow, making her eyes seem wider; as well as a row of striped scars along her thighs. These, say Bushmen, are made to imitate the beauty of zebras, and many women wear them, having been decorated when they were still young. It is a painful procedure. The cuts are made on the thighs and forehead with a knife or ax blade, then charcoal is rubbed in, but the woman told us later that in her case it had been worth the pain and trouble, because, she said, she was extremely ugly and had been made more beautiful.

Her baby's name was Nhwakwe, she told me, and after that we were at a loss for conversation. I offered her a cigarette, which she declined, indicating that it made her cough. I was surprised, for she was the only Bushman I had ever met, man, woman, or child, who did not smoke.

Presently she smiled, pressed her hand to her chest, and said: "Tsetchwe." It was her name.

"Elizabeth," I said, pointing to myself.

"Nisabe," she answered, pronouncing after me and inclining her head graciously. She looked me over carefully without really staring, which to Bushmen is rude. Then, having surely suspected that I was a woman, she put her hand on my breast gravely, and, finding that I was, she gravely touched her own breasts. Many Bushmen do this; to them all Europeans look the same.

"Tsau si" (women), she said.

Then after a moment's pause. Tsetchwe began to teach me a few words, the names of a few objects around us, grass, rock, bean shell, so that we could have a conversation later. As she talked she took a handful of the beans out of her kaross, broke them open, and began to eat them. This is a wonderful, bitter bean, shaped like a lima bean, which grows on tiny bushes in patches throughout the Kalahari. When you eat these beans they burn your tongue, throat, and stomach, but they take away hunger and thirst. Besides the beans in her kaross, Tsetchwe, who began unloading, brought out a large, edible root which she had dug up—she must have been gathering food before we came—and put in the shade of a bush beside her fireplace. Also, she brought out six round green melons which are called *tsama* melons, and which, during the autumn, provide the only liquid available for all the Bushmen in the desert, and for all the game antelope besides. Under the green rind a tsama is very like a watermelon, filled with small oval seeds and very watery in texture, but is itself pale green and smaller, the size of a small cantaloupe. Tsetchwe placed one between her feet and, gripping it firmly with her strong toes, chopped a hole in the top of it with her digging-stick; then, lifting the cap away like the lid of a jack-o'-lantern, she mashed the pulp inside until it was liquid. She put the melon to her mouth and, tipping her head back, drank from it, using her long digging-stick to help push the pulp into her mouth, working it like an enormous chopstick, making a watery noise as she sucked. When Tsetchwe had collected a mouthful of seeds she put the melon down, took an old, dry tsama melon rind from her kaross, and spat the seeds into it to save them, for they can be roasted and eaten like nuts when they are dry. Tsetchwe drank all the liquid in the rind and seemed refreshed as she cast the empty rind over her shoulder and brushed off her mouth and hands.

At last Gai strode back into the werf, followed at a distance by a group of three small boys and, much farther, by three old women who stood waist-deep in bushes, close together like three antelope, craning their necks to see us.

When they noticed Tsetchwe and Ukwane,

they came forward with more confidence, accepted tobacco, and, squatting immediately, began to smoke. It had been months, Ukwane said, since they had used their last tobacco, had been reduced to smoking leaves, and they were very happy to have the tobacco we had given them. Bushmen love to smoke. They say that tobacco, as well as the wild beans, takes away hunger and thirst, and, besides that, it makes their hearts glad. One of the old women, Dasina, who was Tsetchwe's mother, inhaled too deeply and began to faint. Tsetchwe half turned her mother so that everyone would not see her, and, putting an arm around her for support, let the old woman lean on her shoulder. Our interpreter laughed, and Tsetchwe turned to glare. Tsetchwe's back was exactly like her mother's, broad but curved in at the waist, the old woman's a little bloated but Tsetchwe's young and strong.

Another old woman was smoking, too, puffing on a short, wide pipe cut from a leg bone of some large antelope, so big that she had to stuff one end with grass to keep the tobacco inside. She almost unhinged her jaw each time she puffed. She would inhale and spit, cough, and inhale again without a sign of dizziness, and when she saw Dasina faint she too laughed out loudly. Her name, she told us, was Twikwe.

Twikwe was skinny and tall as a man, with long, lanky arms that she flung about in the air, gesturing, and long legs that jerked when she walked. She wore only a short piece of leather that reached from her waist to her thighs, and we could see that she was wrinkled from head to foot, her skin hanging in long, vertical wrinkles down her thighs and belly, like an old apple that has dried. She talked incessantly and loudly, always opening and closing her mouth, and she joked, for Ukwane and the young boys near her laughed at everything she said. She was telling how her husband had outdistanced her as they were running away and was surely running still. Every now and then she stopped her talk to shout out to him, jeering, saying that he was depriving himself of tobacco and should come back; then everyone would listen, but no sound came from him, no answer. He never did come back, and in the weeks we were there we never saw him. Perhaps he was running away from Twikwe, for we later learned that he was living in a valley with his other wife.

REVIEW QUESTIONS

1. How did Gikwe women, in general, view the importance of beauty? Were Tsetchwe's views typical or atypical? Explain.
2. Specifically, what was the diet of the Gikwe? What was their primary source of fluids?
3. Why was smoking tobacco important to the San?
4. Describe the relationship between Gikwe men and women. How would you describe gender roles in their society?

A Nigerian Novelist Portrays the Oppression of Women (1966)

FLORA NWAPA, *Efuru*

Flora Nwapa has been called "the mother of modern African literature." The publication of her first novel, *Efuru,* triggered an outpouring of Nigerian protest literature, much of which was written by women. Their works contributed significantly to social reform movements in Nigeria by offering accurate and sometimes uncomfortably realistic portrayals of the lingering effects of patriarchy and colonialism, the result of more than 150 years of British domination and rule.

Born in Oguta, Nigeria, Florence Nwanzuruaha Nkiru Nwapa (1931–1993) was the daughter of parents who were both teachers. She received university degrees in English and education in Ibadan, Nigeria, and Edinburgh, Scotland, then worked in education and civil service in Nigeria for many years. After the Nigerian civil war, as Minister for Health and Social Welfare in the East Central State, she found homes for two thousand children orphaned by the war. The publication of *Efuru* (1966) and later, *Idu* (1971), thrust her into the international spotlight. *Efuru* in particular was a startlingly honest recreation of life in Nigeria from a woman's perspective, and it had a dramatic effect upon the world literary scene. Nwapa was also the first Nigerian woman to publish in English and the first African woman to have her writing published in London.

Efuru, which takes its title from the main character, deals with the oppression of women in Nigeria, a theme which Nwapa continued in successive novels. It is based on a Nigerian folk story about a woman favored by the lake goddess Uhamiri. The protagonist, Efuru, is thus strong and beautiful but seldom happy. Uhamiri's favorites are allowed few children—a terrible fate in Nigeria, especially in Efuru's rural community. The novel follows Efuru as she suffers through two unhappy marriages and the death of a child. Chapter I, part of which is included here, focuses on the early days of her first marriage. The frank discussion of Efuru's circumcision shocked Western readers, few of whom were aware of the practice. Nwapa's candid revelations inspired many other African women to describe their own experiences, particularly their dissatisfaction with post-colonial violence and authoritarianism.

In the 1970s, dissatisfied with the publicity and distribution efforts of her publisher, Nwapa founded two publishing companies of her own: Tana Press, Ltd., which published adult fiction, and Flora Nwapa Books, which specialized in children's literature. Not only did she publish the rest of her own books herself, but her companies provided other Nigerian women the opportunity to publish their work. At the same time, Nwapa continued to teach, quite often as a visiting professor at colleges and universities around the world, such as at New York University, Trinity College, and the universities of Minnesota and Michigan. In 1982, the Nigerian government presented her with its premier honor, the Order of Niger. Her home town, Oguta, bestowed on her the title of highest chieftain, *Ogbuefi,* a distinction reserved for men of achievement.

'Why does Adizua go to the town so often?' one of the farmers asked.

'Don't you know that he has married a very beautiful woman. How the woman agreed to marry him still remains a mystery to everybody.'

'How? Is the woman from a very good family?'

'The daughter of Nwashike Ogene, the mighty man of valour. Ogene who, single handed, fought against the Aros when they came to molest us. Nwashike himself proved himself the son of his father. He was a great fisherman. When he went fishing, he caught only asa and aja. His yams were the fattest in the whole town. And what is more, no man has ever seen his back on the ground. Ogworo azu ngwere eru ani.'

'So that's the man whose daughter that imbecile married?'

'Yes. The amazing thing is that the father has done nothing about it. He has sent some young men to fetch his daughter, but she did not go with them. And since then he had done nothing about it. If it were in his youthful days, Nwashike would have taught that fool a lesson. Things are changing fast these days. These white people have imposed so much strain on our people. The least thing you do nowadays you are put into prison.'

'I don't envy him,' the other man said. But it was obvious that he was green with envy.

'I give them only three years. By then the woman will know her husband too well to want to stay with him longer. Why does she remain in town and not come to the farm with her husband?'

'She refused to go to the farm. She is trading instead. She said she was not cut out for farm work. And I don't blame her, she is so beautiful. You would think that the woman of the lake is her mother. Her mother died five years ago, she too was a very beautiful woman.'

'After seeing this type of woman,' the other man continued, 'one hisses when one sees one's wife.' The other laughed.

'You have a lovely wife yourself.'

'Yes, I know it but . . . Well let's leave it at that.'

Efuru's husband returned home and was told about his wife's circumcision. 'It must be done now, my son,' his mother told him. 'And this is the time. Let's not leave it until she gets pregnant.' Adizua said it was all right. He could afford the expenses. But he was afraid of Efuru's father. 'Your father must be told, my wife. It won't be fair to have you have your bath without his knowledge. He must be told.'

'He won't be told. It will make him angrier. When we have enough money to pay the dowry, we shall approach elderly men who will help us beg him.'

So it was as Efuru said. Her mother-in-law got everything ready, the camwood, iziziani ufie awusa were bought on Nkwo day. She went to Onicha and bought home-made cloth for her daughter-in-law. When she came back she went to see the woman who would do the circumcision.

'Is that you, my friend?' the woman asked from within.

'Yes, Ugwunwa,' she greeted her.

'O o, and what is yours? I have forgotten it.'

'Omeifeaku.'

'Yes, Omeifeaku. And how is everybody in your home?'

'They are well, and yours?'

'We are well. It is only hunger troubling us.'

'It is good it is only hunger. It is better than ill-health.'

'That's what they say. Ill-health is worse.'

She came out from the room with a mat.

'Sit down here, my friend.' The two elderly women talked on general things for a while. 'I have no kola, please.'

'Don't worry about kola. It is very early. And besides this is Nkwo morning. Nobody gives kola to people on Nkwo morning. I have something important to tell you. You know my son has been married. His wife has not yet had her bath, so we want her to have her bath and that's why I have come. What day will suit you?'

'I am glad to hear this. Is your daughter-in-law pregnant?'

'I don't think so. She told me she was not.'

'Find out from her again. I don't want to do it if she is pregnant. It is risky. If she loses too much blood, it won't be good for her. So find out from her again and bring word tomorrow. Oh, what a pity I have no kola. Wait, let me see.'

She went into her room again. She came out with a bottle of home-made gin, and a ganashi.

'You will like the gin. My daughter cooks it in the farm. When she finishes, she puts it in a canoe in the dead of the night and paddles to town. When they come I hide them at the back of my house and no policeman will see it.'

She filled the ganashi and gave it to her visitor. Efuru's mother-in-law drank it in a gulp and made a noise with her mouth. The woman filled the same ganashi and drank the gin in a gulp also.

'It is a good gin. We shall continue cooking our gin. I don't see the difference between it and the gin sold in special bottles in the shops.'

Efuru's mother-in-law got up to go.

'Thank you very much. I am going.'

'You are going? Thank you. Come tomorrow, go well.'

Efuru's mother-in-law was at the woman's house the next day. She told her that her daughter-in-law was not pregnant.

'That's all right then. I shall come tomorrow morning after the cock crow. Get hot water ready.'

The next morning the woman was at Efuru's. She sat down and Efuru came out and greeted her.

'You are the young wife, my daughter. You are beautiful, my daughter. I will be gentle with you. Don't be afraid. It is painful no doubt, but the pain disappears like hunger. You know what?' and she turned to Efuru's mother-in-law. 'You know Nwakaego's daughter?'

'Yes, I know her.'

'She did not have her bath before she had that baby who died after that dreadful flood.'

'God forbid. Why?'

'Fear. She was afraid. Foolish girl. She had a foolish mother, their folly cost them a son, a good son.'

'How did you know?'

'They came to me early one morning and told me. They wanted it to be done in my house so that people will not know. The dibia had already told them that the baby died because she did not have her bath. I did it for them. She remained in my house for seven days. Is everything ready now?'

'Yes, come this way.'

The woman went to the back of the house and there it was done. Efuru screamed and screamed. It was so painful. Her mother-in-law consoled her. 'It will soon be over, my daughter don't cry.'

Meanwhile Efuru's husband was in his room. He felt all the pain. It seemed as if he was the one being circumcised. The neighbours wondered what was the matter. When they came to the house they saw that the back door was locked and they turned back.

'It's being done now,' one of the neighbours said to the other. 'Oh, yes, that's it, I saw the woman when she came. Efuru is having her bath. Poor girl, it's so painful.'

Efuru lay on her back with her feet apart. She was not crying any more. But it was still very painful.

The woman gave instructions. She prepared a black stuff and put it in a small calabash and left it outside the room where Efuru was lying. 'Sprinkle this on the feet of all the visitors before they come into the room. It will be infected if this is not done. Press it with hot water every morning, and night. If anything goes wrong send for me. Oh, where is my razor?'

Efuru's mother-in-law gave her the sharp razor that did the work. She wrapped it up and tied it at one end of her wrappa.

The next morning Ajanupu the sister of Efuru's mother-in-law came to the house. After eating kola, she cleared her throat.

'Ossai, you have done something. Why was I not told that Adizu's wife was going to have her bath. Why am I treated these days as if I am a stranger and not your sister? Adizua married a wife and you did not tell me. I heard it from outside. Again, Adizua's wife has washed and you have not told me either. What have I done to you?'

'Please, my sister, you have done nothing wrong. You have not offended me in any way. It is my fault and I am very sorry.'

'All right. I am happy I have told you. I don't want to bear any grudge against you. How is Efuru doing?'

'She is in the room: go in and see her.'

She saw the black stuff. There was a feather in it. She took the feather dipped it into the black stuff and sprinkled it on her two feet.

'How are you, my daughter?'

'I am well. Oh, you have come to see us today.'

'Nobody told me. I heard it from outside and so I came. Is it very painful?'

'It is much better now. It was dreadful the first day.'

"Gbonu, my daughter. It is what every woman undergoes. So don't worry.'

Efuru's mother-in-law saw to it that she was very well looked after. She was to eat the best food and she was to do no work. She was simply to eat and grow fat. And above all she was to look beautiful. The camwood was used in dyeing her cloth. She also rubbed it all over her body and the iziziani was used for her face.

She ate whatever she wanted to eat. She did not eat cassava in any form. Only yams were pounded for her. She ate the best fish from the market. It was said that she was feasting. On market days, her mother went to the market and bought her the best. When she prized something in the market other buyers gave her way and asked her how the feasting woman was getting on. She too rubbed some camwood on her hands and feet to tell people that her daughter has been circumcised.

As Efuru's mother-in-law was buying things in the market one day, she heard someone calling:

'Mother of a feasting girl; mother of feasting girl.' She turned and saw that it was her sister, Ajanupu.

'How is she now?'

'She is well, my sister.'

'Has it healed?'

'Yes, it has healed. She had good body.'

'That's very good. The woman who did it has good hands, too. She never has any trouble with all her cases. Unlike Mgbokworo.'

'No, Mgbokworo is not good. She has not actually learnt the operation.'

'What are you buying for your daughter-in-law? Let's see your basin. You have bought so much. By the way is she a good daughter-in-law?'

'You cannot see two like her. She is such a

nice girl. I like her very much; I am glad my son married her.' . . .

Efuru feasted for one month. Her mother-in-law wanted her to continue feasting for two months, but she refused saying that the life was a dull one. She wanted to be up and doing.

'Since you won't continue feasting, we shall talk about going to the market,' her mother-in-law told her one day. 'But if I were you, Efuru, I should continue for another one month. When I did mine, I feasted for three months. I know I cannot do for you all that my own mother did for me, but I will try.'

'No, mother. One month of confinement is enough. We have not got much money, and I want to start trading. Again we have not paid the dowry yet. I shall go to the market on Nkwo day.'

'You are right, my daughter. I was only thinking of what people would say.'

'Never mind what people would say.'

So on Nkwo day, Efuru dressed gorgeously. She plaited her lovely hair very well, tied velvet to her waist and used aka stones for her neck. Her body was bare showing her beautiful breasts. No dress was worn when a young woman went to the market after the period of feasting. Her body was exposed so that the people saw how well her mother or her mother-in-law had cared for her. A woman who was not beautiful on that day, would never be beautiful in her life.

As Efuru was being dressed, a small girl of about eight years old was dressed in similar fashion. Just when the sun was going down Efuru took the girl to the market. They were followed from the house by a few women.

Efuru and the girl went round the market and were greeted by the people. As they were coming, some women asked 'whose daughter is that?'

'Don't you know her? She is the daughter of Nwashike Ogene.'

'She is very beautiful. I have never seen a woman so beautiful. Who is her husband?'

'Her husband is Adizua.'

'Who is Adizua? Who is his father? Is he known?'

'He is not known. And nobody knows why she ever married him, and besides, not a cowrie has been paid on her head.'

'What are you telling me?'

'It is true. The husband has not even gone with his people to Nwashike Ogene.'

'And what has the father done?'

'Nothing so far. What will he do now that he is getting old? If it were in his youth, his daughter would not have dared insult him in this way.'

As the two women were talking, Efuru came near. 'Wait, my daughter, take this,' and one of the women gave her some money.

'You are very beautiful my daughter: take this,' and another woman gave her some money also. Efuru thanked them and went on. When she had gone round the market, she went home without buying anything.

When she got home, she changed her cloth and the little girl changed hers also and they went back to the market, this time to buy little things like fruits, ground-nuts, kola-nuts and so on.

'Ahaa, this is a better cloth, the first one was rather old. This is nicer.' One woman said. Efuru heard this and laughed to herself. She went on buying things. This time her mother-in-law was in the market and she was being congratulated.

'Well done, Ossai. You have looked after her very well. Her cloth is gorgeous, but the first one is better. Why, she should have tied the first one now.'

Efuru heard this also and smiled to herself.

'Who can please the world?' she asked herself. She knew that both cloths were very nice, and what was more they fitted the occasion. They were the cloths her mother left for her. She bought them many years ago and whenever there was a festival or the second burial of a relative, the cloths served very well. She knew that to buy some cloths in the market for the occasion would not do. The older the cloth the better. It showed that in the days gone by your mother could afford those cloths and so her prestige was enhanced, because her family was not among the newly rich, the wealth had been in it for years.

Efuru came home feeling very tired that evening. Many people came to the house to congratulate her and her mother-in-law.

'Everything went on well,' they told them.

'Your daughter's face is good,' they told her, meaning that she was popular with people.

'Your daughter has the face of people,' others told her, meaning the same thing.

'It is a good sign,' they agreed.

But underneath, something weighed Efuru down.

REVIEW QUESTIONS

1. What was Efuru's "bath"? Why do you think it was so important to her mother-in-law and to the other women of the village? How did Efuru's life change afterward?
2. How would you describe the relationship between men and women in Efuru's world? Which gender seems to make most of the decisions?
3. Compare Kikuyu and Gikwe women's attitudes toward physical appearance to those of the women of Efuru's community.
4. In general, how does Flora Nwapa's description of the life of a woman in Africa differ from that of a non-African author—for example, Elizabeth Marshall Thomas?

Two Travel Writers Look at Family Size, Prostitution, and Trains in Cameroon

Dervla Murphy, *Cameroon with Egbert,* 1987
Peter Biddlecombe, *French Lessons in Africa,* 1993

Cameroon, described in the following selections by professional travel writers Dervla Murphy and Peter Biddlecombe, is typical of modern Africa—a mixture of the old and new, the efficient and inefficient. The legacy of colonialism is still very evident, and there are vestiges of three colonial powers in Cameroon's culture. Located on the western coast of central Africa, Cameroon became a German protectorate called Kamerun in 1884. French and British troops occupied the region during World War I, after which it was divided into Western Cameroon, a British mandate, and Eastern Cameroon, a French mandate. Both became United Nations trust territories in 1946 and achieved full independence in 1961. The northwestern part of Cameroon joined Nigeria in 1961, at which time the rest of Western Cameroon merged with Eastern Cameroon to form a federal republic. In 1987 and 1993, when Murphy and Biddlecombe visited Cameroon, the country was aggressively developing its infrastructure.

Dervla Murphy, the author of the first selection, was born in 1931 in Ireland. Her writing career did not begin until age thirty-two, after her mother, for whom Murphy had cared since leaving Trinity College, died of rheumatoid arthritis. In January of 1963, she packed one change of clothing, a pistol, and some small tools and set off for India on a bicycle. Her first book, *Full Tilt: From Ireland to India on a Bicycle,* was published in 1965. Since then Murphy and her daughter Rachel (who started traveling with her mother in 1973 at the age of five) have trekked through many remote and unusual parts of the world—on foot, on bicycles, or astride a pony, horse, or mule. Their experiences are recounted in thirteen additional books on travel, including *Cameroon with Egbert* (an African packhorse the two acquired in Cameroon). Murphy has also written an autobiography and books on Irish history and nuclear warfare. Her writing has been hailed for its lack of pretentiousness, its "relentless honesty," and its focus on people—such as the chief with whom she ate dinner in Ntem and the prostitutes with whom she drank Guinness in Mayo Darlé, described in the following selection.

In contrast, Peter Biddlecombe's travel experiences have hardly been those of someone who prefers a bicycle as a means of transport. A British businessman, he has visited and written about over one hundred different countries. Biddlecombe's first travel book, *French Lessons in Africa: Travels with My Briefcase,* was based on ten years of travel (for unspecified business purposes) from Cameroon and the Congo to Senegal and Zaire. Since its publication in 1993, he has written eight other books, five of them popular accounts of his travels. In the second selection, Biddlecombe describes a surprisingly comfortable train ride from the Atlantic port city of Douala, Cameroon's largest city, inland to Yaoundé, the capital—a distance of approximately 150 miles. Biddlecombe's writing usually focuses on the humorous and amusing aspects of global business travel; his description of train travel in Cameroon is uncharacteristically serious.

CAMEROON WITH EGBERT

. . . This was Ntem, a small village surrounded by big trees. We tethered Egbert on a grassy patch, while seeking the Chief's permission to sleep in the school; rain seemed probable and we now knew our tent was not big enough for two on a wet night. Outside the off-licence an amiable youth greeted us—conveniently, one of the Chief's twenty-nine children, who offered to show me the palace while Rachel remained beer-swigging amidst a jovial welcoming throng.

This was a more imposing palace than Nthambaw's, with an incongruous modern bungalow in front of the mud fortifications. The Chief, too, was more imposing: a dignified courteous man in his mid-fifties who spoke good English and was warmly and wittily welcoming: 'Are you pretending to live a hundred years ago, when there were no vehicles in Cameroon?' Having escorted me back to the off-licence—a mile-long walk—he ordered food, stood us beers and himself had a Top. He too was Muslim.

The Chief's unwonted appearance after dark caused some excitement along the village street and much bowing and cupping of hands. One sensed a strong mutual affection; evidently this Chief's benignly paternalistic attitude was appreciated and he exchanged quips with both sexes and all age groups. Ntem is mainly Christian and its women-folk were out in force, enjoying the Murphy road-show. They particularly enjoyed our statutory gender-confusion session. I had introduced Rachel to the Chief as my daughter and a few moments later, addressing her, he referred to 'your father'. When she respectfully but firmly corrected him he leant forward, scrutinised me by lamp-light and exclaimed, 'Impossible! This is a strong man!'

'It's *not*!' said Rachel. 'It's a strong *woman*!'

Our audience was in paroxysms of mirth, a phrase that applies more exactly to Africans than to any other race I know. They shook and heaved with laughter, seized each other by the shoulders, jumped up and down together and literally fell about in the abandon of their hilarity. Finally the Chief was convinced and made a public announcement, in whatever language Ntem people speak, confirming that this odd bod really *was* female. Whereupon several young women rushed to shake my hand and/or embrace me.

A small boy arrived then with our supper. He offered the dish first to the Chief, who removed its lid and took one symbolic morsel, to prove it wasn't poisoned, before signalling that the rest was for us. In darkness we groped through a thick, highly spiced sauce and found little bundles wrapped in bristly hide. These contained bush-meat (beef) which we were hungry enough to relish despite the bristles.

As we ate, the Chief expounded on family life: 'Some foreigners would like to sell birth-controls in this country but it is wrong to think of economics before children. We love our children, we can't have too many. Ntem has two-and-a-half thousand people and more than one thousand are schoolchildren. So we have built a second schoolroom where you will sleep. We built it without help from government but now we hope they will give us more teachers—and *good* teachers! Bad teachers are worse than nothing. But too many good teachers don't like to live in the bush. I have had difficulties, giving education to twenty-nine children—my daughters also have education. See! There is one speaking good English!' He indicated a comely young woman talking to Rachel. 'But these difficulties are not important. I have seventeen sons and twelve daughters and each one is a gift from God. I am grateful.'

Hearing that I have only one child, the Chief was deeply sympathetic. He obviously felt that his question had been a *faux pas* and hastily changed the subject. This awkward topic of my infertility came up almost daily without its ever occurring to anyone that a personal decision might be involved. For most villagers, *choosing*

to have only one child is literally unthinkable. And the few who can grasp that idea consider it grossly immoral. (Or at least the men do; some women, significantly, are more ambivalent on this matter.) It would have been futile as well as rude to try to explain to the Chief why, in future, women should have no more than two children each. Many Whites look ahead, most Blacks don't. To us, but not to them, the African birth-rate of 47 per 1,000 is menacing. Nowhere else in the world has ever experienced such a population increase: 3.2 per cent per annum, despite one child in seven dying before its fifth birthday. Even without droughts, food production cannot keep pace with such a breeding-rate; an estimated 99 million Africans were starving *before* the 1982 famine. . . .

Like all the (fortunately few) towns on our route, Mayo Darlé seemed to signify a strong African disinclination to come to terms with having been dragged into the Modern Age. These places look like wounds inflicted on the country by some alien force. The contrast with bush villages, away from 'motorable' tracks, could not be more striking; many villages still retain that simple, orderly beauty so much admired by early travellers in West Africa. Nor is this comparison just one more symptom of silly White romanticism. The towns do not provide a more comfortable or convenient way of life than the villages—rather the reverse. If they have an electricity generator (usually they don't) its unreliability means that it is not a mod. con. but a source of dismay and confusion. A post office may occasionally exist but it can take letters a month or two to travel a hundred miles. A health centre may also exist in theory (the French maps are peppered with them), but it will be so understaffed and ill-equipped that it is better to stick with the medicine-men, as most people do. A water source may be closer to each compound, but it will almost certainly be more polluted than rural supplies. And health is further endangered by a hazard (now a deadly hazard) unknown in the villages—prostitution.

Often prostitution is someone's problem exported from a village to a town, as on every continent. Mayo Darlé has a colony of more than two hundred prostitutes to serve passing truckers and while bar-crawling I met dozens (many bars are also brothels). Once I was invited to the two-roomed hut of an articulate Anglophone quartet; all were barren and had been rejected by their husbands, leaving prostitution as the only alternative to starvation.

This was the dark side to the Ntem Chief's moving love for—*reverence* for—children. According to traditional beliefs, a barren woman is a non-person. Her husband will not necessarily reject her, demanding a refund of the bride-wealth, because she may still be useful as a field worker. But the extended family and the local community will make her feel so inadequate—almost *wicked*—that it is often easier to run away. She sees herself as excluded from the tribe/family/clan. When she dies there will be no one to remember her, to maintain contact with her spirit, so she cannot join the living-dead. It will be as though she had never lived. Barrenness has removed her from the river that flows from birth through life to afterlife; it flows on without her. And even while she lives she is non-existent because unfruitful.

All four women in that sad little hut were believing Christians—two Baptists, one Roman Catholic, one Presbyterian—yet none took comfort from their faith. If anything, having been brought up on the ideal of Christian marriage sharpened their grief. Not only had they failed as women, in their traditional role, but they had also failed as Christian partners in a monogamous life-long union. Belonging to 'Mission Christian', as distinct from 'Black Church', families can make rejection even more humiliating; often the barren wife is blamed for leaving her husband with no choice but to sin. These women's reliance on children—especially sons—to confer immortality had remained undiminished by their exposure to the Christian doctrine of individual posthumous rewards or punishments. None could sufficiently comprehend 'the Beatific Vision' to regard it as an adequate consolation prize for childless women. Not myself

believing in the Christian afterlife, I shared their gut-reaction to 'Heaven' and became aware of an ironic closing of a circle. We five women were agreed that immortality has more to do with child-bearing than with 'Heaven' but we had travelled to that meeting-point by different—and opposite—roads.

On another level our conversation was one more reminder of the gulf between individualistic Westerners and most of the rest of mankind. In their own estimation these women had no value as individuals; they saw themselves only as part of a community to which, being female, they should contribute young. Instinctively they were concerned with the survival of the species, to an extent and with an intensity that is no longer necessary. The fulfilment of the individual was not on their agenda.

When I asked what they knew about AIDS the women giggled. There was no problem in Cameroon, only in other places . . . It would have been pointless to remind them that most of their clients came from the 'other places' in question. There was nothing they could do to protect themselves, even had it been possible to convince them that protection was necessary. Cameroon is not in the main danger zone (yet) but the virus has of course arrived and we heard of several deaths in the Kumbo region.

As we talked in that shadowy little room—becoming increasingly uninhibited on '33' and Guinness (they preferred Guinness)—I wondered what would happen to my unfortunate friends, and their many colleagues, when their bodies are no longer saleable. Like most African countries, Cameroon has no social security system; family members are supposed to care for one another and usually do, at least in rural areas. All four women were in their mid-forties and their prices had dropped to 100 CFA (about 20p): the price of a hand of bananas. Many teenagers, they said, could charge 500 CFA and even up to 1,000 CFA (just over £2) if they were *very* fat. I asked why teenagers chose this job and was startled to learn that some are earning their brothers' school fees. Prostitution does not of course carry the same stigma in Africa as in Europe. If times are hard—a crop failure, an expensive ill-ness, storm damage to a compound—it may make economic sense to send a daughter out to earn for a few years, before marriage, even if this leads to her husband paying somewhat reduced bridewealth. Being by then on my third '33' I got lost in the maze of clans and groups now mentioned. Some are openly tolerant of pre-marital sex and see prostitution as nothing more;

others condone it, but furtively; others condemn it and would consider a daughter on the streets the ultimate family disgrace. Yet even from among that last group many modern girls now defy their families and come to the bright (lamp) lights of Mayo Darlé because they want to find 'educated' husbands and graduate to the bril-liant (electric) lights of Douala or Yaoundé.

FRENCH LESSONS IN AFRICA

The railway station on Douala is unbelievably modern, like a cross between a space station and an Ivoirian cathedral. Everything is clean and bright, and so new they have not had time to put up signs. Not only is it impossible to find out which train I need, I can't even find the plat-form. Eventually by asking and asking I get my bearings. I follow an old man, who keeps stop-ping to look at an imaginary watch on his wrist, down a flight of stairs. Halfway down, I spot a dilapidated, filthy, wooden-box railway car-riage and instinctively think all the thoughts I shouldn't think. But another two steps and I see the most modern, most glamorous train I have ever seen. A smart young lady takes my ticket and escorts me to my seat. Am I dreaming?

This is Cameroon's new, up-to-date, priva-tised railway line to Yaounde, the capital in the north, financed by the Canadians and built by the Italians. In the old days there was only a nar-row muddy road linking Douala and Yaounde, which was often closed because of the rains. In 1985 they built a road which cut travelling time to three hours. Now this superb railway.

The train slowly fills up. Every passenger is escorted to their seat and wished a good trip. African trains were never like this. A business-man sitting opposite me sees my amazement.

'It's all privatised,' he whispers. 'Even the recep-tion and hostesses. They all come from a private company.' He buries his head in his papers.

For me Cameroon is a serious country; hard-working, dour, and very staid compared to other francophone nations. Which probably has some-thing to do with their Teutonic heritage. You can buy bread in the market, order a beer in a restaurant or even have a letter typed for you at one of the big open-air typing pools that spring up outside government offices in Yaounde and nobody will say a word to you. They take your money and give you your change without as much as a bonjour or merci. Even the children begging in the streets just shuffle up and stand waiting to be recognised. In other countries, they shout and plead. At the most in Cameroon they will murmur a polite 'Cadeau' and whisper a fragile 'Merci, monsieur'.

It is now 6.15 am. On the dot, the train puffs away from the station. If only my train to Lon-don was like this: beautiful upholstery, no dust, most definitely no cigarettes or ash. The staff are friendly and helpful and courteous. And so are the passengers. The conductor comes along and says bonjour to us. We all bonjour him back. Nothing like the 6.50 from Buxted, East Sussex. Out of the window—which is actually clean; no graffiti or rude words—I can see people hurry-ing to work. They scramble over the tracks, dodge between moving trains and duck between the carriages. Further away, the roads are filling up with buses and cars. Everywhere there are people, some striding out, others shuffling along unwillingly. Few seem to be talking to each other. Douala seems to lack the joie de vivre of other francophone cities. All along the line are flimsy huts and wooden houses. Old cars are piled up everywhere. Enormous puddles flow between the houses and the cars and the junk. The rain must have been heavier than I thought.

The ticket collector comes along, smart in his new uniform. He asks whether we want to visit the Panoramique. 'The dining car, sir. Breakfast is now being served.'

The wooden shacks have given way to lush vegetation. The train is still not going very fast, but it is sounding its horn all the time.

'Our people are not used to trains yet,' says the businessman opposite who can obviously read my thoughts. 'The driver is telling them we are coming. You cannot be too sure.'

We go straight through the first station. Old warehouses slip by on either side. Some more tin shacks. The view is now opening up and I can see right across Douala: tall office buildings, wide, straight roads. The city looks efficient, which is probably half the battle.

Now the train begins to pick up speed. The ticket collector insists on showing us how the little table works. Then he declares that the seats are not good enough and runs off to find us better ones, despite our protests that we are very comfortable. I feel the train definitely going faster; we're heading for open country. Back comes the inspector. He apologises; he can't find any other seats. Then he says that on behalf of the company he would like to treat us to breakfast. Would we do him the honour of joining him? How could anybody refuse an invitation to breakfast by a railway ticket inspector? Usually I'm on my knees pleading with them to serve me.

The restaurant car isn't the Orient Express, but it is bright, clean, almost functional. The service is superb, and no wonder. Standing be-

hind the counter are four girls and two boys. I only have to say, 'coffee' and it is there; croissants too. I wish I had ordered a grand traditional English breakfast, for I'm certain it would have appeared, piping hot, before I could have got the words out. The inspector, beaming with pride, told me again how long it had been operating, how it was quicker than flying to Yaounde and, by the way, had anybody shown us how to operate the sunblinds. . . .

The businessman was now fast asleep. I started to check my papers for my meetings in Yaounde. Suddenly the whole train shuddered and screeched to a halt. My briefcase fell on the floor. Papers flew everywhere. The businessman shot out of his seat and landed on my briefcase smashing it to pieces.

'Another one of those market women,' he grumbled picking himself up. 'Always happens as soon as we get close to Yaounde. The women walk along the railway line. It's easier and quicker than struggling through the bush. Problem is the driver doesn't see them till the last minute.'

'You mean they'll walk to Yaounde and back on the track with all their goods on their head? Isn't it dangerous?'

'Not now everybody knows they are doing it. At first, yes. But now it's all right.'

'Why don't they put fences along the line?'

'Do you know how much that would cost?'

'A lot. But it would save people's lives.'

'And how long do you think the fence would last?'

'A couple of days,' I said, realising the African dimension. It would no sooner be up than it would be torn up and redistributed all over the region—and you would have the problem as before.

'So you agree. It's best to leave things as they are, even if the occasional person gets injured or even killed.'

'I agree,' I said.

The train was now drawing into Yaounde. Stretched either side of us were row after row of sandy tin roofs. We passed the state printing company and a collection of giant oil tanks. By now there were hundreds of men, women, girls streaming across the lines on the way to work. There were probably more on the tracks, jumping over the lines, stumbling over the sleepers and dodging between carriages of trains waiting at red lights, then walking along the road.

'But that must be dangerous,' I said in amazement.

'More dangerous than the roads?'

I couldn't say a word.

REVIEW QUESTIONS

1. In Murphy's selection, what is the chief's attitude toward women, children, and large families? How did Murphy react to his attitudes?
2. Why did the men and women of Ntem—and especially its chief— think Murphy was "infertile"?
3. At the time of Murphy's visit to Cameroon, what were the primary reasons women became prostitutes?
4. Despite their varied religious backgrounds, how did the four female prostitutes in Mayo Darlé view immortality?
5. Why were the prostitutes in Mayo Darlé more at risk for AIDS than elsewhere in Cameroon?
6. Why was Biddlecombe continually surprised by the cleanliness, efficiency, and courteous service on the train from Douala to Yaoundé?
7. What positive changes had resulted from privatization of the railroads in Cameroon? What negative changes?
8. Why did the businessman on the train believe that fences should not be built along the railroad tracks?

A Global Traveler Contrasts Religion and Political Struggle in Ethiopia (1950)

PICO IYER, *Tropical Classical*

Known primarily for his travel writings, Pico Iyer has referred to himself as "a mongrel," one among many people today who exist in several cultures without primarily identifying with any single one. Iyer's visits and writing have been mostly to and about what he calls "remote places," often linked by jet lag in what he once described as "an alternate reality."

Born in England of Indian parents, raised in California, often living in Japan, frequently traveling, Iyer is part of "the universal diaspora," which he has said characterizes the millions who cross international borders every day. He also identifies with the "multiculturalists" in modern Indian letters, such as Salman Rushdie, Bharati Mukherji, Anita Desai, and Amitav Ghosh (all of whom write in English). He feels that these writers—and there are numerous others as well—are "bringing a freshness" in style, tone, and theme to writing. Without losing their Indian heritage, they become global in their interests. Many, like Iyer, have an academic heritage; his father, Raghavan Iyer, was the foremost scholar and authority on the thought of Mahatma Gandhi.

For Iyer, "globalization" extends beyond the marketplace and communications technology to people "whizzing around." One aspect of globalization that fascinates him is the spread of Western pop culture, which has vulgarized non-Western cultures. Many of his voluminous writings reflect this phenomenon (e.g., *Video Night in Kathmandu,* 1988). In addition to his several books, Iyer has had articles published in *Harper's,* the *New York Review of Books,* the *New York Times, Sports Illustrated,* and *Time.*

The following selection focuses on two major characteristics of modern Ethiopia: the results of an almost forty-year struggle between Ethiopia and Eritrea, which is now an independent nation immediately north of Ethiopia, and the central role of Coptic Christianity, or the Ethiopian Orthodox Church. An ancient religion, it was not really acknowledged or even taken seriously by European Christians. Its central belief is one that most of Christianity considers heterodox: the "Monophysite creed," which stresses that Christ has just one nature and not two, the divine but not the human. Iyer's descriptions, however, are not about the theological or philosophical characteristics, but the human.

The final five miles to Lalibela, over unpaved road, the car's wheels spinning in dry creekbeds, the fuel in the cans in back all but suffocating us, took almost three hours. It was, we noted sorrowfully, December 31. "The end of the year in the end of the world!" cried the I.B., with a gaiety brought on by hysteria.

And then, suddenly, we were there, in silence and in mystery. Inside the rock churches, the white figures were everywhere in the dim light, leaning against pillars, standing in front of windows, reading old, leathery, hand-size Bibles, or letting out unearthly mumbled chants that reverberated around the ancient spaces. Sometimes I could see only their eyes in the dark, and hear only their song.

Lean, gaunt-bearded priests with piercing eyes made strange movements with their crosses, and pilgrims slept in empty spaces, and somewhere in the rafters, pigeons whirred. Incense rose up from the shrine, and deacons sang, and figure after figure came into the darkness, kissing the cool stone before coming in. "I weary of writing about these buildings," said the first foreign visitor to describe them, a Portuguese priest in the early sixteenth century, "because it seems to me I shall not be believed."

From time to time in Lalibela, I simply sat on slopes and listened to the sounds around: the chatter of old men with crooks, gathered in the shade; a mother shouting to her child; the voices of other children, playing in the distance. Birds with gorgeous, iridescent turquoise wings—Abyssinian rollers, I later learned—lit up the branches. Often, there was nothing but the calling of the birds and the wind, whistling in my ears.

Occasionally, there were vultures in the trees and bells to summon priests to church. And everywhere, a sense of piety and fervor, a world inscribed by nothing but devotion. "This is Golgotha," said a deacon, pointing to an inner gate. "And this is Nazareth. And there, in the light of the church, are the graves of Abraham, Isaac, and Jacob."

"It isn't Africa," a Swiss medieval historian said over dinner that night, on New Year's Eve. "It's more like a cross between medieval Europe and Arabia. In this village, for example, there are seven thousand people. And one thousand of them are priests. That, too, is medieval: in Europe, in the Middle Ages, one-tenth of the population were priests."

The next day, the I.B. and I got on mules and rode through the dust-colored mountains, over a landscape as majestic and humbling as Monument Valley, the I.B. listening to Dead bootlegs in his Walkman, as we passed peasants, with long black beards, seated under trees, sharing food, and donkeys and cedar trees and olive trees and juniper. All around us, as so often in Ethiopia, it felt as if we were passing through an illuminated Bible from the thirteenth century, except that all the figures moved.

When we arrived in Nakutola'ab, where twenty-five anchorites live in rock caves, we came upon a group of pilgrims—mud-grimed grandfathers and sunken-cheeked women and young girls in pockmarked gowns—all of them clapping and singing their joy, ululating wildly and pounding on drums, in a circle, to vent their pent-up pleasure after arriving at the place that they had been dreaming of all their lives.

I asked one of the men (through a translator) how old he was—a strapping man, tall and lean, his eyes alight with glee. He was seventy, he said, and he had walked twelve days and nights to mark Christmas (celebrated in Ethiopia on January 7) in this sacred site.

"And why do you come here?"

"Because this is heaven. We believe if we are here we go to heaven."

"Then I'll see you in heaven," said the I.B., clapping him on the shoulder, and there were wild shouts of approval and laughs all round. . . .

The other site in Gonder that we inspected closely was the Ethiopian Airlines Office (which pins "Positive Attitude" posters from Fairfield, New Jersey, on its walls). E.T., as the experts call it, has a sterling reputation but is not without its extraterrestrial elements. Its schedules seem to follow the solar calendar, it insists on security checks at every stage of check-in, and in many places, the only terminals in sight are trees.

"Ethiopia is a land where the great unknown yonder still exists in plenty," says the legend on every ticket.

Undeterred, we took our lives in our hands (and out of the hands of our driver, who had taken now to plaintive moans of "I am very suffering") and flew low over the high plateaus toward Bahar Dar. The town itself is a pleasant, palm-fringed settlement along the banks of Lake Tana. The Tisisat are nearby, a rainbow punctually arcing across their rush of water every morning and marking the place where James Bruce excitedly hailed the waters of the Blue Nile. Boys cross the river on papyrus boats, and hoist stalks of sugarcane taller than themselves. On the quiet lake, there are tens of little islands, most of them given over to monasteries, some so strict that no female is allowed to set foot on them (even hens are not permitted). The round, dried-mud churches at their center, three hundred years old, swarm with naive, brightly colored murals bursting with angels and stories from the Bible and even—a typical Ethiopian anachronism—Jesus surrounded by gun-toting men.

That strain was beginning to hit me more and more forcibly. As soon as I went to change my money at a local bank, a security guard came up to frisk me, and to ask me to deposit my camera next to the rifles, laid neatly against the wall outside; an hour later, walking through quiet villages to see the falls, I was accompanied by a sharp-talking teenager and a barefoot peasant with a rifle (whether to ward off bandits or to perform banditry himself, I never knew). Pride is only a hairbreadth from machismo here, and when it does not take the form of guarding Jesus—or General Aidid—with guns, it involves overtaking around blind turns and driving the other man off the road.

The most obvious reason for this is that the country is only just emerging from decades of civil war. Ever since their region was annexed, in 1962, the Eritreans had been crossing the border to fight against central authority in Addis, and then their guerrillas had joined the local rebels to overthrow the Communists. Meanwhile, more than a hundred other ethnic groups were ardently pursuing their rivalries and interests in north and south and east. The result is that everywhere you go in Ethiopia, you see the scars and remnants of thirty years of war: airports are blasted, and their tarmac is littered with wrecked helicopters and junked Aeroflot planes. Rusted tanks line every road, and faded replicas of the hammer and sickle. Once, in Bahar Dar, coming upon a car crash (there are more crashes than cars in Ethiopia, it often seems), I ended up spending a long day in a local hospital, a place of terrible cries and whimpers, where boys with bandaged heads and sunken faces writhed under rough blankets. The doctors were courtly and efficient, but it was not a place where I would like to fall ill. "Are there many car accidents here?" I asked a pretty young nurse. "No," she said, nonchalant. "Usually it is bullet wounds. But that, too, not so often. Usually the people here shoot to kill, not wound. So we let them just go ahead with it." And, smiling, went off to another victim.

We explored Bahar Dar in an old car decorated with pictures of Rambo and Jesus on the windshield, driven by Solomon, with Mikael at his side, both of them breaking into smiles of good-natured perplexity as the I.B. recited a poem about a duck-billed platypus entering the diplomatic service. We visited the U.N. Shoe Shine store and the Marine Bingo Club, and in the evening, we got the manager of the local cinema to screen *The Border* just for us, though the print was so washed out and mutilated that the picture was over in a matter of minutes, and somehow the classic last scene of Freddy Fender singing Ry Cooder's "Across the Borderline" was lost. Nonetheless, it was a cheerful experience, sitting on long wooden benches, like pews, in what looked like a school assembly hall, the boys in the balcony eating egg sandwiches and sipping *shai,* and scarcely missing Freddy Fender.

REVIEW QUESTIONS

1. A Swiss historian told Iyer that Ethiopia wasn't really Africa; it was "a cross between medieval Europe and Arabia." What prompted him to make this remark?
2. What examples in the article indicate the presence of Western pop culture?
3. How would you describe Iyer's general attitude in this article? Explain.

14

Americas and Oceania, 1918 to the Present

From the end of World War I to the present, most travelers to and throughout the Americas and the Pacific islands found a great deal of difference between what they had anticipated and what they experienced. Travel became easier and cheaper with the technological developments of motor cars, ocean cruise ships, and air travel. At the same time these modes of transportation were perfected, increasing numbers of people became wealthier and had the money to indulge themselves in the types of travel that had always been available only to the elites. Particularly peoples from the Eastern Hemisphere came to the West in search of excitement, education, and intellectual stimulation.

The most striking differences between the goals of the traveler and the reality of the conditions in the lands of their destination appear in the accounts of four people who traveled from the United States to other parts of the Americas and Oceania. For instance, Seth Humphrey found the unusual and exotic peoples he sought, but he soon realized that the blessings of British rule he had anticipated had not made great differences in those people's lives. John Clytus traveled to Cuba to escape the racism he endured in the United States, but learned that closed minds can exist in a Communist-led country as well as a capitalist one. Phillips Russell embarked on a safari-type expedition into Meso-America to discover the ruins of the ancient peoples but found the modern Mayas more interesting than tree-covered temples. On the other hand, Charles Baker did not change his opinion of Latin American cuisine as he traveled through South America; instead he chose to glorify the foods and preparation methods he found so he could sell them as exotic meals for the American table.

An examination of the accounts of those who came from Europe, Latin America, and various parts of Asia to the United States shows that this country where streets were supposedly paved with gold was not all it seemed. After years of attempting to gain the support of U.S. Jews for the newly established nation of Israel, Nahum Goldmann found only disappointment because he discovered that the Jews in the United States were much too self-satisfied to be of help. Poranee Natadecha-Sponsel brought to the United States her Asian beliefs in the priority of the family and discreet public behavior, thinking that family unity and polite public behavior were important to Americans also. As a Chinese expatriot, Buwei Yang-Chao, who visited Hawaii, learned that many Americans from different parts of the United States have very diverse priorities and beliefs from one another. Her letters home and other autobiographical writings, however, advise others that there were great differences between the public words and private actions of Americans and that within the family disunity and conflict often existed. Finally, the Mexican artist José Clemente Orozco came to New York City primarily at the invitation of women from wealthy industrialist families who promised to support and promote him and his art. Like the others represented here, he did not find what he expected.

A Mexican Muralist Portrays Life in New York City (1927–1928)

JOSÉ CLEMENTE OROZCO, *The Artist in New York*

The Roaring Twenties in the United States presented opportunities to many foreigners who came to New York City to become part of the new social scene—based upon new fortunes rather than on inherited wealth. Rich industrialist families basked in the glow of an ever-rising stock market and the money to be made from investing in the rebuilding of Europe and the modernization of Latin American nations. These newly prominent families expressed their wealth and social position by spending large sums of money on the arts, everything from classical performers to jazz musicians, and from European cubist artists to Mexican folk art muralists. Before the financial crisis at the end of the 1920s, the city teemed with people spending lavishly and enjoying exciting lives.

Clemente Orozco came to the United States from Mexico in 1926 at the encouragement of several admirers in New York. His work had brought him fame, as well as notoriety, in Mexico City because of his strong support of the Socialists and their goals for the country. A contemporary of Diego Rivera, Orozco competed with him and other Latin American artists for recognition in the United States. In a sense, he was a pawn of the elite, men and women who paid extravagant prices for his sketches and who held showings for his paintings and murals. The following excerpts from his personal letters to his friend Jean Charlot and various women patrons reveal much about Orozco's opinions and reaction to the frenzy of this society.

N.Y. 21 Dec./27

Brother Jean:

This is the first chance I've had to write since I arrived on Friday night, very tired and during a spell of terribly cold weather. . . .

I had to come in as an immigrant, that is, by making statements under oath and paying 10 dollars more, or 18 in all. They lectured me because I stayed for 2 years the last time, instead of 6 months, but I told them it was on account of the Revolution. This time I can live here for as long as I wish. The material life is *very expensive,* more so than before. And I'm not the only one who says this, everyone agrees. To give you a better idea, I'll tell you that what you pay in Mexico in pesos silver, you pay here in dollars plus about 10 percent. It's true that some things are very cheap, clothes, for example, but that is misleading because they are either things you don't need or else they're of poor quality. Anita and Lucy* have a little apartment with two bedrooms, a small living room, and kitchen, and it costs them 78 dollars in one of the cheapest neighborhoods. . . .

N.Y. 3 January 28

Very dear Juan:

. . . The only thing I've been doing is getting settled and wandering through the city, visiting galleries and museums and defending myself from the cold, which is very unpleasant for me after Mexico. . . .

---

*Anita Brenner was an author who wrote about the Mexican art scene. She was the author of *Idols Behind Altars* (1929). Lucy Knox was her roommate.

The show at the Valentine Gallery, the catalog of which I am enclosing, is *vastly better,* divided equally between Matisse and Derain; this is the first time I have seen modern art, art of the present day, without feeling nostalgia for ancient art. Pure painting, without any subterfuges. Grace. Naturalness. Joy. It is a great pleasure to see these pictures, and it makes one feel happy and contented for the rest of the day. Derain's are torsos of women, fleshy and profound. Matisse is color and light, freshness, serenity. These painters are people who live in gardens and meet their ladies for five o'clock tea, they frequent the salons and are acquainted with good society, good drinking, and good beds. We are the revolutionaries, the accursed ones, the starvelings.

Decidedly, here in N.Y., French art means the cream of the cream, it is the ideal, the top, what is most prestigious, the model; to praise something one compares it to the French. That is what is most exquisite.

Perhaps one day we Mexicans may come to have some influence, but it will be in another direction. There is nothing "exquisite" about us; / "Do you know what I mean?"/ . . .

4 Jan. 28

Very dear Jean:

. . . The only thing I am doing now is "getting adjusted." How happy I would be if you were here! There are many interesting things to see, both American and imported. With their money they are bringing Europe over here, stone by stone. Any day now they will set up the Eiffel Tower in Central Park, next to the obelisk. You should see the machines for excavating rock and burying the iron that will support a skyscraper, and 10 minutes away you can see a collection of Grecos and 3,500-year-old Egyptian tombs!

I have just seen: a whole collection of 18th-century art: furniture, tapestries, architectural pieces, Watteau, Fragonard, Boucher, Pater, etc. . . .

You have no idea how funny the /American painters/ are, there are thousands of them. In the Metropolitan Museum there are rooms and rooms, but the curious thing is this: among the /

American/ paintings you suddenly find a Cézanne, then more /Americans/, then another Cézanne and then a Pissarro and then Claude Monet, and in other exhibitions they are mixed in with Picasso and Dufy and other French artists. I don't know why they do this because only a blind man can confuse the one with the other. They have only been able to "catch" or understand (and that only incompletely) very little or almost nothing of the French "theme," that is to say, the /"literature"/ part or what they think is the /"literature"/ of European painting. I assure you that the /American painters/ are a real tragedy. A tragedy that has an enormous lump of gold—a mountain of gold!—tied around its neck. It will collapse and no one will be able to stop it. The real American artists are the ones who make the machines: you have to take off your hat to them. . . .

New York, 22 February 1928
Mrs. A. Charlot Goupil
México

. . . I don't see Anita any more—I have broken off all relations with her—and as to "Friends," they do not exist for me. Here in New York there is only self-interest and deception and bad faith. I am completely alone, relying on my own forces, which happily are still considerable. A foreign country is where one gets to know people best. Here my "friends" have scorned and humiliated me.

This is a very hard struggle. As far as painting is concerned, it is necessary to start over again and get rid of every trace of "Mexican" if one wants to have a personality of his own, because otherwise we shall be forever "Rivera's disciples."[†] . . .

Rents in N. York are high: I have an acquaintance who lives /"uptown,"/ on 198th, and he has a small apartment in a large building like those in Mexico—three little rooms, bath and

---

[†]Orozco refers here to Diego Rivera, the famous Mexican muralist whose work had been recently exhibited in New York and had received a great deal of acclaim. In another letter, Orozco lamented that "despite the fact that it was a ridiculous show," it firmly established the idea that Rivera was "the great creator of everything" and that other Mexican artists were "only his disciples."

kitchenette, all very small, and he pays 75 dollars including heat, with light and gas extra, but it seems that there are some for less in Brooklyn and certain outlying sections. On Sunday I'll send you the classified section of the *Times* to give you an idea. Of course I can help when you come, because I know the city very well. . . .

August 3

Very dear Jean:

. . . I don't talk about exhibitions any more for the simple reason that there aren't any. You have no idea how every bit of activity here stops in the summer, and the little that does go on is so unimportant that it doesn't matter. There are no plays, or concerts, or painting, or anything like that. Newspapers reduce their pages to the bare minimum, and business and everything else slows down. The worst thing is that the "civilized" people go to the country, to Europe, to Mexico, anywhere. By civilized I mean the cultured people and those who have money and spend it on art, in any of its forms. New York is absolutely "dead" at this season, even business. The only entertainment is the movies with old films and very small audiences, all in shirt sleeves. Only those of us who are very "unfortunate" remain here, because even people with limited means go away on vacation.

Sept. 10

Very dear Jean:

I received your letter and I am glad that at least you have some hope now. You must not be discouraged and besides you have to realize that since life in N. York is so busy and complicated, with so many "social" obligations, and with the days so short in winter, there is scarcely enough time to paint, and although it's true that you aren't doing it now, because you aren't in the right frame of mind, you can still do mental work and make little sketches to develop later. If you bring a collection of these, you'll see how useful they will be.

I saw Pach yesterday, he invited me to come to the place where he is spending the summer, a country estate called Amenia, about 100 kilometers north of N. York, owned by some very rich people, the Spingarns. They have a piece of sculpture from some French cathedral, magnificent, they say that it cost them 15,000 dollars. It's a very pretty place. . . .

A week ago I was in Washington. The ambassador knows about painting. The embassy impossible, but converted into a *cantina*—very good wines. Washington is above all the city of snobs and fakes whose money comes from mysterious sources. What statues! Three thousand of them in all sizes, colors, and flavors, they're even in the sewers, from Joan of Arc to Senator X. Final drinking party with the embassy people—hangover the next day—night festival on the eve of Saint Fortunata's day in the Italian section—like those in Mexico. There are no peanuts, but there are snails, which look almost the same, except that they are peanuts (or snails) that move and climb little sticks. . . .

Americans are serious people in winter but in the summer they revert to their childhood and forget about everything, they play golf and go fishing. Coolidge is in Wisconsin now, fishing in a pond that was stocked with fish beforehand, and there is a diver in the pond who attaches the fish to the presidential fishhook. When he is through fishing and summer is over, he will return to the /White House/ to continue harassing the Nicaraguans. Your bosses at the Carnegie are no doubt fishing too, or playing marbles.

Don't be discouraged, and write me.

A very affectionate greeting to the Señora your mother.

Clemente

REVIEW QUESTIONS

1. How did the practical realities of everyday life in New York City affect Orozco's life?
2. What was his opinion of the artistic attitude, or climate, of the wealthy in New York City?

3. What was his opinion of other Mexican artists? Of French and European painters who were glorified in the United States?
4. Why would the elites of New York City want to sponsor such artists? What did they receive for their money? Explain.

A Chinese Doctor Observes Life in the United States (1924, 1938–1939)

BUWEI YANG CHAO, *Autobiography of a Chinese Woman*

Buwei Yang Chao began her book in 1913 as a novel but quickly decided that the real events of her life were more exciting than anything she could imagine. She calls herself a "typical Chinese woman" who grew up in a big family with four generations living in the same house. Among the extraordinary acts of this typical woman, Yang Chao admits to breaking a marriage engagement during a time when it was just not done and being the principal of a school before she went to college. She was also a refugee from her home in the first decade of the twentieth century because of the civil war in China, and she worked as a nurse and doctor for the rebels during the Communist revolution. At that time she was married without a wedding ceremony. Following these events, she visited and lived in Japan for six years and in the United States on three separate occasions for a total of thirteen years. Although she saw herself as a typical Chinese woman, she lived an exceptional life because her intelligence and initiative during a period of enormous change in China offered her many opportunities.

After Buwei Yang Chao studied medicine in Japan and China, she met and married her husband, Yuenren Chao, a linguist who had worked in Europe and the United States. During the continuing revolution in China, those who were born into the elite and wealthy classes moved into the interior to avoid the conflict. Educated professionals and educated Chinese citizens, such as the Chaos, went abroad and sat out the war in comfort and safety, and they often had lucrative occupations in the West. In the late 1930s, Yuenren obtained a visiting professorship at Yale University to teach linguistics, and the family traveled from Beijing to New Haven, Connecticut. This was their second voyage to the United States, and the following excerpt compares several events and sites along their route.

I went to Hawaii in 1938 with nothing but summer clothes. It was only a one-year plan. Yuenren should be able to regain his health after a year on the beaches of Waikiki, and we would then return to Kunming, or, as I fancied, possibly to Nanking. I had little idea that this was to be my longest stay in America.

I shared the common impression of outsiders that Honolulu was not United States, but a United States military outpost in a country inhabited by aboriginal natives and a large China-town population. I have actually heard people from the States ask what kind of money they use over there and what their postage stamps look like. My previous one-day visits had not taught me much. But when I actually lived there, I found that there was much greater approach to harmony between racial groups than anywhere else. I often did the tactless thing of speaking of the white people there as "Americans." But they are all Americans. The white Americans, as against the non-white Americans, are called *haoles,* a *haole,* in the Hawaiian language, meaning a person who does not have to work.

One of my previous impressions which remained with me was the holiday air about the whole place. While the 60-degree mornings and evenings of Kunming stimulate you to work, the constant 75- to 85-degree days of Honolulu send you to the beach, and make you feel like going barefoot all the time. We did have a few chilly days in November, but we all went to have our regular bathing on New Year's Day.

Our house was one of a row of pretty bungalows on Lunalilo Street, with small but comfortable rooms. A tall tree in our neighbor's yard dropped ripe mangoes into our yard, while a still taller tree in our yard dropped ripe coconuts into the other neighbor's yard. When I gossiped with Mrs. Kam, our mangoes neighbor, and Iris called me up to say supper was ready, I could hear her both through the telephone and through the open windows.

Being prepared to stay at Honolulu for a whole year, of course I never visited the Aquarium. I had already "done" the Aquarium as a tourist. I thought that the Hawaiian fish markets must be the richest in the world. I had heard of the fish called *homohomonukunukuapua,* a four-inch little fish, and the *o,*[1] a big, long fish. Would they taste as interesting as they sounded? But when I went to the fish market, I was greatly surprised to find that there was less variety of fish there than in Peiping or Washington, not to say Shanghai or Boston. They had only the usual things like tuna

or flounder and, owing to some special conditions, all the sea food was expensive. Shrimps and lobsters had to be even imported from the mainland.

I found catching sea food more fun than buying sea food. Our neighbors the William Kams had a villa on the north side of the Oahu Island, on the opposite side of Honolulu. They used to take our whole family there in a car to do squidding. Each of us would wade over prickly corals with a glass-bottomed box, into which you could look through the shallow water. If a squid caught hold of you before you caught hold of it, the thing to do was to bite its head with your teeth and its tentacles would release their hold at once. But I never had occasion to bite a squid until after it was properly seasoned and cooked.

Crabbing at night was even more fun than squidding at day. For this I sometimes went with the Kams, sometimes with Mrs. Loo Goon, who had a fishery near Pearl Harbor—the Pearl Harbor before "Pearl Harbor," of course. Mrs. Loo Goon is a remarkable Chinese woman. She was widowed young and had to raise a family of ten children single-handed. She put all her children through college in Hawaii or in the States, got them established, and found time to study Mandarin on the side. I used to meet her at some of the social-service meetings and was often invited to visit her fishery for picnics and crabbing. Once, four of us ladies caught one hundred pounds of crabs in one evening's operation.

I lived idly and a good deal out of doors because I minded the constant summer heat and had no mind for work. But Yuenren found that he had more to stay indoors for than he had expected, though it suited his sedentary habits very well. He had some good students in his language courses, but was bored by his own lectures on the History and Appreciation of Chinese Music. He is fond of "doing something with Chinese music," but frankly unappreciative of Chinese music as it is. In order to find what could be appreciated in the history of Chinese music, he went into such technicalities as Chinese scales and the Chinese discovery of equal temperament one hundred years before the Occidental

---

[1]Pronounced very short, like *o* in *obey.*

discovery. That was of course over the head of most of the students, as it still is over mine.

The children had stiff schedules of their own. Iris and Nova entered Roosevelt High School. This was their third change of reading language, not counting their previous changes of spoken language from English to French and from French to Chinese. Each day for the first few days they would come home with six hundred new words for Daddy to tell them the meanings of. The school newspaper made much of the fact that their favorite subject was mathematics. The reason was of course that mathematics was the subject with the least number of new words.

REVIEW QUESTIONS

1. Which of the activities described in this reading seem the most unusual to you? Why?
2. How did life in Hawaii vary from that in China and the U.S. mainland? What were Chao's responses to the differences?
3. Did Buwei Yang Chao prefer living in Hawaii or Connecticut? Why?
4. What evidence do you find that the Chaos were able to incorporate their Chinese culture into their lives in Hawaii?

A Lithuanian Jewish Activist Comments on Jewish Life in New York City (mid-twentieth century)

The Autobiography of Nahum Goldmann: Sixty Years of Jewish Life

The life of Nahum Goldmann provides great insight into the differences between Jewish intellectuals of Europe and those in the United States before, during and after World War II. Born into a Jewish family in Lithuania in 1895, Goldmann moved to Frankfurt with his mother and father when he was about seven years old. He participated in many Zionist activities during his youth and completed the study of law at Heidelberg. Rather than pursue a legal or academic career, however, Goldmann became a journalist and lecturer during the 1920s. From 1923 to 1932, he worked on the *Encyclopaedia Judaica,* which was to eventually become a comprehensive Jewish encyclopedia. With the rise of Adolph Hitler in 1933, Goldmann moved to Geneva and three years later became a leader in the newly formed World Jewish Congress. During the Second World War and through the middle of the twentieth century, he continued to work for international Zionist organizations in Europe, the United States, and Israel.

Goldmann's anti-Nazi activities in the 1930s eventually forced him to flee Europe entirely and take up residence in the United States. He and his family were in Paris during the fall of 1939 when the French government declared that all German Jewish refugees were enemy aliens and must be jailed. The Goldmanns escaped to Portugal before the Germans invaded France in May 1940, and via a circuitous route through Ireland, Goldmann and his family reached New York City on June 21, 1940. They resided in the United States for the next twenty-four years.

Aided by many supporters in the United States, Goldmann continued his work on behalf of the World Jewish Congress. During the war years, he concentrated on saving European Jews and "solving the problem of Palestine, which was obviously going to come to a head when the war ended." In these activities, he became very familiar with the organizations of Jewish leaders in the United States. The following excerpt from his *Autobiography,* which was compiled in Jerusalem in the late 1960s, presents his opinions and reactions to the Jewish community as seen especially in New York City, both during and after World War II.

Along with many other Jewish leaders, I belong to a generation, the last of its kind, that has played a unique role in Jewish life of the last three decades, a generation rooted in Eastern Europe but educated in the West and combining many features of European culture, Eastern and Western, Jewish and non-Jewish. The most eminent and in a sense the most typical representative of this generation was Chaim Weizmann. It is no accident that its leading members have played a major role in modern Zionism, for one of the characteristics of that movement is that it was based on a synthesis of East and West.

As far as I can tell (the archives of my *shtetl,* or little town, were destroyed in the First World War), I was born on July 10, 1895, in Visznevo, Lithuania. Although I spent no more than my first six years there, I vividly remember those early experiences and have always been aware that the most important influences on the development of my mind and character came from Eastern European Judaism. My parents had left for Germany soon after I was born to start a new life, and I remained in the care of my paternal grandparents. My father studied in Königsberg and Heidelberg but was unable to complete his studies for lack of money. He and my mother finally moved to Frankfurt, and when they were settled, I came to live with them. But those crucial six years of my early childhood were dominated by the intimacy of my grandparents' home

and by the cultural atmosphere of the Visznevo *shtetl.* . . .

The Jews share another characteristic of the general American mentality: the excessive importance they attach to material assets, the dominance of the rich man. Public institutions, especially charitable ones, are, like those in other Anglo-Saxon cultures, far more dependent on private contributions than in Europe, where the state is the major source of support. In America and England, hospitals, universities, schools, and cultural projects are financed to a large extent by private funds. This state of affairs is even more obvious in American Jewry, which lacks any representative organization for dealing with government. Thus the "big giver" almost inevitably and automatically becomes a leader in Jewish life. Let us take one example. In the United States there are no real Jewish community organizations in which the whole Jewish population of a city comes together; there are synagogues supported by their congregations and a multiplicity of Jewish groups and institutions. These usually administer jointly a common welfare fund produced by the numerous fund drives for local and foreign Jewish causes. Since this fund is the backbone of every communal organization, the big giver obviously plays a decisive role. While we must respect and recognize the generosity of many wealthy Jews who year in and year out contribute not only large sums of money but also much time and energy to fund drives, from the sociological point of view, their predominant position in the structure of American Jewry is a disadvantage. It makes organization on a really large scale impossible.

Any organization representing all of American Jewry must, by its very nature, be democratic. The handful of big givers will never assent to this—and it is quite understandable from the human point of view that they should want recognition. The more numerous the separate organizations, the more easily every philanthropist can acquire his own little world in which to be a leader. The result is a harmful splintering of American Jewry, dissipation of energy and money, duplication of effort in many areas, and ultimately a serious lowering of achievement. Instead of fighting over differences in their programs, which would be understandable and creative, the organizations compete for prestige, jockeying for position for themselves and their leaders. This is what makes exaggerated advertising necessary. Dependent on voluntary contributions and fund raising, they must try to attract attention because they have to keep people aware of their importance. This makes long-range political planning incomparably more difficult. You need publicity; whether or not *The New York Times* will publish a report becomes a fundamental problem.

I remember a dinner of the New York Foreign Policy Association in honor of the first visit of Chancellor Adenauer, at which I sat next to Arthur Hays Sulzberger, owner and publisher of *The New York Times.* Although very much a Jew, Mr. Sulzberger was very restrained in Jewish matters, chiefly in order to protect the *Times,* with its great influence, from any charge of favoring Jewish interests, and he took this opportunity to justify the paper's reserve on Jewish questions. I replied: "Mr. Sulzberger, there is one way in which you could do American Jewish life a great service, and it might even be profitable for your paper too. Except for a few special cases, stop publishing all those statements by Jewish organizations and so-called leaders of

American Jewry. This would do a great deal to improve the internal organization of Jewish life in America and to limit the publicity-seeking which accounts for so many of its activities." Unfortunately Sulzberger did not follow my advice, probably because of the many Jews who read his paper.

Another consequence of the multiplicity of organizations is the great bureaucratic apparatus it requires. A whole class of well-paid "professional Jews" has emerged. Since they can devote full time to their work, these officials are steadily gaining the upper hand in the direction of their organizations, even though they are usually not much in evidence from the outside. American Jewry faces the danger of becoming professionalized and bureaucratized, with all the moral and intellectual disadvantages such a process inevitably involves.

One of the consequences of this situation is the quite inadequate, not to say negligible, role the intellectual plays in Jewish life in the United States. The reason for this is certainly not a lack of intelligence among American Jews, who have produced as many scientists, thinkers, and artists as their European counterparts. In fact, they have certainly produced more on a percentage basis, since the higher level of education in America and the prosperity of American Jews permit far more of them to attend universities. The intellectual's lack of influence in Jewish life parallels a similar situation in American life as a whole. But in Jewish life this has a much more detrimental effect, since the Jewish people in the Diaspora lives primarily by its spiritual values and capacities, not by its economic or political power.

Recently, of course, American intellectuals have been acquiring more and more influence. Professors and university students, writers and poets, eminent journalists, play a growing and often vociferous role in American politics—often a role of outspoken criticism and opposition. In this respect Jewish life still lags behind the general trend in America. Except for a few intellectual rabbinical leaders, there are almost no influential figures who do not owe their position to financial contributions and fund-raising activities. How often have I reproached American-Jewish intellectuals for their inadequate participation in Jewish life, only to hear the answer: I'm not a big giver; what part could I play? But the whole thing goes much further. The aloofness of tens and hundreds of thousands of intellectuals impoverishes Jewish life, makes it boring, shallow, and devoid of spiritual impetus.

REVIEW QUESTIONS

1. What strengths and weaknesses did Goldmann observe when introduced to the work of Jewish leaders in the United States?
2. What changes did he want to see among the elite leaders of American Jewry?
3. To what extent are the situations he describes here the result of the capitalist economic structure in the United States?
4. Goldmann acknowledges that his autobiography was written from recollections and memories more than from documents or accounts written over time. How might this have affected the final content and tone of his work?

A Thai Educator Describes Cultural Values in the United States (1990s)

PORANEE NATADECHA-SPONSEL, *The Young, the Rich, and the Famous: Individualism as an American Cultural Value*

Needless to say, the social customs and personal priorities of people in Southeast Asia and North America are extremely different, as this account reveals. The cultures of Southeast Asia have developed over thousands of years, whereas those of the United States have had only a little more than two centuries to form. Consequently, ideas of a person's position in society and the limits to democracy differ considerably. Because of the importance of the extended family, people of the Malay Peninsula and Thailand have few opportunities for personal privacy. An individual's concerns and conditions are part of the family's business, and the family includes all persons in the community who are related by blood, marriage, and friendship over an extended period of time. The business and financial conditions of the individual are also part of this extended family's concerns, and individual attainment of wealth is always subsumed in that of the family. As can be seen in the civilian coup that took control from the military government in 1991–1992, democracy has become an important element in Thailand's culture, but only as tempered by a strong socioeconomic system.

Poranee Natadecha-Sponsel is a Thai and Malay woman from southern Thailand who came to the United States with a B.A. in English and philosophy from Chulalongkorn University in Bangkok. She earned an M.A. in philosophy from Ohio University (Athens, Ohio) in 1973, and her Ed.D. from the University of Hawaii in 1991. She now teaches interdisciplinary courses in women's studies at the Manoa campus of the University of Hawaii. To fit into American society, Natadecha-Sponsel had to adjust her attitude on personal privacy, as well as on many other issues.

"Hi, how are you?" "Fine, thank you, and you?" These are greetings that everybody in America hears and says every day—salutations that come ready-made and packaged just like a hamburger and fries. There is no real expectation for any special information in response to these greetings. Do not, under any circumstances, take up anyone's time by responding in depth to the programmed query. What or how you may feel at the moment is of little, if any, importance. Thai people would immediately perceive that our concerned American friends are truly interested in our welfare, and this concern would require polite reciprocation by spelling out the details of our current condition. We become very disappointed when we have had enough experience in the United States to learn that we have bored, amused, or even frightened many of our American acquaintances by taking the greeting "How are you?" so literally. We were reacting like Thais, but in the American context where salutations have a different meaning, our detailed reactions were inappropriate. In Thai society, a greeting among acquaintances usually requests specific information about the other person's condition, such as "Where are you going?" or "Have you eaten?"

One of the American contexts in which this greeting is most confusing and ambiguous is at the hospital or clinic. In these sterile and ritualistic settings, I have always been uncertain exactly how to answer when the doctor or nurse asks "How are you?" If I deliver a packaged answer of "Fine," I wonder if I am telling a lie. After all, I am there in the first place precisely because I am not so fine. Finally, after debating for some time, I asked one nurse how she expected a patient to answer the query "How are

you?" But after asking this question, I then wondered if it was rude to do so. However, she looked relieved after I explained to her that people from different cultures have different ways to greet other people and that for me to be asked how I am in the hospital results in awkwardness. Do I simply answer, "Fine, thank you," or do I reveal in accurate detail how I really feel at the moment? My suspicion was verified when the nurse declared that "How are you?" was really no more than a polite greeting and that she didn't expect any answer more elaborate than simply "Fine." However, she told me that some patients do answer her by describing every last ache and pain from which they are suffering.

A significant question that comes to mind is whether the verbal pattern of greetings reflects any social relationship in American culture. The apparently warm and sincere greeting may initially suggest interest in the person, yet the intention and expectations are, to me, quite superficial. For example, most often the person greets you quickly and then walks by to attend to other business without even waiting for your response! This type of greeting is just like a package of American fast food! The person eats the food quickly without enjoying the taste. The convenience is like many other American accoutrements of living such as cars, household appliances, efficient telephones, or simple, systematic, and predictable arrangements of groceries in the supermarket. However, usually when this greeting is delivered, it seems to lack a personal touch and genuine feeling. It is little more than ritualized behavior.

I have noticed that most Americans keep to themselves even at social gatherings. Conversation may revolve around many topics, but little, if anything, is revealed about oneself. Without talking much about oneself and not knowing much about others, social relations seem to remain at an abbreviated superficial level. How could one know a person without knowing something about him or her? How much does one need to know about a person to really know that person?

After living in this culture for more than a decade, I have learned that there are many topics that should not be mentioned in conversations with American acquaintances or even close friends. One's personal life and one's income are considered to be very private and even taboo topics. Unlike my Thai culture, Americans do not show interest or curiosity by asking such personal questions, especially when one just meets the individual for the first time. Many times I have been embarrassed by my Thai acquaintances who recently arrived at the University of Hawaii and the East-West Center. For instance, one day I was walking on campus with an American friend when we met another Thai woman to whom I had been introduced a few days earlier. The Thai woman came to write her doctoral dissertation at the East-West Center where the American woman worked, so I introduced them to each other. The American woman greeted my Thai companion in Thai language, which so impressed her that she felt immediately at ease. At once, she asked the American woman numerous personal questions such as, How long did you live in Thailand? Why were you there? How long were you married to the Thai man? Why did you divorce him? How long have you been divorced? Are you going to marry a Thai again or an American? How long have you been working here? How much do you earn? The American was stunned. However, she was very patient and more or less answered all those questions as succinctly as she could. I was so uncomfortable that I had to interrupt whenever I could to get her out of the awkward situation in which she had been forced into talking about things she considered personal. For people in Thai society, such questions would be appropriate and not considered too personal, let alone taboo.

The way Americans value their individual privacy continues to impress me. Americans seem to be open and yet there is a contradiction because they are also aloof and secretive. This is reflected in many of their behavior patterns. By Thai standards, the relationship between friends in American society seems to be somewhat superficial. Many Thai students, as well as other Asians, have felt that they could not find genuine friendship with Americans. For example, I met many American classmates who were very helpful and friendly while we were in the same class. We went out, exchanged phone calls, and did the same things as would good friends in Thailand. But those activities stopped suddenly when the semester ended.

Privacy as a component of the American cultural value of individualism is nurtured in the home as children grow up. From birth they are given their own individual, private space, a bedroom separate from that of their parents. American children are taught to become progressively independent, both emotionally and economically, from their family. They learn to help themselves at an early age. In comparison, in Thailand, when parents bring a new baby home from the hospital, it shares the parents' bedroom for two to three years and then shares another bedroom with older siblings of the same sex. Most Thai children do not have their own private room until they finish high school, and some do not have their own room until another sibling moves out, usually when the sibling gets married. In Thailand, there are strong bonds within the extended family. Older siblings regularly help their parents to care for younger ones. In this and other ways, the Thai family emphasizes the interdependence of its members.

I was accustomed to helping Thai babies who fell down to stand up again. Thus, in America when I saw babies fall, it was natural for me to try to help them back on their feet. Once at summer camp for East–West Center participants, one of the supervisors brought his wife and their ten-month-old son with him. The baby was so cute that many students were playing with him. At one point he was trying to walk and fell, so all the Asian students, males and females, rushed to help him up. Although the father and mother were nearby, they paid no attention to their fallen and crying baby. However, as the students were trying to help and comfort him, the parents told them to leave him alone; he would be all right on his own. The baby did get up and stopped crying without any assistance. Independence is yet another component of the American value of individualism.

Individualism is even reflected in the way Americans prepare, serve, and consume food. In a typical American meal, each person has a separate plate and is not supposed to share or taste food from other people's plates. My Thai friends and I are used to eating Thai style, in which you share food from a big serving dish in the middle of the table. Each person dishes a small amount from the serving dish onto his or her plate and finishes this portion before going on with the next portion of the same or a different serving dish. With the Thai pattern of eating, you regularly reach out to the serving dishes throughout the meal. But this way of eating is not considered appropriate in comparison to the common American practice where each person eats separately from his or her individual plate.

One time my American host, a divorcée who lived alone, invited a Thai girlfriend and myself to an American dinner at her home. When we were reaching out and eating a small portion of one thing at a time in Thai style, we were told to dish everything we wanted onto our plates at one time and that it was not considered polite to reach across the table. The proper American way was to have each kind of food piled up on your plate at once. If we were to eat in the same manner in Thailand, eyebrows would have been raised at the way we piled up food on our plates, and we would have been considered to be eating like pigs, greedy and inconsiderate of others who shared the meal at the table.

Individualism as a pivotal value in American culture is reflected in many other ways. Material wealth is not only a prime status marker in American society but also a guarantee and celebration of individualism—wealth allows the freedom to do almost anything, although usually within the limits of law. The pursuit of material wealth through individual achievement is instilled in Americans from the youngest age. For example, I was surprised to see an affluent American couple, who own a large ranch house and two BMW cars, send their nine-year-old son to deliver newspapers. He has to get up very early each morning to deliver the papers, even on Sunday! During summer vacation, the boy earns additional money by helping in his parents' gift shop from 10 A.M. to 5 P.M. His thirteen-year-old sister often earns money by babysitting, even at night.

In Thailand, only children from poorer families work to earn money to help the household. Middle- and high-income parents do not encourage their children to work until after they have finished their education. They provide economic support in order to free their children to concentrate on and excel in their studies. Beyond the regular schooling, families who can afford it pay for special tutoring as well as training in music, dance, or sports. However, children in low- and middle-income families help their parents with household chores and the care of younger children.

Many American children have been encouraged to get paid for their help around the house. They rarely get any gifts free of obligations. They even have to be good to get Santa's gifts at Christmas! As they grow up, they are conditioned to earn things they want; they learn that "there is no such thing as a free lunch." From an early age, children are taught to become progressively independent economically from their parents. Also, most young people are encouraged to leave home at college age to be on their own. From my viewpoint as a Thai, it seems that American family ties and closeness are not as strong as in Asian families whose children depend on family financial support until joining the work force after college age. Thereafter, it is the children's turn to help support their parents financially.

Modern American society and economy emphasize individualism in other ways. The nuclear family is more common than the extended family, and newlyweds usually establish their own independent household rather than initially living with either the husband's or the wife's parents. Parents and children appear to be close only when the children are very young. Most American parents seem to "lose" their children by the teenage years. They don't seem to belong to each other as closely as do Thai families. Even though I have seen more explicit affectionate expression among American family members than among Asian ones, the close interpersonal spirit seems to be lacking. Grandparents have relatively little to do with the grandchildren on any regular basis, in contrast to the extended family, which is more common in Thailand. The family and society seem to be graded by age to the point that grandparents, parents, and children are separated by generational subcultures that are evidently alienated from one another. Each group "does its own thing." Help and support are usually limited to whatever does not interfere with one's own life. In America, the locus of responsibility is more on the individual than on the family.

REVIEW QUESTIONS

1. What is the tone and attitude with which Natadecha-Sponsel relates the differences in culture she has experienced?
2. What is the tension that seems to exist, according to this author, between Americans' private lives and feelings and what they show to others?
3. Does Natadecha-Sponsel relate individualism to competition and the emphasis upon earning money? In what way?
4. How does the role of personal responsibility differ in these two cultures?

An American Black Experiences Living Conditions in Cuba (1964–1967)

JOHN CLYTUS, *Black Man in Red Cuba*

During the height of the civil rights movement in the United States, John Clytus decided to forsake the hypocrisy of what he called his "Negro-black-Afro-American-colored-revolutionary" existence for the opportunity of equality in Cuba. He had visited Cuba before, in the 1950s, when the U.S.-controlled Fulgencio Batista had led a military dictatorship and Fidel Castro was a young revolutionary in the south of Cuba. Clytus does not tell us how he got to Cuba in 1964, when the United States had placed severe restrictions and prohibitions against any commerce or communication between the two nations, but he details how he was jailed the moment he reached Havana by the Cuban immigration officials, who thoroughly investigated his motives, purposes, and finances before releasing him.

Clytus did not find the racial equality he had anticipated in Havana. He came on a teaching mission and found employment teaching English to Cuban children. He met friends from Mexico and others he had known in Cuba in the 1950s, but he was not accepted by Cuban officials or citizens. During his three years in Cuba, he failed to inspire or interest his students in learning English, so he left that job. He then began to wander from one location to another, surviving as best he could on odd jobs and government handouts. The government controlled his movements and his employment. Earlier in his book, Clytus tells of his relationships with Cubans (men and women, black, colored, and white), which reveal all of the undercurrents of racism he thought he had left in the United States.

By the time he had spent eighteen months in Cuba, he began to try to return to the United States, but he found that leaving Cuba was more difficult than he anticipated. Because the United States had no embassy on the island, any diplomatic assistance had to come from the Swiss embassy, which he was not eager to use because he also found them very prejudicial in their dealings with African-Americans. Since public demonstrations against the Cuban government were forbidden, he decided to demonstrate in the hopes of getting himself deported. As a result, he spent much of his last year in Cuba in jail.

A week later, on a hot Saturday afternoon, I decided that I had given the authorities ample time to take some action on my case. I didn't wait any longer. Unable to find a black marking pencil in any of the stores, I bought an eyebrow pencil, hunted about, and found a piece of cardboard and some string. I made a sign that read, translated: "ON HUNGER STRIKE UNTIL THEY DEPORT ME FROM THIS COUNTRY."

I hung the sign on my neck and went to a park in old Havana and sat down. In a country that tolerated no protest demonstrations, this was equivalent to an uprising. Several times an old man or an old woman pleaded with me to take the sign off before the authorities took my head off, but I ignored them, and they walked away shaking their heads and exclaiming one "Ave Maria" after another.

After about two hours, the police picked me up and turned me over to the G-2 again. I wasn't interrogated until the next day, and the session lasted only about ten minutes. This time, there were two interrogators who cursed, scowled, threatened to pull me apart limb by limb, and then sent me back to my cell.

About twenty minutes later, I was called out again. The same two smiled sweetly and said

that they were going to send me out of the country, that they hoped I had no feelings of ill-will toward them, that they only needed my passport and an address where they could contact me at all times, and that I would be hearing from them in a couple of days. Their parting words were, "Are you happy, now?"

My suspicions were aroused immediately, but I smiled and answered "Yes, very happy." I hoped that they were sincere, but I knew better than to trust them. They wanted to silence me, but they had to be careful about it—they were using the black people and the racial unrest in the States for propaganda.

On the streets during the following days, as in all the days that I had been there, I looked at little black girls with white dolls in their arms and told myself that if I were lucky, I wouldn't have to look at such ridiculous sights much longer. Soon I'd be where I never had to read a white man's newspapers, books, or magazines. In the States, the black publishers could satisfy my demands for literature. Where I would get food, shelter, and clothing might be something else.

In Cuba at this point I was not only left stranded for the latter commodities, I was also down to my last peso and had no way of earning any more. Of course, I could have taught some private English classes, but since I had told the authorities that I'd never work in Cuba again, I wouldn't show weakness by doing so.

Being broke and hungry when I didn't have to be was also a sign of weakness, I decided. With a telephone call, I could have money and food. It was just a question of overcoming pride. But pride wasn't worth a damn if it didn't help me to survive, I told myself, and I went immediately to the phone and called the European. I explained to her that though we were finished as lovers, that needn't be a reason not to remain friends. After telling her of my desperate need of sustenance, she asked what amount I needed.

When I met her at the library, her mood was different from what it had been the last time I had seen her. We had a beer at the Habana Libre, she gave me thirty pesos, and said "Nothing ever really ends."

We were sitting at the bar, and when she said that, her arm touched mine. Inwardly, I recoiled. It was the last time that I saw her.

The following week, a call came from "Comrade" Rodriguez at the Office for Foreign Residents. I expected him to be more helpful than he had been when I had first gone to see him, but when I walked into his office, I saw that his face was as sullen as before.

"We've been taking an interest in your case," he said.

I'll bet you have, I thought. It was twisting his insides to say it; obviously the word had come to him through the Communist hierarchy.

"We've got your papers ready. It's just a question of getting you on a ship," he said.

"How long do you think that'll take?" I asked.

"Possibly this week. We'll call you."

Again a phone call became the most important thing in my life. I went to bed listening for it and woke up listening for it. The week passed.

When two weeks went by and the call did not come, I went back to see Rodriguez. "Trouble with the ship. It's not ready yet. Maybe in two weeks," he said.

I tried to convince myself that these weren't more lies, that the authorities were as anxious to get rid of me as I of them. The two weeks passed and no call came. I accepted the truth. They had no intention of calling me or sending me out of the country. To keep me quiet, they had promised me the trip and, to make me believe they were sincere, were stringing me along on booster promises. They hoped that I would eventually see that I could not beat them, that not working and not eating well I would become demoralized and give up.

They did not know that they were only strengthening my determination to beat them. Having nothing to do day and night weighed dangerously as a demoralizing factor, but I had a routine to follow, boring though it was. I slept until two or three in the afternoon, then went downtown to old Havana to a run-down twenty-five-cent movie house. When I left the movie, I walked the streets or sat on the Prado for a time. Then I went over to Central Park and listened to the Communist propagandists hold forth.

Nightly I listened to them rail and rant against the bad, bad capitalists in the United States and praise the noble, virtuous Russians. According to the ranters, the United States was far behind the Russians in technological advancement. They spoke glowingly of any Russian accomplishment in space and ridiculed any slipup in the space program of the United States. The fire that caused the death of three American astronauts gave them great ammunition to show the incompetence of the *gringos.*

They boasted about the courage of the Russians and all Communist revolutionaries and described the capitalists as cowards. They regularly thumped their chests with the tale that during the October 1962 missile crisis during John F. Kennedy's presidency, the people in the States were shaking in their boots, scared to death, while the revolutionaries in Cuba were dancing in the streets.

According to the speechmakers, the Communist athletes were the greatest, physically and morally, in the world. Cuba's amateur boxers and baseball players, they said, were as good as any of the professionals in the States. The propagandists were particularly loud when their baseball team won the championship in the Caribbean games in Puerto Rico. They failed to mention that their revolutionary "amateurs" had an average age of twenty-five and had been playing baseball for years. At least one of their star pitchers, a thirty-year-old by the name of Alfredo Street, had played professionally.

It made my guts groan, not ever to hear a voice in disagreement, and especially not to be able to dissent myself, but I knew that the moment I was recognized to be a foreigner—especially from Stateside—they would not miss the opportunity to accuse me of being an "imperialist" spy. They would lick their chops over the chance to arouse the easily excitable bystanders to such an emotional pitch that they would have attacked me physically as an enemy against Cuba. I had to keep quiet and listen while poor, uneducated, untraveled men—women were never present—were duped by professional Communist liars.

After listening to this propaganda for several hours each night, I would walk over and sit on one of the benches along the Prado, and watch sad-faced, silent men and women stroll by. Before the revolution, the Prado had been lined by glittering neon lights above luxurious hotels, travel agencies, night clubs, and casinos. This onetime "boardwalk" of Havana was now lined on both sides of the street by a string of empty, dirty, windowless buildings.

I would leave the Prado and walk over to the Malecón and sit there, looking out over the sea and watching the ships in the harbor, weighing my chances of stowing away. When I left, it would be after one in the morning, and by the time that I finally got a bus and went to my room, it would be around four. I would sleep until two or three the next day and then start the routine all over again. I went through this mo-notonous strolling up and down every night that I was not in some jail, except one.

On that night, I lay under the mosquito net over my bed, more or less stoically accepting the beads of sweat on my face and chest and listening to the mosquitoes buzz about the room. I was more agitated than usual, and to see the nightly repetitiousness would have made me worse. A desperate move was shaping itself in my thoughts, a move that could get me shot or get me a long prison term. But, I asked myself, did I deserve freedom if I would not take risks for it?

It had been five months since I had worked. I had been existing mostly on fish soup and rice and bags of galletas and an occasional meal from Ted. He, having been fired from his job for wanting to leave the country, was as critically lassoed as I. From time to time, he got boxes of food from his wife in Canada, though often the hungry postal clerks left him little in a box.

Not being employed, I was no longer allowed to have a ration book, and I only had soap and toothpaste—and that was because one morning as a field worker was running to board a truck, a small package fell from the bundle he was carrying, and I picked it up. It contained a precious bar of soap and a precious tube of toothpaste. I had sold my last suit and the money had been spent. I had just ten centavos left, enough for a bus to take me to the waterfront.

I lay beneath the mosquito net thinking of all these things and that I was truly imprisoned on this island and only a ship, the *Tina,* could save me. I wondered when it was scheduled to sail. I had watched it every day for a week, and ships usually didn't stay more than a week. At this very moment it might be preparing to sail, I thought. I got up, took a wet towel, wiped the sweat from my body, dressed, and left.

REVIEW QUESTIONS

1. How did Clytus believe his situation would be better in the United States than in Cuba? Do you think he was glorifying his opportunities in the United States?
2. How did the people of Havana react to his signs? How did the government?

3. Why did they not deport him immediately, or keep him in jail?
4. If he had been a Cuban coming to the United States, would he have been treated differently than he was by the Cuban authorities?

An American Explorer Describes a Mexican Village (late 1920s)

PHILLIPS RUSSELL, *Red Tiger: Adventures in Yucatan and Mexico*

In the late 1920s, the explorer Phillips Russell and his traveling companions from the United States traveled in the southern part of Mexico and in Chiapas, Tabasco, the Yucatan, and Guatemala. They intended to retrace the 1839 journey of the archaeologists John L. Stephens and Frederick Catherwood. Stephens and Catherwood, also Americans, had made startling discoveries at ancient Mayan sites, and the publication of their work still brings adventurers to Mexico to retrace their steps. The problems Russell and his companions faced were twofold. First, Mexico was in the last stages of its political revolution of 1910, and the ancient cities discovered and drawn by Stephens and Catherwood had long since been obscured by jungle. Second, although the area they traveled was far south of Mexico City, the military was still very much in evidence, and the minor officials the travelers encountered in the cities and villages were very cautious about assisting them.

From the town of Bochil, in the highlands of central Chiapas, it is almost equidistant to Tuxtla Gutiérrez and San Cristóbal de las Casas, an area in which rebels against the national government and foreign-owned industries have been traditionally centered. The pueblo of San Juan, which is also mentioned in this excerpt, was a small village of a few hundred people. The people of this region are primarily of Mayan descent, and today they continue to support the goals of the Zapatistas, modern-day rebels reacting to national restrictions on native landholdings. In 1929 these natives were solidly behind the movement to restore their property ownership to ancient lands. In the late 1920s, as today, they were not more politically active than most people in Mexico, where community and communal activities take precedence over national concerns. They are farmers who value their families, land, and independence above all else. Today, the Mexican town of Bochil in the highlands of central Chiapas has 2,500 residents.

Russell and his traveling companions found few grand Mayan sites because most had been swallowed by the jungle during the revolutionary years. They did, however, encounter much that was traditional in rural, southern Mexico during the early days of the Great Depression. The frescoes to which Russell refers were at that time being composed by the soon-to-be famous Mexican muralists Diego Rivera and José Clemente Orozco. Today, the completed murals can be seen in the National Palace at the central square (Zocolo) in Mexico City, as well as in museums and other sites about the city. Muralists continued the native traditions of painting while incorporating modern themes of Marxist and Socialist thought prominent among Mexico's intelligentsia immediately after the revolution of 1910. Russell's analogy of the frescoes' themes to what he observes in the Mexican village is quite authentic.

Bochil being eleven leagues from Simojovel, we would have to ride hard to reach the former town by nightfall, and we were off early on the same mounts through a wonderfully beautiful country containing vegetation very tropical on the one hand, with orchids and hibiscus glowing in the moist valleys, and more like the temperate zone on the other, the hills being covered with familiar looking pines and hardwood and the roadsides thick with blackberry bushes.

As we proceeded, our one mule, which had been carrying part of the baggage, became restive and repeatedly planted himself at right-angles across the trail, with his forefeet up a slope, as if in an endeavor to throw the weight of his load on his hindquarters. Several times we adjusted his pack, but he became more troublesome than ever, even cries of "Macho!" (Male one!) and beatings about the head failing to make any impression. At length he developed a limp in a forefoot, and we were compelled to halt at a village to attend to him. This was the pueblo of San Juan. As we halted in the little plaza, the mayor, a tall, middle-aged man with humorous blue eyes and streaked red whiskers, came out to greet us. On learning that we should have to shoe the mule, he remarked that it was a day of much heat, that a big storm was coming up, and that we were ill-advised to go farther. If we would remain, he said he would open the city hall and place it at our disposal.

Since the storm did seem to be the most threatening that we had yet seen and promised to become a hurricane, we accepted his invitation and dismounted at the city hall while our two guides went in search of a shoe that would fit the macho's foot. The cabildo was a low stone structure of two rooms, with a wooden veranda and a red tiled roof. In the middle of the plaza was a large round boulder, worn smooth by much

sitting, on which rested a dozen Indians of a type different from any we had previously seen. Their bodies were short and slender, and very muscular. In color they were dark brown, with large noses and projecting mouths. They wore only two garments—a short jacket which did little more than cover their shoulders, and trousers rolled up high on their thighs. Each was smoking a long black puro with an appearance of the sublimest comfort and disinclination to move. They showed interest in our arrival, but did not take the trouble to come closer. When I pointed a small camera at them, an exclamation of horror ran round the group, and they broke and fled like so many brown hares.

A little later we had lunch at a nearby hut kept by a comely woman who had a small daughter, a lovely child of about five years. I asked the mother's permission to make a picture. This she gave, but when I aimed the camera, the child gave a piercing scream and burst into hysterics, with wails that aroused the entire community. The mother vainly tried to soothe her, but even the promise of *dulces,* sweets, failed to interest the screaming child, and I gave it up.

The fear of the camera could be ascribed to the belief in the "evil eye," which is still prevalent among the primitive tribes of Mexico, but it was difficult to account for the extraordinary timidity of the population in other respects. We took a short walk through the village, comprising about twenty huts around which men, women, and children were busy at various occupations, but at our approach they vanished like wild rabbits down a hole, and a peer into their doorways disclosed nothing but darkness and silence.

On the edge of the village the poles of a new hut had been erected and a thatch of grass bundles was just being put on. About fifteen men and youths were at work happily, but when they spied us the whites of their eyes showed large with fear and any sudden movement would have sent them all running. However, after we had stood quietly by for several moments, they decided we were harmless and resumed their work. The rafters of the hut were occupied by the older men, who with strips of fiber tied on the grass bundles tossed to them by the young men on the ground.

Here, after their fear of us had passed entirely, we saw one of the pleasantest phases of communal life in Mexico. Though the house was to be occupied by one individual or family, the work was being done by all the neighbors, each of whom had no doubt enjoyed in the past this form of communal assistance. They were making a picnic of the whole affair, talking and laughing with obvious happiness. They not only exchanged verbal jokes, doubtless at each other's expense, but played practical ones, tossing the bundles about, hitting each other in the face with them, and engaging in pushing contests during which one or more of them fell through the light covering to the ground. Such comedies caused shouts of laughter.

Cornfields are planted by the same method. All the neighbors gather on a certain day and in a long line they march across the field, making holes in the ground with a pointed stick and dropping in the grains, which they cover with a stamp of their bare heels as they pass over. This too is done to the accompaniment of conversation and laughter.

To see the Mexican Indian at such communistic tasks is to realize how completely he has nullified the old Biblical curse bestowed on man in respect to his labor, and how unnecessary is the grim, forbidding silence in which the Nordic white man earns his daily bread. By arousing the communal spirit the Mexican Indian no longer performs work as toil but converts it into play.

And then comes the industrialist and by persuasion or compulsion, takes the docile brown man away from this joyful labor and its spacious solidarity and herds him into gloomy masses, regimented, ticketed, and silenced. Indeed, the curse of industrialism is not its introduction of the machine, with its creation of the uniform man as well as the uniform product, so much as it is its taking from men the right to be happy and talkative at their work. Its effects on the Indian of Mexico, the son of uncircumscribed time and space, are depicted with a terrible power in the frescoes of the Mexican painters Diego Rivera and José Clemente Orozco on the walls of two public buildings in Mexico City.

We had an immediate illustration of the tendency of the local native to work in his own way and in his own time. On the veranda of the cabildo we had seen, upon our arrival, an Indian industriously at work making a ball of heavy twine. In the bend of his knee, he held between calf and thigh a bunch of fibers, from which he plucked selected strands and twisted them into a string by rolling them on his bare thigh. The leg had been worn smooth of hair through this process. He made another string by rolling the fibers in the opposite direction. When he united the two strings they twisted themselves together by natural tension, making a thick, strong twine, of which he apparently had about a mile and intended to make a mile more.

His neighbors of the sitting-down boulder had meantime returned to their post and, the camera being absent, had relighted their puros. With the mayor as interpreter we approached and asked if one or more of them would guide us through the nearby forests, where we had learned there was much jaguar and *tigrillo.* They took the matter under advisement while they puffed their smoke [in the United States these would have cost fifty cents each]. At length one turned to his neighbor and said, "You go." The latter passed the word on to a companion: "You go." And so it went, all around the circle, with no one budging. The consequence was that we got no hunting that day. The man on the veranda continued his second mile of twine.

Alfredo and Pedro had meantime returned with a mule shoe. It was too small for the macho's foot, but that gave them little concern. They simply cut the hoof down to the size of the shoe. Their method of fastening the shoe we found to be the same as that followed generally in the primitive regions of Mexico. They drove in a nail as far as it would go and if the animal reared, that was a sign the nail had touched the quick. It was then withdrawn and driven in again. If the mule did not rear, all was well.

By this time it was too late to resume the road, and we made arrangements to sleep in that room of the cabildo usually reserved for travellers. While we were so engaged, a nomadic family of pottery-sellers arrived and, seeing the cabildo occupied, contented themselves with camping on the ground in front. They lighted a fire on the grass and cooked meat and tortillas which they shared with their numerous dogs. Sly pigs nosed their way among them and occasionally snatched a piece of food from a child. The women then gave a signal for the dogs to clear away the pigs, which they did to a bedlam of squeals.

A billygoat came up and enthusiastically joined the dogs in the chase. A large sow refused to give ground and kept the dogs at bay with her vicious teeth, but the goat routed her by butting her furiously in the rear, each butt being followed by a pronounced "Oof!" from the sow. She eventually checkmated the goat by lying flat on the ground in such a position that the goat's head could not reach her, but she was forced to retreat when the dogs ran up in turn and chewed her tail.

After their meal, the campers spread out their wares on the veranda and waited for trade. Their pottery was of a salmon color, beautifully shaped, but very fragile. Among their offerings were hair combs cut by hand out of mahogany.

These pottery-sellers were apparently natives, but they were distinguished from the local Indians by their unusual hairiness. The Indian of southern and southeastern Mexico is usually smooth of skin, and even the beards of the old men are sparse and straggling, but the arms of these women were hairy from shoulder to fingertip and the backs of their hands were virtually furred.

The village occupying a magnificent situation in a bowl rimmed with violet mountains, the sunset was correspondingly gorgeous, the red rays converting the stony crags and escarpments into pillars of fire. For dinner we had deliciously cooked chicken tamales sent to us from a nearby hut, and a few centavos bought enough pineapples to supply us all, their texture and flavor being incomparably sweeter and more delicate then the fibrous article sold in the markets of the North.

At bedtime we slung our hammocks across one end of the veranda while the nomads disputed the other with dogs and pigs. In the middle of the night a group of porters came up, unstrapped their burdens at our end of the veranda, lighted puros, and began an animated conversation in their own language. Some of them, judging by the laughter, told funny stories; these were invariably related in a high falsetto voice markedly different from the conversational tone. They might have remained talking until daylight, had we not driven them away by rising from our hammocks in the clear moonlight and glaring at them fiercely.

REVIEW QUESTIONS

1. What characteristics of the native people impressed Russell the most? Which the least? Why do you think so?
2. What does Russell think about the temperament and work habits of the village people? Explain with examples.
3. How does Russell reveal his opinion of the worth and extent of "civilization" among the Mayan people he observes?

An American Gourmet Offers Advice About Food in South America (c. 1950)

CHARLES H. BAKER, JR., *The South American Gentleman's Companion: Or, Up & Down the Andes with Knife, Fork, & Spoon*

Among the cultural changes the world experienced after World War II was the amazing speed with which international travel evolved. Europe was not an option for leisurely travel in the 1940s and 1950s, and China and other Asian nations also seemed too unsettled for most travelers from the United States. Africa remained beyond the means of all but the wealthiest traveler; in addition, it was still considered a dangerous and disease-ridden area of the world. Latin America, however, while still exotic and different, was both affordable and accessible to the rising upper-middle-class traveler. Sea cruises and airline flights, with guided tours, became more affordable and available. As Americans became more urbanized in their residences and professional in their occupations, the two-or-three-week summer vacation became a new standard of affluence, and with it the desire to visit foreign lands. Although few could actually go to South America, books such as those of Charles Baker allowed voyeurism and fantasy to become part of the average, working-class, household experience.

By the 1950s, adventurers from the United States came in a new form. The swashbuckling, rugged, Teddy Roosevelt type of foreign adventure had evolved into a much more refined and civilized form of travel that experienced not the rough jungle dangers but the thrills of cultural and culinary experimentation in distant lands. As a free-lance author of food and drink throughout the world during the 1930s through the 1950s, Charles H. Baker fulfilled the nation's need for civilized adventures. He subtitled his second edition of *Gentleman's Companion* "Up & Down the Andes with Knife, Fork & Spoon." Whereas many renowned writers and journalists, such as Ernest Hemingway, wrote of travels that combined the earlier adventurer epics with attention to elements of fine culture, writers such as Baker were unabashed at advising their readers that when dining in the South American style, "do as your intelligent *Latino* host and hostess would automatically contrive: no rushing through your food. . . . above all, *leave all arguments and all politics— domestic, local and world-wide—locked up in your hotel closet.*" Americans who had time and money should focus on enjoying exotic foreign cultures and experiencing the full benefits of a variety of cuisines, prepared and served in extraordinary ways. For these fortunate individuals, travel should include only the most enjoyable of experiences, with no thought of "Russia, taxes, in-laws or atomic bombs." This very pretentious two-volume set of books attempts to do for South American cooking what Auguste Escoffier did for French cuisine only thirty years before—allow the middle class to live like the elite.

FIRST ON OUR FINAL LATIN LIST *marches a crisp business known as almond fingers, or DEDOS de AL-MENDRAS*, which we consumed at a very fancy Buenos Aires high tea.

We don't quite know yet just how the boys worked it but some of those fine Argentine *Caballeros* have managed to rig themselves with a cozy little matinee system which our best *Yanqui lobos* might well study. First off, after 8 or 10 years of marriage and the little woman has presented her husband with 8 or 10 children, she quite reasonably cries, "Hold—enough! Donate me your attention, my brave fertile king. During the extent of our marriage I have denied you nothing—witness these 10 stalwart sons and daughters. During this passage of time you have gone forth into the wide gay world whereas I, in my perpetual delicate estate, have been in happy confinement within my home. There is no jealousy in my heart in your past freedom, but I grow lonely for proper society; for the tea-parties of my female friends. And this is why, my *bravo*, I suggest that you provide yourself with a fine young *querida:* a mistress. Choose one of a culture and refinement befitting our station, of course; and just one other thing: do not escort her into any public place where I or my friends will see her. *Claro?*"

"Claro," he says; and that, my dear children, is how the tea-party system was born, and Park Avenue's matrons take notice!

Well, anyway, after the usual hard 2 hours at the office our *bravo* knocks-off for a light and leisurely snack of *almuerzo*—Latins always take their big meal at night—then he goes to the silk-lined *gabinete* of his sultry young bon-bon for a reasonable *pas seul;* then takes his siesta until 'long about half-past-seven or so, when he goes home soothed and refreshed, dons the black tie and takes his bride—who has between the hours of 5 and 7 given a whacking big hen tea-party to all her friends!—out, or in, to dinner. Simple? . . . But what we really meant you to appreciate was the number and quantity of sweets, cookies, candies and cakes those smart handsome Argentine ladies tuck in endless succession into their little rosebud mouths, and which—along about age 25—start-in to upholster their handsome little hips. . . . *Almond Fingers,* just for instance . . .

Cream 1 lb of sugar with same butter, then add grated (yellow only) rind of 2 or 3 lemons, and finally work smooth with 6 lightly beaten eggs, 2 tbsp cherry brandy, 6 drops almond flavoring. In go 2⅔ cups pastry flour and 1 lb finely-ground blanched almonds. Mix lightly but well; put in refrigerator for 1½ hours. When firm roll thin, brush tops with a little egg white, dust on all the fine-chopped blanched almonds that will stick, and brown at 375°.

REVIEW QUESTIONS

1. What are the author's assumptions about the socioeconomic group to which he is writing?
2. What is his opinion of South American women and society?
3. Do you think this book would appeal to a homemaker in the United States? Why or why not?

An American Writer Describes Life on Tonga (1920s)

SETH K. HUMPHREY, *Loafing Through the Pacific*

After World War I, many Europeans and Americans began to travel to observe the blessings they had bestowed upon their colonies around the world and to find examples of unusual and exotic styles of life. Many travelers believed the tenets of Social Darwinism and capitalism and, having won the "Great War to end all wars," needed to make a modern exploration of the earth's farthest reaches. What they found, as did the writer Seth K. Humphrey, was that many peoples were changed minimally by their experiences with the leading capitalist countries of the world. While Humphrey also authored books on Native American dispossession and U. S. racial problems, he often comments somewhat sarcastically on the adaptations to modernity found among those he visited. For example, on touring the Fiji Islands, Humphrey states that "the white man's coming has reduced the Fijians to a singularly placid, aimless, churchgoing race. In my rambles about these islands for a month I found the Fijians the tamest lot of niggers outside of 'South C'[aro]lina'."

After touring the United States, this American boarded a steamer in Los Angeles and began a fifteen-month tour of the Pacific islands. He began in Hawaii and then proceeded to other islands, large and small, as well as to Canton, Peking (Beijing), Korea, and Japan. In his introduction, Humphrey describes Tonga, the subject of the following excerpt, as the "only native kingdom left in the Pacific; a kingdom without a hotel, but with a twenty-three-year-old native queen, and a brave showing of independence under the quietly steering hand of Great Britain." Actually, Tongan culture dates from about 1000 B.C.E., when Polynesian farming people settled the islands. When they entered the international trade network in the eighteenth century, they had few products that could not be obtained by European traders elsewhere, but over time they began to concentrate upon the production of copra, dried coconut meat used for making coconut oil. Located east of Australia and south of the Fiji Islands, Tonga became one of many pawns of British, French, and United States imperialism in the South Pacific during the nineteenth century. When the Treaty of Versailles ending World War I confirmed the British Protectorate status of Tonga, the islands became the focus of many travelers such as Humphrey.

The Kingdom of Tonga is odd among the nations in other respects. It has no taxes of any sort. No annual struggle here with your conscience and an income-tax sheet, even if you are of the species created subsequent to the pig. Tonga has no public debt; instead, a surplus of eighty thousand pounds sterling is in the royal treasury.

Whence comes the revenue?

From the world's only complete system of ground rents. There is no freehold in the kingdom. Everybody who occupies land pays rent to the government. Not a foot of real estate can be bought or sold in the Friendly Islands.

It is somewhat after the Socialist's ideal—and

the results are as might be expected. On this island's wide stretches of level, rich soil there is
not a plough. . . .

At first sight, the Tongans seemed like modified Samoans. Many heads of frizzy hair, running almost to kinkiness, suggested the infusion
of another race. Their large, dark eyes evinced
the same lively interest in us as newly arrived
Europeans, but with a subtle change in attitude.
Expressed offhand, the difference between the
Samoan and the Tongan gaze is that one is a welcome and the other a scrutiny.

But among themselves there was the same
carefree laughter, disarming enough when cou-
pled with a willingness to assist with the luggage for the expected sixpence or two. Dinky
little flat cars on a miniature railroad, with a
horse for tractive power, soon transferred our effects up the long causeway to the shore.

At the custom house I showed my fumiga-
tion certificate and denied all acquaintance with
beetles. I also had to declare that in my luggage there were no articles of Samoan make—
souvenirs and the like. One article with the
Samoan touch would have "queered" the lot; my
effects, if admitted at all, would have had to be
thoroughly hand-picked and refumigated.

In a kingdom that is without a hotel, the alternative is the kingdom's one and only board-
ing house. Here I settled for a month.

A room with one door opening on a veranda,
and another back into the house; no windows—
not even the usual swinging shutters which give
ventilation when the doors are closed. Strict privacy, then, meant an airtight compartment. In
my Nukualofa home, I was no stickler for strict
privacy.

A shower bath—the only sign of waterworks
about the place—with a pump which the bather
worked with one hand while he did the best he
could with the other. The lack of coördination
reminded me of the old trick of trying to pat the
head and rub the chest at the same time. My
bathing hand had an awkward way of keeping
stroke with the pumper.

A portly Tongan woman as chambermaid,
who did her work to the accompaniment of an
enormous cigarette. Daily she hung out the towels to dry in the sun, until necessity would drive
me to ask for clean ones. We differed slightly as
to how many days a towel ought to serve without a recess at the laundry; but as she differed in
Tongan and I in English, there was no decision.

A table as well supplied as circumstances permitted took care of the inner man; around it,
all the detached white persons in Nukualofa—
New Zealanders, Australians, and a Britisher or
two—made an agreeable company. For a month
I was to live in a growing appreciation of the
courtesy and kindliness of these men and women
from the South. . . .

The almost universal dress in the villages is
the waist-cloth, *lava-lava,* changed here only in
name to *vala*—which is *lava* with the two syllables reversed. At this season it is unusual to see
it worn without other clothing, even by the men.
A temperature under 70—extremely rare in the
daytime—will send the natives into any covering at hand. Against the bitter cold of night—
once while I was in Nukualofa the mercury
dropped to 58—they shut up their houses as
nearly airtight as possible and wind themselves
in tappa cloth.

The Tongans make more copra than the
Samoans. They have to. Every male Tongan at
his sixteenth year is allotted about eight acres
of coconut land, and a little plot in his village
for a *fale.* These, of course, he cannot sell—and
he must pay rent whether he wants the land or
not. It is a gift with a decided string to it.

Land rent, extra clothing, the demands of the
church, and the cost of boards and corrugated
roofing if their tastes happen to run that way—
these compel the Tongans to make an appreciable amount of copra. It is well that they have to,
for in the absence of indentured or imported
labour of any sort the whole commerce of the
Friendly Islands—and the preservation of the
kingdom, for that matter—depends upon the copra turned out by the natives themselves.

The less debilitating climate favours them,
and their allotments assure plenty of coconuts.
Even at that they work only a small fraction of
the time at copra-making. The Tongans are not

forced out of the leisure class by the total of all the shillings required of them. . . .

Another survival of an old Tongan custom is the women's habit of wearing decrepit mats tied around their waists as a sign of mourning. It persists even among the well-dressed native women of Nukualofa. The more shabby and ragged the mat, the greater is the wearer's sorrow for the departed.

Among the villagers living as Tongans have always lived, one thinks no more of this mourning custom than of our wearing of black; but frayed and dingy mats tied around the neat European dresses of girls and women on their way to Sunday morning church in Nukualofa strike rather forcibly at one's sense of the incongruous.

Kolomotua, of all the villages on the island, has no church. This is because the people of Kolomotua go to church in Nukualofa. Every other village of a few *fales* has at least two churches out of the six denominations covering the Friendly Islands.

The Tongans seem to have had about the same religious experience as the Samoans: a decline in chieftainship, a void to be filled, and the rise of a native ministry. They take to religion for obvious reasons, and they pass up the rest of civilization for reasons as obvious.

The inhabitants of the Friendly Islands were once anything but friendly. Warlike, fierce, brave—and as cannibals not far removed in savagery from the Fijians. Now, they all go to church. They *enjoy* it—and without their church they would be holy terrors. But the multitude of native preachers!

Getting contributions from members is a skillfully conducted business. Churches are stirred to rivalry in the matter of collections—not churches of rival denominations, but of the same denomination, and by their own pastors.

Such and such a church has collected so much; shall we let them get ahead of us? No! Then the contest is on.

The giver has the inspiration of publicity. Each donor marches up forward, while songs and chantings stir his emotions to a pitch of fi-

nancial indiscretion, and lays down his money in full view. If it is not up to expectations, the native pastor is rarely backward in voicing his desire that the brother or sister come again. But many a donor gives less at first than he intends to eventually, so as to have the pleasure of one or two more parades to the front.

Raising money for the church stimulates copra-making and trade, and with it comes the eternal question, as in other South Sea islands, whether a church and a preacher for about every one hundred inhabitants are a necessary incumbrance.

But the traders like the copra, and the preachers like the money, and the people like the excitement—and the people are not very busy anyway.

The Tongan takes his Christianity back with him into the old Tongan atmosphere. To the call of the native tom-tom beaten with a club he gathers at a church built like a *fale,* squats on a native mat and listens to a native preacher in his native tongue, sings songs in Tongan set to native music, and works himself into the superstitious fervor of his ancestors.

That's the way he likes it. And as we civilized people have our Christianity served up in forty different ways to suit individual tastes, why criticize the Tongans and Samoans? *Laissez faire.*

There's an indescribable weirdness in the sound of the tom-tom giving its call in the still hours. A log six to eight feet long, hollowed out like a feeding trough and left solid at the ends—this is the Tongan tom-tom. Struck on one edge with a short club, it has just enough resonance to save the sound from being a noise. Even when a church has a bell, as in town, it also has a tom-tom—and the bell-ringer, after a few feeble jerks of the bell, falls upon the tom-tom with a vigour that proclaims his love for it. The *boom, boom, boom,* at night off in the villages takes one as nothing else can back into the primitiveness of the old Tongan days. . . .

In every village are copra-buying stations of rival traders—sometimes only two, oftener several, depending on the amount of copra produced in the district and the individual notions of the traders. They are all pretty much alike: a raised platform thirty to fifty feet square, on which the coconut meat brought in by the natives is spread out to dry; at one corner of it, a small warehouse for weighing, receiving, and storing the copra in its various stages; and the trading store, its shelves laden with tinned goods, bolts of gaily coloured cloth, matches, tinware, and odds of all sorts.

According to a law of the kingdom, all copra must be paid for in cash; then the native pays cash for his purchases in the store. The law fairly shines with wisdom. When the native had to trade his copra direct for goods, he found it confusing business to translate the value of one into the value of the other. Now, he gets the whole proceeds in money which he has learned to count; he can buy what he wants, and where he wants, or go home with his money if he wishes.

This law has taken the chief joy from the lives of unscrupulous traders. This and the fierce competition of these latter days have put most of their kind out of business. If any survive, they tread the thorny path of rectitude. . . .

In Tonga, as in many South Sea islands, kava is the national drink. In Samoa they call it "ava" because there is no *k* in their alphabet, but the beverage is the same.

In the old times, the kava root was first masticated to a savoury pulp by young girls whose mouths were supposed to be notably clean, and the resulting juice—or juices—mixed with water. The white traders liked kava, but their fondness for the drink was clouded by thoughts of the process. So the traders, although not specially given to reforming anything, brought about a reform in the making of kava. Nowadays, the root is pounded into shreds, then tied up in cloths, which are mashed, squeezed, wrung, and twisted in a bucket of water by as many brown hands as can get into it. The improvement in method is largely sentimental. Having observed the new way, I have a leaning toward the old.

I have drunk kava with as much relish as I would drink dishwater, which it resembles more closely than anything else. And what is more to the credit of my heroic nature, I have drunk kava after watching the natives make it. It was because I had to, or give mortal offence.

When used freshly made, as it almost always is, kava is not intoxicating; but because of some drug effect in it the kava-drinking habit grows on the drinker, until, in the case of Tongan natives at least, it becomes a wide-spread dissipation. Heavy drinking brings on a temporary paralysis of the legs—and of the legs only.

Imagine the effect. A man may be dead drunk from the hips down, while his mind is as sober as that of the proverbial judge. Kava is the only beverage which puts the right end of a man out of commission. It makes him safer to be at large than when he is sober.

The after effects of steady indulgence are a general weakening of the system and a scaling off of cuticle. Kava drunkards can be distinguished by whitened patches of skin, especially about the legs.

Kava-drinking opens most native ceremonial gatherings. One might naturally think that the head chief would be the first to drain the coconut bowl; but good form decrees that two subchiefs must first partake of the liquid. This old custom—and indeed the origin of kava itself—is accounted for in their legends.

REVIEW QUESTIONS

1. How does Humphrey compare the customs and habits of the Tongans to those of natives on other islands? Explain.
2. What is the role of copra making on the islands? What is Humphrey's opinion of this industry?
3. What does Humphrey mean when he says that the Tongan "takes his Christianity back with him into the old Tongan atmosphere"? What is his attitude toward this practice?
4. How do the Tongans respond to the imposition of competition in their culture?

15

Europe, 1918 to the Present

The overwhelming theme of Europe in the twentieth century is war and revolution. Justifiably labeled the bloodiest century in human history, this period is dominated by horrific events that resulted in the deaths of as many as—or possibly even more than—100 million people. World War I, the Bolshevik revolution, Stalin's purges, and World War II unleashed violence and social upheaval on an unprecedented level. Sweeping social and political change resulted, especially in areas where casualties were unspeakably high, such as Poland and the Soviet Union. The latter was a particular focus of foreign observers in Europe in this time period, and rightly so. In only sixty years, the Soviet Union transformed itself from serfdom to superpower. Nowhere else in Europe was there such dramatic change, and for this reason four selections on the Soviet Union are included in this chapter.

Foreign observers of Europe in this period could not—and did not—fail to note the toll these cataclysmic events took on the lives of ordinary Europeans. For the first time many of these writers tried to explain what they saw: to analyze the events they witnessed, to account for conditions they observed, to explain the attitudes of the people to whom they spoke. The level of analysis in the writings of post-1918 authors, in fact, contrasts dramatically to the lack of analysis of earlier travelers. This is particularly noticeable in the second half of the century. In an earlier chapter, for example, Jack London vividly described London at the beginning of the century, but he did not connect the grinding poverty he witnessed with the Industrial Revolution. In contrast, in a selection in this chapter, Guido Piovene goes to great lengths to explain the historical and social causes of the so-called sexual revolution in Sweden in the late 1960s and early 1970s. No doubt visitors to Europe in this period had increasingly sophisticated interests and educational backgrounds but surely the drama of the extraordinary changes they witnessed also compelled analysis.

A focus on both the threat of violence and its aftermath is particularly evident in the writings and analyses of twentieth-century observers of Europe. In the 1930s, for example, Haruko Ichikawa visited Spain during a brief lull between the republican overthrow of King Alfonso and the civil war that erupted soon after her visit. She was struck by the contrasts she saw: the apathy of the Spanish people toward their recent revolution and the passion with which they anticipated a bullfight. Likewise, Philip Gibbs traveled to Germany before the outbreak of World War II. A former correspondent in World War I, he had read Hitler's *Mein Kampf* and clearly did not believe the people he interviewed, who insisted that Hitler was a benign and benevolent leader. In much the same way, a twenty-eight-year-old John F. Kennedy described the devastation of Berlin immediately after World War II, and he also viewed with increasing alarm attitudes and behaviors that would lead to the Cold

War. Violence is also the theme underlying the stories of appalling hardships endured by the students and teachers at the Tambov Street school in Leningrad, as they battled—both physically and mentally—a siege that took the lives of nearly one million of the city's residents, over 640,000 by starvation. Finally, the lingering impact of violence and revolution is evident in Hans Magnus Enzensberger's description of Warsaw in 1986, which forty years after World War II had still not recuperated from its effects.

A second theme that characterizes European civilization since the end of World War I is the polarization of ideology between Eastern communism and Western European capitalism. The descriptions of collective agriculture in the Soviet Union by Zara Witkin and W. L. White illustrate this particularly well. Witkin arrived in the Soviet Union passionately motivated to put his engineering skills to use on behalf of the revolution; he departed two years later, a Soviet sympathizer no more and completely disgusted by the waste, apathy, and inefficiency he had seen. Ten years later, White had a totally different experience, but his American biases are still evident. White found much to admire in state-controlled agricultural production, which resulted in adequate food supplies (if one was willing to stand in line) and in low prices for consumers, but he found the Soviet system "silly" when compared to that of the United States. In contrast, life in Western Europe, particularly Great Britain, as described by a writer from India, was almost too good to be true. B. N. Misra was particularly amazed at the size and efficiency of construction equipment, the number of appliances in ordinary homes, and the impact these machines had upon the lives of ordinary people.

Another important theme of nearly all these selections is the role of women. Although none focuses directly on the women's movement itself, students can learn much about the lives of women after the end of World War I from these readings. Particular attention should be paid to William White's description of laws that the Soviets enacted to improve the lives of women, Morris Deutsch's comments on the behavior of French and British women during World War II, Kennedy's observations of women as the victims of both allied bombings of Berlin and its occupation by Soviet troops, Piovene's unconscious inclusion of women as instigators and beneficiaries of sexual freedom in Sweden, and Misra's insightful and surprised observation that the use of machines in Great Britain had made women's lives not easier, but busier and more complex.

Overall, the complexity of Europe in the twentieth century is reflected in the variety of selections in this chapter. Europe is and always has been a region of many different peoples, languages, and beliefs. Students, as they are reading, might ask themselves, "Are the defining characteristics of Europeans their similarities or their differences?"

Two Views of Collective Agriculture in the Soviet Union

An American Engineer in Stalin's Russia:
The Memoirs of Zara Witkin (1932)
W. L. WHITE, Report on the Russians (1944)

One of the policies of Soviet government following the Bolshevik revolution of 1917 was the collectivization of agriculture. In the late 1920s, nearly all productive farmland in the Soviet Union was seized by the state and reorganized along Communist principles, with the goal of increasing food production and improving the lives of the peasants. Much of this land had previously belonged to the great estates of the nobles; some of it, however, belonged to middle-class farmers and small groups of peasants. In the 1930s, in particular, Stalin's push to modernize Russia resulted in the establishment of extremely large government-owned farms, which experienced varying degrees of success, and sometimes none at all. Some of these farms acquired considerable international reputations from the writings of journalists and occasionally tourists. This selection features the observations of two American men who visited collective farms in the Soviet Union.

In the early 1930s, Zara Witkin, a young American engineer, spent two years in the Soviet Union as a consultant and advisor on an assortment of different types of state-sponsored projects. His experience changed his life and his outlook on the world. The son of Russian immigrants to the United States, Witkin had departed for the Soviet Union in 1932 filled with idealistic support for the revolution and absolutely convinced that he could use his skills and knowledge to make a positive difference in the lives of the Russian people. When he returned home two years later, he was bitter, disillusioned, and above all frustrated beyond measure that the Russians did not seem interested in American models of efficient management and design. Nowhere is his attitude more pronounced than in his description of the second largest collective farm in the Soviet Union, the famous State Experimental Farm of Verblud.

Twelve years later, W. L. White, an American journalist, also toured a collective farm in the Soviet Union. His was a much different type of mission than Witkin's. In 1944, U.S. and Soviet forces were allied against the Germans, and White's trip was made to bolster understanding between the two nations. He was accompanied by Eric Johnston, the president of the U.S. Chamber of Commerce. White's observations focused on market conditions in the Soviet Union, particularly prices and the availability of different food items. Thus he also paid a great deal of attention to collective farms and to a state-run greenhouse he visited. It did not occur to White that he and his traveling companions were not allowed to see a complete picture of the Soviet system. Although he admitted they were entertained lavishly, he felt that this treatment was not intended to influence what he wrote, nor were the motives of the Russians "in any way sinister."

The two men, Witkin and White, could not have had more different views of the Soviet people. Witkin found them lazy, inefficient, and apathetic; his irritation with Russian managers and workers is evident on nearly every page of the book he wrote about his experiences, *An American Engineer in Stalin's Russia.* In contrast, in the introduction to the *Report on the Russians,* White says that he liked the Russian people very much. "In many ways they are like Americans," he writes. "They have a fresh and unspoiled outlook which is close to our own." Like Americans, he hints, the Soviets were a "young" nation with a great deal of energy.

AN AMERICAN ENGINEER IN STALIN'S RUSSIA: THE MEMOIRS OF ZARA WITKIN

We intended to make a thorough inspection of the farm. Its management methods were of especial interest to us. To allow ample time for the officials to begin their work and get out the necessary daily orders, we did not appear at the director's office until ten o'clock. It was locked! No one was there! We waited three-quarters of an hour. Then the bookkeeper came. I recalled the reputation of the manager, Margolin, who had been so lauded in descriptions of this farm in several books on Soviet Russia.

A few minutes later the assistant director arrived. It was then about eleven o'clock. This official invited us in. We were seated and he began to tell us about the farm. We asked about the distribution of various crops. He pointed to some maps which hung on the wall. They were in colored crayon showing different crops under cultivation. This graphical study pleased me. It seemed systematic. Here, at least, was a sign of order. We decided to go into the fields to see the cultivation of some particular crop. Spring wheat was selected, shown in green on the map. The assistant director hesitated peculiarly. We pressed our guide for explanation. There was a short, lively colloquy between her and the assistant director. When the conversational smoke cleared, we discovered that the map was two years old and bore no relation to the present crops in the fields! The assistant director could not tell us of their actual position or extent.

"Take us to any part of the farm where work is in progress," I said. "I want to see the methods in use, the machinery employed and the way of handling the farm employees in collective cultivation."

Our guide and the assistant director entered the automobile with us, and we began a strange tour of the farm. We dashed erratically several miles in various directions, but found no one at work! The fields were deserted! The director seemed quite as astonished as we were. Evidently he did not know what work was in progress nor where. An hour was spent in this futile search. Finally, we sighted three tractors at work, and a foreman on horseback. As we drove closer, the foreman rode up to us. The sides of his horse were torn and bleeding. I asked why the animal was ridden in such a condition. The foreman, grinning cynically, informed us that the wounds were caused by the sun! Even our guide seemed disgusted by this callous brutality.

The extraordinary emptiness of the fields amazed us. We were told that plowing was being done at night because of the fierce midday heat. The tractors, therefore, must have carried lights. We asked to see them and were conducted to the spot where the machines were parked. All the headlights were broken! Not one was in operating condition! The assistant director hurried to explain the visible idleness. He said that this was a "rest-day." But some people were at work, we observed. Other excuses for the paralysis which hung over the farm were tentatively put forward. As quickly as we discovered that one was false, another was suggested.

Work was actually at a standstill. That was the fact. There was nothing to do but return to the headquarters of the farm. There, we looked through the machine-stop where tractors and other farm machinery were repaired. It was in indescribable confusion. The floor was piled high with broken parts, metal cuttings and oiled waste. Several machines lay about in various stages of dis-assembly. Lathes, presses and other machines looked dirty and uncared for. It was a disheartening sight.

Across the road, a gang of workers were moving a tractor and wagon out of the field, through an opening in the fence. By amazing maneuvering, the driver of the tractor had managed to get the wagon wheel hooked in the fence. Vociferous debate alternating with sudden hysterical attempts to move the wagon resulted almost in uprooting the fence. This was too much for my silent endurance. I walked over to the men and directed them to get a strong plank. With it we wedged the wagon over so that it cleared the fence opening. Then it was pulled through triumphantly.

By this time it was well past the lunch hour, and we hurried to the dining-room. A toilet, too foul for use, opened directly into it. The odors did not enhance the appetite. On the great Verblud State Experimental Farm of the Soviet Union, we had anticipated some wholesome farm food. Soup, milk and coffee were served to us. The soup was made of the customary sour cabbage. The milk had a peculiar taste. After one swallow we rejected it. The "coffee" was a grain substitute, none too palatable. Soon after the meal we suffered mild stomach disturbances. That was the last straw. We decided to return to Rostov at once and to go on to Dneprostroi.

REPORT ON THE RUSSIANS

In the Soviet Union everything which has any possible food value is either rigidly rationed or else is unobtainable except at fantastic prices.

The Soviet food ration, which she must buy at her assigned grocery store, gives the worker about nine-tenths of what she must have to keep alive and working. For the other tenth, and for any food delicacies she wants, she must look elsewhere.

The first place to look is in the free market or Rynok, where farmers bring produce for sale.

A note here on the farmer. He lives on a collective or state farm, where he does his share of the common work. When the crop is sold, certain overhead expenses must be met, just as in capitalist countries. There are the state taxes, which take a substantial share. His collective probably owes money for farm implements it has bought from the Machinery Trust, and these installments must be paid. The Collective has probably pledged itself to buy a tank for the Red Army, so taking these items together, nine-tenths of what it raises must be sold to the State at the low-pegged official price.

But not all. A small surplus of produce usually remains, and this is distributed among the farmers, who are free either to eat it or bring it to town for sale in the free market, at any price they care to ask. This is also true of what each farmer raises in the small kitchen garden tract which is allotted him. It is supposedly only large enough for his family's needs, but usually something is left over.

In America commission men make the rounds of farm houses in trucks, buying surplus vegetables for resale in town. In the Soviet Union both the farmer and the commission man would get a five-year sentence, because that is exploitation. For the commission man hopes to sell what he buys at a profit, and is thus guilty of exploiting both farmer and the worker. To avoid this crime, the Soviet farmer must take time to hitch up and go to market where he sells personally what he raises, and the hungry housewife may go by subway clear across Moscow to find him.

The Moscow Central Rynok is a large, crowded, fairly clean pavilion, which resembles a farmer's market in any fair-sized American town. The rouble-per-kilo prices I translate into

American dollars and cents per pound. But remember that on this same basis, our Russian warworker gets a total of $20 a week.

With this, at the Rynok, she may buy all the eggs she wants (but with no guarantee of their freshness) at $13.10 a dozen. And bread, too. She probably can't afford a whole loaf but may buy as big a chunk as she wants at the rate of $5.67 per pound. Here is some mutton (or perhaps goat)—a bargain at $11.34 per pound—more than half her week's wages.

Has my lady a sweet tooth? Well, an old peasant woman is selling chunks of sugar beet at 80 cents a pound. But if she wants much of that honey at the next booth, she must save her money for he is asking $15 a pound. It's much sweeter than the watery beet.

Then there are assorted items. Across the way an old lady is selling a calf's head and its four knuckles. She wants $18 for the collection, with the hair on and glassy eyes open, attracting a few flies. . . .

"Today," says Kirilov,* "we visit vegetable factory." This, it develops, is an enormous state-run greenhouse a few kilometers beyond Moscow, which was started a number of years ago by our host, Commissar Mikoyan, when he was head of the Commissariat of Supply. Its purpose was to provide Moscow with a year-round supply of fresh vegetables.

In an open air garden, fresh cucumbers are not ready to pick until the middle of July. This hothouse begins to deliver them in late February.

First, the director. He is small, wiry, and sunburned, a farmer type in any country. Eric starts in with some questions about financing.

Last year they produced 10,000,000 roubles' worth of vegetables, the director tells us, on which they made a profit of 3,000,000, and this was used to enlarge the farm.

These figures are based on the low fixed price at which this farm must sell its vegetables to the

state grocery stores. If they were sold in the free market, the profit would be in terms of billions.

The farm, they tell us, has a production norm, and its workers get a third of everything produced in excess of this, given to them in a vegetable dividend toward the end of the year. This they may either eat or sell in the open market, and is, of course, in addition to their wages of 500 roubles a month for which they work ten hours a day, six days a week. These wages are low by war-plant standards, but remember they may eat or sell vegetables at free market prices—or trade them for clothing. Money is always secondary in the Soviet Union.

Now we begin the tour. First a huge hothouse for tomatoes, where the workers (90 per cent are girls) pick them green at an even size to ripen on frames.

The size of the place is staggering. They tell us there are more than 30,000 square yards under glass. In addition they have 22,000 cold frames, each more than a yard and a half square. We see long vistas of tomato plants. Peak production here is 100,000 pounds of tomatoes a month.

In the next building are long alleys of pumpkins. This I can hardly believe. For with us pumpkins are so cheap that no one would dream of raising them under glass.

This plant is the largest of several other vegetable factories which supply Moscow, they explain, but its production equals that of the others combined. That would allow one pound of tomatoes a month in winter for about 200,000 privileged people out of Moscow's millions.

And the price? The director tells us they get in winter ten times the price of tomatoes raised in summer in the open air. No wonder 30 cents of every dollar is profit, in spite of the fact that they must heat the greenhouses from September to May in this sub-arctic climate.

In America such a spread would bring quick competition: somebody would invest money in railroad cars to bring them up from the south in winter. Certainly in America no one could afford to produce hothouse pumpkins, since they are cheap to raise, keep so well, and are so easy to ship.

---

*Kirilov, a protocol official for the People's Commissariate of Foreign Trade, was guide, host, and traveling companion to White and his group throughout their visit to the Soviet Union.

But here a state monopoly has no competition to uncover its mistakes; instead they can point with pride to their 30 per cent profit.

The plant is clean and seems efficiently run, following the most modern methods. They also show us their live stock which they explain is not for sale, but for the use of members of this co-operative. They have flocks of fine-looking chickens, geese, turkeys, and ducks, all of carefully selected breeds; the pens are immaculate.

No dinner in Russia was better than the honest meal we sat down to in the big dining room. True, the Intourist steward hovered around, uncorking champagne and spooning out caviar. But we could ignore him, for they had good, simple dishes cooked on the farm—cabbage soup, roast pork, roast duck, and homemade dumplings.

These Russians are fine farmers. It is the fault of the system if what they are doing may in part be silly. They are doing it efficiently and well.

REVIEW QUESTIONS

1. Describe the physical conditions of the collective farm at Verblud that Witkin visited.
2. How did various supervisors explain the problems at the farm? Who, if anyone, was to blame? Why?
3. Do you think Witkin's description of Verblud was biased? Why or why not?
4. What did White admire about Soviet agriculture? Why? What faults did he find? Why?
5. Compare and contrast the description of the Soviet Union by Zara Witkin (1930s) with W. L. White's description (1944).
6. How might World War II have affected Soviet attitudes and work habits?

A Japanese Woman Ponders Spanish Attitudes Toward Revolution and Bullfights (1931)

HARUKO ICHIKAWA, *Japanese Lady in Europe*

In 1931 and 1932, Haruko Ichikawa accompanied her husband, Sanki Ichikawa (an eminent Japanese scholar and the recipient of a traveling fellowship), on a trip around the world. Every night she sat up and wrote down "all the things which had cast their shadows" on her mind during the day—a pleasurable task that she likened to developing photos. Her very lengthy diary was published in Japan shortly after their return home; in 1937 it was abridged to approximately half of its original size and translated into English under the title *Japanese Lady in Europe*. Her chapter on Spain was not abbreviated; the following excerpt is as she wrote it.

Ichikawa apologized for her own lack of education in the preface to the English edition. "My education is limited to a girls' high school," she confessed. "If I had deeper knowledge I should have been able to make more interesting observations." Because of what she viewed as a defect, however, she says she strove to make her observations as interesting as possible. She succeeded with a vengeance, and critics of her book credited her with single-handedly changing Western views of Japanese women. In an age when many in the West viewed a Japanese woman as either a quiet and submissive wife or as a "*geisha*-girl who had fallen in love with a *samurai* committing *hara-kiri*," Ichikawa revealed herself to be a woman of sophistication, insight, and imagination.

Ichikawa's chapter on Spain is especially striking. At the time of her visit there, Spain was between crises. In 1931, republican leaders had driven King Alfonso from the country, had begun to write a democratic constitution, and were about to elect a liberal president; in 1934, however, conservatives who supported the monarchy led an uprising against the new government that two years later turned into a brutal civil war. The author captures this moment: the Spain she describes is peaceful, but violence seethes just beneath its surface.

Although it was soon after the Revolution, the revolutionary atmosphere was extremely slight. Mr. C. of the Japanese Legation told us about the first general election in the Republic, which was coming on in a few days, and gave us a lot of information. In short, the common people, having no patience, desired their business conditions to improve at once, so that life would quickly become easier, and politicians, for their part, flattering the showy temperament of the people, excited the populace with the vain prospect of a Republican party which would bring about Paradise after the fall of the Royalist party. But this party could not, after all, do as they promised, so the people at once thought this was no use either and decided that Syndicalism might do some good instead. Their mood was just like that of an invalid who changes his medicine time and again, deceived by advertisements, so we could not bring ourselves to try to understand their views seriously. The general election, which took place on the 28th, was also extremely dull, and I could not see any passion in it although all men of about twenty-three years of age had the franchise. As I came from a country where violent campaigns are fought out, the first general election of Spain gave me the impression that the whole town was too indifferent to it, and I thought it frightfully boring. Women, though having a good opportunity in the Revolution which was going to rebuild everything from the root, made no endeavours, in spite of their hav-

ing no vote while all men over twenty-three years got it, and they took to habitual church-going. I was told that if women had been given the franchise, people would have no end of trouble because of the Catholic party, which would carry matters with a high hand. Their revolution, I was informed, only goes into the flippancy of pageantry at once by choosing, for instance, a "Miss Republica" with beautiful ornaments such as a high comb and mantilla, or by drawing festival carriages about the town carrying labourers in hunting-caps. On the day when we went to Seville, there was a strike of masons taking place, and I heard a gardener saying, with envy, "I've heard that Russian Bolsheviks have told them not to work, giving them two pesetas each. What a good job it is!" Yet I had not seen one poster anywhere which would help such a populace trust the present government. The best way to induce the illiterate people into a revolution is by propaganda in the streets, and as I saw evidence of this in the streets of Russia, which has a genius for this sort of thing, I was very much dissatisfied with Spain. The political upheaval in this country was not really a revolution in which the national spirit of rebirth that had been pent up within broke out and blew off the King, but was nothing but a quarrel between the political parties in which the Republican party won the victory and obtained the rule from the Royalist party, while the Alfonso family collapsed of itself like a fruit that falls after rotting. In a book of geography I once read that Spaniards were idle and fond of having a nap in the daytime, but since I experienced the heat of the day in this country, I thought that a short sleep was unavoidable for people who lived in such a climate. Taking a siesta in the daytime, however, they sit up far into the night, and there is idle talking in the streets even at three o'clock in the morning, thus living in a way which is expressed in a Japanese "haiku" poem, "There shoots a star, and the topic changes on the summer evening bench." So they never seem to be able to take to serious and steady study. Spain, the country of heat, therefore, has a very dim prospective light before her except that she may turn out by chance a transient genius leader, and the cry of "Tanto monta!" (Excelsior) is nothing more than the incoherent utterance of a drunkard. Why was it that the flower of civilization opened, in ancient times, only in hot countries such as Egypt, Greece, Rome and Spain? Was the heat of the sun a little milder in olden times? Now, anyhow, it was hot, hot, hot!

SEEING A BULLFIGHT

As June 28th was the day when Spain was to be re-born, the day of the first general election after the Revolution, we went out into the streets with great expectation to see how it was going on. We had been staying in Madrid, the capital of Spain, and managed to extend our stay to be there on that day, for that purpose. But with much disappointment and dissatisfaction we came back to our hotel, where the porter brought us entrance tickets for a bull fight which was going to take place in the afternoon. I dropped off to sleep while thinking it very interesting that there was a difference of a few shillings in the charge for seats according to the amount of sun and shade on them. I slept like mud during the noon-day hours, as people should do in Rome as the Romans do, and we did not go out until four o'clock. To my surprise there was a great change in the appearance of the streets. They were all hurry and bustle. The way in which the people were making for the bullfight-ring was like that of blood throbbing upward to the head of a man who was going to suffer cerebral haemorrhage. Then we too changed into two of the blood corpuscles, and were pushed along in the stream of humanity.

Climbing up the stone-steps under the seats of the ring, we suddenly came inside, and felt with a shock that Rome was living, it was so much like the Coliseum. In the centre was a wide sandy area surrounded by a fence about four feet high, and along the outer side of the fence there was a space of six feet around it, and rows of stone seats for fifteen thousand spectators spread in the shape of a mortar. Above it was the blue sky, and the afternoon sunshine was dividing the large amphitheatre into two parts, dyeing it light and shade, purple and gold.

People came pouring in and seated themselves on the stone seats, after putting cushions on them. Behind us, there was a throne, and on the seats near it, Spanish beauties with blood-coloured nails were seated, having gorgeous shawls hung on the rails in front of them, and moving their large fans to and fro. Everything was Roman—exactly Roman. Nero was going to appear in the throne.

Were not the people around us shouting noisily, "Give the Christians to the lions"? *Baedeker* says, "When ladies are of the party it is advisable to sit in the upper rows in case they should faint." "But not I," I thought to myself, and remembered the story of Monte Cristo, who saw the cruel spectacle of hanging a criminal in order to train his heart.

Towards five o'clock there was no room at all in the spectators' seats. On the other side of the arena, fans and white handkerchiefs were fluttering almost hurting my eyes. Looking around, I saw that all eyes had a feverish glitter. One could see even by their dresses that most of the spectators were simply absorbed in the sport, for the admittance fee was as much as ten shillings, while they were most of them poor folk. How many days do they have to work in order to get that sum of money? The population of Madrid is eight hundred thousand, and the ring holds fifteen thousand seats. The fights take place twice a week, and there are two hundred rings in the whole country . . . My mind was for a time shaking off the excited feeling of a character in *Quo Vadis,* and looking round with critical eyes. And when the trumpet announcing the opening of the sport sounded at five o'clock to the minute, I thought with a cold smile that the improvement of Spain had gone no further than to open bullfights punctually. . . .

REVIEW QUESTIONS

1. How does Ichikawa describe the reaction of ordinary Spaniards to the revolution?
2. Compare and contrast this reaction to the enthusiasm with which the Spanish people anticipated the bullfight. How does the author explain this?
3. How does Ichikawa feel about the weather in Spain? What significance does she assign to it?
4. Were the bullfight and the revolution linked in the mind of Ichikawa? Did the bullfight or any aspects of it have any important symbolism for her? If so, what?

An American Reporter Talks to People in Berlin About the Nazis (1934)

PHILIP GIBBS, *European Journey*

In the Introduction to *European Journey,* Philip Gibbs describes the purpose of his trip through central Europe sixteen years after the end of World War I, which he had seen firsthand as a war correspondent in France. He wanted to see how Europe had changed since the war, especially how the common people had fared. "My mission was not to interview statesmen and politicians," he says, "—one knows in advance what they will say—but to get in touch with the common folk whose lives are unrecorded and whose ideas are unexpressed." Traveling by automobile, Gibbs and two companions started from Paris and drove through Switzerland, Italy, Austria, Hungary, Germany, and the Saar. It was the spring and summer of 1934. Adolf Hitler had just come to power, and Germany was finally beginning to recover from the disastrous economic aftermath of the Great War (World War I).

In the following excerpt, Gibbs interacts with native Germans, as well as tourists and a foreign resident of Berlin. No one he interviewed—not the commander of a group of Hitler Youth, the American wife of a German native, a group of English tourists, nor the musician who claimed Hitler as a friend—viewed Hitler's policies or activities with alarm. Gibbs, however, saw much in Berlin that he found "not exactly reassuring."

I went about Berlin keeping my eyes and ears open, talking to many people of different classes, trying to penetrate somewhat into the hidden spirit of this Nazi revolution. It was not easy to get a clear line of conviction. There were many inconsistencies and many mysteries. There had been a Jewish persecution carried out in the early days of Hitler's triumph with great brutality, according to many accounts by credible witnesses. Jewish intellectuals were still being dismissed from their posts. But the stores of Tietz and Wertheim were open, and many of their assistants were Jews. I saw Jews moving about their business unmolested, though with uneasy eyes.

Hitler proclaimed his desire for peace. He offered friendship to France, and any form of disarmament to the lowest level, if France would agree to German equality.

Goering, even, denied that he had any belief in war or any intention of preparing for war. Had he not been in the last war? he asked. Did people think he was a madman? (It did not occur to him that the answer would be "Yes"!) Was it not ridiculous? he asked.

Baldur von Schirach, a young man of twenty-eight in command of the Hitler Jugend, declined to admit that the youth of Germany had any warlike spirit or purpose because they marched about in uniform, like boy scouts. It was to build a new world of comradeship and not to destroy the world that they submitted to a little discipline and showed their ardour for service.

But it was curious that whenever I picked up a German magazine it was stuffed with pictures of soldiers in steel helmets and pictures of the World War. There seemed to be a new and morbid interest in the life of trenches and dugouts, in great guns and aërial bombs and all the machinery of death.

In the very centre of Unter den Linden there was, during my visit to Berlin, an exhibition called *Der Front.* All day long German boys had their noses glued to the windowpanes. German students with their girls paid a mark to go inside. Now and again a middle-aged German and his wife stared at the windows, hesitated for a

moment, and then went in. It was a war exhibition, devoted to the instruments of slaughter— trench mortars, machine guns, aerial torpedoes, large-sized shells, lurid pictures of battle by sea, land and air. A guide showed a young German girl how to work a machine gun. She was very much amused by this demonstration. *"Ausgeseichnet!"* she exclaimed, as though a machine gun were a charming piece of mechanism which might be nice in the home.

Why all this revival of interest in things which the rest of the world—England, anyhow—was trying to forget?

I asked the question of a young Nazi, who was highly intelligent and very sincere, I thought.

"It's difficult to explain," he answered. "But it's not at all what foreigners think. You see, in England and France you were proud of your soldiers after the war. It was your victory. You put up war memorials. You had your two minutes' silence. You had your poppy day. But in Germany it was all too painful at first, and our returning soldiers were insulted by Communists and Social Democrats. They had their badges torn from their shoulders, and their Iron Crosses were grabbed. No one remembered the heroism of the German troops and all their victories and sufferings. Now at last, under Hitler, we wish to remember. We're proud to remember the courage of our fathers and all they went through in those frightful years. It's a revival of German pride in heroic achievement, but not a revival of the war spirit, or the wish for another war, which we all know would be the end of European civilisation. You won't find a single Nazi who has war in his mind—except perhaps as a menace of war against Germany itself. I assure you that is true."

He believed it was true.

An American lady who had long been married to a German came to tea with me at the Fürstenhof. We talked freely about the German situation and mentality, until I noticed that several young waiters were listening with their ears cocked.

"Most people in England, and everybody in

France," I told her, "believe Germany is preparing for a new war."

She was astounded and shocked.

"But that is impossible! It's ridiculous! Why should they believe such an absurdity?"

I gave her some of the reasons. Every news reel in every cinema showed German youth drilling, marching, parading. There was a conviction that Germany was re-arming secretly and that every German was a soldier. Hitler's book *Mein Kampf* was not exactly reassuring. All that stuff about absorbing the other Nordic peoples and extending the German Kultur over Holland, Denmark, Sweden, parts of Hungary, Austria, and Czecho-Slovakia was alarming. The Hitler régime had begun with brutality against the Jews. The spirit of the bully was exalted by the Nazi creed. Men like Rosenberg, with his wild, mystical nonsense about the Germanic race and the old paganism, were preaching a cult against intellectualism and proclaiming the coming reign of instinct and biological force. It was a denial of all civilised ideals. It was deliberately a hark-back to barbarism. There was a book by a man named Banse, a professor with an official appointment as a university instructor. It was written in the spirit of blood lust. It exalted war. It called upon the German people to smash France and England in the fulfilment of a divine destiny. There was a lot of rubbish like that.

The lady who had lived many years of married life in Germany listened to my words attentively. She was very much surprised.

"My German friends laugh at Rosenberg's nonsense," she said. "Do you think they take it seriously? As for that man Banse, I have never heard of him, and I doubt whether the people I know have ever heard of him. As for all this marching and drilling, it means nothing as far as war is concerned. Germans like it, just as the English like football and cricket. They love to go marching along, singing songs and feeling fit. It gives them a sense of *Kamaradschaft,* which is a great need in the minds of young Germans. I

know so many of these young Nazis. They talk very freely to me, because I am the wife of a German and therefore, in their minds, German. They never talk of wanting war. On the contrary, they hate the idea of it. If ever they speak of war it is because they have a fear that France and her allies will force it upon them and march through Germany. Naturally they feel that they must defend the Fatherland. Wouldn't any other nation feel the same? Wouldn't England, if it were threatened with invasion?"

It was then that I became aware of several young waiters of the Fürstenhof listening with their ears cocked.

"We had better get into a quiet corner," I suggested. "We are having an audience."

We retired and continued our talk. She was a very knowledgeable lady. She knew Herr Hitler and admired him.

"He is all for peace," she assured me. "Foreigners don't believe in his sincerity. But I'm certain that he wants to make a friendship with France. It is his strongest wish. And you must admit that he has said so publicly several times. Why doesn't France accept the offer?"

I found others in Berlin who believed in Hitler's sincerity—some of them English people who were in close touch with him. They sized him up as a simple-minded man, fanatical, of course, and with the obstinacy of a fanatic, but sentimental, emotional, and honest. His head, they said, had not been turned by power. On the contrary, he had abandoned some of his wild ideas and the verbal fury of the demagogue. He was becoming a statesman. He was anxious to preserve peace in Europe. His claim for equality in arms down to any level or up to any level was, after all, just. Its justice had been admitted—and then repudiated—by England and France. He was a very pleasant person to meet—perfectly modest and unassuming—rather gentle even. They liked him. . . . It was before the thirtieth of June, when he was not so gentle with those who had been his comrades.

REVIEW QUESTIONS

1. Compare the attitudes of native Germans toward Hitler with those of the foreigners Gibbs interviewed and with the attitudes of Gibbs himself.
2. What activities did Gibbs observe in Berlin that he found, as he later said, "not exactly reassuring"?
3. What does this excerpt from *European Journey* tell you about the author's political beliefs and sympathies?

A Russian-Born Foreign Correspondent Reports on the Experiences of Schoolchildren During the Siege of Leningrad (1943)

ALEXANDER WERTH, *Russia at War*

Alexander Werth was born in St. Petersburg and spent the first seventeen years of his life there. In 1918, his parents escaped the Bolshevik revolution and moved to Great Britain, where he went to college. His long career as a journalist, political observer, commentator, and educator took him from Scotland to France to the Soviet Union, and from London to New York. He was a widely recognized expert on modern European politics and history, and the author of seventeen books on France and the Soviet Union. The first of his works, *France in Ferment,* was published in 1934; the last, *Russia: Hopes and Fears,* appeared shortly before his death in 1969.

Werth was particularly famous for his keen and insightful observations of Soviet people and politics. Sent to the Soviet Union in 1941, he was the Moscow correspondent for London's *Sunday Times* and wrote "Russian Commentaries" for the British Broadcasting Corporation during and after World War II. All in all, Werth spent seven years in the Soviet Union (which he persistently called "Russia"), traveling either alone or with small groups of reporters. Speaking Russian "like a native"—which he was, after all—he was able to talk "freely and informally" to literally thousands of soldiers and civilians, and even to a few captured Germans. In the introduction to *Russia at War,* Werth says, "I think I may say that one of my chief qualifications for writing this story of the war years in Russia is that I was there." He believed he was the only surviving Westerner who lived in Russia through the entire war and who kept a day-to-day record of everything he saw, heard, and experienced.

Of Werth's eight books on the Soviet Union, *Russia at War* is perhaps his most famous and most significant. It primarily tells the "human story" of the Soviet war against the Germans, although it provides political and military context for the struggle as well. "In the fearful days of 1941–42," he writes, "and in the next two and a half years of hard and costly victories, I never lost the feeling that this was a genuine People's War; first, a war waged by a people fighting for their life against terrible odds, and later a war fought by a fundamentally unaggressive people, now roused to anger and determined to demonstrate their own military superiority." *Russia at War* makes it clear that it was unquestionably the Red Army that defeated the Germans, at the cost of 20 to 27 million Russian dead, more than two-thirds of them civilians.

This selection features an interview with a schoolmaster and essays by teenagers who survived the horrific 900-day siege of Leningrad (St. Petersburg), in part by clinging doggedly to familiar routines of school and study. Werth talked with them in September of 1943, before the siege was officially lifted but after the blockade had been broken in January and Russian troops were managing to bring some welcome supplies into the city. For the 640,000 people who had already died of starvation, however, they were too late. Particularly difficult had been the winter of 1941–1942, during which rations in Leningrad were cut to 1,087 calories per day for manual laborers, 581 for office workers, 466 for adult dependents, and 684 for children. These were official figures, which Werth called "an optimistic exaggeration." Most people did not have as much to eat as the figures indicate. Unusually cold weather, even for Russia, also exacerbated problems: by December there was almost no fuel, electricity, or running water. Nor was there even hope of relief by surrendering. Hitler had ordered that Leningrad be "wiped off the face of the earth," reasoning that the city would be too dangerous for victorious German troops to enter. When Russian troops finally drove the Germans back, some 33 percent of the city's presiege population had starved, frozen, or been killed by enemy shells and bombs—nearly one million people. The stories of the students and their teacher, documented by Werth, vividly underscore the quiet courage and everyday heroism of ordinary Russian people who triumphed over death and despair in one of the worst episodes in human history.

Another striking memory is my visit to a secondary school in Tambov Street, in a modern and heavily shelled part of the city, three or four miles from the front. It was run by an elderly man, Tikhomirov, a "Teacher of Merit of the USSR," who had started as an elementary teacher back in 1907. This school was one of the few that had not closed down even at the height of the famine. On four occasions it had been heavily damaged by German shells; but the boys had cleared away the glass, bricked up the walls that had been smashed, and had put plywood in the windows. During the last shelling in May, a woman-teacher had been killed in the yard of the school.

The boys were typical Leningrad children; eighty-five per cent of the boys' fathers were still at the Leningrad Front, or had already been killed there, while many others had died in the Leningrad famine, and nearly all their mothers—if still alive—were working in Leningrad factories, or on transport, or on wood-cutting, or in civil defence. The boys all had a passionate hatred for the Germans, but were fully convinced by now that these *svolochi* (bastards) would be destroyed outside Leningrad before long. They had mixed feelings about Britain and America; they knew London had been bombed; that the RAF was "bombing the hell out of the Fritzes"; that the Americans were supplying the Red Army with a lot of lorries, and that they (the boys) were getting American chocolate to eat; but "there was still no Second Front."

The headmaster, Comrade Tikhomirov, told

me how they had "stuck it, and stuck it fairly well. We had no wood, but the Leningrad Soviet gave us a small wooden house not far away for demolition, so we could use the timber for heating. The bombing and shelling was very severe in those days. We had about 120 pupils then—boys and girls—and we had to hold our classes in the shelter. Not for a day did the work stop. It was very cold. The little stoves heated the air properly only a yard around them, and in the rest of the shelter the temperature was below zero. There was no lighting, apart from a kerosene lamp. But we carried on, and the children were so serious and earnest that we got better results than in any other year. Surprising, but true. We had meals for them; the army helped us to feed them. Several of the teachers died, but I am proud to say that all the children in our care survived. Only it was pathetic to watch them during those famine months. Towards the end of 1941, they hardly looked like children any more. They were strangely silent . . . They would not walk about; they would just sit. But none of them died; and only some of those pupils who had stopped coming to school, and stayed at home, died, often together with the rest of the family . . ."

Tikhomirov then showed me an extraordinary document, which he called "our Famine Scrapbook," containing copies of many children's essays written during the famine, and much other material. It was bound in purple velvet, and the margins composed of rather conventional children's watercolours depicting soldiers, tanks, planes and the like; these surrounded little typewritten sheets—copies of typical essays written during the famine. One young girl wrote:

Until June 22 everybody had work and a good life assured to him. That day we went on an excursion to the Kirov Islands. A fresh wind was blowing from the Gulf, bringing with it bits of the song some kids were singing not far away. "Great and glorious is my native land." And then the enemy began to come nearer and nearer our city. We went out

to dig big trenches.* It was difficult, because a lot of the kids were not used to such hard physical labour. The German General von Leeb was already licking his chops at the thought of the gala dinner he was going to get at the Astoria.† Now we are sitting in the shelter round improvised stoves, with our coats and fur caps and gloves on. We have been knitting warm things for our soldiers, and have been taking round their letters to friends and relatives. We have also been collecting non-ferrous metal for salvage . . .

Valentina Solovyova, an older girl of sixteen, wrote:

June 22! How much that date means to us now! But then it just seemed an ordinary summer day . . . Before long, the House Committee was swarming with women, girls and children, who had come to join the civil defence teams, the anti-fire and anti-gas squads . . . By September the city was encircled. Food supplies from outside had stopped. The last evacuee trains‡ had departed. The people of Leningrad tightened their belts. The streets began to bristle with barricades and anti-tank hedgehogs. Dugouts and firing points—a whole network of them—were springing up around the city.

As in 1919, so now, the great question arose: "Shall Leningrad remain a Soviet city or not?" Leningrad was in danger. But its workers had risen like one man for its defence.

---

*The German invasion of the Soviet Union began on June 22, 1941. Over one million volunteers, including schoolchildren, immediately began constructing defenses in and around Leningrad. By the time shelling of the city began on September 4, they had dug 340 miles of antitank ditches and 15,875 miles of open trenches, and they had erected 400 miles of barbed-wire defenses, 190 miles of obstacle defenses (made from felled trees and other materials), and 5,000 wooden or concrete firing walls.
†The Astoria was a famous luxury hotel in Leningrad.
‡Fewer than 190,000 people were evacuated from a city of approximately 3,000,000 before the railroad lines were cut. Approximately 150,000 were "resident foreigners" from the Baltic states; only 40,000 were native residents of Leningrad.

Tanks were thundering down the streets. Everywhere men of the civil guard were joining up . . . A cold and terrible winter was approaching. Together with their bombs, enemy planes were dropping leaflets. They said they would raze Leningrad to the ground. They said we would all die of hunger. They thought they would frighten us, but they filled us with renewed strength . . . Leningrad did not let the enemy through its gates! The city was starving, but it lived and worked, and kept on sending to the front more of its sons and daughters. Though knocking at the knees with hunger, our workers went to work in their factories, with the air-raid sirens filling the air with their screams . . .

This from another essay on how the schoolchildren dug trenches while the Germans were approaching Leningrad:

In August we worked for twenty-five days digging trenches. We were machine-gunned and some of us were killed, but we carried on, though we weren't used to this work. And the Germans were stopped by the trenches we had dug . . .

Another girl of sixteen, Luba Tereshchenkova, described how work continued at the school even during the worst time of the blockade:

In January and February terrible frost also joined in the blockade and lent Hitler a hand. It was never less than thirty degrees of frost! Our classes continued on the "Round the Stove" principle. But there were no reserved seats, and if you wanted a seat near the stove or under the stove pipe, you had to come early. The place facing the stove door was reserved for the teacher. You sat down and were suddenly seized by a wonderful feeling of well-being: the warmth penetrated through your skin, right into your bones; it made you all weak and languid; you just wanted to think of nothing, only to slumber and drink

in the warmth. It was agony to stand up and go to the blackboard. . . At the blackboard it was so cold and dark, and your hand, imprisoned in its heavy glove, went all numb and rigid and refused to obey. The chalk kept falling out of your hand, and the lines were all crooked . . . By the time we reached the third lesson there was no more fuel left. The stove went cold and a horrid icy draught started blowing down the pipe. It became terribly cold. It was then that Vasya Pugin, with a puckish look on his face, could be seen slinking out and bringing in a few logs from Anna Ivanovna's emergency reserve; and a few minutes later, we could again hear the magic crackling of wood inside the stove . . . During the break nobody would jump up because nobody had any desire to go into the icy corridors.

And this from another essay:

The winter came, fierce and merciless. The water pipes froze, and there was no electric light, and the tram-cars stopped running. To get to school in time, I had to get up very early every morning, for I live out in the suburbs. It was particularly difficult to get to school after a blizzard, when all roads and paths are covered with snowdrifts. But I firmly decided to complete my school year . . . One day, after standing in a bread queue for six hours (I had to miss school that day, for I had received no bread for two days) I caught a cold and fell ill. Never had I felt so miserable as during those days. Not for physical reasons, but because I needed the moral support of my school-mates, their encouraging jokes . . .

None of the children who continued to go to school died, but several of the teachers did. The last section of the Famine Scrapbook, introduced by a title page with a decorative funeral urn painted in purple watercolour, was written by Tikhomirov, the headmaster. It was a series of obituary notes of the teachers who were either killed in the war or had died of hunger. The assistant headmaster was "killed in action." Another was "killed at Kingisepp," in that terrible battle of Kingisepp where the Germans broke through towards Leningrad from Estonia. The maths teacher "died of hunger"; so did the teacher of geography. Comrade Nemirov, the teacher of literature, "was among the victims of the blockade," and Akimov, the history teacher, died of malnutrition and exhaustion despite a long rest in a sanatorium to which he was taken in January. Of another teacher Tikhomirov wrote: "He worked conscientiously until he realised he could no longer walk. He asked me for a few days' leave in the hope that his strength would return to him. He stayed at home, preparing his lessons for the second term. He went on reading books. So he spent the day of January 8. On January 9 he quietly passed away." What a human story was behind these simple words!

I have described conditions in Leningrad as I found them in September 1943, when the city was still under frequent and often intense shellfire. This shelling continued for the rest of the year, and it was not till January 1944 that the ordeal of Leningrad finally ended. During the previous weeks a large Russian armed force was transferred under cover of night to the "Oranienbaum bridgehead" on the south bank of the Gulf of Finland; and this force, under the command of General Fedyuninsky, struck out towards Ropsha, where it was to meet the troops of the Leningrad Front striking towards the southwest. During that first day of the Russian breakthrough no fewer than 500,000 shells were used to smash the German fortifications. About the same time, the Volkhov army group also came into motion, and, within a few days, the Germans were on the run, all the way to Pskov and Estonia. On January 27, 1944 the blockade officially ended.

REVIEW QUESTIONS

1. In addition to moral support and camaraderie, what did the Tambov Street school provide for its students? How did this help them survive the siege of Leningrad?
2. How did the students participate in the Soviet war effort? What was the result of their hard work?
3. Comrade Tikhomirov, the headmaster, told Werth that student academic performance was better during the worst year of the siege than in any other year. Why do you suppose this was true?
4. Werth noted, with surprise, that none of the "ultra-patriotic essays" in the school's "Famine Scrapbook" mentioned Joseph Stalin. Speculate as to the reason for this peculiar omission.
5. The obituary pages of the Famine Scrapbook list the deaths of six teachers, and Werth mentioned a seventh. Why would teachers have felt so strongly obligated to continue working in such hazardous and unpleasant conditions? Would your high school or college teachers have responded to a similar situation in the same way? Why or why not?

An American Soldier Writes Home from Europe During World War II (1945)

MORRIS DEUTSCH, *"Letter to Margie"*

Unlike most of the authors included in this volume, Morris Deutsch was an "ordinary man." He grew up and lived in New York City and its suburbs. After serving in the U.S. armed forces in World War II, he became a lawyer and eventually an amateur art collector. The following letter describing his experiences in the war, as well as his opinions about Londoners, Parisians, and Germans, was found by relatives following his death in 1993. It has not been published previously.

Aug. {illegible date} 1945

Dear Margie,

. . . Paris is a wonderful city of beautiful public buildings, wide boulevards that sweep across the city and are lined with trees, lovely parks and side walk cafés that dot every street and liven them up with colorful awnings and umbrellas. The city is alive and the very air is electrifying and smells of Paris. I visited all the places of tourist interest like the Eiffel Tower, the Arc de Triomphe, the Louvre, the Jardin [garden] of the Tuilleries, the Place de La Concorde and Bastille, the book stalls along the Seine, Notre Dame Cathedral and the Sacre Coeur and I don't remember what all else. I saw the shows at the Follies Bergere and the Casino de Paris, both of which were excellent. They are something like our Broadway Revues except that their stage settings are much more daring and imaginative, the skits more risque and suggestive, every scene employs a bed in one form or another, and the girls for the most part are bare breasted and one girl in the Follies wore a g-string no bigger than an American six cent postage stamp. The audience was mostly military, but the pantomime was excellent, and usualy someone would come out and explain in English what the scene was all about. Both theaters were lovely with large lounges and a bar in the lobby where it only cost an arm and a leg and two quarts of blood for a shot of cognac.

The center of the nightlife in Paris, besides a few high class cafe's on the Champs Elysees was in Monmarte. The main street there was the Rue Pigalle known as Pig Alley to all the G.I.'s. There are reputed to be 80,000 licensed prostitutes in Paris and altho some can be found in every cafe in the city, I'd venture to say more than that number ply the trade in Pigalle. The street is lined with cafe's jammed with soldiers and girls, drinks and music, and it's a movie producers dream of what Paris should look like to a soldier on furlough. The place is impossible of description. The sight of all these girls hustling on every street corner, but openly and suggestively is amazing. The French themselves don't seem to pay it any attention. They just calmly go about their business. The French take a lot more liberal view of sex than we do and the amateur competition was high.

The women of Paris are singularly attractive. They go in a great deal for makeup and fancy hairdoes. I've seen hair dyed every color under the sun in Paris except green and I'm sure some girl must have had that except that I missed her. Despite shortages in material their clothes are very attractive and they know how to wear them. The sight of these mademoiselles pedaling down the boulevards their skirts flying in the wind is a sight for sore G.I. eyes. In Paris you can see the oddest combinations of male and female, and the general run of women are taller than the men. A casual observer would never guess that there existed a shortage of food and clothes and that no one knew where this winters coal was to come from.

We left France for Germany several weeks before V-E day but never ran into any action. We went through Aachen and Cologne, swung south thru Bonn, stopped over night in Weimar where I visited Buchenwald (later saw Dachau) what places. You have probably seen pictures of them back home. And we were in Pretzfeld when the war ended.

We are now located in Herrsching, about 25 miles south and west of Munich. We live in a hotel on a beautiful lake in the Bavarian mountains, and the snow caps of the Alps can be seen in the distance. I share a room with two other men. We each have an individual bed, there is running water in the room and a radio. D.P.'s [displaced persons] do all the cleaning and K.P. We get swell food and eat off plates in the hotels dining room. We have a civilian baker and generally get ice cream three times a week. We get all the beer we can drink and a liquor ration of two bottles of cognac, four wine and four champagne a month. . . .

Despite the lifting of the ban on fraternization I still haven't spoken to any Germans. There are several French and Hungarian D.P.'s here and I confine my friendships to these people. I can manage to make myself understood in both languages. My particular girlfriend here happens to be a Hungarian girl and I can get along in that language ok. I was sorry to see the ban on fraternization lifted as too many of the soldiers are becoming friendly with the German men. I can readily understand their making friends with the women, but it gripes me to see them becoming friendly with the other sex. At least when the ban was on a guy had to keep his romancing under cover and that forced him to limit his attentions to the girl. But now he gets to know her family and all that sort of stuff and I don't like it.

These people are absolutely the most arrogant, selfish, greedy, stupid and unmoral people in the world. They talk about the French women, they are only immoral, but these women have no morals at all. This place is a bathing resort and the women are sun worshippers and flaunt their

practically naked bodies all over the beach. Changing from street clothes to a bathing suit on the beach is just the ordinary thing. Some newspaper writers said it was being done just to tease the Americans, but now that it is no longer verbotten [prohibited] that would hardly seem to be good reasoning, and besides that nearly every one of them is on the make. And after you strike up an acquaintance with one of them, no further persuasion is needed, the fact that she is going to sleep with you is just in the ordinary course of events. Most of the married ones their husbands are missing and unheard from, and the men have long since been drained away and the single girls figure there just will never be enough men around what with the killed, wounded, missing and prisoners of war. The stories some of these guys tell about these German women is almost unbelievable. Not all of the D.P.'s were in concentration camps and those that weren't had it made as far as women were concerned. If a census of all the illegitimate children in Germany were made the figure would reach an astonishing total.

This Hungarian girl I go with has been living here for three years and knows all the gossip about every one in town. If her [illegible word] is an indication of what went on all over Germany, this country is sure a mess. Whenever we are down at the beach or walking thru town and we pass anyone, I get the lowdown. This one never was married and has two children, this one lived with a Frenchman, or a Serb, or a Hungarian or whatever he was, this one is married but her husband hasn't been home for three years and she has two children, etc. Several of the men have German girlfriends who are [sleeping?] with their husbands. You figure it out.

The attitude of the majority is the same. They are not sorry for anything that they did, Hitler was a good man and under him the country prospered (that they had a war time economy and he gave them license to steal they don't figure) and they can't see why the United States had to butt in for in the first place. The only thing they are sorry for is that they lost the war and they don't blame Hitler for their sorry plight today, they blame us. Food is scarce now and will be scarcer this winter. Personally, I hope that they all starve. Question them about the concentration camps, atrocities etc., and nobody knows a damn thing.

I think that we ought to get the hell out of this country and leave the Germans to the tender mercies of the Russians and the French. They are in mortal fear of the Russians and the French [illegible word] them no love. In France, if a German wearing a uniform fell into the hands of the F.F.I.[1] he was a dead duck. Those French soldiers don't believe in taking SS prisoners alive. The SS troops used to hide out in the woods until they could find some American soldiers to surrender to.

Thats the whole story briefly. If there is anything particular you'd like to know just ask me questions. As far as the point system of discharge is concerned, I'm a long way from out. I have five battle stars (Normandy, Northern France,

the Rhineland, the Ardennes and Central Germany) which with my service in the States and over seas total up to the grand sum of 77. Originally we were to be in the occupation army, but that's been changed. Just what the score is now or what the future holds in store, neither Deponent [?] nor anyone else seems to know. I hope that we stay here for a while because if we go home now it's the CBI[2] for sure and I'm tired of roaming, all I want is out.

[Deutsch typed the letter above, but added the following paragraph by hand]

Since I wrote this we've had some startling news: the atomic bomb, Russia's entry into the war, and now the Japanese surrender. Things sure look good and maybe I'll be home in [a] couple, three or four months. Otherwise [illegible word or phrase] well.

Love
Morris

---

[1]The French resistance (Forces françaises de I'Intérieur).

[2]The China-Burma-India theater of the war.

REVIEW QUESTIONS

1. How would you characterize Deutsch's attitude toward Paris and the French? What evidence supports your opinion?
2. What aspects of these foreign cultures did Deutsch like the most? The least? Explain.
3. Deutsch obviously disliked Germans. Did he make a convincing case for his opinion? Why or why not?

An American Reporter Inspects Conditions in Germany in the Summer of 1945

Prelude to Leadership: The European Diary of John F. Kennedy

Shortly after the surrender of the Axis powers, John F. Kennedy (president of the United States from 1960 to 1963) traveled to Europe on assignment as a reporter for the Hearst newspapers. At twenty-eight, he was already a veteran of World War II in the Pacific and a Harvard graduate whose senior thesis, *Why England Slept,* had become a best-seller. The relatively terse sentences of his travel diary, first published in basically a reporter's notebook, reveal the mind of a young man of experience, insight, and compassion. Written in 1945, the diary was not published until 1995.

Kennedy began his trip by spending two months in San Francisco observing the meetings that gave birth to the United Nations. From there he traveled to Britain, Ireland, and France, ending his trip in Germany. Excerpted here are his observations of occupied Berlin. Pay close attention not just to Kennedy's descriptions of a war-torn city and his opinions of the defeated Germans, but also to the conduct of the Russians and the Allies, especially his fellow Americans.

GERMANY

July 29, 1945

With Secretary of the Navy Forrestal and others of his party, we left Paris at about three o'clock in the Secretary's C54 plane for Berlin.

In flying over Germany, the small towns and fields looked peaceful, but in the larger cities like Frankfurt the buildings are merely of the sods. All the centers of the big cities are of the same ash gray color from the air—the color of churned up and powdered stone and brick. Railroad centers are especially badly hit, but the harvest seems to be reasonably good and the fields appear as though they were being worked fully.

At the field at Berlin where we arrived, Prime Minister Attlee came in just ahead of us. There was a large crowd, and he inspected the same Guard of Honor which Prime Minister had inspected only a few days before. We drove immediately to Potsdam through miles of Russian soldiers. They were stationed on both sides of the road at about 40 yard intervals—green-hatted and green-epauleted—Stalin's personal and picked guard. They looked rugged and tough, unsmiling but with perfect discipline. As the cars drove by, they presented arms.

We stopped in front of the President's house which was in a peaceful Potsdam square untouched by war. It was small but surrounded by our own M.P.'s, evidently influenced by the Russians because they saluted and stood at attention like Marines.

Here, as in all the rest of Germany, the Army discipline was perfect—a far cry from the laxity of Paris. Outside the President's house were the plain-clothes men of the American Secret Service. They looked big and tough and equally as unsmiling as the Russians.

The Secretary talked to the President for a few minutes, and then we drove to a house on the Kleine Wann See—a beautifully furnished house on a wonderful location along a beautiful lake. It was untouched by bombs, but during the evening as we drove along the lake in a speed boat, many of the houses in this residential section were badly hit.

Notes

The Russian Army in Berlin now is the second Russian Army to be in occupation. The first army, which was the fighting army, had been withdrawn by the time we arrived. The Russians gave the first army a 72-hour pass after they had taken the city, and raping and looting was general. What they didn't take, they destroyed. When that army had been withdrawn, the second Russian Army was given the same leave and the same privileges, but since that time the discipline has been better. The Russians have been taking all the able-bodied men and women and shipping them away. Prisoners that we released are taken up and sent back to Russia.

All the children under fifteen or women over fifty and old men are dumped into the American zone and thus become an American responsibility.

(Feeding)

There are approximately 900,000 originally in the American zone. The French have been added to the occupation forces at the expense of the British who now have 200,000 fewer to feed. But it means that the Americans now have 200,000 extra mouths to feed as the Americans are supplying food for the French district.

(Note)

There seems to be a general feeling here that the Germans hoped that the Germany Army would stop fighting in the West and permit the Allies to come in before the Russians. As far as the Russian treatment of the Germans, most admit that it was as bad as the propaganda had told them it would be. Raping was general. The Russians stole watches in payment and cameras were second choice. The Russians have recently been paid and they are very free with their money. The standard price for watches brought some Americans over $400. The official rate of exchange is 10 marks to the dollar.

One opinion here is that the Russians are never going to pull out of their zone of occupation but plan to make their part of Germany a Soviet Socialist Republic. The question, therefore, is whether the other three occupying forces can afford to leave their zones. So far, the British seem to be encouraging a German economic revival. (The new British government may change this.)

The French who are in the Rhine area will probably want to continue to take large portions of German production. The United States will probably want to pull out—the present plan is to keep an occupying army of 400,000. If a split among the Big Four develops as far as long-time administrative procedure, it will be serious. Germany will be unable to build and maintain communications, roads, canals, trade, coal, and food. If we don't withdraw and allow them to administer their own affairs, we will be confronted with an extremely difficult administrative problem. Yet, if we pull out, we may leave a political vacuum that the Russians will be only too glad to fill.

IMPRESSIONS OF BERLIN RUINS

The devastation is complete. Unter der Linden and the streets are relatively clear, but there is not a single building which is not gutted. On some of the streets the stench—sweet and sickish from dead bodies—is overwhelming.

The people all have completely colorless faces—a yellow tinge with pale tan lips. They are all carrying bundles. Where they are going, no one seems to know. I wonder whether they do.

They sleep in cellars. The women will do anything for food. One or two of the women wore lipstick, but most seem to be trying to make themselves as unobtrusive as possible to escape the notice of the Russians.

The Russians were short, stocky, and dour looking. Their features were heavy and their uniforms dirty.

Hitler's Reich Chancellery was a shell. The walls were chipped and scarred by bullets, showing the terrific fight which took place at the time of its fall. Hitler's air-raid shelter was about 120 feet down into the ground—well furnished but completely devastated. The room where Hitler was supposed to have met his death showed scorched walls and traces of fire. There is no complete evidence, however, that the body that was found was Hitler's body. The Russians doubt that he is dead.

TALK WITH COL. HOWLIE, CHIEF OF AMERICAN MILITARY GOVERNMENT IN BERLIN

On our arrival in Berlin, the American group was viewed with profound distrust. The Russians did not let them take over for the first few days using as their excuse—that they had to have time to evacuate. The Col. thinks, however, that it was because they wanted to continue their looting.

The Colonel ordered his staff to move in one morning. When the Russians arrived at their offices, they found the Americans already there. After a few protests, they retired. Now things are working reasonably smoothly.

All decisions have to be unanimous between the four occupying forces. They run the city as a unit—they work disputes over until the decision is unanimous.

Up until now the food for the American zone is delivered by the Americans to the edge of the Russian zone in the West, which extends 200 miles west of Berlin. Then the Russians transport it to Berlin. After August fifteenth, when the bridges and roads are fixed, the United States will bring their food in directly.

The basic ration is 1½ pounds a day—approximately 1,200 calories (2,000 considered by the health authorities for normal diets—the ration is only 900 calories in Vienna).

The British ship in about 9,000 tons of coal a day for the city which is used for public utilities and for the services of the occupying forces. During this winter the situation may be extremely severe. The Colonel thinks that the Russians may be hard pressed. If they are, they undoubtedly will take the food meant for the civilians. This may present a problem for us because the Americans cannot feed their civilians better than those in the Russian zone because this would cause an influx from all over Berlin.

The Russians have pretty well plundered the country, have been living off it—and therefore, although they control the food basket of Germany, they may never be able to develop their quota for this winter.

The Russian staff work, according to the Colonel, is sloppy. When they make appointments, they may not keep them. Ordinarily, this is not due to indifference to the Americans but merely because they are home drunk in bed. The Colonel says that Americans have to talk tough and know their facts. He does feel, however, that the suspicion between the Russians and the Americans has lessened since the occupation began.

CONVERSATION WITH A GERMAN GIRL

This girl is about twenty-two, speaks some English, and is a Roman Catholic. She said it was difficult to get to Catholic church after the Nazis came to power, though it was possible. She thought the Germans were going to win the war but the first victories were just "shiny."

She thought the future of Germany is "melancholy." After finishing her secondary school education, she worked for a year doing manual labor. The work was extremely hard. She then returned to the University and as the war got increasingly severe, she went to the western front and worked with a search-light crew. She felt

that the war was lost in 1942 when American planes came over.

When the Russians came, she and her two sisters were taken down to the cellar. Her clothes were "taken out"—she gave them all her rings, cried, waved a bottle of wine. Her "face was blue." She demonstrated by swinging a bottle at me. I can quite believe that no Russian would want to rape her. She says the Russians let them go untouched. When the Russians saw the Holy Mother's picture and the Crucifix on the wall, they said, "You must be anti-Nazi if you're a Catholic."

People did not realize what was going on in the concentration camps. In many ways the "SS" were as bad as the Russians. The feeding in Berlin was extremely well organized, even in the most severe blitz.

Her brother was killed on the Eastern front and her fiance is in an Italian prisoner-of-war camp. She feels that Russia and the United States will fight when Russia is ready. They now know that our equipment is far superior.

She feels that that war would be the ruination of Germany which would be the common battleground.

Note

SS was enlarged in 1942 because Himmler wanted to increase his own power. Their brutality was, therefore, diluted by forced recruits.

Note

According to our naval experts, the bombing of Germany was not effective in stopping their production and production increased three-fold during 1942–44.

Note

One of the debatable questions now in Berlin is whether Berlin will ever be built up again into a large city. If Germany remains divided into four administrative units as she is now, Berlin will remain a ruined and unproductive city. In any case, it will be many years before Berlin can clear the wreckage and get the material to rebuild.

REVIEW QUESTIONS

1. How did Kennedy feel toward the defeated Germans? Do you think his views are typical of most Americans in this time period? Why or why not?
2. The editor of Kennedy's diary, Deirdre Henderson, claimed that Kennedy described the origins of the Cold War in the diary. What in these entries might justify her claim?
3. Did what Kennedy see in Berlin make him optimistic or pessimistic about the future of Europe? Explain.

An Italian Correspondent Looks at Sexual Freedom in Sweden (1969)

GUIDO PIOVENE, *In Search of Europe: Portraits of the Non-Communist West*

Count Guido Piovene (1907–1974) was born and raised in northern Italy, particularly the cities of Vicenza and Milan. From an aristocratic family, he was provided with an education that focused on humanistic and liberal values. A journalist, novelist, and travel writer with an international reputation, Piovene emphasized the theme of travel in everything he wrote.

Between 1969 and 1972, Piovene traveled through Europe as a correspondent for Italy's most prominent daily newspaper, *La Stampa.* His assignment was to discover common values, ideologies, and traditions that would justify a "United Europe," a movement that had its origins in the late 1940s with the creation of the Organization for European Economic Cooperation, an outgrowth of the Marshall Plan. In 1957, the European Economic Community (the Common Market) had formed, and many Europeans were considering the need for co-operation that went beyond economic concerns.

Piovene's observations became a book called *In Search of Europe: Portraits of the Non-Communist West,* from which the following excerpt on Sweden is taken. The chief strengths of Piovene's writing, according to one critic, were the result of his "faculty to grasp the essence of a place, an event, a foreign country" and his ability to repudiate mistaken opinions. This selection certainly justifies this statement. At a time when a great deal of world attention—both positive and negative—was focused on the sexual "revolution" in Sweden, Piovene demonstrated that Swedish sexual behavior in the 1960s and 1970s was actually more traditional than revolutionary.

. . . Sweden is a didactic country, not a licentious one. I have not seen the famous film in which three eminent scientists, a doctor, a sociologist, and a psychologist, teach young and old couples "how to do it" and "how not to do it" by a series of examples that leave nothing to the imagination, the purpose being to prevent the unhappiness that comes from inexperience or inhibition. But I know that young Swedes watch the spectacle with great seriousness, in silence, without batting an eyelash, exactly as though they were in school.

It should be noted that sexual freedom at a very young age is in the tradition of a country that was agricultural until recent times, one in which premarital relations and experimentation before making a choice were a custom approved by the family; now what was once permitted in a cruder form by habit, is rationalized and propagandized. The peasant mentality, with the end of agricultural society, comes together and is reconciled with that of an advanced industrial world. The only true religion of almost all the Swedes, tranquilly settled in a nonreligious civilization except for some possibly tragic exceptions, remains the first and pre-Christian one: that of nature. I should also note that one of the chief Swedish vices is timidity; their education tends to break psychological ties, and even relations between married couples sometimes end for this reason, to be replaced by estrangement.

The public airing of sex carries with it no inclination to desecrate it, as in other countries. It is not desecrated, because there is nothing sacred about it to be combatted in the public mind. Matters regarding sex are explained in the schools rapidly, precisely, and matter-of-factly. It is symptomatic that the drive against moralism comes from above and not below: that is, from the government and not the teachers. It seems that up until a while ago a number of teachers, explaining the facts "objectively," recommended a certain abstinence for very young people. These moralistic and subjective intrusions are now censured and forbidden. The opinion of scientists, psychologists, sociologists, ethnographers, and the authorities has coincided with that of student organizations, and in particular of high school students. Only information must be given, plus a relativistic idea: laws and moral standards vary according to place, time, the kind of society and culture—and so does the age to begin. So it is necessary to present all the norms, not to recommend any one of them. With premarital relations permitted, one must examine birth-control precautions and abortion with the same objectivity; parents are advised not to be irra-

tional and pretend that their own daughters are any different from others. Among Swedish youth I do not observe the same audacious love for children that I found in England alongside emancipation; the prevailing mood is, "If we are to have a baby we must first make sure that it will have a better future than our own." The birth rate is low.

In practice, say the statistics, virginity, female or male, is not lost any earlier or later in Sweden than in other countries. Adventures are no easier than elsewhere; the principal reason for unions is to escape from the national Swedish incubus, solitude. This leads, if anything, to a certain stability. One cannot say that family ties are really in crisis. In a country suffering from solitude, where relationships of friendship and acquaintanceship are scarce, those of kinship sometimes represent the only emotional protection, and also present no burden to the budget. Divorce sometimes takes place only for economic reasons, and constitutes one of those passive evasions of which I have spoken. The income of married couples adds up to increase the percentage taken by taxes; many therefore get divorced while continuing to live together. This leads to curious scenes in the course of introductions: "This is my friend Mrs. So-and-so." "What? Isn't she your wife?" "She was, but now she's my friend."

More interesting and useful is the tendency, which will surely be developed in the future, of legalizing the union of unmarried couples. Marriages in Sweden are celebrated by a minister of the cult; many nonreligious people reject the hypocrisy of the nuptial ceremony. Marriage today, writes the minister of justice, Herman Kling, is "a voluntary relationship between independent persons." The present coercive laws refer to a time in which the man worked and the woman was dependent on him. While keeping the marriage tradition secure if required, there is still no need to grant it privileges, only to remain neutral before different forms of cohabitation.

The wish to demolish restrictions where sex is concerned is today a universal fact. But in Sweden it presents an aspect that elsewhere does not exist or is barely hinted at (for example, as in Holland). The greatest sexual freedom is an obligation, an interest, and a technique of the government, supported by intellectuals and students; it is something to be imposed on the backward and timid; it firmly excludes middle ways, which it judges irrational, not without that authoritarian emphasis that distinguishes a government of the enlightened. We may wonder at the reason for this new kind of integralism. The answer may be that it is just and democratic, and that Sweden, aspiring to the role of "most democratic country" on our continent, indeed that of school and model of democracy, would like to apply its principles with the most rigid consistency. One can also say that the most important part of sexual freedom, independently of the use that may be made of it, is political, educational, conceptual. It is an item, one of the principal ones, of the "Swedish philosophy," of a Swedish way of thinking. Swedish democracy is more a "system" than any of the other various European ways of governing, it therefore requires a philosophy and a moral sentiment sufficiently uniform to sustain it, and also a certain degree of disguised authoritarianism, which finds its center in the schools and in the minds of young people. The relative nature of moral rules is here marvelously illustrated. Swedish sex education, directed primarily to the mind, does not provoke disorders, and brings everyone together on a subject of great importance. It is a safeguard of the system just like the restrictions and inhibitions of Victorian England. The totally naked and the totally dressed, in different times and places, have the same duty and the same effect.

REVIEW QUESTIONS

1. How does Piovene explain Sweden's matter-of-fact approach to sex? Does he approve of this attitude? Why or why not?
2. Piovene frequently alludes to Sweden's institutionalization of sex. What effect did this have on the Swedish people?
3. A contemporary critic called Piovene's book "a diagnosis of shortcomings that afflict the entire 'civilized' world." Does this description fit his analysis of Sweden? Why or why not?

An Indian Civil Servant Observes the Use of Machines in Liverpool (1982)

B. N. MISRA, *Inside United Kingdom and Europe*

B. N. Misra was born in 1923 in the Indian state of Orissa. Educated in India, where he eventually received an M.A. in English from Allahabad University, he had a long and distinguished career at several Indian universities, in both teaching and administration. Eventually Misra entered government service in the Ministry of Education, retiring in 1981; he and his wife took their first trip to Europe the following year. They toured extensively in the United Kingdom, and they also visited Holland, Belgium, Luxembourg, Germany, and France. It was the United Kingdom, however, that made the biggest impression on him. "Our experiences in the U.K.," said Misra after his return to India in 1983, "left an indelible impression on my mind." Friends, listening with interest to his experiences, urged him to write a book on the subject. Subsequently, *Inside United Kingdom and Europe* was published in 1987.

Unlike many foreign travelers to the United Kingdom, Misra chose not to focus on the standard tourist experience: cathedrals, castles, and art museums. Instead, he and his wife were fascinated with the daily lives of ordinary people, particularly the friends with whom they were staying and other Indian immigrants in England. Notice, in particular, Misra's interest in excavation equipment and household appliances.

USE OF MACHINES IN DAILY LIFE

As in other nations of the West, machines were used in the U.K. for various activities. At Croxteth Park, Liverpool, we saw construction of houses. It was very near our house. So we had plenty of time to observe it. We noticed that levelling of land, digging the earth for laying the foundation of the house, were all done with the help of machines. I noticed also how with the help of machines the excavated earth was deposited at a distance. The machine had a palm and fingers like a man's, though much bigger in size. When the earth was being lifted and removed by the machine it appeared as if a giant in the Arabian Nights had come and was doing the bidding of his master, who wielded a magic wand. This was so interesting that my wife did not tire of seeing it for hours. Then came bricks with the help of machines. Only two or three men were found working at the site. But they were very sincere and were doing their work well though there was none to supervise their work. Very often engineers themselves built the houses. After the laying of bricks was complete a prefabricated roof was lifted by a crane and put over the brickwork. Thereafter the tiles were laid on the roof. Last of all was the laying of waterpipes and the electric connection. The entire construction work was completed within a fortnight. It appears incredible to us. Houses in our country are completed after months of labour with the help of a multitude of masons and workers. It was surprising how houses could be completed within such a short time and with so few men. We saw the use of machines there inside the house in the daily activities. A Hoover vacuum cleaner was used to clean the house and remove the dust once a week, on a Saturday or on a Sunday. Since it was an electrical machine the inside of the house could be cleaned and dusted with minimal labour. In the kitchen were the fridge and freezer. In our country the fridge has come into vogue at last but there is virtually no use of the freezer. Foodstuffs, particularly fish and meat, can be preserved in the freezer for about six months without their going stale. Washing machines were used for cleaning clothes. After putting soap powder and dirty linen in their respective places in the machine the clothes were cleaned merely by switching on the machine. If the machine was timed the drier dried the clothes after the lapse of the stipulated time. There was a separate arrangement in the washing machine for cleaning woollen and synthetic clothes. There were also shops with washing machines. Those machines could be hired and used there by women who did not have washing machines at home. Such women for a small sum could get their clothes cleaned and dried within a short period of time. There was no necessity for them to wait and watch the cleaning of their clothes. There were dishwashers for cleaning the dishes in the kitchen. In cooking there was frequent use of machines. When the water boiled in the kettle the electric machine would be automatically switched off. It was very easy to cook with the help of electric grills and ovens. In those machines the cooking could be timed and cooked food would be ready without the necessity of waiting for the cooking to be over. The machine, so timed, stopped after the stipulated length of time. In the market half-cooked food or food fully cooked was available. For all these reasons getting a meal ready was not a problem. It did not take more than half an hour to prepare a meal. So the housewife got a lot of time for doing other things in the house. The situation is very different for us, where a lady has to spend the better part of the day in the kitchen for getting meals ready.

In spite of such conveniences due to the use of machines the women, I found, were busy throughout the day. They took the children to the school or to the hospital. They went to the shopping centre or the Bank. They cleaned the house and even painted it. Most of the assistants in shops and offices, I found, were women. Work done earlier by men was being done by women. In comparison middle class women in our country have to do less work. Even now servants and maids are available for employment in our country. But I found they were a dream in England. I noticed women very active there. They walked so fast that it was more like running. It was difficult to keep pace with them. Our women feel tired after a short walk and they walk so slowly it cannot stand comparison with the pace of women abroad. When I alighted from the plane at the Heathrow airport and carried our large suitcases with considerable difficulty I realised then how dependent we are. Later on I came to see how the people there did all work by themselves. They were not dependent like us. Our neighbour, who was elderly, was a teacher in the local college. In digging the earth for flower-beds, in fencing the garden and in the laying of the lawn, he did not need any help. He did it all by himself. He could also make a beautiful shelf for his living room without assistance from anybody.

I remember one experience in particular. Umesh had bought a new house. There was a lawn in front of the house but there was no lawn at the rear. So turf was bought for laying the lawn. It cost Rs. 250 in Indian currency. The neat machine-cut turf was in piles of uniform length and breadth. After the strips of turf were stretched on the ground small quantities of sand filled up the gaps in between them. Thereafter the turf was watered. After a fortnight it was a splendid lawn and none could guess it was newly planted. Before the laying of the turf the ground had been ploughed with a small mechanical plough, which had been hired for £ 16.10 or roughly Rs. 250 in Indian currency. After the turf had been laid it was necessary to fence it. The fencing consisted of wooden planks neatly cut and painted and put together, resembling a wall. In between those planks concrete poles had to be put for which it was necessary to dig deep holes. So help had to be hired. John agreed that day to do this work. He was available because he was unemployed at that time. He worked for four hours and dug a few holes. Later on Umesh secured the poles with packings of cement and metal. John had come for work that day at 10 A.M. on his motor bike. He left his car at home. He worked for a couple of hours and at 12 noon was invited to join us for lunch. He was very friendly and courteous. After he had finished woak he was paid as his wages £ 16 or Rs. 250 in Indian currency. After he left we discussed regarding his earnings. For such labourers the monthly incame worked out to Rs. 8,000. Most of the labouress had their own house and car. From these and other things one would conclude they were comfortable in life.

REVIEW QUESTIONS

1. Which machine or appliance does Misra seem to regard as particularly useful? Why?
2. Why does Misra admire English construction workers?

3. According to the author, what impact did machines and appliances have on the lives of British women? Does he approve of the result? Why or why not?
4. What particular contrasts between life in the United Kingdom and in India does Misra emphasize? Which lifestyle do you think he preferred? Why?

A German Essayist Describes Warsaw (1986)

Hans Magnus Enzensberger, *Europe, Europe*

The author of this selection, Hans Magnus Enzensberger, was born in 1929 in Bavaria and grew up in Nuremberg. He was educated at the Universities of Freiburg, Hamburg, and Erloangen, and at the Sorbonne. Considered by most to be Germany's most important living poet, he is also a well-known essayist, journalist, and cultural critic.

In 1986, Enzensberger traveled through Sweden, Italy, Hungary, Portugal, Poland, and Spain, making careful observations of what he saw. Unlike Guido Piovene, whose writing sought to find cultural similarities that might encourage European unity, Enzensberger believed that the essence of Europe was diversity and complexity, and he saw little hope of unity. Indeed, only two years after his book was published, a wave of nationalism washed over Europe that resulted in the breakup of the Soviet Union, Czechoslovakia, and Yugoslavia.

Europe, Europe has been described by critics as "witty and engaging" and as revealing "profound aspects of the continent." These statements might be true of the work as a whole, but only the latter comment can be applied to Enzensberger's chapter on Poland, "Polish Incidents." Here Enzensberger's usual wit deserted him when he sat down to describe Poland in the mid-1980s. He found nothing in Warsaw particularly amusing; rather, he saw the Poles and their surroundings as a tragic people and a doomed place, obsessed and oppressed by their past.

Warsaw, Saturday/Sunday

After ten at night, the huge main arteries of the Polish capital are completely deserted, the department store show-cases and the windows in the granite façades are dark. There has been a wooden fence at the intersection of Jerusalem Boulevard and Marszałkowska, in the center of town, for years. The sparse traffic curves around the building site. The needle point of the Palace of Culture disappears into a heavy layer of fog, half haze, half smog, that lies over Warsaw. The sidewalks here are seventy-five feet wide. The few people still out and about look lost on these endless, wet, thoroughfares. Old women, shift workers, pensioners, young people stagger by wrapped in padded jackets, yards apart from each other, stare at the mannequins in the store windows, muttering curses under their breath. An empty bottle smashes on the pavement. No one pays any attention to these isolated ghosts. They waver but don't fall down. Not even the militia is around at this hour.

Where are the 1.6 million inhabitants of the

Polish capital hiding? There are not many places of refuge in the city's center. Restaurants are few and they close early. The Shanghai is a drafty, inhospitable hall. The lighting is weak, the food is half cold, and there are no Chinese dishes; the few customers are in a hurry to get home. There's no taxi at the taxi stand. The people in line look resigned. Most of the citizens of Warsaw have stayed home, in the endless highrises that cover the Masovian plain and that are so remote that they're called "the Falklands."

The empty boulevards and squares of the city are built over a necropolis. After the Warsaw Uprising in autumn 1944, more than 150,000 dead were left in the ruins. The survivors were deported. The Germans were already beaten, but they did their utmost to erase every memory of the city from the face of the earth. The remaining ruins were scrupulously and professionally blown up. Almost all the public buildings—the churches, the palaces, the university, what was left of the royal castle—were razed. The electric cables were even torn out of the ground. Hitler seemed to have achieved his goal of making the city uninhabitable forever.

Today the monstrous palaces of Stalinism tower above this *tabula rasa.* Their pasted-on façades proclaim the triumph of yet another foreign power. They cover up the emptiness but the void shines through. The traces of an older settlement can be found only in a few back courts—rotten, dilapidated, cramped tenements, pockmarked by war.

It's almost half a century since this city, this heap of rubble, was liberated. But walking through it, I can still almost feel on my tongue that smell of fire and carbolic acid, soot, and rubble that everyone who lived through 1945 remembers. In Warsaw memory is not repressed. Here destruction and shortages, oppression and self-defense have turned to stone. Forty years after the armistice it is the only city in Europe still living in the postwar period.

When Poles talk about "the war," they don't mean just the German-Soviet attack of 1939 and the years of the occupation, they also mean the course of action their own army took in December 1981. It's difficult to sum up in a single phrase what happened then. State of emergency? But the Jaruzelski government regards the situation that is forcibly brought to an end as the emergency. Martial law? But this coup had nothing to do with law. State of siege? But who was the besieger, if not the Polish people?

The Constitution of the People's Republic did not provide for such an eventuality. It had been unimaginable to the Stalinists. So in order to give his intervention a constitutional veneer, the general had to fall back on the provisions for defense in wartime. However, this solution had one disadvantage: the regime was forced to formally declare war on its own population. Even though the "state of war" was lifted years ago, the shock can still be felt on the deserted streets at night.

Warsaw, Monday

After walking aimlessly through the unfamiliar city for two days, I'm pretty exhausted. I'm living in a district where the ministries are concentrated: heavy industry, energy, mining. This is where the iron men, the party whips of an industrialization that long ago became a nightmare, have their offices. Concentration, centralization. Mountains of paperwork bury the projects of forced accumulation: flooded mines and bankrupt steelworks, monuments to megalomania and wasteful exploitation. The administrators of the catastrophe sit in their honeycombs, breakfast in shirtsleeves, and make phone calls.

The big department stores are a few streets farther on. Shopping is hard, exhausting, boring work. Only someone who is very well informed and has considerable stamina is up to it. The customers, mainly women, give the impression of being highly trained experts. Not poverty but lack dominates life here. Anger or despair would be misplaced. A sharp wit and unflagging patience are the virtues required for survival. The individual counters are either empty or overflowing, depending on what's unavailable and what "*they*'ve thrown down"—an expression imported from the Soviet Union. Scarce consumer goods suddenly appear, no one knows when, where, or why, as if they'd dropped from the sky. People jump on them like a dog on a bone. Today there's dishwashing liquid, which is being poured into canisters and bottles the customers have brought with them, and shapeless balls of toilet paper.

Prices are completely nebulous. The streetcar costs almost nothing, telephone calls just as little, but on the black market the prices are all reckoned in thousands and millions. Presumably the officially controlled prices are supposed to "control" something or to camouflage the frantic inflation of the zloty, but the result is chaotic. A second currency is necessary to fix the real value of a commodity or service. The dollar serves as the economic yardstick in Poland. Regardless of fluctuations, it has assumed the status of an unshakable, almost metaphysical certainty. The state long ago gave up trying to fight its spell and has now become the country's largest black marketeer. Its agencies quite openly advertise luxury tours to Paris, Miami, and Egypt—payable in dollars. The passersby who read these offers are not surprised. They are used to being mocked. Nine million Poles live abroad. Who would want to stop them from helping their friends and relatives at home? Who would cast the first stone? Does the elegant old lady coming out of the PEWEX shop with a heavy shopping bag look like a racketeer? All she has bought is laundry detergent and toothpaste, coffee for her daughter, and chocolate for her nephew. PEWEX is the name of the state's ubiquitous black-market centers. The letters stand for "State Enterprise for Internal Export Trade"—a designation expressive of the madness that has become method here.

If there were no parks, one would have to fear for the mental health of the citizens of Warsaw. But escape from the city's oppressive architecture is never more than ten minutes' walk away. The parks are the city's idyllic side. Time stands still here. Broad avenues, ponds, mossy steps leading down to the river flats, pensioners sunk deep in thought, lots of baby carriages, castles with barred shutters, secluded pavilions, swans, and weeping willows. Urban Warsaw consists not of stone but of vegetation.

The Old Town is another place of refuge. It's not only the largest but also the most marvelous forgery in the world. In 1945 Warsaw was at its lowest point. Everything was lacking, money, materials, food, machinery, and no one even knew what a dollar looked like. Yet the city's inhabitants had nothing better to do than rebuild these seventeenth-, eighteenth-, and nineteenth-century streets with their bare hands on a scale of one to one, a perfect replica down to the last inch. A quixotic venture of heroic dimensions. The Poles anticipated the reconstruction of Europe with their achievement. Its success is demonstrated by the fact that the boldness of the decision has become invisible over the years. Residents and visitors walk across the squares and down the alleyways just as they do in any other Old Town of Europe, whether it's Santiago, Stockholm, or Bergamo. The past seems to have caught up with these walls. They are coated with a secondary patina. Already there's not enough money to repair them. Only someone who looks closely is overcome by a kind of historical vertigo when he asks himself whether this gutter or that door handle is old-old or new-old. Not only did the soaring ambition of the project anticipate all the contradictions of preservation, the Poles also showed a whole continent what it means to reconstruct one's own history.

Warsaw, Tuesday

"And that broad, flat river is the Vistula. No current: the surface flows smoothly. Yellow sandbars almost break the surface. Small ships wait at the riverbank. The sun throws the pattern of the bridge's ironwork across the water. The far bank is sandy, grass-covered. Laborers idling, railroad tracks, steaming locomotives. It takes a long time to walk across this bridge, which is used by so many poor people . . . Now I have arrived in a humble district that, like all gray, disorderly, lively places, pleases me—I slip past churches and palaces far too easily. This is Praga. Peasant women in loose, floral-pattern linen skirts, dragging baskets . . . There's a broad avenue on the right. Terrible pavement, little houses with dirty fronts. A crack opens up between two houses: the entrance to the market stalls; small, red, wooden booths for fruit, clothes, boots. The vendors are almost all Jews. Sometimes a whole family stands behind a little table . . . So many suffering faces, white-parchment complexions, women with untidy hair, elderly women with thick lips, large eyes, and loose cheeks of a terrible ugliness."

Sixty years later, the suburb on the other bank seems unchanged, poor but alive, just as Alfred Döblin described it. Only the Jews are no longer there. Kreuzberg, Prenzlauer Berg, Wedding, and Lichtenberg—what are these Berlin remnants compared to Praga, the only quarter of Warsaw dominated not by postwar but by prewar times? Faces here are marked by an older vitality, indissolubly mixed with an older misery. On Ząbokowska, where the balconies had already fallen from the façades a generation ago, rusty steel supports protrude from bare brick walls. In the nearby market, old women stand for hours with a cap or a shirt, the only thing they have to sell, pressed to their breast. Proletarian poverty leavened with the criminal energy of the deviant, a terrain of smugglers, whores, and drunks. The tiny shop window of the hatmaker: dust on pastel-colored creations, melancholy reminiscence of the time when Warsaw was known as the Paris of the East. Beside it, a shabby little hairdresser's and a cobbler's. In a back court, among the garbage cans

and enclosed by fire walls, a madonna beneath a painted sky-blue canopy. She is wreathed in garlands of little lightbulbs that are left burning night and day. On small lace mats, whole pyramids of tin cans holding fresh flowers. Two mangy cats have settled down in front of this domestic altar.

A couple of streets farther on, an old factory—a sooty brick building with castellated turrets. Over the years, the supporting scaffolding in front of the blank windows has itself become dilapidated. With the help of my pocket dictionary, I decipher the sign at the door, "Warsaw State Plants of the Alcoholic Spirits Industry," as well as the banner hanging across the front of the factory, "The alliance between workers and peasants—foundation of Poland's progress."

At the bus stop on Wileńska, a drunk, a man in his thirties with a mustache and a boxer's build, is blustering with rage. I don't know why, but he's got it in for me. The militia calm him down with difficulty. A student explains to me why he had been shouting, "I'm a worker, I've got a right to make a noise!" It was my red scarf* that had provoked his outburst.

---

*Red scarves were worn by members of paramilitary groups that supported existing communist regimes in Eastern Europe. Membership was primarily honorary, but it was understood that these groups might be called on as reserve forces, and they were allowed to carry weapons in parades and at other times. Thus, wearing a red scarf was symbolic of zealous support for communism.

REVIEW QUESTIONS

1. Enzensberger says that as he walked through the streets of Warsaw, he could still almost feel on his tongue "that smell of fire and carbolic acid, soot, and rubble that everyone who lived through 1945 remembers." What prompted him to make this statement?

2. How did ordinary Poles cope with the economic and political realities described by the author in this selection?

3. Compare Enzensberger's description of Warsaw in 1986 with White's description of Moscow in 1931. Why was Warsaw, forty years after the end of World War II, still basically a war-torn city?

Web Resources

General History Sites

World History Archives

http://www.hartford-hwp.com/archives/index.html   Contains a collection of documents for teaching and understanding world history from a working-class perspective. It is associated with Gateway to World History, which offers general resources for the study of world history.

Internet History Sourcebook Project

http://www.fordham.edu/halsall/   Includes hundreds of excerpts from primary sources sorted by chronological period, area, and topic.

Exploring Ancient World Cultures

http://eawc.evansville.edu/index.htm   Includes an on-line textbook provided by the University of Evansville.

Diotima

http://www.stoa.org/diotima/   Includes materials for the study of women and gender in the ancient world, including images, excerpts from primary sources, on-line course materials, and scholarly articles (accepted only after peer review).

American History

General Site

http://www.academic.marist.edu/history/links/hisamer.htm

From Revolution to Reconstruction

http://odur.let.rug.nl/~usa/   A list of web sites on American history from the colonial period until modern times.

Women's Suffrage

http://www.history.rochester.edu/class/suffrage/home.htm

Cold War Links

http://www.stmartin.edu/~dprice/cold.war.html

The National Civil Rights Museum Web Site

http://www.civilrightsmuseum.org

The Vietnam War

http://www.historicaltextarchive.com

American Women's History

http://www.mtsu.edu/~kmiddlet/history/women/wom-mm.html

Distinguished Women of Past and Present

http://www.DistinguishedWomen.com/

European History

General Site

http://www.academic.marist.edu/history/links/hiseuro.htm

Worlds of Late Antiquity

http://ccat.sas.upenn.edu/jod/wola.html   A home page for miscellaneous materials relating to the culture of the Mediterranean world in late antiquity (roughly 200–700 C.E.).

Classics and Mediterranean Archaeology Home Page

http://rome.classics.lsa.umich.edu/welcome.html

The Ancient City of Athens

http://www.indiana.edu/~kglowack/athens/

Medieval & Renaissance Europe—Primary Historical Documents

http://library.byu.edu/~rdh/eurodocs/medren.html

Discoverer's Web Page

http://www.win.tue.nl/~engels/discovery/

Argos

http://argos.evansville.edu/   Provides a limited area search engine for information on ancient and medieval history and culture.

The Perseus Project

http://www.perseus.tufts.edu/   The best site on the web for Greek History. Also features images related to Roman history, with some Latin texts and their English translations.

The Ancient World Web

http://www.julen.net/ancient/   Provides links to over 1,100 web sites on ancient history.

Romarch

http://acad.depauw.edu/romarch/index.html   Emphasizes Roman art and archaeology. It also features the *Journal of Roman Archaeology*, a large index of maps, and an on-line discussion group.

Russian History

Russian History

http://www.academic.marist.edu/history/links/hisruss.htm   A general site for Russian history.

Russian History

http://www.departments.bucknell.edu/russian/chrono.html   Links major events in Russian history to explanatory and related materials on the web.

African History

General Site

http://www.historicaltextarchive.com

Africa, the Cradle of Civilization

http://library.thinkquest.org/C002739/index2.shtm

History of Africa's Countries-African Cultures

http://africancultures.about.com/culture/africancultures/library/extras/history/blhistory.htm

Internet Sites for the History of Africa

http://personal.ecu.edu/wilburnk/netah.htm

Latin American History

Lords of the Earth

http://www.mayaLords.org/#aztec   Deals with the archeology and anthropology of the Americas.

Asian History

Harappa

http://www.harappa.com/welcome.html

The Ancient Near East

http://eawc.evansville.edu/nepage.htm

Chinese History: To The Qing Dynasty

http://www.usc.edu/isd/locations/ssh/eastasian/toqing.htm

Chinese History

http://www.mrdowling.com/613chinesehistory.html

Other Related Chinese History Links

http://www.freesaves.com/china/related_links.htm

History of India

http://www.historyofindia.com/home.html

Information on India

http://adaniel.tripod.com/history.htm

East and Southeast Asia: An Annotated Directory of Internet Resources

http://newton.uor.edu/Departments&Programs/AsianStudiesDept/japan-history.html
General sources by region or country.

History on Film

Ancient History in the Movies

http:www.fordham.edu/halstall/ancient/asbookmovies.html.   Includes links to movie sites on medieval and modern history.

List of Sources

Chapter 1

p. 3: Reprinted with the permission of The Free Press, an imprint of Simon & Schuster Adult Publishing Group, from *Chinese Civilization and Society: A Sourcebook,* edited by Patricia Buckley Ebrey. Copyright © 1981 by The Free Press. p. 7: From *The History of the Great and Mighty Kingdom of China and the Situation Thereof,* compiled by the Padre Juan Gonzalez de Mendoza, edited by Sir George T. Staunton, Bart. p. 9: From John Bell, *A Journey from St. Petersburg to Pekin,* J.L. Stevenson, ed. Copyright 1966 Barnes & Noble, Inc. p. 13: From *An Embassy to China,* edited by J.L. Cranmer-Byng. Copyright © 1963 Archon Books. p. 16: From "Toyotomi Hideyoshi, "Letter to the Viceroy of the Indies," in *Sources of Japanese Tradition, Vol. I,* compiled by Ryusaku Tsunoda, Wm. Theodore de Bary, and Donald Keene. Copyright © 1958 Columbia University Press. Reprinted with permission of the publisher. p. 18: From François Caron and Joost Schouten, *A True Description of the Mighty Kingdoms of Japan & Siam.* Copyright © 1935.

Chapter 2

p. 29: From *The Travels of Ludovico di Varthema in Egypt, Syria, Arabia Deserta and Arabia Felix, in Persia, India, and Ethiopia.* Translated from the original Italian edition of 1510, with a preface, by John Winter Jones, Esq. p. 35: From *The Baburnama: Memoirs of Babur, Prince and Emperor,* edited by Wheeler M. Thackston, translated by Wheeler M. Thackston. Copyright © 1996 by Smithsonian Institution. Used by permission of Oxford University Press, Inc. p. 39: From *The A'In-I Akbari* by Abu'L-Fazl Allami. Translated from the original Persian by H. Blochmann, M.A. p. 41: Reprinted with permission from "The Indian Letters of 'Il Fantastico'," by Pietro Della Valle from *The Travels of Pietro della Valle in India,* 1614-26, from *The Great Travelers, Volume I,* edited by Milton Rugoff, © 1960, pp. 44–45, 47–50, 50–51. p. 51: From François Valentin's *Description of Ceylon,* translated by Sinnappah Arasaratnam. Copyright © 1978. Reprinted by permission of David Higham Associates.

Chapter 3

p. 62: From *The Discovery of River Gambra* by Richard Jobson, edited by David P. Gamble and P.E.h. Hair. Copyright © 1999. Reprinted by permission of David Higham Associates. p. 66: Reprinted with permission from Fr. Gaspar de Santo Bernardino, OFM, *Itinerario de India,* as appeared in G.S.P. Freeman-Grenville, *The East African Coast.* Copyright © 1962, pp. 155–156, 157, 158–160, 160–162. p. 73: From *Barbot on Guinea: The Writings of Jean Barbot on West Africa,* 1678-1712, Volume II. Copyright © 1992. Reprinted by permission of David Higham Associates. p. 79: From *The Interesting Narrative of the Life of Olaudah Equiano,* written by himself, edited by Robert Allison. Copyright © 1995. p. 82: Reprinted with permission from Joseph Crassons de Medeuil, France, *Ministère de la Marine,* as appeared in G.S.P. Freeman-Grenville, *The East African Coast.* Copyright © 1962, pp. 192-197.

Chapter 4

p. 88: From *Andre Thevet's North America: A Sixteenth-Century View,* trans. by Roger Schlesinger and Arthur P. Stabler. Copyright © 1986. Reprinted by permission of the author. p. 91: *The Florentine Codex: General History of the Things of New Spain,* by Fray Bernardino de Sahagun, *Book 10: The People,* trans. from the Aztec by Charles E. Dibble and Arthur J.O. Anderson, part XI, © 1961, pp. 165-167, 174-175, 176-179. Reprinted with permission. p. 95: From Fray Diego Duran, *Aztecs: The History of the Indies of New Spain,* trans. Doris Heyden and Fernando Horcasitas. Copyright © 1964 Orion Books. Reprinted by permission of Penguin Publishing. p. 104: From *The Captivity of Hans Stade of Hesse, in A.D. 1547-1555, Amont the Wild Tribes of Eastern Brazil,* translated by Albert Tootal, Esq. p. 108: From *Expeditions into the Valley of the Amazons,* 1539, 1540, 1639. Translated and edited, with notes, by Clements R. Markham, F.R.G.S. p. 111: From *The Voyages of Pedro Fernandez de Quiros, 1595 to 1606,* translated and edited by Sir Clements Markham. Reprinted by permission of David Higham Associates. p. 115: From *La Australia Del Espiritu Santo: The Journal of Fray Martín de Munilla O.F.M* , translated and edited by Celsus Kelly, O.F.M. Copyright © 1966. Reprinted with permission. p. 117: From *Early Voyages to Terra Australis now called Australia,* edited, with an introduction by R.H. Major, Esq.

Chapter 5

p. 123: Reprinted with permission from Giovanni Della Casa, *Galateo,* translated by Konrad Eisenbichller and Kenneth Bartlett. Copyright © 1986 Center for Reformation and Renaissance Studies. p. 126: From *The Travels of Antonio de Beatis: Germany, Switzerland, and The Low Countries, France and Italy, 1517–1518,* translated by J.R. Hale and J.M.A. Lindon. Copyright © 1979. Reprinted with permission of David Higham Associates. p. 140: As appeared in Lady Mary Wortley Montagu, Turkish Embassy Letters. Copyright © 1993. Text edited and annotated by Malcolm Jack. p. 145: Excerpts from Donald Keene, *The Japanese Discovery of Europe, 1720–1830,* Revised Edition. Copyright © 1952, 1969 by Donald Keene. Reprinted with the permission of Stanford University Press, *www.sup.org*

Chapter 6

p. 152: As appeared in *Moving Pictures, More Borneo Travel,* compiled by Victor T. King. Copyright © 1999. p. 162: Reprinted with the permission of The Free Press, an imprint of Simon &

Schuster Adult Publishing Group, from *Chinese Civilization and Society: A Sourcebook,* edited by Patricia Buckley Ebrey. Copyright © 1981 by The Free Press. **p. 167:** From *Modern Japanese Literature,* edited by Donald Keene. Copyright © 1956 by Grove Press, Inc. Used by permission of Grove/Atlantic, Inc.

Chapter 7

p. 198: From Keki Daruwalla, *Apparition in April.* Copyright © 1971.

Chapter 8

p. 207: Reprinted with permission from Joseph Crassons de Medeuil, France, *Ministère de la Marine,* as appeared in G.S.P. Freeman-Grenville, *The East African Coast.* Copyright © 1962, pp. 192–197. **p. 227:** From Mohandas K. Gandhi, *An Autobiograpy: The Story of My Experiments with Truth* by Mohandas K. Gandhi, translated by Mahadev Desai. Copyright © 1988 by Navajivan Press. Reprinted with permission.

Chapter 9

p. 223: From *The Journals of Lewis and Clark,* edited by Bernard DeVoto. Copyright © 1953 by Bernard DeVoto, renewed 1981 by Avis DeVoto. Reproduced by permission of Houghton Mifflin Company. All rights reserved. **p. 253:** As appeared in Pavel N. Golovin, *Civil and Savage Encounters: The Worldly Travel letters of an Imperial Russian Navy Officer,* translated and annotated by Bail Dmytryshyn and E.A.O. Crownhart-Vaughan. **p. 256:** From *The Japanese in America,* ed. Charles Lanman (New York: University Publishing Company, 1872), pp. 66–72, 82–85, 94–100.

Chapter 10

p. 264: From *The Memoirs of Fray Servando Teresa de Mier* by Fray Servando Teresa de Mier, edited by Susana Rotker, translated by Helen Lane. Copyright © 1998 by Oxford University Press, Inc. Used by permission of Oxford University Press, Inc. **p. 267:** Rai San-yo, "Dutch Ship (poem), 1818," as appeared in *The Japanese Discovery of America: A Brief History with Documents,* edited and with an introduction by Peter Duus, © 1997. **p. 267:** Reprinted by permission of the Harvard University Asia Center from Bob Tadashi Wakabayashi, *Anti-Foreignism and Western Learning in early Modern Japan: The New Theses of 1825* (Cambridge, MA.: Council on East Asian Studies, Harvard University, 1986), pp. 149–150, 200–209, 211. Copyright © 1986 The President and Fellows of Harvard College. **p. 273:** Copyright © 1974 Oxford University Press. Reprinted from *The First Chinese Embassy to the West: The Journals of Kuo Sung-T'ao, Liu Hsi-Hung and Chang Te-Yi,* translated and annotated by J.D. Frodsham (1974) by permission of Oxford University Press.

Chapter 11

p. 295: *An African Student in China* by Emmanuel John Hevi. Copyright © 1962 by Greenwood Press. Reproduced with permission of Greenwood Publishing Group, Inc., Westport, CT. **p. 298:** From *Report from a Chinese Village* by Jan Myrdal, translated by Maurice Michael. Copyright © 1965 by William

Heineman Ltd. Used by permission of Pantheon Books, a division of Random House, Inc. **p. 303:** From *Red Azalea* by Anchee Min. Copyright © 1994 by Anchee Min. Used by permission of Pantheon Books, a division of Random House, Inc. **p. 306:** From Nikos Kazantzakis, *Japan China,* translated from the Greek by George C. Pappageotes. Copyright © 1963. **p. 309:** From *Over a Bamboo Fence* by Margery Finn Brown. Copyright © 1951, 1979 by Margery Finn Brown. Reprinted by permission of HarperCollins Publishers, Inc. **p. 313:** From Nguyen Long with Harry H. Kendall, *After Saigon Fell: Daily Life Under the Vietnamese Communists.* Copyright © 1981. Reprinted by permission of the Institute of East Asia Studies. **p. 317:** Copyright © 1994 by Cleo Odzer. Reprinted by permission from Patpong Sisters, published by Arcade Publishing, New York, New York.

Chapter 12

p. 322: From Colette Modiano, *Turkish Coffee and the Fertile Crescent.* Copyright © 1974. Published by Michael Joseph, London, England. **p. 325:** From *Guests of the Sheik* by Elizabeth Warnock Fernea. Copyright © 1965 by Elizabeth Warnock Fernea. Reprinted by permission of Doubleday, a division of Random House. **p. 327:** From Ella K. Maillart, *The Cruel Way.* Copyright © 1986. Published by Beacon Press. **p. 330:** From Anthony Weller, *Days and Nights on the Grand Trunk Road.* Copyright © 1997 by Anthony Weller. Reprinted by permission of the author. **p. 334:** From Margaret W. Andres, John L. Baker, and Fritz Blackwell, eds., *Letters from Chittagong: An American Forestry Couple's Letters Home, 1952-1954.* Copyright © 1992. Reprinted with permission. **p. 337:** From *Sketches from My Past: Encounters with India's Oppressed* by Mahadevi Varma, translated by Neera Kuckreja Sohoni. Copyright © 1994 by Neera Kuckreja Sohoni. Reprinted with the permission of Northeastern University Press. **p. 342:** From Nayantara Sahgal, Prison and Chocolate Cake. Copyright © 1954. Reprinted by permission of the author. **p. 347:** From Mark Tully, *No Full Stops in India.* Copyright © 1991. Reprinted with permission.

Chapter 13

p. 354: From Julian Huxley, *Africa View.* Copyright © 1931. **p. 357:** From *The Autobiography of an Unknown South African* by Naboth Mokgatle. Copyright © 1971 by the Regeants of the University of California. Reprinted by permission of the University of California Press. **p. 362:** "Marrakech," by George Orwell (Copyright © George Orwell) by permission of Bill Hamilton as the Literary Executor of the Estate of the Late Sonia Brownell Orwell and Secker & Warburg Ltd. **p. 365:** From Elizabeth Marshall Thomas, "The Shy People of the Kalahari," in *The Great Travelers, Volume I,* edited by Milton Rugoff, © 1960, pp. 44–45, 47–50, 50–51. Reprinted by permission of the author. **p. 369:** Reprinted from Flora Nwapa, *Efura.* Copyright © 1966 Harcourt Education Ltd. Reprinted by permission. **p. 374:** From the book *Cameroon with Egbert.* Copyright © 1990 by Dervla Murphy. Reprinted with the permission of The Overlook Press. **p. 374:** From Peter Biddlecombe, *French Lessons in Africa: Travels with My Briefcase Through French Africa.* Copyright © 1993. Reprinted by permission of Time Warner